THE
CHESS-PLAYER'S
HANDBOOK

The Chess-Player's Handbook

First published in 1847 by H. G. Bonh, London, and
then in 1985 by B. T. Batsford, London

This edition published in 1994 by Senate, an imprint of
Studio Editions Ltd, Princess House, 50 Eastcastle Street,
London W1N 7AP, England

ISBN 1 85958 005 X
Printed and bound in Guernsey by
The Guernsey Press Co Ltd

THE CHESS-PLAYER'S HANDBOOK

HOWARD STAUNTON

FOREWORD BY
RAYMOND KEENE
INTERNATIONAL GRANDMASTER

SENATE

FOREWORD.

HOWARD STAUNTON is the only English player ever to have been recognised as the world's strongest; he lent his name to the style of chess pieces now in use in all major tournaments; he inaugurated the English tradition of chess literature and organised the very first international tournament, London 1851.

Nevertheless, English chessplayers have been unnecessarily reserved in their attitude to Staunton, who should properly be regarded as the founder of our national school. The Russians have the great Tchigorin, who has been elevated by their writers into the exalted position of spiritual founder of the Soviet school of chess. The Germans have Tarrasch and they have not been slow to stress his status as a chess teacher of world prestige. The French have Philidor. The Austrian Steinitz is regarded as the 'founder of modern chess' and the Americans have several heroes, some of whom have been magnified into legendary figures. Denmark has given some recognition to Nimzowitsch who took refuge in Scandinavia in the 1920's. The Dutch have Euwe.

Staunton's *Chess Player's Handbook* appeared in 1847. In his article 'Writers who have changed chess history' Harry Golombek ranks this work as number two in a series of five throughout the ages, which began with Philidor's *Analyse des Echecs* and continued with Lasker's *Commonsense in Chess*, Réti's *New Ideas in Chess* and Nimzowitsch's *My System*. It immediately became the standard textbook of English chessplayers and remained so for over half a century, being republished twenty-one times between 1847 and 1935.

RAYMOND KEENE
INTERNATIONAL GRANDMASTER

PREFACE.

WIDE as is the field of theory which comprehends the manifold varieties of openings and endings in the game of Chess, its every part has been explored in modern times with so much skill and perseverance, that little now remains for a follower in this walk beyond the adaptation and arrangement of materials which have been garnered by his predecessors. The pretensions of this treatise can therefore take no lofty ground. Adopting the common basis founded by the earlier writers, Lopez, Salvio, Greco, Cozio, Lolli, &c., and superadding the important discoveries brought to light in the works of Bilguer and Jaenisch, I have aimed only at producing an instructive compendium available by the large majority of English players to whom those works are inaccessible. In my labours of collation and compression, I have not, however, indolently acquiesced in the opinions of those distinguished authorities, but have subjected every variation they have given to the test of repeated investigation, and hence it will be found that I have occasionally deviated from the course prescribed by them, and ventured on a route which they have overlooked. For these digressions, put forth without the advantage of revision by other players, I may reasonably solicit the indulgence that should be shown to any one who devotes himself to a task so difficult as that of devising new combinations in openings which have already undergone the ordeal of laborious examination by the most penetrating and industrious intellects.

In a work of this description, intended as well for the general as the scientific reader, it was thought desirable to adhere to the notation in common use among the players of this country, but in a more elaborate and expansive treatise, it would certainly be desirable, perhaps indispensable, to adopt such a modification of the system as would admit of tabular demonstrations. Who that has ever attempted the wearisome exertion of threading his way through the ramifications of a leading opening from an English book, can ever forget the bewilderment and confusion which its endless references to "Variations 1, 2, 3," and " A, B, C," and "Games 5, 6, and 7," have occasioned him? And yet such references for the most part are needful, and indeed inseparable, from our method of recording the moves in columns, rather than on tables. Mindful of these obstacles to the progress of the student, I have been at some pains to lessen his difficulties in the present work. In the first place, by discarding all unnecessary variations, and abridging, where curtailment was practicable, the remainder; and secondly, by distinguishing the accredited methods of attack and defence from the subordinate or doubtful ones, by a difference of type. Thus the reader who has not leisure to pursue an opening through its several deviations, and is content to follow the moves which have been pronounced the best, has only to play over the column of larger type, and may reserve for a future opportunity the study of the many beautiful and suggestive variations which are given in the smaller letter.

By these means much of the irksomeness complained of in the practice of playing from book may be avoided, and I have hopes that the mere learner will be enabled in a short time to master an opening of " The Handbook," variations and all, and derive not only profit but even pleasure from the task.

I must not omit the present opportunity to acknowledge the profound obligations this volume is under to its great namesake "The Handbuch" of Bilguer and V. der Laza, a production—whether considered in reference to its research, its suggestiveness, or the methodical completeness of its arrangement,—which stands unrivalled and alone.

Nor can I forego the gratification of tendering my warmest thanks to Messrs. Angas and Finley, of Durham, for their invaluable assistance in the shape of translations and corrections, and to my esteemed friend the Rev. H. Bolton, and to those gentlemen who have kindly seconded his efforts, for the series of exquisite problems which so appropriately concludes the work.

H. S.

London, June, 1847.

CONTENTS.

BOOK III.

THE KING'S BISHOP'S OPENING.

BOOK IV.

THE KING'S GAMBIT.

BOOK V.

BOOK VI.

ENDINGS OF GAMES.

The
Chess-Player's Handbook.

BOOK I.

INTRODUCTION.

CHAPTER I.

DESCRIPTION OF THE CHESS BOARD AND MEN —
ARRANGEMENT OF THE MEN — THE KING — THE
QUEEN—THE ROOKS OR CASTLES—THE BISHOPS—
THE KNIGHTS — AND THE PAWNS — THEIR MOVE-
MENTS, POWERS, METHOD OF CAPTURING AN
ADVERSE MAN, ETC.

THE game of Chess, the most fascinating and intellectual
pastime which the "wisdom of antiquity" has bequeathed
to us, is played by two persons, each having at command
a little army of sixteen men, upon a board divided into
sixty-four squares, eight on each of the four sides. The
squares are usually coloured white and black, or red and
white, alternately; and custom has made it an indispensable
regulation in this country, that the board shall be so placed
that each player has a white square at his right-hand corner.*

---

* This arrangement is merely conventional. In the earlier ages of
chess, the board was simply divided into sixty-four squares, without any
difference of colour; and there is good reason for believing that the
chess-men were then alike in form and size, and distinguishable only by
an inscription or sign on each.

The following diagram represents the board with all the men arranged in proper order for the commencement of a game :—

No. 1.

BLACK.

WHITE.

Each player, it will be observed, has eight superior Pieces or officers, and eight minor ones which are called Pawns; and for the purpose of distinction, the Pieces and Pawns of one party are of a different colour to those of the other.

The eight superior Pieces, on each side, are—

A King . . . . ♔ ♚

A Queen . . . . ♕ ♛

Two Rooks, or Castles . . . . .
    (as they are indiscriminately called)

Two Bishops . . . . ,

Two Knights . . . . . .

And each of these Pieces has his Pawn or Foot-
    soldier . . . .

making in all an array of sixteen men on each side.

On beginning a game, these Pieces and Pawns are disposed in the manner shown on the foregoing diagram. The King and Queen occupy the centre squares of the first or "royal" line, as it is called, and each has for its supporters a Bishop, a Knight, and a Rook, while before the whole stand the Pawns or Foot-soldiers in a row. (To prevent a common error among young players, of misplacing the King and Queen on commencing a game, it is well to bear in mind that at the outset the white King always stands on a black square, and the black King on a white one). The Pieces on the King's side of the board are called the King s, as King's Bishop, King's Knight, King's Rook; and the Pawns directly in front of them, the King's Pawn, King's Bishop's Pawn, King's Knight's Pawn, and King's Rook's Pawn The Pieces on the Queen's side are, in like manner, called the Queen's Bishop. Queen's Knight. and Queen's Rook; and the Pawns before them, Queen's Bishop's Pawn, Queen's Knight's Pawn, and Queen's Rook's Pawn.

MOVEMENT OF THE PIECES AND PAWNS.

A knowledge of the moves peculiar to these several men is so difficult to describe in writing, and so comparatively easy to acquire over the chess-board, from any competent person, that the learner is strongly recommended to avail himself of the latter means when practicable: for the use, however, of those who have no chess-playing acquaintance at command, the subjoined description will, it is hoped, suffice.

THE KING.

The King can move one square only at a time (except in "Castling," which will be explained hereafter), but he can make this move in any direction, forwards, backwards, laterally, or diagonally.* He can take any one of the adversary's men which stands on an adjoining square to that he occupies, provided such man is left unprotected, and he has the peculiar privilege of being himself exempt from capture. He is not permitted, however, to move into check, that is, on to any square which is guarded by a Piece or Pawn of the enemy, nor can he, under any circumstance, be played to an adjacent square to that on which the rival King is stationed. Like most of the other Pieces, his power is greatest in the middle of the board, where, without obstruction, he has the choice of eight different squares. At the sides, he may play to any one of five, but when in the angles of the board, three squares only are at his command.

THE QUEEN.

The Queen is by much the most powerful of the forces. She has the advantage of moving as a Rook, in straight lines, forwards, backwards, and sideways, to the extent of the board in all directions, and as a Bishop, diagonally, with the same range. To comprehend her scope of action, place her alone in the centre of the board; it will then be seen that she has the command of no less than twenty-seven squares, besides the one she stands on. (See diagram No. 4.)

* The original movement of the King, or "Rey," as he was first called in Europe, appears to have been very limited, since he was restricted from moving at all, except by the necessity of extricating himself from an adverse check. About the beginning of the thirteenth century, he had the power of playing one square directly, but was not permitted to move or capture angularly; this limitation, however, lasted but a short period, and then the Rey had the privilege of moving and taking in any direction, as at present, but his range of action never extended beyond one square. (See an interesting article "On the Moves and Powers of the Chessmen of our Ancestors," &c., &c.—*Chess-Player's Chronicle*, vol. iii. p. 61.)

THE ROOK.

The Rook, or Castle, is next in power to the Queen. He moves in a straight line, forwards, backwards, or sideways, having a uniform range, on a clear board, of fourteen squares, exclusive of the one he occupies.—(See *Castling*, page 19.)

THE BISHOP.

The Bishop moves diagonally forwards or backwards, to the extent of the board. It follows, therefore, that he travels throughout the game only on squares of the same colour as the one on which he stands when the game begins, and that each player has a Bishop running on white squares, and one on black squares. When placed on a centre square of a clear board, he will be found to have a range of thirteen squares.

THE KNIGHT.

The action of the Knight is peculiar, and not easy to describe. He is the only one of the Pieces which has the privilege of leaping over another man. The movements of the others are all dependent on their freedom from obstruction by their own and the enemy's men. For example, when the forces are duly ranged in order of battle before the commencement of the game, the Knight is the only one of the eight capital Pieces which can be played before the Pawns are moved—King, Queen, Bishop, and Rook are all hemmed in by the rank of Pawns, which they cannot overleap; but the Knight, having the liberty of springing over the heads of other men, can be brought into the field at once. In this case, as his move is one square *in a straight line*, and *one in an oblique direction*, if the King's Knight were to begin the game, he must be played either to King's Rook's third square, or to King's Bishop's third square ; and if the Queen's Knight commenced, he must be moved to Queen's Rook's third square, or to Queen's Bishop's third square.

The following diagram will serve, perhaps, to make his action better understood. (See also pages 12 and 43, for a description of the powers and peculiarities of this Piece.)

No. 2.

BLACK.

WHITE.

In this position we have the Knight surrounded by Pawns in a way which would render any other Piece immoveable. A King, Queen, Rook, or Bishop, so encompassed by their own forces, could never stir until one of the men were moved to make an outlet; and, if thus shut in by *adverse* Pawns, could escape only by being enabled to capture one or other of them. But the Knight clears such impediments at a bound, and can here be played to any one of the eight white squares around. It is worth remarking, that if he is stationed on a *white* square in the centre of the board, he has then eight *black* squares at his choice; because, from the peculiarity of his move, it is impossible for him to spring from a white square to a white one, or from a black square to a black one. On placing him on any square at the side of the board, it will be seen that his scope of action is much diminished, and when standing on either of the four corners, or Rook's squares, as they are called, he has then only two squares to which he can leap.

THE PAWN.

The Pawn moves only one square at a time, and that *straight forward*, except in the act of capturing, when it takes one step diagonally to the right or left file on to the square occupied by the man taken, and continues on that file until it captures another man. A power has been conceded to it, however, in latter times, of going *two steps when first played* in the game, *provided no hostile Pawn commands the first square over which he leaps*, but, in that case, the adverse Pawn has the option of taking him in his passage, *as if he had moved one step only* (see the diagram, No. 9). A Pawn is the only one of the forces *which goes out of his direction to capture*, and which has not the advantage of moving backwards; but it has one remarkable privilege, by which on occasions it becomes invaluable, *whenever it reaches the extreme square of the file on which it travels, it is invested with the title and assumes the power of any superior Piece, except the King, which the player chooses*. From this circumstance it frequently happens that one party, by skilful management of his Pawns, contrives to have two, and sometimes even three, Queens on the board at once, a combination of force which of course is irresistible.*

* The regulation which enjoins a plurality of Queens is not, however, by any means of general prevalence. In Italy, at the present day, the Pawn, on reaching the 8th square, is replaced by a second Queen, whether the former one is on the board or not; but this was not always the case there, and according to Major Jaenisch, throughout the whole of the North of Europe, in Russia, in Scandinavia, in Germany, as well as in the classic Italian authors, Del Rio, Lolli, and Ponziani, the rule obtains that a Pawn having reached the 8th square, is exchanged for a Piece from among those the player has lost. Two Queens, two Bishops of the same colour, three Rooks, three Knights, are not permitted; and if a player advances a Pawn to an extreme square of the board, it must remain inactive till one of his Pieces is taken by the enemy, upon which it instantly assumes the rank of that Piece, and is brought into action again.—(See the Introductory Article on the Laws of the Game of Chess, in the "Analyse Nouvelle," &c., vol. i. p. 28.)

ON CAPTURING AN ADVERSE MAN.

The "Pieces," by which title the eight superior officers are technically designated, in contradistinction to the "Pawns," all take in the same direction in which they move. This act consists in removing the adverse Piece or Pawn from the board, and placing the captor on the square the former occupied. To make this clear, we will begin with the King, and show his mode of capturing an adverse man.

No. 3.

BLACK.

WHITE.

Supposing the above to be the position of the men towards the conclusion of a game, and it being either party's turn to play, he could take the adverse Pawn from the board, and place his King on the square it occupied; and by doing so, the King would not depart from the order of his march, which, as we have before said, permits him to move *one step* in every direction. In each of these instances we have placed the Pawn in *front* of the King, but he would be equally entitled to take it were it standing on any other of the eight squares immediately surrounding him, *always provided it was not sustained or guarded by some other Piece or Pawn.*

The next diagram will exhibit the power of the Queen in capturing an enemy.

No. 4.

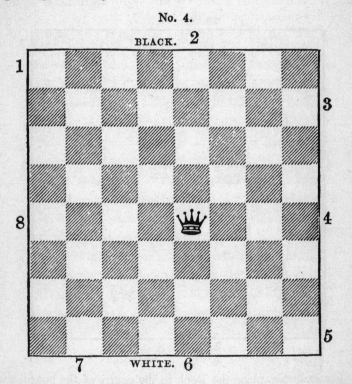

Thus placed in the middle of the board, the range of the Queen is immense. She has here the option of taking any one of eight men at the extremity of the board, on the squares respectively numbered 1, 2, 3, 4, 5, 6, 7, and 8, should her line of march be unobstructed; and if these men were nearer, on any of the intermediate squares, she would be equally enabled to take any one of them at her choice. Like all

the other Pieces and Pawns she effects the capture by removing
the man from the board, and stationing herself on the vacated
square.

The Rook has the same power in taking as the Queen,
forwards, backwards, and sideways, but he cannot, like her,
take any man diagonally.

No. 5.

BLACK. 1

4   2

WHITE. 3

For example, place the Rook in the centre of the board, and
an opposing man on each of the squares numbered, and the
Rook has the power of taking any one of the four; and he
has the same power if the Pieces are one or two squares closer
to him, or immediately surrounding him, in the direction indicated by the four figures.

The BISHOP takes, as he moves, diagonally, either forwards or backwards, his range extending, on unobstructed

squares, to the extent of the diagonal line on which he travels.*

No. 6.

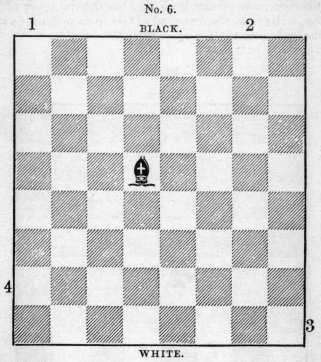

BLACK.

1   2

4   3

WHITE.

* In the thirteenth century, we find the Bishop, then termed *Alfyn*, **a** corruption from its Eastern name, *al Phil*, the Elephant, had its present diagonal movement, but was restricted in its march to the third square from that on which it stood; thus, supposing White's King's Bishop to stand on his own third square, he could then capture any Piece or Pawn standing on his Queen's square, or Queen's fifth square, and his King's Rook's square, or his King's Rook's fifth square; but as he was not permitted to move to a greater or less number of squares, he had no power over an enemy which stood either closer or more removed than the third square. To compensate for this limited action, the *Alfyn* had the peculiarity bestowed on him of vaulting over another Piece in the manner somewhat of the Knight. For example :—place White's King's Bishop as before on his own third square, with a Black Bishop at Black's King's fifth, and a Black Pawn at his Queen's fourth, in this, or any similar position, the White Bishop could not capture the Black one, but could overleap him and take the Pawn, and then be out of the range of the Black Bishop's action. (See the article on the Moves, &c.. of the Pieces in the thirteenth century, before referred to.)

The KNIGHT, as we have seen before, moves one square forward and one obliquely, his action being a combination of the shortest move of the Rook and the shortest move of the Bishop. His power and method of taking an opponent's man will be seen from the diagram subjoined.

No. 7.

BLACK.

WHITE.

In this situation, in the centre of the board, he would have the power of taking any one of the men stationed on the squares numbered, by removing the man and placing himself on the vacant square.*

* There is no evidence we believe to show that the Knight has undergone any variation in action or power, since the first introduction of chess into Europe. His move appears to be supplementary to the range of the other forces, and to comprehend just those squares of the board over which none of them, similarly placed, would have command.

The Pawn, as we have previously observed, is the only man which captures in a direction different from his line of march. He is permitted to move only one square forward at a time, and is not allowed to take any Piece or Pawn which may impede his path. If, however, he meet with any of the adverse force on a point diagonal, one step either to the right or left of the square he occupies, he is at liberty to capture that man and take his place on the next file; for example,—

No. 8.

BLACK.

WHITE.

Suppose, at the opening of the game, White begins by playing King's Pawn to King's fourth square (see the article on Notation, p. 16). Black may reply in the same manner with King's Pawn to King's fourth square, and neither Pawn can do more than remain an obstruction to the onward march of the other, but if Black answer instead with King's Bishop's Pawn to Bishop's fourth, or as in the diagram, with Queen's Pawn to Queen's fourth, then White, if he choose, may take the adverse Pawn from the board and place his own in its stead. To exemplify another peculiarity of the Pawn, suppose White in this situation to prefer playing the Pawn on to King's fifth square, instead of taking the Pawn, the following would be the aspect of the board :—

No. 9.

BLACK.

WHITE.

If, now, Black choose to play King's Bishop's Pawn to King's Bishop's fourth, White has the option of taking that Pawn (in passing, as it is called), just as if Black, instead of playing it two steps, had moved it to King's Bishop's third square only; White, in fact, might arrest it in its leap over the King's Bishop's third square. take it off the board, and station his King's Pawn on the said Bishop's third square, as in an ordinary case of capture. But if he omit to exercise this power at once, he is not allowed to do so after another move has been made.*

This privilege of the Pawn to take, in passing, another Pawn which attempts to advance two steps when first moved, is so very imperfectly understood by young practitioners, and is the cause of so much error and misunderstanding among them, that every one should comprehend it thoroughly before he begins to play a game in earnest.

---

* The following instructive observations on the subject of the Pawn's moving two steps, and his power of taking an adverse Pawn which attempts to pass him, are extracted from Major Jaenisch's " Analyse Nouvelle," &c.

" To be able properly to judge the question relative to the taking of a Pawn *en passant*, or *passar battaglia* of the Italians, we must recollect that at the origin of the game, the Pawns advanced but one square only; and this is still the general usage in the East. Besides, the nature of the Pawn itself indicates it. It is evident, it was with the intention of augmenting the value of this, the weakest but the most interesting of the chess forces, and to avoid by that means a languid opening, that it was permitted to march two steps on the first move, when it was tacitly supposed no enemy was yet within reach. It was subsequently perceived that some Piece of the enemy might often command the square over which the Pawn leaps, and that to permit this leap was in some sort to violate the rights of that Piece ; but whether from generous disregard of the Pawn, or indulgence for its weakness, it was generally agreed to permit it this licence. The aspect of things changed when the question came to be discussed, if this violation of the rights of the attacking Piece conceded to the Pawn at its first move, could be equally exercised *vis à vis* of another Pawn : in other words, if the *passar battaglia* with regard to a Piece, could be tolerated with respect to a Pawn of the adversary which had arrived at his fifth square. Upon this point the opinions of chess-players were divided ; the majority of amateurs, the great players of Spain and Portugal at their head, (Iberia was then the classic land of chess), decided that the Pawn could not be permitted *vis à vis* of an equal, what was tolerated as to a Piece. That the permission of *passar battaglia* as to an attacking Piece, could have no other object than to give animation to the game, in aiding the weakness of the Pawn ; that this object would not only be unattained, but that a directly contrary effect would be produced if the legitimate rights of the Pawn advanced to its fifth square should be violated. It is thus, at least, that we explain the motives that led the players of the Iberian Peninsula (according to the testimony of Ruy Lopez), and later those of France, England, and Germany, to establish the rule of taking the Pawns in passing, which heightens powerfully the interest of the game, in giving additional force to the Pawns, the ' soul of chess,' as they are called by Philidor." (Jaenisch, vol. i. p. 34.)

CHAPTER II.

THE NOTATION ADOPTED TO DESCRIBE THE MOVES OF THE MEN.

THERE is no portion of an elementary work on Chess of so much importance to the learner, and none which requires more resolute mastering than this.

The notation may be called the language of the game, and a knowledge of it is absolutely indispensable to every one who is himself ambitious of excelling, or who is desirous of appreciating the excellencies of other players.   How many thousands of amateurs are there who have never played a single game or opening through from books in their lives, and who debar themselves from the primary source of enjoyment, and indeed improvement, which chess affords, simply because they will never be at the pains of acquiring the key to studying printed games?   Others, again, have contrived to pick up sufficient acquaintance with some particular system adopted by one writer, or in one country, to play over a printed game from that notation with tolerable accuracy, but cannot be induced to devote the requisite time and attention for the attainment of any other.   Now, as the method of describing the movements of the chess-men differs materially in different countries, your true chess-player will never be content till he has acquired knowledge enough of these systems to decipher all the most important, such as those of Germany, France, and England, with facility.   It is best to begin, however, with one of these, and learn that accurately first.   Accordingly, we shall here proceed to explain only the method adopted throughout this country in describing the moves, &c., reserving a dissertation upon the most popular systems in use abroad for another part of the Treatise.

Having marshalled the men in battle order, as shown in the first diagram, you will observe that each party has two *ranks* of men, on the first of which stand the superior Pieces, and on the next the eight Pawns.   The eight squares which compose the first rank are each distinguished by the name of the Piece which occupies it when the men are first arranged.   There are, therefore, the King's square, the King's Bishop's square, King's

Knight's square, and King's Rook's square, and in like manner, the Queen's square, Queen's Bishop's square, Queen's Knight's and Queen's Rook's squares. The *files*, that is, the row of squares running from top to bottom of the board, are also named by the Pieces occupying the first square in each *file*. Thus each of the superior officers has a file or row of eight squares running from his end of the board to the corresponding Piece of the enemy, and every one of these eight squares takes its name from such officer. The following diagram will serve to show the designation of the various squares:—

No. 10.

BLACK.

Q R's sd.	Q Kt's sd.	Q B's sd.	Q's sd.	K's sd.	K B's sd.	K Kt's sd.	K R's sd.
Q R's 8th.	Q Kt's 8th.	Q B's 8th.	Q's 8th.	K's 8th.	K B's 8th.	K Kt's 8th.	K R's 8th.
Q R's 2d.	Q Kt's 2d.	Q B's 2d.	Q's 2d.	K's 2d.	K B's 2d.	K Kt's 2d.	K R's 2d.
Q R's 7th.	Q Kt's 7th.	Q B's 7th.	Q's 7th.	K's 7th.	K B's 7th.	K Kt's 7th.	K R's 7th.
Q R's 3d.	Q Kt's 3d.	Q B's 3d.	Q's 3d.	K's 3d.	K B's 3d.	K Kt's 3d.	K R's 3d.
Q R's 6th.	Q Kt's 6th.	Q B's 6th.	Q's 6th.	K's 6th.	K B's 6th.	K Kt's 6th.	K R's 6th.
Q R's 4th.	Q Kt's 4th.	Q B's 4th.	Q's 4th.	K's 4th.	K B's 4th.	K Kt's 4th.	K R's 4th.
Q R's 5th.	Q Kt's 5th.	Q B's 5th.	Q's 5th.	K's 5th.	K B's 5th.	K Kt's 5th.	K R's 5th.
Q R's 5th.	Q Kt's 5th.	Q B's 5th.	Q's 5th.	K's 5th.	K B's 5th.	K Kt's 5th.	K R's 5th.
Q R's 4th.	Q Kt's 4th.	Q B's 4th.	Q's 4th.	K's 4th.	K B's 4th.	K Kt's 4th.	K R's 4th.
Q R's 6th.	Q Kt's 6th.	Q B's 6th.	Q's 6th.	K's 6th.	K B's 6th.	K Kt's 6th.	K R's 6th.
Q R's 3d.	Q Kt's 3d.	Q B's 3d.	Q's 3d.	K's 3d.	K B's 3d.	K Kt's 3d.	K R's 3d.
Q R's 7th.	Q Kt's 7th.	Q B's 7th.	Q's 7th.	K's 7th.	K B's 7th.	K Kt's 7th.	K R's 7th.
Q R's 2d.	Q Kt's 2d.	Q B's 2d.	Q's 2d.	K's 2d.	K B's 2d.	K Kt's 2d.	K R's 2d.
Q R's 8th.	Q Kt's 8th.	Q B's 8th.	Q's 8th.	K's 8th.	K B's 8th.	K Kt's 8th.	K R's 8th.
Q R's sq.	Q Kt's sq.	Q B's sq.	Q's sq.	K's sq.	K B's sq.	K Kt's sq.	K R's sq.

WHITE.

Here it is seen that White names every square on the board, in accordance with its relative position to one of his eight

Pieces, and that Black does the same. Hence follows an anomaly. Black's *first* squares are White's *eighth*, and *vice versâ*. This irregularity is avoided by the notation which was generally adopted in this country until lately. That was founded upon the true principle of the chess-board being divided into two parts, one of which belonged to White and the other to Black. All beyond the four first squares of every file was the territory of the adversary. Instead, therefore, of describing a Piece as at "King's sixth," or "King's Rook's seventh," or "Queen's sixth," it was said to be at "adverse King's third," or "adverse King's Rook's second," or "adverse Queen's third," &c. There can be no question that this was more correct than the present mode, but it was thought less concise, and has latterly gone quite out of use both here and in France.

Before proceeding further, it will be desirable for the student to familiarise himself with the respective moves of the Pieces, names of the squares, &c. A very little practice will enable him to do so, especially with the aid of any friend acquainted with them. He should, in the first place, accustom himself to the setting up the men in order of battle; after a few repetitions of the process, and comparing their position with the diagram on the second page, he will soon have no difficulty whatever in arranging them correctly without referring to the book. It will then be well to clear the board of all but a single Piece, and practise with that until perfect in its movements; another, and then another, may be added, until the action of every one is as familiar as the alphabet.

Suppose, as a first exercise, you begin by placing your Queen on her square (*i. e.*, her first square), then play her to Q's 5th square, then (diagonally, observe) to Q. Rook's 8th square, then to King's Rook's 8th square, then to Q. R's square, and then home again to her square. It is proper to mention that the directions for moving a Piece are not usually printed in full, and that according to the modern abbreviations in the present and other chess-books, these several instructions would be given thus :—

1. Q. to her sq.
2. Q. to her 5th.
3. Q. to her R's 8th.
4. Q. to K. R's 8th.
5. Q. to her R's sq.
6. Q. to her sq.

As a next exercise, put the Queen's Bishop on his square, beside the Queen, and play him as follows :—

1. Q. B. to K. R's 6th.
2. Q. B. to K. B's 8th.
3. Q. B. to Q. R's 3rd.
4. Q. B. to his sq.

To these two Pieces now add the Queen's Knight, on his own square, and play as follows :—

1. Q. Kt. to Q's 2nd.
2. Q. Kt. to K's 4th.
3. Q. Kt. to K. B's 6th.
4. Q. Kt. to K's 8th.
5. Q. Kt. to Q. B's 7th.
6. Q. Kt. to Q. Kt.'s 5th.
7. Q. Kt. to Q. B's 3rd.
8. Q. Kt. to his sq.

By taking all the Pieces in succession thus, you will speedily obtain sufficient knowledge of their movements to commence the opening of a game; but before attempting this, it is needful for you to be acquainted with the technical terms in use among chess-players, and the code of laws which governs the game.

CHAPTER III.

TECHNICAL TERMS IN USE AMONG CHESS PLAYERS.

CASTLING.

ALTHOUGH, as a general rule, the move of the King is restricted to one square at a time, he has the privilege, under certain conditions, once in the game, of moving in conjunction with either of the Rooks two squares. This peculiar movement is called *Castling*, and, in this country, it is performed in the following manner :—If a player wishes to castle on his King's side of the board, he moves the King to K. Kt. s sq., and then places the K's Rook on K. B's square. If he castle on the Queen's side, he plays his King to Q. B's sq., and Q's Rook to Q's sq. The object of this compound move is generally to place the royal Piece in safety, and at the same time bring the Rook from the corner square into better play.

The conditions under which a player is permitted to castle are:—1st. The King must not be in check. 2nd. The King must not have moved. 3rd. The Rook must not have moved. 4th. The King must not pass over or on to any square attacked by an enemy's man. And 5th. There must be no Piece, either of his own or the adversary's, between the King and the Rook.

In exemplification of the importance of castling, to escape from an attack, and to retort one on the adversary, see, presently, the diagram No. 11.

CHECK AND CHECKMATE.

The King is said to be in *check* when he is attacked by any Piece or Pawn, for it being a fundamental law of chess that the King can never be taken, whenever any direct attack upon him is made, he must be warned of his danger by the cry of *check*, and the player is then compelled either to remove his King *out* of *check*, or parry the check by interposing a man between the King and the attacking Piece, or capture the checking man.

When he can do none of these three things, he is *checkmated*, and the game won by the other side. (See diagram No. 12, at the end of this Chapter.) When the King is directly attacked by the Piece played, it is a *simple* check; but when the Piece moved does not itself give check, but unmasks another which does, it is called a *discovered check*. (See diagram No. 13.) The third species of check is named the *double check*, where the King is attacked both by the Piece moved and the one discovered. The fourth description is called *perpetual check*, a case which arises when a player has two or more squares on which he can give check, and his opponent can only parry one check by affording an opportunity for another. If the first player then persists in the repetition of these particular checks, the game must be abandoned as drawn. (See diagram No. 14.)

DOUBLED PAWN.

When two Pawns of the same colour are on the same file, the front one is called a *doubled Pawn*.

DRAWN GAME.

When neither party can give checkmate, the game is drawn. This may arise from several causes, as:—1st. *Perpetual check*. 2nd. Where there is not sufficient force to effect a mate, as a King and a Knight only, or a King and two Knights, &c., &c. 3rd. Where one party has force sufficient, but is ignorant of the proper mode of applying it, and thus fails to checkmate his helpless adversary within the fifty moves prescribed by the 22nd law. 4th. Where both parties persist in repeating the same move from fear of each other. 5th. Where both parties are left with the same force at the end, as a Queen against a Queen, a Rook against a Rook, and the like, when, except in particular cases, the game should be resigned as a drawn battle. And 6th. When one of the Kings is *stalemated*.

EN PRISE.

When a Piece or Pawn is in a situation to be taken by the enemy, it is said to be *en prise*. To put a Piece *en prise*, is to play it so that it may be captured.

THE EXCHANGE.

When a player gains a Rook for a Bishop or a Knight, it is termed *winning the exchange*.

FALSE MOVE.

Any illegal move, such as castling when the King has been moved or is in check, moving a Rook diagonally, or a Bishop like a Knight, is called a false or an " impossible" move.

FOOL'S MATE.

This is the simplest of all checkmates, being accomplished in two moves in the following manner:—

WHITE.	BLACK.
1. K. Kt. P. to K. Kt.'s 4th.	1. K. P. to K's 4th.
2. K. B. P. to K. B's 4th.	2. Q. to K. R's 5th, check-mate.

It cannot possibly be given by the first player.

FORCED MOVE.

When a player has one only legal move at command, it is said to be a *forced move*.

GAMBIT.

This word is derived from an Italian phrase in wrestling, and signifies a movement by which the adversary is tripped up. In chess, this is attempted by the first player putting a Pawn *en prise* of the enemy early in the game, by which he is enabled more rapidly and effectually to develope his superior Pieces. There are several gambits, but the most important, and one which includes many others, is the King's gambit, commenced as follows:—

WHITE.	BLACK.
1. K. P. to K's 4th.	1. K. P. to K's 4th.
2. K. B P. to B's 4th.	2. P. takes K. B. P.

The Pawn offered by the first player here at his second move is called the Gambit Pawn, and when taken by the adversary the opening becomes a gambit.

The varieties of the gambits are often designated by the names of the players who invented or first brought them into vogue—as the *Muzio* gambit, the *Salvio* gambit, the *Allgaier* gambit. the *Lopez* gambit; while others obtain their names from the opening moves of the first player, as the King's Bishop's gambit, which begins thus:—

WHITE.	BLACK.
1. K. P. to K's 4th.	1. K. P. to K's 4th.
2. K. B. P. to B's 4th.	2. P. takes P.
3. K. B. to Q. B's 4th,	

and is so called because the K's Bishop is played out at the 3rd move instead of the K's Knight.

There is also the Queen's gambit, of which the opening moves are—

WHITE.	BLACK.
1. Q. P. to Q's 4th.	1. Q. P. to Q's 4th.
2. Q. B. P. to B's 4th.	2. P. takes P.

The gambits are the most brilliant and animated of all the openings. full of hair-breadth 'scapes and perilous vicissitudes, but affording an infinitude of beautiful and daring combinations.

" GIUOCO PIANO,"

A solid and instructive modification of the King's Knight's game, is of all others the most generally practised by the leading players. The opening moves are:—

WHITE.	BLACK.
1. P. to K's 4th.	1. P. to K's 4th.
2. K. Kt. to B's 3rd.	2. Q. Kt. to B's 3rd.
3. K. B. to Q. B's 4th.	3. K. B. to Q. B's 4th.

TO INTERPOSE.

When the King is checked, or any valuable Piece in danger from the attack of an enemy, you are said to *interpose* a man when you play it between the attacked and attacking Piece.

ISOLATED PAWN.

A Pawn which stands alone, without the support and protection of other Pawns, is termed an *isolated* Pawn.

J'ADOUBE.

A French expression, signifying " I arrange," or " I replace," which is used by a player when he touches a man merely to adjust its position on the board, without intending to play it. (See the 7th law.)

MINOR PIECES.

The Bishop and Knight, in contradistinction to the **Queen** and Rook, are called *minor Pieces*.

THE OPPOSITION.

An important manœuvre in playing the King, by which one player is enabled to occupy certain key squares, and thus compel the adverse King to abandon a favourable position.

PARTY.

From the French *partie*. Frequently used by modern writers instead of the word " game."

PASSED PAWN.

A Pawn is said to be a *passed* one when the adversary has no Pawn to obstruct its march on the same file, or on either of the next files to the right or left.

PION COIFFÉ, OR MARKED PAWN.

This is a description of odds but rarely given, and only when there is a vast disparity between the skill of the players. It consists in one party placing a *cap* or ring on one of his Pawns, and undertaking to checkmate his opponent with that particular Pawn. He is not allowed to *Queen* the Pawn, and if he loses it, or happens to checkmate his opponent with any other man, he forfeits the game. The Pawn usually *capped* is the King's Knight's, because it can be more readily and effectually surrounded by protecting Pieces.

TO QUEEN A PAWN, OR TO ADVANCE A PAWN TO QUEEN.

When a player has contrived to advance a Pawn to the eighth or last square of the file, it assumes the rank and power of a Queen, or any other Piece he chooses, and he is then said to have *queened* his Pawn. (See the 21st law.)

SCHOLAR'S MATE.

A checkmate occasionally given at the opening of a game by a practised player to one but little tutored in the science. The following are the moves :—

WHITE.	BLACK.
1. P. to K's 4th.	1. P. to K's 4th.
2. K. B. to Q. B's 4th.	2. K. B. to Q. B's 4th.
3. Q. to K. R's 5th.	3. Q. P. one.
4. Q. takes K. B. P., giving checkmate.	

SMOTHERED MATE

A checkmate which is sometimes given by the Knight when the adverse King is hemmed in, or *smothered*, by his own forces. (See diagram No. 16.)

STALEMATE.

When one party has his King so circumstanced that, not being at the moment in check, he cannot play him without going into check, and at the same time has no other Piece or Pawn to move instead, he is said to be *stalemated*, and the game is considered drawn. (See diagram No. 17.)

TAKING A PAWN EN PASSANT, OR IN PASSING.

It has been shown before, in speaking of the action of the Pawn, that he is limited in his march to one square forward at a time, when not capturing, and one square forward diagonally, either to the right or left, when he takes an adversary, but that he has the privilege, on being first played in the game, to advance two squares, unless in so doing he pass a square which is attacked by a hostile Pawn; in which case the opponent may, at his option, permit him to make the two steps forward, and there remain, or may capture him in his passage in the same way as if he had moved but one step. (See diagram No. 9.)

THE OPERATION OF "CASTLING."*—(See page 19.)

No. 11.

BLACK.

WHITE.

In this situation the white King is threatened with what is called "a discovered check," that is, his opponent, by removing the Bishop would *discover* check from the Queen, a proceeding, in the present instance, which would speedily involve the loss of the game to White. Not being at the moment in check, however, and having moved neither King nor Rook, and there being no *intervening* Piece between the

---

* The practice of castling is a European innovation of comparatively modern origin. In the oriental nations, the birthplace of chess, castling is unknown, and the earliest authors upon the game in Europe, Damiano (1512), and Lopez (1561), have no allusion to it, but mention only the "leap of the King," a peculiar privilege derived from the Eastern game, which permits the King, on his being first played, provided he has not been checked, to move and even make a capture like a Knight.

King and his own Rook, White is enabled to castle, giving check to the adverse King at the same time, and win the game easily, for Black has no square to which he can move his King without going into check, and is consequently obliged to interpose his Q. at K. B's second, or K. B's third square, in either case being checkmated in two more moves, as you will soon be able to see.

CHECKMATE.

No. 12.

BLACK.

WHITE.

The above position represents the appearance of the forces on each side towards the end of a game, and will assist to explain the application of two or three of the technical terms described in the present Chapter, as well as to exhibit the King in a situation of checkmate. You already understand that the moves at chess are played by each party alternately;

in this case it is White's turn to play, and he will checkmate
his antagonist in two moves. Place the chess-men on your
board exactly in the order they stand in the diagram; having
done this, suppose yourself to be playing the White men, and
take the Black King's Pawn with your Queen, in the manner
before shown, *i. e.*, by taking the Pawn from the board and
stationing your Queen on the square it occupied. By this
act, you not only take his Pawn, but you attack his King,
and must apprise him of his danger by calling "*check*."
He has now two ways only of parrying this check. It is
clear he cannot move his King, because the only two squares
to which he could move without going into check are occupied
by his own men; he is forced then either to take the Queen
with his K. B's Pawn, or to interpose the Bishop at King's
second square. If he take the Queen with his K. B's Pawn,
you must reply by playing your King's Bishop (which you
will know by the colour of the diagonal on which he travels)
to K. Kt.'s sixth square, crying "check." Examine the
position attentively and you will find that Black has no
square to which he can move his King, the only vacant one
being attacked by your Queen's Bishop, that he has nothing
wherewith to take the Bishop that has given check, and
neither Piece nor Pawn with which to interpose between it
and his King, and that, consequently, he is not only checked,
but *checkmated*. In like manner, if, at his first move, instead
of capturing your Queen, he interpose his Bishop at King's
second square, you immediately take the Bishop with your
Queen, who is protected by her Bishop, and say "checkmate."

DISCOVERED CHECK.

This is a striking though simple instance of the power of a
discovered check. Arrange your chess-men as in the diagram,
and you will find that if White has now to play, although he
is so much inferior to his opponent in force, he can win the
game in two moves. If indeed there were no Rook on the
board, he would do so on the first move by playing his Rook
to Q. B's eighth square, discovering check with the Bishop;
Black would then be unable to interpose his Queen, because,
in so doing, he must leave his King attacked by the Rook,

No. 13.

BLACK.

WHITE.

and he would, consequently, be checkmated at once. In the position under consideration, however, you must observe that the Bishop is attacked by the Black Rook, and if White were to play his Rook in the way just spoken of, Black could take the Bishop with his Rook, and would ultimately win the game. Under these circumstances, White must play his Rook to K. Kt.'s sixth square, discovering check equally with the Bishop, and at the same time preventing his capture by the Rook. As Black cannot remove his King, nothing remains for him but to interpose the Queen at her Kt.'s second square, whereupon White takes the Rook, giving checkmate, since the Queen is already occupied in parrying the Bishop's check, and the King is unable to stir.

PERPETUAL CHECK.

No. 14.

BLACK.

WHITE.

This position is only a modification of the preceding one, but it will enable you to understand what is meant by *perpetual check* as well as the most elaborate arrangement of the men could do. Place the men on your chess-board according to the diagram, suppose yourself to be playing the white Pieces, and that it is your turn to move. Your adversary, you will observe, has the advantage in point of force, but this is counterbalanced by the situation, which enables you to draw the game. To do this, you must first play your Queen to one of the three squares where she will check the King, *i. e.*, to K's 4th, Q's 5th, or Q. B's 6th; it is indifferent which, say, therefore, Q. to K's 4th (check). Black has no option, his King cannot move, he must interpose his Queen. If now you were to take the Queen you would lose the game, on account of his two Pawns; but instead of doing so, you play the Queen to King's 8th sq., giving check. The black Queen must again interpose; you repeat the check at K's 4th, Black can only parry it with his Queen, and you may persist in giving the same two checks, *ad infinitum.* In such cases, the game is resigned as " drawn by *perpetual check.*"

ANOTHER EXAMPLE OF PERPETUAL CHECK.

No. 15.

BLACK.

WHITE.

In this instance, which is given by Mendheim, White is much inferior to his opponent in numerical strength, but from the peculiarity of the situation he is enabled to draw the game. Endeavour to discover how this is accomplished, beginning by playing the Rook to K. B's 8th square, giving check, &c.

SMOTHERED MATE.

No. 16.

BLACK.

WHITE.

This is a familiar example of *smothered mate*, which you will find can be effected by no other Piece than the Knight. White's first move is, Queen to her 5th square, checking. Black is obliged to retreat his King to the R's sq., because, were he to play him to his B's sq., the Q. would checkmate at once. Upon the King retiring, White gives check with his Kt. at K. B's 7th; this brings the King back again to Knight's sq., and affords to White an opportunity of giving *double check*, which he does by moving the Knight to K. Rook's 6th, checking with both Q. and Knight; as before, the King must go to Rook's sq.; and now follows a beautiful move—White plays his Queen down to *K. Kt.'s 8th* (next square to the Black King), giving check; the King cannot take on account of the

Knight; he is compelled, therefore, to capture with his Rook, and the Knight then gives the *smothered mate* at K. B's 7th square.

STALEMATE.

No. 17.

BLACK.

WHITE.

Here you observe that White has the great advantage of a Queen against a Rook; but with all this, and the move to boot, it is impossible for him to do more than draw the game. It is evident that he cannot move his Queen from the front of his King on account of exposing him to check with the Rook. If he move his King, Black takes the Queen, and the game is drawn. And lastly, if he take the Rook with his Queen, he places the adverse King in the position before described of *stalemate.*

CHAPTER IV.

ON THE RELATIVE VALUE OF THE CHESS FORCES.

AN attempt to establish a scale of powers whereby the relative values of the several men could be estimated with mathematical exactitude, although it has frequently engaged the attention of scientific minds, appears to be an expenditure of ingenuity and research upon an unattainable object. So ever varying, so much dependent on the mutations of *position* which every move occasion, and on the augmented power which it acquires when combined with other forces, is the proportionate worth of this with that particular man, that it would seem to be beyond the reach of computation to devise a formula by which it can be reckoned with precision. But still an approximation to correctness has been made, and the result arrived at gives the following as the ultimate respective values:—

Pawn .... = 1.00
Knight .... = 3.05
Bishop .... = 3.50
Rook .... = 5.48
Queen......................... = 9.94

The King, from the nature of the game, which does not admit of his being exchanged or captured, is invaluable, and he is not, therefore, included in the calculations.

The Pawn, it is seen, is the least valuable of all the men, the Knight being worth at least three Pawns.

The Bishops and Knights are practically considered of equal value, although there is a difference in the estimate here given.

A Rook is of the value of five Pawns and a fraction, and may be exchanged for a minor Piece and two Pawns. Two Rooks may be exchanged for three minor Pieces.

The Queen is usually reckoned equal, in average situations, to two Rooks and a Pawn, but towards the end of a game she is hardly so valuable as two Rooks.

These comparative values may be of service to the student

in general cases of exchanging men, but he will find in practice the relative worth of his soldiers is modified by so many circumstances of time, opportunity, and position, that nothing but experience can ever teach him to determine accurately in every case " which to give up and which to keep."

CHAPTER V.

THE LAWS OF THE GAME.

THE following Laws, with some trifling variations, have been in general use for the last fifty years. They have recently been revised by a committee of the London Chess Club, established in 1807; and are now universally adopted by all the chess clubs of Great Britain.

I.

The chess-board must be so placed that each player has a white corner square nearest his right-hand. If the board have been improperly placed, it must be adjusted, provided *four* moves on each side have not been played, but not afterwards.

II.

If a Piece or Pawn be misplaced at the beginning of the game, either player may insist upon the mistake being rectified, if he discover it before playing his fourth move, but not afterwards.

III.

Should a player, at the commencement of the game, omit to place all his men on the board, he may correct the omission before playing his fourth move, but not afterwards.

IV.

If a player, undertaking to give the odds of a Piece or Pawn, neglect to remove it from the board, his adversary, after *four* moves have been played on each side, has the choice of proceeding with or recommencing the game.

V.

When no odds are given, the players must take the first move of each game alternately, drawing lots to determine who shall begin the first game. If a game be drawn, the player who began it has the first move or the following one.

VI.

The player who gives the odds has the right of moving first in each game, unless otherwise agreed. Whenever a Pawn is given, it is understood to be always the King's Bishop's Pawn.

VII.

A Piece or Pawn touched must be played, unless at the moment of touching it the player say "*J'adoube*," or words to that effect; *but if a Piece or Pawn be displaced or overturned by accident, it may be restored to its place.*

VIII.

While a player holds the Piece or Pawn he has touched, he may play it to any other than the square he took it from; but, having quitted it, he cannot recall the move.

IX.

Should a player take one of his adversary's Pieces or Pawns, without saying "*J'adoube*," or words to that effect, his adversary may compel him to take it; but if it cannot be legally taken, he may oblige him to move the King; should his King, however, be so posted that he cannot be legally moved, no penalty can be inflicted.

X.

Should a player move one of his adversary's men, his antagonist has the option of compelling him—1st, to replace the Piece or Pawn and move his King; 2nd, to replace the Piece or Pawn and take it; 3rd, to let the Piece or Pawn remain on the square to which it had been played, as if the move were correct.

XI.

If a player take one of his adversary's men with one of his own that cannot take it without making a false move, his antagonist has the option of compelling him to take it with a Piece or Pawn that can legally take it, or to move his own Piece or Pawn which he touched.

XII.

Should a player take one of his own men with another, his adversary has the option of obliging him to move either.

XIII.

If a player make a false move, i. e., play a Piece or Pawn to any square to which it cannot legally be moved, his adversary has the choice of three penalties; viz., 1st, of compelling him to let the Piece or Pawn remain on the square to which he played it; 2nd, to move correctly to another square; 3rd, to replace the Piece or Pawn and move his King.

XIV.

Should a player move out of his turn, his adversary may choose whether both moves shall remain, or the second be retracted.

XV.

When a Pawn is first moved in a game, it may be played one or two squares; but in the latter case the opponent has the privilege of taking it *en passant* with any Pawn which could have taken it had it been played one square only. A Pawn cannot be taken *en passant* by a Piece.

XVI.

A player cannot castle in the following cases :—

1. If the King or Rook have been moved.
2. If the King be in check.
3. If there be any Piece between the King and Rook.
4. If the King pass over any square attacked by one of the adversary's Pieces or Pawns.

Should a player castle in any of the above cases, his adversary has the choice of three penalties; viz., 1st, of insisting that the move remain; 2nd, of compelling him to move the King; 3rd, of compelling him to move the Rook.

XVII.

If a player touch a Piece or Pawn that cannot be moved without leaving the King in check, he must replace the Piece or Pawn and move his King; but if the King cannot be moved, no penalty can be inflicted.

XVIII.

If a player attack the adverse King without saying "Check," his adversary is not obliged to attend to it; but if the former, in playing his next move, were to say "Check," each player must retract his last move, and he that is under check must obviate it.

XIX.

If the King has been in check for several moves, and it cannot be ascertained how it occurred, the player whose King is in check must retract his last move and free his King from the check; but if the moves made subsequent to the check be known, they must be retracted.

XX.

Should a player say "Check," without giving it, and his adversary, in consequence, move his King, or touch a Piece or Pawn to interpose, he may retract such move, provided his adversary have not completed his last move.

XXI.

Every Pawn which has reached the eighth or last square of the chess-board, must be immediately exchanged for a Queen or any other Piece the player may think fit, even though all the Pieces remain on the board. It follows, therefore, that he may have two or more Queens, three or more Rooks, Bishops, or Knights.

XXII.

If a play remain, at the end of the game, with a Rook and Bishop against a Rook; with both Bishops only; with Knight and Bishop only, &c., he must checkmate his adversary in fifty moves on each side at most, or the game will be considered as drawn; the fifty moves commence from the time the adversary gives notice that he will count them. The law holds good for all other checkmates of Pieces only, such as Queen, or Rook only, Queen against a Rook, &c., &c.

XXIII.

If a player agree to checkmate with a particular Piece or Pawn, or on a particular square, or engage to force his adversary to stalemate or checkmate him, he is not restricted to any number of moves.

XXIV.

A stalemate is a drawn game.

XXV.

If a player make a false move, castle improperly, &c., &c., the adversary must take notice of such irregularity before he touches a Piece or Pawn, or he will not be allowed to inflict any penalty.

XXVI.

Should any question arise, respecting which there is no law, or in case of a dispute respecting any law, the players must refer the point to the most skilful disinterested bystanders, and their decision must be considered as conclusive.

[I cannot permit the present opportunity to pass without expressing a hope that the time is not far distant when the advancing intelligence of chess-players will prompt their leading authorities in Europe to unite for the purpose of abolishing the several crude collections of ambiguities which are now received as the " Laws of Chess," and to establish in their stead one general and comprehensive code of regulations, in the interpretation of which there shall be neither doubt nor difficulty, and which shall be worthy of the period and of a game which aspires almost to the dignity of science.]

Chapter VI.

GENERAL RULES AND OBSERVATIONS.

CONCERNING THE KING.

It is mostly advisable to castle the King pretty early in the game, and to do so on the King's side, because he is less subject to an attack, and better able to repel one on that side than the other—nevertheless, it frequently happens, that a player by castling on the Queen's side, is enabled to make a formidable assault on the adverse King, by throwing forward his King's flank Pawns. When the Queens are exchanged off early in the game, it is often well to move the King to K. B's 2nd square, and in that way bring the Rooks into play, instead of castling, because there is then less danger to the King, and he may become a valuable auxiliary during the remainder of the fight. In castling, move the King before you touch the Rook.

Be fearful, when castled on the King's side, of permitting an adverse Knight to gain safe possession of your King's Bishop's 4th square, and remember that it is seldom prudent in an inexperienced player to advance the Pawns on the side his King has castled.

Be cautious of playing your Queen in front of your King. Never subject yourself to a *discovered check*. It is better when check is given to your King to interpose a man that attacks the checking Piece than with one that does not. Beware of giving useless checks to your adversary's King, but when, by checking, you can oblige him to move, and thus deprive him of the right to castle, it is generally good play to do so. It is sometimes useful to give a series of checks, and even sacrifice a Piece, to force the King into the middle of the board, where he may be subjected to the attacks of your other men.

Do not in all cases take an enemy's Pawn which stands before your King,—it may serve sometimes as a protection to him ; and bear in mind that towards the termination of a game, especially when the superior Pieces have been taken off the field, the King should be made to compensate for his previous inactivity, by being busily engaged. The fate of the game is then dependent for the most part on the skill displayed in the management of the King.

CONCERNING THE QUEEN.

The Queen is so powerful and important a Piece at chess that she should rarely be employed to defend or attack any point if you can do it as well with a subordinate.

It is not good to play the Queen out into the game at the beginning, because she can be attacked by inferior Pieces, and is compelled to retire with the loss of many moves.

Be careful, too, when about to capture a distant Pawn or Piece, that you do not remove your Queen too far from the immediate point of action. A clever player will often permit you to win a Pawn with the Queen, that he may prevent her returning in time to rescue your King from his attack. The power of the Queen is wonderfully greater when she is aided and protected by other Pieces than when she goes forth unsupported; it is generally injudicious, therefore, to make an attack with her unless in combination with some other of your forces.

CONCERNING THE ROOK.

The Rook is a most important officer, yet few players even among the best avail themselves sufficiently of his power. He has seldom much scope for action in the early part of the engagement, but when the field is thinned no time should be lost in bringing him into action. You should then endeavour to *double* your Rooks, that is, to place them one before the other on the same file: in this situation, mutually sustaining one another, their potency on a clear field is equal to the Queen's.

It is usually good play to get command of an open file, that is to say, a file which is occupied by no other man, by stationing a Rook at one end of it. When you have thus gained possession of the file, should your opponent try to dispossess you of it, by playing one of his Rooks on the same file, it is frequently better to defend with your other Rook than to take his or remove your own. You will often embarrass your adversary, too, if you can manage to post a Rook on his second rank, say at your King's 7th or Queen's 7th square. In this position he generally makes an attack on the Pawns unmoved, and compels the enemy to lose time in defending them, while you can bring more forces into action.

One of the strongest reasons for playing out your Pieces early in the battle, is, that while at home they are not only themselves inactive, but they utterly retard the movements of your Rooks. In an unskilfully developed game it is a common occurrence to see the victory won before the defeated player's Rooks have ever moved.

CONCERNING THE BISHOP.

When the game is opened by each party with King's Pawn to King's 4th square, the *King's Bishop* is somewhat superior to the *Queen's*, because it can be sooner brought into play, and may be made to bear immediately on the King's weak point, his Bishop's Pawn. It is desirable therefore generally to exchange your Queen's Bishop or Queen's Knight for the adversary's King's Bishop. The King's Bishop should rarely or never be played to the Queen's 3rd square before the Queen's Pawn is moved. His best position, as we have remarked above, is to Queen's Bishop's 4th square, where he attacks the opponent's King's Bishop's Pawn. If your antagonist then challenges an exchange of Bishops by moving his Queen's Bishop to King's 3rd square, it is not always prudent to accept it, because although you may double the Pawns on his King's file, you at the same time afford him an open range for his King's Rook when he has castled. The best play in such a case is, therefore, to retreat your King's Bishop to *Queen's Knight's 3rd square*.

Be careful, as a general rule, in an open game, not to move your Queen's Pawn *one* square *before* you bring out the King's Bishop, as by so doing you leave him but the *King's 2nd square* on which to move, and there his position is defensive rather than attacking.

If strong in Pawns towards the conclusion of the game, endeavour to get rid of the enemy's Bishops, because they can impede the march of your Pawns more readily than either the Rooks or Knights.

When the other men are exchanged off, and you remain with a Bishop and two or three Pawns, it is often proper to keep your Pawns on squares of a different colour to those on which your Bishop travels, as he can then prevent the opposing King from approaching them. If, however, you have the worst of the game, it is mostly better then to keep them on the same colour as the Bishop, that he may defend them.

Supposing you have *Pawns only* at the end of a game, and the adversary has a Bishop, it is generally advisable to move the Pawns as soon as possible to squares of a different colour to the diagonals he moves on.

Do not indiscriminately exchange your Bishops for Knights, or *vice versâ*. Two Bishops at the finish of a game are stronger than two Knights, and one Knight generally more useful than a single Bishop.

CONCERNING THE KNIGHT.

The Knight is at once the most striking and most beautiful of all the Pieces. The singularity of its evolutions, by which it is enabled to overleap the other men and wind its way into the penetralia of the adverse ranks, and if attacked leap back again within the boundary of its own, has rendered it the favourite Piece of leading players in every country.

The assault of the Knight is more subtle and dangerous than that of any other Piece, because he attacks without putting himself *en prise*, and his attack can never be resisted by the interposition of another man.

At the commencement of a game, the best place for the King's Knight is at *K. B's 3rd sq.;* it there attacks your adversary's K's Pawn, if it has been moved two squares, and offers no impediment to the playing out your King's Bishop, and prevents the adversary from placing his Queen on your King Rook's 4th sq., where she would often be a source of restraint and danger to your King. Many persons prefer playing the K. Kt. to *K's 2nd* at the second move, from the mistaken notion that the K. B's P. should be moved before the Knight is played to Bishop's 3rd; this is an error, and generally leads to a very bad game.

When you have brought out your *Q. Kt.* to *B's* 3rd, it is frequently advisable, at a proper opportunity, to get him round by K's 2nd sq. to the *K. Kt.'s 3rd*, where he exercises a very important influence, by threatening, whenever the square is left unguarded, to post himself on *K. B's 5th.*

A Knight with three or four Pawns, at the end of a game, has an advantage over a Bishop with an equal number of Pawns, because he can leap from white to black, and thus attack the Pawns on either coloured squares, whereas the Bishop can attack them only when they move on squares of the colour of his diagonals. In similar circumstances, however, he is not so useful in defending as a Bishop or a Rook, since if forced to remove he ceases to defend, while the Rook or Bishop may retreat and still protect.

CONCERNING THE PAWNS.

Struck by the scope and power of the higher Pieces, young players commonly overlook the homely Pawns, or deem them scarcely worthy of regard, and are amazed to learn that the combinations of these simple elements are among the most refined and arduous studies of the science. Yet such is the fact, and without a thorough comprehension of their quiet but remarkable predominance in almost every circumstance of the game, it is impossible for any one to attain a high degree of excellence.

It is generally advantageous for your Pawns to occupy the middle of the board, because when there they greatly retard the movements of the opposing forces. The King's Pawn and Queen's Pawn, at their fourth squares, are well posted, but it is not easy to maintain them in that position, and if you are driven to advance one of them, the power of both is much diminished. It is well, therefore, not to be too eager to establish two Pawns abreast in the centre until you are fully able to sustain them there.

When you have two Pawns abreast, the King and Queen's, for instance, at their fourth squares, should the adversary attack one of them with a Pawn, it is occasionally better to advance the Pawn that is attacked another step, than to take the Pawn.

The Pawns, however, should seldom be far advanced, unless they can be properly sustained by the Pieces. Pawns at their fourt squares are therefore mostly more powerful than at their six h.

The King's Bishop's Pawn having no support but that of the King, is usually the point to which the first attack is directed, and more than ordinary care should be taken to preserve it. It is rarely good play to move the King's Bishop's Pawn to Bishop's 3rd early in the game.

As a general rule, it is not advisable to move King's Knight's Pawn or Queen's Knight's Pawn early in the game. The former played to K. Kt.'s 3rd square will often allow your adversary to play his Queen's Bishop to your King's Rook's 3rd square, a dangerous move when you have castled on King's side.

After castling, it is generally proper not to move the Knight's Pawn that is before your King, until you are obliged.

In a diagonal line of Pawns you should endeavour to preserve the Pawn at the head of them. Pawns, when united, have great strength ; but when separated, their power is sensibly lessened.

A passed Pawn is mostly serviceable when supported by another Pawn.

A doubled Pawn is not in all cases a disadvantage, especially if it is united with other Pawns. The worst kind of doubled Pawn is one on a Rook's file ; while the most advantageous is the King's Bishop's Pawn doubled on the King's file, because it strengthens your middle Pawns and opens a file for your King's Rook.

The Pawn being less important than a Piece, it is usually better to defend with it than with a Piece. For the same reason it is likewise better to protect a Pawn with a Pawn than with a Piece. No Piece can interpose between the attack of a Pawn, it can therefore frequently check the King with great advantage.

Be cautious generally of advancing the Pawns far on either side, till you see on which your opponent castles ; and remember, when approaching the end of a game, where you have Pawns, or even a Pawn, against a minor Piece, that *you may win*, but that your opponent, except in very rare cases, cannot, and that two Pawns in any situation can *protect themselves* against the adverse King.

We shall conclude the present Chapter with an attempt to define mathematically the action and powers of the chessmen, taken from "The Chess-Player's Chronicle," vol. ii. p. 383.

MATHEMATICAL DEFINITIONS OF THE MOVES AND POWERS OF THE CHESS-MEN.

The moves and attacking powers of the several Pieces are determined by line, direction, and limit.

The lines of movement and attack on the chess-board are threefold, viz.:—

1. The sides of squares.
2. The diagonals of squares.
3. The diagonals of parallelograms of six squares, i. e., 3 by 2.

The directions of movement and attack are fourfold—forward, backward, lateral, and diagonal.

The limits of movement and attack are threefold:—

1. When confined to adjacent squares.
2. Extending over the whole board.
3. Confined to the opposite squares of parallelograms, 3 by 2.

The lines of movement and attack are coincident for all the Pieces except the Pawns, whose line of motion is one square forward along the side, and their line of attack one square forward diagonally.

The KING's line of motion and attack is one square in every direction, forward and backward, lateral and diagonal.

The QUEEN's line of motion and attack are all along both the sides and the diagonals of squares in every direction, to the extremity of the board: thus combining those of the Rook and Bishop.

The ROOK's line of motion and attack is along the sides of squares in every direction, to the extremity of the board.

The BISHOP's line of motion and attack is along the diagonals of squares in every direction, to the extremity of the board.

The KNIGHT's line of motion and attack is along the diagonals of parallelograms, 3 by 2, in every direction, to the opposite square.

CHAPTER VII.

MAXIMS AND ADVICE FOR AN INEXPERIENCED PLAYER.

THERE is nothing that will improve you so much as playing with good players; never refuse, therefore, when any one offers you odds, to accept them: you cannot expect a proficient to feel much interest in playing with you upon *even* terms, and as you are sure to derive both amusement and instruction from him, it is but fair that he should name the conditions. It will soon happen that you yourself will be able to give odds to many amateurs whom you meet; when this is the case, avoid, if possible, playing them *even*, or you are likely to acquire an indolent, neglectful habit of play, which it will be very difficult to throw off. When you cannot induce such players to accept odds, propose to play for a small stake; and they will soon be glad to take all the advantages you can offer. Be always careful, before beginning a game, that the men on both sides are properly arranged.

Never permit your hand to hover over the board, or indeed to approach it, until you have completely made up your mind what Piece to move; a contrary habit begets a feeling of indecision that is fatal to success. Play invariably according to the laws of the game, neither taking back a move yourself, nor allowing your opponent to recall one. Do not exhibit impatience when your adversary is long in making his move. His slowness is a tacit compliment to your skill, and enables you to play with proportionate quickness, because while he is meditating on his next step you can take advantage of the time to consider what shall be your rejoinder; besides, it is absolutely necessary for every one desirous of excelling at chess to play slowly. Mr. Lewis aptly remarks, " It is no doubt desirable to play well and quickly, but I scarcely ever knew a very good player who was not also a slow one; and indeed, how can it well be otherwise? A fine player examines occasionally from five to twenty or more moves on each side: can this be done in a moment? It is easy enough to play quick against inferior play; but against equal and very good play one cannot play quick without losing."

Learn to play indifferently either with the white or black men. Do not play too many games at a sitting—and never suffer the loss of a game to occasion you much disquietude. Think of how many thousand games a Philidor must have lost before he attained his highest excellence; besides, the loss of one well-fought game with a fine practitioner will do more towards your improvement than the gain of ten light skirmishes with weaker players than yourself. Endeavour to play all your Pieces equally well. Many young players have a predilection for a particular Piece, as the Knight or the Queen, and lose both time and position in trying to prevent exchanges of their favourite. In opening your game, endeavour to bring your superior officers into action speedily, but avoid all premature attacks. Take care not to play a Piece to a square where it impedes the action of another, and beware of venturing an unsupported Piece in the adversary's game.

If subjected to a violent attack, you may often disconcert your opponent by compelling the exchange of two or three Pieces. When, however, you are about to exchange officers, you must calculate not only their ordinary value, but their peculiar worth in the situation in question; for example, a Rook is generally more valuable than a Knight or a Bishop; but it will happen, that by exchanging a Rook for one of the latter you may greatly improve your game.

It is mostly good play to exchange the Pieces off when you are superior in power, so that when you have the odds of a Piece given to you by a finished player, you should endeavour to exchange as often as you can consistently with safety.

When an exchange of two or more Pieces appears inevitable, look closely to see whether it is better for you to take first or to compel your opponent to do so. When one of the enemy is *completely* in your power, do not be too eager to make the capture—there may perhaps be a move of importance which you can make before you take him. Beware also of snatching hastily a proffered man, it may be only given as a bait to catch a more important advantage from you.

If at the end of a game you remain with Pawns against a Knight and find it difficult to evade his repeated checks, recollect that by placing your King on the same diagonal as the Knight, with but one intervening square between them, that you cannot again be checked under three moves.

When you have lost a game which has cost you great attention, it is a good practice to play it over afterwards in private, and endeavour to discover where the error occurred through which your opponent gained his first advantage. This custom will improve both your memory and your play.

Comparing small things with great ones, never forget that in chess, as in modern warfare, one of the most important stratagems is the art of gaining *time* upon the enemy. In this respect, as indeed in many others, the broad principles which are laid down by the highest military authorities as the basis of operations in a campaign are applicable to the management of your forces on the chess field. From the *Traité de Grand Tactique* of General Jomini, we gather that the art of war, as exemplified by Buonaparte, consisted in the proper application of three combinations—first, the art of disposing the lines of operation in the most advantageous manner; secondly, in a skilful concentration of the forces with the greatest possible rapidity upon the most important point of the enemy's line of operations; and thirdly, that of combining the simultaneous employment of this accumulated force upon the position against which it is directed. No player of great skill can fail to see that we have here the key to the basis of offensive movements in the battle of chess. Nor, to carry on the parallel, are the principles which direct defensive operations on the grander field in any degree less capable of application. "It is an acknowledged principle," says another able writer on the subject, "that the base of a plan of attack should form the best possible line of defence; and this fundamental rule cannot be violated with impunity, since nothing is more embarrassing than a sudden transition from offensive to defensive operations, when false measures or an unfortunate turn of affairs may have overset the plans of an assault."

With every allowance for the amazing disparity in the importance of the individuals and the magnitude of the objects at stake, there is an analogy observable, too, in the abilities requisite for the command of armies and the perfectly first-rate manœuvring of the mimic warriors of the chess-board. The commander of an army must possess not less a profound acquaintance with the general principles which regulate the conduct of a long and tedious campaign, than with those that are called into requisition in actual conflict. He must be able equally to arrange the plan of preliminary operations—to act at once and with decision in cases of the most pressing emergency, and on the occurrence of the most unforeseen events—to judge of the importance of a position and of the strength of an intrenchment—to discover from the slightest indications the designs of the enemy, while his own are impenetrable—and at the same time to preside with unshaken self-possession over the tumult of the battle-field, and the raging fury of an assault. The qualifications of a really finished chess-player, however less in degree, are somewhat similar in kind. To a perfect mastery of the difficult art of selecting and occupying, with the utmost rapidity, a "good position," he must add a thorough knowledge of all the complicated varieties of stratagems and snares which he is called upon alternately to invent and to defeat. He must, in short, to some extent, display the same energies on the smaller scale which are so indispensable on the grander one.

Marshal Saxe, a great general, (and an enthusiastic lover of chess by the way) in his summary of the attributes required in a commander-in-chief, gives him genius, and courage, and health. The first of these qualities is unquestionably called for in the highest order of chess skill; and if by courage is implied, not so much mere physical bravery as entire self-possession, promptitude of decision, and undaunted perseverance; and by health is meant the preservation of a sound mind, to which a sound body is so important an adjunct, then indeed both courage and health will be found to exercise a powerful influence upon the success of the chess-player, as well as upon the fortunes of a Marlborough or a Wellington.

These comparisons might be extended to more minute particulars, but the general analogy observable may suffice to show you that great mental activity is called into requisition, and much attention and perseverance are necessary for the attainment of the highest excellence, even in the strategy of chess-playing.

CHAPTER VIII.

ON THE SEVERAL OPENINGS OR BEGINNINGS OF GAMES.

BEFORE proceeding to the consideration of the various methods of commencing the game, it is advisable for you to recur to the preceding Chapters, which treat of the arrangement of the men—the moves of the men—their relative powers—the technical terms in use among players—and the laws of the game. When you have familiarized yourself with these, it will be time for you to direct your attention to that most important feature in the game of chess—the art of opening the game.

There are several modes of beginning the game, but the following are the principal :—

1st. Each player begins by moving his *King's Pawn tc King's 4th square*, and the first player then moves *King's Knight* to *King's Bishop's 3rd square*. This is called the *King's Knight's opening*.

2nd. Each player commences by moving his *King's Pawn to King's 4th square*, and then he who has the first move plays *King's Bishop to Queen's Bishop's 4th square*. This is known as the *King's Bishop's opening*.

3rd. Each player opens with *King's Pawn to King's 4th square*, and the first plays *Queen's Bishop's Pawn to Bishop's 3rd square*. This is termed the *Queen's Bishop's Pawn's opening*.

4th. Each player begins with *King's Pawn to King's 4th square*, and the first follows with *King's Bishop's Pawn to Bishop's 4th square*. This is called the *King's gambit*.

Of these four openings on *the King's side* there are many modifications, of which each has its appropriate appellation; there are also several openings began on the Queen's side, all of which will be duly treated of in the following pages; but the four above-named are those most generally practised, and with them you should be thoroughly conversant before advancing further.

CHAPTER IX.

PRELIMINARY GAME.

PREPARATORY to the investigation of the several openings treated of in the following Chapters, it may not be uninstructive to give a short game which shall exhibit the application of some technical phrases in use at chess, and at the same time show a few of the most prominent errors into which an inexperienced player is likely to fall.

In this game, as in all the analyses which follow, the reader will be supposed to play the White Pieces and to have the first move, although, as it has been before remarked, it is advisable for you to accustom yourself to play with either Black or White, for which purpose it is well to practise the attack, first with the White and then with the Black Pieces.

WHITE.
BLACK.
1. K's P. to K's 4th.*   1. K's P. to K's 4th.

When the men are first arranged in battle order, it is seen that the only Pieces which have the power of moving are the Knights, and that to liberate the others it is indispensably necessary to move a Pawn. Now, as the King's Pawn, on being moved, gives freedom both to the Queen and to the King's Bishop, it is more frequently played at the beginning of the game than any other. You will remember, in speaking of the Pawns it was shown that on certain conditions they have the privilege of going either one or two steps when they are first moved.

2. K's B. to Q. B's 4th.   2. K's B. to Q. B's 4th.

Thus far the game illustrative of the *King's Bishop's* opening is correctly began. Each party plays his King's Bishop thus, because it attacks the most vulnerable point of the adverse position, viz., the *King's Bishop's Pawn*.

3. Q. B's Pawn to B's 3rd.   3. Q's Knight to B's 3rd.

In playing this Pawn your object is afterwards to play Queen's Pawn to Queen's 4th square, and thus establish your Pawns in the centre; but Black foresees the intention and thinks to prevent its execution by bringing another Piece to bear upon the square.

4. Q's Pawn to Q's 4th.   4. Pawn takes Q's Pawn.
5. Q. B's Pawn takes Pawn.   5. K's B. takes Pawn.

Here you have played without due consideration. Black's third move of Queen's Knight to Bishop's 3rd square was a bad one, and afforded you an opportunity of gaining a striking advantage, but omitting this, you have enabled him to gain a

---

* This is a slight departure from the notation commonly adopted by modern chess authors in England, who describe the moves of the Pawns by the number of steps they make, as *King's Pawn two squares, Queen's Bishop's Pawn one square;* a method, however, which is found embarrassing in the case of two Pawns on the same file. The present mode is not liable to this objection, and appears to be equally expressive and more consistent and uniform with the description of the movements of the Pieces.

valuable Pawn for nothing. Observe, now, your reply to his third move was good enough, (4. Queen's Pawn to Queen's 4th square), but when he took your Pawn with his, instead of taking again, you ought to have taken his *King's Bishop's Pawn* with your Bishop, giving check: the game would then most probably have gone on thus:—

5. *K's B. takes K. B's Pawn* (ch.)	5. *K. takes Bishop.*
6. *Queen to K. R's 5th (check).*	6. *K. to his B's square.*
7. *Queen takes K's Bishop* (check).	

In this variation, you see Black has lost his King's Bishop's Pawn, and what is worse, *has lost his privilege of castling*, by being forced to move his King; and although for a moment he had gained a Bishop for a Pawn, it was quite clear that he must lose a Bishop in return by the check of the adverse Queen at King's Rook's 5th square. It is true that he need not have taken the Bishop, but still his King must have moved, and White could then have taken the King's Knight with his Bishop, having always the better position.

But now to proceed with the actual game:—

6. K's Knight to K. B's 3rd.	6. Queen to K. B's 3rd.

Bringing out the Knight is good play; you not only threaten to win his Bishop, but you afford yourself an opportunity of castling whenever it may be needful. Black would have played better in retiring the Bishop from the attack to Queen's Knight's 3rd square than in supporting it with the Queen.

7. Knight takes Bishop.	7. Queen takes Knight.

Both parties played well in their last moves. You rightly took off the Bishop, because supported by the Queen he menaced your Queen's Knight's Pawn, and Black properly retook with his Queen instead of the Knight, because having a Pawn ahead, it was his interest to exchange off the Queens.

8. Q's Knight to Q's 2nd.	8. K's Knight to B's 3rd.

You played correctly here in not exchanging Queens, and also in protecting your Bishop and your King's Pawn, both of which were attacked by the adverse Queen; but all this might have been done without impeding the movements of any of your Pieces, by simply playing Queen to King's 2nd sq.; as it is, the Knight entirely shuts your Queen's Bishop from

the field.   Black properly brings another Piece to the attack
of your King's Pawn :—

  9. K. B's Pawn to B's 3rd.   9. Q's Knight to King's 4th.

In protecting the King's Pawn with your K. Bishop's Pawn,
you are guilty of a very common error among young players;
as you improve, you will find that it is rarely good play to
move the K. Bishop's Pawn to the third square—in the present instance, for example, you have deprived yourself of the
power of castling, at least for some time, since the adverse
Queen now commands the very square upon which your King,
in castling on his own side, has to move.   Black's last move is
much more sensible.   He again attacks your Bishop, and by
the same move brings his Q's Knight into co-operation with
the King's, on the weak point of your position :—

  10. Pawn to Q. Kt.'s 3rd.   10. Q. takes Queen's Rook.

This is a serious blunder indeed.   In your anxiety to save the
threatened Bishop, which you feared to withdraw to Q. Kt.'s
3rd sq., on account of the adverse Knight's giving check at
your Queen's 3rd square, you have actually left your Q's
Rook *en prise !*   Black takes it, of course, and having gained
such an important advantage, ought to win easily.

  11. Castles, (*i. e.*, plays K. to   11. Q's Kt. takes Bishop.
    his Kt.'s sq., and Rook
    to K. B.'s sq.)
  12. Kt. takes Kt.   12. Castles.
  13. Q. to her 2nd.   13. Q. B's Pawn to B's 4th.

Your last move is very subtle; finding the mistake that Black
had committed in not retreating his Queen directly after winning the Rook, you determine, if possible, to prevent her
escape by gaining command of all the squares she can move
to.   Seeing the danger, Black throws forward this Pawn to
enable him, if possible, to bring the Queen off, by playing her
to her 5th sq., giving check.

  14. Bishop to Q. Kt.'s 2nd.   14. Q. takes Q. R's Pawn.

This move of the Bishop is well timed; it does not, to be
sure, prevent the Queen from escaping for a move or two, but
it gives you an attack, and very great command of the field.

  15. Q. to K. Kt.'s 5th.   15. Knight to K.'s sq.

Very well played on both sides.   By playing the Queen to K.
Kt.'s 5th, you threatened to win his Knight by at once taking

it with your Bishop, which he could not retake without opening check on his King. Instead of so moving, you might
have played the Knight to Q. Rook's 5th sq., in which case,
by afterwards moving the Rook to Q. Rook's square, it would
have been impossible for his Queen to get away.

| 16. Q. to King's 3rd. | 16. K. R's Pawn to R's 3rd. |

You prudently retreated your Queen to guard her Knight's
Pawn, which it was important to save, on account of its protection to the Knight. Black played the King R's Pawn to
prevent your Queen returning to the same post of attack.

| 17. K. R's P. to R's 3rd. | 17. K. to his R's sq. |

Here are two instances of what is called "lost time" at chess,
neither move serving in the slightest degree to advance the
game of the player. That you should have overlooked the
opportunity of gaining the adverse Queen was to be expected.
Similar advantages present themselves in every game between
young players, and are unobserved.

| 18. K. B's Pawn to B's 4th. | 18. Q. Kt.'s Pawn to Kt.'s 3rd. |

Again you have failed to see a most important move; you
might have taken the K. Rook's Pawn with your Queen,
giving check safely, because Black could not take your Queen
without being in check with your Bishop. All this time, too,
your opponent omits to see the jeopardy his Queen is in, and
that as far as practical assistance to his other Pieces is con-
cerned, she might as well be off the board.

| 19. K. Kt.'s Pawn to Kt.'s 4th. | 19. Q. Kt.'s Pawn to Q. Kt.'s 4th. |

Your last move is far from good. By thus attacking your
Knight, Black threatens to win a Piece, because upon playing
away the Knight you must leave the Bishop unprotected.

| 20. Pawn to K. Kt.'s 5th. | 20. Pawn takes Knight. |

Although your Knight was thus attacked, it might have been
saved very easily. In the first place, by your taking the adversary's Q. B's Pawn, threatening to take his King's Rook, on
his removing which, or interposing the Q's Pawn, you could
have taken the Pawn which attacked your Knight; or, in the
second place, by moving your Queen to her 2nd square. In
the latter case, if Black ventured to take the Knight, you
would have won his Queen by taking the K. Kt.'s Pawn with
your Bishop, giving check, and thus exposing his Queen to

yours. Black would have been obliged to parry the check,
either by taking the Bishop or removing his King, and you
would then have taken his Queen. This position is very
instructive, and merits attentive examination.

21. B. to Q. B's 3rd.	21. Pawn takes Q. Kt.'s Pawn.
22. Pawn to K. R's 4th.	22. Pawn to Q. Kt.'s 7th.

In such a position, the advance of your King's flank Pawns is
a process too dilatory to be very effective.

23. Pawn to K. B's 5th.	23. Pawn to Q. Kt.'s 8th, becoming a Queen.

Now the fault of your tortoise-like movements with the Pawns
becomes fatally evident. Black has been enabled to make a
second Queen, and has an overwhelming force at command.

24. Rook takes Queen.	24. Queen takes Rook (check).

You had no better move than to take the newly-elected Queen,
for two Queens must have proved irresistible.

25. King to his Kt.'s 2nd.	25. Kt. to Queen's 3rd.
26. K. Kt.'s Pawn to Kt.'s 6th.	26. P. takes Pawn.
27. P. takes Pawn.	27. Bishop to Q. Kt.'s 2nd.

Here you have given another remarkable instance of lost
opportunity. At your last move you might have redeemed
all former disasters by checkmating your opponent in two
moves. Endeavour to find out how this was to be accomplished.

28. K. R's Pawn to R's 5th.	28. Knight takes King's Pawn.
29. Bishop to King's 5th.	29. Kt. to K. Kt.'s 4th (discovering check).

Up to Black's last move you had still the opportunity of
winning the game before mentioned.

30. King to Kt.'s 3rd.	30. K's Rook to B's 6th (ch.)
31. King to R's 4th.	31. Q. to K. Bishop's 4th.

At this point you were utterly at the mercy of your antagonist, but fortunately he wanted the skill to avail himself properly of his vast superiority in force and position, or he might
have won the game in half a dozen different ways.

32. Q. takes Rook.	32. Q. takes Queen.
33. B. takes K. Kt.'s Pawn (ch.)	33. King takes Bishop.

This was your last chance, and its success should serve to

convince you that in the most apparently hopeless situations of the game there is often a latent resource, if we will only have the patience to search it out. By taking the Bishop, Black has left your King, *who is not in check*, no move without going into check, and as you have neither Piece nor Pawn besides to play, you are *stalemated*, and the game is DRAWN.

If thoroughly acquainted with the information contained in the preceding Chapters, you may now proceed to the consideration of the openings; before you do this, however, it is necessary to apprise you that without a great abridgment of the notation adopted in the foregoing game, it would be impossible to compress within the limits of this work one-third of the variations which are required to be given. The following abbreviations will therefore be used throughout the remainder of our HANDBOOK :—

K.	for King.
Q.	Queen.
R.	Rook.
B.	Bishop.
Kt.	Knight.
P.	Pawn.
sq.	square.
adv.	adversary's.
ch.	check or checking.
dis. ch.	discovering check.

The word "square" is only used to distinguish the first row of squares on which the superior Pieces stand at the commencement—thus, we say, Kt. to K's 2nd, and omit the word square; but if the Kt. were played to K's *first* square or R's *first* square, the move would be described not as Kt. to K's or R's first square, but "Kt. to K's or R's square."

END OF BOOK I.

SYNOPSIS OF BOOK II.

The following are the specific appellations given to the most important varieties of attack and defence which are included under the generic denomination of the KING'S KNIGHT'S OPENING.

THE DAMIANO GAMBIT :—

1. $\dfrac{\text{P. to K's 4th.}}{\text{P. to K's 4th.}}$ 2. $\dfrac{\text{K. Kt. to B's 3rd.}}{\text{P. to K. B's 3rd.}}$

PHILIDOR'S DEFENCE :—

1. $\dfrac{\text{P. to K's 4th.}}{\text{P. to K's 4th.}}$ 2. $\dfrac{\text{K. Kt. to B's 3rd.}}{\text{P. to Q's 3rd.}}$

PETROFF'S DEFENCE :—

1. $\dfrac{\text{P. to K's 4th.}}{\text{P. to K's 4th.}}$ 2. $\dfrac{\text{K. Kt. to B's 3rd.}}{\text{K. Kt. to B's 3rd.}}$

THE COUNTER GAMBIT IN THE KNIGHT'S OPENING :—

1. $\dfrac{\text{P. to K's 4th.}}{\text{P. to K's 4th.}}$ 2. $\dfrac{\text{K. Kt. to B's 3rd.}}{\text{P. to K. B's 4th.}}$

THE GUIOCO PIANO :—

1. $\dfrac{\text{P. to K's 4th.}}{\text{P. to K's 4th.}}$ 2. $\dfrac{\text{K. Kt. to B's 3rd.}}{\text{Q. Kt. to B's 3rd.}}$ 3. $\dfrac{\text{K. B. to Q. B's 4th.}}{\text{K. B. to Q. B's 4th.}}$

CAPTAIN EVANS' GAMBIT :—

1. $\dfrac{\text{P. to K's 4th.}}{\text{P. to K's 4th.}}$ 2. $\dfrac{\text{K. Kt. to B's 3rd.}}{\text{Q. Kt. to B's 3rd.}}$ 3. $\dfrac{\text{K. B. to Q. B's 4th.}}{\text{K. B. to Q. B's 4th.}}$

4. $\dfrac{}{\text{P. to Q. Kt.'s 4th.}}$

THE TWO KNIGHTS' DEFENCE :—

1. $\dfrac{\text{P. to K's 4th.}}{\text{P. to K's 4th.}}$ 2. $\dfrac{\text{K. Kt. to B's 3rd.}}{\text{Q. Kt. to B's 3rd.}}$ 3. $\dfrac{\text{K. B. to Q. B's 4th.}}{\text{K. Kt. to B's 3rd.}}$

THE KNIGHT'S GAME OF RUY LOPEZ :—

1. $\dfrac{\text{P. to K's 4th.}}{\text{P. to K's 4th.}}$ 2. $\dfrac{\text{K. Kt. to B's 3rd.}}{\text{Q. Kt. to B's 3rd.}}$ 3. $\dfrac{\text{K. B. to Q. Kt.'s 5th.}}{}$

THE QUEEN'S PAWN'S GAME, OR SCOTCH GAMBIT :—

1. $\dfrac{\text{P. to K's 4th.}}{\text{P. to K's 4th.}}$ 2. $\dfrac{\text{K. Kt. to B's 3rd.}}{\text{Q. Kt. to B's 3rd.}}$ 3. $\dfrac{\text{P. to Q's 4th.}}{}$

AND

THE QUEEN'S BISHOP'S PAWN'S GAME IN THE KNIGHT'S OPENING :—

1. $\dfrac{\text{P. to K's 4th.}}{\text{P. to K's 4th.}}$ 2. $\dfrac{\text{K. Kt. to B's 3rd.}}{\text{Q. Kt. to B's 3rd.}}$ 3. P. to Q. B's 3rd.

BOOK II.

The King's Knight's Opening.

CHAPTER I.

WHITE.	BLACK.
1. P. to K's 4th.	1. P. to K's 4th.
2. K's Kt. to B's 3rd.	

Your second move gives the name to this opening, which is one of the most popular and instructive of all the various methods of commencing the game. The Kt., it will be observed, at once attacks the adverse Pawn, and the defence, recommended by the best authors and the leading players of Europe, is for Black to reply 2. Q's Kt. to B's 3rd. He has, however, many other ways of playing, and as the examination of these comparatively simple variations will serve to prepare you for the more complex and elaborate combinations of the best defences, it will be advisable to consider them previously. In the first place, then, Black may sustain his Pawn by playing—

1. P. to K. B's 3rd.
2. K's B. to Q's 3rd.
3. Q. to K. B's 3rd.
4. P. to Q's 3rd.

or, in the second place, he may leave it unprotected, and play—

5. K's Kt. to B's 3rd.
6. K's B. to Q. B's 4th.
7. P. to K. B's 4th.
8. P. to Q's 4th.

He has thus eight different modes of play at his command, besides the move of Q's Kt. to B's 3rd, in answer to your second move of K's Kt. to B's 3rd. Each of these will form the subject of a separate game.

GAME THE FIRST.

WHITE.	BLACK.
1. P. to K's 4th.	1. P. to K's 4th.
2. K's Kt. to B's 3rd.	2. P. to K. B's 3rd.*
3. Kt. takes K's P.	3. P. takes Kt.

After this capture of the Knight, Black's game is hopeless.
His best move is 3. Q. to K's 2nd, as will be shown hereafter.

| 4. Q. to K. R's 5th (ch.) | 4. P. to K. Kt.'s 3rd. |

This is his best move; if instead of it he play K. to his 2nd,
you obtain a speedy victory; thus,—

	4. K. to his 2nd.
5. Q. takes K's P. (ch.)	5. K. to B's 2nd.
6. B. to Q. B's 4th (ch.)	6. P. to Q's 4th (best)
7. B. takes Q's P. (ch.)	7. K. to Kt.'s 3rd.
8. P. to K. R's 4th.	8. K's B. to Q's 3rd.
9. P. to K. R's 5th (ch.)	9. K. to R's 3rd.
10. P. to Q's 4th (dis. ch.)	10. P. to K. Kt.'s 4th.
11. P. takes P. (in passing, dis. ch.)	11. K. takes P

And you give mate in two moves.

5. Q. takes K's P. (ch.)	5. Q. to K's 2nd.
6. Q. takes R.	6. K's Kt. to B's 3rd.

He might also play—

	6. Q. takes P. (ch.)
7. K. to Q's sq. (best)	7. P. to Q's 4th.
8. B. to Q. Kt.'s 5th (ch.)†	8. K. to Q's sq. (best)
9. R. to K's sq.	9. Q's B. to Kt.'s 5th (ch.)
10. P. to K. B's 3rd.	

And you win easily.

7. P. to Q's 4th (best)	7. Q. takes P. (ch.)
8. Q's B. to K's 3rd.	8. Q. takes Q. B's P.

He had better have returned with his Q. to K's 2nd again.

9. Q. takes Kt.	9. Q. takes Q. Kt.'s P.
10. K's B. to Q. B's 4th.	10. K's B. to Q. Kt.'s 5th (ch.)

Here, too, it would have been prudent for him to check with
the Q., and then bring her to the succour of the King.

* This move occurs in the old work of Damiano, who gives some ingenious variations on it. Lopez, and later authors, have hence entitled it
" Damiano's Gambit."

† Better than taking the Kt. with Q., on account of Black's check,
with Q's B. at K. Kt.'s 5th, by which he would draw the game.

11. Q's Kt. to Q's 2nd.	11. Q. takes R. (ch.)
12. K. to his 2nd.	12. Q. takes K's R.,

and you give mate in two moves.

The foregoing variations are dependent on Black's taking the Kt., which is very bad play. His proper move, under the circumstances, is 3. Q. to K's 2nd, as in the following example:—

WHITE.	BLACK.
1. P. to K's 4th.	1. P. to K's 4th.
2. K's Kt. to B's 3rd.	2. P. to K. B's 3rd.
3. K's Kt. takes P.	3. Q. to K's 2nd.
4. K's Kt. to B's 3rd (best)	4. P. to Q's 4th.

It would be bad play to check with your Q. at K. R's 5th after his move of 3. Q. to K's 2nd, because he would interpose the K. Kt.'s P., and if you took this Pawn with your Knight, he might first take K's P. (ch.), with his Queen, and then capture your Knight with her.

5. P. to Q's 3rd.	5. P. takes K's P.
6. P. takes P.	6. Q. takes P. (ch.)
7. B. to K's 2nd.	7. Q's B. to K. B's 4th.
8. Kt. to Q's 4th.	8. Q's Kt. to B's 3rd.
9. Kt. takes B.	9. Q. takes Kt.
10. Castles.	10. B. to Q's 3rd.
11. B. to Q's 3rd.	

You have an excellent position.

GAME THE SECOND.

WHITE.	BLACK.
1. P. to K's 4th.	1. P. to K's 4th.
2. K's Kt. to B's 3rd.	2. K's B. to Q's 3rd.

This mode of defending the Pawn is highly objectionable, because it imprisons both the Queen's Pawn and Bishop.

3. B. to Q. B's 4th.	3. K's Kt. to B's 3rd.
4. P. to Q's 4th.	4. Q's Kt to B's 3rd.

If he take the K's P. with the Kt., you must win a Piece; for example,—

	4. Kt. takes K's P.
5. P. takes P.	5. B. to Q. B's 4th.
5. Q. to her 5th.	6. B. takes K. B's P. (ch.)

7. K. to his 2nd.	7. Castles.
8. Q. takes Kt.	8. B. to Q. Kt.'s 3rd.
9. Kt. to K. Kt.'s 5th,	

Followed by R. to B's sq., and the attack must be irresistible.

5. P. takes K's P.	5. B. takes P.

If instead of this he take the P. with Kt., your advantage is more speedy and decided. (*e. g.*)

	5. Kt. takes P.
6. Kt. takes Kt.	6. B. takes Kt.
7. P. to K. B's 4th.	7. B. to Q's 3rd.
8. P. to K's 5th.	8. Q. to K's 2nd.
9. Q. to K's 2nd.	

And you gain a Piece.

6. K's Kt. to his 5th.	6. Castles.
7. P. to K. B's 4th.	7. B. to Q's 5th.
8. P. to K's 5th.	8. Q. to K's 2nd.

If in place of 8. Q. to K's 2nd, he retire the Kt., you win by playing the Q. to K. R's 5th.

9. Q. to K's 2nd.	9. K's Kt. to K's sq.
10. B. to Q's 5th.	10. K's B. to Q. Kt.'s 3rd.

By moving the B. to Q's 5th, you threatened to take off the Kt., and then to play Q. to K's 4th, offering mate or to win the Bishop.

11. Q's Kt. to B's 3rd.	11. P. to K. R's 3rd.

In reply, you may now play P. to K. R's 4th, having a capital game. If instead of 11. P. to R's 3rd, he play 11. Q's Kt. to Q's 5th, you move 12. Q. to her 3rd, then B. to Q's 2nd, and finally castle on the Q's side. If, however, in lieu of that move he play 11. B. to Q. R's 4th, you can move 12. B. to Q's 2nd, and presently castle on the Q's side; and lastly, if he play 11. K. to R's sq., then you take your Queen to K. R's 5th, and he cannot save the game.

GAME THE THIRD.

WHITE.	BLACK.
1. P. to K's 4th.	1. P. to K's 4th.
2. K's Kt. to B's 3rd.	2. Q. to K. B's 3rd.

It is seldom good to bring the Q. into play early in the game, unless for some decisive blow, because she is so easily assailable by the opponent's minor Pieces, and in attacking her he brings his forces into action.

3. K's B. to Q. B's 4th.   3. Q. to K. Kt.'s 3rd.

Black now attacks two undefended Pawns, but he can take neither without ruinous loss to him; for suppose on your playing P. to Q's 3rd, to protect the K's P., he ventures to take the K. Kt.'s P., you immediately take the K. B's P. with your Bishop (ch.). If he then take the Bishop with his King, you attack his Queen with your Rook, and on her retiring to R's 6th, you win her by K's Kt. to his 5th (ch.). On the other hand, you can leave the King's Pawn, and castle safely.

4. Castles.   4. Q. takes K's P
5. K's B. takes B's P. (ch.)   5. K. to Q's sq.

It is quite obvious that he would lose his Queen by the check of the Knight, if he took the Bishop, and if, instead of moving the K. to Q's sq., he places him on K's 2nd, the following moves will show that you win without much difficulty:—

	5. K. to his 2nd.
6. R. to K's sq.	6. Q. to K. B's 5th.
7. R. takes P. (ch.)	7. K. takes B.*
8. P. to Q's 4th.	8. Q. to K. B's 3rd.
9. Kt. to his 5th (ch.)	9. K. to Kt.'s 3rd.
10. Q. to her 3rd (ch.)	10. K. to R's 4th.
11. P. to K. Kt.'s 4th (ch.)	

And checkmate next move.

6. Kt. takes K's P.   6. K's Kt. to B's 3rd.

If he take the Kt., you will play R. to K's sq., compelling him either to take it with his Q. or be mated.

7. K's R. to K's sq.   7. Q. to K. B's 4th.
8. K's B. to K. Kt.'s 6th.   8. Q. to K's 3rd.
9. Kt. to B's 7th (ch.), and gains the Queen.

At this opening, when Black, as above, plays Q. to K. B's 3rd, for his second move, you may also get a good game by playing for your third move 3. Q's Kt. to B's 3rd, instead of 3. K's B. to Q. B's 4th.

* if 7. K. to B's 3rd, you reply with P. to Q's 4th, attacking the Q. with your Q's B., and then with P. to R's 3rd, winning her.

GAME THE FOURTH.

PHILIDOR'S DEFENCE.

WHITE.	BLACK.
1. P. to K's 4th.	1. P. to K's 4th.
2. K. Kt. to B's 3rd.	2. P. to Q's 3rd. *

This way of defending the K's P. is less objectionable than any of the three preceding ones, but it is not so good as 2. Q. Kt. to B's 3rd.

3. P. to Q's 4th.	3. P. to K. B's 4th.

Your third move is the best you can make at this point, although you may also play 3. K. B. to Q. B's 4th without disadvantage. (*e. g.*)

---

* Damiano's defence to the K. Kt.'s opening was 2. Q. Kt. to B's 3rd, the very move adopted by the best players and recommended by the chief authors of the present day. His successor, Ruy Lopez, rejected this defence, considering that White by playing 3. K's B. to Q. Kt.'s 5th obtained an advantage; and he proposed instead for Black's second move 2. P. to Q's 3rd. As this move, however, consigns the K's Bishop to a long inaction, later analyses have in turn discarded the P. to Q's 3rd, and returned again to the move of Damiano. In the year 1749 Philidor published his "Analyse du Jeu des Echecs;" and he there maintains, that 2. P. to Q's 3rd is not only a good move, but that it gives the second player so strong a game as to render unadvisable White's second move of K's Kt. to B's 3rd. Philidor's opinion is grounded upon the belief that Black is enabled to establish his Pawns in the centre. His third game involves this particular defence, but in the subsequent editions of his "Analyse, &c.," 1777 and 1790, he observes himself that this third game is faulty. It is in reference to this game, in a note to which Philidor takes occasion to censure the playing 2. K's Kt. to B's 3rd by the first player, that the celebrated Modenese says: "the bold assertion that it is bad at the second move to play K's Kt. to B's 3rd square, always surprised me, seeing that the author attempts to prove this by a worse move on the part of the second player, who is made to defend the King's Pawn with the Queen's Pawn, instead of with the Q's Kt., as the most approved writers recommend. I call this move worse, inasmuch as it confines the King's Bishop, which cannot speedily be placed in any attacking position, which it would be at Q's B's 4th sq.; and because it often happens that you are obliged to advance the Q's Pawn two squares, for which object you must here employ two moves, when one only might have sufficed. And, lastly, because by defending with the Q's Kt. at B's 3rd sq. you bring a Piece into play, in a situation to act much better than it could be expected to do at its own square. Hence it is seen in practice, that he who defends at

3. K's B. to Q. B's 4th.	3. P. to Q. B's 3rd. *
4. P. to Q's 4th (best)	4. P. to Q's 4th.
5. P. takes Q's P.	5. P. to K's 5th.
6. Kt. to K's 5th.	6. P. takes P.
7. B. to Q. Kt.'s 5th (ch.)	7. B. to Q's 2nd.
8. Kt. takes B.	8. Kt. takes Kt.

The game is equal : and hence it will presently be apparent that your 3rd move of P. to Q's 4th is better for you than 3. K. B. to Q. B's 4th.

4. Q's P. takes P.	4. K. B's P. takes P.
5. Kt. to K. Kt.'s 5th.	5. P. to Q's 4th.
6. P. to K's 6th.	6. Kt. to K. R's 3rd.
7. P. to K. B's 3rd.	7. Q. Kt. to B's 3rd.

Your move of 7. P. to K. B's 3rd is invented by Von H. der Laza. Instead of it, Lewis recommends you to check with your Q. at K. R's 5th, then retreat the Queen to K. R's 3rd, and afterwards play 9. P. to Q. B's 4th. H. der Laza says, however, that Black may in that case, after 7. P. to K. Kt.'s 3rd and 8. Q. to K. B's 3rd, move, 9. P. to Q's 5th, and equalize the positions.

If Black, in answer to your 7th move, play 7. K's P. takes P., or 7. K's B. to K's 2nd, the following moves will show that you gain an advantage.

In the first place,

	7. K's P. takes B's P.
8. Q. takes B's P.	8. R. to K. Kt.'s sq.
9. Q's Kt. to B's 3rd (best)	9. P. to Q. B's 3rd.
10. Q. to K. B's 7th (ch.)	10. Kt. takes Q.
11. P. takes Kt. (ch.)	

Taking the R., and becoming a Q. next move.

In the second place,

	7. K's B. to K's 2nd.
8. P. takes K's P.	8. B. takes Kt.
9. Q. to R's 5th (ch.)	9. P. to K. Kt.'s 3rd.

---

the second move his King's Pawn with Q's Pawn has at least a weak and constrained game for a long time. For reasons akin to these, the same move, when recommended by Lopez, was condemned by the celebrated academies of chess at Naples, who adopted that of the Q's Kt.; and I am satisfied in my Treatise to follow in their steps.''

* Far better than 3. P. to K. B's 4th, as advised by Philidor. For the result of which, see the Variation of Game the Seventh, at page 97.

10. Q. takes B.	10. Q. takes Q.
11. B. takes Q.	11. Kt. is moved.
12. P. takes Q's P.	

And you ought to win.

8. B. to Q. Kt.'s 5th.	8. Q. to her 3rd.
9. Q. Kt. to B's 3rd.	9. Q. B. takes K's P.

If you play 9. B. P. takes P., the game becomes very critical for both, and you do not obtain any marked superiority.

10. K. Kt. takes B.	10. Q. takes Kt.

You might also play 10. Q's Kt. takes K's P. and still obtain the better position. For example :—

10. Q's Kt. takes K's P.	10. Q. to K's 4th (best)
11. P. to K. B's 4th.	11. Q. to K. B's 4th.
12. Q's Kt. to K. Kt.'s 3rd.	12. Q. to K. Kt.'s 3rd.
13. Q. to K's 2nd.	13. K. to Q's 2nd.
14. B. takes Kt. (ch.)	14. P. takes B.

And you have the superior situation.

11. Q. takes Q's P.	11. Q. takes Q.
12. Kt. takes Q.	12. Castles.
13. P. takes K's P.	

You have a Pawn more than Black, and a better position.

VARIATION OF THIS ATTACK,

Commencing at White's 7th move.

BLACK.

WHITE.

In this position, instead of playing 7. P. to K. B's 3rd, as advised by H. der Laza, or Q. to K. R's 5th, by Lewis and others, you may move 7. Q. Kt. to B's 3rd, which leads to many brilliant and difficult strokes of play.

WHITE.	BLACK.
7. Q's Kt. to B's 3rd.	7. P. to Q. B's 3rd.

This is considered by all the leading writers Black's best move. If he play instead 7. K. B. to Q. Kt.'s 5th, the result is clearly in your favour. *(e. g.)*

	7. K's B. to Q. Kt.'s 5th.
8. Q. to K. R's 5th (ch.)	8. K. to B's sq.
9. Kt. to K. B's 7th.	9. Q. to K's sq.
10. Q. takes Q's P.	10. Kt. takes Kt.
11. P. takes Kt.	11. Q. to Q. B's 3rd.
12. K's B. to Q. B's 4th,	

And you retain the P. and have a fine position.

In reply to his seventh move two methods of play are at your command.

In the first place,

8. K. Kt. takes K. R's P.	8. Q. B. takes K's P. (best)

If he take the Kt. you check with your Q. at K. R's 5th, and win easily.

9. Kt. takes K's B.	9. K. takes Kt.
10. Q. Kt. takes K's P.	10. Kt. to K. Kt.'s 5th.
11. K. Kt. to K. Kt.'s 5th, with the better game.	

In the second place,

8. K's Kt. takes K's P.	8. P. takes Kt.

The sacrifice of the Kt. here forms the subject of some of the very interesting games which were published a few years back under the title of "A Selection of Games actually played by Philidor and his contemporaries, &c., by G. Walker."

9. Q. to K. R's 5th (ch.)	9. P. to K. Kt.'s 3rd.
10. Q. to K's 5th.	10. K. R. to Kt.'s sq.
11. B. takes K's Kt.	11. B. takes B.
12. Q. R. to Q's sq.	12. Q. to K's 2nd.

The move now given to White by Bilguer, Von H. der Laza, and other leading authors, and which is also played in the games above mentioned, is 13. K. B. to Q. B's 4th, whereupon Black replies with 13. K. B. to Kt.'s 2nd, then takes the Kt. (ch.), and gets a decided advantage. There is another move, however, for you, 13. Kt. takes K's P., the value of which appears to have been never fairly tested, although the variations springing from it give rise to some beautiful play.

13. Kt. takes K's P.	13. Q's B. takes P.

This appears to be his best move; 13. K's B. to Kt.'s 2nd is obviously bad, on account of 14. Kt. to Q's 6th (ch.), and when the King moves to B's sq., 15. Q. to K. B's 4th (ch.). If, instead of taking Pawn with the Bishop, he play 13. Q. takes P., the following moves show clearly that the game is in your favour.

	13. Q. takes K's P.
14. Q. to her 4th.	14. Q. to K's 2nd.

(If he play 14. B. to K. Kt.'s 2nd, you check at Q. B's 7th, and then, whether he interpose the Kt. or Q. or B., by playing B. to Q. B's 4th, you win; if 14. R. to B's sq., you can attack his Q. with the Bishop, and have an irresistible game.)

15. B. to K's 2nd.

Castling afterwards, and with his King so exposed, you must win.

He has the choice, however, at his 14th move, of another not very obvious mode of playing, which seems to prolong his defence considerably: this is,

14. P. to Q. Kt.'s 4th.

(By this move your threatened check at Q's 8th becomes useless, because it cannot in this case be followed at the proper moment by B. to Q. B's 4th. The correct reply for you now appears to be)—

15. B. to K's 2nd.	15. B. to Q's 2nd.

(This, or Kt. to Q's 2nd, is his best move, but in every case you gain a Piece in return for the one before given up, with a Pawn more, and at least an equal position.)

16. B. to K. Kt.'s 4th.	16. Q. to K's 2nd.
17. Castles.	17. B. takes B.
18. Kt. to Q's 6th (ch.)	18. K. to B's sq.
19. Q. takes B.	

You afterwards attack the Q. with your K. R., and nothing can withstand your position.

14. R. to Q's 6th.   14. Q. B. to K. B's 4th.

If instead of this, he play 14. K. to B's 2nd, you take the
Bishop, and if the Q. retake, play B. to Q. B's 4th, winning
his Q. next move. If he move 14. B. to K. B's 2nd, you win
his Q. and B., or mate in three moves. If he play 14. B. to
Q's 2nd, you can check with the Kt., should he then go with
his K. to B's sq., you take K. R's P. (ch.), (he cannot take the
Kt. without losing his Q.), then again check at B's 6th with
the Kt., then take Q. with Q. (ch.), and R. with Kt. (ch.),
winning the K's Bishop, and remaining with equal Pieces,
a better situation, and two Pawns more than he has. But if
he play 15. K. to Q's sq., instead of to B's sq., your best
move apparently is, to check with the Kt., exchange Queens,
then take the Rook with the Kt. (ch.), and afterwards taking
the K's B., have a Pawn more, and a better position. In lieu
of moving the Bishop, either to K. B's 2nd or to Q's 2nd, he
may play it to Q's 4th, in which case you simply take it with
your Rook, winning a Piece if he take Q. with Q ; or, if he
prefer to take the R., you check with your Kt. at B's 6th,
then exchange Queens, afterwards winning both K's R. and
Bishop.

15. Kt. to B's 6th (ch.)   15. K. to B's sq. (best)
16. R. to Q's 8th (ch.)   16. K. to B's 2nd.

Should he take the R. you answer with 17. Kt. takes K. R's
P. (ch.), and then B. to Q. B's 4th (ch.).

17. B. to Q. B's 4th (ch.)   17. B. to K's 3rd (best)
18. Kt. takes R., and wins.

Or you may exchange Queens and Bishops, and then take the
Rook.

VARIATION OF THE DEFENCE IN THIS OPENING,
Beginning at Black's 3rd move.

WHITE.	BLACK.
1. P. to K's 4th.	1. P. to K's 4th.
2. K. Kt. to B's 3rd.	2. P. to Q's 3rd.
3. P. to Q's 4th.	3. K. Kt. to B's 3rd.

This third move of Black's is much less dangerous for him
than the one recommended by Philidor of 3. P. to K. B's 4th,
which has just been examined; but even this gives him an
irksome, defensive position for very many moves.

4. Q. B. to K. Kt.'s 5th.   4. Q. B. to K. Kt.'s 5th.

He may also play 4. P. takes P. ; but that too would be advantageous to you; for example,—

	4. P. takes P.
5. Q. takes P.	5. B. to K's 2nd.
6. Q's Kt. to B's 3rd.	6. Castles.
7. Castles, on Q's side,	

Having a better position than he has.

5. P. takes K's P.	5. B. takes Kt.
6. Q. takes B.	6. P. takes P.
7. Q. to her Kt.'s 3rd.	7. P. to Q. Kt.'s 3rd.

If instead of this he play 7. Q. Kt. to Q's 2nd, you equally reply with 8. K. B. to Q. B's 4th.

8. K. B. to Q. B's 4th.	8. Q. to Q's 2nd.
9. B. takes Kt.	9. P. takes B.
10. Q's Kt. to B's 3rd.	10. K's B. to K. Kt.'s 2nd.
11. Q's R. to Q's sq.	11. Q. to K's 2nd.
12. B. to Q. Kt.'s 5th (ch.)	12. P. to Q. B's 3rd.

If he move his King you can play 13. Q. to her 5th, and have a winning situation.

13. Kt. to Q's 5th,

with an excellent game.

ANOTHER VARIATION OF THE DEFENCE,

Beginning also from Black's 3rd move.

WHITE.	BLACK.
1. P. to K's 4th.	1. P. to K's 4th.
2. K's Kt. to B's 3rd.	2. P. to Q's 3rd.
3. P. to Q's 4th.	3. Q's B. to K. Kt.'s 5th.

There is one other defence he may adopt here besides this and the two moves before analyzed, viz., 3. P. takes P., which deserves examination.

	3. P. takes P.
4. Q. takes P.	4. Q's Kt. to B's 3rd.
5. K's B. to Q. Kt.'s 5th.	5. Q's B. to Q's 2nd.
6. Q. to Q's sq.	6. Kt. to K's 4th.

(He can play 6. Kt. to his 5th, and you must reply with 7. K's B. to Q. B's 4th.)

7. Kt. takes Kt.

And whether he take Kt. or B., by playing your Q. to her 5th, you gain at least a Pawn.

4. P. takes P.	4. B. takes Kt.
5. Q. takes B.	5. P. takes P.

Bilguer and H. der Laza prefer P. takes B. for your 5th move, following it up thus :—

5. P. takes B.	5. Q's P. takes P.
6. Q. takes Q. (ch.)	6. K. takes Q.
7. P. to K. B's 4th, &c.	

Taking with the Queen, however, appears to me a stronger move, although in either case the advantage is on your side.

6. B. to Q. B's 4th.	6. Q. to K. B's 3rd.
7. Q. to her Kt.'s 3rd.	7. P. to Q. Kt.'s 3rd.
8. Q's Kt. to B's 3rd.	8. P. to Q. B's 3rd.
9. Castles.	9. B. to Q's 3rd.
10. P. to K. B's 4th.	10. P. takes P.

You may now obtain a capital attack by playing 11. P. to K's 5th, and if he take the P. with B., moving your Kt. to K's 4th; or, if he take with Q., you may take K. B's P. with B., giving check, and have an excellent game.

11. Q's B. takes P.	11. B. takes B. (best)

If he give check with Q., instead of taking the B., you retreat the King, his best move is then to take B. with B. ; you need not at the moment retake, but rather play B. takes K. B's P. (ch.), and you will thus get an overpowering attack.

12. P. to K's 5th.	12. B. takes K. R's P. (ch.)

If instead of this move he play Q. to K. R's 3rd, you may first take K. B's P. (ch.), and then play P. to K. Kt.'s 3rd; but the attack perhaps is hardly so vigorous or secure as that obtained by first advancing the P. to K's 5th.

SUMMARY OF THE FOREGOING VARIATIONS IN PHILIDOR'S DEFENCE.

The result of the preceding analysis serves to prove that Q's P. one, as the second move of Black, is not a tenable defence; since, play as he can afterwards, if the best moves are adopted by the first player, he will always have a very insecure or a very constrained game.

GAMES

ILLUSTRATIVE OF THE PRECEDING ANALYSES.

(From the *Chess-Player's Chronicle*.)

GAME I.—(By Philidor.)

WHITE.	BLACK.
1. P. to K's 4th.	1. P. to K's 4th.
2. K's Kt. to B's 3rd.	2. P. to Q's 3rd.
3. P. to Q's 4th.	3. P. to K. B's 4th.
4. P. takes K's P.	4. K. B's P. takes K's P.
5. Kt. to Kt.'s 5th.	5. P. to Q's 4th.
6. P. to K. B's 4th. *	6. K's B. to Q. B's 4th.
7. P. to Q. B's 4th.	7. P. to Q. B's 3rd.
8. Q's Kt. to B's 3rd.	8. K's Kt. to K's 2nd.
9. P. to K. R's 4th.	9. P. to K. R's 3rd.
10. K's Kt. to R's 3rd.	10. Castles.
11. Q's Kt. to Q. R's 4th.	11. B. to Q. Kt.'s 5th (ch.)
12. B. to Q's 2nd.	12. B. takes B. (ch.)
13. Q. takes B.	13. P. to Q's 5th.
14. P. to Q. B's 5th.	14. P. to Q. Kt.'s 4th.
15. P. takes P. (in passing)	15. Q. R's P. takes P.
16. P. to Q. Kt.'s 3rd.	16. Q's B. to K's 3rd.
17. B. to K's 2nd.	17. Kt. to K. B's 4th.
18. K's Kt. to his sq.	18. K's Kt. to Kt.'s 6th.
19. K's R. to his 2nd.	19. P. to K's 6th.
20. Q. to her Kt.'s 2nd.	20. P. to Q's 6th.
21. B. to K. B's 3rd.	21. K's R. takes P.
22. Castles on Q's side.	22. K's R. takes Kt.
23. P. takes K's R.	23. Q's R. takes P.
24. P. to Q. R's 3rd.	24. R. to Q. B's 5th (ch.)
25. K. to Q. Kt.'s sq.	25. R. to Q. B's 7th.
26. Q. to Kt.'s 4th.	26. Q's Kt. to R's 3rd.
27. Q. to K. B's 4th.	27. Q. Kt. to B's 4th.
28. Q. takes K's Kt.	

And Black mates in two moves.

GAME II.—Between Messrs. Attwood and Wilson, contemporaries of Philidor.

WHITE. (Mr. A.)	BLACK. (Mr. W.)
1. P. to K's 4th.	1. P. to K's 4th.
2. K's Kt. to B's 3rd.	2. P. to Q's 3rd.

---

* This is not the proper move; he should play 6. P. to K's 6th.

3. P. to Q's 4th.
4. Q's P. takes P.
5. Kt. to Kt.'s 5th.
6. P. to K's 6th.
7. Q's Kt. to B's 3rd.
8. K's Kt. takes K's P.
9. Q. to K. R's 5th (ch.)
10. Q. to K's 5th.
11. B. takes Kt.
12. R. to Q's sq.
13. K's B. to Q. B's 4th.
14. Q. takes K's P.
15. Q's Kt. to his 5th.
16. B. takes P. (ch.)
17. B. takes Kt. (ch.)
18. Q. takes Q. B's P. (ch.)
19. Q. takes R. (ch.)
20. P. takes B. (ch.)
21. Q. checks, and wins.

3. P. to K. B's 4th.
4. K. B's P. takes P.
5. P. to Q's 4th.
6. K's Kt. to R's 3rd.
7. P. to Q. B's 3rd.
8. P. takes Kt.
9. P. to K. Kt.'s 3rd.
10. R. to K. Kt.'s sq.
11. B. takes B.
12. Q. to K's 2nd.
13. K's B. to Kt.'s 2nd.
14. K's R. to B's sq. *
15. P. takes Kt.
16. Kt. to B's 3rd.
17. P. takes B.
18. Q's B. to Q's 2nd.
19. Q. to her sq.
20. K. to his 2nd.

GAME III.—M. De la Bourdonnais plays without seeing the Chess-board, against M. Boncourt.

WHITE. (M. De la B.)

1. P. to K's 4th.
2. K's Kt. to B's 3rd.
3. K's B. to Q. B's 4th.
4. P. to Q's 3rd.
5. Q's Kt. to B's 3rd.
6. Castles.
7. Q. to K's 2nd.
8. K's B. to Q. Kt.'s 3rd.
9. Q's Kt. to Q's sq.
10. P. takes P.
11. K's B. to Q. B's 4th.
12. Q. takes B.
13. P. takes P.
14. Q. to K's 2nd.
15. K's Kt. to Q's 4th.
16. Q's Kt. to K's 3rd.
17. Kt. takes Kt.
18. Kt. to K. B's 5th.
19. Q's B. to K's 3rd.
20. Kt. to Q's 4th.
21. P. to K. B's 4th.
22. P. to K. R's 3rd.

BLACK. (M. B.)

1. P. to K's 4th.
2. P. to Q's 3rd.
3. P. to K. B's 4th.
4. P. to Q. B's 3rd.
5. K's B. to K's 2nd.
6. K's Kt. to B's 3rd.
7. P. to Q. Kt.'s 4th.
8. P. to Q. Kt.'s 5th.
9. K. B's P. takes P.
10. Q's B. to R's 3rd.
11. B. takes B.
12. P. to Q's 4th.
13. P. takes P.
14. P. to K's 5th.
15. Q. to her 2nd.
16. Q's Kt. to B's 3rd.
17. Q. takes Kt.
18. K's B. to his sq.
19. Q. to her 2nd.
20. K's B. to Q's 3rd.
21. Castles on K's side.
22. P. to K. R's 4th.

---

* Black should have taken the Kt. with his Bishop (ch.).

23. Q's R. to Q's sq.	23. K's B. to Q. B's 4th.
24. P. to K. B's 5th.	24. Q's R. to K's sq.
25. P. to Q. B's 4th.	25. P. takes P. *en passant.*
26. P. takes P.	26. Q's R. to K's 4th.
27. P. to Q. B's 4th.	27. B. takes Kt.
28. B. takes B.	28. R. takes P.
29. R. takes R.	29. Q. takes R.
30. B. takes Kt.	30. Q. takes B.
31. P. takes P.	31. Q. to K's 4th.
32. P. to Q's 6th.	32. P. to K's 6th.
33. P. to Q's 7th.	33. R. to Q's sq.
34. Q. to her B's 4th (ch.)	34. K. to R's 2nd.
35. R. to Q's 5th.	35. Q. to her R's 8th (ch.)
36. K. to R's 2nd.	36. P. to K. Kt.'s 3rd.
37. Q. to her B's 5th.	37. Q. to K. B's 3rd.
38. Q. takes K's P.	38. R. to K. B's sq.
39. R. to K's 5th.	39. Q. to her 3rd.
40. P. to K. Kt.'s 3rd.	40. R. to K. B's 2nd.

Drawn game.

GAME IV.—Between Mr. Buckle and Captain Kennedy.

WHITE. (Capt. K.)	BLACK. (Mr. B.)
1. P. to K's 4th.	1. P. to K's 4th.
2. K's Kt. to K. B's 3rd.	2. P. to Q's 3rd.
3. P. to Q's 4th.	3. P. takes P.
4. Q. takes P.	4. K's Kt. to B's 3rd.
5. Q's B. to K. Kt.'s 5th.	5. K's B. to K's 2nd.
6. Q's Kt. to B's 3rd.	6. Castles.
7. Castles.	7. Q's Kt. to B's 3rd.
8. Q. to Q's 2nd.	8. Q's B. to K's 3rd.
9. K's Kt. to Q's 4th.	9. Q's Kt. takes K's Kt.
10. Q. takes Kt.	10. P. to Q. B's 4th.
11. Q. to Q's 2nd.	11. Q. to Q. R's 4th.
12. P. to Q. R's 3rd.	12. P. to Q. Kt.'s 4th.
13. Q's B. takes Kt.	13. K's B. takes B.
14. Kt. to Q's 5th.	14. Q. takes Q.
15. R. takes Q.	15. Q's B. takes Kt.
16. R. takes B.	16. K's R. to Q's sq.
17. B. takes Q. Kt.'s P.	17. Q's R. to Q. Kt.'s sq.
18. P. to Q. R's 4th.	18. P. to Q. R's 3rd.
19. B. takes Q. R's P.	19. B. takes Q. Kt.'s P. (ch.)
20. K. to Q's 2nd.	20. Q's R. to Q. Kt.'s 5th.
21. B. to Q. Kt.'s 5th.	21. Q's R. takes K's P.
22. P. to Q. B's 3rd.	22. P. to Q. B's 5th.*
23. K's R. to Q. Kt.'s sq.	23. B. to Q. R's 6th.
24. P. to K. B's 3rd.	24. Q's R. to K. R's 5th.

* The only move he has to save the Bishop.

25. P. to K. R's 3rd.	25. K's R. to Q. Kt.'s sq.
26. K's R. to K's sq.	26. K. to K. B's sq.
27. K's R. to K's 4th.	27. R. takes R.
28. K. B's P. takes R.	28. K. to K's 2nd.
29. R. to Q's 4th.	29. R. to Q. B's sq.
30. R. takes Q. B's P.*	30. R. takes R.
31. B. takes R.	31. P. to K. R's 4th.
32. P. to Q. R's 5th.	32. P. to K. R's 5th.
33. P. to Q. R's 6th.	33. B. to Q. B's 4th.

And after many more moves the game was declared drawn.

GAME V.—Between Mr. Horwitz and Mr. Staunton.

WHITE. (Mr. S.)	BLACK. (Mr. H.)
1. P. to K's 4th.	1. P. to K's 4th.
2. K's Kt. to B's 3rd.	2. P. to Q's 3rd.
3. P. to Q's 4th.	3. P. takes P.
4. Kt. takes P.	4. K's Kt. to B's 3rd.
5. Q's Kt. to B's 3rd.	5. K's B. to K's 2nd.
6. K's B. to K's 2nd.	6. Castles.
7. P. to K. B's 4th.	7. P. to Q. B's 4th.
8. K's Kt. to B's 3rd.	8. Q's Kt. to B's 3rd.
9. Castles.	9. Q's B. to K. Kt.'s 5th.†
10. Q's B. to K's 3rd.	10. P. to Q. R's 3rd.
11. P. to Q. R's 3rd.	11. B. takes Kt.
12. B. takes B.	12. Q's R. to Q. B's sq.
13. Kt. to K's 2nd.	13. Q. to her B's 2nd.‡
14. Kt. to K. Kt.'s 3rd.	14. K's R. to K's sq.§
15. P. to Q. B's 3rd.	15. Q's R. to Q's sq.
16. Q. to her B's 2nd.	16. B. to his sq.
17. Q's R. to Q's sq.	17. P. to Q. Kt.'s 3rd.
18. P. to Q. Kt.'s 4th.	18. Q's Kt. to Q. R's 2nd.
19. P. to Q. B's 4th.	19. P. takes Kt.'s P.
20. P. takes P.	20. P. to Q's 4th.‖

---

* This Pawn ought to have been taken with Bishop.

† With the hope of planting his Kt. at Q's 5th.

‡ Intending presently, if an opportunity occur, to play Q's Kt. to Q's 5th, and, after the exchanges, take Q. B's P. with his Q.

§ Had he played the Kt. over to Q's 5th, before protecting the B., he would have lost at least a Pawn.

‖ The exchange of Pawns, with the subsequent advance of this Pawn, appears, at first sight, a skilful conception, and one that must turn the scale in favour of the second player. Upon examination, however, it turns out to have been made without any consideration of the move White had in store, which renders the whole combination worse than nugatory.

21. Q. to K. B's 2nd.*	21. Q's Kt. to Q. B's sq.†
22. Q. B's P. takes Q's P.	22. B. takes Kt.'s P.
23. P. to K's 5th.	23. K's Kt. to Q's 2nd.
24. P. to Q's 6th.	24. Q. to Kt.'s sq.
25. B. to Q. B's 6th.	25. P. to K. Kt.'s 3rd.‡
26. Kt. to K's 4th.	26. R. to K's 3rd.
27. Q. to K. R's 4th.	27. Q's Kt. to Q. R's 2nd.
28. B. takes K's Kt.	28. R. takes B.
29. Kt. to K. Kt.'s 5th.	29. P. to K. R's 4th.
30. Kt. takes R.	30. P. takes Kt.
31. P. to K. B's 5th.	31. P. to Q. R's 4th.
32. P. takes K's P.	32. R. to K. Kt.'s 2nd.
33. P. to K's 7th.	

And Black resigns.

---

* This rejoinder was certainly not foreseen by Black when he played on the Q's Pawn.

† He would have got an equally bad position by taking the K's P. with P.

‡ As the sacrifice of the Q's Kt. at this crisis had many advocates when the game was over, it may be well to examine briefly the consequences of that move. Suppose, then, instead of " P. to K. Kt.'s 3rd," that Black had played—

25. Q's Kt. takes Q's P.

White then has several ways of playing.

IN THE FIRST PLACE.

26. B. takes K's Kt.	26. Q's R. takes B.
27. K. to R's sq.	27. Q's R. to K's 2nd. [1]
28. P. takes Kt.	28. R. takes B.
29. P. to Q's 7th, winning easily.	

IN THE SECOND PLACE.

26. R. takes Q's Kt.	26. B. takes R.
27. P. takes B.	27. Q. takes P.
28. B. takes Kt.	28. R. takes B.
29. B. takes P., and White ought to win.	

IN THE THIRD PLACE.

26. P. takes Q's Kt.	26. R. takes B.
27. Q. takes R.	27. B. to Q. B's 4th.
28. Q's R. to Q's 4th.	28. Kt. to K. B's 3rd.
29. K's R. to Q's sq.	29. R. takes P.
30. Kt. to K. B's 5th.	30. B. takes R.
31. R. takes B., retaining a Piece more than Black.	

---

[1] If he support the Q's R., White may at once take off the Kt.

CHAPTER II

GAME THE FIFTH.

PETROFF'S DEFENCE.

WHITE.	BLACK.
1. P. to K's 4th.	1. P. to K's 4th.
2. K's Kt. to B's 3rd.	2. K's Kt. to B's 3rd.

This mode of defence is touched on by Damiano, and has been examined, subsequently, by Lopez (1584), pp. 119, 125; Selenus, pp. 25, 267; Cozio (first edition), 212, 214, 312; Greco (Hirshel's edition), p. 36; Ponziani (1782), p. 103; Lolli, pp. 183, 184; Allgaier, tab. iii.; Lewis (first edition), pp. 25, 81, (second edition) 8, 83; Treatise (1844), pp. 111—115; Walker (1841), p. 46; (1846), pp. 46—50; but never received the consideration it was entitled to until Mr. Petroff, the celebrated Russian player, introduced it again a few years back. It has since undergone a complete analysis at the hands of Major Jaenisch, who for some time recommended it as Black's best move, an opinion, however, which he lately qualified, believing now that it gives him a somewhat inferior position to his opponent.

3. P. to Q's 4th.	3. P. takes P.

Your third move was suggested by Mr. Petroff. It is perhaps less attacking, Major Jaenisch observes, than taking the K's P. with the Kt. (as in Variation III.), but it leads to many beautiful variations. In reply, Black in place of taking P. with P., may take it with the Kt. (See Variation I.)

4. P. to K's 5th.	4. Kt. to K's 5th (best)

He may here play Kt. to Q's 4th, or Q. to K's 2nd; if the latter, the following moves are likely to occur:—

	4. Q. to K's 2nd.
5. Q. to K's 2nd (best)	5. K's Kt. to Q's 4th.
6. Kt. takes P.	6. P. to Q's 3rd.
7. P. takes P.	7. Q. takes Q. (ch.)
8. B. takes Q.	8. K's B. takes P.
9. Castles.	9. Castles.
10. P. to Q. B's 4th.	10. K's Kt. to K. B's 5th.
11. K's B. to his 3rd.	11. P. to Q. B's 3rd.

12. Q's Kt. to B's 3rd.   12. Q's Kt. to Q's 2nd.
13. Q's Kt. to K's 4th.   13. K's B. to Q. B's 2nd.

And the game is quite even.

5. Kt. takes P.   5. P. to Q's 3rd (best)

Instead of taking the Pawn with your Kt., you may play
5. K's B. to Q's 3rd.   (See Variation II.) He might also
play 5. P. to Q's 4th, or 5. B. to Q. B's 4th, without danger.

6. P. takes P.   6. K's B. takes P.
7. K's B. to Q. B's 4th.   7. K's B. to Q. B's 4th.
8. Q's B. to K's 3rd.   8. Castles.

Instead of this move he might take the Kt.

9. Castles.   9. Q's Kt. to Q's 2nd.

The game is equal.

VARIATION I.,

Commencing at Black's 3rd move.

WHITE.	BLACK.
1. P. to K's 4th.	1. P. to K's 4th.
2. K. Kt. to B's 3rd.	2. K. Kt. to B's 3rd.
3. P. to Q's 4th.	3. Kt. takes P.
4. K's B. to Q's 3rd.	4. P. to Q's 4th.
5. Kt. takes K's P.	5. Kt. to Q's 3rd.

Black may play 5. P. to Q. B's 4th, and the result would be
an even game.

6. P. to Q. B's 4th.	6. P. takes P.
7. K's Kt. takes P.	7. Q's B. to K's 3rd.
8. Kt. to K's 3rd.	8. B. to K's 2nd.
9. Castles.	9. Castles.

You have the move, and somewhat the advantage of position.

VARIATION II.,

Beginning at White's 5th move.

WHITE.	BLACK.
1. P. to K's 4th.	1. P. to K's 4th.
2. K. Kt. to B's 3rd.	2. K. Kt. to B's 3rd.
3. P. to Q's 4th.	3. P. takes P.
4. P. to K's 5th.	4. Kt. to K's 5th.

In the former example you now took the P. with the Kt., perhaps your best move, but the following may also be played without harm :—

5. K's B. to Q's 3rd.	5. K's Kt. to Q. B's 4th.
6. Kt. takes P.	6. P. to Q's 3rd.
7. P. takes P.	7. K's B. takes P.
8. Castles.	8. Castles.

It would not be a good move for Black, instead of castling, to take your K. R's P. (ch.), and then to take the Kt., on account of your check with the B., which would leave his Q. exposed to capture.

VARIATION III.,

Beginning at White's 3rd move.

WHITE.	BLACK.
1. P. to K's 4th.	1. P. to K's 4th.
2. K's Kt. to B's 3rd.	2. K's Kt. to B's 3rd.
3. Kt. takes K's P.	3. Kt. takes P.

Black may now adopt the defence given in Cozio, and which has latterly been brought into vogue by Jaenisch, viz., 3. P. to Q's 3rd. (See Variation IV.)

4. Q. to K's 2nd.	4. Q. to K's 2nd.

If he retreat the Kt. instead of this move, you evidently win his Q. by playing your Kt. to Q. B's 6th (dis. ch.).

5. Q. takes Kt.	5. P. to Q's 3rd.
6. P. to Q's 4th.	6. P. to K. B's 3rd.
7. P. to K. B's 4th.	7. Q's Kt. to Q's 2nd.

If he take the Kt. you gain a Pawn. (*e. g.*)

	7. Q's P. takes Kt.
8. B's P. takes P.	8. P. takes P.
9. Q. takes P., &c.	

8. Q's Kt. to B's 3rd.	8. Q's P. takes Kt.

He may, however, take with the Bishop's Pawn, but the result is also in your favour, as the following moves will show :—

	8. K. B's P. takes Kt.
9. K. B's P. takes P.	9. P. takes P.
10. Q's Kt. to Q's 5th.	10. Kt. to K. B's 3rd.

(If instead of this he move 10. Q. to her sq., you take P. with P.)

11. B. to Q. Kt.'s 5th (ch.)	11. P. to Q. B's 3rd.
12. Kt. takes Kt. (ch.)	12. P. takes Kt. (best)
13. B. takes P. (ch.)	13. K. to Q's sq. (best)
14. Q's B. to Q's 2nd.	14. P. to Q. R's 4th.*
15. Castles on Q's side.	15. P. takes B.
16. Q. takes Q. B's P.	16. Q's R. to his 3rd.

(If he play 16. Q's B. to Kt.'s 2nd, you take the Q. R's P. with your Bishop (ch.), and follow that by 17. P. takes K's P. (dis. ch.), and win.)

17. B. takes P. (ch.)	17. R. takes B.
18. P. takes P. (dis. ch.)	18. B. to Q's 2nd.
19. P. to K's 6th.	19. B. to K. R's 3rd (ch.)
20. K. to Kt.'s sq.	20. R. to Q. R's 2nd.
21. R. takes B. (ch.)	21. R. takes R.
22. P. takes R.	

Winning the other R. also, or giving immediate mate.

9. Q's Kt. to Q's 5th.	9. Q. to her 3rd.
10. Q's P. takes P.	10. P. takes P.
11. P. takes P.	11. Q. to her B's 3rd.

If he take the P. with his Q., you exchange Queens, and then gain the Q's R. by 12 Kt. takes Q. B's P. (ch.). If he take the P. with the Kt., you win the Kt. by 12. Q's B. to K. B's 4th.

12. K's B. to Q. Kt.'s 5th.	12. Q. to her B's 4th.

It is quite clear that by taking the Bishop Black loses his Queen.

13. P. to Q. Kt.'s 4th.

Winning the Q. At his 12th move, Black might prolong the game by playing 12. Q. to K. Kt.'s 3rd, but in that case you would take 13. Q. B's P. with the Kt. (ch.), then take Q. with Q., and afterwards Q's R. with Kt.

VARIATION IV.,

Beginning at Black's 3rd move.

WHITE.	BLACK.
1. P. to K's 4th.	1. P. to K's 4th.
2. K's Kt. to B's 3rd.	2. K's Kt. to B's 3rd.
3. Kt. takes K's P.	3. P. to Q's 3rd.

* Better than taking the Bishop.

This defence is found in Cozio, p. 312, but it was reserved for Jaenisch to exhibit the full importance of its bearing upon the opening. (See Palamède (1842), pp. 107, 108, and "Analyse des Ouvertures," vol. ii.)

4. Kt. to K. B's 3rd.	4. Kt. takes K's P.
5. P. to Q's 4th.	5. P. to Q's 4th.

Your move of 5. P. to Q's 4th, is considered by Jaenisch as the best. If instead you play 5. Q. to K's 2nd, the adversary also moves 5. Q. to K's 2nd, and the positions are strictly equal.

6. K's B. to Q's 3rd.	6. K's B. to K's 2nd.

Black's 6th move is commended by Jaenisch.—If he play 6. P. to Q. B's 4th, you reply with P. to Q. B's 4th. If 6. K. B. to Q's 3rd, the following moves will demonstrate that the opening is in your favour.

	6. K. B. to Q's 3rd.
7. Castles.	7. Castles.
8. P. to Q. B's 4th.	8. Q. B. to K's 3rd.
9. Q. to her B's 2nd.	9. P. to K. B's 4th.

(In the careful and elaborate analysis of this opening presented by Major Jaenisch, your move of 9. Q. to her B's 2nd, preparatory to playing her to Kt.'s 3rd, appears to have been overlooked. It first occurs in the admirable game won by the Pesth club, in correspondence with the Paris club; and its success in that case has doubtless had its effect in modifying the opinion M. Jaenisch at first entertained of the defence.)

10. Q. to her Kt.'s 3rd.

And you have a very fine game.

These moves form the opening of the game alluded to, which will be found complete at the end of this Chapter.

7. Castles.	7. Q. Kt. to B's 3rd.
8. P. to Q. B's 4th.	8. Q. B. to K's 3rd.
9. P. to Q. R's 3rd.	9. Castles.

You are now enabled to play Q. to her B's 2nd, and obtain a good attacking situation.

The foregoing variations of this opening are chiefly taken from Jaenisch's analysis. Those which follow are derived from the masterly work of Bilguer and H. der Laza.

ANOTHER VARIATION,

Beginning at the 3rd move of White.

WHITE.	BLACK.
1. P. to K's 4th.	1. P. to K's 4th.
2. K. Kt. to B's 3rd.	2. K. Kt. to B's 3rd.
3. K. B. to Q. B's 4th.	3. Kt. takes P.

You may also play 3. Q. Kt. to B's 3rd, to which Black would respond with 3. K. B. to Q. Kt.'s 5th, and the result, after a few moves, would be an even game. In reply to your 3rd move of K. B. to Q. B's 4th, if Black play 3. Q. Kt. to B's 3rd, the opening is resolved into a position of the "Two Knights' Game," where it is brought about by

1. P. to K's 4th.	1. P. to K's 4th.
2. K. Kt. to B's 3rd.	2. Q. Kt. to B's 3rd.
3. K. B. to Q. B's 4th.	3. K. Kt. to B's 3rd.

In this situation, by moving 4. K. Kt. to his 5th, you obtain the advantage, as will be shown in the examination of the "Two Knights' Game."

4. Q. to K's 2nd.	4. P. to Q's 4th.

If you play 4. Kt. takes K. P., Black answers with 4. P. to Q's 4th, and, upon your retreating the B. to Q. Kt.'s 3rd, he moves Q. to K. Kt.'s 4th, having the better game, as will be seen in the analysis of the King's Bishop's game, where the same position occurs from

1. P. to K's 4th.	1. P. to K's 4th.
2. K. B. to Q. B's 4th.	2. K. Kt. to B's 3rd.
3. K. Kt. to B's 3rd.	3. Kt. takes P.

&c., &c.

5. Kt. takes K. P.	5. K. B. to Q. B's 4th (best)
6. P. to Q's 3rd.	6. B. takes K. B. P. (ch.)

Your move, 6. P. to Q's 3rd, is better than castling. If he take with Kt. instead of the B., the following moves will show the advantage you must gain.

	6. Kt. takes K. B. P.
7. Kt. to Q. B's 6th (dis. ch.)	7. K. to Q's 2nd.
8. Kt. takes Q.	8. R. to K's sq.
9. Q. takes R. (ch.)	9. K. takes Q.
10. B. takes Q. P.	10. Kt. takes R.
11. Kt. takes K. B. P.	11. Kt. to K. B's 7th.
12. P. to K. R's 3rd.	

And the Kt. cannot escape without loss.

Instead, however, of taking the K. B. P. either with Bishop or Knight, Black can play 6. Q. P. takes B., a move which is given by Bilguer and H. der Laza, but hardly followed up with their customary acumen. (See Variation A.)

7. K. to Q's sq. (best)   7. B. to Q. Kt.'s 3rd.

He might likewise castle at his 7th move, and if you played 8. K. B. to Q. Kt.'s 5th, move B. to Q's 5th.

8. Kt. takes K. B. P.   8. Q. B. to K. Kt.'s 5th.

If he take the Knight with his King, you capture his Knight and win without much trouble. (e. g.)

	8. K. takes Kt.
9. Q. takes Kt.	9. Q. B. to K's 3rd.
10. R. to B's sq. (ch.)	10. K. to his 2nd.
11. B. to K. Kt.'s 5th (ch.)	11. K. to Q's 2nd.
12. K. B. takes Q. P.	12. Q. takes Q. B.
13. Q. takes B. (ch.)	13. K. to Q's sq.
14. B. takes Q. Kt. P.	

And you must win of course.

9. Kt. takes Q.	9. B. takes Q. (ch.)
10. K. takes B.	10. Kt. to K. B's 7th.
11. R. to K. B's sq.	11. P. takes B.
12. Kt. to K's 6th.	12. P. takes P. (ch.)
13. P. takes P.	13. K. to his 2nd.
14. Kt. takes K. Kt. P.	14. R. to K. Kt.'s sq.

You might also have taken the Q. B. P. with your Kt., and upon his taking it with B. have taken Kt. with R., but the move in the text seems preferable.

15. Kt. to K. B's 5th (ch.)	15. K. to his 3rd.
16. Q. B. to K's 3rd.	16. B. takes B.

If he take the Kt. P. with Rook instead of taking the Bishop, you can take B. with B., and on his capturing the B., play Kt. to K's 3rd, winning a Piece. He may, however, take the Kt. with his King, whereupon you take Kt. with Rook (ch.), then exchange Bishops, and have a Pawn more and a superior position.

17. Kt. takes B.	17. Kt. to K. Kt.'s 5th.

The positions are equal, but you have a Pawn more.

VARIATION (A.)

Beginning at Black's 6th move.

BLACK.

WHITE.

In the previous example, the consequences of Black's taking the K. B. P. at his 6th move, both with B. and Kt., were shown; it remains to be seen whether he may not acquire a better game by simply taking the B. with Q. P. at this point.

WHITE.	BLACK.
	6. Q. P. takes B.
7. Q. takes Kt.	7. Castles.
8. Q. takes doubled P.	8. Q. to K's 2nd.
9. P. to K. B's 4th.	9. Q. Kt. to B's 3rd.
10. Q. to K's 4th.	

Thus far the moves are those laid down by Bilguer and H. der Laza. They now make Black take the Kt. with Kt., the Queens are exchanged, and the game dismissed as equal. It would appear, however that if Black, instead of exchanging Knights, play 10. K. R. to K's square, he may obtain a very embarrassing attack. In reply, you must not 11. take Kt. with Kt., or he wins your Queen.

The most feasible move for you apparently is K. to Q's square, or Q. Kt. to Q's 2nd. (See the next Variation.) K. to B's square is obviously bad. Suppose in the first place you play

11. K. to Q's sq.   11. Q. to K. R's 5th.

He now threatens a dangerous check with his Q. B. at K. Kt.'s 5th. If you try to escape the consequences by playing 12. P.

to K. Kt.'s 3rd, the subjoined moves show he ought to win the game.

12. P. to K. Kt.'s 3rd.	12. Q. to K. R's 4th (ch.)

Should you interpose the Q. at K. B's 3rd, he wins a Piece by taking the Knight with Rook ; if you play Q. to K's 2nd, he equally gains the Knight by exchanging Queens, and then moving P. to K. B's 3rd; and if you move K. to Q's 2nd, the following is likely to be the termination :—

13. K. to Q's 2nd.	13. Kt. takes Kt.
14. P. takes Kt.	14. R. takes P.

Winning easily.

Instead, however, of playing 12. P. to K. Kt.'s 3rd, you might at that moment move Q. Kt. to Q's 2nd.

12. Q. Kt. to Q's 2nd.	12. Q. to K. R's 4th (ch.)
13. Q. Kt. to K. B's 3rd (best)	13. Q. B. to K. Kt.'s 5th,

and now, play as you can, Black must gain a decided advantage by taking the K. Kt. with Kt., &c.

VARIATION,

Beginning at White's 11th move.

BLACK.

WHITE.

11. Q's Kt. to Q's 2nd.	11. Q. to K. R's 4th (ch.)
12. P. to K. Kt.'s 3rd.	12. Q. to K. R's 4th.
13. Q. Kt. to K. B's 3rd.	13. Q. B. to K. B's 4th.
14. Q. to K's 2nd (best)	14. Q. B. to K. Kt.'s 5th.
15. K. R. to B's sq.	15. Q. Kt. to Q's 5th.

And Black must win.

GAMES

ILLUSTRATIVE OF THE PRECEDING ANALYSES.

(From the *Chess-Player's Chronicle*.)

GAME I.—Played by correspondence between Paris and Pesth.

WHITE. (Pesth.)	BLACK. (Paris.)
1. P. to K's 4th.	1. P. to K's 4th.
2. K's Kt. to B's 3rd.	2. K's Kt. to B's 3rd.*
3. K's Kt. takes K's P.	3. P. to Q's 3rd.
4. K's Kt. to B's 3rd.	4. Kt. takes K's P.
5. P. to Q's 4th.	5. P. to Q's 4th.
6. K's B. to Q's 3rd.	6. K's B. to Q's 3rd.
7. Castles.	7. Castles.
8. P. to Q. B's 4th.	8. Q's B. to K's 3rd.
9. Q. to her B's 2nd.†	9. P. to K. B's 4th. ‡
10. Q. to Q. Kt.'s 3rd.§	10. Q's P. takes P.

---

* The reply to Pesth's second move was the occasion of a very animated discussion in the French camp, which terminated in the abrupt secession of M. Deschapelles from their councils. This distinguished player was opposed, justly we think, to the adoption of K. Kt. to B's 3rd, a move newly brought into vogue by the Russian amateurs, MM. Petroff and Jaenisch, and which their subsequent analyses have condemned; but instead of recommending the acknowledged and well-tried answer, " Q. Kt. to B's 3rd," he strangely enough insisted on the substitution of another bizarre move, " P. to K. B's 4th," still more prejudicial to the interests of the second player. After a good deal of controversy, in the course of which the veteran proffered to play the defence single-handed against the whole Commission, the majority decided in favour of " K. Kt. to B's 3rd," and M. Deschapelles quitted the club. An able analysis of the disputed move was afterwards published by the Committee, and left no doubt of their propriety in rejecting it.

† There is nothing like actual play for testing the value of new suggestions. In the elaborate examination of this pet opening by M. Jaenisch, the present move, which is a very probable and a very important one, appears to have been quite overlooked. M. Jaenisch makes the first player move Q. to her Kt.'s 3rd at once.

‡ If this be the best move left for Black, their Monarch totters already.

§ These moves result from a profound investigation of the opening. The sort of *coup de repos*, to await the advance of the enemy's K. B. P., was a master touch.

11. Q. takes Q. Kt.'s P.*	11. P. to Q. B's 3rd.
12. K's B. takes K's Kt.	12. K. B's P. takes B.
13. K's Kt. to his 5th.	13. Q's B. to K. B's 4th.
14. Q's Kt. to B's 3rd.	14. Q. to her 2nd.†
15. Q. takes Q.	15. Q's Kt. takes Q.
16. K's Kt. takes K's P.	16. K's B. to Q. B's 2nd.
17. K's R. to K's square.	17. Q's R. to Q. Kt.'s square.
18. K's R. to K's 2nd.	18. Kt. to Q. Kt.'s 3rd.‡
19. K's Kt. to Q. B's 5th.	19. K's B. to Q's 3rd.
20. K's Kt. to K's 4th.	20. K's B. to Q. B's 2nd.§
21. K's Kt. to Q. B's 5th.	21. K's B. to Q's 3rd.
22. K's Kt. to K's 4th.	22. K's B. to Q. B's 2nd.
23. K's Kt. to Q. B's 5th.	23. K's B. to Q's 3rd.
24. K's Kt. to K's 4th.	24. K's B. to Q. B's 2nd.
25. K's Kt. to Q. B's 5th.	25. K's B. to Q's 3rd.
26. K's Kt. to K's 4th.	26. K's B. to Q. B's 2nd.
27. K's Kt. to Q. B's 5th.	27. Q's B. to Q's 6th.
28. K's R. to K's 3rd.	28. Q's B. to his 7th.
29. K's Kt. to K's 6th.	29. R. to K. B's 2nd.
30. Kt. takes B.	30. R. takes Kt.
31. K's R. to K's 2nd.‖	31. B. to Q's 6th.
32. Q's B. to K. B's 4th.	32. B. takes R.
33. B. takes R.	33. R. to K's square.
34. B. takes Kt.	34. P. takes B.
35. R. to K's square.	35. B. to K. R's 4th.
36. R. takes R. (ch.)	36. B. takes R.
37. Kt. to K's 4th.	37. P. to Q. Kt.'s 4th.
38. P. to Q. R's 3rd.	38. B. to K. Kt.'s 3rd.
39. P. to K. B's 3rd.¶	39. K. to K. B's 2nd.
40. K. to B's 2nd.	40. K. to his 3rd.

---

* This and many moves to come form connecting links in the admirable combination of the Hungarians, and were evidently foreseen when the Q. was played to her B's 2nd.

† Is there anything better to be done by Black at this juncture? B. to Q. B's square would compel the Queen to take the Rook. But *cui bono?* Could she then be caught? We doubt it.

‡ With the view to plant the Kt. at Q's 4th.

§ The same moves, Kt. to Q. B's 5th and B. to Q. B's 2nd, were persisted in for weeks by both parties. Pesth having the first game virtually won, were content to draw this without further trouble. In the end, Paris, as they must lose equally whether they drew or lost the present party, decided on venturing another move.

‖ All this denotes an admirable insight of the position. White see clearly that every exchange now strengthens the advantage they have acquired.

¶ Not only protecting the Kt., but affording a speedier route for the King to sustain his Pawns.

41. K. to his 3rd.
42. P. to K. Kt.'s 4th.
43. Kt. to Q. B's 3rd (ch.)
44. P. to K. B's 4th.
45. P. to K. B's 5th.
46. Kt. to K's 4th (ch.)
47. K. to K. B's 4th.
48. K. to his 5th.
49. P. to K. R's 4th.
50. P. to K. Kt.'s 5th.
51. P. takes P.
52. P. to K. Kt.'s 6th.‡

41. P. to K. R's 3rd.
42. K. to Q's 4th.
43. K. to Q's 3rd.
44. B. to K's square.*
45. Q's B. to Q's 2nd.
46. K. to his 2nd.
47. B. to K's square.†
48. B. to K. B's 2nd.
49. B. to Q's 4th.
50. P. takes P.
51. B. to K. Kt.'s square.

Paris surrendered.

GAME II.—Skilfully conducted *Partie* played in 1837, by M. Petroff, against three Russian Amateurs in council together.

WHITE. (M. Petroff.)
1. P. to K's 4th.
2. K's Kt. to B's 3rd.
3. P. to Q's 4th.
4. K's B. to Q's 3rd.
5. Kt. takes K's P.
6. Castles.
7. P. to Q. B's 4th.
8. P. to K. B's 4th.
9. Q's B. to K's 3rd.
10. P. takes Q's P.
11. Q's Kt. to B's 3rd.
12. Q's R. to Q. B's square.
13. B. takes Kt.
14. Q's Kt. to his 5th.
15. Kt. takes B.

BLACK. (Amateurs.)
1. P. to K's 4th.
2. K's Kt. to B's 3rd.
3. Kt. takes K's P.
4. P. to Q's 4th.
5. K's B. to Q's 3rd.
6. Castles.
7. P. to K. B's 4th.
8. P. to Q. B's 3rd.
9. Q's B. to K's 3rd.
10. P. takes P.
11. Q's Kt. to B's 3rd.
12. K's R. to B's 3rd. §
13. K. B's P. takes B.
14. Kt. to K's 2nd.
15. Q. takes Kt.

----

* B. to Q's 6th would permit the White to play their Q. Kt.'s P. one square, with advantage.

† The Black have no resource left.

‡ Longer resistance would be frivolous and vexatious, and the Frenchmen with good grace resign.

§ This unfortunate counter attack is admirably taken advantage of by M. Petroff.

16. P. to K. Kt.'s 4th.	16. P. to K. Kt.'s 3rd.*
17. P. to K. B's 5th.†	17. P. takes P.
18. B. to K. Kt.'s 5th.	18. K's R. to B's square.
19. B. to K. R's 6th.	19. K's R. to Q. B's square.‡
20. Q. to her 2nd.§	20. Q. to her square.
21. R. takes R.	21. R. takes R.
22. P. takes P.	22. Kt. takes P.
23. Q. to K. Kt.'s 2nd (ch.)	23. K. to R's square.
24. R. takes Kt.	24. Q. to K. Kt.'s square
25. R. to B's 6th.	25. B. to K. R's 6th.
26. Q. to K. Kt.'s 3rd.	26. Q. takes Q.
27. P. takes Q.	

On this move, the Amateurs abandoned the game.

FIRST DEFENCE.

WHITE.	BLACK.
20. Q. to her 2nd.	20. Kt. to K. Kt.'s 3rd.
21. R. takes R. (ch.)	21. R. takes R.
22. P. takes P.	22. Kt. takes Kt.
23. Q. to K. Kt.'s 5th (ch.)	23. Kt. to Kt.'s 3rd.
24. P. takes Kt.	24. Q. to her 2nd.
25. R. to K. B's 7th.	25. R. checks.
26. K. to B's 2nd.	26. R. to B's 7th (ch.)
27. K. to his 3rd.	Lost game.

SECOND DEFENCE.

WHITE.	BLACK.
20. Q. to her 2nd.	20. R. takes R.
21. Q. to Kt.'s 5th (ch.)	21. Kt. to Kt.'s 3rd.
22. Kt. takes Kt.	22. R. to Q. B's 2nd (best)
23. Kt. to Kt.'s 7th (dble. ch.)	23. K. to B's 2nd.
24. P. takes K. B's P.	24. Q. takes Kt. (best)
25. P. takes B. (dble. ch.)	25. K. takes P.
26. Q. to Kt.'s 4th (ch.)	26. K. to Q's 3rd.
27. B. checks.	27. K. to Q. B's 3rd.
28. R. to Q. B's square (ch.)	28. K. to Kt.'s 4th.
29. R. takes R.	

And wins.

---

* They do not appear to have had a better move.

† Well played.

‡ It would have been better to leave the Rook *en prise*, and advance the Pawn to King's Bishop's 5th.

§ After this move, the game of Black was beyond redemption; but as the situation is interesting, we shall give in two variations the two systems of defence which seem practicable, beside that actually adopted.

GAME III.—Between Von. H. der Laza and Major Jaenisch.

WHITE. (V. H. L.)	BLACK. (M. J.)
1. P. to K's 4th.	1. P. to K's 4th.
2. K's Kt. to B's 3rd.	2. K's Kt. to B's 3rd.
3. Kt. takes K's P.	3. P. to Q's 3rd.
4. Kt. to K. B's 3rd.	4. Kt. takes K's P.
5. P. to Q's 3rd.	5. Kt. to K. B's 3rd.
6. P. to Q's 4th.	6. P. to Q's 4th.
7. P. to K. R's 3rd.	7. K's B. to Q's 3rd.
8. Q's B. to K's 3rd.	8. Castles.
9. K's B. to K's 2nd.	9. Q. to K's 2nd.
10. P. to Q. B's 3rd.	10. P. to Q. B's 4th.
11. Q. to her B's 2nd.	11. Q's Kt. to B's 3rd.
12. Q's Kt. to Q's 2nd.	12. Q's B. to K's 3rd.
13. Q's P. takes P.	13. K's B. takes P.
14. B. takes B.	14. Q. takes B.
15. Q's Kt. to his 3rd.	15. Q. to her Kt.'s 3rd.
16. Castles on K's side.	16. Q's R. to Q. B's square.
17. Q. to her 2nd.	17. K's R. to Q's square.
18. Q's R. to Q's square.	18. P. to Q. R's 3rd.
19. K's R. to K's square.	19. K's R. to Q's 2nd.
20. K's B. to Q's 3rd.	20. Q's R. to Q's square.
21. Q's Kt. to Q's 4th.	21. Q's R. to K's square.
22. K's R. to K's 2nd.	22. K's R. to K's 2nd.
23. Q's R. to K's square.	23. P. to K. R's 3rd.
24. Q. to K. B's 4th.	24. Q's Kt. to Q's square.
25. B. to K. B's 5th.	25. Q. to her B's 4th.
26. K's Kt. to K's 5th.	26. B. takes B.
27. Q's Kt. takes B.	27. Kt. to K's 3rd.
28. Kt. takes R. (ch.)	28. R. takes Kt.
29. Q. to K. B's 5th.	29. P. to Q's 5th.
30. K's R. to Q. B's 2nd.	30. P. to Q's 6th.
31. Q. takes Q's P.	31. Q's Kt. to K. B's 5th.
32. Q. to her 4th.	32. Q. takes Q.
33. P. takes Q.	33. K's Kt. to Q's 4th.
34. P. to Q. R's 3rd.	34. P. to K. Kt.'s 4th.
35. Kt. to K. B's 3rd.	35. R. takes R. (ch.)
36. Kt. takes R.	36. K. to Kt.'s 2nd.
37. R. to Q. B's 5th.	37. P. to Q. Kt.'s 3rd.
38. R. to B's 6th.	38. Q's Kt. to K's 3rd.
39. R. to Q's 6th.	39. K's Kt. to K. B's 5th.
40. Kt. to Q. B's 2nd.	40. K's Kt. to Q's 6th.
41. R. takes Q. Kt.'s P.	

And Black surrendered.

CHAPTER III.

GAME THE SIXTH.

WHITE.	BLACK.
1. P. to K's 4th.	1. P. to K's 4th.
2. K's Kt. to B's 3rd.	2. K's B. to Q. B's 4th.

This mode of answering your second move is very poor and inefficient, and affords you an opportunity of bringing your Pieces into action speedily.

3. Kt. takes K's P.	3. Q. to K's 2nd.
4. P. to Q's 4th.	4. B. to Q. Kt.'s 3rd.

He has three other ways of playing at his choice, 4. B. to Q's 3rd, 4. P. to Q's 3rd, and 4. P. to K. B's 3rd, each of which shall be briefly examined. In the first place, suppose—

	4. B. to Q's 3rd.
5. P. to K. B's 4th.	5. P. to K. B's 3rd.
6. Kt. to Q. B's 4th.	6. Q. takes P. (ch.)
7. K. to B's 2nd.	7. Q's Kt. to B's 3rd.*
8. K's B. to Q's 3rd.	8. Q. takes Q's P. (ch.)
9. Q's B. to K's 3rd.	9. Q. to her 4th.
10. B. to K. Kt.'s 6th (ch.), and you take the Q. next move.	

In the second place,—

	4. P. to Q's 3rd.
5. Kt. takes K. B's P.	5. Q. takes K's P. (ch.)†
6. Q's B. to K's 3rd.	6. K. takes Kt.
7. P. takes B.	7. P. takes P.
8. Q. to K. R's 5th (ch.)	8. K. to B's sq.
9. Q. takes doubled P. (ch.), and you have a fine game.	

The third variation consists in his playing—

	4. P. to K. B's 3rd.
5. Q. to K. R's 5th (ch.)	5. P. to K. Kt.'s 3rd.
6. Kt. takes Kt.'s P.	6. Q. takes K's P. (ch.)
7. K. to Q's sq.	7. Q. takes Kt.
8. Q. takes B.	

You have much the better game.

---

* He might also take K. B's P. with his B., but the result would be in your favour.

† If he take the Kt. with Q., you take his B. with P., and have a P. more and a better position.

Having seen the results of these methods of play, we may now proceed with the original game, from which we deviated after the 4th move.

5. K's B. to Q. B's 4th.   5. K's Kt. to B's 3rd.
6. B. takes B's P. (ch.)   6. K. to B's sq.
7. B. to Q. Kt.'s 3rd.   7. Kt. takes K's P.
8. Castles,

and you have an excellent position.

GAME THE SEVENTH.

COUNTER GAMBIT IN THE KNIGHT'S OPENING.

WHITE.   BLACK.
1. P. to K's 4th.   1. P. to K's 4th.
2. K. Kt. to B's 3rd.   2. P. to K. B's 4th.*

Your best move is now to take the Pawn with the Kt.; but you may also play advantageously K's B. to Q. B's 4th. If, instead of either of these moves, you take the Pawn with K's Pawn, Black will have the better game.

3. K's Kt. takes P. (best)   3. Q. to K. B's 3rd (best)

---

* In the admirable German treatise on the openings, began by Von Bilguer and ultimately so well concluded by Von H. der Laza, the following remarks are made upon this opening, which there is designated "THE COUNTER GAMBIT IN THE KNIGHT'S GAME." "During the summer of the year 1839, five of the best chess-players in Berlin, amongst whom were Von Bilguer, the deceased author of this work, and Von H. der Laza, its editor, agreed to meet weekly, and to select this opening as the subject of their investigations." (The most important variations resulting from these inquiries will be found in the present Chapter.) . . . . "The principal authors who have turned their attention to this *début* are,—Lewis, 1st Ed. (1842) pp. 84, 88; Lewis's Treatise, pp. 117, 122, 236, 239; Walker (1841), p. 186; Greco (Hirshell), pp. 112, 116; Cozio, i. pp. 280, 285, 288, 350, 353; Cozio, ii. pp. 342, 350, 354; Ponziani (1782), p. 105, and in the Palamède of 1843, pp. 19, 26, with the specific title of 'Gambit en second.'" M. Deschapelles, in the match by correspondence between Paris and Pesth, had recommended the move 2. P. to K. B's 4th as the best defence against K's Kt. to B's 3rd of the first player. It was, however, rightly rejected by the committee, and K's Kt. to B's 3rd adopted instead.

The idea of this game is traceable to Damiano, but Greco appears to be the true originator.

If he play 3. Q. to K's 2nd, the subjoined moves show you will get the advantage :—

	3. Q. to K's 2nd.
4. Q. to K. R's 5th (ch.)	4. P. to K. Kt.'s 3rd.
5. Kt. takes Kt.'s P.	5. Q. takes K's P. (ch.)
6. B. to K's 2nd (best)	6. K's Kt. to B's 3rd.
7. Q. to R's 3rd (best)	7. P. takes Kt.*
8. Q. takes R.	8. Q. takes K. Kt.'s P.
9. R. to K. B's sq.	9. K. to B's 2nd.
10. Q. to R's 4th,	

With the better game.

4. P. to Q's 4th.	4. P. to Q's 3rd.

He may also take the K's P. with P. (See the Fourth Variation.)

5. Kt. to Q. B's 4th.	5. P. takes K's P.
6. Q. Kt. to B's 3rd.	6. P. to Q. B's 3rd, or First Variation.

This sixth move of Black gives rise to some extremely delicate manœuvring, in which, without the greatest exactness on White's part, he may lose a Knight.

7. Q's Kt. takes K's P. (best)	7. Q. to K's 3rd.
8. Q. to K's 2nd.	8. P. to Q's 4th.
9. Q's Kt. to Q's 6th (ch.)	9. K. to Q's 2nd.

If he play 9. K. to Q's sq., these moves are likely to follow :—

	9. K. to Q's sq.
10. Q's Kt. takes Q. Kt.'s P. (ch.)	10. K. to Q. B's 2nd. †
11. Q. takes Q.	11. Q's B. takes Q.
12. K's Kt. to Q. R's 5th.	12. K. to Kt.'s 3rd (best)
13. Q's B. to Q's 2nd.	13. Q's Kt. to Q's 2nd.
14. P. to Q. Kt.'s 4th,	

And afterwards Q's Kt. to B's 5th, with a superior game.

Observe here, that it is far from indifferent which Kt. you check with. If you play 9. K's Kt. to Q's 6th (ch.), he may move K. to Q's sq. You reply with 10. Q's B. to K. Kt.'s 5th (ch.); he then moves K. to Q. B's 2nd, and wins one of the Knights. At your 10th move, however, instead of checking with the B. you may play 10. Q's Kt. to K. Kt.'s 5th; Black

---

* If R. to Kt.'s sq., White replies with Q. Kt. to B's 3rd, or Q. P. to Q's 3rd, and then Kt. to K. B's 4th.

† If he play otherwise the Knight will secure a retreat.

cannot then take the other Kt. on account of 11. Kt. to B's 7th (ch.), winning the Queen, but he would take your Q. with Q. (ch.), and the game would probably go on thus :—

11. B. takes Q.	11. B. takes Kt.
12. Kt. to K. B's 7th (ch.)	12. K. to his 2nd.
13. Kt. takes R.	13. K's B. to Q's 3rd.
14. B. to Q's 3rd.	14. K's Kt. to B's 3rd.
15. Kt. to K. Kt.'s 6th.	15. P. takes Kt.
16. K's B. takes P., and	

White ought not to win.

10. Q's Kt. to K. B's 7th.	10. Q's P. takes K's Kt.
11. Q. takes Q. (ch.)	11. K. takes Q.
12. K's B. takes P. (ch.)	12. K. to his 2nd.
13. Kt. takes R.	13. Q's B. to K's 3rd.
14. K's B. to Q's 3rd.	14. K's Kt. to B's 3rd.
15. Q's B. to K. Kt.'s 5th.	15. Q's B. to K. Kt.'s sq.
16. Castles, with a fine game.	

Should he, for his 15th move, instead of Q's B. to K. Kt.'s sq., play P. to K. Kt.'s 3rd, you may give up the Knight for the two Pawns; but in the present position the Knight need not be lost.

FIRST VARIATION,

Beginning at Black's 6th move.

BLACK.

WHITE.

WHITE.	BLACK.
	6. Q's B. to K. B's 4th.
7. P. to K. Kt.'s 4th.	7. Q's B. to K. Kt.'s 3rd.
8. K's B. to Kt.'s 2nd.	8. P. to Q. B's 3rd.
9. B. takes K's P.	9. B. takes B.
10. Q's Kt. takes B.	10. Q. to K's 3rd.
11. Q. to K's 2nd.	11. P. to Q's 4th.
12. K's Kt. to Q's 6th (ch.)	

If now Black take the Knight with his Bishop, you retake with the Q's Kt. (ch.), then exchange Queens, and win the Q. Kt.'s P. He may, however, move 12. K. to his 2nd, whereupon you check with K's Kt. at K. B's 5th, and afterwards liberate your other Kt.

SECOND VARIATION,

Beginning at Black's 6th move.

Arrange the men according to the preceding diagram again.

WHITE.	BLACK.
	6. K's Kt. to K's 2nd.
7. P. to Q's 5th.	7. Q. to K. Kt.'s 3rd.

If at his 7th move he play Q's B. to K. B's 4th, you again attack the B. with K. Kt.'s P., and then play K's B. to Kt.'s 2nd.

8. Q. to her 4th.	8. Q's B. to K. B's 4th.
9. Q's Kt. to his 5th, gaining a Pawn.	

THIRD VARIATION,

From Black's 6th move.—(See preceding diagram.)

WHITE.	BLACK.
	6. Q. to K. Kt.'s 3rd.
7. P. to K. B's 3rd (best)	7. K's Kt. to B's 3rd.
8. P. takes K's P.	8. Kt. takes P.
9. Q. to K's 2nd.	9. Q's B. to K. B's 4th.
10. K's Kt. to Q's 2nd.	10. Q's Kt. to B's 3rd.
11. K's Kt. takes Kt.	11. Kt. takes Q's P.
12. Q. to her 3rd, having won a Piece.	

Black's error in this last variation is not taking the K. B's P. with P. at his 7th move. If he take the P. you still have a considerable advantage in position, but he avoids the loss of any of his men. (*e. g.*)

	7. P. takes K. B's P.
8. Q. takes P.	8. K's Kt. to B's 3rd.
9. K's B. to Q's 3rd.	9. Q. to K. Kt.'s 5th.
10. Q. to K's 3rd (ch.)	10. B. to K's 2nd.
11. Castles, with the bet-	
ter game.	

FOURTH VARIATION OF THIS GAME,

Beginning at Black's 4th move.

WHITE.	BLACK.
1. P. to K's 4th.	1. P. to K's 4th.
2. K's Kt. to B's 3rd.	2. P. to K. B's 4th.
3. Kt. takes K's P.	3. Q. to K. B's 3rd.
4. P. to Q's 4th.	4. P. takes K's P.
5. K's B. to Q. B's 4th.	5. P. to Q. B's 3rd.

If instead of this, he move 5. K's Kt. to K's 2nd, the game is likely to proceed thus :—

	5. K's Kt. to K's 2nd.
6. Q's Kt. to B's 3rd.	6. Q. to K. B's 4th.
7. Q's Kt. to his 5th.	7. Q's Kt. to R's 3rd.
8. K's Kt. to B's 7th,	

Winning at least the Rook, for if he attempt to save it, he must lose the Q. by 9. Kt. to Q's 6th (ch.), &c.

6. B. to B's 7th (ch.)	6. K. to his 2nd.

Should he move the K. to Q's sq., you can take the Kt., and if he retake with his R., play 9. Q's B. to K. Kt.'s 5th, winning the Q. in two moves.

7. P. to K. R's 4th.	7. P. to K. R's 3rd.
8. Q. to K. R's 5th.	8. K. to Q's 3rd.
9. Q's B. to K. Kt.'s 5th.	9. P. takes B.
10. Q. takes R.,	

and you have an easy game.

ANOTHER VARIATION,

Beginning at the 3rd move of White.

WHITE.	BLACK.
1. P. to K's 4th.	1. P. to K's 4th.
2. K's Kt. to B's 3rd.	2. P. to K. B's 4th.
3. K's B. to Q. B's 4th.	3. P. takes K's P.

Black might also play 3. P. to Q's 3rd, and the position would be the same as in one of the modifications of "Philidor's defence of the Knight's Opening."—In that case the game would probably be followed thus:—

	3. P. to Q's 3rd.
4. P. to Q's 4th (best)	4. P. takes K's P.

(If he take the Q's P. instead, you play 5. K. Kt. to his 5th, and have a much better game than he has.)

5. Kt. takes P.	5. P. takes Kt.

(If the Kt. is not taken, you have evidently an excellent position.)

6. Q. to K. R's 5th (ch.)	6. K. to Q's 2nd.

(By interposing the K. Kt. P. he would lose his Rook, and if he played the King to his 2nd, you checkmate him in two moves.)

7. Q. to K. B's 5th (ch.)	7. K. to Q. B's 3rd.
8. Q. takes P. at K's 5th.	8. P. to Q. R's 3rd.

(This is his only move to avert immediate mate.)

9. P. to Q's 5th (ch.)	9. K. to Kt.'s 3rd.

(If he move the K. to B's 4th, mate follows in four moves.)

10. B. to K's 3rd (ch.)	10. B. to Q. B's 4th.

(Should he play 10. P. to Q. B's 4th, you take the P. in passing, and then move Q. Kt. to B's 3rd, secure of the game.)

11. B. takes B. (ch.)	11. K. takes B.
12. P. to K. Kt.'s 4th (ch.)	12. K. takes P.

(If he take the Bishop, you may mate him in four moves.)

13. Kt. to Q's 2nd.	13. P. to Q. Kt.'s 4th.

(If 13. K. to B's 4th, he will be mated in three moves.)

14. R. to Kt.'s sq. (ch.)	14. K. to R's 4th.

(It is indifferent where he plays.)

15. Q. to her 4th.	15. Q. to her 3rd.
16. Kt. to Kt.'s 3rd. (ch.)	

And you win.

4. Kt. takes P.	4. Q. to K. Kt.'s 4th.

You would play badly at move 4, in taking the K's Kt. with your Bishop. (*e. g.*)

4. B. takes Kt.	4. R. takes B.
5. Kt. takes K's P.	5. Q. to K. Kt.'s 4th.
6. Kt. to his 4th.	6. P. to Q's 4th.

And he has the better position.

5. Kt. to K. B's 7th (best)   5. Q. takes K. Kt.'s P.

Instead of 5. Kt. to B's 7th, you might play P. to Q's 4th, and if he took the K. Kt.'s P., move Q. to K. R's 5th (ch.), having a strong attack.

6. R. to K. B's sq.	6. P. to Q's 4th.
7. Kt. takes R.	7. P. takes B.

If you take the Q's P. with B., instead of capturing the Rook, Black, as the annexed moves prove, will have the better game.

7. B. takes Q's P.	7. Q's B. to K. R's 6th.
8. Q. to K's 2nd.	8. K's Kt. to B's 3rd.
9. K's B. to Q. B's 4th (best)	9. Q's Kt. to B's 3rd.
10. Kt. takes R.	10. Q's Kt. to Q's 5th.

And Black should win.

8. Q. to K. R's 5th. (ch.)	8. P. to K. Kt.'s 3rd.
9. Q. takes K. R's P.	9. Q's B. to K's 3rd.
10. Q. takes K. Kt.'s P. (ch.)	10. Q. takes Q.
11. Kt. takes Q.	

and you have " the exchange" and a Pawn advantage.

The foregoing examples will suffice to show that in this opening you obtain a decided superiority by answering Black's 2nd move, P. to K. B's 4th, either with 3. K's Kt. takes K's P. or 3. K's B. to Q. B's 4th. But the result is not so clearly in your favour, if in place of one of these moves you substitute 3. P. takes K. B's P., as you will see by the following variations.

VARIATION OF THIS GAME,

Beginning at White's 3rd move.

WHITE.	BLACK.
1. P. to K's 4th.	1. P. to K's 4th.
2. K. Kt. to B's 3rd.	2. P. to K. B's 4th.
3. P. takes P.	3. P. to Q's 3rd.

This is Black's best mode of taking advantage of your bad 3rd move, P. takes P. He may also play 3. Q. to K. B's 3rd without danger; for example,—

	3. Q. to K. B's 3rd.
4. Q. to K's 2nd.	4. Q. Kt. to B's 3rd.
5. P. to Q's 4th.	5. P. to Q's 3rd.
6. P. takes P.	6. P. takes P.
7. Q. B. to K. B's 4th.	7. K. B. to Q's 3rd.
8. P. to K. Kt.'s 4th.	8. K. Kt. to K's 2nd.
9. Q. B. to K. Kt.'s 5th.	9. Q. to K. B's 2nd.
10. P. to K. R's 3rd.	10. P. to K. R's 4th.
11. K. B. to K. Kt.'s 2nd.	11. P. takes P.
12. P. takes P.	12. R. takes R.
13. K. B. takes R.	13. P. to K. Kt.'s 3rd.
14. B. takes K. Kt.	14. Q. takes B.

(If instead of taking the Kt., you play 14. P. to K. B's 6th, he will move 14. K. Kt. to his sq., and win the Pawn and a better position; and if you take P. with P., he takes again with his Kt., having a fine game.)

| 15. P. takes K. Kt. P. | 15. B. takes K. Kt. P. |

And he has the advantage.

| 4. P. to Q's 4th. | 4. P. to K's 5th. |
| 5. Kt. to his 5th. | 5. Q. B. takes P. |

You may also play 5. Q. to K's 2nd, but that would hardly be so good as the move given.

6. Q. to K's 2nd.	6. P. to Q's 4th.
7. Q. to her Kt.'s 5th (ch.)	7. Q. Kt. to B's 3rd.
8. Q. takes Q. Kt. P.	8. Q. Kt. takes Q. P.
9. B. to Q. Kt.'s 5th (ch.)	9. Kt. takes B.
10. Q. takes Kt. (ch.)	10. Q. to her 2nd.
11. Q. to Q. Kt.'s 7th.	11. Q. R. to B's sq.
12. Q. takes Q. R. P.	12. P. to K. R's 3rd.
13. Kt. to K. R's 3rd.	13. B. takes Kt.
14. K. Kt. P. takes B.	14. Q. takes P.

And he has the superiority in position.

GAME THE EIGHTH.

WHITE.	BLACK.
1. P. to K's 4th.	1. P. to K's 4th.
2. K's Kt. to B's 3rd.	2. P. to Q's 4th.

This defence may be adopted without much danger, but if you take his proffered Pawn with P. at your 3rd move, your position is slightly better than Black's.

| 3. P. takes P. (best) | 3. Q. takes P. |

This appears to be his best reply. If instead of taking the Pawn, he play 3. P. to K's 5th, the result will be as follows:—

	3. P. to K's 5th.
4. Q. to K's 2nd.	4. Q. to K's 2nd.
5. Kt. to Q's 4th.	5. K's Kt. to B's 3rd.
6. Q's Kt. to B's 3rd.	6. Q. to K's 4th.
7. K's Kt. to B's 3rd.	7. Q. to K's 2nd.
8. K's Kt. to his 5th.	8. Q's B. to K. B's 4th.
9. Q. to her Kt.'s 5th (ch.)	

And you must gain some advantage.

4. Q's Kt. to B's 3rd.	4. Q. to K's 3rd.
5. B. to Q. Kt.'s 5th (ch.)	5. B. to Q's 2nd.
6. Castles.	6. B. takes B.
7. Kt. takes B.	7. K's B. to Q's 3rd.
8. R. to K's sq.	8. P. to K. B's 3rd.

You might also play 8. K's Kt. takes K's P., and the next move place K's R. at K's sq., threatening to take Q. B's P. with the Kt.

9. P. to Q's 4th.	9. P. to Q. B's 3rd.
10. Q's P. takes P.	10. P. takes P.
11. K's Kt. takes P.	

Winning of course.

Your success in this variation results from your 3rd move of P. takes P.; if instead of this you take the K's P. with the Knight, it is not so evident that any marked advantage would accrue to you; for instance,—

WHITE.	BLACK.
1. P. to K's 4th.	1. P. to K's 4th.
2. K's Kt. to B's 3rd.	2. P. to Q's 4th.
3. Kt. takes K's P.	3. Q. to K's 2nd (best)

This is considered his best move; if 3. P. takes P. the game proceeds thus:—

	3. P. takes P.
4. K's B. to Q. B's 4th.	4. Q. to K. Kt.'s 4th (best)
5. P. to Q's 4th.	5. Q. takes K. Kt.'s P.
6. R. to K. B's sq.	6. B. to K's 3rd (best)

(If he play 6. B. to K. R's 6th, you may take K. B's P. with your B. (ch.), and then return the B. to Q. B's 4th.)

7. P. to Q's 5th.	7. B. to K. R's 6th.
8. Q's B. to K. B's 4th.	

The game is equal.

4. P. to Q's 4th.

5. Kt. to his 4th.

4. P. to K. B's 3rd.

5. B. takes Kt.

There is a beautiful but not sound variation on your move at this point, the invention of Mr. Cochrane, which is to leave the K's Kt. and play 5. Q's Kt. to B's 3rd. (See the game " between Messrs. Cochrane and Staunton," in which this occurs, at the end of the present Chapter.)

6. Q. takes B.

7. Q. takes Q. (ch.)

6. Q. takes P. (ch.)

7. P. takes Q.

There is no advantage on either side.

From these variations you will gather that when Black adopts the defence of 2. P. to Q's 4th in this game, your best answer is 3. P. takes Q's P., and that any other reply will lead to about an even game.

———

GAMES

ILLUSTRATIVE OF THE PRECEDING VARIATIONS.

(From the *Chess-Player's Chronicle.*)

GAME I.—Between Messrs. Cochrane and Staunton.

WHITE. (Mr. Cochrane.)	BLACK. (Mr. Staunton.)
1. P. to K's 4th.	1. P. to K's 4th.
2. K. Kt. to B's 3rd.	2. P. to Q's 4th.
3. Kt. takes K. P.	3. Q. to K's 2nd.
4. P. to Q's 4th.	4. P. to K. B's 3rd.
5. Q. Kt. to B's 3rd.	5. P. takes K. Kt.
6. Kt. takes Q. P.	6. Q. to K. B's 2nd.
7. K. B. to Q. B's 4th.	7. Q. B. to K's 3rd.
8. Castles.	8. P. to Q. B's 3rd.
9. P. to K. B's 4th.	9. P. takes Kt.
10. B. P. takes P.	10. Q. to her 2nd.
11. K. P. takes P.	11. B. takes P.
12. P. to K's 6th.	12. Q. to her B's 3rd.
13. Q to K. R's 5th (ch.)	13. P. to K. Kt.'s 3rd.
14. Q. takes B.	14. K. Kt. to K's 2nd.
15. Q. to K's 5th.	15. Q. takes B.
16. Q. takes R.	16. Kt. to K. B's 4th.
17. Q. B. to K. R's 6th.	17. Q. to her Kt.'s 5th.
18. Q. takes B. (ch.)	18. Q. takes Q.
19. B. takes Q.	19. K. takes B.
20. P. to K. Kt.'s 4th.	

Black surrenders.

GAME II.—Between MM. Jaenisch and Petroff.

(From the same work.)

WHITE. (M. Jaenisch.)	BLACK. (M. Petroff.)
1. P. to K's 4th.	1. P. to K's 4th.
2. K. Kt. to B's 3rd.	2. P. to Q's 4th.
3. K. Kt. takes P.	3. Q. to K's 2nd.
4. P. to Q's 4th.	4. P. to K. B's 3rd.
5. Kt. to B's 3rd.	5. P. takes P.
6. K. Kt. to Q's 2nd.	6. P. to K. B's 4th.
7. K. B. to K's 2nd.	7. Q. Kt. to B's 3rd.
8. K. Kt. to Q. Kt.'s 3rd.	8. K. Kt. to B's 3rd.
9. Castles.	9. Q. to K. B's 2nd.
10. P. 'o Q. B's 4th.	10. Q. B. to Q's 2nd.
11. Q. B. to K. B's 4th.	11. Castles.
12. Q. Kt. to B's 3rd.	12. P. to K. R's 3rd.
13. P. to Q. R's 3rd.	13. P. to K. Kt.'s 4th.
14. Q. B. to Q's 2nd.	14. P. to K. B's 5th.
15. P. to Q's 5th.	15. Q. Kt. to K's 4th.
16. K. Kt. to Q's 4th.	16. K. B. to Q. B's 4th.
17. Q. B. to K's sq.	17. K. R. to Kt.'s sq.
18. P. to Q. Kt.'s 4th.	18. K. B. to K's 2nd.
19. P. to K. B's 3rd.	19. P. to K's 6th.
20. Q. to her Kt.'s 3rd.	20. P. to K. Kt.'s 5th.
21. P. to Q. B's 5th.	21. P. takes K. B. P.
22. Kt. takes P.	22. Kt. takes Kt. (ch.)
23. B. takes Kt.	23. Kt. to K. Kt.'s 5th.
24. Q. to her B's 4th.	24. K. to Kt.'s sq.
25. Q. to K's 4th.	25. Q. R. to K's sq.
26. P. to Q's 6th.	26. Q. B. to his 3rd.
27. Q. to her 4th.	27. B. takes B.
28. R. takes B.	28. B. to K. Kt.'s 4th.
29. Q. Kt. to his 5th.	29. P. to Q. B's 3rd.
30. P. to Q's 7th.	30. Q. R. to K's 3rd.
31. B. to K. Kt.'s 3rd.	31. P. takes Q. Kt.*
32. B. takes B. P. (ch.)	32. Kt. to K's 4th.
33. B. takes Kt. (ch.)	33. R. takes B.
34. Q. takes R. (ch.)	34. K. to R's sq.
35. R. takes Q.	35. P. to K's 7th.
36. Q. to K's 8th (ch.)	36. R. takes Q.
37. P. takes R., becomes a Queen (ch.), and wins.	

---

* If Black had taken the B. with K. B. P. at this point, the following moves show that he would have equally lost :—

	31. P. takes B.
32. Q. takes Kt.	32. P. takes P. (ch.)
33. K. to R's sq.	33. Q. takes Q. P.
34. Q. to K. Kt.'s 3rd (ch.), and wins.	

CHAPTER IV.

GAME THE NINTH.

THE GUIOCO PIANO.

AN attentive examination of the eight separate methods of reply to your second move of K's Kt. to B's 3rd in the antecedent games, will have enabled you to understand that four at least of these defences, viz.: P. to K. B's 3rd, B. to Q's 3rd, Q. to B's 3rd, and B. to Q. B's 4th, are untenable and injurious for the game of the second player, and that the remaining four, if not absolutely bad for him, are unsatisfactory, because against the best attack, they leave the balance of advantage in favour of the party playing first.

It is now time to consider the consequences to both parties when Black, abandoning the objectionable or uncertain modes of play he has hitherto adopted, shall answer with the move which the best authorities at length concur in recommending as the proper one, i. e., 2. Q's Kt. to B's 3rd. Upon his playing thus, you have the choice of three good moves: in the first place, to play 3. K's B. to Q. B's 4th, as in the present game; secondly, 3. P. to Q's 4th; and thirdly, P. to Q. B's 3rd. The two latter of which will form the subjects of games hereafter.

WHITE.	BLACK.
1. P. to K's 4th.	1. P. to K's 4th.
2. K's Kt. to B's 3rd.	2. Q's Kt. to B's 3rd.
3. K's B. to Q. B's 4th.	3. K's B. to Q. B's 4th.

It is generally admitted that Black's 3rd move is the best he can adopt; and the opening now formed is that which the Italians have entitled the "Guioco Piano;"* an opening, less attacking than many others, but one perfectly safe for both players, and therefore always in request, and which usually generates games of the most solid and instructive kind.

* The leading works to be consulted on this important opening, are Lolli, pp. 46, 162, 264; Ponziani, 1782, p. 53; Stamma, 1745, pp. 7—19; Lewis (1st Ed.), pp. 94—125; (2nd Ed.), pp. 90—120, 152—170; also in his last Treatise, 1844, pp. 148—189; Mauvillon, 1829; Bilguer's Handbuch, 1843; and the immense collection of games in the Chess-Player's Chronicle, vol. i. to vii.

Instead of this move, he may however play 3. K's Kt.
to B's 3rd, or 4. P. to K. B's 4th, both of which will be subsequently examined; 4. Q's P. one is obviously bad for him,
by shutting in his K's B., and 4. Q. to K. B's 3rd, a move too
frequently adopted by young players, will be touched upon
incidentally in the analysis of the former two.

4. P. to Q. B's 3rd.	4. K's Kt. to B's 3rd (best)

Your move of 4. P. to Q. B's 3rd is the one most played at
this point, because it makes an outlet for your Q. to her
Kt.'s 3rd, and enables you at the proper moment to advance
the Q's P. to the 4th sq.; but 4. Q's Kt. to B's 3rd, or
4. P. to Q's 3rd (see Game 15th), though less immediately
attacking, may also be made with advantage. You may likewise castle at this moment (see Game 14th). Black's answer
of 4. K's Kt. to B's 3rd, is the oldest and best defence he
can adopt. It is to be found as far back as the time of
Damiano, 1512, and modern authorities agree in acknow-
ledging it to be the most secure reply at Black's command.
Instead of this move, however, it has been shown in the
"Handbuch" of Bilguer and H. der Laza, that he may,
without any very marked disadvantage, play either 4. Q. to
K's 2nd, or 4. K's B. to Q. Kt.'s 3rd (see Game 13th), both of
which will be considered presently, together with 4. P. to
Q's 3rd (see Game 11th), the move commended by the great
Italian players, and subsequently by Lewis, but which cer-
tainly appears less effective than bringing out the K's Kt.

5. P. to Q's 4th.	5. P. takes P.

The question as to which is your best 5th move, has long
occupied the attention of the leading writers. Mr. Lewis has
a preference for 5. P. to Q's 3rd; but he remarks, it is difficult to decide (see Game 10th); and Bilguer and H. der
Laza recommend you to castle—the result of which shall
be shown in Variation III. If instead of any one of these
three ways, you play 5. Kt. to Kt.'s 5th, the following moves
will show that your opponent gains the advantage of position:

5. K's Kt. to his 5th.	5. Castles.
6. P. to K. B's 4th.	6. P. to Q's 4th (best)
7. P. takes Q's P. (best)	7. Kt. takes P.
8. B. takes Kt.	8. Q. takes B.
9. Q. to K. B's 3rd.	9. K's R. to Q's sq. (best)

If you play 9. Q. to K. R's 5th, Black plays 9. Q's B. to K. B's 4th, and the second player should win. Black's 9th move, K's R. to Q's sq., first occurs in a game between the writer and Mr. Horwitz, and it appears to be a satisfactory reply to the attack.

6. P. to K's 5th.	6. P. to Q's 4th (best)

You might have played 6. P. takes P., a move the German masters recommend, and the consequences from which will be shown in Variation II. You may also play 6. P. to Q. Kt.'s 4th, and upon the Bishop retreating, take 7. P. with P.; in that case, Black must not take the Kt.'s P. with Kt., on account of your playing P. to K's 5th, which would then give you a capital game.

Black plays the best move he has. If instead, he move 6. Q. to K's 2nd, you castle; if 6. K's Kt. to his 5th, you may take K. B's P. with B., checking, and when the K. takes B., play Kt. to his 5th (ch.), or better perhaps than taking the K. B's P., take Q's P. with P. But, as recommended by some authors, he may play 6. K's Kt. to K's 5th, which will form the subject of Variation I.

7. K's B. to Q. Kt.'s 5th.	7. K's Kt. to K's 5th.

If at move 7. you take the Kt. with K's P., he takes your B. with P., and if then you play 8. P. takes K. Kt.'s P., he replies with 8. K's R. to Kt.'s sq., and has the better game.

8. B. takes Kt. (ch.)	8. P. takes B.
9. P. takes P.	9. B. to Q. Kt.'s 3rd.

Black may check with his B. here; but that is hardly so good as the move given. (e. g.)

	9. B. to Q. Kt.'s 5th (ch.)
10. B. to Q's 2nd.	10. B. takes B. (ch.)
11. Q's Kt. takes B.	11. P. to K. B's 4th.

You may now play 12. Q's R. to Q. B's sq., having a slight advantage of position.

10. Castles.	10. Q's B. to K. Kt.'s 5th.
11. Q's B. to K's 3rd.	11. Castles.

The game is equal.

VARIATION I.,

Beginning at Black's 6th move.

WHITE.	BLACK.
1. P. to K's 4th.	1. P. to K's 4th.
2. K's Kt. to B's 3rd.	2. Q's Kt. to B's 3rd.

3. K's B. to Q. B's 4th.	3. K's B. to Q. B's 4th.
4. P. to Q. B's 3rd.	4. K's Kt. to B's 3rd.
5. P. to Q's 4th.	5. P. takes P.
6. P. to K's 5th.	6. K's Kt. to K's 5th.
7. K's B. to Q's 5th.	7. Kt. takes K. B's P.

If you play 7. Q. to K's 2nd, he moves 7. P. to Q's 4th, and on your playing 8. P. takes P. in passing, he moves 8. Q's B. to K. B's 4th, with a better position; and if you move 7. P. takes P., he then checks with his B., and the game is equal.

8. K. takes Kt.	8. P. takes P. (dis. ch.)
9. K. to Kt.'s 3rd.	9. P. takes Q. Kt.'s P.

The King, at your 9th move, has three squares to move to, each of which has its advocates; the Italian authors recommend K. to his own sq.; Jaenisch, Ghulam Kassim, and Mendheim prefer the move in the text; and Petroff advises K. to B's sq. It may be well to examine the first and last before proceeding with the other.

In the first place then suppose,—

9. K. to his sq.	9. P. takes Q. Kt.'s P.
10. Q's B. takes P.	10. Q's Kt. to K's 2nd.
11. K. B. to K's 4th.	11. P. to Q's 4th.
12. P. takes P. in passing.	12. Q. takes P.
13. Q. takes Q.	13. P. takes Q.
14. Q's Kt. to B's 3rd.	14. Q's B. to K. B's 4th.
15. K. to his 2nd.	

White appears to me to have the advantage.

In the second place suppose you play,—

9. K. to B's sq.	9. P. takes P.
10. Q's B. takes P.	10. Castles.
11. Q's Kt. to Q's 2nd.	11. P. to Q's 3rd.
12. Q's Kt. to K's 4th.	12. Q's Kt. to K's 2nd.
13. Q's Kt. takes B.	13. P. takes Kt.
14. B. to K's 4th.*	14. Q's B. to K. B's 4th.
15. Q. to her B's 2nd.	15. B. takes B.
16. Q. takes B.	16. Q. to her 4th.
17. Kt. to K. Kt.'s 5th.	

His best move apparently is to take your Q., and you have then I think the better game.

---

* Not B. takes K. B's P. (ch.), because he would of course take with his K.

10. Q's B. takes P.	10. Q's Kt. to K's 2nd.
11. Q. to her B's 2nd.	11. P. to Q's 3rd.

Ghulam Kassim, in his copious analysis of this position, recommends you to play 11. P. to K. R's 3rd, or 11. K's B. to K's 4th, and in both cases his variations end in giving the advantage to White. Jaenisch prefers, but I think without sufficient reason, 11. K's R. to K's sq.; the move in the text of 11. Q. to her B's 2nd, strikes me as at least equal to any of the others.

12. B. to K's 4th.	12. Kt. to K. Kt.'s 3rd.
13. Q's Kt. to Q's 2nd.	13. P. to Q. B's 3rd.
14. Q's R. to Q's sq.	

And the game appears to me in your favour.

Remember that at your move 14, you must not, instead of playing Q's R. to Q's sq., take the Kt. with your B., and afterwards play 15. Q's Kt. to K's 4th, because after taking your B. with K. R's P., he might move Q's B. to K. B's 4th, and thus prevent you moving your Kt. advantageously.

VARIATION II.,

Beginning at White's 6th move.

WHITE.	BLACK.
1. P. to K's 4th.	1. P. to K's 4th.
2. K's Kt. to B's 3rd.	2. Q's Kt. to B's 3rd.
3. K's B. to Q. B's 4th.	3. K's B. to Q. B's 4th.
4. P. to Q. B's 3rd.	4. K's Kt. to B's 3rd.
5. P. to Q's 4th.	5. P. takes P.
6. P. takes P.	6. B. to Q. Kt.'s 5th (ch.)

In the former example, you advanced the K's P. on the Kt., but the present move is advocated among the German players, and may be played without danger. Black's best reply is to check with his B.

7. B. to Q's 2nd.	7. B. takes B. (ch.)

If you interpose Q's Kt. at B's 3rd, the following moves will occur:—

7. Q's Kt. to B's 3rd.	7. Kt. takes K's P.
8. Castles.	8. B. takes Kt.
9. P. takes B.	9. P. to Q's 4th.

And he has an equal position and a P. more.

8. Q's Kt. takes B.	8. P. to Q's 4th.
9. P. takes P.	9. Kt. takes P.
10. Q. to her Kt.'s 3rd.	10. Q's Kt. to K's 2nd.

The game is even.

VARIATION III.,

Beginning at White's 5th move.

WHITE.	BLACK.
1. P. to K's 4th.	1. P. to K's 4th.
2. K's Kt. to B's 3rd.	2. Q's Kt. to B's 3rd.
3. K's B. to Q. B's 4th.	3. K's B. to Q. B's 4th.
4. P. to Q. B's 3rd.	4. K's Kt. to B's 3rd.
5. Castles.	5. Kt. takes K's P.

Castling at this crisis is unanimously condemned by the Italian triumvirate, Lolli, Ponziani (second edition), and the anonymous Modenese;* but as the present variation shows, it may be adopted with perfect safety.

Upon Black's 5th move the authorities of Italy and of Germany are at issue, the Italians, with one accord, denouncing the move 5. Kt. takes P., on account of White playing 6. Q. to K's 2nd, and recommending instead that Black should castle also; whilst Messrs. Bilguer and H. der Laza, on the contrary, pronounce 5. Kt. takes K's P. to be the best move of all for the second player. The result of the other mode of play may be seen in the following variation :—

---

* We must be careful of attaching too much importance to the opinions of the earlier authorities and the distinguished writers of the Italian School—their theory of openings being founded upon principles of play so different to ours, as to render it frequently a useless and sometimes a very treacherous guide. In the time of Damiano and Lopez, Castling appears to have been unknown, at least in Spain and a great part of Europe, and the method of performing this operation in Italy, where it is supposed to have originated, has been subjected to so many variable restrictions, and has been, and is, so dissimilar to the uniform and regular mode proposed by Greco, and now adopted throughout England, Germany, and France, that any system of openings dependent on the one, must be in some degree inapplicable to the other. Another peculiarity in the game of the Italian School, which must also tend to qualify the value of their theories to us, is that the Pawn in making two steps at his first move, can never be taken by a hostile Pawn in passing, but is privileged "*passar battaglia*," to pass the enemy untouched.

	5. Castles.
6. P. to Q's 4th.	6. B. to Q. Kt.'s 3rd (best)
7. P. takes P.	7. K's Kt. takes K's P.
8. P. to Q. Kt.'s 4th.	8. K. to R's sq. (best)
9. P. to Q. R's 4th.	9. P. to Q. R's 3rd.
10. B. to Q's 5th.	10. P. to K. B's 4th.
11. Q's R. to his 2nd.	

And you have the better game.

Q. to K's 2nd.	6. P. to Q's 4th.

You may also play 6. B. to Q's 5th, and make an even game; for instance,—

6. B. to Q's 5th.	6. K. Kt. to B's 3rd.
7. B. takes Q. Kt.	7. Q. Kt. P. takes B.
8. Kt. takes K. P.	

Your game is at least as good as Black's.

7. B. to Q. Kt.'s 5th.	7. Castles.
8. B. takes Q. Kt.	8. P. takes B.
9. Kt. takes K. P.	9. Q. B. to Kt.'s 2nd.
10. P. to Q's 4th.	10. K. B. to Q. Kt.'s 3rd.

There is no advantage on either side.

At your 6th move in this game it is not good, I think, instead of Q. to K's 2nd, or B. to Q's 5th, to play P. to Q's 4th, as the following moves seem to give your opponent the better game :—

6. P. to Q's 4th.	6. P. takes P.
7. R. to K's sq.	7. P. to Q's 4th.
8. P. takes P.	8. B. to Q. Kt.'s 5th.
9. B. to Q's 2nd.	9. Castles.
10. B. takes B.	10. Kt. takes B.
11. Q. to her Kt.'s 3rd.	11. P. takes B.
12. Q. takes Kt.	12. Kt. to Q's 3rd.

Black can sustain his Pawn.

GAME THE TENTH.

WHITE.	BLACK.
1. P. to K's 4th.	1. P. to K's 4th.
2. K's Kt. to B's 3rd.	2. Q's Kt. to B's 3rd.
3. K's B. to Q. B's 4th.	3. K's B. to Q. B's 4th.
4. P. to Q. B's 3rd.	4. K's Kt. to B's 3rd.
5. P. to Q's 3rd.	5. P. to Q's 3rd.

Your 5th move is preferred to P. to Q's 4th by some players, as safer, though less attacking. (For the result of 5. K. Kt. to Kt.'s 5th, see Game VI., between Messrs. Horwitz and Staunton, at the end of the Chapter.) If Black reply with 5. K's Kt. to his 5th, you can take the K. B's P., checking, and if the K. take the B., you check with the K's Kt., and take his Kt. with your Q.; if he refuse to take your B. with his K., you play Q's B. to K. Kt.'s 5th, having the better game. In reply to your 5th move, he may also play 5. P. to Q's 4th, when the following moves are likely to ensue :—

	5. P. to Q's 4th.
6. P. takes Q's P.	6. K's Kt. takes P.
7. Q. to her Kt.'s 3rd.	7. Q's B. to K's 3rd.
8. Q. takes Q. Kt.'s P.	8. K's Kt. to K's 2nd.
9. B. takes B.	9. P. takes B.

Your game is better than Black's.

6. P. to Q's 4th.	6. P. takes P.
7. P. takes P.	7. B. to Q. Kt.'s 3rd.
8. Q's Kt. to B's 3rd.	8. Q's B. to K. Kt.'s 5th.
9. P. to Q's 5th.	9. Q's Kt. to K's 4th.

The game is equal.

GAME THE ELEVENTH.

WHITE.	BLACK.
1. P. to K's 4th.	1. P. to K's 4th.
2. K's Kt. to B's 3rd.	2. Q's Kt. to B's 3rd.
3. K's B. to Q. B's 4th.	3. K's B. to Q. B's 4th.
4. P. to Q. B's 3rd.	4. P. to Q's 3rd.

Black's move of 4. P. to Q's 3rd is sanctioned by the approval of Mr. Lewis, who appears to prefer it to the more generally adopted one of K's Kt. to B's 3rd. It may be made, I think, without any positive disadvantage, but I agree with the German writers in believing the latter more advisable.

5. P. to Q's 4th.	5. P. takes P.
6. P. takes P.	6. B. to Q. Kt.'s 5th (ch.)

He may also play 6. B. to Q. Kt.'s 3rd, without danger. (*e.g.*)

	6. B. to Q. Kt.'s 3rd.
7. P. to K. R's 3rd.	7. K's Kt. to B's 3rd.
8. Q's B. to K. Kt.'s 5th.	8. P. to K. R's 3rd.

9. B. takes Kt.*	9. Q. takes B.
10. B. to Q. Kt.'s 5th.	10. Castles.
11. B. takes Kt.	11. P. takes B.
12. Castles.	12. P. to Q. B's 4th.
13. P. to K's 5th.	13. Q. to K. Kt.'s 3rd.

And Black's game is fully equal to yours.

At your 6th move, instead of immediately taking the Pawn, you may play 6. P. to Q. Kt.'s 4th, and when the Bishop retires, take the P. with Q. B's P., and in that case Black must not take the Kt.'s P. with Kt., or he will lose a Piece.

7. B. to Q's 2nd.	7. B. takes B. (ch.)

An interesting variation arises here from your moving the K. to B's sq., instead of interposing the Bishop. (See Var. I.)

8. Q's Kt. takes B.	8. K's Kt. to B's 3rd.
9. Q. to her Kt.'s 3rd.	9. Castles.
10. Castles.	10. Q's Kt. to R's 4th.
11. Q. to her B's 2nd.	11. Kt. takes B.
12. Q. takes Kt.	12. Kt. takes K's P.
13. Kt. takes Kt.	13. P. to Q's 4th.
14. Q. to K's 2nd.	14. P. takes Kt.
15. Q. takes P.	

There is little difference in the positions, but your men are better disposed for immediate action, and you have the advantage of a Knight against a Bishop.

VARIATION I.,

Beginning at White's 7th move.

WHITE.	BLACK.
1. P. to K's 4th.	1. P. to K's 4th.
2. K's Kt. to B's 3rd.	2. Q's Kt. to B's 3rd.
3. K's B. to Q. B's 4th.	3. K's B. to Q. B's 4th.
4. P. to Q. B's 3rd.	4. P. to Q's 3rd.
5. P. to Q's 4th.	5. P. takes P.
6. P. takes P.	6. B. to Q. Kt.'s 5th (ch.)
7. K. to his B's sq.	7. Q's B. to K. Kt.'s 5th.

The ingenious move of K. to his B's sq. at this moment,

---

* It would be imprudent to move 9. B. to R's 4th, and when the Kt.'s P. was pushed to Kt.'s 4th, to give up the B. for the two Pawns, because Black would play R. to K. B's sq., with a safe game.

instead of interposing either the Kt. or B., was first introduced
by Mr. Lewis, and although great pains have been taken by
the latest writers to prove it unsound, I believe it may be
made, not only with safety, but with advantage to your game.

8. Q. to her R's 4th.	8. B. takes Kt.

In place of 8. Q. to her R's 4th, you might first play P. to
Q's 5th, and proceed as follows :—

8. P. to Q's 5th.	8. B. takes Kt.
9. Q. to R's 4th.	9. B. takes K's P.
10. P. takes Kt.	10. P. to Q. Kt.'s 4th.
11. B. takes Q. Kt.'s P.	11. B. takes Q's Kt.
12. Q. takes K's B.	12. B. to K. B's 4th.

The game is even.

Instead of either 8. P. to Q's 5th, or 8. Q. to her R's 4th, you may get
an excellent game by playing 8. Q. to K. Kt.'s 3rd.

9. P. takes B.	9. Q. to her 2nd.
10. K's B. to Q. Kt.'s 5th.	10. Castles.

If you play 10. P. to Q's 5th, he moves the Kt. to K's 4th,
and when you have taken his B. with Q., he checks at K. R's
6th, and afterwards takes the doubled P. with his Queen.

11. K. to Kt.'s 2nd.

And it appears to me that White has an unquestionable
advantage. Instead of this move, the best authorities, even
including Mr. Lewis, make you take the Kt. with B. Black
retakes with his Q., and, as in doing so, he attacks your Q's
B., an exchange of Queens takes place, and the game is
equal; but by first moving the K. to Kt.'s 2nd, you avoid the
necessity of this exchange, and, I believe, must win a Piece by
force. When, however, you play 7. K. to B's sq., Black
is not compelled to reply with 7. Q's B. to K. Kt.'s 5th,
although it is apparently his best move; he may play 7. Q. to
her 2nd, or 7. K's B. to Q. R's 4th, as in the following
examples. In the first instance :—

	7. Q. to her 2nd.
8. Q. to her R's 4th.	8. B. to Q. R's 4th.
9. Q's Kt. to Q. R's 3rd.	9. K's B. to Q. Kt.'s 3rd.

(You would play badly to move 9. P. to Q's 5th, as he would answer
with 9. Q's Kt. to K's 4th.)

10. K's B. to Q. Kt.'s 5th.	10. P. to Q. R's 3rd.
11. P. to Q's 5th.	11. P. takes B.
12. Q. takes R.	12. Kt. to Q. R's 4th.
13. P. to Q. Kt.'s 4th.	

You have the better game.

If at his last move he play 12. Q. Kt. to K's 2nd, you answer with Q's B. to K's 3rd.

In the second instance :—

	7. K's B. to Q. R's 4th.
8. Q. to her R's 4th.	8. Q's B. to Q's 2nd.
9. P. to Q's 5th.	9. Q's Kt. to Q's 5th.

If he play 9. Kt. to K's 4th, you speedily ensure an advantage. (*e. g.*)

	9. Q's Kt. to K's 4th.
10. Q. takes K's B.	10. Kt. takes B.
11. Q. to her B's 3rd.	11. B. to Q. Kt.'s 4th.
12. Q. takes K. Kt.'s P.	

With a superior game.

10. Q. takes K's B.	10. Kt. to Q. B's 7th.
11. Q. to her B's 3rd.	11. Kt. takes Q's R.
12. P. to Q. Kt.'s 3rd.	12. Q. to K. B's 3rd.
13. B. to Q. Kt.'s 2nd, or P. to K's 5th.	

And you have the better game.

At the 8th move of this last variation, Black would do better perhaps to play 8. P. to Q. R's 3rd, instead of Q's B. to Q's 2nd; for example,—

	8. P. to Q. R's 3rd.
9. P. to Q's 5th.	9. P. to Q. Kt.'s 4th.
10. Q. to her R's 3rd.	10. P. takes B.
11. P. takes Kt.	11. B. to Q. Kt.'s 3rd.
12. Q. to her B's 3rd.	

You have a slight advantage.

GAME THE TWELFTH.

WHITE.	BLACK.
1. P. to K's 4th.	1. P. to K's 4th.
2. K. Kt. to B's 3rd.	2. Q. Kt. to B's 3rd.
3. K. B. to Q. B's 4th.	3. K. B. to Q. B's 4th.
4. P. to Q. B's 3rd.	4. P. to K. B's 4th.

Black's 4th move in this game is extremely hazardous, and if properly answered, must always serve to assist the first player's attack.

| 5. P. to Q's 4th. | 5. K. B. P. takes K. P. |

He may likewise play 5. P. takes Q. P., but the advantage will be equally on your side. (*e. g.*)

| | 5. P. takes Q. P. |
| 6. K. Kt. to his 5th. | 6. P. to Q's 4th. |

7. B. takes Q. P.	7. P. takes K. P.
8. B. takes K. Kt.	8. R. takes B.
9. Q. to K. R's 5th (ch.)	9. P. to K. Kt.'s 3rd.
10. Q. takes K. R. P.	10. Q. to her 4th.
11. P. to Q. B's 4th.	11. Q. takes P.

(If he check with the B. first, you play 12. B. to Q's 2nd.)

12. Q. Kt. to Q's 2nd.	12. B. to Q. Kt.'s 5th.
13. K. Kt. takes K. P.	

And you have an excellent game.

6. K. Kt. takes K. P.	6. B. to Q. Kt.'s 3rd.
7. Q. to K. R's 5th (ch.)	7. P. to K. Kt.'s 3rd.
8. B. to K. B's 7th (ch.)	8. K. to B's sq.
9. Q. B. to K. R's 6th (ch.)	9. Kt. takes B.
10. Q. takes Kt. (ch.)	10. K. to his 2nd
11. B. takes Kt.'s P.	11. Kt. takes Kt.
12. Q. to K. Kt.'s 5th (ch.)	

And you must win.

———

GAME THE THIRTEENTH.

As was remarked at the opening of the Chapter, Black for his 4th move, instead of K's Kt. to B's 3rd, may play without much danger either 4. Q. to K's 2nd, or 4. B. to Q. Kt.'s 3rd. In the first place, suppose,—

WHITE.	BLACK.
1. P. to K's 4th.	1. P. to K's 4th.
2. K's Kt. to B's 3rd.	2. Q's Kt. to B's 3rd.
3. K's B. to Q. B's 4th.	3. K's B. to Q. B's 4th.
4. P. to Q. B's 3rd.	4. Q. to K's 2nd.
5. P. to Q's 4th.	5. B. to Q. Kt.'s 3rd.

If for his 5th move he takes P. with P., you castle, and have an undoubted superiority of position ; for example —

	5. P. takes P.
6. Castles.	6. Kt. to K's 4th.
7. Kt. takes Kt.	7. Q. takes Kt.
8. P. to K. B's 4th.	8. P. takes Q. B's P. (dis. ch.)
9. K. to R's sq.	9. P. takes Q. Kt.'s P.
10. P. takes Q.	10. P. takes Q's R. (becoming a
11. Q. to her 5th.	Queen.)

And you ought to win easily.

6. P. takes K's P.	6. Kt. takes P.
7. Kt. takes Kt.	7. Q. takes Kt.
8. Castles.	8. P. to Q's 3rd.
9. K. to R's sq.	9. Q's B. to K's 3rd.

In the German "Handbuch," the game is here dismissed as equal. I cannot help thinking it a little in your favour.

In the second place,—

	4. K. B. to Q. Kt.'s 3rd.
5. P. to K's 4th.	5. P. to Q's 3rd.

If he play 5. Q. to K's 2nd, the position is the same as in the variation first given.

6. P. takes P.	6. P. takes P.
7. Q. takes Q. (ch.)	7. K. takes Q.
8. B. takes K. B's P.,	

and you have the better game.

This phase of the Guioco Piano Game, where the second player moves his Q. to K's 2nd on his 4th move, has been very fully analysed in the little work before mentioned, by Ghulam Kassim, and will be further illustrated by the games appended to this Chapter.

GAME THE FOURTEENTH.

WHITE.	BLACK.
1. P. to K's 4th.	1. P. to K's 4th.
2. K's Kt. to B's 3rd.	2. Q's Kt. to B's 3rd.
3. K's B. to Q. B's 4th.	3. K's B. to Q. B's 4th.
4. Castles.	4. P. to Q's 3rd.

Castling at your 4th move appears to me at least as good a move as playing P. to Q. B's 3rd. Black's response is recommended by Ponziani and most leading writers since, as the best he can make. If, instead, he play 4. K's Kt. to B's 3rd, the following moves are likely to occur:—

	4. K's Kt. to B's 3rd.
5. K's R. to K's sq.	5. Castles.
6. P. to Q. B's 3rd.	6. K's R. to K's sq.*

---

* He may also play P. to Q's 3rd.

7. P. to Q's 4th.	7. B. to Q. Kt.'s 3rd.*
8. Kt. to Kt.'s 5th.	8. R. to K's 2nd.

I prefer your game.

5. P. to Q. B's 3rd.	5. Q's B. to K. Kt.'s 5th.
6. Q. to her Kt.'s 3rd.	6. Q's B. takes Kt.

If, in place of taking the Knight, he play 6. Q. to her 2nd, you must not take K. B's P. with your B., but Q. Kt.'s P. with your Q., as follows:—

	6. Q. to her 2nd.
7. Q. takes Q. Kt.'s P.	7. Q's R. to Kt.'s sq.
8. Q. to R's 6th.	8. B. takes K's Kt.
9. P. takes B.	9. R. to Q. Kt.'s 3rd.
10. Q. to Q. R's 4th.	10. Q. to K. R's 6th.
11. B. to K's 2nd (best)	

And you have a P. more and a good position.

7. B. takes K. B's P. (ch.)	7. K. to K. B's sq.
8. K. Kt.'s P. takes Q's B.	8. Q. to K. B's 3rd.
9. K's B. to K. R's 5th.	9. P. to K. Kt.'s 3rd.
10. K's B. to Kt.'s 4th.	10. B. to Q. Kt.'s 3rd.
11. Q. to her sq.	

You have the better game.

If, instead of retreating the Bishop at his 10th move, he play 10. P. to K. R's 4th, you play 11. B. to K. R's 3rd, and should he take the doubled Pawn, you then move B. to K. Kt.'s 2nd, and subsequently win a Piece by taking the Q. Kt.'s P. with your Queen.

GAME THE FIFTEENTH.

WHITE.	BLACK.
1. P. to K's 4th.	1. P. to K's 4th.
2. K. Kt. to B's 3rd.	2. Q. Kt. to B's 3rd.
3. K. B. to Q. B's 4th.	3. K. B. to Q. B's 4th.
4. P. to Q's 3rd.	4. P. to Q's 3rd.

Your present 4th move may be played at least as advantageously, I think, as P. to Q. B's 3rd, but you must not follow it

----

* He would play ill to take the Pawn.

with 5. K. Kt. to his 5th. You may also move 4. Q. Kt. to
B's 3rd, or 4. P. to Q's 4th, but the latter is not good; and
you can now, by playing 4. P. to Q. Kt.'s 4th, form the celebrated Evans' Gambit, for which see the next Chapter.

5. P. to Q. B's 3rd.   5. Q. to K. B's 3rd.

Black may here move 5. K. Kt. to B's 3rd, or 5. K. B. to
Q. Kt.'s 3rd, without any disadvantage; but if he play 5. Q. B.
to K. Kt.'s 5th, you answer with 6. Q. to her Kt.'s 3rd, and
have a better position.

6. Q. B. to K. Kt.'s 5th.	6. Q. to K. Kt.'s 3rd.
7. Castles.	7. Q. B. to K. Kt.'s 5th.
8. Q. Kt. to Q's 2nd.	8. K. Kt. to K. R's 3rd.
9. P. to Q. Kt.'s 4th.	9. K. B. to Q. Kt.'s 3rd.
10. P. to Q. R's 4th.	10. P. to Q. R's 4th (best)
11. P. to Q. Kt.'s 5th.	11. Kt. to Q's sq.

If he play Kt. to K's 2nd, you take him with the Bishop, and
still confine his game by moving B. to Q's 5th.

12. K. B. to Q's 5th.

The game is in your favour.

GAMES

ILLUSTRATIVE OF THE " GUIOCO PIANO."

(From the *Chess-Player's Chronicle*.)

GAME I.—Between Mr. Horwitz and Mr. Staunton.

WHITE. (Mr. H.)	BLACK. (Mr. S.)
1. P. to K's 4th.	1. P. to K's 4th.
2. K. Kt. to B's 3rd.	2. Q. Kt. to B's 3rd.
3. K. B. to Q. B's 4th.	3. K. B. to Q. B's 4th.
4. P. to Q. B's 3rd.	4. K. Kt. to B's 3rd.
5. P. to Q's 4th.	5. P. takes P.
6. P. to K's 5th.	6. P. to Q's 4th.
7. K. B. to Q. Kt.'s 5th.	7. K. Kt. to K's 5th.
8. P. takes P.	8. B. to Q. Kt.'s 3rd.
9. Castles.	9. Castles.
10. P. to K. R's 3rd.	10. P. to K. B's 3rd.
11. Q. Kt. to B's 3rd.	11. P. takes K. P.
12. B. takes Kt.	12. P. takes B.

13. K. Kt. takes P.	13. Q. B. to Q. R's 3rd.
14. Q. Kt. to K's 2nd.*	14. P. to Q. B's 4th.†
15. B. to K's 3rd.	15. P. takes P.

---

* We should have taken off the Knight in preference. Black then, as his best move, would probably have taken the Knight (for taking the Rook would be dangerous, on account of "Q. Kt. to K. Kt.'s 5th"), and then the game might have proceeded thus :—

WHITE.	BLACK.
14. Q. takes Kt.	14. Q. P. takes Kt.
15. Q. to her Kt.'s 3rd (ch.)	15. Q. to her 4th.
16. Q. takes Q.	16. P. takes Q.
17. K. R. to Q's square.	&c. &c.

The position, however, would even then have been much in favour of the second player, from the commanding situation of his two Bishops.

† This is stronger play, we believe, than taking the Q. Kt. After advancing the doubled Pawn, Black remarked that, had his position been less favourable, and the advantages springing from this move less obviously certain, he should have much preferred the more enterprising play of taking the K. B. P. with his Kt.,—a sacrifice, as he demonstrated in an after game, which leads to many strikingly beautiful situations—for example :—

WHITE.	BLACK.
	15. Kt. takes K. B. P.
16. R. takes Kt.	16. R. takes R.
17. K. takes R.	17. Q. to K. R's 5th (ch.)
(In the first back game, White now played)	(Whereupon Black mated him prettily enough, as follows)—
18. K. to his B's square.	18. R. to K. B's square (ch.)
19. K. Kt. to B's 3rd.	19. B. takes Q. P.
20. Q. to K's square.	20. R. takes Kt. (ch.)

(White's only move, unless he give up the Q. for Bishop.)

21. P. takes R.	21. Q. takes K. R. P. Mate.

In a second back game, instead of "K. to B's square," White played—

WHITE.	BLACK.
18. P. to K. Kt.'s 3rd.	18. Q. takes K. R. P.
19. K. Kt. to B's 3rd, or (A.)	19. R. to K. B's square.
20. Q. Kt. to K. B's 4th.	20. B. takes Q. P. (ch.)
21. Q. takes B. (ch.)	21. Q. to K. B's 8th.
22. K. to his 3rd.	22. R. to K's square (ch.)

(If Kt. to K's 5th, White loses his Q., therefore)

23. K. to Q's 2nd.	23. Black may now take the Kt. or play R. to K's 5th, in either case having a winning game.

16. B. takes P.*	16. B. takes Kt.
17. Q. takes B.	17. B. takes B.
18. Kt. to Q. B's 6th.	18. Q. to K. B's 3rd.†
19. Kt. takes B.	19. Q. takes Kt.
20. Q. R. to Q's square.	20. Q. to her B's 4th.
21. Q. R. to Q. B's square.	21. Q. to her Kt.'s 3rd.
22. P. to Q. Kt.'s 3rd.	22. Kt. to K. Kt.'s 6th.
23. Q. to her 3rd.	23. Kt. takes K. R.

And after a few more moves, White surrendered.

GAME II.—Between Mr. Horwitz and Mr. Staunton.

WHITE. (Mr. S.)	BLACK. (Mr. H.)
1. P. to K's 4th.	1. P. to K's 4th.
2. K. Kt. to B's 3rd.	2. Q. Kt. to B's 3rd.
3. K. B. to Q. B's 4th.	3. K. B. to Q. B's 4th.
4. P. to Q. B's 3rd.	4. P. to Q's 3rd.
5. P. to Q's 4th.	5. P. takes P.
6. P. takes P.	6. B. to Q. Kt.'s 3rd.
7. Q. Kt. to B's 3rd.	7. Q. B. to K. Kt.'s 5th.
8. Q. B. to K's 3rd.	8. K. Kt. to B's 3rd.
9. P. to Q. R's 3rd.	9. Castles.
10. K. B. to K's 2nd.	10. K. R. to K's sq.
11. P. to Q's 5th.	11. Q. Kt. to K's 4th.
12. Kt. takes Kt.	12. Q. B. takes K. B.
13. Q. takes B.	13. R. takes Kt.
14. B. takes K. B.	14. Q. R. P. takes B.
15. Castles on K's side.	15. Kt. takes K. P.

(A.)

19. Q. Kt. to K. B's 4th.	19. B. takes Q. P. (ch.)

(If White take the B. he loses his Q. in three moves, therefore)

20. K. to B's 3rd.[1]	20. R. to K. B's square.
21. Q. takes B. (ch.)	21. Q. to K. R's 8th (ch.)

(If now the K. be played to B's 2nd, or K's 3rd, Black wins the Q., therefore)

22. K. to Kt.'s 4th.	22. B. to his square (ch.)

And Black wins.

(There are many other variations, but these will suffice to show the resources of the attack.)

* This move loses a clear Piece. Play as he could, however, the game was irredeemable.

† A move White overlooked, unfortunately, when he took the P. with Bishop.

---

[1] He may also play B. to K's 3rd, upon which Black can check with his Q., and afterwards take Kt. with B., having the better game.

16. Kt. takes Kt.	16. P. to K. B's 4th.
17. P. to K. B's 3rd.	17. P. takes Kt.
18. P. takes P.	18. Q. to K's 2nd.
19. Q. R. to K's sq.	19. Q. R. to K's sq.
20. K. R. to K. B's 4th.	20. P. to K. R's 3rd.*
21. Q. to K. B's 3rd.†	21. R. takes Q. P.
22. Q. R. to K. B's sq. ‡	22. R. to K's 4th.
23. K. R. to K. B's 7th.	23. Q. to K's 3rd.§
24. K. R. takes Q. B. P.	24. R. takes K. P.
25. R. takes Q. Kt. P.	25. P. to Q's 4th.
26. P. to K. R's 3rd.‖	26. R. to K's 8th.
27. R. takes R.	27. Q. takes R. (ch.)
28. Q. to K. B's sq.¶	28. Q. to K's 6th (ch.)
29. Q. to K. B's 2nd.	29. Q. to her B's 8th (ch.)
30. K. to R's 2nd.	30. R. to K. B's sq.
31. Q. to her 4th.	31. R. to K. B's 3rd.**
32. Q. takes P. (ch.)	32. K. to R's 2nd.
33. Q. to K's 5th.	33. R. to K. Kt.'s 3rd.††
34. R. to K's 7th.	34. Q. to her 7th.

* Black would have gained no advantage by taking the Q. P. at this juncture, or by advancing his P. to K. Kt.'s 4th, to attack the Rook. The move in the text was not made without due deliberation, and we believe it the best on the board.

† White designedly gives up the Queen's Pawn, to get a counter attack with his combined forces.

‡ Queen to her Knight's 3rd would have been worse than useless.

§ Had he gone to Queen's square, to protect his threatened Pawn, White would have won the King's Knight's Pawn. (e. g.)

WHITE.	BLACK.
	23. Q. to Q's sq.
24. R. takes K. Kt. P. (ch.)	24. K. takes R.
25. Q. to K. B's 7th (ch.)	25. K. to R's sq.
26. K. R. to K. B's 6th.	26. R. to K. R's 4th.[1]
27. Q. takes K. R.	27. Q. takes R.
28. Q. takes R. (ch.), &c.	

‖ A most important move. Black dare not now advance his Q. P. on account of Q. to B's 7th (ch.), which would enable White to double his Rooks on the adversary's K. Kt. P., and thus win easily.

¶ K. to R's 2nd would have been very bad play, because Black would have checked with his Q. at K's 4th; and if then the Queen were interposed, he would have taken the Q. and played R. to K's 6th (ch.), and afterwards R. to Q. Kt.'s 6th.

** He could not save all the Pawns attacked.

†† Threatening to take the K. Kt. P. with his Rook, and then check with the Queen at her Bishop's 3rd.

---

[1] If R. to K's 3rd, White takes R. with R., &c.

35. Q. to K's 4th.	35. Q. to her 3rd (ch.)
36. R. to K's 5th.	36. K. to Kt.'s sq.
37. Q. to her 5th (ch.)	37. Q. takes Q.
38. R. takes Q.	38. K. to B's 2nd.
39. R. to Q. Kt.'s 5th.	39. K. to his 2nd.
40. P. to K. Kt.'s 4th.	40. K. to Q's 2nd.
41. K. to Kt.'s 3rd.	41. K. to Q. B's 3rd.
42. R. to K's 5th.	42. R. to Q's 3rd.
43. R. to K's 3rd.	43. K. to Q. B's 4th.
44. P. to K. R's 4th.	44. P. to K. Kt.'s 3rd.
45. K. to B's 4th.	45. K. to Q's 5th.
46. R. to K's 4th (ch.)	46. K. to Q's 4th.
47. R. to K's 8th.	47. R. to K. B's 3rd (ch.)
48. K. to his 3rd.	48. K. to Q. B's 5th.
49. R. to K's 4th (ch.)	49. K. to Q's 4th.
50. R. to K. B's 4th.	50. R. to Q. B's 3rd.
51. R. to Q. Kt.'s 4th.	51. R. to K's 3rd (ch.)
52. K. to Q's 3rd.	52. R. to K. B's 3rd.
53. R. to Q. Kt.'s 5th (ch.)*	53. K. to Q. B's 3rd.
54. R. to K's 5th.	54. K. to Q's 3rd.
55. R. to Q. Kt.'s 5th.	55. K. to Q. B's 3rd.
56. R. to Q. Kt.'s 4th.	56. R. to B's 6th (ch.)
57. K. to his 2nd.	57. R. to K. R's 6th.
58. R. to K. B's 4th.	58. R. takes K. R. P.
59. R. to B's 6th (ch.)	59. K. to Kt.'s 4th.
60. R. takes K. Kt. P.	60. R. to R's 7th (ch.)
61. K. to B's 3rd.	61. R. takes Q. Kt. P.
62. R. takes K. R. P	62. R. to Q. Kt.'s 6th (ch.)
63. K. to B's 4th.	63. R. takes Q. R. P.
64. P. to Kt.'s 5th.	64. R. to Q. R's 8th.
65. R. to K. R's 4th.	65. K. to Q. B's 4th.
66. P. to Kt.'s 6th.	66. R. to Q. R's 2nd.
67. K. to his B's 5th.	67. P. to Kt.'s 4th.
68. R. to K. Kt.'s 4th.	68. P. to Kt.'s 5th.†
69. P. to Kt.'s 7th.	69. R. takes P.
70. R. takes R.	70. P. to Kt.'s 6th.
71. K. to his 4th.	71. K. to Kt.'s 5th.
72. K. to Q's 3rd.	

And Black surrenders.

---

* K to his 3rd would have been better.

† This was ill-judged. He should have played R. to K. Kt.'s 2nd, or Q. R's square.

GAME III.—Between Mr. Horwitz and Mr. Staunton.

WHITE. (Mr. H.)	BLACK. (Mr. S.)
1. P. to K's 4th.	1. P. to K's 4th.
2. K. Kt. to B's 3rd.	2. Q. Kt. to B's 3rd.
3. K. B. to Q. B's 4th.	3. K. B. to Q. B's 4th.
4. P. to Q. B's 3rd.	4. K. Kt. to B's 3rd.
5. P. to Q.'s 3rd.	5. P. to Q's 3rd.
6. K. Kt. to his 5th.	6. Castles.
7. P. to K. B's 4th.	7. P. to Q's 4th.
8. P. takes Q. P.	8. K. Kt. takes P.
9. B. takes Kt.	9. Q. takes B.
10. Q. to K. B's 3rd.*	10. K. R. to Q's sq.†
11. Q. takes Q.	11. R. takes Q.
12. K. to his 2nd.‡	12. Q. B. to K. Kt.'s 5th (ch.)
13. K. Kt. to B's 3rd.	13. Q. R. to Q's sq.
14. P. to Q's 4th.§	14. P. takes Q. P.
15. P. to Q. B's 4th.	15. Q. R. to K's sq. (ch.)
16. K. to B's 2nd.‖	16. K. R. to Q's 2nd.
17. Q. Kt. to Q's 2nd.	17. P. to Q's 6th (dis. ch.)
18. K. to his Kt.'s 3rd.	18. Q. B. takes Kt.
19. Kt. takes B.	19. Q. R. to K's 7th.
20. B. to Q's 2nd.	20. K. R. to Q's 3rd.
21. Q. R. to Q's sq.	21. K. R. to K. Kt.'s 3rd (ch.)
22. K. to R's 3rd.¶	22. K. R. to his 3rd (ch.)
23. Kt. to K. R's 4th.	23. B. to K's 2nd.
24. P. to K. Kt.'s 3rd.	24. Kt. to Q's 5th.

---

* This variation of the " Guioco Piano" is little known. It is briefly touched on in M. Heydebrant's " Handbuch des Schachspiels," but the first player there moves his Q. to K. R's 5th, whereupon Black replies with Q. B. to K. B's 4th, and the *début* is dismissed as favourable for the defence. On the first occasion when Mr. Horwitz played this opening, we were of opinion that his move of Q. to K. B's 3rd was decidedly preferable to Q. to K. R's 5th ; but the counter move hit upon by his antagonist in the present game shows clearly, we think, that the opening in any case is disadvantageous to the first player.

† From this point we look upon the game as virtually lost for White.

‡ Probably his best move. Had he played P. to Q. Kt.'s 4th, Black might have taken it with his Kt., and upon the B. P. retaking, have moved K. B. to Q's 5th, winning the exchange.

§ As good a move, perhaps, as he had on the board. By playing K. R. to Q's sq., he would evidently have lost a Piece.

‖ Well conceived. Tempting Black to open the discovered check, which would cost him " the exchange."

¶ Interposing the Kt. and then pushing the K. B. P. on the Rook afterwards, would have been unwise, on account of B. to Q's 3rd (ch.), &c.

25. B. to Q. B's 3rd.	25. Kt. to K's 3rd.*
26. K. to his Kt.'s 4th.	26. B. takes Kt.
27. P. takes B.	27. Q. R. to K's 5th.
28. K. R. to K. B's sq.	28. K. R. to Kt.'s 3rd (ch.)
29. K. to B's 5th.	29. Q. R. to K's 6th.
30. P. to K. R's 5th.	30. K. R. to Kt.'s 7th.
31. P. to K. R's 4th.	31. Kt. to Q. B's 4th.†
32. K. R. to K's sq.‡	32. P. to K. Kt.'s 3rd (ch.)

And then Black mates in two moves.

GAME IV.—Between M. St. Amant and Mr. Staunton.

WHITE. (Mr. S.)	BLACK. (M. St. A.)
1. P. to K's 4th.	1. P. to K's 4th.
2. K. B. to Q. B's 4th.	2. K. B. to Q. B's 4th.
3. K. Kt. to B's 3rd.	3. Q. Kt. to B's 3rd.
4. P. to Q. B's 3rd.	4. Q. to K's 2nd.
5. P. to Q's 4th.	5. P. takes P.§
6. Castles.	6. Q. Kt. to K's 4th.
7. Kt. takes Kt.	7. Q. takes Kt.
8. P. to K. B's 4th.	8. P. takes Q. B. P. (dis. ch.)
9. K. to R's sq.	9. Q. to her 5th.||
10. Q. to her Kt.'s 3rd.	10. Kt. to K. R's 3rd.
11. Q. Kt. takes P.	11. Castles.
12. P. to K. R's 3rd.¶	12. P. to Q. B's 3rd.
13. P. to K. B's 5th.	13. Q. to K. B's 3rd.
14. P. to K's 5th.**	14. Q. to K. R's 5th.
15. Q. B. takes Kt.	15. Q. takes Q. B.
16. Kt. to K's 4th.	16. B. to Q's 5th.
17. Kt. to Q's 6th.	17. Q. to K. R's 4th.
18. B. takes K. B. P. (ch.)	18. R. takes B.
19. P. to K. Kt.'s 4th.	19. B. takes K. P.††

---

* Threatening, if White took the Q. P., to win a Piece.

† He might also have played K. Kt. P. one (ch.), and after the exchange of Pawns when the K. was driven to his B's 6th, have taken K. B. P. with the Kt. The move in the text, however, appears as effectual as any.

‡ If B. to K's 5th, Black rejoined with Kt. to Q's 2nd, &c.

§ The proper move is B. to Q. Kt.'s 3rd. Taking the Pawn gives an immediate advantage to White.

|| The ill consequences attendant on taking the Q. Kt. P. with P. have been shown in the preceding analysis.

¶ If White play P. to K. B's 5th at this point, his opponent may move Kt. to K. Kt.'s 5th, threatening to play afterwards Q. to K. Kt.'s 8th ch.), and then mate with his Kt. at B's 7th.

** From this move the attack is very lively and interesting.

†† There appears to be nothing better, bad as this is.

20. Q. R. to K's sq.	20. Q. takes K. R. P. (ch.)
21. Q. takes Q.	21. B. takes Kt.
22. R. to K's 8th (ch.)	22. B. to his sq.
23. K. R. to K's sq.	23. P. to Q's 4th.
24. Q. R. to Q's 8th.	24. R. to Q's 2nd.
25. K. R. to K's 8th.	25. R. takes Q. R.
26. R. takes R.	26. P. to Q. Kt.'s 3rd.
27. Q. to K's 3rd.	27. Q. B. to Kt.'s 2nd.
28. R. takes R.	28. B. takes R.
29. Q. to K's 6th (ch.)	29. K. to R's sq.
30. Q. to K. B's 7th.	

Black resigns.

GAME V.—In the match by correspondence between Mr. Mendheim and the Amateurs of Breslau.

WHITE. (Berlin.)	BLACK. (Breslau.)
1. P. to K's 4th.	1. P. to K's 4th.
2. K. Kt. to B's 3rd.	2. Q. Kt. to B's 3rd.
3. K. B. to Q. B's 4th.	3. K. B. to Q. B's 4th.
4. P. to Q. B's 3rd.	4. K. Kt. to B's 3rd.
5. P. to Q's 4th.	5. P. takes P.
6. P. to K's 5th.	6. K. Kt. to K's 5th.
7. K. B. to Q's 5th.	7. Kt. takes K. B. P.
8. K. takes Kt.	8. P. takes P. (dis. ch.)
9. K. to his sq.	9. P. takes Q. Kt. P.
10. Q. B. takes P.	10. Q. to K's 2nd.
11. B. takes Q. Kt.	11. Q. P. takes B.
12. Q. to her B's 2nd.	12. Q. B. to K's 3rd.
13. Q. Kt. to Q's 2nd.	13. Castles on Q's side.
14. K. to K's 2nd.	14. P. to K. Kt.'s 3rd.
15. Q. Kt. to K's 4th.	15. K. B. to Q. Kt.'s 3rd.
16. Q. to her R's 4th.	16. Q. B. to Q's 4th.
17. K. R. to Q. B's sq.	17. P. to K. B's 4th.
18. Q. Kt. to Q's 2nd.	18. Q. B. takes K. Kt. (ch.)
19. Kt. takes Q. B.	19. P. to K. Kt.'s 4th.
20. K. R. to K. B's sq.	20. Q. R. to Q's 4th.
21. Q. R. to Q's sq.	21. P. to K. Kt.'s 5th.
22. Kt. to Q's 2nd.	22. Q. to K's 3rd.

At this point the Breslau party, by taking K. P. with Rook (ch.), must have won without difficulty, but the game was prolonged to the 59th move, and won by Mr. Mendheim. For the remaining moves see Bilguer's "Handbuch," p. 128.

GAME VI.—Between Mr. Popert and another fine player of London.

WHITE. (Mr. P.)	BLACK. (Mr. —)
1. P. to K's 4th.	1. P. to K's 4th.
2. K. Kt. to B's 3rd.	2. Q. Kt. to B's 3rd.

3. K. B. to Q. B's 4th.	3. K. B. to Q. B's 4th.
4. P. to Q. B's 3rd.	4. K. Kt. to B's 3rd.
5. Castles.*	5. K. Kt. takes P.
6. P. to Q's 4th.	6. P. to Q's 4th.
7. K. B. to Q. Kt.'s 5th.	7. P. takes Q. P.
8. P. takes P.	8. K. B. to Q's 3rd.
9. K. Kt. to K's 5th	9. B. takes Kt.
10. P. takes B.	10. Castles.
11. P. to K. B's 4th.	11. P. to K. B's 4th.
12. Q. Kt. to B's 3rd.	12. Q. B. to K's 3rd.
13. Q. B. to K's 3rd.	13. P. to Q. R's 3rd.
14. B. takes Kt.	14. P. takes B.
15. Q. R. to Q. B's sq.†	15. Q. to K's sq.
16. Q. to her B's 2nd.‡	16. Q. R. to Kt.'s sq.
17. Kt. takes Kt.	17. K. B. P. takes Kt.
18. Q. takes Q. B. P.	18. Q. R. takes Q. Kt. P.
19. Q. takes Q.	19. R. takes Q.
20. P. to K. B's 5th.§	20. B. to his sq.
21. Q. R. takes P.	21. Q. R. to K's 7th.
22. B. to Q's 4th.	22. Q. R. to Q's 7th.
23. B. to Q. B's 3rd.	23. R. to Q's 6th.
24. P. to K. B's 6th.	24. P. takes P.
25. P. takes P.	25. Q. B. to K's 3rd.
26. R. to K. Kt.'s 7th (ch.)	26. K. to R's sq.
27. B. to K's 5th.	27. B. to K. Kt.'s sq.
28. R. to K's 7th.	28. B. to K. B's 2nd.

White now checkmates in two more moves.

GAME VII.—Between Mr. Buckle and Mr. Harrwitz.

WHITE. (Mr. B.)	BLACK. (Mr. H.)
1. P. to K's 4th.	1. P. to K's 4th.
2. K. Kt. to B's 3rd.	2. Q. Kt. to B's 3rd.
3. K. B. to Q. B's 4th.	3. K. B. to Q. B's 4th.
4. Castles.	4. K. Kt. to B's 3rd.
5. Q. Kt. to B's 3rd.	5. P. to Q's 3rd.
6. P. to K. R's 3rd.	6. Castles.
7. P. to Q's 3rd.	7. Q. B. to K's 3rd.
8. K. B. to Kt.'s 3rd.	8. Q. Kt. to K's 2nd.
9. Q. Kt. to K's 2nd.	9. Q. Kt. to K. Kt.'s 3rd.

---

* Castling before moving the Q. B. P., and before the adverse K. Kt. is in the field, appears safer play.

† Threatening to exchange the Kt., and then take Q. B. P. with the Rook.

‡ Intending again to take the Kt., and thus win a Pawn.

§ Well played, the advance of this Pawn secures to him an irresistible attack.

10. Q. Kt. to K. Kt.'s 3rd.
11. P. to Q. B's 3rd.
12. P. to Q's 4th.
13. Q. P. takes B.
14. Q. takes P.
15. P. takes B.
16. Kt. to K. B's 5th.*
17. P. takes Kt. P.
18. P. to Q. B's 4th.
19. B. takes K. Kt.
20. K. R. to Q's sq.†
21. Q. takes Q. B. P.
22. Q. takes Q.
23. Kt. to Q's 6th.
24. K. to B's sq.
25. P. to Q. Kt.'s 4th.
26. P. to Q. B's 5th.
27. Q. R. to R's 4th.
28. K. R. to Q. R's sq.
29. R. takes P.
30. R. takes R.
31. R. to Q. Kt.'s 7th.‡
32. Kt. takes R.
33. K. to K's 2nd.
34. K. to Q's 2nd.
35. Kt. to R's 5th.
36. Kt. to K. Kt.'s 3rd.
37. K. to Q. B's 3rd.
38. Kt. takes Kt.
39. P. to K. R's 4th.
40. P. to K. B's 3rd.
41. P. to K. R's 5th.
42. P. takes P.
43. P. to K. Kt.'s 4th.
44. P. to Q. Kt.'s 4th.
45. P. to Q. Kt.'s 5th.
46. P. to Q. Kt.'s 6th.
47. P. to Q. Kt.'s 7th.
48. P. becomes a Queen.

10. P. to Q. B's 3rd.
11. P. to Q's 4th.
12. Q. P. takes K. P.
13. P. takes Kt.
14. Q. B. takes K. B.
15. K. Kt. to Q's 4th.
16. P. to Q. Kt.'s 3rd.
17. Q. takes P.
18. K. Kt. to K. B's 5th.
19. Q. Kt. takes B.
20. Q. to Q. B's 2nd.
21. K. R. to Q. B's sq.
22. R. takes Q.
23. Kt. to K's 7th (ch.)
24. Kt. to Q's 5th.
25. P. to K. B's 4th.
26. Q. R. to Q. Kt.'s sq.
27. P. to K. Kt.'s 3rd.
28. Kt. to Q. B's 7th.
29. R. takes R.
30. Kt. takes Q. Kt. P.
31. R. takes R.
32. K. to B's 2nd.
33. K. to K's 2nd.
34. K. to Q's 2nd.
35. Kt. to R's 3rd.
36. K. to Q. B's 3rd.
37. Kt. takes P.
38. K. takes Kt.
39. P. to K. R's 3rd.
40. P. to K. Kt.'s 4th.
41. P. to K's 5th.
42. K. B. P. takes P.
43. K. to Q's 4th.
44. K. to K's 4th.
45. K. to K. B's 5th.
46. P. to K's 6th.
47. K. to B's 6th.

And wins.§

---

* This is a very attacking position for the Kt., and generally occasions great embarrassment to an adversary.

† Prudently taking possession of an "open file."

‡ White plays with remarkable care and judgment here.

§ The termination of this game is an improving lesson in Pawn play.

CHAPTER V.

GAME THE FIRST.

(CAPTAIN EVANS' GAMBIT.)

THIS ingenious and interesting variation of the Guioco Piano opening, was invented some years ago by Captain Evans, and has deservedly attained a high degree of favour among players of all classes from the period of its introduction. Its deviation from the generic opening, with which it accords for the first three moves on each side, consists in the sacrifice of the K. Kt. P. at the 4th move, whereby the first player is enabled not only to establish his Pawns in the centre of the board, but promptly bring both Queen and Queen's Bishop to the attack of the adverse King.

The leading works to be consulted upon the Evans' Gambit, are Lewis, 1834, pp. 133–150; 1844, pp. 216–229; Walker, 1841, pp. 66–80; 1846, pp. 88–102. The games between La Bourdonnais and McDonnell, Cochrane and Staunton, and others, in the " Chess-Player's Chronicle."

WHITE.	BLACK.
1. P. to K's 4th.	1. P. to K's 4th.
2. K. Kt. to B's 3rd.	2. Q. Kt. to B's 3rd.
3. K. B. to Q. B's 4th.	3. K. B. to Q. B's 4th.
4. P. to Q. Kt.'s 4th.	4. B. takes Q. Kt. P. (best)

On the advance of the Pawn, Black is obliged to take it with Bishop or Knight, or otherwise retreat his Bishop. The consequences of taking with the Kt. will be shown in Variation I. If he decline to take, and retire his B. to Q. Kt.'s 3rd, your best play is not to push the Pawn on the Kt. and afterwards take the K's P., because he would first play the Kt. to Q. R's 4th, and when you took the Pawn, move Q. to K. B's 3rd sq., attacking your Kt. and threatening checkmate. Your safest play, therefore, instead of P. to Q. Kt.'s 5th, would be P. to Q. R's 4th, or to castle.

5. P. to Q. B's 3rd.	5. B. to Q. R's 4th.

Instead of so playing, he may retire his B. to K's 2nd, or Q's 3rd, or Q. B's 4th ; and it may be well to show you here the best modes of play in each of the former cases, reserving the last for a variation presently. In the first place, suppose—

	5. B. to K's 2nd.
6. Q. to her Kt.'s 3rd.	6. K. Kt. to R's 3rd.
7. P. to Q's 4th.	7. Q. Kt. to Q. R's 4th.

(If he castle at his 7th move, or take Q. P., you take his K. Kt. with
your Q. B.)

8. Q. to R's 4th.	8. Kt. takes B.
9. Q. takes Kt.	9. K. Kt. to his 5th.
10. P. to K. R's 3rd.	10. K. Kt. to B's 3rd.
11. P. takes K. P.	

If he move the Kt. to K. R's 4th,' you play P. to K. Kt.'s 4th, winning
it, and if he return it home, you have clearly the better game.

In the second place, suppose—

	5. B. to Q's 3rd.
6. Castles.	6. K. Kt. to B's 3rd.
7. P. to Q's 4th.	7. Kt. takes K. P.
8. P. takes P.	8. B. takes P.

(If he take with the Kt., you play 9. R. to K's sq.)

| 9. Kt. takes B. | 9. Kt. takes Kt. |
| 10. Q. to her 5th. | |

And you must win a Piece.

As an additional exemplification of the error of retreating
the B. to Q's 3rd, see the game at the end of this Chapter
between Horwitz and Kieseritzky.

In the third place, he may retreat his 5. B. to K. B's 4th,
as in Variation II.

| 6. Castles. | 6. P. to Q's 3rd (best) |

He may also play 6. K. Kt. to B's 3rd, but as that defence
involves many series of moves, it will form the subject of a
distinct game.   (See Game the 2nd.)

| 7. P. to Q's 4th. | 7. P. takes P. |

He might instead play 7. B. to Q. Kt.'s 3rd, and you would
then take P. with P., exchange Queens, and gain a Pawn; or
he might for his 7th move play—

	7. K. Kt. to B's 3rd.
8. Q. to Q. R's 4th.	8. P. takes Q. P. (best)
9. P. to K's 5th.	9. K. Kt. to his 5th.
10. Q. B. P. takes P.	10. Q. B. to Q's 2nd.

(If he castles, you win a Piece by P. to K. R's 3rd, and afterwards P. to
Q's 5th.)

| 11. Q. to her R's 3rd. | 11. K. B. to Q. Kt.'s 3rd. |
| 12. Q. B. to K. Kt.'s 5th. | 12. P. to K. B's 3rd. |

13. P. takes Q. P.	13. P. takes P.
14. R. to K's sq. (ch.)	14. Q. Kt. to K's 2nd.
15. Q. B. to K. B's 4th.	15. K. B. to Q. B's 2nd.
16. Q. Kt. to B's 3rd.	

And you must win.

8. P. takes P.	8. B. to Q. Kt.'s 3rd.

You may take P. with Kt., instead of with P., and Black's best reply is then, perhaps, K. Kt. to K's 2nd. If for his 8th move he play Kt. to K. B's 3rd, you answer with 9. P. to K's 5th.

9. B. to Q. Kt.'s 2nd.	9. K. Kt. to B's 3rd.

In practice I have found the best move at this point to keep up the attack was 9. Q. B. to R's 3rd; P. to K. R's 3rd, as practised formerly, appears to lose time, and give an advantage to Black. If, instead of 9. K. Kt. to B's 3rd, he play 9. Q. B. to K. Kt.'s 5th, the game may probably go on as follows :—

	9. Q. B. to K. Kt.'s 5th.
10. K. B. to Q. Kt.'s 5th.	10. P. to Q. R's 3rd.
11. K. B. to Q. R's 4th.	11. P. to Q's 4th.
12. P. takes P.	12. Q. takes P.
13. Q. Kt. to B's 3rd.	13. B. takes K. Kt.
14. Kt. takes Q.	14. B. takes Q.
15. Kt. takes K. B.	15. P. takes Kt.
16. Q. R. takes B.	

And play as he can, you have a winning advantage.

10. P. to Q's 5th.	10. Q. Kt. to K's 2nd.

If you play instead, 10. P. to K's 5th, he takes P. with P., and on your moving B. to Q. R's 3rd, he answers with Q. B. to K's 3rd, and your attack is gone. His move 10. Q. Kt. to K's 2nd, is far better than 10. Kt. to his sq., or 10. Kt. to Q. R's 4th.

11. B. takes K. Kt.	11. P. takes B.

It is not safe, in this position, for you to play 11. P. to K's 5th, in lieu of taking the Kt., although it looks a tempting move.

12. K. Kt. to Q's 4th.	12. B. takes Kt.

He may also play 12. Kt. to K. Kt.'s 3rd, or castle; but, in any case, the greater freedom of your men appears to me to fully counterbalance the doubtful advantage of his doubled Pawn.

VARIATION I.,

Beginning at Black's 4th move.

WHITE.	BLACK.
1. P. to K's 4th.	1. P. to K's 4th.
2. K. Kt. to B's 3rd.	2. Q. Kt. to B's 3rd.
3. K. B. to Q. B's 4th.	3. K. B. to Q. B's 4th.
4. P. to Q. Kt.'s 4th.	4. Q. Kt. takes Kt. P.
5. P. to Q. B's 3rd.	5. Kt. to Q. B's 3rd.

It is not advisable for you to take the K. P. instead of dislodging the Kt., because he would at once play 5. Q. to K. B's 3rd, and if you then, to protect the Kt. and avert the threatened mate, played 6. P. to Q's 4th, he could take the Q. P. with his B., and you could not take the B. without losing your Queen. By playing 5. P. to B's 3rd, you obtain equally the same position as if he had taken the Gambit Pawn with the Bishop, and afterwards retired him to Q. B's 4th, as in the next variation.

VARIATION II.,

Beginning at Black's 5th move.

BLACK.

WHITE.

5. B. to Q. B's 4th.

You observe, upon Black's retreating his B. thus, the situation is precisely that at the end of the variation just given.

In the German "Handbuch" it is remarked, that if Black's intention is to retire his B. finally to Q. Kt.'s 3rd, it is indifferent whether at his 5th move he play him to Q. R's 4th, or to Q. B's 4th, but if he purpose to adopt the defence of K. Kt. to B's 3rd, at his 6th move, (as in the next game,) then the moving him to Q. B's 4th is objectionable. Major Jaenisch opposes it, however, because he thinks it admits of the immediate and effectual advance of White's P. to Q's 4th. My opinion is, that B. to Q. B's 4th is the better move for Black, unless, as before observed, he intend to adopt the defence in the next game, for the Pawn can be as safely played to Q's 4th on the following move by you, when the Bishop stands at Q. R's 4th, as when he is at B's 4th, and indeed in play I have found it better so to play the Pawn at once, instead of castling; besides, when his Bishop stands at R's 4th, you can more advantageously play your Queen to her Kt.'s 3rd, without the fear of her being dislodged by the adverse Kt. going to Q. R's 4th sq.

| 6. P. to Q's 4th. | 6. P. takes P. |

Instead of playing 6. P. to Q's 4th, the customary move has been castling. (See Variation III.)

| 7. P. takes P. | 7. B. to Q. Kt.'s 3rd. |

Instead of taking 7. P. with P., you may castle now, and if he take your Q. B. P., you will obtain a still more powerful attack by playing 8. P. to K's 5th. If Black at his 7th move, instead of retiring the Bishop, gives check at Q. Kt.'s 5th, your best move is 8. K. to B's sq., and if then he play 8. Q. to K's 2nd, you can move 9. P. to Q. R's 3rd, and afterwards play 10. Q. R. to his 2nd.

| 8. Castles. | 8. P. to Q's 3rd. |
| 9. P. to Q's 5th. | 9. Q. Kt. to K's 2nd. |

This is his best square for the Kt.; if he play him to K's 4th, you take him with your Kt., and can presently move Q. B. to Q. R's 3rd, and embarrass the adverse game considerably; and if he move him to Q. R's 4th, you play first Q. B. to Q. Kt.'s 2nd, and then K. B. to Q's 3rd.

| 10. Q. B. to Q. Kt.'s 2nd. | 10. K. Kt. to B's 3rd. |

And the position is the same as in the former variation, where he played 5. B. to Q. R's 4th. At your 10th move you may play Q. B. to R's 3rd with at least as much advantage as to Kt.'s 2nd.

VARIATION III.,

Beginning at White's 6th move.

WHITE.	BLACK.
1. P. to K's 4th.	1. P. to K's 4th.
2. K. Kt. to B's 3rd.	2. Q. Kt. to B's 3rd.
3. K. B. to Q. B's 4th.	3. K. B. to Q. B's 4th.
4. P. to Q. Kt.'s 4th.	4. B. takes Kt. P.
5. P. to Q. B's 3rd.	5. B. to Q. B's 4th.
6. Castles.	6. P. to Q's 3rd.

If, at this stage, instead of 6. P. to Q's 3rd, he play 6. K. Kt. to B's 3rd, you ensure a fine attacking game, as follows :—

	6. K. Kt. to B's 3rd.
7. P. to Q's 4th.	7. P. takes P.
8. P. takes P.	8. B. to Q. Kt.'s 3rd, or (A.)
9. P. to K's 5th.	9. K. Kt. to his sq.

(He appears to have no better defence ; for if he play 9. P. to Q's 4th, you take his Kt. and then check with your Rook; if he play 9. Kt. to Kt.'s 5th, you can take 10. K. B's P. (ch.); if to K's 5th, you move K. R. to K's sq.; and, finally, if to K. R's 4th, you may play K. Kt. to his 5th.)

10. P. to Q's 5th.	10. Q. Kt. to R's 4th.

(If he play the Kt. to K's 2nd, you may move P. to Q's 6th.)

11. Q. B. to K. Kt.'s 5th.	11. P. to K. B's 3rd.

(Should he, instead, play 11. K. Kt. to K's 2nd, you advance 12. P. to Q's 6th.)

12. P. takes P.	12. K. Kt. takes P.

(If he play 12. P. takes P., you move Kt. to K's 5th, and win.)

13. P. to Q's 6th.	13. Kt. takes K. B. (best)
14. Q. to K's 2nd (ch.)	14. K. to B's sq.

You have a far better game.

(A.)

	8. B. to Q. Kt.'s 5th.
9. P. to K's 5th.	9. Kt. to K's 5th.
10. Q. to K's 2nd.	10. Kt. to Q. B's 6th.
11. Kt. takes Kt.	11. B. takes Kt.
12. Kt. to Kt.'s 5th.	12. B. takes R.

(If he move 10. Castles, you may play 11. Q. to K. R's 5th, or Q. to her 3rd, with a winning game.)

12. B. takes K. B. P. (ch.)	12. K. to B's sq.
13. Q. B. checks.	13. P. to Q's 3rd.

(If he interpose the Kt., you move Q. to K. B's 3rd.)

14. P. takes P.	14. P. takes P.
15. B. takes P. (ch.)	15. Kt. to K's 2nd.
16. Q. B. to Q. R's 3rd.	16. K. B. to Q. B's 6th.
17. Q. to K. B's 3rd.	

Winning easily.

There are other variations; but these will suffice to show that K. Kt. to B's 3rd, at the 6th move, when his B. is at Q. B's 4th, is a bad move for Black.

Let us now resume the original game.

7. P. to Q's 4th.	7. P. takes P.
8. P. takes P.	8. B. to Q. Kt.'s 3rd.
9. Q. B. to Q. R's 3rd.	9. K. Kt. to B's 3rd.

If you play 9. Q. B. to Q. Kt.'s 2nd, or 9. P. to Q's 5th, the position will in a move or two become the same as in a previous example. Should he reply at his 9th move, Q. B. to K. Kt.'s 5th, you play 10. Q. to her Kt.'s 3rd, with a good game.

10. P. to K's 5th.	10. P. takes P.
11. Q. to her Kt.'s 3rd.	

And your game is preferable to Black's.

GAME THE SECOND.

WHITE.	BLACK.
1. P. to K's 4th.	1. P. to K's 4th.
2. K. Kt. to B's 3rd.	2. Q. Kt. to B's 3rd.
3. K. B. to Q. B's 4th.	3. K. B. to Q. B's 4th.
4. P. to Q. Kt.'s 4th.	4. B. takes Kt. P.
5. P. to Q. B's 3rd.	5. B. to Q. R's 4th.
6. Castles.	6. K. Kt. to B's 3rd.

His move of 6. Kt. to B's 3rd, may be adopted more safely when his B. is at Q. R's 4th, than at the B's 4th.

7. K. Kt. to his 5th.	7. Castles.

You might also play 7. P. to Q's 4th, as in Variation I.

8. P. to K. B's 4th.	8. P. to Q's 4th.

Black has several other ways of playing. If he move 8. P. to K. R's 3rd, you take 9. K. B. P. with Kt., and on his taking Kt. with R., you take R. with B. (ch.), you then take K. P. with P., he retakes with Q. Kt., and by checking with your Q. at K. R's 5th, you win one of the Knights, and have a conquering game.

If he play 8. K. P. takes B. P., you advance 9. P. to Q's 4th, and if then he attack your Kt. with K. R. P., you leave the Kt. to be taken, and capture P. with Q. B. If he move 8. K. Kt. takes K. P., you take 9. K. B. P. with Kt., then 10. R. with B. (ch.), and afterwards play 11. Q. to K. B's 3rd, and have the better game. He may however, at his 8th move, play P. to Q's 3rd, as in the following:—

	8. P. to Q's 3rd.
9. P. to Q's 3rd.	9. P. to K. R's 3rd.
10. P. to K. B's 5th.	10. P. takes Kt.
11. Q. B. takes P.	11. B. to Q. Kt.'s 3rd (ch.)
12. K. to R's sq.	12. Q. Kt. to R's 4th.
13. Q. to K's sq.	13. Kt. takes K. B.
14. P. takes Q. Kt.	14. R. to K's sq.
15. Q. to K. R's 4th.	15. K. B. to K's 6th (best)
16. B. takes B.	16. Kt. to K. R's 2nd.
17. Q. to K. Kt.'s 3rd.	

You have a fine situation.

9. P. takes Q. P.	9. K. Kt. takes P.
10. P. to Q's 4th.	10. P. to K. R's 3rd.

You may also play 10. Q. B. to Q. R's 3rd, but Black will get the better game. (*e. g.*)

10. Q. B. to R's 3rd.	10. Kt. takes K. B. P.
11. R. takes Kt.	11. Q. takes Kt.
12. R. to K. B's sq.	12. B. to Kt.'s 3rd (ch.)
13. P. to Q's 4th.	13. Kt. to Q. R's 4th.

(It is of little importance whether you play 13. K. to R's sq., or as in the text.)

14. Q. B. takes R.	14. Kt. takes K. B.
15. B. to Q. B's 5th.	15. B. takes B.
16. P. takes B.	16. Q. B. to K's 3rd.

The game is in Black's favour.

11. Q. to her Kt.'s 3rd.	11. P. takes Kt
12. B. takes Kt.	12. K. P. takes B. P.
13. P. to K. Kt.'s 3rd.	13. Kt. to K's 2nd.

Black has the advantage.

VARIATION I.,

Beginning at White's 7th move.

BLACK.

WHITE.

In this situation, instead of playing 7. Kt. to Kt.'s 5th, you can move as follows:—

WHITE.	BLACK.
7. P. to Q's 4th.	7. P. takes P.

In place of taking the P., Black may castle, and apparently preserve his advantage. (See Game the Third.) If he take K. P. with Kt., you get the better game; for example,—

	7. Kt. takes K. P.
8. R. to K's sq.	8. P. to Q's 4th, or (A.)

(If, at your 8th move, you take P. with Pawn, he may castle safely.)

9. R. takes Kt.	9. P. takes R.
10. K. Kt. to his 5th.	10. Castles.
11. Q. to K. R's 5th.	11. P. to K. R's 3rd.
12. Kt. takes K. B. P.	12. R. takes Kt.
13. B. takes R. (ch.)	13. K. to B's sq.
14. B. to Q. R's 3rd (ch.)	

And you must win.

(A.)

	8. Kt. takes Q. B. P.
9. Kt. takes Kt.	9. B. takes Kt.
10. Q. to her Kt.'s 3rd.	10. B. takes K. R.
11. K. B. takes P. (ch.)	11. K. to B's sq.
12. Q. B. to K. Kt.'s 5th.	12. Q. Kt. takes P.
13. Q. to K's 3rd.	13. Kt. to K. B's 4th (best)

(If, instead of Q. to K's 3rd, you play 13. Q. to Q. R's 3rd (ch.), Black will obtain the better game by first interposing his B. at Q. Kt.'s 5th, and then playing 14. P. to Q. B's 4th.)

14. Q. to her R's 3rd (ch.)	14. Kt. to K's 2nd.
15. Kt. takes K. P.	15. P. to Q's 3rd.
16. Q. to K. B's 3rd.	16. B. takes K. B. P. (ch.)
17. K. takes B.	17. Q. B. to K. B's 4th.
18. K. B. to K's 6th.	18. P. takes Kt.
19. B. takes B.	19. Q. to her 5th (ch.)
20. K. to Kt.'s 3rd.	20. K. to his sq.

(If, at his 20th move, he take the B. with Kt., you mate in six moves.)

21. R. to Q's sq.	21. Q. takes R. (best)
22. Q. takes Q.	22. Kt. takes B. (ch.)
23. K. to Kt.'s 4th.	23. P. to K. Kt.'s 3rd.
24. Q. to her 5th.	

You ought to win.

(These latter variations are from a clever analysis of Black's 8th move, by Mr. G. Waller, of the Dublin club, which may be found at length in vol. vii. p. 353, of the "Chess-Player's Chronicle.")

Let us again refer to the diagram, and after making the 7th move on each side, proceed with the game.

8. P. to K's 5th.	8. K. Kt. to K's 5th.
9. Q. to her Kt.'s 3rd.	9. Castles.
10. Q. B. to Q. R's 3rd.	10. P. to Q's 3rd.
11. Q. B. P. takes P.	11. K. B. to Q. Kt.'s 3rd.
12. Q. to K's 3rd.	12. Q. B. to K. B's 4th.
13. B. to Q's 5th.	

And you win a Piece.

GAME THE THIRD.

Varying from the preceding at Black's 7th move.

WHITE.	BLACK.
1. P. to K's 4th.	1. P. to K's 4th.
2. K. Kt. to B's 3rd.	2. Q. Kt. to B's 3rd.
3. K. B. to Q. B's 4th.	3. K. B. to Q. B's 4th.
4. P. to Q. Kt.'s 4th.	4. B. takes Kt. P.
5. P. to Q. B's 3rd.	5. B. to Q. R's 4th.
6. Castles.	6. K. Kt. to B's 3rd.
7. P. to Q's 4th.	7. Castles.
8. P. takes K. P.	8. Kt. takes K. P.

If you play 8. Q. B. to K. Kt.'s 5th, he can reply with 8. P. to K. R.'s 3rd; but when you then retreat the B. to K. R's

4th, he ought not to advance P. to K. Kt.'s 4th, because you might advantageously give up your K. Kt. for the two Pawns. He should rather play P. to Q's 3rd.

9. Q. to Q. B's 2nd.   9. P. to Q's 4th.

And he has the better game. If, at your 9th move, you play Q. B. to R's 3rd, his best answer appears to be 9. P. to Q's 3rd; and if 9. K. B. to Q's 3rd, then he may safely advance P. to Q's 4th.

GAMES

ILLUSTRATIVE OF CAPTAIN EVANS' GAMBIT.

(From the *Chess-Player's Chronicle*.)

GAME I.—Between Messrs. Cochrane and Staunton.

WHITE. (Mr. S.)	BLACK. (Mr. C.)
1. P. to K's 4th.	1. P. to K's 4th.
2. K. Kt. to B's 3rd.	2. Q. Kt. to B's 3rd
3. K. B. to Q. B's 4th.	3. K. B. to Q. B's 4th
4. P. to Q. Kt.'s 4th.	4. B. takes Q. Kt. P.
5. P. to Q. B's 3rd.	5. B. to Q. R's 4th.
6. Castles.	6. B. to Q. Kt.'s 3rd.
7. P. to Q's 4th.	7. P. takes P.
8. P. to K's 5th.*	8. P. to Q's 4th.
9. P. takes P. in passing.	9. Q. takes P.
10. R. to K's sq. (ch.)	10. Q. B. to K's 3rd.
11. Q. B. to Q. R's 3rd.	11. Q. to her 2nd.
12. Kt. to K. Kt.'s 5th.	12. P. takes P.
13. Kt. takes Q. B.†	13. Q. takes Q.
14. Kt. takes Kt. P. (double ch.)	14. K. to Q's 2nd.
15. R. takes Q. (ch.)	15. K. to B's sq.
16. Q. Kt. takes P.	16. K. B. to Q's 5th.
17. R. takes B.	17. Kt. takes R.
18. B. takes K. B. P.	18. K. Kt. to R's 3rd.
19. K. B. to Q. Kt.'s 3rd.	19. Kt. takes B.
20. Q. R. P. takes Kt.	20. K. to Q's 2nd.

---

* This variation, which was played, for the first time, in the present game, attracted the attention of the celebrated Indian player, Ghulam Kassim, who took the pains to analyse it very carefully, and forwarded the result to the writer. His analysis will be found in the "Chess-Player's Chronicle," vol. vi. p. 47.

† This is an instructive situation.

21. R. to Q's sq. (ch.)	21. K. to Q. B's 3rd.
22. K. Kt. to K's 6th.	22. P. to Q. Kt.'s 3rd.
23. R. to Q. B's sq.	23. K. to Q. Kt.'s 2nd.
24. Q. Kt. to Kt.'s 5th.	24. P. to Q. B's 4th.
25. P. to Q. Kt.'s 4th.	25. K. to B's 3rd.
26. Q. Kt. to Q. B's 7th.	26. Q. R. to Q. B's sq.
27. P. takes P.	27. P. to Q. Kt.'s 4th.
28. Q. Kt. to Q. R's 6th.	

White wins.

GAME II.—Between Mr. Horwitz and M. Kieseritzky.

WHITE. (Mr. H.)	BLACK. (M. K.)
1. P. to K's 4th.	1. P. to K's 4th.
2. K. Kt. to B's 3rd.	2. Q. Kt. to B's 3rd.
3. K. B. to Q. B's 4th.	3. K. B. to Q. B's 4th.
4. P. to Q. Kt.'s 4th.	4. B. takes Kt. P.
5. P. to Q. B's 3rd.	5. B. to Q. R's 4th.
6. Castles.	6. P. to Q's 3rd.
7. P. to Q's 4th.	7. P. takes P.
8. P. takes P.	8. B. to Q. Kt.'s 3rd.
9. Q. B. to Kt.'s 2nd.	9. K. Kt. to B's 3rd.
10. Q. Kt. to Q's 2nd.	10. Castles.
11. P. to Q's 5th.	11. Q. Kt. to K's 2nd.
12. B. takes K. Kt.	12. P. takes B.
13. Kt. to K. R's 4th.	13. Kt. to K. Kt.'s 3rd.
14. Q. to K. R's 5th.*	14. Q. to K's 2nd.†
15. K. Kt. to B's 5th.	15. B. takes Kt.
16. P. takes B.	16. Kt. to K's 4th.
17. Q. R. to K's square.	17. Q. R. to K's square.‡
18. Q. R. to K's 4th.	18. K. to Kt.'s 2nd.§
19. Q. R. to K. R's 4th.	19. K. R. to his square.
20. Q. to K. R's 6th (ch.)	20. K. to Kt.'s square.
21. Q. R. to K. R's 3rd.‖	21. Kt. to K. Kt.'s 5th.
22. Q. to K. B's 4th.¶	22. P. to K. R's 4th.**
23. R. to K. Kt.'s 3rd.	23. K. to B's square.

---

* The opening of this game is admirably played by Mr. Horwitz.

† Very tame and inefficient.

‡ After this move, with common care on White's part, Black's game was irrecoverable.

§ It is difficult to imagine a more deplorable situation than poor Black's at this point.

‖ A very good move, but Kt. to K's 4th we believe to be a better.

¶ This inconceivable blunder loses White a won game. If he had simply played Q. to K. R's 5th, Black might with good grace have given up the *partie*.

** It is worth remarking, that if White, on his last move, instead of playing the Q., had tried to confine the Kt., by placing his R. at K. Kt.'s

24. P. to K. R's 3rd.	24. Q. to K's 4th.
25. Q. takes Q.*	25. Kt. takes Q.
26. B. to Q. Kt.'s 3rd.	26. P. to K. R's 5th.
27. R. to Q. B's 3rd.	27. B. to Q. R's 4th.
28. R. to B's 2nd.	28. K. R. to Kt.'s square.
29. K. to R's 2nd.	29. B. to Q. Kt.'s 3rd.
30. P. to K. B's 4th.	30. Kt. to Q's 6th.
31. R. to Q. B's 3rd.	31. Q. R. to K's 7th.

And White abandoned the contest.

GAME III.—Played by Messrs. Perigal and Pulling consulting against Mr. Popert.

WHITE. (The Allies.)	BLACK. (Mr. Popert.)
1. P. to K's 4th.	1. P. to K's 4th.
2. K. Kt. to B's 3rd.	2. Q. Kt. to B's 3rd.
3. K. B. to Q. B's 4th.	3. K. B. to Q. B's 4th.
4. P. to Q. Kt.'s 4th.	4. B. takes Kt. P.
5. P. to Q. B's 3rd.	5. B. to Q. B's 4th.
6. Castles.	6. P. to Q's 3rd.
7. P. to Q's 4th.	7. P. takes P.
8. P. takes P.	8. B. to Q. Kt.'s 3rd.
9. Q. Kt. to B's 3rd.†	9. Kt. to K. B's 3rd.
10. P. to K's 5th.	10. P. takes P.
11. Q. B. to R's 3rd.	11. Q. Kt. to R's 4th.‡
12. K. R. to K's sq.§	12. Kt. takes B.
13. Q. to her R's 4th (ch.)	13. P. to Q. B's 3rd.
14. Q. takes Kt.	14. Q. B. to K's 3rd.
15. R. takes K. P.	15. Q. to her 2nd.

3rd, he would have lost all his advantage, because, in that case, Black could have taken K. B. P. with his B. (*e. g.*)

WHITE.	BLACK.
22. R. to Kt.'s 3rd.	22. B. takes K. B. P. (ch.)
23. K. R. takes B., or (A.)	23. Q. to K's 8th (ch.)
24. K. R. to K. B's square.	24. Q. takes Q. R.

(A.)

23. K. to R's square.	23. B. takes Q. R.

And must win.

* This was compelled; had White attempted to evade it, by moving his Q. to K. B's 3rd, Black would have answered with Kt. to K. R's 7th, and when the K. took it, have played P. to K. R's 3rd, winning the exchange at least.

† This is not the customary move, but it may be adopted without disadvantage, and requires great care in answering.

‡ The position of White's Q. Kt. completely foils the usual defence at this point of Q. B. to K's 3rd.

§ This is all very cleverly played.

16. R. takes B. (ch.)*	16. P. takes R.
17. Kt. to K's 5th.	17. Q. to her B's sq.
18. R. to K's sq.	18. K. Kt. to Q's 4th.
19. Kt. takes Kt.	19. Q. B. P. takes Kt.
20. Q. to Kt.'s 5th (ch.)	20. K. to Q's sq.

And White mated in two more moves.

GAME IV.—Between M. Kieseritzky and Mr. Horwitz.

WHITE. (Mr. H.)	BLACK. (M. K.)
1. P. to K's 4th.	1. P. to K's 4th.
2. K. Kt. to B's 3rd.	2. Q. Kt. to B's 3rd.
3. K. B. to Q. B's 4th.	3. K. B. to Q. B's 4th.
4. P. to Q. Kt.'s 4th.	4. B. takes P.
5. P. to Q. B's 3rd.	5. B. to Q's 3rd.†
6. Castles.	6. Q. to K's 2nd.
7. P. to Q's 4th.	7. Q. Kt. to Q's square.
8. P. takes P.	8. B. takes P.
9. Kt. takes B.	9. Q. takes Kt.
10. Q. to Q's 3rd.	10. K. Kt. to B's 3rd.
11. P. to K. B's 4th.	11. Q. takes K. P.
12. Q. takes Q.	12. Kt. takes Q.
13. K. R. to K's square.	13. P. to K. B's 4th.
14. Q. Kt. to Q's 2nd.	14. Q. Kt. to K's 3rd.
15. Kt. takes Kt.	15. P. takes Kt.
16. R. takes P.	16. P. to K. Kt.'s 3rd.
17. Q. B. to R's 3rd.	17. K. to B's 2nd.
18. Q. R. to K. B's square.	18. P. to Q's 3rd.
19. P. to K. Kt.'s 4th.	19. K. R. to Kt.'s square.
20. Q. R. to K's square. ‡	

And Black resigns.

GAME V.—Between Messrs. Walker and Slous.

WHITE. (Mr. S.)	BLACK. (Mr. W.)
1. P. to K's 4th.	1. P. to K's 4th.
2. K. Kt. to B's 3rd.	2. Q. Kt. to B's 3rd.
3. K. B. to Q. B's 4th.	3. K. B. to Q. B's 4th.
4. P. to Q. Kt.'s 4th.	4. B. takes Q. Kt. P.
5. P. to Q. B's 3rd.	5. B. to Q. R's 4th.
6. Castles.	6. K. Kt. to B's 3rd.
7. K. Kt. to his 5th.	7. Castles.
8. P. to K. B's 4th.	8. P. to Q's 4th.

---

* The attack is kept up with uncommon spirit and ability.
† This is not at all a commendable defence to the Evans' Gambit.
‡ A lively well-played game, on the part of Mr. Horwitz.

9. P. takes Q. P.	9. K. Kt. takes P.
10. Q. B. to Q. R's 3rd.	10. Kt. takes K. B. P.
11. R. takes Kt.	11. Q. takes Kt.
12. R. to K. B's sq.	12. B. to Q. Kt.'s 3rd (ch.)
13. P. to Q's 4th.	13. Q. B. to K's 3rd.
14. B. takes B.	14. P. takes B.
15. R. takes R. (ch.)	15. R. takes R.
16. B. takes R.	16. K. takes B.
17. Kt. to Q's 2nd.	17. P. takes P.
18. Kt. to Q. B's 4th.	18. P. takes Q. B. P. (dis. ch.)
19. Kt. takes B.	19. Q. R. P. takes Kt.
20. Q. to Q's 7th.	20. Q. to K's 2nd.
21. R. to K. B's sq. (ch.)	21. K. to Kt.'s sq.
22. Q. to Q. B's 8th (ch.)	22. Kt. to Q's sq.
23. R. to Q's sq.	23. P. to Q. B's 7th.
24. R. takes Kt. (ch.) *	24. K. to B's 2nd.
25. R. to K. B's 8th (ch.)	25. Q. takes R.
26. Q. takes B. P. (ch.)	26. Q. to K's 2nd.
27. Q. takes B. P.	27. Q. to her B's 4th (ch.)

And Black wins.

CHAPTER VI.

THE TWO KNIGHTS' DEFENCE.

THIS, like the Evans' Gambit, and the Queen's Pawn
Game or Scotch Gambit, is a variation merely of the Guioco
Piano; the second player, instead of moving at his 3rd move,
K. B. to Q. B's 4th, bringing out his K. Kt. to B's 3rd. It is
said to have been invented by Gianutio (1597), and is also
noticed by Greco (1615); but the specific title of "The Two
Knights' Game" (Zweispringerspiel) it owes to M. Bilguer,
who, some years ago, published a small work, exclusively

* The position now is extremely interesting and instructive. By taking
the Kt. with his Rook, apparently an easy winning move, White loses the
game, while by taking with the Queen he must have won it; for example,—

24. Q. takes Kt. (ch.)	24. Q. takes Q.

(If he move the King, White checks with his R. at K. B's sq., and then
takes the Q.)

25. R. takes Q. (ch.)	25. K. to B's 2nd.
26. R. to Q's 7th (ch.)	26. K. is moved.
27. R. takes Q. B. P.	

And wins of course.

devoted to the analysis of this one opening,* the greater part
of which was afterwards incorporated in his "Handbuch."
The chief writers to be consulted upon this offset of the
Guioco Piano, are—Gianutio (translated by Sarratt, 1817),
pp. 21—32; Salvio (1723), pp. 81—83; Ponziani (1782),
p. 105; Lolli, pp. 173, 266; Allgaier, tab. iii.; Lewis, 2nd
edition, pp. 60—90; and his Treatise (1844), pp. 123—128;
Walker (1846), pp. 84, 87; and the German "Handbuch,"
pp. 147—160.

GAME THE FIRST.

WHITE.	BLACK.
1. P. to K's 4th.	1. P. to K's 4th.
2. K. Kt. to B's 3rd.	2. Q. Kt. to B's 3rd.
3. K. B. to Q. B's 4th.	3. K. Kt. to B's 3rd.

It is this move of Black which has caused the variation to be
distinguished as "The Two Knights' Game," both his Knights
being brought into action at the very outset of the contest.

4. K. Kt. to his 5th.	4. P. to Q's 4th.

If in place of 4. P. to Q's 4th, he play 4. Q. Kt. to R's 4th,
or Q. to K's 2nd, you take K. B. P. with the B. (ch.); but he
may play 4. K. Kt. takes K. P., for the result of which refer
to the next game.

5. P. takes P.	5. K. Kt. takes P.

He may also play 5. Q. Kt. to Q. R's 4th, when the following
moves are likely to ensue:—

	5. Q. Kt. to R's 4th.
6. B. to Q. Kt.'s 5th (ch.)	6. B. to Q's 2nd.

(If Black here play 6. P. to Q. B's 3rd, you must take P. with P., and
when he retakes with P., your only move is Q. to K. B's 3rd, any
other leaves you with an inferior game. This variation is important,
but seems to have escaped the writers who have examined the opening.)

7. Q. to K's 2nd.	7. K. B. to Q's 3rd.
8. B. takes B. (ch.)	8. Q. takes B.
9. P. to Q. B's 4th.	

And you remain with a P. more, and a better position.

---

* "Das Zweispringerspiel im Nachzuge." Berlin, 1839.

6. K. Kt. takes K. B. P.   6. K. takes Kt.

Lolli strongly recommends P. to Q's 4th for your 6th move, but there is now no doubt that the move in the text is preferable.

7. Q. to K. B's 3rd (ch.)   7. K. to his 3rd.

This is his only play to keep the Kt.

8. Q. Kt. to Q. B's 3rd.   8. Q. Kt. to K's 2nd.

If he play 8. Q. Kt. to his 5th, the following moves show you must gain a speedy advantage :—

               8. Q. Kt. to his 5th.

9. Q. to K's 4th.   9. P. to Q. B's 3rd.

(Generally speaking, it is advisable in this opening to keep your Queen immoveable on the K. B's file, as then she exercises the greatest influence on Black's game. The present instance, however, is an exception ; Black has made a bad move, and to take advantage of it, you may safely play the Q. thus,)—

10. P. to Q's 4th.   10. Q. to her 3rd.

(You might also play advantageously 10. P. to Q. R's 3rd, and afterwards P. to Q's 4th. If Black, at his 10th move, play K. B. to Q's 3rd, or Q. to K. B's 3rd, you can dislodge his Q. Kt. with Q. R. P., and then take the other Kt. with Kt.)

11. P. to K. B's 4th.   11. P. to Q. Kt.'s 4th.
12. K. B. P. takes P.   12. Q. to her 2nd.
13. Castles.   13. P. takes K. B.

And you now give checkmate in seven moves.

9. P. to Q's 4th.   9. P. to Q. B's 3rd.

It is evident he cannot take the Pawn without your winning the Kt. by Q. to K's 4th (ch). He may, however, play 9. P. to K. R's 3rd, to prevent your subsequently moving Q. B. to K. Kt.'s 5th; let us suppose,—

              9. P. to K. R's 3rd.

10. Castles.   10. P. to Q. B's 3rd.
11. K. R. to K's sq.   11. P. to K. Kt.'s 4th.

(If he play instead of this 11. K. to Q's 3rd, you take P. with P., and then move P. to K's 6th. He may, however, play Kt. to K. Kt.'s 3rd, or P. to Q. Kt.'s 4th ; but in each case to your advantage.)

12. R. takes P. (ch.)   12. K. to Q's 2nd.
13. B. takes Kt.   13. Kt. takes B.
14. Q. Kt. takes Kt.   14. P. takes Kt.
15. R. takes P. (ch.)   15. B. to Q's 3rd.
16. P. to Q. B's 4th.

You have the better game.

10. Q. B. to K. Kt.'s 5th.	10. P. to K. R's 3rd.

Should he play 10. P. takes Q. P., you can castle on Q's side, and then check with K. R.; if he play 10. K. to Q's 2nd or 3rd, you may take P. with P., and afterwards castle on Q's side.

11. Q. B. takes Kt.	11. B. takes B.
12. Castles on Q's side.	12. K. R. to B's sq.
13. Q. to K's 4th.	13. Q. to her 3rd.
14. K. R. to K's sq.	14. R. to K. B's 4th.
15. P. to K. Kt.'s 4th.	15. B. to Kt.'s 4th (ch.)
16. K. to Kt.'s sq.	16. R. to B's 5th.
17. Q. to K. R's 7th.	17. B. to K. B's 3rd.
18. P. takes P.	18. B. takes P.
19. B. takes Kt. (ch.)	19. P. takes B.
20. Kt. takes P.	

And you must win easily.

GAME THE SECOND.

WHITE.	BLACK.
1. P. to K's 4th.	1. P. to K's 4th.
2. K. Kt. to B's 3rd.	2. Q. Kt. to B's 3rd.
3. K. B. to Q. B's 4th.	3. K. Kt. to B's 3rd.
4. K. Kt. to his 5th.	4. K. Kt. takes K. P.
5. B. takes K. B. P. (ch.)	5. K. to his 2nd.

You would play badly in taking the Kt. instead of the K. B. P., because Black would reply with 5. P. to Q's 4th, recovering the lost Piece, with no inferiority of position. And you would also play ill to take the K. B. P. with your Kt., instead of with the Bishop; for example,—

5. Kt. takes K. B. P.	5. Q. to K. R's 5th.
6. Castles.	6. K. B. to Q. B's 4th.

(In lieu of castling, you might play 6. P. to K. Kt.'s 3rd, 6. Q. to K's 2nd, or 6. R. to K. B's sq., but in any of these cases the result would be against you.)

7. P. to Q's 4th.	7. B. takes Q. P.

(If you play 7. P. to K. Kt.'s 3rd, he may take the K. Kt. P. with his Kt., and win without much difficulty. You may also play 7. Kt. takes K. R., but in this case also by first taking K. B. P. with his Kt., and then the Rook with his B., Black would have a much better game than you.)

8. Kt. takes K. R.	8. Kt. takes K. B. P.
9. B. to K. B's 7th (ch.)	9. K. to B's sq.

(If you take Kt. with R., instead of checking with the B., the game shortly becomes still more unfavourable for you.)

10. K. R. takes Kt.	10. Q. takes R. (ch.)
11. K. to R's sq.	11. P. to Q's 3rd.
12. K. B. to Q's 5th.	12. Q. B. to K. Kt.'s 5th.
13. K. B. to his 3rd.	13. Q. B. takes K. B.
14. P. takes B.	14. K. to Kt.'s sq.

And he ought to win.

We may now resume the original game, which we left at the 5th move.

6. P. to Q's 3rd.	6. Kt. to K. B's 3rd.

If he were to take your Kt., you evidently gain his Q. for the three minor Pieces; if he play 6. Kt. to Q's 3rd, you also win the Q. by first playing Kt. to K's 6th, and then checking with your Bishop.

7. B. to Q. Kt.'s 3rd.	7. P. to Q's 4th.
8. P. to K. B's 4th.	8. Q. B. to K. Kt.'s 5th.
9. Q. to her 2nd.	9. P. to K. R's 3rd.
10. P. takes K. P.	10. Q. Kt. takes P.
11. Q. to K's 3rd.	11. P. takes Kt.
12. Q. takes Kt. (ch.)	12. K. to B's 2nd.
13. Castles.	13. B. to Q's 3rd.
14. Q. takes Q. P. (ch.)	

And you must win.

GAMES

ILLUSTRATIVE OF THE TWO KNIGHTS' GAME.

GAME I.—Between Von H. der Laza and Mr. M.

WHITE. (V. H. d. L.)	BLACK. (Mr. M.)
1. P. to K's 4th.	1. P. to K's 4th.
2. K. Kt. to B's 3rd.	2. Q. Kt. to B's 3rd.
3. K. B. to Q. B's 4th.	3. K. Kt. to B's 3rd.
4. K. Kt. to his 5th.	4. P. to Q's 4th.
5. P. takes P.	5. Kt. takes P.
6. Kt. takes K. B. P.	6. K. takes Kt.
7. Q. to K. B's 3rd (ch.)	7. K. to his 3rd.
8. Q. Kt. to B's 3rd.	8. Q. Kt. to K's 2nd.
9. P. to Q's 4th.	9. P. to Q. Kt.'s 4th.

10. Kt. takes P.	10. P. to Q. B's 3rd.
11. Kt. to Q. B's 3rd.	11. Q. to her Kt.'s 3rd.
12. P. takes K. P.	12. Q. B. to Kt.'s 2nd.
13. Kt. to K's 4th.	13. Q. to Kt.'s 5th (ch.)
14. Q. B. to Q's 2nd.	14. Q. takes K. B.
15. Q. to K. Kt.'s 4th (ch.)	15. K. takes P.
16. P. to K. B's 4th (ch.)	16. K. to Q's 5th.
17. P. to Q. B's 3rd (ch.)	17. Kt. takes B. P.
18. B. takes Kt. (ch.)	18. K. takes Kt.
19. P. to B's 5th (dis. ch.)	19. K. to Q's 4th.
20. Castles on Q's side (ch.)	20. K. to B's 4th.
21. P. to Q. Kt.'s 4th (ch.)	21. K. to Kt.'s 4th.
22. P. to Q. R's 4th (ch.)	22. K. takes P.
23. Q. takes Q.	23. Kt. to Q's 4th.
24. K. to Q. Kt.'s 2nd, and wins.	

GAME II.—Between two members of the Berlin Chess Club.

WHITE. (Mr. M.)	BLACK. (Mr. H.)
1. P. to K's 4th.	1. P. to K's 4th.
2. K. Kt. to B's 3rd.	2. Q. Kt. to B's 3rd.
3. B. to Q. B's 4th.	3. K. Kt. to B's 3rd.
4. K. Kt. to his 5th.	4. P. to Q's 4th.
5. P. takes P.	5. K. Kt. takes P.
6. Kt. takes K. B. P.	6. K. takes Kt.
7. Q. to K. B's 3rd (ch.)	7. K. to his 3rd.
8. Q. Kt. to B's 3rd.	8. Q. Kt. to K's 2nd.
9. P. to Q's 4th.	9. P. to Q. B's 3rd.
10. P. takes P.	10. Q. Kt. to K. Kt.'s 3rd.
11. Castles.	11. K. B. to Q. Kt.'s 5th.
12. Kt. takes Kt.	12. P. takes Kt.
13. K. R. to Q's sq.	13. Kt. to K's 2nd.*
14. Q. B. to K. Kt.'s 5th.	14. K. R. to B's sq.
15. B. takes Kt.	15. K. takes B.
16. Q. to her Kt.'s 3rd.	16. K. B. to Q. B's 4th.
17. R. takes Q. P.	17. B. takes K. B. P. (ch.)
18. K. to R's sq.	18. Q. to her Kt.'s 3rd.
19. Q. to her R's 3rd (ch.)	19. K. to his sq.
20. Q. to R's 4th (ch.)	20. K. to his 2nd.
21. Q. R. to Q's sq.	21. R. to K. B's 4th.
22. R. to Q's 7th (ch.)	22. K. to B's sq.
23. K. R. to Q's 8th (ch.)	23. K. to his 2nd.
24. Q. R. to Q's 7th (ch.) †	24. B. takes R.
25. Q. takes B., mate.	

---

* Better to take the Bishop with Pawn, and give up the Queen.
† He might have mated the King on the move at K's 8th.

CHAPTER VII.

THE KNIGHT'S GAME OF RÙY LOPEZ.

THIS is the appellation by which the German "Handbuch" designates that modification of the King's Knight's Opening, where the first player, at his 3rd move, instead of playing K. B. to Q. B's 4th, moves it to Q. Kt.'s 5th, as advised by Ruy Lopez, in the second chapter of his " *Libro de la Invencion liberal y Arte del Juego del Axedres*," a variation which seems to merit a more favourable judgment than has been passed on it by the generality of subsequent writers.

GAME THE FIRST.

WHITE.	BLACK.
1. P. to K's 4th.	1. P. to K's 4th.
2. K. Kt. to B's 3rd.	2. Q. Kt. to B's 3rd.
3. K. B. to Q. Kt.'s 5th.	3. K. Kt. to B's 3rd.

By playing your Bishop thus you again threaten to win his King's Pawn. His best reply, according to the German writers, is the move in the text, but he has the choice of other moves, the most important of which are 3. K. B. to Q. B's 4th, 3. Q. to K. B's 3rd, and 3. P. to Q. R's 3rd. (See Game the Second.) If instead of these he play 3. P. to Q's 3rd, he confines his King's Bishop, and subjects himself to the disadvantage of a badly doubled Pawn; and should he play 3. Q. Kt. to Q's 5th, the superiority, in a few moves, will be on your side. (*e. g.*)

	3. Q. Kt. to Q's 5th.
4. Kt. takes Kt.	4. P. takes Kt.
5. P. to Q's 3rd.	5. B. to Q. B's 4th.
6. Q. to K. R's 5th.	6. Q. to K's 2nd.
7. Q. B. to K. Kt.'s 5th.	7. B. to Q. Kt.'s 5th (ch.)
8. P. to Q. B's 3rd.	8. P. takes P.
9. P. takes P.	9. Q. to her B's 4th.
10. B. to Q. B's 4th.	

You have the better game.

4. Q. to K's 2nd.	4. K. B. to K's 2nd.

This appears your best move; P. to Q's 4th, P. to Q's 3rd, Q. Kt. to B's 3rd, and castling, lead apparently to an even game only.

If Black venture now to play 4. K. B. to Q. B's 4th, the position shortly becomes still more favourable for you; let us suppose,—

	4. K. B. to Q. B's 4th.
5. B. takes Kt.	5. Q. P. takes P.
6. Kt. takes K. P.	6. Q. to her 5th.
7. Kt. to Q's 3rd.	7. B. to Q. Kt.'s 3rd.
8. P. to K. B's 3rd.	

Followed presently by P. to Q. B's 3rd and K. Kt. to K. B's 2nd.

| 5. P. to Q. B's 3rd. | 5. P. to Q's 3rd. |

If instead of this move you too eagerly attempt to win his Pawn, he may reduce the game to an equality; for example,—

5. B. takes Q. Kt.	5. Q. P. takes B.
6. Kt. takes K. P.	6. Q. to her 5th.
7. Kt. to B's 3rd.	7. Q. takes K. P.

&c., &c.

6. P. to Q's 4th.	6. P. takes P.
7. Kt. takes P.	7. B. to Q's 2nd.
8. Kt. takes Q. Kt.	8. B. takes Kt.
9. B. takes B. (ch.)	9. P. takes B.

And his Bishop is locked, and the position altogether in your favour.

GAME THE SECOND.

WHITE.	BLACK.
1. P. to K's 4th.	1. P. to K's 4th.
2. K. Kt. to B's 3rd.	2. Q. Kt. to B's 3rd.
3. K. B. to Q. Kt.'s 5th.	3. K. B. to Q. B's 4th.

As was before observed, he may also play 3. Q. to K. B's 3rd and P. to Q. R's 3rd; if the former, you immediately bring out your Q. Kt., and have then an opportunity of presently commencing a vigorous attack. If he play the latter, I do not think it advisable to take off the Q. Kt., as is generally done, because that leads infallibly to a game without advantage on either side; but I believe it better to withdraw the Bishop to Q. R's 4th, with the view to prevent as long as possible the safe advance of Black's Queen's Pawn. If he then drive your Bishop to Q. Kt.'s 3rd, it will be well posted, and his game be still a little embarrassed.

4. P. to Q. B's 3rd.	4. Q. to K. B's 3rd.

Instead of so playing, he may move 4. P. to Q's 3rd, the result of which will be shown in Variation I.; he may also play, as advised by some authorities, 4. K. Kt. to K's 2nd, upon which the game is likely to be pursued as follows:—

	4. K. Kt. to K's 2nd.
5. Castles.	5. P. to Q. R's 3rd.
6. B. to Q. R's 4th.	6. Castles.
7. P. to Q's 4th.	7. P. takes P.
8. P. takes P.	8. B. to Q. Kt.'s 3rd.
9. P. to Q's 5th.	9. Q. Kt. to his sq.

You have an unquestionable advantage from position.

5. Castles.	5. K. Kt. to K's 2nd.
6. P. to Q's 4th.	6. P. takes P.
7. Q. B. to K. Kt.'s 5th.	7. Q. to K. Kt.'s 3rd.
8. B. takes K. Kt.	8. Q. Kt. takes B.
9. P. takes P.	9. B. to Q. Kt.'s 3rd.
10. Q. Kt. to B's 3rd.	10. Castles.

Your game is a little better developed.

The defence in the above variation is that commended by Ponziani, who remarks that if White, at his 5th move, take Q. Kt. with B., Black answers with 5. Q. takes B., and if then White move 6. P. to Q's 4th, Black takes K. P. with Q. (ch.), and has the advantage. If at your 5th move you advance P. to Q's 4th, Black must beware of the following variation:—

5. P. to Q's 4th.	5. P. takes P.
6. P. to K's 5th.	6. Kt. takes P.
7. Q. to K's 2nd.	

And he loses a Piece.

VARIATION I.,

Beginning at Black's 4th move.

WHITE.	BLACK.
1. P. to K's 4th.	1. P. to K's 4th.
2. K. Kt. to B's 3rd.	2. Q. Kt. to B's 3rd.
3. K. B. to Q. Kt.'s 5th.	3. K. B. to Q. B's 4th.
4. P. to Q. B's 3rd.	4. P. to Q's 3rd.
5. P. to Q's 4th.	5. P. takes P.
6. P. takes P.	6. B. to Q. Kt.'s 5th (ch.)
7. K. to his 2nd.	7. P. to Q's 4th.

At your 7th move you might also play K. to B's sq., or interpose either Bishop or Q's Kt., and in any of these cases have a superior game.

If Black, instead of his present move, should play 7. P. to Q. R's 3rd, you must take his Kt. (ch.), and then play Q. to her R's 4th (ch.), winning the Bishop. If he play 7. Q. B. to Q's 2nd, you may also play 8. Q. to R's 4th, winning.

8. Q. to her R's 4th.	8. P. takes K. P.
9. B. takes Kt. (ch.)	9. P. takes B.
10. Q. takes P. (ch.)	10. Q. B. to Q's 2nd.
11. Q. takes K. P. (ch.)	

And the game is much in your favour.

GAMES

ILLUSTRATIVE OF RUY LOPEZ'S KNIGHT'S GAME.

The two following games, with notes, are from the Berlin Chess Journal.

WHITE. (Mr. Hanstein.)	BLACK. (V. H. der Laza.)
1. P. to K's 4th.	1. P. to K's 4th.
2. K. Kt. to B's 3rd.	2. Q. Kt. to B's 3rd.
3. K. B. to Q. Kt.'s 5th.	3. K. B. to Q. B's 4th.
4. P. to Q. B's 3rd.	4. K. Kt. to K's 2nd.
5. Castles.	5. Castles.
6. P. to Q's 4th.	6. P. takes P.
7. P. takes P.	7. B. to Q. Kt.'s 3rd.
8. P. to Q's 5th.	8. Q. Kt. to his sq.
9. P. to Q's 6th.*	9. P. takes P.†
10. Q. takes P.	10. K. B. to Q. B's 2nd.
11. Q. to her 3rd.‡	11. P. to Q's 4th.
12. Q. Kt. to B's 3rd.	12. P. takes P.

---

* The present move is stronger, and affords a more lasting attack, than 9. K. Kt. to B's 3rd.

† Black may here play Q. Kt. to his 3rd, which White would follow with—

10. P. takes Q. B. P.	10. Q. or B. takes P.
11. Q. Kt. to B's 3rd,	

with a superior game.

‡ At this point, Jaenisch, vol. ii. p. 75, leaves the game, considering White's position as the better. The same move, 11. Q. to her 3rd, occurs in the game which follows this; it affords the adversary, however, an opportunity to disentangle his game by playing P. to Q's 4th, and with cor-

13. Q. takes P.*	13. Q. Kt. to B's 3rd.
14. K. R. to Q's sq. †	14. Q. to K's sq.
15. K. Kt. to his 5th.‡	15. Q. B. to K. B's 4th.
16. B. takes Kt.	16. P. takes B.
17. Q. to K. R's 4th.	17. Kt. to Q's 4th.
18. Kt. takes Kt.	18. P. takes Kt.
19. Q. B. to K's 3rd.§	19. Q. to her Kt.'s 4th.
20. B. to Q's 4th.	20. K. R. to K's sq.
21. Kt. to K. B's 3rd.	21. P. to K. B's 3rd.
22. B. takes K. B. P. ‖	22. P. takes B.
23. Q. takes B. P.	23. B. to K. Kt.'s 3rd.
24. Q. R. to Q. B's sq.	24. B. to Q. Kt.'s 3rd.
25. P. to K. R's 3rd.	25. K. R. to K's 7th.
26. Kt. to Q's 4th.	26. Q. takes P.
27. Q. to her B's 6th.¶	27. K. R. to K's sq. **

---

rect play would most likely lead to a drawn battle. A much stronger move, although it may not appear so theoretically, would be Q. to her R's 3rd; for in that case, Black could nct advance his P. to Q's 4th, as White would gain an advantage by answering with K. R. to Q's sq., which would give to Black a very confined position. Indeed it is not difficult to see, that after the move recommended, of Q. to her R's 3rd, Black's game affords no satisfactory defence for a length of time; and we must repeat that the playing K. B. to Q. B's 4th, by the second player, at his third move, is not to be commended.

* If the Knight takes this Pawn, Black gains an advantage by Q. B. to K. B's 4th.

† Instead of this move, White plays in the next game Q. B. to K. Kt.'s 5th.

‡ To separate the Pawns on the Queen's side.

§ If the Rook take the Pawn, the Queen gives mate; and if, instead of playing the Bishop to K's 3rd, he were played to K. B's 4th, Black might exchange Bishops, and then support his Q. P. by moving B. to K's 3rd.

‖ A bold sacrifice to be ventured in an actual game.

¶ The only saving move, and one which at the same time imperils Black.

** This is the best move. K. R. takes K. B. P. would perhaps have been good, but K. B. takes Kt. would have lost the game. (*e. g.*)

27. Q. to her B's 6th.	27. B. takes Kt.
28. Q. takes R. (ch.)	28. K. to Kt.'s 2nd (best)
29. R. to B's 7th (ch.)	29. K. to R's 3rd.[1]
30. Q. to K. B's 8th (ch.)	30. K. to R's 4th.
31. Q. to K. B's 3rd (ch.)	31. K. takes P.[2]
32. K. R. takes B. (ch.), &c.	

---

[1] Interposing the Bishop would cost a Piece.
[2] Or mate follows in two moves.

28. Q. takes Q. P. (ch.)		28. K. to R's sq. *
29. Q. R. to B's 6th. †		29. B. to K's 5th. ‡
30. Q. to her 6th.		30. B. takes Kt. §
31. R. takes B.		31. K. R. to K's 3rd.
32. Q. takes R.		32. Q. takes R.
33. Q. to K. B's 6th (ch.)		33. Q. takes Q.
34. R. takes Q.		34. R. to Q. Kt.'s sq. ‖
35. P. to K. B's 3rd.		35. B. to Q's 4th.
36. P. to Q. R's 3rd.		36. R. to Kt.'s 3rd. ¶
37. R. takes R.		37. P. takes R.
38. K. to B's 2nd.		38. K. to Kt.'s 2nd.
39. K. to his 3rd.		39. K. to B's 3rd.
40. K. to B's 4th.		40. B. to Q. B's 3rd.
41. K. to Kt.'s 4th.		41. B. to K's sq.
42. K. to B's 4th.		42. B. to K. Kt.'s 3rd.
43. K. to Kt.'s 4th.		43. P. to K. R's 4th (ch.)
44. K. to B's 4th.		44. B. to K. B's 4th.
45. P. to K. Kt.'s 4th.		45. B. to K. Kt.'s 3rd.
46. P. takes P.		46. B. takes P.
47. P. to Q. R's 4th. **		47. B. to K's sq.
48. P. to Q. R's 5th.		48. P. takes P. ††
49. K. to his 3rd.		

And the game was resigned as a drawn battle.

---

* Interposing the B. would lead to perpetual check.

† Q. R. to B's 4th would also have been good, but the move in the text is more beautiful, as it involved a snare, into which Black fell, and enabled White to save the game.

‡ Black could not resist the temptation of winning the Rook for Bishop, and thus overlooked the perpetual check. The strongest move for him was Q. R. to Q's sq.

§ If the other Bishop takes the Rook, White gives perpetual check.

‖ We recommend the study of the terminating moves, which were extremely difficult for both parties. They prove the possibility of positions occurring where two Pawns not even moved can draw the game against a Bishop.

¶ Black would have had a better chance of winning by not exchanging Rooks.

** Most important, because the Bishop might otherwise have prevented the Pawn advancing to compel the Black Pawn to take.

†† If Black does not take the Pawn, White would win. (?)   As it is, the game must be drawn, even if White had no Pawns, since the Pawn on R's file can never reach the 8th sq.

Between the same Players.

(The first thirteen moves on each side in this game were the same as in the preceding one.)

WHITE. (Mr. Hanstein.)	BLACK. (V. H. der Laza.)
14. Q. B. to K. Kt.'s 5th.	14. P. to K. B's 3rd.*
15. Q. R. to Q's sq.	15. Q. to K's sq.
16. K. R. to K's sq.	16. Q. to K. Kt.'s 3rd.†
17. B. takes Kt.	17. Kt. takes B.
18. Q. takes Q.	18. P. takes Q.
19. Q. Kt. to Q's 5th. ‡	19. B. to Q. R's 4th.
20. B. to Q's 2nd.	20. B. takes B.
21. Q. R. takes B.	21. B. to K. Kt.'s 5th.
22. K. Kt. to Q's 4th.	22. Q. R. to K's sq.
23. R. takes R.	23. R. takes R.
24. P. to K. B's 3rd.	24. Kt. takes Kt.
25. R. takes Kt.	25. B. to K's 3rd.
26. R. to K's 4th.	26. K. to B's 2nd.
27. Kt. to B's 7th.	27. R. to K's 2nd.
28. Kt. to Q. Kt.'s 5th.	28. R. to Q's 2nd.§
29. Kt. to Q. B's 3rd.	

After the twenty-ninth move, the game was resigned as drawn.

GAME III.—Between Captain Kennedy and Mr. Lowe.

WHITE. (Capt. K.)	BLACK. (Mr. L.)
1. P. to K's 4th.	1. P. to K's 4th.
2. K. Kt. to B's 3rd.	2. Q. Kt. to B's 3rd.
3. K. B. to Q. Kt.'s 5th.	3. K. B. to Q. B's 4th.
4. P. to Q. B's 3rd.	4. Q. to K's 2nd.

---

* If Black play Q. B. to K. B's 4th, White could gain a Pawn by taking the K. Kt. with Q. B.

† By playing Q. to K. R's 4th, he might have avoided getting a doubled Pawn, which, however, is not here a serious disadvantage. He could not take the Bishop with Pawn, on account of the other Bishop taking his Q. Kt.

‡ The Bishop on K. Kt.'s 5th is left *en prise* for the fifth time, but still cannot be taken. This move of the Knight was necessary to prepare a better retreat for the Bishop.

§ Had he played Q. R. P., White would have won a Pawn by playing—

29. Kt. to Q's 6th (ch.)	29. K. to B's sq.
30. Kt. takes P.	30. R. takes Kt.
31. R. takes B., &c.	

5. Castles.	5. P. to Q's 3rd.
6. P. to Q's 4th.	6. P. takes P.
7. P. takes P.	7. B. to Q. Kt.'s 3rd.
8. P. to Q's 5th.	8. P. to Q. R's 3rd.
9. Q. to Q. R's 4th.	9. Q. R. P. takes B.
10. Q. takes Q. R.	10. Kt. to Q. R's 2nd.
11. Q. B. to K's 3rd.	11. P. to Q. B's 4th.
12. Q. P. takes P. *en passant.*	12. B. takes B.
13. K. B. P. takes B.	13. Q. Kt. P. takes P.
14. K. Kt. to Q's 4th.	14. Q. to Q. B's 2nd.
15. P. to Q. Kt.'s 4th.	15. K. Kt. to B's 3rd.
16. P. to Q. R's 4th.	16. Castles.
17. Q. R. P. takes P.	17. B. to Q. R's 3rd.*
18. Q. takes R. (ch.)	18. K. takes Q.
19. Q. R. takes B. †	19. Q. B. P. takes P.
20. Q. Kt. to Q's 2nd.	20. Q. to Q. B's 6th.
21. K. Kt. to K. B's 5th. ‡	21. P. to K. Kt.'s 3rd.
22. Q. Kt. to his sq.	22. Q. to Q. Kt.'s 6th.
23. K. Kt. takes Q. P.	23. Q. takes K. P. (ch.)
24. K. to R's sq.	24. K. Kt. to K. Kt.'s 5th.
25. Q. R. to Q. R's 2nd.	25. K. Kt. to K's 4th.
26. K. Kt. takes K. B. P.	26. Kt. takes Kt.
27. Q. R. to K. B's 2nd.	27. Q. Kt. to Q. B's 3rd.
28. Q. R. takes K. Kt. (ch.)	28. K. to Kt.'s sq.
29. Q. R. to K. B's 3rd.	29. Q. takes K. P.
30. Kt. to Q. B's 3rd.	30. Q. takes Q. Kt. P.
31. Kt. to Q's 5th.	31. Q. to Q's 3rd.
32. Kt. to K. B's 6th (ch.)	32. K. to R's sq.
33. Kt. to K's 8th.	

And wins.

Chapter VIII.

THE QUEEN'S PAWN GAME, OR SCOTCH GAMBIT,

Is an opening upon which but little information can be gathered from the earlier writers. Lolli has devoted some consideration to a few of its more important variations; but it was not till the occasion of the great match by correspondence, between the London and Edinburgh Chess Clubs, when each party adopted this opening in one of their games, that its merits began to be appreciated. Since that period it has undergone a searching and complete analysis, and is now

* An ingenious move.
† White has a full equivalent for his lost Queen.
‡ Very well played.

acknowledged throughout Europe to be one of the most excellent and suggestive methods of commencing a game which has ever been invented. The chief authors to be consulted on "THE QUEEN'S PAWN GAME" are—Ghulam Kassim, in an interesting little work published at Madras, in 1829, under the title of "Analysis of the Muzio Gambit, &c.," 4to., p. 64; Lewis, Jaenisch, Bilguer and V. H. der Laza, Walker, and the "Chess-Player's Chronicle."

GAME THE FIRST.

WHITE.	BLACK.
1. P. to K's 4th.	1. P. to K's 4th.
2. K's Kt. to B's 3rd.	2. Q's Kt. to B's 3rd.
3. P. to Q's 4th.	3. Kt. takes P.

It is from your third move the opening derives its name of "The Queen's Pawn Game." Upon the advance of this Pawn, Black is compelled to take it, or have a very bad position, and this is one of the advantages the present gambit possesses over the ordinary ones, in most of which the defensive player may refuse the offered Pawn with perfect safety. Black has now the option of taking it either with his Knight or Pawn, and as the respective variations are distinct in character from each other, it will be as well to examine them separately. In this game your opponent takes the Pawn with his Knight, which Lolli commends as preferable to taking with the Pawn. Modern authors are at issue with the Italian on this point, and seem to concur in opinion that 3. P. takes P. is the proper mode of play.

4. Kt. takes Kt.	4. P. takes Kt.

You may also take P. with Kt., and preserve a slight advantage of position, as will be shown in a variation on your 4th move presently.

5. Q. takes P.	5. Kt. to K's 2nd.

He may prefer playing 5. Q. to K. B's 3rd, and the following shows the probable result.

	5. Q. to K. B's 3rd.
6. P. to K's 5th.	6. Q. to K. Kt.'s 3rd.*
7. Q's Kt. to B's 3rd.	7. Q. takes Q. B's P.

---

* If he play 6. Q. to her Kt.'s 3rd, you reply with 7. Q's B. to K's 3rd.

8. B. to Q's 3rd.	8. B. to Q. B's 4th.
9. Q. takes B.	9. Q. takes B.
10. Q's Kt. to his 5th.	10. Q. to K's 5th (ch.)
11. B. to K's 3rd.	11. Q. takes K. Kt.'s P.
12. Kt.. takes B's P. (ch.)	12. K. to Q's square.
13. Q. to K. B's 8th (ch.)	13. K. takes Kt.
14. R. to Q. B's sq. (ch.), and wins.	

6. K's B. to Q. B's 4th.	6. Kt. to Q. B's 3rd.

If instead of this, you play 6. Q's B. to K. Kt.'s 5th, he may answer with 6. Kt. to Q. B's 3rd, just the same, and you have little, if any, advantage in the game.

7. Q. to her 5th.	7. Q. to K. B's 3rd (best)
8. Castles.	8. B. to K's 2nd.

You have a better opened game, but the superiority is not important. At his 8th move he may play, instead of B. to K's 2nd, P. to Q's 3rd, which you can answer with 9. K's B. to Q. Kt.'s 5th, and then 10. Q's Kt. to B's 3rd, having a good opening.

VARIATION I.,

Beginning at White's 4th move.

WHITE.	BLACK.
1. P. to K's 4th.	1. P. to K's 4th.
2. K's Kt. to B's 3rd.	2. Q's Kt. to B's 3rd.
3. P. to Q's 4th.	3. Kt. takes P.
4. Kt. takes P.	4. Kt. to K's 3rd.

If he play 4. K's B. to Q. B's 4th, you proceed thus :—

	4. K's B. to Q. B's 4th.
5. K's B. to Q. B's 4th.*	5. Kt. to K's 3rd (best)
6. B. takes Kt.	6. K. B's P. takes B.†
7. Q. to K. R's 5th (ch.)	7. P. to K. Kt.'s 3rd.
8. Kt. takes P.	8. Kt. to K. B's 3rd.
9. Q. takes B.	

And you have gained a P. and the better situation.

5. K's B. to Q. B's 4th.	5. K's Kt. to B's 3rd.

If he play 5. P. to Q's 3rd, you check with your B. at Q. Kt.'s 5th, then take the interposed Q. B's P. with Kt., and upon

---

* You must not play 5. Kt. takes K. B's P., on account of 5. Q. to K. R's 5th.

† If he take the B. with Q's P., you exchange Queens, and then take K. B's P. with Kt. (ch.), winning the R.

his taking your Kt. as his best, you take the P. with B. (ch.), and afterwards the R., and although you give up two minor Pieces for the R. and Pawns, your game will be preferable to his. But he may also, at his 5th move, play P. to Q. B's 3rd, and, as the subjoined variation shows, maintain a good defence.

	5. P. to Q. B's 3rd.
6. B. takes Kt.*	6. Q. to R's 4th (ch.)

(You may castle without any disadvantage, instead of taking the Kt.)

7. Q's Kt. to B's 3rd.	7. Q. takes K's Kt.
8. B. to Q. Kt.'s 3rd.	8. B. to Q. B's 4th.
9. Castles.	

The positions are about equal.

6. Castles.	6. P. to Q's 3rd.
7. Kt. to K. Kt.'s 4th.	7. B. to K's 2nd.

Your game is less confined than his, but you have very little advantage.

If at his 6th move, instead of P. to Q's 3rd, he play 6. Kt. takes K's P., the game would probably be carried on thus :—

	6. Kt. takes K's P.
7. Kt. takes K. B's P.	7. K. takes Kt.
8. B. takes Kt. (ch.)	8. K. takes B.
9. Q. to K. Kt.'s 4th (ch.)	

And you afterwards gain the Kt., and have a winning position.

Having examined the consequences arising from Black's taking your Queen's Pawn *with the Knight* at his third move in this game, the next will be devoted to the variations which spring from his taking it with the King's Pawn.

GAME THE SECOND.

WHITE.	BLACK.
1. P. to K's 4th.	1. P. to K's 4th.
2. K's Kt. to B's 3rd.	2. Q's Kt. to B's 3rd.
3. P. to Q's 4th.	3. P. takes P.

In the preceding game it was remarked that later authors, in opposition to Lolli, regarded this as Black's better way of taking the Pawn.

* A powerful attack may now be got by taking the K. B's P. with Kt. (See game between Messrs. Cochrane and Walker, at the end of the present Chapter.)

You have now two modes of proceeding, either to retake the Pawn with your Kt. at once, or leave it to bring out your King's B., and thus be enabled to castle, and get the rest of your forces into action speedily. The latter is by far the more general practice, and gives rise to situations of greater beauty and diversity than the former; we will first, therefore, proceed to consider the consequences of this line of operation, and afterwards examine those attendant on the immediate capture of the Pawn.   (See Game the Sixth.)

4. K's B. to Q. B's 4th.	4. K's B. to Q. B's 4th.

Authorities are divided on the subject of Black's 4th move, some advocating the check with the Bishop, and others the move shown here; an analysis of the variations springing from both will follow (for the former, see next game), so that you may compare and judge between them.   There are also three other moves at his command, viz., 4. P. to Q's 3rd, K. Kt. to B's 3rd, and 4. Q. to K. B's 3rd, each of which shall be subsequently examined.   (See Variations III and IV.)

5. P. to Q. B's 3rd.	5. P. to Q's 6th.

You might also play K. Kt. to his 5th (See Variation I.), or castle at this point, as in Variation II.; both of these moves will be examined hereafter. Black's 5th move is that formerly advised as best by the chief writers; if instead he should play 5. P. takes P., you may take the K. B's P. with your B. (ch.), and if he take B. with K., you play Q. to her 5th (ch.), and then take his B.   He may, however, adopt the move suggested by Jaenisch of 5. K's Kt. to B's 3rd, and resolve the game into a position of the "Guioco Piano," which we arrive at in that game by these moves:—

1. P. to K's 4th.	1. P. to K's 4th.
2. K's Kt. to B's 3rd.	2. Q's Kt. to B's 3rd.
3. K's B. to Q. B's 4th.	3. K's B. to Q. B's 4th.
4. P. to Q. B's 3rd.	4. K's Kt. to B's 3rd.
5. P. to Q's 4th.	5. P. takes P.

The result of which is considered an even game. (See the "Guioco Piano.")

6. P. to Q. Kt.'s 4th.	6. B. to Q. Kt.'s 3rd.
7. P. to Q. Kt.'s 5th.	7. Q. to K's 2nd.

For your 7th move the best writers have heretofore recommended Q. to her Kt.'s 3rd, in which case the following moves ensue :—

7. Q. to her Kt.'s 3rd.	7. Q. to K. B's 3rd.
8. Castles.	8. P. to Q's 3rd.
9. B. takes doubled P.	9. Q's B. to K's 3rd.
10. Q. to her B's 2nd.*	10. Kt. to K's 2nd.
11. Q's B. to Kt.'s 2nd.†	11. Q's Kt. to K's 4th.
12. Kt. takes Kt.	12. P. takes Kt.

You have still a little attack, but the advantage on your side is very slight.

The move of 7. P. to Q. Kt.'s 5th occurs in a game lately played between the writer and Mr. Harrwitz, and has been sanctioned in practice since by some of the best players in the country; if Black, in reply, play 7. Kt. to Q. R's 4th, or Kt. to his sq., his Kt. for some moves is inactive, and White has time to develope his forces; if he answer with 7. Kt. to K's 2nd, White plays Q. to her Kt.'s 3rd, and should win. The move adopted by Mr. Harrwitz, of 7. Q. to K's 2nd, appears the best.

8. Castles.	8. Kt. to K's 4th.
9. Kt. takes Kt.	9. Q. takes Kt.
10. Q. to her Kt.'s 3rd.	10. Q. to K. B's 3rd, or
11. P. to K's 4th.	K's 2nd.

You have a fine game.

---

* Better than P. to Q. B's 4th.

† This move is given in the German "Handbuch," but White, it appears to me, may try the subjoined with safety :—

11. B. to K. Kt.'s 5th.	11. Q. to K. Kt.'s 3rd.
12. P. to Q. Kt.'s 5th.	12. Q's Kt. to K's 4th.[1]
13. Kt. takes Kt.	13. P. takes Kt.
14. B. takes Kt.	14. K. takes B.

You now play K. to R's sq. and have the better game.

---

[1] If he retreat, or go to Q. R's 4th, you first take K's Kt. with Q's Bishop, then advance P. to K's 5th, exchange the Pieces, and afterwards take P. with P.

VARIATION I.,

Beginning at White's 5th move.

BLACK.

WHITE.

5. K's Kt. to his 5th.	5. K's Kt. to R's 3rd (best)

This is his best move; if he play 5. Q's Kt. to K's 4th, you proceed as in the present case, but with a more favourable game.

6. Kt. takes K. B's P.	6. Kt. takes Kt.

If instead of taking the Kt., he now play 6. B. to Q. Kt.'s 5th (ch.), the result will be to your advantage.

	6. B. to Q. Kt.'s 5th (ch.)
7. P. to Q. B's 3rd.	7. P. takes P.
8. P. takes P,	8. B. takes P. (ch.)
9. Q's Kt. takes B.	9. Kt. takes K's Kt.
10. B. takes Kt. (ch.)	10. K. takes B.
11. Q. to K. R's 5th (ch.)	

And you have a fine attacking position.

This variation is admirably exemplified in the game between Mr. Cochrane and M. Deschappelles, at the end of the Chapter.

7. B. takes Kt. (ch.)	7. K. takes B.
8. Q. to K. R's 5th (ch.)	8. P. to K. Kt.'s 3rd.
9. Q. takes B.	9. P. to Q's 3rd.

He might also play 9. Q. to K's 2nd, which would probably be followed up thus:—

	9. Q. to K's 2nd.
10. Q. to her B's 4th (ch.)	10. Q. to K's 3rd.
11. Q. to K's 2nd.	11. P. to Q's 4th.

12. P. to K. B's 3rd.	12. K's R. to K's sq.
13. Castles.	13. K. to Kt.'s 2nd.
14. Q. to K. B's 2nd.	14. P. takes K's P.
15. P. takes P.	

The game is in your favour.

10. Q. to her Kt.'s 5th.	10. P. to Q. R's 3rd.
11. Q. to her 3rd.	11. K. to Kt.'s 2nd.
12. Castles.	12. Q's B. to K's 3rd.
13. P. to Q. B's 3rd.	13. Q. to K. B's 3rd.
14. B. to Q's 2nd.	

You appear to me to have the better game.

VARIATION II.,

Beginning at White's 5th move.—(See the preceding diagram.)

5. Castles.	5. P. to Q's 3rd.

If at this point he move 5. Q. to K. B's 3rd, the result will be somewhat in your favour; for example,—

	5. Q. to K. B's 3rd.
6. P. to Q. B's 3rd.	6. P. to Q's 3rd.
7. P. to Q. Kt.'s 4th.	7. B. to Q. Kt.'s 3rd.
8. B. to Q. Kt.'s 2nd.	8. Kt. to K's 4th.
9. Kt. takes Kt.	9. P. takes Kt.
10. P. takes P.	10. B. takes P.
11. B. takes B.	11. P. takes B.
12. P. to K's 5th.	12. Q. to her Kt.'s 3rd.
13. P. to Q. R's 4th.	13. P. to Q. R's 4th.
14. P. takes P.	14. R. takes P.
15. Kt. to Q. R's 3rd.	

And although short of Pawns, your Pieces will soon be in powerful co-operation with each other, and give you the stronger game.

6. P. to Q. B's 3rd.	6. P. takes P.

He may also play without danger 6. P. to Q's 6th.

7. Q's Kt. takes P.	7. K's Kt. to K's 2nd.

If instead he move 7. Q's B. to K's 3rd, you get the better game, as follows:—

	7. Q's B. to K's 3rd.
8. B. takes B.	8. P. takes B.
9. K's Kt. to his 5th.	9. Q. to her B's sq.
10. Q. to K. R's 5th (ch.)	10. P. to K. Kt.'s 3rd.
11. Q. to K. Kt.'s 4th.	11. P. to K's 4th.
12. Kt. to K's 6th.	12. K's Kt. to B's 3rd.

13. Q. to K. R's 3rd.   13. K. to his 2nd.
14. Q's Kt. to Q's 5th (ch.)   14. Kt. takes Kt.
15. P. takes Kt., &c.

8. K's Kt. to his 5th.   8. Kt. to K's 4th.

And he has at least as good a game as you have.   This variation serves to prove that your castling on the 5th move is less
advisable than the move of 5. P. to Q. B's 3rd.

VARIATION III.,

Beginning at Black's 4th move.

WHITE.	BLACK.
1. P. to K's 4th.	1. P. to K's 4th.
2. K's Kt. to B's 3rd.	2. Q's Kt. to B's 3rd.
3. P. to Q's 4th.	3. P. takes P.
4. K's B. to Q. B's 4th.	4. P. to Q's 3rd.

Black now relinquishes the defence of the P. he has gained,
but he also, in some degree, neutralizes your attack.

At this point, in the opinion of V. H. der Laza, he may
also equalize the game by playing 4. K. Kt. to B's 3rd, a
variation which this able writer pursues as follows :—

	4. K's Kt. to B's 3rd.
5. Kt. takes P., or (A.)	5. Kt. takes K's P.
6. B. takes K. B's P. (ch.)	6. K. takes B.
7. Q. to K. R's 5th (ch.)	7. P. to K. Kt.'s 3rd.
8. Q. to her 5th (ch.)	8. K. to Kt.'s 2nd.
9. Kt. takes Q's Kt.	9. Q. to K. R's 5th.

(Another move suggested by V. H. der Laza for Black, viz., 9. **Q. to**
K's sq., I think preferable to the one made.)

10. Q. to her 4th (ch.)   10. K. to Kt.'s sq.
11. Kt. to K's 5th.

I certainly think White has the better game.

(A.)

5. P. to K's 5th.	5. Kt. to K. Kt.'s 5th.
6. B. takes K. B's P. (ch.)	6. K. takes B.
7. Kt. to K. Kt.'s 5th (ch.)	7. K. to Kt.'s sq.
8. Q. takes Kt.	8. P. to K. R's 3rd.

These are the moves of the able writer mentioned ; if I am not mistaken,
White should rather play 8. Q. to K. B's 3rd, instead of taking the Kt.
immediately.

V. H. d. L's variation proceeds thus :—

9. K's Kt. to B's 3rd.   9. P. to Q's 3rd.
10. Q. to K's 4th.   10. P. takes K's P.

11. Kt. takes K's P.	11. Kt. takes Kt.
12. Q. takes Kt.	12. K. to R's 2nd.
13. Castles.	13. P. to K. Kt.'s 3rd.
14. K's R. to Q's sq.	14. B. to K. Kt.'s 2nd.
15. Q. to K. Kt.'s 3rd.	15. P. to Q. B's 3rd.
16. P. to Q. B's 3rd.	16. Q. to K's 2nd.

And it is remarked in the German " Handbuch," " Black has not a bad game."

5. P. to Q. B's 3rd.   5. P. takes P.

If you castle at this moment, Black will play 5. Q's B. to K. Kt.'s 5th, and sustain his P. In reply to your move of 5. P. to Q. B's 3rd, Black may play 5. Q's Kt. to K's 4th, whereupon you may take the P. with P., and when he takes your B., you can check with the Q. at her R's 4th, and then take the Kt. In the German " Handbuch," Black is made to play 5. Q's B. to K. Kt.'s 5th; but there is evidently some mistake in the calculations, because although after a few moves the game is pronounced equal, Black in reality is minus a Piece. He may, however, seemingly, move 5. K's Kt. to B's 3rd, instead of taking the P. with P., but in that case also, your Pieces have greater freedom than his.

6. Q's Kt. takes P.

You have certainly the advantage in position.

VARIATION IV.,

Beginning also at Black's 4th move.

WHITE.	BLACK.
1. P. to K's 4th.	1. P. to K's 4th.
2. K's Kt. to B's 3rd.	2. Q's Kt. to B's 3rd.
3. P. to Q's 4th.	3. P. takes P.
4. K's B. to Q. B's 4th.	4. Q. to K. B's 3rd.

This was a defence adopted by McDonnell against La Bourdonnais. It is ingenious, but it gives an irksome and restrained position to Black for a long time.

5. Castles.   5. P. to Q's 3rd.

If he play 5. K's B. to Q. B's 4th, you answer with 6. P. to K's 5th, and upon the Q. being moved to K. Kt.'s 3rd or K. B's 4th, you play K's R. to K's sq., threatening to win her by Kt. to K. R's 4th.

6. P. to Q. B's 3rd.	6. P. to Q's 6th.

It would be bad play for him to take P. with P., because he would bring your Q's Kt. into effective action. He might, however, play 6. Q's B. to K. Kt.'s 5th, with some plausibility. (*e. g.*)

	6. Q's B. to K. Kt.'s 5th.
7. Q. to her Kt.'s 3rd.	7. Castles on Q's side.
8. Q's B. to K. Kt.'s 5th.	8. Q's Kt. to Q. R's 4th.
9. Q. to her Kt.'s 5th.	9. Q. to K. Kt.'s 3rd.
10. K's Kt. to K. R's 4th, &c.	

7. Q. takes P.	7. Q. to K. Kt.'s 3rd.
8. Q's B. to K. B's 4th.	8. B. to K's 2nd.
9. Q's Kt. to Q. R's 3rd.	9. P. to Q. R's 3rd.
10. Q's Kt. to Q. B's 2nd.	10. K's Kt. to R's 3rd.

Your game is better opened, but there is no very striking disparity in the positions.

GAME THE THIRD.

WHITE.	BLACK.
1. P. to K's 4th.	1. P. to K's 4th.
2. K's Kt. to B's 3rd.	2. Q's Kt. to B's 3rd.
3. P. to Q's 4th.	3. P. takes P.
4. K's B. to Q. B's 4th.	4. B. to Q. Kt.'s 5th (ch.)

Black's 4th move, as was remarked in the preceding game, has long been a *vexata quæstio* among chess-players; the majority are of opinion that, if followed by taking the adverse Q. B's P. and Q. Kt.'s P., it compromises Black's game irredeemably; but some few believe the two gained Pawns to be a sufficient equivalent for the disadvantage of position. It appears to me that the check may be given without much danger, but that by taking *both* the Pawns, Black subjects himself to an attack for which his superiority of force but poorly compensates.

5. P. to Q. B's 3rd.	5. P. takes P.
6. Castles.	6. P. to Q. B's 7th.

Instead of castling, Mr. Cochrane brought into vogue a very novel and ingenious mode of continuing the attack by now taking P. with Q. Kt.'s P. (See the next game.)

For the consequences of Black's taking the second Pawn at this point, refer to Game the Fifth.

If instead of either move, he play 6. P. to Q's 3rd, or 6. Q. to K. B's 3rd, I think you obtain a slightly better game. (*e. g.*) In the first place, suppose,—

	6. P. to Q's 3rd.
7. P. to Q. R's 3rd.	7. B. to Q. R's 4th.
8. P. to Q. Kt.'s 4th.	8. B. to Q. Kt.'s 3rd.
9. Q. to her Kt.'s 3rd.	9. Q. to K. B's 3rd.
10. Q's Kt. takes P.	10. Q's B. to K's 3rd.

(You might also attack the Q. with your Q's B., and afterwards take the P. with Q's Kt.)

11. Q's Kt. to Q's 5th.	11. B. takes Kt.

(He would play ill in taking your Q's R., on account of 12. Q's B. to Kt.'s 2nd.)

12. B. takes B.	12. K's Kt. to K's 2nd.
13. Q's B. to K. Kt.'s 5th.	13. Q. to Kt.'s 3rd.
14. Q's B. takes K's Kt.	14. K. takes B
15. Kt. to K. R's 4th.	15. Q. to K. B's 3rd.
16. Kt. to K. B's 5th (ch.)	16. K. to his sq. or B's sq.
17. Q's R. to B's sq.	17. Kt. to Q's sq.
18. P. to Q. Kt.'s 5th.	

And the gained P. is hardly an equivalent for the confinement of his Pieces.

In the second place,—

	6. Q. to K. B's 3rd.
7. P. to K's 5th.	7. Q. to K. Kt.'s 3rd.
8. P. takes P.	8. B. to Q. B's 4th.
9. Q. to K's 2nd.	9. Q's Kt. to Q's sq.
10. Kt. to K. R's 4th.	10. Q. to her B's 3rd.

His game is ill developed.

7. Q. takes P	7. P. to Q's 3rd.
8. P. to Q. R's 3rd.	8. B. to Q. B's 4th.
9. P. to Q. Kt.'s 4th.	9. B. to Q. Kt.'s 3rd.

If he play 9. B. to Q's 5th, you take him with the Kt., and then move Q. to her B's 3rd; if he move 9. Kt. to Q's 5th, you likewise take him, and afterwards take K. B's P. with your B. (ch.).

10. Q's B. to Kt.'s 2nd.	10. K's Kt. to B's 3rd.

The game is about even.

GAME THE FOURTH.
MR. COCHRANE'S ATTACK.

WHITE.	BLACK.
1. P. to K's 4th.	1. P. to K's 4th.
2. K's Kt. to B's 3rd.	2. Q's Kt. to B's 3rd.
3. P. to Q's 4th.	3. P. takes P.
4. K's B. to Q. B's 4th.	4. K's B. checks.
5. P. to Q. B's 3rd.	5. P. takes P.
6. P. takes P.	6. B. to Q. R's 4th.

Your move of 6. P. takes P., unless opposed with uncommon care, will give you a very powerful attack.

| 7. P. to K's 5th. | 7. P. to Q's 4th (best) |

P. to K's 5th is the move adopted by Mr. Cochrane; I have found 7. Castling (see Var. I.) more advantageous, because it prevents the advance of Black's P. to Q's 4th. If Black play 7. P. to Q's 3rd, he has a bad opening. (See the game between Messrs. Cochrane and Popert, at the end of the present Chapter.) He may move, however, 7. K's Kt. to K's 2nd, as commended by Jaenisch. (*e. g.*)

	7. K's Kt. to K's 2nd.
8. Q's B. to Q. R's 3rd.	8. Castles.
9. Castles.	9. K. to R's sq.

(If he play 9. P. to Q's 4th, you take the P. in passing, and the positions are about equal.)

| 10. R. to K's sq. | |

He has a P. more, but your position is very superior.

| 8. Q. takes P. | 8. Q. takes Q. |

You may also take P. with P. in passing, or P. with K's B. at your 8th move.   In the first place,—

| 8. P. takes P. in passing. | 8. Q. takes P. |
| 9. Q. to her Kt.'s 3rd. | 9. Q's B. to K's 3rd. |

(Instead of Q. to her Kt.'s 3rd, you can likewise play 9. Q's B. to Q. R's 3rd, or take Q. with Q., but in either case the game is a little in Black's favour.)

10. Castles.	10. K's Kt. to K's 2nd.
11. Q's B. to Q. R's 3rd.	11. B. takes K's B.
12. Q. takes B.	12. Q. to her 4th.
13. Q. takes Q.	13. Kt. takes Q.
14. R. checks.	14. K's Kt. to K's 2nd.
15. Kt. to K's 5th.	15. Kt. takes Kt.
16. R. takes Kt.	16. Castles on Q's side.

And you dare not take either Piece, so Black preserves the Pawn.

if at the 16th move you take K's Kt. with B., he answers with P. to K. B's 3rd.

In the second place,—

8. B. takes Q's P.	8. K's Kt. to K's 2nd.
9. B. takes Q's Kt. (ch.)	9. K's Kt. takes B.
10. Q. takes Q. (ch.)	10. Kt. takes Q.
11. B. to Q. Kt.'s 2nd.	11. Q's B. to K. Kt.'s 5th.
12. Q's Kt. to Q's 2nd.	

Even game.

9. B. takes Q.	9. K's Kt. to K's 2nd.
10. K's B. takes Q's Kt. (ch.)	10. Kt. takes B.
11. Q's B. to K. B's 4th.	11. Castles.
12. Castles.	12. K's R. to K's sq.
13. P. to K. R's 3rd.	

The game is equal.

VARIATION I.

BLACK.

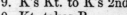

WHITE.

Moves 1 to 6 on each side as before.

WHITE.	BLACK.
7. Castles.	7. P. to Q's 3rd.

If he play 7. K's Kt. to K's 2nd, you may move K's Kt. to his 5th, and if then he play 8. Q's Kt. to K's 4th, you can take K. B's P. with Kt., &c., checking afterwards with Q. at K. R's 5th, and then taking the Bishop.

8. P. to K's 5th.	8. Q's B. to K's 3rd.

If he venture to take 8. P. with P., you win by 9. B. takes K. B's P. (ch.), and when the K. takes B., Kt. takes K's P. (ch.), &c.; the King then has no safe place of refuge.

9. B. takes B.   9. P. takes B.
10. Q. to her Kt.'s 3rd.   10. Q. to B's sq.
11. P. takes Q's P.   11. P. takes P.
12. K's Kt. to his 5th,

Followed by R. to K's sq., and you appear to me to have a better game than Black.

GAME THE FIFTH.

WHITE.	BLACK.
1. P. to K's 4th.	1. P. to K's 4th.
2. K's Kt. to B's 3rd.	2. Q's Kt. to B's 3rd.
3. P. to Q's 4th.	3. P. takes P.
4. K's B. to Q. B's 4th.	4. K's B. checks.
5. P. to Q. B's 3rd.	5. P. takes P.
6. Castles.	6. P. takes Q. Kt.'s P.

La Bourdonnais and most leading players concur in decrying this second capture of Black's, but hitherto no one has pointed out the way to win against it.

7. Q's B. takes P.   7. K's B. to his sq.

I believe this to be the best defence of his Kt.'s P. he has. Instead of retreating the Bishop, he may play 7. K. to B's sq., the move advised in the German "Handbuch" (See Var. I.), 7. P. to K. B's 3rd, and 7. K's Kt. to B's 3rd. The effect of playing either of the latter moves may be shown before proceeding further. In the first place then, suppose—

	7. P. to K. B's 3rd.
8. P. to K's 5th.	8. P. takes P.

(You may likewise play 8. Q. to her Kt.'s 3rd, and 8. Kt. to K. Kt.'s 5th, in both cases with a fine attack. If Black, instead of taking the P. with P., take it with his Kt., you take Kt. with Kt., and then play Q. to her Kt.'s 3rd.)

9. K's Kt. takes P.	9. Q's Kt. takes Kt.
10. Q's B. takes Kt.	10. K's Kt. to B's 3rd.
11. Q. to her R's 4th.	11. Q. to K's 2nd.

(If he play 11. B. to K's 2nd, you can then move your K's R. to K's sq., and if 11. P. to Q. B's 4th, you may play 12. P. to Q. R's 3rd, and then Q's R. to his 2nd.)

12. Q's B. takes Kt.	12. P. takes B.
13. P. to Q. R's 3rd.	13. B. to Q. B's 4th.
14. Q's Kt. to B's 3rd.	

You have a fine game.

In the next place—

	7. K's Kt. to B's 3rd.
8. K's Kt. to his 5th.	8. Castles.
9. P. to K's 5th.	9. K's Kt. to his 5th.

(If he move 9. Kt. to K's sq., you must reply with 10. Q. to K. R's 5th, having an easy game. He may also play 9. P. to Q's 4th, or 9. P. to K. R's 3rd, and in each case you can take his Kt. with the P., and will have the better game.)

10. Q. takes Kt.	10. P. to Q's 4th.
11. P. to K's 6th.	11. P. takes K's B.
12. Kt. takes K. B's P.	12. R. takes Kt.
13. P. takes R. (ch.)	

And you win.

Now to resume the original game.

8. Q's Kt. to B's 3rd.	8. K's Kt. to R's 3rd.

I believe your 8th move to be better than either Q. to her 5th or P. to K's 5th, (both of which, with careful play on Black's part, should result in a drawn game), and that after this *sortie* of your Q's Kt., the board affords no satisfactory defence for the second player.

9. P. to K's 5th.	9. K's B. to K's 2nd.
10. Q's Kt. to K's 4th.	10. Castles.
11. Q. to her 2nd.	11. P. to Q's 3rd.
12. Kt. to K. B's 6th (ch.)	

You have an excellent attack.

VARIATION I.,
Beginning at Black's 7th move.

BLACK.

WHITE.

Moves 1 to 7 as before.

WHITE.	BLACK.
	7. K. to B's sq.
8. P. to K's 5th.	8. Q. to K's 2nd.
9. P. to Q. R's 3rd.	9. B. to Q. B's 4th.

He has the choice of two evils, either to play thus, and permit you to bring out the Q's Kt., or to move his B. to Q. R's 4th, and occupy the only attacking sq. which is open to his Q's Kt.

10. Q's Kt. to B's 3rd.	10. P. to Q's 3rd.
11. Q's Kt. to Q's 5th.	11. Q. to her 2nd.
12. R. to K's sq.	12. P. takes K's P.
13. Q's B. takes P.	13. Kt. takes B.
14. Kt. takes Kt.	14. Q. to her sq.
15. Kt. takes K. B's P.	

And you must win.

The foregoing is an analysis of the most important combinations which proceed from your playing B. to Q. B's 4th at the 4th move, instead of taking the Pawn with your Kt. The next consideration must be the consequences to be looked for from the latter course of action.

GAME THE SIXTH.

WHITE.	BLACK.
1. P. to K's 4th.	1. P. to K's 4th.
2. K's Kt. to B's 3rd.	2. Q's Kt. to B's 3rd.
3. P. to Q's 4th.	3. P. takes P.
4. Kt. takes P.	4. Q. to K. R's 5th.

The move of 4. Kt. takes P., I believe to have been censured without good cause, and that it may be made with perfect security. The chief objection advanced against it, is the counter move by Black of Q. to K. R's 5th; a manœuvre which is highly ingenious certainly, and has been approved by every writer of eminence from the time of its introduction, but which I have the temerity to think has been somewhat over estimated. The usual modes of opposing this move of the Queen have been by playing 5. Q. to her 3rd, or 5. Q's Kt. to B's 3rd, and the result in each case is favourable for Black, as you will see in the following examples. Firstly—

5. Q. to her 3rd.	5. K's Kt. to B's 3rd.

(He may also play as advised by Jaenisch, 5. Q's Kt. to K's 4th, and
obtain a fine game.)

6. Kt. takes Q's Kt.	6. Q's P. takes Kt.
7. P. to K's 5th.	7. K's B. to Q. B's 4th.
8. Q's B. to K's 3rd.	8. B. takes B.

(If you take the Kt. at your 8th move, he will win your Q. at least.)

9. Q. takes B.	9. Kt. to his 5th.
10. Q. to K's 2nd.	10. Q. to K's 2nd.
11. P. to K. B's 4th.	11. Q. to her Kt.'s 5th (ch.)

And he has the better game.

Secondly—

5. Q's Kt. to B's 3rd.	5. K's B. to Q. Kt.'s 5th.
6. Q. to her 3rd.	6. B. takes Kt. (ch.)
7. P. takes B.	7. K's Kt. to B's 3rd.

He has the advantage.

These were the accepted methods of replying to Black's 4th
move, until a few months ago Mr. Horwitz originated another
mode, which is, I think, deserving more attention than it has
received; this is—

5. K's Kt. to Q. Kt.'s 5th.　　　5. K's B. to Q. B's 4th.

In an interesting article on the Scotch Gambit, in the "Berlin
Schachzeitung," for October, 1846, we find this move of Mr.
Horwitz's is reviewed, and the writer, in answer to it, suggests
that Black may take the K's P. (ch.), and afterwards establish
a good defence (the result of this way of play will be shown in
Var. I.); he is of opinion, too, in common with most players
here, that the move in the text of 5. K's B. to Q. B's 4th,
entirely foils the previous device of White. Upon this point
I am disposed to differ with him. The game now proceeds as
follows :—

6. Q. to K. B's 3rd.　　　　　　6. Q's Kt. to Q's 5th.

Black's 5th and 6th moves were suggested by some members
of the London Club, and have been supposed by those who
have examined them, including the writer of the article just
spoken of and Mr. Horwitz himself, to compel the exchange
of Knights, and thus completely nullify the first attack. I
believe, however, that the exchange of Pieces is not imperative, and that this play of the B. and Kt., so far from weakening your game, adds much to its power. In proof, I venture
to submit the following train of play :—

7. Kt. takes Q. B's P. (ch.)   7. K. to Q's sq. (best)
8. Q. to K. B's 4th.   8. Kt. takes Q. B's P. (ch.)

He has apparently no stronger move.

9. K. to Q's sq.   9. Q. takes Q.

Any other play would be still more disadvantageous to him.

10. B. takes Q   10. Kt. takes Q's R.
11. Kt. takes Q's R.

I believe the best answering moves have been made by Black, and now, upon surveying the aspect of the board, there can be no question, I apprehend, that your game is much superior. The Kt. which has captured your Rook, he can never extricate, while, to secure yours in the same position, he must lose many moves, and thus afford you ample time for the development of your remaining forces.

VARIATION,

Beginning at Black's 5th move.

WHITE.	BLACK.
1. P. to K's 4th.	1. P. to K's 4th.
2. K's Kt. to B's 3rd.	2. Q's Kt. to B's 3rd.,
3. P. to Q's 4th.	3. P. takes P.
4. Kt. takes P.	4. Q. to K. R's 5th.
5. Kt. to Q. Kt.'s 5th.	5. Q. takes K's P. (ch.)

This is the other mode of play for Black proposed by the German writer, and he pursues it thus :—

6. B. to K's 2nd.   6. K. to Q's sq.

If he take the K. Kt.'s P., you move K's B. to his 3rd, &c., and if instead of moving his King, he play 6. K's B. to Q's 3rd, you take the B. with your Q., and must win "the exchange." He may, however, play another move, viz., 6. K's B. to Kt.'s 5th (ch.), the consequences of which it may be well to examine briefly.

                                    6. K's B. to Q. Kt.'s 5th (ch.)
7. B. to Q's 2nd.   7. K. to Q's sq.
8. Castles.

In this situation I think, in opposition to the able writer mentioned, that Black's game is vastly inferior to yours, and that with his King so circumstanced, the loss of your Pawn is actually an advantage, since it affords so much scope for the attack of the Rooks.

7. Castles.	7. P. to Q. R's 3rd.
8. Q's Kt. to B's 3rd.	8. Q. to K's sq.

This is the retreat proposed by the German critic; if the Q. be moved to K's 4th, you first play Q's Kt. to Q's 5th, and if then he take the other Kt., you reply with Q's B. to K. B's 4th, and have a better game.

9. K's Kt. to Q's 4th.

And again, I believe, with the strangely changed positions of his King and Queen, and the facility afforded you for bringing the Pieces into immediate action, that the game is very much in your favour.

GAME THE SEVENTH.

Varying from the preceding at Black's 4th move.

WHITE.	BLACK.
1. P. to K's 4th.	1. P. to K's 4th.
2. K's Kt. to B's 3rd.	2. Q's Kt. to B's 3rd.
3. P. to Q's 4th.	3. P. takes P.
4. Kt. takes P.	4. K's B. to Q. B's 4th.

This is probably his strongest move; he may, though, play 4. Kt. takes Kt., and resolve the game into a position of a former example, which we arrive at there by—

1. P. to K's 4th.	1. P. to K's 4th.
2. K's Kt. to B's 3rd.	2. Q's Kt. to B's 3rd.
3. P. to Q's 4th.	3. Kt. takes P.
4. Kt. takes Kt.	4. P. takes Kt.
5. Q. takes P.	

5. Kt. takes Q's Kt.	5. Q. to K. B's 3rd.
6. Q. to K. B's 3rd.	6. Q. takes Q.
7. P. takes Q.	7. Q. Kt.'s P. takes Kt.
8. Q's B. to K. B's 4th.	8. P. to Q's 3rd.
9. K's B. to Q. B's 4th.	9. Q's B. to K's 3rd.
10. Q's Kt. to Q's 2nd.	

And the game is in every respect equal.

GAMES

ILLUSTRATIVE OF THE QUEEN'S PAWN OR SCOTCH GAMBIT.

(From the *Chess-Player's Chronicle*.)

GAME I.—Played in the celebrated match between the London and Edinburgh Chess Clubs, 1826.

WHITE. (Edinburgh.)	BLACK. (London.)
1. P. to K's 4th.	1. P. to K's 4th.
2. K. Kt to B's 3rd.	2. Q. Kt. to B's 3rd.
3. P. to Q's 4th.	3. Kt. takes P.
4. Kt. takes Kt.	4. P. takes Kt.
5. Q. takes P.	5. K. Kt. to K's 2nd.
6. K. B. to Q. B's 4th.	6. Kt. to Q. B's 3rd.
7. Q. to her 5th.	7. Q. to K. B's 3rd.
8. Kt. to Q. B's 3rd.*	8. K. B. to Q. Kt.'s 5th.
9. Q. B. to Q's 2nd.	9. P. to Q's 3rd.
10. K. B. to Q. Kt.'s 5th.	10. Q. B. to Q's 2nd.
11. Q. to her B's 4th.	11. K. B. to Q. B's 4th.
12. Castles on K's side.	12. Castles on K's side.
13. Q. to her 3rd.†	13. Kt. to K's 4th.
14. Q. to K. Kt.'s 3rd.	14. B. takes B.
15. Kt. takes B.	15. P. to Q. B's 3rd.
16. Kt. to Q. B's 3rd.	16. Kt. to Q. B's 5th.
17. B. to K. Kt.'s 5th.	17. Q. to K. Kt.'s 3rd.
18. P. to Q. Kt.'s 3rd.	18. P. to K. B's 3rd.
19. B. to Q. B's sq.	19. Q. takes Q.
20. K. R. P. takes Q.	20. B. to Q's 5th.
21. P. takes Kt.	21. B. takes Kt.
22. Q. R. to Kt.'s sq.	22. P. to Q. Kt.'s 3rd.
23. K. R. to Q's sq.	23. Q. R. to K's sq.
24. Q. R. to Q. Kt.'s 3rd.	24. B. to Q. R's 4th.
25. P. to K. B's 3rd.	25. P. to K. B's 3rd.
26. P. takes P.	26. Q. R. to K's 7th.‡
27. P. to K. Kt.'s 4th.	27. Q. R. takes Q. B. P.

---

* Castling would have been better play, because Black would then have had no favourable opportunity of bringing their K. B. into the field.

† Kt. to Q's 5th looks a tempting move, but it would have been a very bad one for them. (*e. g.*)

13. Kt. to Q's 5th.	13. Q. to K. R's 5th.
14. Kt. takes Q. B. P.	14. Q. R. to Q. B's sq.
15. Kt. to Q's 5th.	15. Kt. to K's 4th.
16. Q. to K's 2nd.	16. Q. B. to K. Kt.'s 5th.
17. Q. to K's sq.	17. Kt. to K. B's 6th (ch.)

And Black win.

‡ They should have taken the P. with K's Rook.

28. B. to K. B's 4th.	28. Q. R. takes Q. B. P.
29. B. takes Q. P.	29. K. R. to K s sq.
30. Q. R. to his 3rd.	30. P. to K. R's 3rd.
31. B. to Q. B's 7th.	31. R. to K's 2nd.
32. K. R. to Q's 8th (ch.)	32. K. to R's 2nd.
33. R. to Q. B's 8th.	33. Q. R. to B's 8th (ch.)
34. K. to his R's 2nd.	34. K. R. to K's 8th.
35. K. to his R's 3rd.	35. R. to K. R's 8th (ch.)
36. B. to K. R's 2nd.	36. B. to Q. B's 6th.*
37. P. to K. B's 4th.	37. B. to Q's 7th.
38. P. to K. Kt.'s 3rd.	38. B. to Q. R's 4th.†
39. Q. R. to K's 3rd.‡	39. Q. R. to Q. B's 2nd.
40. P. to K. Kt.'s 5th.	40. K. R. takes B. (ch.)
41. K. to his Kt.'s 4th.	41. P. to K. R's 4th (ch.)
42. K. to B's 3rd.	42. K. R. to B's 7th (ch.)
43. K. to his 4th.	43. P. to K. Kt's 3rd.
44. K. R. to Q. B's 7th (ch.)	44. K. to his Kt.'s sq.
45. K. to his 5th.	45. Q. R. to Q. B's 4th (ch.)
46. K. to B's 6th.	46. Q. R. takes P. (ch.)
47. K. takes P.	47. Q. R. to K. B's sq.
48. K. R. to K. Kt.'s 7th (ch.)	48. K. to R's sq.
49. K. to R's 6th.	49. B. to Q. Kt.'s 5th.
50. Q. R. to K's 6th.	50. Q. R. to K. B's 4th.
51. K. R. to R's 7th (ch.)	51. K. to his Kt.'s sq.
52. Q. R. to K. Kt.'s 6th (ch.)	52. K. to B's sq.
53. Q. R. takes B. P.	53. Q. R. to Q. B's 4th.
54. Q. R. to K. B's 6th (ch.)	54. K. to his sq.

---

* From the subjoined variation it appears that they would not have improved their game by the move of B. to Q's 7th.

	36. B. to Q's 7th.
37. Q. R. to R's 4th.	37. B. to K's 6th.
38. Q. R. to K's 4th.	38. B. to K. Kt.'s 8th.
39. Q. R. to K's 8th.	39. R. takes B. (ch.)
40. K. to Kt.'s 3rd.	

And White must win.

† If Black had played their Rook to Q. B's 7th, the opposing party would have moved P. to K. Kt.'s 5th. (e. g.)

	38. R. to Q. B's 7th.
39. P. to K. Kt.'s 5th.	39. P. takes P., or (A.)
40. Q. R. takes Q. R. P.	

And White wins.

(A.)

	39. K. R. takes B.
40. K. to his Kt.'s 4th.	

Black cannot save the game.

‡ This is admirably played.

55. P. to K. Kt.'s 6th.	55. Q. R. to Q. B's 6th.
56. P. to K. Kt.'s 4th.	56. B. to K. B's sq. (ch.)
57. R. takes B. (ch.)	57. K. takes R.
58. P. to K. Kt.'s 7th (ch.)	58. K. to B's 2nd.
59. R. to K. R's 8th.	59. Q. R. to B's 3rd (ch.)
60. K. to his R's 7th.	

And Black resigned.

GAME II.—Between Messrs. Cochrane and Walker.

WHITE. (Mr. C.)	BLACK. (Mr. W.)
1. P. to K's 4th.	1. P. to K's 4th.
2. K. Kt. to B's 3rd.	2. Q. Kt. to B's 3rd.
3. P. to Q's 4th.	3. Kt. takes P.
4. Kt. takes P.	4. Kt. to K's 3rd.
5. B. to Q. B's 4th.	5. P. to Q. B's 3rd.
6. Castles.	6. K. Kt. to B's 3rd.
7. Kt. takes K. B. P.*	7. K. takes Kt.
8. B. takes Kt. (ch.)	8. K. takes B.
9. P. to K's 5th.	9. Kt. to Q's 4th.
10. P. to Q. B's 4th.	10. Kt. to Q. Kt.'s 3rd.
11. K. to R's sq.	11. P. to K. R's 4th.
12. P. to K. B's 4th.	12. P. to K. Kt.'s 3rd.
13. P. to K. B's 5th (ch.)	13. K. takes K. P.
14. B. to K. B's 4th (ch.)	

And Black lost the game.

GAME III.—Between Messrs. Cochrane and Deschappelles.

WHITE. (Mr. C.)	BLACK. (M. D.)
1. P. to K's 4th.	1. P. to K's 4th.
2. K. Kt. to B's 3rd.	2. Q. Kt. to B's 3rd.
3. P. to Q's 4th.	3. P. takes P.
4. K. B. to Q. B's 4th.	4. K. B. to Q. B's 4th.
5. K. Kt. to Kt.'s 5th.	5. Q. Kt. to K's 4th.†
6. K. B. takes B. P. (ch.)	6. Q. Kt. takes B.
7. Kt. takes Kt.	7. B. to Q. Kt.'s 5th (ch.)
8. P. to Q. B's 3rd.	8. P. takes P.
9. P. takes P.	9. K. B. takes P. (ch.)
10. Q. Kt. takes B.	10. K. takes Kt.
11. Q. to her 5th (ch.)	11. K. to B's square.

---

* We are indebted to Mr. Cochrane for this ingenious variation from the ordinary opening.

† This is not the correct move, he should have played K. Kt. to R's 3rd.

12. Q. B. to R's 3rd (ch.)	12. P. to Q's 3rd.
13. P. to K's 5th.	13. Q. to K. Kt.'s 4t
14. P. takes P.*	14. Q. takes Q.
15. P. takes P. (dis. ch.)	15. K. to B's 2nd.
16. Kt. takes Q.	16. Q. B. to Q's 2nd.
17. Castles on K's side.	17. Q. R. to Q. B's square.
18. B. to Q's 6th.	18. K. to his 3rd.
19. Q. B. to K. Kt.'s 3rd.	19. Q. B. to his 3rd.
20. Q. R. to Q's square.	20. B. takes Kt.
21. K. R. to K's square (ch.)	21. K. to B's 3rd.
22. Q. R. takes B.	22. K. Kt. to R's 3rd.
23. Q. R. to his 5th.	23. Kt. to K. B's 4th.
24. Q. R. to Q. B's 5th.	24. Kt. takes B.
25. K. R. P. takes Kt.	25. K. to B's 2nd.
26. K. R. to Q's square.	26. K. R. to K's square.
27. K. R. to Q's 3rd.	27. K. R. to K's 2nd.
28. Q. R. to K. B's 5th (ch.)	28. K. to his square.†
29. Q. R. to Q's 8th (ch.)	29. R. takes R.
30. R. to K. B's 8th (ch.)	30. K. takes R.
31. P. takes R., becoming a Q. (ch.)	

And White wins.

Game IV.—Between Messrs. Popert and Staunton.

WHITE. (Mr. S.)	BLACK. (Mr. P.)
1. P. to K's 4th.	1. P. to K's 4th.
2. K. Kt. to B's 3rd.	2. Q. Kt. to B's 3rd.
3. P. to Q's 4th.	3. P. takes P.
4. K. B. to Q. B's 4th.	4. K. B. checks.
5. P. to Q. B's 3rd.	5. P. takes P.
6. Castles.	6. P. to Q. B's 7th.
7. Q. takes P.	7. P. to Q's 3rd.
8. P. to Q. R's 3rd.	8. B. to Q. R's 4th.
9. P. to Q. Kt.'s 4th.	9. B. to Q. Kt.'s 3rd.
10. Q. B. to Q. Kt.'s 2nd.	10. K. Kt. to B's 3rd.
11. P. to K's 5th.	11. P. takes P.
12. Kt. takes P.	12. Kt. takes Kt.
13. B. takes Kt.	13. Castles.
14. Q. Kt. to B's 3rd.	14. Kt. to K. Kt.'s 5th.
15. Q. B. to K. Kt.'s 3rd.	15. Q. to K. Kt.'s 4th.
16. Q. R. to K's sq.	16. Q. B. to K. B's 4th.
17. Q. to her Kt.'s 3rd.	17. P. to Q. B's 3rd.‡

---

* The termination of this game is very ingeniously played by Mr. Cochrane.

† K. to his 3rd would have saved the game.

‡ Highly ingenious, the object being to tempt White to attack the Rook, that Black might be enabled to take the K. B. P.

18. B. to Q's 6th.	18. Kt. takes K. B. P.
19. B. takes K. R.*	19. Q. B. to K. R's 6th.†
20. K. B. takes K. B. P. (ch.)	20. K. takes Q. B.
21. B. to Q's 5th.‡	21. Q. B. P. takes B.
22. Q. takes P.	22. Q. to K. B's 3rd.
23. P. takes B.	23. Kt. takes P. (double check.)
24. K. to Kt.'s 2nd.	24. Kt. to K. B's 7th.
25. Kt. to K.'s 4th.	25. Q. to K. Kt.'s 3rd (ch.)
26. Q. to K. Kt.'s 5th.	26. Q. to her B's 3rd.
27. R. takes Kt. (ch.)	27. B. takes R.
28. K. takes B.	28. K. to Kt.'s sq.

White wins.

GAME V.—Between Messrs. Cochrane and Popert.

WHITE. (Mr. C.)	BLACK. (Mr. P.)
1. P. to K's 4th.	1. P. to K's 4th.
2. K. Kt. to B's 3rd.	2. Q. Kt. to B's 3rd
3. P. to Q's 4th.	3. P. takes P.
4. K. B. to Q. B's 4th.	4. B. checks.
5. P. to Q. B's 3rd.	5. P. takes P.
6. P. takes P.	6. B. to Q. R's 4th.
7. P. to K's 5th.	7. P. to Q's 3rd.§
8. Q. to her Kt.'s 3rd.	8. Q. to K's 2nd.
9. Castles.	9. Q. P. takes P.
10. Q. B. to Q. R's 3rd.	10. Q. to K. B's 3rd.
11. Q. Kt. to Q's 2nd.	11. Q. B. to K. B's 4th.
12. K. Kt. takes P.	12. Kt. takes Kt.
13. Q. to Kt.'s 5th (ch.)	13. Q. Kt. to B's 3rd.
14. K. R. to K's sq. (ch.)	14. Q. B. to K's 3rd.
15. B. takes B.	15. P. takes B.
16. Q. takes Q. Kt. P.‖	16. R. to Q's sq.
17. Q. takes Kt. (ch.)	17. K. to his B's 2nd.
18. Kt. to K's 4th.	18. Kt. to K's 2nd.
19. Kt. to K. Kt.'s 5th (ch.)	19. Q. takes Kt.
20. Q. takes K. P. (ch.)	

And White wins.

---

* If he had taken the Kt., Black would have had a fine position of offence.

† This is very skilful, nothing but the nicest care can save White's game.

‡ The only move apparently to avert the threatened defeat.

§ In the analysis of this opening it is shown that the better move is—
7. P. to Q's 4th.

‖ This game is admirably played by Mr. Cochrane.

GAME VI.—Between Messrs. Horwitz and Staunton.

WHITE. (Mr. H.)	BLACK. (Mr. S.)
1. P. to K's 4th.	1. P. to K's 4th.
2. K. Kt. to B's 3rd.	2. Q. Kt. to B's 3rd.
3. P. to Q's 4th.	3. P. takes P.
4. Kt. takes P.	4. Q. to K. R's 5th.*
5. K. Kt. to Q. Kt.'s 5th.†	5. Q. takes P. (ch.) ‡
6. B. to K's 2nd.	6. Q. to K's 4th. §
7. P. to K. B's 4th.	7. Q. to her B's 4th.
8. Kt. takes Q. B. P. (ch.)	8. K. to Q's sq.
9. Kt. takes R.	9. K. Kt. to B's 3rd.
10. Q. Kt. to B's 3rd.	10. K. B. to K's 2nd.
11. Q. to her 2nd.	11. R. to K's sq.
12. Q. Kt. to Q. R's 4th.	12. Q. to K. B's 4th.

* This move, which was introduced by a brilliant amateur of the London Chess Club, a few years ago, has been approved by the best writers, Bilguer, Lewis, Jaenisch, &c., since, as the most effectual way of wresting the attack from the opening player; but an examination of the highly ingenious rejoinder, devised by Mr. Horwitz, will have the effect, if we mistake not, of considerably weakening the reliance of players upon this favourite variation in future.

† This is the counter move invented by Mr. Horwitz. He had long felt assured, he tells us, that the fourth move of Black was unsound, and, after much pondering and analysis, it occurred to him that Kt. to Q. Kt.'s 5th might be satisfactorily opposed to it. The following moves will serve to show the effect this move is likely to have upon the subsequent game of the second player. Suppose,—

WHITE.	BLACK.
	5. Q. takes P. (ch.)

(It is with this object Black plays his Q. out.)

6. B. to K's 2nd.	6. K. B. to Q's 3rd, or (A.)
7. Q. takes K. B.	7. Q. takes K. B. (ch.) (best)
8. K. takes Q.	8. P. takes Q.
9. Kt. to Q. B's 7th (ch.)	

Winning the exchange.

(A.)

	6. K. to Q's sq.
7. Castles.	7. Q. R. P. one.
8. Q. Kt. to B's 3rd.	8. Q. to K's 4th.
9. Q. Kt. to Q's 5th.	9. P. takes Kt.
10. Q. B. to K. B's 4th.	10. Q. to her 5th.
11. Q. B. takes P. (ch.)	11. K. to his sq.
12. Kt. to Q. Kt.'s 6th.	

‡ He plays in evident unconsciousness of the perils with which his opponent's new attack surrounds him.

§ Throwing away the game at once.

13. Castles.	13. Kt. to K's 5th.
14. Q. to her 3rd.	14. Q. to K's 3rd.
15. P. to K. B's 5th.	15. Q. to K. B's 3rd.
16. Q. B. to K. B's 4th.	16. K. B. to Q's 3rd.
17. B. takes B.	17. Kt. takes B.
18. Q. R. to Q's sq.	18. Q. Kt. to Q. Kt.'s 5th.
19. Q. takes Kt.	19. Q. takes Q.
20. R. takes Q.	20. R. takes B.
21. P. to Q. B's 3rd.	21. Kt. to Q. B's 7th.
22. P. to K. B's 6th.	22. P. to K. Kt.'s 3rd.
23. K. R. to Q's sq.	23. Kt. to K's 6th.
24. Q. R. to Q's 2nd.	24. R. takes K. Kt. P. (ch.)
25. Q. R. takes R.	25. Kt. takes K. R.
26. R. to K's 2nd.	26. P. to Q. Kt.'s 3rd.
27. R. to K's sq.	27. P. to Q. Kt.'s 4th.
28. Q. Kt. to B's 5th.	28. Kt. takes Q. Kt. P.
29. R. to K's 7th.	29. P. to Q's 3rd.
30. Kt. to Kt.'s 7th (ch.)	30. B. takes Kt.
31. R. takes B.	31. Kt. to Q. B's 5th.
32. R. takes K. B. P.	32. Kt. to K's 4th.
33. R. takes Q. R. P.	

And wins.

———

GAME VII.—Between Mr. B. Greville and Capt. Kennedy.

WHITE. (Capt. K.)	BLACK. (Mr. B. G.)
1. P. to K's 4th.	1. P. to K's 4th.
2. K. Kt. to B's 3rd.	2. Q. Kt. to B's 3rd.
3. P. to Q's 4th.	3. P. takes P.
4. Kt. takes P.	4. K. B. to Q. B's 4th.*
5. Kt. takes Kt.	5. Q. to K. B's 3rd.
6. Q. to her 2nd.	6. Q. P. takes Kt.
7. Q. Kt. to B's 3rd.	7. Q. B. to K's 3rd.
8. K. B. to Q's 3rd.	8. Castles on Q's side.
9. Q. to K. B's 4th.	9. P. to K. R's 3rd.
10. Q. takes Q.	10. Kt. takes Q.
11. Castles.	11. P. to K. Kt.'s 4th.
12. Kt. to K's 2nd.	12. P. to K. Kt.'s 5th.
13. P. to Q. Kt.'s 3rd.	13. K. R. to Kt.'s sq.†
14. Q. B. takes P.	14. Kt. to K. R's 4th.
15. Kt. to B's 4th.	15. P. to K. Kt.'s 6th.‡

———

* This perhaps is the strongest way of replying to White's move of Kt. takes P.

† The sacrifice of the P. here to gain an opening on the adverse K. Rook's file, is the conception of an adept in chess strategy.

‡ This and the subsequent moves of Mr. Greville are of the very first order of fine play.

16. Kt. takes Kt.	16. P. takes K. B. P. (ch.)
17. K. to R's square.	17. R. to K. R's sq.
18. B. to K. Kt.'s 5th.	18. Q. R. to K. Kt.'s sq.
19. Kt. to K. Kt.'s 7th.*	19. K. B. to Q's 3rd.
20. P. to K. R's 3rd.	20. Q. B. takes K. R. P.
21. P. takes B.	21. Q. R. takes Kt.
22. R. takes P.	22. K. R. takes P. (ch.)
23. K. to Kt.'s square.	23. Q. R. takes B. (ch.)
24. R. to K. Kt.'s 2nd.	24. B. to Q. B's 4th (ch.)
25. K. to B's square.	25. K. R. to his 8th (ch.)
26. K. to his 2nd.	26. Q. R. takes R. (ch.)
27. K. to B's 3rd.	27. Q. R. to B's 7th (ch.)
28. K. to Kt.'s 3rd.	28. K. R. takes R.

And Black wins.

GAME VIII.—Between Mr. B. Greville and M. Kieseritzky.

WHITE. (Mr. B. G.)	BLACK. (M. K.)
1. P. to K's 4th.	1. P. to K's 4th.
2. K. Kt. to B's 3rd.	2. Q. Kt. to B's 3rd.
3. P. to Q's 4th.	3. P. takes P.
4. K. B. to Q. B's 4th.	4. B. to Q. Kt.'s 5th (ch.)
5. P. to Q. B's 3rd.	5. P. takes P.
6. Castles.	6. P. takes P.
7. Q. B. takes P.	7. K. to B's square.†
8. P. to K's 5th.	8. P. to Q's 3rd.
9. Q. to her Kt.'s 3rd.	9. K. Kt. to R's 3rd.
10. P. takes P.	10. P. takes P.
11. P. to Q. R's 3rd.	11. B. to Q. R's 4th.
12. Q. Kt. to B's 3rd.	12. K. B. to Q. Kt.'s 3rd.
13. Q. Kt. to Q's 5th.	13. Q. Kt. to Q. R's 4th.
14. Q. to her B's 3rd.‡	14. K. Kt. to B's 4th.
15. K. B. to Q's 3rd.	15. P. to K. B's 3rd.
16. Q. R. to K's square.§	16. Q. Kt. to Q. B's 3rd.

---

* With the view to play his B. to K. B's 6th if Black took the Kt.
† This is inferior, we think, to returning the Bishop home again.
‡ The attack is sustained with a good deal of vigour and ingenuity.
§ Threatening to take off the K. Kt., and then plant the Rook at K's 7th. The young player will comprehend the importance of the Rook being so placed from the annexed moves, which are probable when the Rook is played thus. Let us suppose White had now to move,—

B. takes Kt.	B. takes B.
R. to K's 7th.	Q. R. to B's sq.
Q. to her 2nd.	Kt. or R. attacks both Q. and B.
R. takes K. B. P.	Kt. or R. takes Q.
B. takes K. Kt. P. (ch.)	

and then White mates with the Kt. next move.

17. Kt. takes K. B.	17. Q. R. P. takes Kt.
18. K. Kt. to his 5th.*	18. Q. R. to his 4th.
19. B. takes Kt.	19. R. takes B.
20. Kt. to K's 6th (ch.)	20. B. takes Kt.
21. R. takes B.	21. R. to K's 4th.
22. Q. to K. R's 3rd.	22. R. to Q. Kt.'s 4th.
23. B. to Q. R's square.	23. K. to B's 2nd.
24. P. to K. B's 4th.	24. P. to K. R's 3rd.
25. K. R. to K's square.	25. P. to Q's 4th.†
26. Q. to K. R's 5th (ch.)	26. P. to K. Kt.'s 3rd.
27. Q. to K's 2nd.	27. Kt. to K's 4th.
28. P. takes Kt.	28. K. takes R.
29. P. takes P. (dis. ch.)	

Black surrenders.

CHAPTER IX.

THE QUEEN'S BISHOP'S PAWN GAME IN THE KING'S KNIGHT'S OPENING.

THIS is an offshoot of the King's Knight's Opening, so full of interest and variety, that its omission in many of the leading works on the game is truly unaccountable. Ponziani has briefly touched on it, and proposed an ingenious sort of counter-gambit in Black's reply of 3. P. to K. B's 4th, and Major Jaenisch has given some attention to its salient features, but it deserves, and, if we mistake not, will yet attain a higher place in the category of legitimate openings than has hitherto been assigned to it.

GAME THE FIRST.

WHITE.	BLACK.
1. P to K's 4th.	1. P to K's 4th.
2. K. Kt. to B's 3rd.	2. Q. Kt. to B's 3rd.
3. P. to Q. B's 3rd.	3. P. to K. B's 4th.

Black's 3rd move is the counter-gambit suggested by Ponziani. Instead of this move he may play P. to Q's 4th, as in Variation I., or 3. K. Kt. to B's 3rd, or 3. B. to Q. B's 4th, the result of his adopting either of which will be shown in the next game.

---

* Well played.   Black dare not capture the Kt.
† After this move the game is quite irretrievable.

4. P. to Q's 4th.	4. P. takes K. P.

You may likewise play, though not so advantageously, 4. B. to Q. Kt.'s 5th. (*e.g.*)

4. B. to Q. Kt.'s 5th.	4. P. takes K. P.
5. B. takes Kt.	5. Q. P. takes B.
6. Kt. takes P.	6. Q. to K. Kt.'s 4th.

He must win your K. Kt. P., and will be better situated than you are.

If in place of either, you take the K. B. P. with P., the following moves will show that Black gets the better game:—

4. P. takes P.	4. P. to Q's 3rd.
5. P. to K. Kt.'s 4th.	5. P. to K. R's 4th.
6. K. Kt. to his sq.	6. P. takes P.
7. Q. takes P.	7. K. Kt. to K's 2nd.
8. K. B. to Q's 3rd.	8. P. to K. Kt.'s 3rd.

And you must lose the Pawn and have an inferior position.

5. Kt. takes K. P.	5. K. Kt. to B's 3rd.
6. K. B. to Q. Kt.'s 5th.	6. P. to Q. R's 3rd.

Your move of 6. B. to Q. Kt.'s 5th, is an effectual bar to the advance of the Q. P., and appears to me to give you an undeniable advantage in position. Instead of this move, the German " Handbuch," which only cursorily notices the opening, recommends you to take Kt. with Kt., which gives an equal game. (*e. g.*)

6. Kt. takes Q. Kt.	6. Q. Kt. P. takes Kt.
7. Q. B. to K. Kt.'s 5th.	7. P. to Q's 4th.

&c.

7. B. takes Q. Kt.	7. Q. Kt. P. takes B.

If he retake with Q. P., the game may be pursued thus:—

	7. Q. P. takes B.
8. Q. B. to K. Kt.'s 5th.	8. K. B. to Q's 3rd.
9. Q. Kt. to Q's 2nd.	9. Q. B. to K. B's 4th.

10. Q. to her Kt.'s 3rd, with an excellent position.

8. Q. B. to K. Kt.'s 5th.	8. Q. R. to Kt.'s sq

Black has no good move; if he play 8. K. B. to K's 2nd, you reply with 9. B. takes Kt., and then check with the Q. at K. R's 5th; if he move 8. B. to Q. Kt.'s 2nd, you may play 9. Q. to her Kt.'s 3rd, and win a Piece; and if he play 8. K. B. to Q's 3rd, you can answer with 9. Q. Kt. to Q's 2nd, and have an excellent position.

9. P. to Q. Kt.'s 4th.	9. Q. B. to Kt.'s 2nd.

Thus far the moves are those occurring in a game between

Mr. Harrwitz and the writer. White now played 10. Q. to her R's 4th, and the game proceeded thus:—

10. Q. to her R's 4th.	10. P. to Q's 4th.
11. Castles.	11. P. to K. R's 3rd.

(At the 11th move, White would play badly to take the Q. B. P., on account of 11. Q. to her 2nd.)

12. B. to K. R's 4th.	12. Q. to her 3rd.
13. B. to K. Kt.'s 3rd.	

Winning in a few moves.

You may, however, instead of moving the Queen, play at your 10th move thus:—

10. Castles.	10. P. to Q's 4th.
11. P. to K. B's 3rd.	11. B. to K's 2nd.

If he play 11. P. to K. R's 3rd, you answer 12. B. takes Kt., and if he then retake with his Q., you can take P. with P., and have a splendid game. Should he however prefer taking the B. with K. Kt. P., the following moves are likely to occur; let us suppose,—

	11. P. to K. R's 3rd.
12. B. takes Kt.	12. P. takes B.
13. P. takes K. P.	13. P. takes Kt.
14. Q. to K. R's 5th (ch.)	

And then checkmates in five moves.

12. P. takes K. P.	12. Castles (best)
13. Q. Kt. to Q's 2nd.	

And you have a clear Pawn more, and a much better game than he has.

If he now attempt to regain the P. by taking P. with Kt., you must exchange Rooks, and then you can win easily.

VARIATION I.,

Beginning at Black's 3rd move.

WHITE.	BLACK.
1. P. to K's 4th.	1. P. to K's 4th.
2. K. Kt. to B's 3rd.	2. Q. Kt. to B's 3rd.
3. P. to Q. B's 3rd.	3. P. to Q's 4th.
4. K. B. to Q. Kt.'s 5th.	4. P. takes K. P.

If instead of taking the P. he play 4. Q. B. to K. Kt.'s 5th, the result must be favourable to you; for example,—

	4. Q. B. to K. Kt.'s 5th.
5. Q. to her R's 4th.	5. B. takes Kt.
6. B. takes Kt. (ch.)	6. P. takes B.

7. Q. takes P. (ch.)	7. K. to his 2nd.
8. P. takes B.	

You have a winning game.

5. Kt. takes K. P.	5. Q. to K. Kt.'s 4th.

He may also play 5. Q. to her 4th, and, if you move 6. Q. to Q. R's 4th, follow with 6. K. Kt. to K's 2nd.

6. Q. to her R's 4th.	6. Q. takes Kt.

He has apparently no stronger move—taking the K. Kt. P. would be disastrous to him.

7. B. takes Kt. (ch.)	7. K. to Q's sq.
8. Q. takes K. P.	

Gaining a Pawn and a superior position.

GAME THE SECOND.

WHITE.	BLACK.
1. P. to K's 4th.	1. P. to K's 4th.
2. K. Kt. to B's 3rd.	2. Q. Kt. to B's 3rd.
3. P. to Q. B's 3rd.	3. K. Kt. to B's 3rd.

As was before remarked, he has also the choice of playing 3. K. B. to Q. B's 4th, for which see Variation I., in the present game.

4. P. to Q's 4th.	4. K. Kt. takes K. P.
5. P. takes K. P.	5. P. to Q's 4th.

These are the opening moves of a game between Messrs. Kieseritzky and Horwitz. If Black, for his 5th move, play K. B. to Q. B's 4th, your rejoinder should be also K. B. to Q. B's 4th, and not, as recommended by Jaenisch, 6. Q. to her 5th, and then if he either castle or take your K. B. P., by playing Q. to her 5th, you win a Piece. He may, however, play 5. P. to Q's 3rd, as advised by Jaenisch, apparently without disadvantage.

6. K. B. to Q. Kt.'s 5th.	6. K. B. to Q. B's 4th.
7. K. Kt. to Q's 4th.	7. B. takes Kt.

If he decline the Kt. and play 7. Q. to her 2nd, you win a Piece by 8. P. to K. B's 3rd. If he play 7. B. to Q's 2nd, you may pursue the game as follows:—

	7. B. to Q's 2nd.
8. B. takes Kt.	8. P. takes B.

(Should he take B. with B., you can play Q. to K. Kt.'s 4th, threatening to win the Kt. by P. to K. B's 3rd.)

9. Castles.	9. Castles.
10. P. to K. B's 3rd.	10. K. Kt. to Kt.'s 4th.
11. P. to K. B's 4th.	11. Kt. to K's 4th.
12. P. to K. B's 5th.	

And you have certainly a good game.

8. P. takes B.   8. Castles.

You can now take off his Kt. and castle, and then play Q. to K. R's 5th, preparatory to advancing P. to K. B's 3rd, having a slight advantage. This position may also occur in the ordinary Guioco Piano, where it is brought about by—

1. P. to K's 4th.	1. P. to K's 4th.
2. K. Kt. to B's 3rd.	2. Q. Kt. to B's 3rd.
3. K. B. to Q. B's 4th.	3. K. B. to Q. B's 4th.
4. P. to Q. B's 3rd.	4. K. Kt. to B's 3rd.
5. P. to Q's 4th.	5. P. takes P.
6. P. to K's 5th.	6. P. to Q's 4th.
7. B. to Q. Kt.'s 5th.	7. K. Kt. to K's 5th.
8. K. Kt. takes P.	8. B. takes Kt.
9. P. takes B.	9. Castles.
10. B. takes Q. Kt.	10. P. takes B.

&c., &c.

VARIATION I.,

Beginning at Black's 3rd move.

WHITE.	BLACK.
1. P. to K's 4th.	1. P. to K's 4th.
2. K. Kt. to B's 3rd.	2. Q. Kt. to B's 3rd.
3. P. to Q. B's 3rd.	3. K. B. to B's 4th.
4. P. to Q. Kt.'s 4th.	4. B. to Q. Kt.'s 3rd.
5. P. to Q. Kt.'s 5th.	5. Q. Kt to R's 4th.
6. Kt. takes K. P.	6. Q. to K's 2nd.
7. P. to Q's 4th.	7. P. to Q's 3rd.

These moves occur in the opening of a game between Messrs. Horwitz and Harrwitz:—

8. B. to Q. R's 3rd.	8. P. to K. B's 3rd.
9. Kt. to K. B's 3rd.	9. Q. takes K. P. (ch.)

You may also retreat the Kt. to his 4th, and interpose him at K's 3rd, when the Q. takes K. P.

10. B. to K's 2nd.	10. K. Kt. to R's 3rd.
11. Castles.	11. Castles.
12. K. B. to Q's 3rd.	

And you have an undoubted advantage of situation.

GAMES

ILLUSTRATIVE OF THE QUEEN'S BISHOP'S PAWN GAME IN THE KING'S KNIGHT'S OPENING.

GAME I.—Between Messrs. Harrwitz and Staunton.

WHITE. (Mr. S.)	BLACK. (Mr. H.)
1. P. to K's 4th.	1. P. to K's 4th.
2. K. Kt. to B's 3rd.	2. Q. Kt. to B's 3rd.
3. P. to Q. B's 3rd.	3. P. to K. B's 4th.
4. P. to Q's 4th.	4. K. B. P. takes P.
5. Kt. takes P.	5. K. Kt. to B's 3rd.
6. K. B. to Q. Kt.'s 5th.	6. P. to Q. R's 3rd.
7. B. takes Kt.	7. Q. Kt. P. takes B.
8. Q. B. to K. Kt.'s 5th.	8. Q. R. to Q. Kt.'s sq.
9. P. to Q. Kt.'s 4th.	9. Q. B. to Kt.'s 2nd.
10. Q. to Q. R's 4th.	10. P. to Q's 4th.
11. Castles.*	11. P. to K. R's 3rd.
12. Q. B. to K. R's 4th.	12. Q. to her 3rd.
13. B. to K. Kt.'s 3rd.†	13. K. R. to K. Kt.'s sq.
14. Q. Kt. to Q's 2nd.	14. Q. R. to Q. B's sq.
15. Q. Kt. to his 3rd.	15. Kt. to Q's 2nd.
16. Q. Kt. to R's 5th.	16. Kt. to Kt.'s 3rd.
17. Q. to B's 2nd.	17. Q. B. to Q. R's sq.
18. P. to K. B's 3rd.‡	18. P. takes P.
19. R. takes P.	19. Q. to K's 3rd.
20. Q. R. to K's sq.	20. K. B. to K's 2nd.
21. K. Kt. takes Q. B. P.	21. Q. takes R. (ch.)§
22. B. takes Q.	22. B. takes Kt.
23. Q. to K. Kt.'s 6th (ch.)	23. K. to Q's sq.
24. Kt. takes B. (ch.)	

And wins.

---

* The following moves will show the probable result of taking the P. with Kt.:—

11. Kt. takes Q. B. P.	11. Q. to her 2nd.
12. P. to Q. Kt.'s 5th.	12. R. to Q. R's sq.

(His best move ; if P. takes P., then White plays Q. to her R's 7th.)

13. Q. to her sq.	13. P. takes P., or B. takes Kt.

And White has little if any advantage.

† Threatening to win the K. R. by moving the Kt. to K. B's 7th or Kt.'s 6th.

‡ This is much stronger than taking the Q. B. P. with the K. Kt.

§ He has no better move—the game is beyond hope.

GAME II.—Between Mr. Horwitz and Captain Evans.

WHITE. (Capt. E.)	BLACK. (Mr. H.)
1. P. to K's 4th.	1. P. to K's 4th.
2. K. Kt. to B's 3rd.	2. Q. Kt. to B's 3rd.
3. P. to Q. B's 3rd.	3. P. to K. B's 4th.
4. P. to Q's 4th.	4. P. takes Q. P.*
5. P. to K's 5th.	5. P. takes Q. B. P.
6. Q. Kt. takes P.	6. K. B. to Q. Kt.'s 5th.
7. Q. B. to K. Kt.'s 5th.	7. K. Kt. to K's 2nd.
8. K. B. to Q. B's 4th.	8. P. to Q's 4th.
9. P. takes P. in passing.	9. Q. takes P.
10. Q. to K's 2nd.	10. Q. Kt. to Q's 5th.
11. Kt. takes Kt.	11. Q. takes Kt.
12. Castles.†	12. Q. B. to Q's 2nd.
13. Q. Kt. to Q's 5th.	13. Castles on Q's side.‡
14. Q. B. takes Kt.	14. B. takes B.
15. Kt. takes B. (ch.)	15. K. to Kt.'s sq.
16. K. R. to Q's sq.	16. Q. to K. R's 5th.
17. B. to Q. Kt.'s 3rd.	17. Q. to K. R's 3rd.
18. R. to Q's 2nd.	18. P. to K. B's 5th.
19. Q. R. to Q's sq.	19. P. to K. B's 6th.
20. Q. takes P.	20. P. to Q. R's 3rd.
21. R. takes B.	21. R. takes R.
22. R. takes R.	22. Q. to her B's 8th (ch.)
23. Q. to her sq.	23. Q. takes Kt. P.
24. R. to Q's 8th (ch.)	24. R. takes R.
25. Q. takes R. (ch.)	25. K. to R's 2nd.
26. Kt. to Q. B's 6th (ch.)	

And White mates in four moves.

GAME III.—Between Capt. Evans and Mr. Henderson.

WHITE. (Capt. E.)	BLACK. (Mr. H.)
1. P. to K's 4th.	1. P. to K's 4th.
2. K. Kt. to B's 3rd.	2. Q. Kt. to B's 3rd.
3. P. to Q. B's 3rd.	3. P. to Q's 4th.
4. K. B. to Q. Kt.'s 5th.	4. Q. B. to K. Kt.'s 5th.
5. Q. to her R's 4th.§	5. Q. to her 3rd.

---

* In the previous game the King's Pawn was taken.

† White has now an overwhelming attack.

‡ The loss of a Piece eventually was inevitable, and Black did wisely in giving it up at once, to bring his other forces into action.

§ If Black, at his 4th move, take P. with P., this move is the best reply.

6. Kt. takes K. P.*	6. Q. takes Kt.
7. B. takes Q. Kt. (ch.)	7. P. takes B.
8. Q. takes P. (ch.)	8. K. to his 2nd.
9. P. to K. B's 3rd.	9. R. to Q's sq.
10. P. to Q's 4th.†	10. Q. to K's 3rd.
11. Q. takes Q. B. P. (ch.)	11. R. to Q's 2nd.
12. Q. to Q. B's 5th (ch.)	12. K. to his sq.
13. Q. to Q. B's 8th (ch.)	13. R. to Q's sq.
14. Q. takes Q. (ch.)	14. B. takes Q.
15. P. to K's 5th. ‡	15. P. to K. B's 4th.
16. Kt. to Q's 2nd.	16. Kt. to K. R's 3rd.
17. Kt. to Q. Kt.'s 3rd.	17. Kt. to K. B's 2nd.
18. P. to K. B's 4th.	18. B. to K's 2nd.
19. P. to K. R's 4th.	19. Kt. to K. R's 3rd.
20. K. to his 2nd.	20. B. to Q's 2nd.
21. K. to his B's 3rd.	21. B. to Q. Kt.'s 4th.
22. P. to K. Kt.'s 3rd.	22. B. to Q's 6th.
23. Kt. to Q's 2nd.	23. Kt. to K. Kt.'s 5th.
24. K. R. to K's sq.	24. P. to K. R's 3rd.
25. P. to Q. Kt.'s 3rd.	25. R. to Q. B's sq.
26. B. to Q. Kt.'s 2nd.	26. P. to K. Kt.'s 4th.§
27. P. to K. R's 5th.	27. P. takes B. P.
28. P. takes P.	28. R. to K. Kt.'s sq.
29. R. to K. R's sq.	29. K. to B's 2nd.
30. R. to K. R's 3rd.	30. K. to his 3rd.
31. R. to Q. B's sq.	31. R. to K. Kt.'s 2nd.
32. P. to Q. B's 4th.	32. P. takes P.
33. Kt. takes P.	33. B. to K's 5th (ch.)
34. K. to his 2nd.	34. B. to K. Kt.'s 7th.
35. R. to K. Kt.'s 3rd.	35. B. to K's 5th.
36. P. to Q. R's 3rd.	36. Q. R. to K. Kt.'s sq.
37. Q. R. to K. Kt.'s sq.	37. B. to K. R's 5th.
38. R. to K. R's 3rd.	38. B. to K. B's 7th.
39. R. to Q. B's sq.‖	39. Q. B. to K. Kt.'s 7th.
40. R. to Q's 3rd.	40. B. to K. R's 5th.
41. Kt. to Q's 6th.	41. Kt. to K. B's 7th.
42. K. R. to Q. B's 3rd.	42. Kt. to K's 5th.
43. P. to Q's 5th (ch.)	43. K. takes P.
44. R. to Q's 3rd (ch.)	44. K. to K's 3rd.
45. Kt. takes Kt.	45. P. takes Kt.
46. R. to Q's 6th (ch.)	46. K. to B's 4th.

---

* A little premature; P. to Q's 4th first, would have strengthened the attack.

† This is not a judicious move.

‡ White has still three excellent Pawns for the Piece given up.

§ The power of forcing an opening here, adds greatly to the chances of Black's success.

‖ There is nothing to be gained by taking the Kt. with the Rook.

47. P. to K's 6th.	47. B. to K. B's 6th (ch.)
48. K. to his 3rd.	48. R. to K. Kt.'s 7th.
49. R. to Q. B's 5th (ch.)	49. K. to K. Kt.'s 5th.
50. R. to Q's 2nd.	50. R. takes R.
51. K. takes R.	51. K. takes K. B. P.
52. B. to K's 5th (ch.)	52. K. to K. Kt.'s 5th.
53. K. to his 3rd.	53. B. to K. Kt.'s 4th (ch.)
54. K. to Q's 4th.	54. P. to K's 6th.
55. R. to Q. B's sq.	55. R. to Q's sq. (ch.)
56. K. to Q. B's 3rd.	56. R. to Q. B's sq. (ch.) *

And Black wins.

GAME IV.—Played between Messrs. Horwitz, Harrwitz, and Von Carnap, against Messrs. Perigal, Jones, and Captain Evans, in consultation.

WHITE. (Messrs. H., H., & V. C.)	BLACK. (Messrs. P., J., & E.)
1. P. to K's 4th.	1. P. to K's 4th.
2. K. Kt. to B's 3rd.	2. Q. Kt. to B's 3rd.
3. P. to Q. B's 3rd.	3. K. Kt. to B's 3rd.
4. P. to Q's 4th.	4. P. to Q's 3rd.
5. P. to Q's 5th.	5. Q. Kt. to K's 2nd.
6. Q. Kt. to R's 3rd.	6. P. to Q. B's 3rd.
7. Q. B. to K. Kt.'s 5th.†	7. K. Kt. takes K. P.
8. B. takes Q. Kt.	8. B. takes B.
9. P. takes P.	9. Castles.
10. Q. to Q's 5th.	10. Kt. to Q. B's 4th.
11. P. to Q. Kt.'s 4th.	11. P. takes Q. B. P.
12. Q. takes Q. B. P.	12. Q. B. to Q. Kt.'s 2nd.
13. Q. to Kt.'s 5th.	13. Q. B. to R's 3rd.
14. Q. to B's 6th.	14. R. to Q. B's sq.
15. Q. to her 5th.	15. Q. B. to Kt.'s 2nd.
16. Q. to her sq.	16. Kt. to K's 5th.‡
17. Q. Kt. to his sq.	17. Q. to Q. Kt.'s 3rd.
18. Q. to Q. B's 2nd.	18. Q. takes Q. Kt. P.
19. K. B. to Q's 3rd.	19. Kt. takes Q. B. P.
20. B. takes K. R. P. (ch.)	20. K. to R's sq.
21. Castles.	21. Kt. to K's 5th.
22. Q. to her 3rd.	22. K. takes B.
23. Q. Kt. to Q's 2nd.	23. Q. R. to Q. B's 6th.
24. Q. to K's 2nd.	24. Kt. takes Kt.
25. Kt. takes Kt.	25. Q. to Q. B's 4th.

---

* This is an interesting and well-contested game.

† Where is the prospective equivalent for the P. now sacrificed?

‡ Already Black have so manifest an advantage, that with ordinary care the game is their own.

26. Q. R. to Q. Kt.'s sq.	26. Q. to B's 3rd.
27. P. to K. B's 4th.	27. R. to K's 6th.
28. Q. to K. Kt.'s 4th.	28. P. to K. B's 4th.
29. Q. to K. R's 5th (ch.)	29. K. to Kt's sp.
30. Kt. to B's 3rd.	30. P. takes P.
31. K. R. to Q. B's sq.	31. Q. to K's 5th.
32. P. to Q. R's 4th.	32. R. to K's 7th.
33. K. to R's sq.	33. R. takes K. Kt. P.
34. R. to K. B's sq.*	34. R. to K. Kt.'s 5th.
35. Q. to R's 3rd.	35. B. to K. R's 5th.
36. P. to Q. R's 5th.	36. K. R. to B's 3rd.
37. P. to Q. R's 6th.	37. Q. B. to his 3rd.
38. Q. R. to Q. Kt.'s 8th (ch.)	38. K. to R's 2nd.
39. R. to Q. Kt.'s 3rd.	39. R. to K. R's 3rd.

And Black resigns,

GAME V.—Played by Mr. Perigal and Capt. Evans, consulting against Mr. Harrwitz and Von Carnap.

WHITE. (Messrs. P. and E.)	BLACK. (Messrs. H. and C.)
1. P. to K's 4th.	1. P. to K's 4th.
2. K. Kt. to B's 3rd.	2. Q. Kt. to B's 3rd.
3. P. to Q. B's 3rd.	3. P. to Q's 4th.
4. K. B. to Q. Kt.'s 5th.	4. P. takes P.
5. Kt. takes K. P.	5. Q. to her 4th.
6. Q. to Q. R's 4th.†	6. K. Kt. to K's 2nd.
7. P. to K. B's 4th.	7. P. takes P. in passing.
8. Kt. takes P.	8. P. to Q. R's 3rd.
9. K. B. to Q. B's 4th.	9. Q to K's 5th (ch.)
10. K. to B's 2nd.	10. Q. B. to K's 3rd.‡
11. P. to Q's 3rd.	11. Q. to K. B's 4th.§
12. B. takes B.	12. P. takes B.
13. K. R. to K's sq.	13. Castles.
14. P. to Q's 4th.	14. K. Kt. to his 3rd.
15. Q. to her Kt.'s 3rd.	15. P. to K's 4th.
16. K. to his Kt.'s sq.	16. P. takes P.
17. Q. B. to K. Kt.'s 5th.	17. K. Kt. to K's 2nd.
18. P. takes P.	18. P. to K. R's 3rd.
19. B. takes Kt.	19. B. takes B.
20. Q. Kt. to B's 3rd.	20. Q. Kt. takes P.

---

* Q. R. takes B. would perhaps prolong the defence.

† The attack and defence of this opening are both ably conducted.

‡ It is obvious that if Black had not played with caution, they must have lost their Q. by the B. taking K. B. P.

§ Promising to advance the Q. Kt. P. on the Q. and B.

|| This looks attacking, but it is presently seen to be a weak move.

21. Kt. takes Kt.	21. B. to Q. B's 4th.*
22. R. to K. B's sq.	22. R. takes Kt.
23. K. to R's sq.†	23. Q. to her 2nd.‡
24. K. R. to K. B's 7th.	24. Q. to K. Kt.'s 5th.
25. P. to K. R's 3rd.	25. Q. to K. Kt.'s 3rd.§
26. Kt. to Q's 5th.	26. Q. R. to Q's 7th.‖
27. R. takes P. (ch.)	27. K. to Q's sq.
28. Kt. to K. B's 4th.	28. Q. to her 3rd.
29. R. takes B.	29. Q. takes Kt.
30. Q. takes Q. Kt. P.	30. Q. R. to Q's 2nd.
31. Q. to B's 8th (ch.)	31. K. to his 2nd.
32. Q. R. to K's sq. (ch.)	32. K. to B's 3rd.
33. Q. takes Q. R.	33. K. to his Kt.'s 3rd.
34. Q. to her 3rd (ch.)	34. K. to B's 3rd.
35. R. to B's 6th (ch.)	35. K. to B's 2nd.
36. Q. to K. Kt.'s 6th (ch.)	36. K. to Kt.'s sq.
37. R. to B's 8th (ch.)	

And wins.

GAME VI.—Between Messrs. Horwitz and Harrwitz.

WHITE. (Mr. Horwitz.)	BLACK. (Mr. Harrwitz.)
1. P. to K's 4th.	1. P. to K's 4th.
2. K. Kt. to B's 3rd.	2. Q. Kt. to B's 3rd.
3. P. to Q. B's 3rd.	3. K. B. to Q. B's 4th.
4. P. to Q. Kt.'s 4th.	4. K. B. to Q. Kt.'s 3rd.
5. P. to Q. Kt.'s 5th.	5. Q. Kt. to R's 4th.
6. K. Kt. takes K. P.	6. Q. to K's 2nd.
7. P. to Q's 4th.	7. P. to Q's 3rd.
8. Q. B. to R's 3rd.	8. P. to K. B's 3rd.
9. K. Kt. to K. B's 3rd.	9. Q. takes K. P. (ch.)
10. K. B. to K's 2nd.	10. K. Kt. to R's 3rd.
11. Castles.	11. Castles.
12. K. B. to Q's 3rd.	12. Q. to K. Kt.'s 5th.
13. Q. B. to Kt.'s 4th.	13. Q. to K's 3rd.
14. K. R. to K's sq.	14. Q. to K. B's 2nd.
15. P. to Q's 5th.	15. K. Kt. to his 5th.

* Unquestionably Black have now the advantage both of force and position.

† The proper move: White would be mated at once if they took the Q.

‡ Q. to K. R's 4th we believe to be preferable.

§ Here also we should rather have gone to R's 4th, with the view presently of playing Q. to K's 4th, and B. to Q's 3rd, and because the Q. at R's 4th prevented the Kt. from being moved to K's 2nd or Q's 5th.

‖ This move is the result of imperfect calculation. They should rather have played B. to Q's 3rd.

16. K. R. to K. B's sq.	16. K. Kt. to K's 4th.
17. Kt. takes Kt.	17. B. P. takes Kt.
18. Q. Kt. to Q's 2nd.	18. Q. takes Q. P.
19. Kt to Q. B's 4th.	19. P. to K's 5th.
20. Kt. takes B.	20. Q. R. P. takes Kt.
21. K. B. to Q. B's 2nd.	21. Q. takes Q.
22. B. takes Q.	22. B. to K's 3rd.
23. B. to Q. B's 2nd.	23. K. R. to K's sq.
24. B. takes K. P.	24. B. to Q. B's 5th.
25. K. R. to K's sq.	25. P. to Q's 4th.
26. B. to K. B's 3rd.	26. B. takes Q. R. P.
27. K. R. to Q's sq.	27. B. to Q. Kt.'s 6th.
28. B. takes Q. P. (ch.)	28. B. takes B.
29. R. takes B.	29. Kt. to Q. B's 3rd.
30. Q. R. to Q. B's sq.	30. Kt. takes B.
31. P. takes Kt.	31. Q. R. to his 7th.
32. P. to K. R's 3rd.	32. K. R. to K's 7th.
33. Q. R. takes Q. B. P.	33. P. to K. R's 3rd.
34. K. R. to Q's 8th (ch.)	34. K. to R's 2nd.
35. K. R. to Q's 7th.	35. K. R. takes B. P.
36. K. R. takes Kt. P. (ch.)	36. K. to R's sq.
37. Q. R. takes Q. Kt. P.	37. K. R. to Q. Kt.'s 7th.
38. K. R. to K. Kt.'s 6th.	38. P. to K. R's 4th.
39. K. R. to K. Kt.'s 5th.	39. P. to K. R's 5th.
40. Q. R. takes Q. Kt. P.	40. K. to R's 2nd.
41. K. R. to K. Kt.'s 4th.	41. Q. R. checks.
42. K. to R's 2nd.	42. R. to Q. R's 5th.
43. K. R. takes P. (ch.)	43. K. to Kt.'s 2nd.
44. K. R. to Q. B's 4th.	

And wins.

END OF BOOK II.

SYNOPSIS OF BOOK III.

THE KING'S BISHOP'S OPENING,

WITH ITS SEVERAL MODIFICATIONS, VIZ. :—

1st. THE GAME OF THE TWO KINGS' BISHOPS :—

1. P. to K's 4th. / P. to K's 4th.   2. K. B. to Q. B's 4th. / K. B. to Q. B's 4th.

2nd. THE ITALIANS' DEFENCE :—

1. P. to K's 4th. / P. to K's 4th.   2. K. B. to Q. B's 4th. / K. B. to Q. B's 4th.   3. P. to Q. B's 3rd. / Q. to K. Kt.'s 4th.

3rd. McDONNELL'S DOUBLE GAMBIT :—

1. P. to K's 4th. / P. to K's 4th.   2. K. B. to Q. B's 4th. / K. B. to Q. B's 4th.   3. P. to Q. Kt.'s 4th. / B. takes Kt. P.

4. P. to K. B's 4th.

4th. THE LOPEZ GAMBIT :—

1. P. to K's 4th. / P. to K's 4th.   2. K. B. to Q. B's 4th. / K. B. to Q. B's 4th.   3. Q. to K's 2nd. / P. to Q's 3rd.

4. P. to K. B's 4th.

5th. THE KING'S KNIGHT'S DEFENCE :—

1. P. to K's 4th. / P. to K's 4th.   2. K. B. to Q. B's 4th. / K. Kt. to B's 3rd.

6th. THE COUNTER GAMBIT :—

1. P. to K's 4th. / P. to K's 4th.   2. K. B. to Q. B's 4th. / P. to K. B's 4th.

7th. THE QUEEN'S BISHOP'S PAWN'S DEFENCE :—

1. P. to K's 4th. / P. to K's 4th.   2. K. B. to Q. B's 4th. / P. to Q. B's 3rd.

THE QUEEN'S BISHOP'S PAWN'S OPENING :—

1. P. to K's 4th. / P. to K's 4th.   2. P. to Q. B's 3rd.

BOOK III.

The King's Bishop's Opening.

CHAPTER I.

THE KING'S BISHOP'S OPENING

Is an important and interesting method of commencing the game, and, according to Philidor, the best that the opening player can select, inasmuch as it requires no initiatory sacrifice, and permits the Pawns to advance without obstruction from their officers. Later authors, however, differ materially from Philidor in his estimate of the King's Bishop's Opening, and general opinion now is in favour of beginning with the King's Knight, as the stronger and more lasting manner of attack.

Most writers concur in recommending 2. K. B. to Q. B's 4th also, as Black's best reply to the Bishop's Opening; but Jaenisch and the authors of the German "Handbuch" unanimously recommend 2. K. Kt. to B's 3rd in preference. Upon this point the latter remark: "We support our opinion not only by the authority of the 'Nouvelle Analyse,' in which Jaenisch advises the play of the Kt., but by the experience of our friends, the best players of Berlin, who, in two of their games by correspondence, against Magdeburg (1833) and against Posen (1839), played the move 2. K. Kt. to B's 3rd, in reply to 2. K. B. to Q. B's 4th, and won them both."

The leading works to be consulted upon this old and favourite opening are—Lopez, p. 82; Greco (Hirschel's ed.), pp. 56, 100; Ercole del Rio, pp. 37, 63; Ponziani, 1782, p. 112; Cozio (1st vol.), pp. 236, 276, 322, 323, 345; (2nd vol.), p. 301; Pratt's Philidor, 1825, p. 63; De la Bourdonnais, pp. 16, 110; Jaenisch (vol. i.), pp. 136—151; "Palamède," 1842, p. 241; Lewis's "Treatise," 1844, pp. 33—92; Walker, 1846, pp. 105—123; and the collection of games in the "Chess-Player's Chronicle," vol. i. to vii.

GAME THE FIRST.

WHITE.	BLACK.
1. P. to K's 4th.	1. P. to K's 4th.
2. K. B. to Q. B's 4th.	2. K. B. to Q. B's 4th.

Black has the choice of three good moves and several indifferent ones, in reply to your second move. The unexceptionable answers are 2. K. B. to Q. B's 4th, also 2. K. Kt. to B's 3rd, and 2. P. to K. B's 4th; and upon the two former opinions are so nicely balanced, that it is difficult, and perhaps unimportant, to decide between them. The first of these moves will form the subject of the present Chapter, and the second shall be examined in the next; and 2. P. to K. B's 4th, with those which are more objectionable, will be treated of in Chapter III.

3. P. to Q. B's 3rd.	3. K. Kt. to B's 3rd.

Instead of P. to Q. B's 3rd, you might play 3. K. Kt. to B's 3rd, and if Black then defended his Pawn with Q. Kt., his best move, you have the Guioco Piano opening. (See Game the Sixth.) Black has, in the present *début*, an infinite variety of apparently good moves at his command; and this circumstance would tend to show, I think, that your move of 3. P. to Q. B's 3rd, although the acknowledged "classical" play, handed down to us from Philidor, is not the best the board affords. He may, without much danger, make the move in the text, or Q. to K's 2nd; or, as the Italians recommend, Q. to K. Kt.'s 4th; or P. to Q's 4th, the defence of Mr. Lewis; or Q. Kt. to B's 3rd (See Games Second, Third, Fourth, and Fifth), each of which will be examined in its turn. If, instead of any one of these, he play 3. Q. to K. R's 5th, or 3. P. to Q's 3rd, you speedily obtain an advantage; *e. g.*, in the first place,—

	3. Q. to K. R's 5th.
4. Q. to K's 2nd.	4. K. Kt. to B's 3rd.
5. P. to Q's 4th.	5. B. to Kt.'s 3rd, or (A.)
6. P. takes P.	6. Kt. takes K. P.
7. P. to K. Kt.'s 3rd.	7. B. takes K. B. P. (ch.)
8. Q. takes B.	8. Kt. takes Q.
9. P. takes Q.	9. Kt. takes R.
10. B. to Q's 5th.	10. Q. Kt. to B's 3rd.
11. Q. B. to K. B's 4th.	

Gaining the K. Kt. directly, and having the better game.

(A.)

| | 5. P. takes Q. P. |
| 6. P. to K's 5th. | 6. Kt. to his sq. |

(If he play the Kt. to K's 5th or R's 4th, you move 7. P. to K. Kt.'s 3rd, and win him.)

7. K. Kt. to B's 3rd.	7. Q. to K. Kt.'s 5th.
8. B. takes K. B. P. (ch.)	8. K. to B's sq. (best)
9. P. to K. R's 3rd.	9. Q. to B's 4th.

(By taking the Kt. P. he loses his Q.)

| 10. B. takes K. Kt. | 10. R. takes B. |
| 11. P. takes P. | |

You have a much better game than Black.

In the second place :—

	3. P. to Q's 3rd.
4. P. to Q's 4th.	4. P. takes P.
5. P. takes P.	5. B. to Kt.'s 5th (ch.)
6. Q. Kt. to B's 3rd.	6. B. takes Kt. (ch.)
7. P. takes B.	7. K. Kt. to K's 2nd.
8. Q. to K. R's 5th.	8. Castles.
9. Q. B. to K. Kt.'s 5th.	9. P. to K. Kt.'s 3rd.

(If he play 9. P. to K. R's 3rd, you may move 10. K. Kt. to B's 3rd, leaving your B. to be taken.)

| 10. Q. to K. R's 4th. | 10. K. R. to K's sq. |
| 11. B. takes K. B. P. (ch.) | |

And you win easily.

Having disposed of these unsafe defences, we can now continue the regular game :—

| 4. P. to Q's 4th. | 4. P. takes P. |

If Black, for his 4th move, play B. to Q's 3rd, you take P. with P., and then advance P. to K. B's 4th. He may, however, play another move, viz., 4. B. to Q. Kt.'s 3rd, and the game proceed thus :—

| | 4. B. to Q. Kt.'s 3rd. |
| 5. P. takes P. | 5. Kt. takes P. |

And by playing 6. Q. to her 5th, or B. takes K. B. P. (ch.), you gain a striking advantage.

| 5. P. to K's 5th. | 5. P. to Q's 4th. |

He may also play 5. K. Kt. to K's 5th, or 5. Q. to K's 2nd; but in either case the result after a few moves will be in your favour. For example, in the first place,—

| | 5. Kt. to K's 5th. |
| 6. Q. to K's 2nd. | 6. P. to Q's 4th. |

(You may with equal advantage play 6. B. takes K. B. P. (ch.)

7. P. takes P. in passing.	7. Castles.
8. P. takes Q. B. P.	8. Q. takes P.
9. Q. takes Kt.	

And you have gained a Piece.

In the second place :—

	5. Q. to K's 2nd.
6. P. takes P.	6. B. to Q. Kt.'s 5th (ch.)
7. K. to B's sq.	7. Kt. to K's 5th.

(Your move of the King is much better than interposing a Piece.)

8. Q. to K. Kt.'s 4th.	8. P. to K. B's 4th.

(If he play 8. Kt. to K. B's 3rd, you reply with 9. Q. takes K. Kt. P.; if he move 8. Kt. to Q's 3rd, you play 9. K. B. to K's 2nd ; and if he play 8. P. to Q. B's 3rd, you take the Kt., and in every case must have the better game.)

9. Q. to R's 5th (ch.)	9. P. to K. Kt.'s 3rd.
10. Q. to R's 6th.	10. P. to Q. B's 3rd.
11. P. to K. B's 3rd.	11. P. to Q's 4th.
12. B. to K's 2nd.	

Winning the Kt.

6. P. takes Kt.	6. P. takes B.

If you retreat the B. to Q. Kt.'s 3rd, or check with him at Q. Kt.'s 5th, the result, according to the best authorities, is an even game; but taking the Kt. appears to me to yield you a slight advantage.

7. P. takes K. Kt. P.	7. R. to K. Kt.'s sq.

If he check with his Q. first, you may interpose Q. B. at K's 3rd.

Instead of taking the K. Kt. P. at this point, you may play 7. Q. to K. R's 5th, but not, I think, with the same advantage. For instance :—

7. Q. to K. R's 5th.	7. Castles.

(Castling is his best move.)

8. Q. takes B.	8. R. to K's sq. (ch.)
9. K. Kt. to K's 2nd.	9. P. to Q's 6th.
10. Q. B. to K's 3rd.	10. P. takes Kt.
11. Q. Kt. to Q's 2nd.	11. Q. Kt. to R's 3rd.
12. Q. takes doubled P.	12. Q. takes P.
13. Q. takes P. at K's 2nd.	

The game is about even.

8. Q. to K. R's 5th.	8. Q. to K's 2nd (ch.)
9. K. to Q's sq.	9. R. takes P.
10. K. Kt. to B's 3rd.	10. Q. Kt. to B's 3rd.

11. K. R. to K's sq.	11. Q. B. to K's 3rd.
12. R. takes B.	12. Q. takes R.
13. Q. takes B.	13. P. to Q. Kt.'s 3rd.
14. Q. to her Kt.'s 5th.	14. R. takes K. Kt. P.

In the German " Handbuch" the game is now dismissed as favourable to Black ; but in what his advantage consists is not clear. I certainly prefer your game. You can now take P. with P., and presently develope your forces, having a Piece more than your opponent, and very little inferiority of position.

GAME THE SECOND.

WHITE.	BLACK.
1. P. to K's 4th.	1. P. to K's 4th.
2. K. B. to Q. B's 4th.	2. K. B. to Q. B's 4th.
3. P. to Q. B's 3rd.	3. Q. to K's 2nd.
4. K. Kt. to B's 3rd.	4. P. to Q's 3rd (best)

If he take the K. B. P. (ch.) instead, you get the better game. (*e. g.*)

	4. B. takes B. P. (ch.)
5. K. takes B.	5. Q. to her B's 4th (ch.)
6. P. to Q's 4th.	6. Q. takes B.
7. Kt. takes K. P.	7. Q. to K's 3rd.
8. K. R. to K's sq., &c.	
5. P. to Q's 4th.	5. P. takes P.

He may also retire his B. to Q. Kt.'s 3rd, with a safe though somewhat confined game.

6. Castles.	6. P. takes Q. B. P.

Mr. Jaenisch gives this as Black's best move.

7. P. to Q. Kt.'s 4th.	7. B. to Q. Kt.'s 3rd.

Your 7th move is a suggestion of Mr. Petroff, and serves to increase the power of your attack. If he take the offered P. with his B., the game is likely to proceed as follows :—

	7. B. takes P.
8. Q. to R's 4th (ch.)	8. Q. Kt. to B's 3rd.
9. K. B. to Q. Kt.'s 5th.	9. P. to Q. B's 7th (best)
10. B. takes Kt. (ch.)	10. K. to B's sq. (best)

(If he retreat the K. to Q's sq., you may take B. with Q., he replies with P. takes Q. Kt. (becoming a Q.), you take this Q. with the Q. R., he then takes the B., and you move Q. to her B's 3rd, with a fine attacking game.)

11. B. takes Q. Kt. P.	11. Q. B. takes B.
12. Q. takes K. B.	12. P. takes Kt. (becoming a Q.)
13. Q. R. takes Q.	13. B. takes K. P.
14. K. R. to K's sq.	14. P. to K. B's 4th (best)
15. Kt. to Kt.'s 5th.	15. Q. to her 2nd.
16. Kt. takes B.	16. P. takes Kt.
17. Q. takes K. P.	

And you must at least regain a Pawn, and have a good position.

8. Q. Kt. takes P.	8. K. Kt. to B's 3rd.

If instead of this move he play 8. B. to K's 3rd, you move 9. Q. Kt. to Q's 5th, and bring the game to a position similar to one in the Scotch Game, favourable to the first player. If he play 8. B. to K. Kt.'s 5th, you answer also with 9. Q. Kt. to Q's 5th, and afterwards P. to Q. R's 4th. The move in the text is given by Jaenisch, Bilguer, and H. der Laza, as Black's best.

9. Q. Kt. to Q's 5th.	9. Kt. takes Kt.

You may play, but with less benefit, I think, 9. Q. B. to K. Kt.'s 5th; for example,—

9. Q. B. to K. Kt.'s 5th.	9. Q. B. to K's 3rd.
10. Q. Kt. to Q's 5th.	10. B. takes Kt.
11. P. takes B.	11. Castles.
12. R. to K's sq.	12. Q. to her sq.

And he has a Pawn more, and no inferiority of situation.

10. P. takes Kt.	10. Castles.
11. Q. B. to Q. Kt.'s 2nd.	11. Q. B. to K. Kt.'s 5th.
12. K. R. to K's sq.	12. Q. to her sq.

Your attack is hardly an equivalent for his extra Pawn.

GAME THE THIRD.

THE ITALIANS' DEFENCE.

WHITE.	BLACK.
1. P. to K's 4th.	1. P. to K's 4th.
2. K. B. to Q. B's 4th.	2. K. B. to Q. B's 4th.
3. P. to Q. B's 3rd.	3. Q. to K. Kt.'s 4th.

This defence of Black's is the favourite of the three great Italian masters, Del Rio, Lolli, and Ponziani, and is given by Jaenisch as the best he can adopt. (See "Analyse Nouvelle des Ouvertures," &c., pp. 167—185.)

4. Q. to K. B's 3rd.	4. Q. to K. Kt.'s 3rd (best)

This move of your Queen, which is given by Del Rio, is generally acknowledged by all authors to be the best you can adopt. Instead of it, Mr. Petroff has proposed 4. K. to B's sq., a move of remarkable ingenuity, but which, if correctly opposed, is, in the end, disadvantageous to your game, as the following moves will demonstrate :—

4. K. to B's sq.	4. Q. to K's 2nd.

(By this retreat Black utterly disconcerts the meditated attack; almost any other play would afford you an opportunity of developing your game with rapidity and effect, but this proves the move of your King to be subtle, but not sound.)

5. P. to Q's 4th.	5. B. to Q. Kt.'s 3rd.
6. K. Kt. to B's 3rd.	6. P. to Q's 3rd.

And from the unfortunate position of your King, Black has the better game.

5. K. Kt. to K's 2nd.	5. P. to Q's 3rd.

Instead of so playing, he can move 5. Q. Kt. to B's 3rd, or 5. K. Kt. to B's 3rd. In the first place,—

	5. Q. Kt. to B's 3rd.
6. P. to Q's 3rd.	6. P. to Q's 3rd.
7. B. to K's 3rd.	7. B. to Q. Kt.'s 3rd.
8. Q. Kt. to Q's 2nd.	8. K. Kt. to K's 2nd.

Even game.

In the second case,—

	5. K. Kt. to B's 3rd.
6. P. to Q's 4th.	6. P. takes P.

(If he decline the Pawn, you take P. with P., and have the better game.)

7. P. to K's 5th.	7. Kt. to K's 5th.
8. P. takes P.	8. B. checks.

(You would do wrong to take the K. B. P. with your B. (ch.) at the 8th move.)

9. Q. Kt. to B's 3rd.

And you have the advantage of position.

6. P. to Q's 4th.	6. B. to Q. Kt.'s 3rd.

His best move; if he attack your Queen with his Q. B., you may take K. B. P. with B. (ch.); and if he take P. with K. P., you obtain a better opened game.

7. P. takes P.	7. P. takes P.
8. K. Kt. to his 3rd.	8. K. Kt. to B's 3rd.
9. P. to K. R's 3rd.	

The game is equal.

GAME THE FOURTH.

LEWIS'S COUNTER GAMBIT.

WHITE.	BLACK.
1. P. to K's 4th.	1. P. to K's 4th.
2. K. B. to Q. B's 4th.	2. K. B. to Q. B's 4th.
3. P. to Q. B's 3rd.	3. P. to Q's 4th.

Black's counter move in this variation we owe to the invention of Mr. Lewis. At one time it was held to be invincible; and even now, after passing the ordeal of rigid analysis, it is acknowledged to be an ingenious and beautiful *début*, and one which may be adopted with security, as leading to an even game.

4. B. takes P.	4. K. Kt. to B's 3rd.

If you take the Pawn with Pawn, instead of Bishop, he answers with 4. B. takes K. B. P. (ch.), and if your King takes, he plays Q. to K. R's 5th (ch.), &c.

5. Q. to K. B's 3rd.	5. Castles.

Your present move is recommended as your best by the German "Handbuch," but the obvious and ordinary move for you is 5. Q. to her Kt.'s 3rd, which leads to many highly instructive situations; for example, in the first place,—

5. Q. to her Kt.'s 3rd.	5. Castles.
6. B. takes Q. Kt. P.	6. B. takes B.
7. Q. takes B.	7. Q. to her 6th.
8. Q. takes R.	8. Q. to her R's 3rd.
9. P. to Q's 4th.	9. Q. Kt. to Q's 2nd.
10. Q. takes R. (ch.)	10. B. takes Q.
11. P. to K. B's 3rd.	11. P. takes Q. P.
12. P. takes P.	12. Q. to Q's 6th.

Black has the better game.

Secondly,—

5. Q. to her Kt.'s 3rd.	5. Castles.
6. B. takes Q. Kt. P.	6. B. takes B.
7. Q. takes B.	7. Q. to her 6th.
8. Q. takes R.	8. P. to Q. B's 3rd.
9. Q. to Kt.'s 7th.	9. Q. takes K. P. (ch.)
10. Kt. to K's 2nd.	10. Q. takes K. Kt. P.
11. K. R. to B's sq.	11. Kt. to Kt.'s 5th.
12. P. to Q's 4th.	12. P. takes P.
13. P. takes P.	13. Kt. takes K. R. P.
14. Q. Kt. to Q's 2nd.	

And by this move you obtain the better game.

Thirdly,—

    5. Q. to her Kt.'s 3rd.   5. Castles.
    6. K. Kt. to B's 3rd.   6. P. to Q. B's 3rd.

(If instead he take the B. with Kt., you retake with your Q., and the
    game in a few moves becomes quite even.)

    7. B. takes K. B. P. (ch.)   7. R. takes B.
    8. Kt. takes K. P.   8. Q. to K's 2nd.

(Should he take K. B. P. with B. (ch.), you must play K. to B's sq.)

    9. Q. takes R. (ch.)   9. Q. takes Q.
    10. Kt. takes Q.   10. K. takes Kt.
    11. P. to Q's 4th.

        And you have a fine game.

    6. P. to Q's 4th.   6. P. takes P.
    7. Q. B. to K. Kt.'s 5th.   7. P. takes P.
    8. Q. Kt. takes P.   8. Q. Kt. to Q's 2nd.
    9. Castles.   9. P. to Q. B's 3rd.
    10. B. to Q. Kt.'s 3rd.   10. Q. to K's 2nd.

        The game is even.

GAME THE FIFTH.

    WHITE.   BLACK.
    1. P. to K's 4th.   1. P. to K's 4th.
    2. K. B. to Q. B's 4th.   2. K. B. to Q. B's 4th.
    3. P. to Q. B's 3rd.   3. Q. Kt. to B's 3rd.

The move of 3. Q. Kt. to B's 3rd, may be played with safety,
I believe, provided Black retreats his B. to Q. Kt.'s 3rd, when
your Q. P. is thrown forward; but if he take the P., you certainly have the advantage.

    4. P. to Q's 4th.   4. B. to Q. Kt.'s 3rd (best)
    5. K. Kt. to K's 2nd.   5. K. Kt. to B's 3rd.
    6. Q. to her 3rd.   6. Castles.
    7. P. to K. B's 4th.   7. P. takes Q. P.
    8. P. to K's 5th.   8. P. to Q's 4th.
    9. B. to Q. Kt.'s 3rd.   9. K. Kt. to K's 5th.
    10. Q. B. P. takes P.   10. P. to K. B's 4th.
    11. Q. Kt. to B's 3rd.   11. Q. B. to K's 3rd.

        And the game is even.

GAME THE SIXTH.

WHITE.	BLACK.
1. P. to K s 4th.	1. P. to K's 4th.
2. K. B. to Q. B's 4th.	2. K. B. to Q. B's 4th.
3. K. Kt. to B's 3rd.	3. P. to Q's 3rd.

I quite concur with Major Jaenisoh in opinion that your move of K. Kt. to B's 3rd is more vigorous and attacking than P. to Q. B's 3rd, and that it has not been sufficiently appreciated by authors. As he observes, you evade by this move the powerful defence of the Italian writers, 3. Q. to K. Kt.'s 4th, and that of Mr. Lewis, 3. P. to Q's 4th, involving a long and complicated series of defensive manœuvres, the slightest error in which would be dangerous to your success, and which, when played with perfect accuracy, seems to lead only to an equal game.

In addition to the present move, you have the choice for your third step of the following moves:—1st, Q. to K's 2nd, which will be treated of under the head of "The Lopez Gambit" (see Game 13th); 2ndly, of Q. to K. B's 3rd; 3rdly, of Q. to K. Kt.'s 4th; 4thly, of Q. to K. R's 5th; 5thly, of P. to Q's 4th; 6thly, of P. to Q. Kt.'s 4th; and lastly, of P. to K. B's 4th, each of which shall be examined in detail as we proceed.

If Black, in answer to 3. K. Kt. to B's 3rd, play 3. Q. Kt. to B's 3rd, the opening becomes the Guioco Piano. His present move, Jaenisch cites as the best, now his K. B. is in the field. He may, however, play also 3. K. Kt. to B's 3rd, and the game then be followed thus:—

		3. K. Kt. to B's 3rd.
4. Kt. takes P.		4. Kt. takes P.
5. B. takes P. (ch.)		5. K. to B's sq.
6. Q. to B's 3rd.		6. B. takes P. (ch.)
7. K. to his 2nd.		7. P. to Q's 3rd.
8. Q. takes Kt.		8. P. takes Kt.
9. R. to B's sq.		

And you have a fine game.

4. P. to Q. B's 3rd.	4. K. Kt. to B's 3rd.

I have found in play that 4. P. to Q's 4th gave me a free well opened game, preferable to any obtained by the move in the text.

Black, instead of bringing out his K. Kt., might retreat his

B. to Q. Kt.'s 3rd, or play Q. to K's 2nd, with a safe though
confined position. If he play 4. Q. B. to K's 3rd, you take
B. with B., and then move Q. to her Kt.'s 3rd. If he venture
the counter-gambit 4. P. to K. B's 4th, you retort with P. to
Q's 4th, having a much better game; and lastly, if he move
4. Q. B. to K. Kt.'s 5th, you play 5. Q. to her Kt.'s 3rd,
winning at least a Pawn.

5. P. to Q's 4th.	5. P. takes P.
6. P. takes P.	6. B. to Q. Kt.'s 5th (ch.)

He may also retreat his B. to Q. Kt.'s 3rd, as in the following
example :—

	6. B. to Q. Kt.'s 3rd.
7. Q. Kt. to B's 3rd.	7. Q. B. to K. Kt.'s 5th.

(If he castle instead, you move 8. K. B. to Q's 3rd.)

8. Q. B. to K's 3rd.	8. Castles.
9. K. B. to Q's 3rd.	9. Q. Kt. to B's 3rd.
10. K. B. to Q. B's 2nd.	10. B. takes K. Kt.
11. K. Kt. P. takes B.	

And his King will be exposed to a dangerous attack from your Rooks on
the open K. Kt.'s file.

7. B. to Q's 2nd.	7. B. takes B. (ch.)
8. Q. Kt. takes B.	8. P. to Q's 4th.

If he take 8. K. P. with his Kt., you play 9. B. takes
K. B. P. (ch.); but if he castles instead, you then move
9. K. B. to Q's 3rd.

9. P. takes P.	9. Kt. takes P.
10. Q. to her Kt.'s 3rd.	10. P. to Q. B's 3rd.
11. Castles.	11. Castles.

You have the move, and your Pieces are in better play.

GAME THE SEVENTH.

WHITE.	BLACK.
1. P. to K's 4th.	1. P. to K's 4th.
2. K. B. to Q. B's 4th.	2. K. B. to Q. B's 4th.
3. Q. to K. B's 3rd.	3. K. Kt. to B's 3rd.

Your Queen is ill-placed in occupying the square on which
your K. Kt. should stand, and this mode of attack is not to
be advised.

4. P. to K. Kt.'s 4th.	4. P. to Q's 4th.

If you played instead 4. Q. to K. Kt.'s 3rd, Black could have castled, or he might have played 4. P. to Q's 3rd, leaving you to take the K. Kt. P., the consequences of which have been already seen in the analysis of the K. Kt.'s opening, p. 63.

5. K. B. takes Q. P.   5. Q. B. takes P.

You could have taken P. with P., but would not have improved your game by it.

6. Q. to Q. Kt.'s 3rd.   6. K. Kt. takes K. B.
7. P. takes Kt.   7. K. B. to Q. Kt.'s 3rd.

If you take the Q. Kt. P. at the 7th move, he may win your Q. by moving K. Kt. to Q. Kt.'s 3rd, and then Q. B. to his sq.

8. Q. to K. Kt.'s 3rd.   8. Q. to K. B's 3rd.

Black has the better game.

GAME THE EIGHTH.

WHITE.	BLACK.
1. P. to K's 4th.	1. P. to K's 4th.
2. K. B. to Q. B's 4th.	2. K. B. to Q. B's 4th.
3. Q. to K. Kt.'s 4th.	3. Q. to K. B's 3rd.

The present *sortie* of your Queen is equally objectionable with 3. Q. to K. B's 3rd, and may, like that, be very shortly dismissed.

4. P. to Q's 4th.	4. B. takes P.
5. K. Kt. to B's 3rd.	5. Q. Kt. to B's 3rd.
6. Q. to K. Kt.'s 3rd.	6. P. to Q's 3rd.
7. Q. B. to K. Kt.'s 5th.	7. Q. to K. Kt.'s 3rd.
8. Q. Kt. to Q's 2nd.	8. P. to K. R's 3rd.

Black has the advantage.

GAME THE NINTH.

WHITE.	BLACK.
1. P. to K's 4th.	1. P. to K's 4th.
2. K. B. to Q. B's 4th.	2. K. B. to Q. B's 4th.
3. Q. to K. R's 5th.	3. Q. to K's 2nd.

Q. to K. R's 5th is less exceptionable than the former places for her, yet this is not a good move. Black's best reply is Q. to K's 2nd, but he may also defend his K. B. P., and at the same time attack yours, by playing 3. Q. to K. B's 3rd. (*e. g.*)

	3. Q. to K. B's 3rd.
4. K. Kt. to B's 3rd.	4. P. to Q's 3rd.
5. Q. Kt. to B's 3rd.	5. K. Kt. to K's 2nd.

Even game.

4. K. Kt. to B's 3rd.	4. P. to Q's 3rd.
5. K. Kt. to his 5th.	5. K. Kt. to B's 3rd.
6. Q. takes K. B. P. (ch.) (best)	6. Q. takes Q.

You would not at all improve your game by taking the P. with your B. instead of the Q.; for example,—

6. B. takes K. B. P. (ch.)	6. K. to Q's sq.
7. Q. to K. R's 4th.	7. K. R. to B's sq.

(If you retire your Q. elsewhere at move 7., he wins a Piece by **7. P. to K. R's 3rd.**)

8. K. B. to Q. B's 4th.	8. K. Kt. to his 5th.
9. Castles.	9. R. takes K. B. P.

And Black's game is superior to yours.

7. B. takes Q. (ch.)	7. K. to his 2nd.

You may take the Q. with your Kt. instead, as follows :—

7. Kt. takes Q.	7. R. to K. B's sq.
8. Kt. to his 5th.	8. P. to K. R's 3rd.
9. Kt. to K. B's 3rd.	9. Kt. takes K. P.
10. Castles.	10. Kt. takes K. B. P.
11. R. takes Kt.	11. B. takes R. (ch.)
12. K. takes B.	12. P. to K's 5th.

Winning the Kt., and having the better game.

8. B. to Q. B's 4th.	8. P. to K. R's 3rd.
9. Kt. to K. B's 3rd.	9. Kt. takes K. P.

You have no advantage.

GAME THE TENTH.

WHITE.	BLACK.
1. P. to K's 4th.	1. P. to K's 4th.
2. K. B. to Q. B's 4th.	2. K. B. to Q. B's 4th.
3. P. to Q's 4th.	3. B. takes P.

Your 3rd move in this game comes under the category of premature attacks, the result of which, when they are properly opposed, must always be a loss of time or material to the maker. In the present case you sacrifice a Pawn without any chance of obtaining an equivalent, either in position or otherwise.

4. K. Kt. to B's 3rd.	4. Q. Kt. to B's 3rd.

If you play 4. P. to Q. B's 3rd, he would reply with B. to Q. Kt.'s 3rd, and not to Q. B's 4th, because of your being then enabled to take K. B. P. with B. (ch.), &c.

5. P. to Q. B's 3rd.	5. B. to Q. Kt.'s 3rd.
6. K. Kt. to his 5th.	6. K. Kt. to R's 3rd.
7. Q. to K. R's 5th.	7. Castles.

You have other modes of play, which we omit for want of space, but in all Black maintains in security the Pawn gained.

GAME THE ELEVENTH.

McDonnell's Double Gambit.

WHITE.	BLACK.
1. P. to K's 4th.	1. P. to K's 4th.
2. K. B. to Q. B's 4th.	2. K. B. to Q. B's 4th.
3. P. to Q. Kt.'s 4th.	3. B. takes Kt. P.
4. P. to K. B's 4th.	4. P. to Q's 4th.

Instead of advancing your K. B. P., which forms what is called the "double gambit," an attacking but rather perilous sort of opening for the first player, you can reduce the game to an Evans' Gambit by moving 4. P. to Q. B's 3rd, and then K. Kt. to B's 3rd.

If Black, in lieu of P. to Q's 4th, should take K. B. P. with P., you answer with K. Kt. to B's 3rd, and get a powerful attack. (e. g.)

	4. P. takes K. B. P.
5. K. Kt. to B's 3rd.	5. Q. to K's 2nd.
6. Q. to K's 2nd.	6. K. Kt. to B's 3rd.
7. P. to K's 5th.	7. K. Kt. to R's 4th.
8. P. to Q. B's 3rd.	8. B. to Q. R's 4th.
9. P. to Q's 4th.	9. B. to Q. Kt.'s 3rd.
10. P. to K. Kt.'s 4th.	10. P. takes P. in passing.

The move hitherto given as your 10th is Q. B. to Q. R's 3rd, to which Black answers 10. P. to Q. B's 4th, and the attack is at end.

If Black, instead of taking the Pawn, move 10. P. to Q's 4th, the following few moves will prove, I think, that you still have a better game:—

	10. P. to Q's 4th.
11. B. takes Q. P.	11. P. to Q. B's 3rd (best)

You may now take Q. B. P. with B. (ch.), then take the K. Kt., afterwards recovering the P., and with your fine centre of Pawns have the advantage.

11. Kt. to his 5th.

And you preserve a fine attack.

5. P. takes Q. P.	5. P. to K's 5th.

If you take the Q. P. with your B. instead, he still maintains an advantage; for instance,—

5. B. takes Q. P.	5. P. to Q. B's 3rd.
6. P. to Q. B's 3rd.	6. P. takes B.
7. P. takes B.	7. P. takes K. P.
8. P. takes K. P.	8. Q. to her 5th.
9. Q. to her B's 2nd.	9. Q. B. to K. B's 4th.

He has the better position.

6. K. Kt. to K's 2nd.	6. K. Kt. to B's 3rd.
7. Castles.	7. Castles.
8. Q. Kt. to B's 3rd.	8. P. to Q. B's 3rd.
9. P. takes P.	9. Q. Kt. takes P.
10. K. to R's sq.	10. Q. B. to K. Kt.'s 5th.

Your game is inferior to his.

GAME THE TWELFTH.

WHITE.	BLACK.
1. P. to K's 4th.	1. P. to K's 4th.
2. K. B. to Q. B's 4th.	2. K. B. to Q. B's 4th.
3. P. to K. B's 4th.	3. B. takes K. Kt.

Your present 3rd move is not commendable, because it is needlessly hazardous, and throws upon you at once the onus of defence.

Black plays rightly in taking the Kt.; if he take P. with P. instead, you may play 4. P. to Q's 4th, and if he then checks with his Queen, the game is resolved into a species of K. B's gambit, the advantage of position being much in your favour.

4. Q. to K. R's 5th.	4. Q. to K's 2nd.

If instead of this sally with your Queen, you take the **Kt.**

with your Rook, he answers with 4. Q. to K. R's 5th (ch.), and proceeds as follows :—

	4. Q. to K. R's 5th (ch.)
5. P. to K. Kt.'s 3rd.	5. Q. takes K. R. P.
6. K. to B's sq.	6. P. to Q's 4th.

He has evidently a better game.

5. R. takes B.	5. P. to Q's 3rd.
6. P. to K. B's 5th.	6. K. Kt. to B's 3rd.
7. Q. to K. Kt.'s 5th.	7. K. Kt. takes K. P.
8. Q. takes K. Kt. P.	8. Q. to K. B's 3rd.
9. K. B. takes K. B. P. (ch.)	9. K. to his 2nd.
10. Q. takes Q. (ch.)	10. Kt. takes Q.
11. K. B. to Q. Kt.'s 3rd.	11. Q. B. takes P.

The game is in Black's favour.

GAME THE THIRTEENTH.

THE LOPEZ GAMBIT.

WHITE.	BLACK.
1. P. to K's 4th.	1. P. to K's 4th.
2. K. B. to Q. B's 4th.	2. K. B. to Q. B's 4th.
3. Q. to K's 2nd.	3. P. to Q's 3rd.

The move of your Queen thus is far better than any of the three previous marches. In this position you threaten at once to take Black's K. B. P. with your B., and if he retake the B., to play the Q. to her B's 4th (ch.), and then capture his Bishop in return. At the same time, you have an opportunity, when Black, foreseeing the menaced danger, attempts to guard against it, to advance your P. to K. B's 4th, and thus form a gambit more advantageous to you in some respects than the ordinary King's Gambit. This opening is first found in the old work, " *Libro de la Invencion liberal y Arte del Juego del Axedres*," of Ruy Lopez (1561), and is usually named after its inventor, "The Lopez Gambit."

In reply to your move of 3. Q. to K's 2nd, Black has at his command three good methods of play; viz., 3. P. to Q's 3rd, 3. Q. to K's 2nd, and 3. Q. Kt. to B's 3rd, each of which has its advocates, and shall receive a separate examination.

4. P. to K. B's 4th.	4. Kt. to K. B's 3rd.

Instead of 4. Kt. to K. B's 3rd, Black may play 4. B. takes

K. Kt., or 4. P. takes P., but in either case the game will be
in your favour; for example, in the first place,—

	4. K. B. takes K. Kt.
5. R. takes B.	5. K. Kt. to B's 3rd.

(Taking the Pawn at this point would be detrimental to him.) See (A.)

6. P. to Q's 3rd.	6. Q. to K's 2nd.

(If he play instead 6. Q. B. to K. Kt.'s 5th, you move 7. Q. to K. B's 2nd.)

7. Q. Kt. to B's 3rd.	7. Q. Kt. to B's 3rd.

(He may move 7. Q. B. to K's 3rd, upon which you exchange Bishops
and advance P. to K. B's 5th.)

8. Q. B. to K's 3rd.	8. P. takes K. B. P.
9. Q. B. takes P.	9. Kt. to Q's 5th.
10. Q. to K. B's 2nd.	10. Q. Kt. to K's 3rd.
11. P. to K. Kt.'s 4th.	

You have the advantage.

(A.)

	5. P. takes B. P.
6. P. to Q's 4th.	6. P. to K. Kt.'s 4th.

(You may also play 6. P. to Q's 3rd, and if he answer with 6. P. to
K. Kt.'s 4th, play as in this case) :—

7. P. to K. Kt.'s 3rd.	7. P. takes P.
8. B. takes K. B. P. (ch.)	8. K. takes B.

(If he refuse to take the B., and play his K. to B's sq , you can take the
P. with the R., and should win.)

9. Q. to K. R's 5th (ch.)	9. K. to Kt.'s 2nd.

(If he play 9. K. to B's sq., or K. to his 2nd, you equally take the P. with
your Q. B., and have an obvious advantage.)

10. B. takes Kt. P.	10. Q. to her 2nd.

(Should he take the R. P., you give checkmate in four moves; and if he
interpose the Kt., you check with your B. at K. R's 6th, and win
easily.\

11. R. takes P.	11. K. to B's sq.
12. K. R. to B's 3rd (ch.)	

And you must clearly force the game in a few moves.

In the second place,—

	4. P. takes B. P.
5. K. Kt. to B's 3rd.	5. P. to K. Kt.'s 4th.
6. P. to Q's 4th.	6. B. to Q. Kt.'s 3rd.
7. P. to K. R's 4th.	7. P. to K. Kt.'s 5th.

(If he attempt to sustain the Kt. P. with K. B. P., you take the Kt. P.
with your Kt.)

8. Kt. to his 5th.	8. Kt. to K. R's 3rd.
9. Q. B. takes P.	

And you have an excellent game.

You can now return to and pursue the former scries of moves, which we left at Black's 4th move.

5. K. Kt. to B's 3rd.	5. Q. to K's 2nd.
6. P. to Q's 3rd.	6. Q. B. to K. Kt.'s 5th.
7. P. takes P.	7. P. takes P.
8. Q. B. to K. Kt.'s 5th.	8. Q. Kt. to Q's 2nd.
9. Q. Kt. to Q's 2nd.	9. Castles on Q's side.
10. Castles on Q's side.	

The positions are equal

GAME THE FOURTEENTH.

WHITE.	BLACK.
1. P. to K's 4th.	1. P. to K's 4th.
2. K. B. to Q. B's 4th.	2. K. B. to Q. B's 4th.
3. Q. to K's 2nd.	3. Q. to K's 2nd.

Black's defence here is perfectly safe, and with correct play on both sides, the result, I think, must be an even game.

4. P. to K. B's 4th.	4. K. Kt. to B's 3rd.
5. K. Kt. to B's 3rd.	5. P. to Q's 3rd.
6. Q. Kt. to B's 3rd.	6. P. to Q. B's 3rd.
7. P. to Q's 3rd.	7. Q. B. to K. Kt.'s 5th.
8. P. to K. B's 5th.	8. Q. Kt. to Q's 2nd.
9. Q. B. to K. Kt.'s 5th.	9. P. to K. R's 3rd.
10. Q. B. to K. R's 4th.	10. P. to K. Kt.'s 4th.

You may either take the Pawn in passing, or play Q. B. to K. B's 2nd. The game is quite even.

GAME THE FIFTEENTH.

WHITE.	BLACK.
1. P. to K's 4th.	1. P. to K's 4th.
2. B. to Q. B's 4th.	2. B. to Q. B's 4th.
3. Q. to K's 2nd.	3. Q. Kt. to B's 3rd.

Black's 3rd move in this example is perhaps the best defence of all. It is originally given by Lopez, but was little known until its introduction by M. Calvi, in his valuable series of lessons in the Palamède." (See "Palamède" of June, 1842, for a comprehensive and elegant analysis of the Lopez Gambit.)

4. P. to Q. B's 3rd.	4. K. Kt. to B's 3rd.

Instead of playing your Q. B. P., you might take the adverse K. B. P. with your B. (ch.). (See Variation.)

5. P. to K. B's 4th.	5. B. takes K. Kt.
6. R. takes B.	6. Castles.
7. P. to Q's 3rd.	7. P. to Q's 4th.

You may also take P. with P., and the following moves are then likely to occur:—

7. P. takes P.	7. Q. Kt. takes P.
8. K. B. to Q. Kt.'s 3rd.	8. K. Kt. takes K. P.
9. Q. takes Kt.	9. R. to K's sq.
10. K. to Q's sq.	10. P. to Q's 4th.
11. Q. takes Q. P.	11. B. to K. Kt.'s 5th (ch.)
12. K. to B's 2nd.	12. Q. to K. B's 3rd.

And although you have a Piece more, Black must win.

8. K. B. takes Q. P.	8. K. Kt. takes B.
9. P. takes Kt.	9. P. takes K. B. P.
10. Q. B. takes P.	10. R. to K's sq.

If, instead of taking the P., you play 10. Q. to K. B's 3rd, Black answers with 10 Kt. to K's 4th. His move in the text, of R. to K's sq., is much better than playing 10. Q. takes P.

11. B. to K's 3rd.	11. Kt. to K's 4th.
12. P. to K. R's 3rd.	12. B. to K. B's 4th.
13. P. to Q's 4th.	13. B. to Q's 6th.

And by afterwards moving the Kt. to Q. B's 5th, Black must win at least a Piece.

VARIATION,

Beginning at White's 4th move.

WHITE.	BLACK.
1. P. to K's 4th.	1. P. to K's 4th.
2. K. B. to Q. B's 4th.	2. K. B. to Q. B's 4th.
3. Q. to K's 2nd.	3. Q. Kt. to B's 3rd.
4. K. B. takes K. B. P. (ch.)	4. K. takes B.
5. Q. to her B's 4th (ch.)	5. P. to Q's 4th.
6. Q. takes B.	6. P. takes K. P.

If you take the Q. P. with P. instead of capturing the Bishop,
Black may then take your K. B. P. (ch.), and afterwards
move Q. Kt. to Q. R's 4th.

7. Q. to her B's 4th (ch.)	7. Q. B. to K's 3rd.
8. Q. takes P.	8. K. Kt. to B's 3rd.

And you have an inferior game.

GAMES
ILLUSTRATIVE OF THE PRECEDING ANALYSES.
(From the *Chess-Player's Chronicle*.)

GAME I.—Played some years since between Messrs. Popert
and Staunton.

WHITE. (Mr. S.)	BLACK. (Mr. P.)
1. P. to K's 4th.	1. P. to K's 4th.
2. K. B. to Q. B's 4th.	2. K. B. to Q. B's 4th.
3. P. to Q. B's 3rd.	3. P. to Q's 3rd.*
4. K. Kt. to B's 3rd.†	4. K. Kt. to B's 3rd.
5. P. to Q's 4th.	5. P. takes P.
6. P. takes P.	6. B. checks.
7. B. to Q's 2nd.	7. B. takes B. (ch.)
8. Q. Kt. takes B.	8. Castles.‡
9. B. to Q's 3rd.	9. Kt. to Q. B's 3rd.
10. P. to Q. R's 3rd.	10. Q. B. to K. Kt.'s 5th.
11. Q. to Q. B's 2nd.	11. P. to K. R's 3rd.
12. Q. R. to Q. B's sq.	12. P. to Q's 4th.
13. P. to K's 5th.	13. B. takes Kt.
14. Kt. takes B.	14. Kt. to K. R's 4th.
15. P. to K. Kt.'s 3rd.	15. P. to K. Kt.'s 3rd.
16. P. to Q. Kt.'s 4th.	16. Q. to Q's 2nd.§
17. Q. to Q's 2nd.	17. K. to R's 2nd.
18. Castles.	18. Q. R. to K's sq.
19. Q. R. to B's 3rd.	19. Kt. to Q's sq.
20. Kt. to K. R's 4th.	20. P. to Q. B's 3rd.
21. P. to K. B's 4th.	21. P. to K. B's 4th.
22. P. to K. Kt.'s 4th.	22. Kt. to K. Kt.'s 2nd.
23. P. takes B. P.	23. K. Kt. takes P.
24. Kt. takes Kt.	24. P. takes Kt.
25. K. to R's sq.	25. K. R. to K. Kt.'s sq.

---

* Not so good a move as K. Kt. to B's 3rd, or Q. to K. Kt.'s 4th.
† P. to Q's 4th would perhaps have been stronger play.
‡ P. to Q's 4th is a better move at this point.
§ Intending, if the Q. Kt. P. should be played on his Kt., to move
Q. to K. Kt.'s 5th.

26. Q. R. to Q. B's sq.	26. Q. to K. B's 2nd.
27. Q. to Q. B's 2nd.	27. Q. R. to K. B's sq.
28. K. R. to K. Kt.'s sq.	28. Kt. to K's 3rd.
29. R. takes R.	29. K. takes R.
30. R. to K. Kt.'s sq. (ch.)	30. K. to R's sq.
31. Q. to K. B's 2nd.	31. Q. to K. R's 4th.*
32. B. to K's 2nd.	32. Q. to K. B's 2nd.
33. Q. to K. R's 4th.	33. Q. to K. R's 2nd.
34. B. to K. R's 5th.	34. Kt. takes Q. P.
35. R. to K. Kt.'s 3rd.	35. P. to Q. Kt.'s 3rd.
36. B. to K. Kt.'s 6th.†	36. Q. to K. Kt.'s 2nd.
37. B. to K. B's 7th.	37. R. takes B.‡
38. R. takes Q.	38. K. takes R.
39. K. to Kt.'s 2nd, and wins.	

GAME II.—Between two London Amateurs.

WHITE.	BLACK.
1. P. to K's 4th.	1. P. to K's 4th.
2. K. B. to Q. B's 4th.	2. K. B. to Q. B's 4th.
3. P. to Q. B's 3rd.	3. Q. to K. Kt.'s 4th.
4. Q. to K. B's 3rd.	4. Q. to K. Kt.'s 3rd.
5. K. Kt. to K's 2nd.	5. P. to Q's 3rd.
6. P. to Q's 4th.	6. P. takes P.
7. P. takes P.	7. B. to Q. Kt.'s 3rd.
8. P. to K's 5th.	8. K. Kt. to K's 2nd.
9. P. to K's 6th.	9. P. to K. B's 3rd.
10. Q. Kt. to B's 3rd.	10. Castles.
11. K. Kt. to K. B's 4th.	11. Q. to K's sq.
12. Q. R. to Q's sq.	12. Q. Kt. to Q. B's 3rd.
13. Q. R. to Q's sq.	13. K. to R's sq.
14. P. to K. R's 4th.	14. Q. Kt. to Q's sq.
15. P. to K. R's 5th.	15. P. to K. B's 4th.
16. Q. Kt. to Q's 5th.	16. Q. B. takes P.
17. Kt. takes Kt.	17. Q. takes Kt.
18. Kt. to K. Kt.'s 6th (ch.)	18. P. takes Kt.
19. P. takes P. (dis. ch.)	

And White gives checkmate in three moves.

GAME III.—Played between the London and Edinburgh Chess Clubs in 1824.

EDINBURGH.	LONDON.
1. P. to K's 4th.	1. P. to K's 4th.
2. B. to Q. B's 4th.	2. B. to Q. B's 4th.
3. P. to Q. B's 3rd.	3. Q. to K's 2nd.

* A lost move.
† It would have been more decisive if played to K. B's 7th at once.
‡ If the Q. takes B., mate follows in three moves.

4. K. Kt. to B's 3rd.	4. P. to Q's 3rd.
5. P. to Q's 3rd.	5. K. Kt. to B's 3rd.
6. Q. to K's 2nd.*	6. Castles.
7. Q. B. to K. Kt.'s 5th.	7. P. to K. R's 3rd.†
8. Q. B. to K. R's 4th.	8. Q. B. to K's 3rd.
9. K. B. to Q. Kt.'s 3rd.	9. B. takes B.
10. Q. R. P. takes B.	10. Q. Kt. to B's 3rd.
11. Q. Kt. to Q's 2nd.	11. Q. to K's 3rd.
12. P. to Q. Kt.'s 4th.	12. B. to Q. Kt.'s 3rd.
13. B. takes Kt.	13. Q. takes Kt.
14. Q. Kt. to Q. B's 4th.	14. Q. to K's 3rd.
15. K. Kt. to R's 4th.	15. Kt. to K's 2nd.
16. P. to K. Kt.'s 4th.	16. Kt. to K. Kt.'s 3rd.‡
17. Kt. takes Kt.	17. P. takes Kt.
18. Castles on K's side.	18. K. R. to B's 5th.
19. P. to K. R's 3rd.	19. Q. R. to K. B's sq.
20. Kt. takes B.	20. Q. R. P. takes Kt.
21. P. to K. B's 3rd.	21. Q. to K. B's 3rd.
22. K. to Kt.'s 2nd.	22. P. to Q. B's 3rd.
23. K. R. to B's 2nd.	23. P. to Q. Kt.'s 4th.
24. Q. to K's 3rd.	24. P. to K. R's 4th.
25. K. to Kt.'s 3rd.	25. Q. to K. Kt.'s 4th.§
26. Q. R. to K's sq.	26. K. to R's 2nd.‖
27. Q. to K's 2nd.	27. Q. R. to K. R's sq.
28. Q. to K's 3rd.	28. K. to Kt.'s sq.
29. K. R. to his 2nd.	29. K. R. P. takes P.
30. R. P. takes P.¶	30. R. takes B. P. (ch.)
31. K. takes R.**	31. Q. takes Q. (ch.)
32. K. takes Q.	32. R. takes R.
33. R. to Q. R's sq.	33. R. to R's 6th (ch.)
34. K. to his 2nd.	34. R. to R's 7th (ch.)
35. K. to his 3rd.	35. R. to R's 6th (ch.)

The game was declared drawn.

GAME IV.—Played some years ago between Mr. Staunton
and one of the finest players in Europe.

WHITE. (Mr. S.)	BLACK. (Mr. —)
1. P. to K's 4th.	1. P. to K's 4th.
2. B. to Q. B's 4th.	2. B. to Q. B's 4th.

---

* Castling would perhaps have beeen better play.
† A little like lost time.
‡ P. to Q's 4th would certainly have been a stronger move.
§ Threatening to win the adverse Q.
‖ Q. to K. R's 3rd appears a good mode of continuing the attack.
¶ If they had taken with K. B. P., London would have played Q. to
K. R's 5th (ch.), and then taken K. Kt. P. with the K. R.
** Much better than taking with the Q.

3. P. to Q. B's 3rd.	3. Q. Kt. to B's 3rd.
4. K. Kt. to B's 3rd.	4. P. to Q's 3rd.*
5. P. to Q's 4th.	5. P. takes P.
6. P. takes P.	6. B. to Q. Kt.'s 3rd.
7. Castles.	7. Q. B. to K. Kt.'s 5th.
8. Q. to her Kt.'s 3rd.	8. Q. B. to K. R's 4th.
9. P. to K's 5th.	9. P. takes P.
10. P. takes P.	10. K. Kt. to K's 2nd.
11. P. to K's 6th.	11. Castles.
12. P. takes P. (ch.)	12. K. to R's sq.
13. K. Kt. to K. Kt.'s 5th.	13. Q. Kt. to Q's 5th.
14. Q. to K. R's 3rd.	14. B. to K. Kt.'s 3rd.
15. Q. Kt. to Q. R's 3rd.	15. K. Kt. to K. B's 4th.
16. Q. B. to K. B's 4th.	16. Q. to K. B's 3rd.
17. Q. R. to K's sq.	17. K. Kt. to R's 3rd.
18. K. Kt. to K's 6th.	18. B. to K. B's 4th.
19. Kt. takes R.	19. K. Kt. takes P.†
20. Kt. takes K. R. P.	20. B. takes Kt.
21. Q. to her 7th.	21. Q. takes B.
22. B. takes Kt.	22. B. to K. B's 4th.
23. R. to K's 8th (ch.)	23. R. takes R.
24. Q. takes R. (ch.)	24. K. to R's 2nd.
25. Q. to K. Kt.'s 8th (ch.)	25. K. to R's 3rd.
26. Q. to K. R's 8th (ch.)	26. B. to K. R's 2nd.
27. B. to K. Kt.'s 8th.	

Black resigned in a few moves.

GAME V.—THE LOPEZ GAMBIT.—Between Messrs. De la Bourdonnais and Mc Donnell.

WHITE. (M. De la B.)	BLACK. (Mr. Mc D.)
1. P. to K's 4th.	1. P. to K's 4th.
2. K. B. to Q. B's 4th.	2. K. B. to Q. B's 4th.
3. Q. to K's 2nd.	3. K. Kt. to B's 3rd.
4. P. to Q's 3rd.	4. Q. Kt. to B's 3rd.
5. P. to Q. B's 3rd.	5. Q. Kt. to K's 2nd.
6. P. to K. B's 4th.	6. P. takes P.‡
7. P. to Q's 4th.	7. K. B. to Kt.'s 3rd.
8. Q. B. takes P.	8. P. to Q's 3rd.
9. K. B. to Q's 3rd.	9. Q. Kt. to K. Kt.'s 3rd.
10. Q. B. to K's 3rd.	10. Castles.
11. P. to K. R's 3rd.	11. K. R. to K's sq.
12. Q. Kt. to Q's 2nd.	12. Q. to K's 2nd.

* The position is that of the Guioco Piano,—Black should have brought out his K. Kt. to B's 3rd.

† Had he taken the Q., White would have won easily.

‡ In this opening it is not advisable for the second player to take the gambit P. with his K. P.

13. Castles on Q's side.	13. P. to Q. B's 4th.
14. K. to Kt.'s sq.	14. P. takes P.
15. P. takes P.	15. P. to Q. R's 4th.
16. K. Kt. to B's 3rd.	16. Q. B. to Q's 2nd.
17. P. to K. Kt.'s 4th.	17. P. to K. R's 3rd.
18. Q. R. to K. Kt.'s sq.	18. P. to Q. R's 5th.
19. P. to K. Kt.'s 5th.	19. P. takes P.
20. B. takes P.	20. P. to Q. R's 6th.
21. P. to Q. Kt.'s 3rd.	21. Q. B. to his 3rd.
22. Q. R. to K. Kt.'s 4th.	22. K. B. to Q. R's 4th.
23. P. to K. R's 4th.	23. B. takes Q. Kt.
24. Kt. takes B.	24. Q. R. to his 4th.
25. P. to K. R's 5th.	25. R. takes B.
26. R. takes R.	26. Kt. to K. B's 5th.
27. Q. to K. B's 3rd.	27. Kt. takes B.
28. P. to Q's 5th.	28. Kt. takes Q. P.
29. K. R. to K. Kt.'s sq.*	29. Kt. to B's 6th (ch.)
30. K. to R's sq.	30. B. takes K. P.
31. R. takes K. Kt. P. (ch.)	31. K. to R's sq.
32. Q. to K. Kt.'s 3rd.	32. B. to K. Kt.'s 3rd
33. K. R. P. takes B.	33. Q. to K's 8th (ch.)
34. R. takes Q.†	34. R. takes R. (ch.)
35. Q. takes R.	35. Kt. takes Q.
36. R. to R's 7th (ch.)	36. K. to Kt.'s sq.
37. P. takes K. B. P. (ch.)	37. K. takes R.
38. P. one, becoming a Queen.	38. Kt. mates.

GAME VI.—THE LOPEZ GAMBIT.

WHITE.	BLACK.
1. P. to K's 4th.	1. P. to K's 4th.
2. K. B. to Q. B's 4th.	2. K. B. to Q. B's 4th.
3. Q. to K's 2nd.	3. Q. Kt. to B's 3rd.
4. B. takes K. B. P. (ch.)	4. K. takes B.
5. Q. to her B's 4th (ch.)	5. P. to Q's 4th.

---

* This portion of the game is full of interest and instruction, and is remarkably well played.

† White loses the game by this move. The following variation, by the writer, was published some years since, and seems to prove that White might have won easily from this point :—

	33. Q. to K's 8th (ch.)
34. Kt. to Q. Kt.'s sq.	34. Q. takes Q.
35. R. to K. R's 7th (ch.)	35. K. to his Kt.'s sq.

(If White take the Queen instead of checking with his R., he loses the game.)

36. P. takes K. B. P. (ch.)	36. K. takes R.
37. R. to K. R's sq. (ch.)	37. K. to Kt.'s 2nd.
38. P. takes R., becoming a Q., and wins.	

6. Q. takes B.	6. P. takes P.
7. Q. to her B's 4th (ch.)	7. Q. B. to K's 3rd.
8. Q. takes P.	8. K. Kt. to B's 3rd.
9. Q. to K. R's 4th.	9. Q. Kt. to Q's 5th.
10. Q. Kt. to R's 3rd.	10. P. to K's 5th.
11. P. to Q. B's 3rd.	11. P. to K. Kt.'s 4th.*
12. Q. takes K. Kt. P.	12. K. R. to K. Kt.'s sq.
13. Q. to K's 3rd.	13. Q. Kt. to K. B's 4th.
14. Q. to K's 2nd.	14. R. takes K. Kt. P.
15. Q. Kt. to B's 2nd.	15. Q. to her 3rd.
16. Q. Kt. to K's 3rd.	16. Kt. takes Kt.
17. Q. P. takes Kt.	17. Q. R. to K. Kt.'s sq.
18. Q. to K. B's sq.	18. Q. R. to Q's sq.
19. Q. to K's 2nd.	19. Kt. to his 5th.
20. Kt. to R's 3rd.	20. Kt. to K's 4th.
21. Kt. to K. B's 4th.	21. Kt. to K. B's 6th (ch.)
22. K. to his B's sq.	

And Black can checkmate in six moves.

GAME VII.—Between Messrs. Cochrane and Staunton.

WHITE. (Mr. S.)	BLACK. (Mr. C.)
1. P. to K's 4th.	1. P. to K's 4th.
2. B. to Q. B's 4th.	2. B. to Q. B's 4th.
3. K. Kt. to B's 3rd.	3. Q. Kt. to B's 3rd.
4. P. to Q. Kt.'s 4th.†	4. B. takes Q. Kt. P.
5. P. to Q. B's 3rd.	5. B. to Q. R's 4th.
6. Castles.	6. B. to Q. Kt.'s 3rd.
7. P. to Q's 4th.	7. P. takes Q. P.
8. K. Kt. takes P.	8. Kt. takes Kt.
9. P. takes Kt.	9. P. to Q's 3rd.
10. P. to Q. R's 4th.	10. P. to Q. B's 3rd.
11. P. to Q. R's 5th.	11. K. B. to Q. B's 2nd.‡
12. Q. to her Kt.'s 3rd.	12. Q. to K's 2nd.
13. Q. B. to Q. R's 3rd.	13. Q. to K. B's 3rd.
14. Q. Kt. to Q. B's 3rd.	14. Q. to K. Kt.'s 3rd.
15. Q. Kt. to K's 2nd.	15. K. Kt. to K. R's 3rd.
16. P. to K's 5th.	16. P. to Q's 4th.
17. K. B. to Q's 3rd.	17. Kt. to K. B's 4th.
18. Q. to her Kt.'s 4th.	18. K. B. to Q's sq.

---

* The game from this point forward is admirably conducted by Black.

† We have now the same position brought about which occurs in the Evans' Gambit.

‡ If he had taken the P., Black, by taking the K. B. P. with his B. checking, and when the K. took the B., playing Q. to K. R's 5th (ch.), would have gained a more valuable P. in return, and have deprived his opponent of the privilege of castling.

19. Q. to her Kt.'s sq.	19. Q. to K. R's 4th.
20. Kt. to K. Kt.'s 3rd.	20. Kt. takes Kt.
21. K. B. P. takes Kt.	21. K. B. takes Q. R. P.
22. K. B. to K. B's 5th.	22. K. B. to Q. Kt.'s 3rd.
23. Q. to her Kt.'s 4th.	23. Q. to K. Kt.'s 4th.
24. K. B. takes Q. B.	24. Q. R. takes B.
25. P. to K's 6th.	25. P. takes P.

White announced mate in eight moves.

GAME VIII.—Between Messrs. Walker and Daniels.

WHITE. (Mr. W.)	BLACK. (Mr. D.)
1. P. to K's 4th.	1. P. to K's 4th.
2. B. to Q. B's 4th.	2. B. to Q. B's 4th.
3. P. to Q. B's 3rd.	3. P. to Q's 4th.
4. B. takes Q. P.	4. K. Kt. to B's 3rd.
5. Q. to her Kt.'s 3rd.	5. Castles.
6. K. Kt. to B's 3rd.	6. P. to Q. B's 3rd.*
7. B. takes K. B. P. (ch.) †	7. R. takes B.
8. Kt. takes K. P.	8. Q. to K's 2nd.
9. Q. takes R. (ch.)	9. Q. takes Q.
10. Kt. takes Q.	10. K. takes Kt.
11. P. to Q's 4th.	11. B. to Q. Kt.'s 3rd.
12. P. to K. B's 3rd.	12. Q. B. to K's 3rd.
13. Q. B. to K's 3rd.	13. Q. Kt. to R's 3rd.
14. K. to B's 2nd.	14. Q. Kt. to B's 2nd.
15. Q. Kt. to Q's 2nd.	15. P. to K. Kt.'s 3rd.
16. P. to K. Kt.'s 4th.	16. K. to Kt.'s 2nd.
17. P. to K. R's 4th.	17. R. to K's sq.
18. P. to K. R's 5th.	18. Q. B. to K. B's 2nd.
19. P. takes P.	19. Q. B. takes P.
20. Q. R. to K. Kt.'s sq.	20. Q. Kt. to K's 3rd.
21. Q. Kt. to Q. B's 4th.	21. B. to Q. B's 2nd.
22. P. to K's 5th.	22. K. Kt. to Q's 4th.
23. B. to K. R's 6th (ch.)	23. K. to B's 2nd.
24. K. to Kt.'s 3rd.	24. P. to Q. Kt.'s 4th.
25. Kt. to K's 3rd.	25. Kt. takes Kt.
26. B. takes Kt.	26. P. to Q. B's 4th.
27. P. to K. B's 4th.	27. P. takes P.
28. P. takes P.	28. Q. B. to Q's 6th.
29. P. to K. B's 5th.	

Black resigns.

---

* This is not advisable. It would be better to take B. with Kt.

† The notion of this sacrifice originated with Messrs. Henderson and Williams, of Bristol, during an examination of the present opening.

GAME IX.—Played by correspondence between Berlin and Posen.

WHITE. (Posen.)	BLACK. (Berlin.)
1. P. to K's 4th.	1. P. to K's 4th.
2. B. to Q. B's 4th.	2. K. Kt. to B's 3rd.
3. K. Kt. to B's 3rd.	3. Kt. takes P.
4. Kt. takes P.	4. P. to Q's 4th.
5. K. B. to Q. Kt.'s 3rd.	5. Q. to K. Kt.'s 4th.
6. Kt. takes K. B. P.	6. Q. takes K. Kt. P.
7. K. R. to B's sq.	7. Q. Kt. to B's 3rd.
8. P. to Q. B's 3rd.	8. K. Kt. to Q. B's 4th.
9. P. to Q's 4th.	9. Kt. takes B.
10. K. Kt. takes K. R.	10. Q. to K's 5th (ch.)
11. Q. to K's 2nd.	11. Q. takes Q. (ch.)
12. K. takes Q.	12. Kt. takes R.
13. K. R. to K. Kt.'s sq.	13. Q. B. to K. B's 4th.
14. Q. Kt. to Q's 2nd.	14. Castles.
15. Kt. to K. B's 3rd.	15. R. to K's sq. (ch.)
16. B. to K's 3rd.	16. Q. Kt. to Q. B's 7th.
17. K. Kt. to K. B's 7th.	17. Kt. takes B.
18. P. takes Kt.	18. P. to K. Kt.'s 3rd.
19. P. to K. R's 4th.	19. R. to K's 2nd.
20. K. Kt. to K's 5th.	20. Kt. takes Kt.
21. Kt. takes Kt.	21. K. B. to K. Kt.'s 2nd.
22. Kt. to K. B's 3rd.	22. R. to K's 5th.
23. P. to K. R's 5th.	23. K. B. to R's 3rd.

And Berlin wins.

GAME X.—Between V. H. der Laza and Dr. B.

WHITE. (Dr. B.)	BLACK. (V. H. d. L.)
1. P. to K's 4th.	1. P. to K's 4th.
2. B. to Q. B's 4th.	2. K. Kt. to B's 3rd.
3. P. to Q's 4th.	3. P. takes Q. P.
4. P. to K's 5th.	4. P. to Q's 4th.
5. B. to Q. Kt.'s 3rd.	5. Kt. to K's 5th.
6. K. Kt. to B's 3rd.	6. B. checks.
7. P. to Q. B's 3rd.	7. P. takes P.
8. Castles.	8. P. takes Q. Kt. P.
9. Q. B. takes P.	9. Q. B. to K's 3rd.
10. K. Kt. to Q's 4th.	10. P. to Q. B's 4th.
11. Kt. takes B.	11. P. takes Kt.
12. P. to K. B's 3rd.	12. K. Kt. to his 4th.
13. P. to B's 4th.	13. Kt. to K's 5th.
14. P. to B's 5th.	14. P. to Q. B's 5th.
15. B. to Q. R's 4th (ch.)*	15. Q. Kt. to B's 3rd.

---

* Q. to K. R's 5th (ch.), appears a stronger move.

16. P. takes K. P.*	16. B. checks.
17. B. to Q's 4th.	17. Q. to her Kt.'s 3rd.
18. B. takes B.	18. Q. takes B. (ch.)
19. K. to R's sq.	19. Kt. to K. B's 7th (ch.)
20. R. takes Kt.	20. Q. takes R.
21. Q. Kt. to B's 3rd.	21. Castles on K's side.
22. Kt. takes Q. P.	22. Q. R. to K's sq.
23. P. to K's 7th.	23. K. R. to K. B's 4th.
24. B. to Q. B's 2nd.	24. K. R. takes P.
25. P. to K. R's 3rd.	25. Kt. takes P.
26. Kt. takes Kt. (ch.)	26. Q. R. takes Kt.

White surrenders.

CHAPTER II.

GAME THE FIRST.

THE KING'S KNIGHT'S DEFENCE IN KING'S BISHOP'S OPENING.

WHITE.	BLACK.
1. P. to K's 4th.	1. P. to K's 4th.
2. K. B. to Q. B's 4th.	2. K. Kt. to B's 3rd.

K. Kt. to B's 3rd is the defence most highly approved by
Jaenisch and the writers of the German "Handbuch," who
consider it so powerful a retort, as to wrest from White at
once the advantage of the move, and thus prove the comparative feebleness of the long-established method of beginning
the attack with B. to Q. B's 4th at the second move.

Although of opinion that playing the Kt. is a safe defence,
I am not prepared to estimate it as so much superior to the
old move of B. to Q. B's 4th, as these able writers assume it
to be, especially since I find in their admirable analyses of the
two defences, that the result, with the best play on both sides,
is in either case an equal game. The chief works deserving
consultation upon this particular opening, are—Greco (Hirshell's edition), pp. 63—105; Lolli, pp. 189—201; Cozio
(1st vol.), pp. 326, 345; (2nd vol.), pp. 102, 313, 318, 344;
Ponziani (1782), p. 79; Allgaier (Tab. iii.); Bledow (1843),
pp. 3—23, 80; Lewis (1844), pp. 37—39; Walker (1846),

* Again, checking with the Queen seems preferable.

p. 111; "Palamède" (1842), (2nd vol.), pp. 100—145; the German "Handbuch;" and the collection of openings and games in the "Chess-Player's Chronicle."

| 3. P. to Q's 4th. | 3. P. takes P. |

3. P. to Q's 4th is the move which forms the centre gambit of Ponziani, a mode of play which is censured by Jaenisch, but which may yet, I think, be adopted by you with perfect security, if not with any striking advantage. Instead of so playing, you have the choice of 3. P. to Q's 3rd, or P. to K. B's 4th, 3. K. Kt. to B's 3rd, and 3. Q. Kt. to B's 3rd, each of which will be examined in the present Chapter. (See the next and the two succeeding games.) In answer to your third move in the text, Black may play 3. P. to Q. B's 3rd without danger, or 3. K. Kt. takes P., but the result in the latter case would be favourable to your game. (*e. g.*)

	3. Kt. takes K. P.
4. P. takes P.	4. B. to Q. B's 4th.
5. B. takes K. B. P. (ch.)	5. K. to B's sq.

(If K. take B., you play Q. to her 5th (ch.), and then take the Kt.)
6. Q. to K. B's 3rd.
You have the better game.

| 4. P. to K's 5th. | 4. P. to Q's 4th. |

You may also, for your 4th move, take the P. with your Q.; the game then, in a few moves, becoming equal; for example,—

4. Q. takes P.	4. Q. Kt. to B's 3rd.
5. Q. to K's 3rd.	5. B. to Q. Kt.'s 5th (ch.)
6. B. to Q's 2nd.	6. Castles.

You have certainly no disadvantage.

| 5. B. to Q. Kt.'s 3rd. | 5. Kt. to K's 5th. |

Neither taking the Kt. nor checking with the Bishop is advisable for you at this point. It is much better to retire the latter to Kt.'s 3rd.

| 6. K. Kt. to K's 2nd. | 6. P. to Q. B's 4th. |

If you move 6. K. Kt. to B's 3rd, Black will have the superior game; for suppose,—

6. K. Kt. to B's 3rd.	6. K. B. to Q. Kt.'s 5th (ch.)
7. P. to Q. B's 3rd.	7. P. takes P.
8. Castles.	8. P. takes P.
9. Q. B. takes P.	9. Q. B. to K's 3rd.

And he has the advantage.

7. P. to K. B's 3rd.	7. Kt. to K. Kt.'s 4th.
8. Kt. to K. B's 4th.	8. P. to Q. B's 5th.
9. B. to R's 4th (ch.)	9. Q. Kt. to B's 3rd.
10. B. takes Kt. (ch.)	10. P. takes B.
11. Q. takes doubled P.	11. Kt. to K's 3rd.
12. Kt. takes Kt.	12. K. B. P. takes Kt.
13. Castles.	13. P. to Q. B's 4th.

These moves are given by Jaenisch and the "Handbuch," and White is now made to play 14. Q. to K. B's 2nd, after which the game is speedily dismissed as favourable for Black. This retreat of the Queen, which would be feasible enough if Black, at his 12th move, take the Kt. with the Q. B., appears to me unnecessary, and much inferior to playing her to K. Kt.'s 4th, where she would be well stationed, and for some time could act as a powerful constraint upon the development of Black's forces.

GAME THE SECOND.

WHITE.	BLACK.
1. P. to K's 4th.	1. P. to K's 4th.
2. K. B. to Q. B's 4th.	2. K. Kt. to B's 3rd.
3. P. to Q's 3rd.	3. K. B. to Q. B's 4th.

Your present move is less immediately attacking than 3. P. to Q's 4th, but it is thought preferable by some players.

4. K. Kt. to B's 3rd.	4. P. to Q's 3rd.

You might now get a menacing, but somewhat hazardous, game, by playing 4. P. to K. B's 4th, and pursuing it as follows :—

4. P. to K. B's 4th.	4. P. to Q's 4th.

(If he play this P. one sq., you reply with 5. P. to Q. B's 3rd.)

5. B. takes Q. P.	5. Kt. takes B.

(It is much better to take the Q. P. with Bishop, than with the K. P.)

6. P. takes Kt.	6. Q. takes P.
7. K. Kt. to B's 3rd.	7. P. takes P.
8. B. takes P.	8. Castles.

Black has a good game, and will have a better if you take the Q. B. P. At your 7th move, instead of K. Kt. to B's 3rd, you might play Q. to K. B's 3rd, and equalize the positions.

5. P. to Q. B's 3rd.	5. Castles.
6. P. to Q. R's 4th.	6. P. to Q. R's 4th.

The game is even.

GAME THE THIRD.

WHITE.	BLACK.
1. P. to K's 4th.	1. P. to K's 4th.
2. K. B. to Q. B's 4th.	2. K. Kt. to B's 3rd.
3. P. to K. B's 4th.	3. P. to Q's 4th.

Your 3rd move is censured by Calvi, but it may be played apparently without any dangerous consequences, and with mutually correct moves afterwards, must lead to an equal game.

Black's best reply, I believe, is to throw forward his Q. P., as above; if he play, as some authorities advise, 3. Kt. takes K. P., you must not move 4. Q. to K. B's 3rd, on account of 4. P. to Q's 4th, but you may play 4. P. to Q's 3rd, and the game would probably be followed thus:—

	3. Kt. takes K. P.
4. P. to Q's 3rd.	4. Q. to K. R's 5th (ch.)
5. P. to K. Kt.'s 3rd.	5. Kt. takes K. Kt. P.
6. K. Kt. to B's 3rd.	6. Q. to K. R's 4th.

(If he play 6. Q. to K. R's 3rd, you take K. P. with P., and pursue the attack as in the present case.)

7. R. to K. Kt.'s sq.	7. Kt. to K. B's 4th.
8. R. to Kt.'s 5th.	8. Q. to K. R's 6th.
9. B. takes K. B. P. (ch.)	9. K. takes B.
10. R. to K. R's 5th.	10. Q. to K. Kt.'s 7th.

(He obviously loses his Q. by taking the Rook, or going to Kt.'s 5th with her.)

11. R. takes Kt. (ch.)	11. K. to his sq.

(The German "Handbuch" here makes White, for his 12th move, take P. with R. (ch.), Black interposing his B., and the game is given up as equal; but, I believe, you have an advantage, considering that Black's King has moved, by playing)—

12. R. to K. Kt.'s 5th.	12. Q. to R's 6th (best)
13. R. to K. Kt.'s 3rd.	13. Q. to R's 4th (best)
14. Q. to K's 2nd.	

I prefer your game.

4. P. takes Q. P.	4. P. takes B. P.
5. P. to Q's 4th.	5. B. to K. Kt.'s 5th.

If you play 5. Q. to K's 2nd (ch.), he answers with 5. B. to K's 2nd, and the positions are even.

6. K. Kt. to B's 3rd.

There is no advantage on either side.

GAME THE FOURTH.

WHITE.	BLACK.
1. P. to K's 4th.	1. P. to K's 4th.
2. B. to Q. B's 4th.	2. K. Kt to B's 3rd.
3. K. Kt. to B's 3rd.	3. Kt. takes K. P.

You have also, as was previously observed, beside the present move, and the two moves just examined, the option of playing here 3. Q. Kt. to B's 3rd, by which you may obtain an opening fully equal to your opponent's, as may be briefly shown before proceeding further; suppose then,—

3. Q. Kt. to B's 3rd.	3. K. B. to Q. B's 4th.
4. K. Kt. to B's 3rd.	4. P. to Q's 3rd.

The game is even.

Black's move of 3. Kt. takes K. P. is extolled by Jaenisch and the German " Handbuch," as the veritable mode of play. If instead, he move 3. Q. Kt. to B's 3rd, you have the " Two Knights' Opening," a game very favourable for the first player (see page 142).

4. P. to Q's 3rd.	4. Kt. to Q's 3rd.

For the result of your playing 4. Q. to K's 2nd, see Petroff's defence to the Knight's opening, page 82, where this position occurs. We have there remarked that if, for your 4th move, you take K. P. with Kt., Black replies with 4. P. to Q's 4th, and, when the B. retreats, by moving Q. to K. Kt.'s 4th, he will have the better game. The following variation will show this clearly :—

4. Kt. takes K. P.	4. P. to Q's 4th.
5. B. to Q. Kt.'s 3rd.	5. Q. to K. Kt.'s 4th.
6. Q. to K's 2nd.	6. Q. takes K. Kt. P.

(He may also with advantage take the Kt.)

7. R. to K. B's sq.	7. Q. B. to K's 3rd.
8. P. to Q's 3rd.	8. Kt. to K. B's 3rd.

(If you check with the Q. at Kt.'s 5th, and then capture the Kt. P., Black wins easily by playing Q. B. to K. R's 6th.)

9. Q. B. to K. B's 4th.	9. K. B. to Q's 3rd.
10. Q. Kt. to B's 3rd.	10. Q. Kt. to Q's 2nd.
11. Castles.	11. Kt. takes Kt.
12. B. takes Kt.	12. K. B. takes B.
13. Q. takes B.	13. P. to Q. B's 3rd.
14. R. to K. Kt.'s sq.	14. Q. takes B. P.
15. Q. R. to K. B's sq.	15. Q. to K. R's 5th

| 16. R. takes K. Kt. P. | 16. Q. to K. R's 3rd (ch.) |
| 17. R. to K. Kt.'s 5th. | 17. K. R. to Kt.'s sq. |

Black has an advantage.

Let us now return to the original theme, and proceed from the 4th move.

5. Kt. takes K. P.	5. Kt. takes B.
6. Kt. takes Kt.	6. P. to Q's 4th.
7. Kt. to K's 5th.	7. K. B. to Q's 3rd.
8. P. to Q's 4th.	8. Castles.
9. Castles.	9. P. to K. B's 3rd.
10. Kt. to K. B's 3rd.	

Neither party can boast of advantage.

Chapter III.

COUNTER GAMBIT IN THE KING'S BISHOP'S OPENING.

This ingenious reply to the Bishop's opening, which consists in Black's moving K. B. P. to B's 4th sq. at his 2nd move, first occurs in the valuable games of Greco; it has been subsequently examined by Cozio, Allgaier, Lewis, Jaenisch, who has devoted great attention to it, the German "Handbuch," and the "Chess-Player's Chronicle."

GAME THE FIRST.

WHITE.	BLACK.
1. P. to K's 4th.	1. P. to K's 4th.
2. K. B. to Q. B's 4th.	2. P. to K. B's 4th.

You have now the choice of refusing or accepting the gambit; the former is the more judicious mode of operating, and the consequences arising from it will be shown in this game, while the result of your accepting the gambit shall be considered in the next.

| 3. P. to Q's 3rd. | 3. K. Kt. to B's 3rd. |

This, according to Jaenisch and the German "Handbuch," is your best move for declining the gambit. You may, however, with advantage play 3. P. to Q's 4th, or 3. K. Kt. to B's 3rd, or 3. P. to Q. B's 3rd, as in Variation I.; or 3. K. B. takes Kt., as in Variation II.

| 4. P. to K. B's 4th. | 4. K. P. takes P. |

If instead of this move you play 4. K. Kt. to B's 3rd, Black can answer with 4. P. to Q. B's 3rd, and the game proceed thus:—

4. K. Kt. to B's 3rd.	4. P. to Q. B's 3rd.
5. Castles.	5. Q. to B's 2nd.
6. K. Kt. to his 5th.	6. K. B. to Q. B's 4th.
7. K. to R's sq.	7. P. to K. R's 3rd.
8. Kt. to K. B's 7th.	8. R. to K. B's sq.
9. P. to K. B's 4th.	9. P. to Q's 3rd.

He has the better game.

| 5. Q. B. takes P. | 5. P. takes K. P. |

Black may play 5. P. to Q's 4th, but still the advantage will be with you. (*e. g.*)

	5. P. to Q's 4th.
6. P. takes Q. P.	6. Kt. takes P.
7. Q. to K's 2nd (ch.)	7. Kt. to K's 2nd.
8. K. Kt. to B's 3rd.	

&c., &c.

6. Q. P. takes P.	6. Q. to K's 2nd.
7. P. to K's 5th.	7. P. to Q's 3rd.
8. Q. to K's 2nd.	8. P. takes P.
9. B. takes P.	9. P. to Q. B's 3rd.
10. K. Kt. to B's 3rd.	

You have a better developed opening.

Variation I.,

Beginning at White's 3rd move.

WHITE.	BLACK.
1. P. to K's 4th.	1. P. to K's 4th.
2. K. B. to Q. B's 4th.	2. P. to K. B's 4th.
3. P. to Q's 4th.	3. P. takes Q. P. (best)

Your move of 3. P. to Q's 4th is more attacking than 3. P. to Q's 3rd, and gives you I think an advantage in the opening. At this point you may also adopt 3. P. to Q. B's 3rd or 3. K. Kt. to B's 3rd without danger. In the first place,—

3. P. to Q. B's 3rd.	3. K. Kt. to B's 3rd.
4. P. to Q's 4th.	4. Kt. takes K. P.
5. P. takes K. P.	5. Q. Kt. to B's 3rd.
6. Q. to her 5th.	6. Q. to K's 2nd.

The game is about even.

In the second place,—

3. K. Kt. to B's 3rd.	3. P. to Q. B's 3rd.
4. P. to Q's 4th.	

You have a better opening.

4. Q. takes P.	4. Q. Kt. to B's 3rd.

You may likewise play 4. B. takes Kt., followed by 5. Q. takes P., or, which I think best, 4. B. takes Kt., and then 5. P. takes K. B. P. For example, in the first place,—

4. B. takes Kt.	4. R. takes B.
5. Q. takes P.	5. Q. Kt. to B's 3rd.
6. Q. to her B's 4th.	6. Q. Kt. to K's 2nd.

If he retreat the Rook, you still play

7. Q. Kt. to B's 3rd.

And have, I think, a slight advantage.

In the second place,—

4. B. takes Kt.	4. R. takes B.
5. P. takes K. B. P.	5. Q. to K. B's 3rd.
6. K. Kt. to K's 2nd.	

And again your game appears to me to be safer than his.

5. Q. to K's 3rd.	5. P. takes P.
6. Q. takes P. (ch.)	6. Q. to K's 2nd.

The game is even.

VARIATION II.,

Beginning also at White's 3rd move.

WHITE.	BLACK.
1. P. to K's 4th.	1. P. to K's 4th.
2. K. B. to Q. B's 4th.	2. P. to K. B's 4th.
3. B. takes K. Kt.	3. R. takes B.
4. P. takes P.	4. P. to Q's 4th.

You may here also play 4. Q. Kt. to B's 3rd, and the game proceed thus :—

4. Q. Kt. to B's 3rd.	4. Q. to K. B's 3rd.
5. Q. Kt. to Q's 5th.	5. Q. to her B's 3rd.
6. Q. to R's 5th (ch.)	6. P. to K. Kt.'s 3rd.
7. Q. takes Q. R. P.	7. K. R. to Kt.'s 2nd.
8. Q. to K. R's 4th.	8. Q. takes Q. B. P.
9. Kt. to B's 6th (ch.)	9. K. to his B's 2nd.
10. K. P. takes P.	10. Q. takes P. at K. B's 4th.
11. Kt. to Q's 5th.	

You have the better position.

5. Q. to K. R's 5th (ch.)	5. P. to K. Kt.'s 3rd.

If you play 5. P. to K. Kt.'s 4th, Black will soon get an advantage; for example,—

5. P. to K. Kt.'s 4th.	5. P. to K. R's 4th.
6. P. to K. R's 3rd.	6. P. takes P.
7. P. takes P.	7. P. to K. Kt.'s 3rd.

&c., &c.

| 6. P. takes P. | 6. R. takes P. |
| 7. K. Kt. to B's 3rd. | 7. Q. Kt. to B's 3rd. |

If you take the K. R. P. at your 7th move, he replies with Q. to K. B's 3rd, and has the more favourable game.

Should Black now answer with 7. Q. B. to K. Kt.'s 5th, you pursue the game as follows:—

| | 7. Q. B. to K. Kt.'s 5th. |
| 8. Q. takes K. R. P. | 8. Q. to K. B's 3rd. |

(It would not be good play for him to move 8. R. to K. Kt.'s 2nd.)

9. Q. to K. R's 4th.	9. B. takes Kt.
10. Q. takes Q.	10. R. takes Q.
11. P. takes B.	11. Q. Kt. to B's 3rd.

I prefer your game.

8. Q. takes K. R. P.	8. Q. to K. B's 3rd.
9. P. to Q's 3rd.	9. K. B. to Q. B's 4th.
10. B. to K's 3rd.	10. B. takes B.
11. P. takes B.	11. R. takes K. Kt. P.

The positions are equal.

———

GAME THE SECOND.

WHITE.	BLACK.
1. P. to K's 4th.	1. P. to K's 4th.
2. K. B. to Q. B's 4th.	2. P. to K. B's 4th.
3. P. takes P.	3. K. Kt. to B's 3rd.

Your present 3rd move is less advantageous for you than either of those before examined.

| 4. P. to Q's 4th. | 4. P. takes P. |

You can also play 4. P. to K. Kt.'s 4th, forming a kind of King's gambit, but as the following moves show, you will be unable to sustain the Pawn eventually.

4. P. to K. Kt.'s 4th.	4. P. to Q's 4th.
5. B. to K's 2nd.	5. K. B. to Q. B's 4th.
6. P. to Q's 3rd.	6. P. to K. R's 4th.

(If you move 6. P. to K. Kt.'s 5th. Black may leave his Kt. *en prise*, and take the doubled P. with his Q. B.)

7. P. to K. Kt.'s 5th.	7. Kt. to Kt.'s 5th.
8. B. takes Kt.	8. P. takes B.
9. Q. takes P.	9. Castles.
10. Q. B. to K's 3rd.	10. Q. B. takes P.
11. Q. to K. Kt.'s 3rd.	11. P. to Q's 5th.
12. B. to Q's 2nd.	12. P. to K's 5th.

He has a good game.

5. Q. takes P.	5. P. to Q's 4th.
6. K. B. to Q's 3rd.	6. Q. Kt. to B's 3rd.
7. Q. to K's 3rd (ch.)	7. K. to B's 2nd.
8. K. Kt. to K's 2nd.	8. B. to Q. Kt.'s 5th (ch.)
9. P. to Q. B's 3rd.	9. R. to K's sq.
10. Q. to K. Kt.'s 3rd.	10. K. B. to Q's 3rd.

His game is better developed.

CHAPTER IV.

THE QUEEN'S BISHOP'S PAWN'S DEFENCE IN THE KING'S BISHOP'S OPENING.

WHITE.	BLACK.
1. P. to K's 4th.	1. P. to K's 4th.
2. K. B. to Q. B's 4th.	2. P. to Q. B's 3rd.

This mode of play by Black is not to be commended, as it enables you to develope your men with speed, and consigns his to a long inaction. The chief writers who have treated of this variation are—Cozio (1st vol.), pp. 127, 169, 304; (2nd vol.), pp. 284, 320; Ponziani (1782), p. 80; Philidor (1790), pp. 16, 24, 188, 192; Bertin, p. 45; Lewis (1844), pp. 33—37; Jaenisch (1st vol.), pp. 105—108.

3. Q. to K's 2nd.	3. K. Kt. to B's 3rd.

The move of Q. to K's 2nd is better than 2. P. to Q's 4th, which Philidor recommends; for the latter see the Variation

4. P. to K. B's 4th.	4. P. to Q's 3rd.

If he play 4. B. to Q. B's 4th, you answer with 5. P. takes K. P., and on his taking the K. Kt., you retake B. with R., and have a good position. He may, however, move 4. P. takes B. P., upon which you proceed as follows:—

5. P. to K's 5th.	5. Kt. to Q's 4th.
6. P. to Q's 4th.	6. B. to K's 2nd.
7. B. takes Kt.	7. K. B. to K. R's 5th (ch.)
8. P. to K. Kt.'s 3rd.	8. P. takes P.

9. B. takes K. B. P. (ch.)   9. K. takes B.
10. Q. to K. B's 3rd (ch.) 10. K. to his sq.
11. P. takes P.   11. B. to K's 2nd.

You have an excellent position.

5. P. takes P.	5. P. takes P.
6. K. Kt. to B's 3rd.	6. K. B. to Q's 3rd.
7. P. to Q's 4th.	7. P. takes P.
8. P. to K's 5th.	8. Castles.
9. Castles.	9. K. B. to Q. B's 4th.

If he play 9. K. R. to K's sq., you equally acquire an advantage. For, suppose,—

                    9. K. R. to K's sq.
10. Kt. to his 5th.   10. R. takes P.
11. Kt. takes K. B. P. 11. R. takes Q.
12. Kt. takes Q. (dis. ch.) 12. K. to R's sq.
13. B. takes R.

And you must win.

10. Q. to her 3rd.	10. Kt. to Q's 4th.
11. Kt. to his 5th.	11. P. to K. Kt.'s 3rd.
12. Kt. to K's 4th.	12. B. to K's 2nd.
13. B. takes Kt.	13. P. takes B.
14. Kt. to B's 6th (ch.)	14. B. takes Kt.
15. P. takes B.	

You have a fine game.

VARIATION,

Beginning at White's 3rd move.

WHITE.	BLACK.
1. P. to K's 4th.	1. P. to K's 4th.
2. K. B. to Q. B's 4th.	2. P. to Q. B's 3rd.
3. P. to Q's 4th.	3. K. Kt. to B's 3rd.

K. Kt. to B's 3rd is Black's best move; if he play instead 3. P. to Q's 4th, or 3. P. takes P., the following variations are likely to arise; in the first place,—

                    3. P. to Q's 4th.
4. P. takes Q. P.   4. Q. B. P. takes P.
5. B. checks.   5. B. to Q's 2nd.
6. B. takes B. (ch.) 6. Kt. takes B.
7. P. takes K. P.   7. Kt. takes P.
8. Q. to K's 2nd.   8. Q. to K's 2nd.
9. Q. Kt. to B's 3rd. 9. Castles.
10. Q. B. to K. B's 4th. 10. Kt. to Q. B's 3rd.
11. Castles.

Your game is preferable.

In the second place,—

	3. P. takes P.
4. Q. takes P.	4. P. to Q's 3rd.
5. P. to K. B's 4th.	5. Q. B. to K's 3rd.
6. K. B. to Q's 3rd.	6. P. to Q. B's 4th.
7. Q. to her B's 3rd.	7. Q. Kt. to B's 3rd.
8. K. Kt. to B's 3rd.	8. K. Kt. to B's 3rd.
9. P. to K. B's 5th.	9. Q. B. to Q's ·2nd.
10. Castles.	

Your game is less confined than his.

4. P. takes K. P.   4. Q. to Q. R's 4th (ch.)

Instead of so playing you may proceed thus:—

4. K. Kt. to B's 3rd.	4. P. to Q's 4th.
5. P. takes K. P.	5. Kt. takes K. P.
6. B. to Q's 3rd.	6. P. to K. B's 4th.

The game is even.

5. P. to Q. B's 3rd.	5. Q. takes K. P.
6. B. to Q's 3rd.	6. K. B. to Q. B's 4th.
7. P. to K. B's 4th.	7. Q. to K's 2nd.
8. P. to K's 5th.	

The game is in your favour.

GAMES
ILLUSTRATIVE OF THE PRECEDING ANALYSES.

GAME I.—Between Messrs. Stanley and Rousseau.

WHITE. (Mr. S.)	BLACK. (Mr. R.)
1. P. to K's 4th.	1. P. to K's 4th.
2. K. B. to Q. B's 4th.	2. K. Kt. to B's 3rd.
3. Q. Kt. to B's 3rd.	3. K. B. to Q. B's 4th.
4. K. Kt. to B's 3rd.	4. P. to Q's 3rd.
5. P. to K. R's 3rd.	5. Castles.
6. P. to Q's 3rd.	6. Q. B. to K's 3rd.
7. K. B. to Q. Kt.'s 3rd.	7. Q. Kt. to B's 3rd.
8. Q. Kt. to K's 2nd.	8. Q. to K's 2nd.
9. Q. Kt. to K. Kt.'s 3rd.	9. Q. Kt. to Q's 5th.
10. Kt. takes Kt.	10. B. takes Kt.
11. P. to Q. B's 3rd.*	11. B. to Q. Kt.'s 3rd.
12. Castles.	12. P. to Q's 4th.†
13. Q. B. to K. Kt.'s 5th.	13. P. to Q. B's 3rd.

---

* White gains a move by this exchange of Pieces.
† P. to K. R's 3rd would have been better play.

14. Kt. to K. R's 5th.	14. P. takes K. P.
15. P. takes P.	15. B. takes B.
16. Q. to K. B's 3rd.*	16. Q. B. to his 5th.
17. B. takes Kt.	17. Q. to K's 3rd.
18. Kt. takes K. Kt. P.	18. Q. B. to K's 7th.
19. Kt. takes Q.	19. B. takes Q.
20. Kt. takes R.	

Black surrenders.

GAME II.—Between Messrs. Horwitz and Schulten.

WHITE. (Mr. S.)	BLACK. (Mr. H.)
1. P. to K's 4th.	1. P. to K's 4th.
2. K. B. to Q. B's 4th.	2. K. Kt. to B's 3rd.
3. Q. Kt. to B's 3rd.	3. P. to Q. Kt.'s 4th.
4. B. takes Kt. P.	4. B. to Q. B's 4th.
5. P. to Q's 3rd.	5. P. to Q. B's 3rd.
6. B. to Q. B's 4th.	6. Q. to her Kt.'s 3rd.
7. Q. to K's 2nd.	7. P. to Q's 4th.
8. P. takes P.	8. Castles.
9. Q. Kt. to K's 4th.	9. Kt. takes Kt.
10. P. takes Kt.	10. B. takes K. B. P. (ch.)†
11. Q. takes B.	11. Q. to Kt.'s 5th (ch.)
12. Q. B. to Q's 2nd.	12. Q. takes K. B.
13. Q. to K. B's 3rd.	13. P. to K. B's 4th.
14. P. takes K. B. P.	14. B. takes P.
15. Q. to her Kt.'s 3rd.	

And Black mated by force in three moves.‡

GAME III.—Between Messrs. Horwitz and Kieseritzky.

WHITE. (M. K.)	BLACK. (Mr. H.)
1. P. to K's 4th.	1. P. to K's 4th.
2. K. B. to Q. B's 4th.	2. K. Kt. to B's 3rd.
3. K. Kt. to B's 3rd.	3. Kt. takes P.
4. P. to Q's 3rd.	4. K. Kt. to K. B's 3rd.
5. K. Kt. takes P.	5. P. to Q's 4th.
6. Q. to K's 2nd.	6. Q. B. to K's 3rd.
7. K. B. to Q. Kt.'s 3rd.	7. K. B. to Q's 3rd.
8. P. to K. B's 4th.	8. Castles.

* This is very finely played, and is an example to young players of the importance of gaining time at chess. Had White paused in his attack to recover the lost Bishop, the adversary might have succeeded in dislodging one or other of the Pieces by which he is beleaguered, or in bringing his own forces to the rescue, and then have ultimately retrieved the game.

† Black plays capitally now to the end.

‡ It is rarely in actual play one sees so pretty a mate.

9. Castles.	9. Q. Kt. to Q's 2nd.
10. Q. Kt. to Q. B's 3rd.	10. K. B. to Q. B's 4th (ch.)
11. K. to R's sq.	11. Q. Kt. takes Kt.
12. P. takes Kt.	12. Kt. to K. Kt.'s 5th.
13. Q. B. to K. B's 4th.	13. P. to Q. B's 3rd.
14. Q. Kt. to K's 4th.*	14. Q. P. takes Kt.
15. K. B. takes Q. B.	15. K. Kt. to K. B's 7th (ch.)
16. R. takes Kt.	16. K. B. takes R.
17. K. B. to Q. Kt.'s 3rd.	17. Q. to her 5th.†
18. Q. R. to K. B's sq.	18. P. to K's 6th.
19. P. to K. Kt.'s 3rd.	19. Q. R. to Q's sq.
20. Q. B. to K. Kt.'s 5th.	20. Q. R. to Q's 2nd.
21. K. P. to K's 6th.	21. P. takes P.
22. B. takes P. (ch.)	22. K. to R's sq.
23. Q. takes K. P.‡	23. Q. takes Q.
24. B. takes Q.	24. Q. R. to K's 2nd.
25. Q. B. to Q. B's 5th.	25. Q. R. takes K. B.
26. B. takes K. R.	26. R. to K's 7th.
27. K. to Kt.'s 2nd.	27. B. to Q's 5th (ch.)
28. K. to R's 3rd.	28. R. takes Q. B. P.
29. B. to Q. R's 3rd.	29. P. to K. R's 3rd.
30. K. to Kt.'s 4th.	30. B. takes Q. Kt. P.
31. B. to Q's 6th.	31. B. to K. B's 3rd.
32. P. to K. R's 4th.	32. R. takes Q. R. P.
33. K. to K. B's 5th.	33. K. to K. R's 2nd.
34. K. to K's 6th.	34. R. to Q's 7th.
35. R. to K. B's 3rd.	35. P. to Q. R's 4th.
36. K. to Q's 7th.	36. R. to Q. B's 7th.
37. P. to Q's 4th.	37. B. takes P.

And White resigns.

GAME IV.—Between Dr. Bledow and Von Bilguer.

WHITE. (Dr. B.)	BLACK. (V. B.)
1. P. to K's 4th.	1. P. to K's 4th.
2. K. B. to Q. B's 4th.	2. P. to K. B's 4th.
3. P. to Q's 3rd.	3. K. Kt. to B's 3rd.
4. K. Kt. to B's 3rd.	4. P. takes K. P.
5. P. takes P.	5. Kt. takes P.
6. Q. to her 5th.	6. Kt. to Q's 3rd.
7. Kt. takes K. P.	7. P. to Q. B's 3rd.
8. Q. to K. B's 7th.	8. Kt. takes Q.
9. B. takes Kt. (ch.)	9. K. to his 2nd.

---

* This is pretty, but not sound.

† A good move. If White play P. to Q. B's 3rd, Black takes Q. P. with P.

‡ He would have been mated in two moves, on taking the R. with his B.

10. Q. B. to K. Kt.'s 5th (ch.)	10. K. to Q's 3rd.
11. B. takes Q.	11. K. takes Kt.
12. P. to K. B's 4th (ch.)	12. K. to his B's 4th.
13. Q. B. to K. Kt.'s 5th.	13. K. B. checks.
14. P. to Q. B's 3rd.	14. K. R. to B's sq.
15. K. B. to Q. Kt.'s 3rd.	15. P. to K. R's 3rd
16. K. B. to Q. B's 2nd (ch.)	16. K. to Kt.'s 5th.
17. K. B. to Q's sq. (ch.)	17. K. to B's 4th.
18. P. to K. Kt.'s 4th (ch.)	18. K. to Kt.'s 3rd.
19. B. to Q. B's 2nd (ch.)	19. K. to B's 2nd.
20. Q. B. to K. R's 4th.	20. K. B. to K's 2nd.
21. Q. B. to K. Kt.'s 3rd.	21. P. to Q's 4th.
22. P. to K. B's 5th.	22. Kt. to Q's 2nd.
23. Kt. to Q's 2nd.	23. K. B. to his 3rd.
24. Kt. to K. B's 3rd.	24. R. to K's sq. (ch.)
25. K. to his B's 2nd.	25. Kt. to Q. B's 4th.
26. K. R. to K's sq.	26. Q. B. to Q's 2nd.
27. P. to Q. Kt.'s 4th.	27. Kt. to K's 5th (ch.)
28. R. takes Kt.*	28. P. takes R.
29. B. to Q. Kt.'s 3rd (ch.)	29. K. to B's sq.
30. B. to Q's 6th (ch.)	30. B. to K's 2nd.
31. Kt. to K's 5th.	31. P. to K. Kt.'s 4th.†
32. P. to K. B's 6th.‡	32. P. to K's 6th (ch.)
33. K. to Kt.'s sq.	

Black resigns.

GAME V.—Between V. H. der Laza and a Member of the Berlin Chess Club.

WHITE. (Mr. —)	BLACK. (V. H. d. L.)
1. P. to K's 4th.	1. P. to K's 4th.
2. B. to Q. B's 4th.	2. P. to K. B's 4th.
3. B. takes K. Kt.	3. R. takes B.
4. P. takes P.	4. P. to Q's 4th.
5. Q. to K. R's 5th (ch.)	5. P. to K. Kt.'s 3rd.
6. P. takes P.	6. R. takes P.
7. P. to K. R's 3rd.	7. Q. to K. B's 3rd.
8. K. Kt. to B's 3rd.	8. Q. Kt. to B's 3rd.
9. Q. Kt. to B's 3rd.	9. Q. B. to K's 3rd.
10. K. Kt. to R's 4th.	10. Q. Kt. to Q's 5th.
11. Kt. takes R.	11. Kt. takes Q. B. P. (ch.)
12. K. to Q's sq.	12. P. takes Kt.
13. Q. to K. R's 7th.	13. Kt. takes Q. R.

---

* The terminating moves are admirably played by Dr. Bledow.

† It is quite evident that on taking the B., mate would have followed next move.

‡ Beautifully played.

14. Q. takes Q. B. P.
15. Q. takes Q. Kt. P.
16. Kt. to Q. Kt.'s 5th.
17. K. to K's 2nd.
18. K. to Q's sq.
19. Q. to her B's 6th.
20. Kt. to B's 7th (ch.)
21. Kt. to Q. Kt.'s 5th.
22. R. to K's sq.
23. K. to K's 2nd.

14. Q. to K. B's 4th.
15. R. to Q's sq.
16. Q. to Q. B's 7th (ch.)
17. Q. to K's 5th (ch.)
18. R. to Q's 2nd.
19. Q. B. to K. B's 4th.
20. K. to B's 2nd.
21. Q. takes K. Kt. P.
22. Q. B. to his 7th (ch.)*
23. Q. to K's 5th (ch.)

And Black wins.

GAME VI.—Played between two Amateurs of the London Chess Club.

WHITE.

1. P. to K's 4th.
2. B. to Q. B's 4th.
3. Q. to K's 2nd.
4. P. to Q. B's 3rd.
5. P. to K. B's 4th.
6. P. to K. B's 5th.
7. P. takes P.
8. B. checks.
9. B. takes B. (ch.)
10. P. to Q's 4th.
11. K. Kt. to R's 3rd.
12. Castles.
13. Kt. to K. B's 4th.
14. Q. to K. B's 2nd.
15. Q. to K's 2nd.
16. Kt. takes Q. P.
17. K. to R's sq.
18. Q. takes K. P.
19. Q. to K. B's 3rd.
20. B. to K. Kt.'s 5th.
21. B. to Q's 2nd.
22. Q. Kt. to R's 3rd.
23. Q. Kt. to Q. B's 4th.
24. Q. Kt. takes P.
25. P. to Q. B's 4th.
26. K. Kt. to Q. Kt.'s 6th (ch.)
27. Q. takes P.

BLACK.

1. P. to K's 4th.
2. P. to Q. B's 3rd.
3. Q. to Q. B's 2nd.
4. K. Kt. to B's 3rd.
5. P. to Q's 3rd.
6. P. to Q's 4th.
7. P. takes P.
8. B. to Q's 2nd.
9. Q. Kt. takes B.
10. P. to K's 5th.
11. Castles.
12. B. to Q's 3rd.
13. P. to K. R's 3rd.
14. K. Kt. to his 5th.
15. P. to K. R's 4th.
16. B. takes K. R. P. (ch.)
17. Q. to her 3rd.
18. K. R. to K's sq.
19. P. to K. Kt.'s 3rd.
20. P. to K. B's 3rd.
21. P. to K. Kt.'s 4th.
22. P. to Q. R's 4th.
23. Q. to her B's 3rd.
24. Q. to Kt.'s 4th.
25. Q. to R's 5th.
26. Kt. takes Kt.

Mate.

---

* Q. to K. B's 6th (ch.), followed by B. to B's 7th, would have been more expeditious

CHAPTER V.

QUEEN'S BISHOP'S PAWN'S OPENING,

Is the designation given, in this country, to the opening wherein, after both players have moved their King's Pawn to K's 4th sq., White, instead of bringing out a Piece, prepares at once to occupy, with his Pawns, the centre of the board. This mode of commencing the battle was probably a favourite in the earlier days of European chess play, as Ruy Lopez has devoted more than ordinary space and attention to it in his often-quoted work of the sixteenth century. It is noticed also by Allgaier, Stamma, and Philidor, and to its condemnation by the latter, we are, perhaps, indebted for the elaborate analysis it has undergone by the celebrated Italian school, and which proves that, although this mode of beginning the game affords but few opportunities for striking or intricate combinations, it may be adopted with perfect safety. The leading works which treat of the Q. B. P's opening, besides the authors before-named, are—Ponziani (1782), pp. 85, 86, 98; Sarratt (1808), pp. 1, 72—76, 90; Lewis (1844), pp. 259 —270; Jaenisch (vol. i.), pp. 94—101; the German " Handbuch," and the " Chess-Player's Chronicle."

GAME THE FIRST,

WHITE.	BLACK.
1. P. to K's 4th.	1. P. to K's 4th.
2. P. to Q. B's 3rd.	2. P. to Q's 4th (best)

It was this reply of Black's which induced both Allgaier and Philidor to decry the opening as bad for White; but subsequent examination has shown that, despite this formidable counter-move, he may pursue the game without disadvantage. If Black, instead of 2. P. to Q's 4th, play the move given by earlier writers, viz., 2. K. Kt. to B's 3rd, the positions, in a few moves, would be equal. (See the next game.) He may also play 2. P. to K. B's 4th, but with still less benefit to his game, or 2. K. B. to Q. B's 4th, in which case the game would shortly resolve itself into some position, before examined, in the King's Knight's opening.

3. K. Kt. to B's 3rd.	3. P. takes K. P.

He can also play with safety 3. K. Kt. to B's 3rd. (See the

Variation.) Your third move we owe to Del Rio. Philidor
gives 3. P. takes P., which is much inferior. (*e. g.*)

3. P. takes P.	3. Q. takes P.
4. P. to Q's 4th.	4. Q. Kt. to B's 3rd.
5. Q. B. to K's 3rd.	5. Q. B. to K. B's 4th.
6. P. to Q. B's 4th.	6. Q. to her R's 4th (ch.)
7. B. to Q's 2nd.	7. Q. to her Kt.'s 3rd.
8. P. takes P.	8. Q. Kt. to Q's 5th.

He has a capital attack.

4. Kt. takes K. P.	4. K. B. to Q's 3rd.

Del Rio advises, for your 4th move, Q. to Q. R's 4th (ch.),
and supposes it would give you the superiority; but in this
he errs, as the subjoined variation will show.

4. Q. to her R's 4th (ch.)	4. P. to Q. B's 3rd.
5. Q. takes K. P.	5. K. B. to Q's 3rd.
6. K. B. to Q. B's 4th.	6. K. Kt. to B's 3rd.

(If you move 6. P. to Q's 4th, he plays 6. P. to K. B's 4th with
advantage.)

7. Q. to K's 2nd.	7. P. to K's 5th.
8. P. to Q's 3rd.	8. Castles.
9. P. takes P.	9. Kt. takes P.
10. Q. B. to K's 3rd.	10. Q. B. to K. B's 4th.

The game is even.

5. Kt. to Q. B's 4th.	5. Q. B. to K's 3rd.

If you check with your Q. at the 5th move, and then take
the K. P., Black first interposes the Q. B. P., and afterwards moves Q. to K's 2nd.

6. P. to Q's 4th.	6. P. takes P. in pass-
7. B. takes P.	ing.

The positions are equal.

VARIATION,

Beginning at Black's 3rd move.

3. K. Kt. to B's 3rd.

This move is given by Jaenisch, who thought it a novelty, but
it had previously occurred in the games between Mr. Cochrane and the writer.

4. P. to Q's 4th.	4. Kt. takes P.

You can also without danger, I think, take K. P. with Kt.,
instead of playing 4. P. to Q's 4th.

5. Kt. takes P.	5. K. B. to Q's 3rd.
6. K. Kt. to Q's 3rd.	6. P. to Q. B's 4th.
7. P. takes P.	7. Kt. takes P.
8. Q. B. to K's 3rd.	8. Kt. takes Kt. (ch.)
9. B. takes Kt.	9. Q. Kt. to B's 3rd.
10. Castles.	10. Castles.

Neither party has the advantage.

GAME THE SECOND.

WHITE.	BLACK.
1. P. to K's 4th.	1. P. to K's 4th.
2. P. to Q. B's 3rd.	2. K. Kt. to B's 3rd.
3. P. to Q's 4th.	3. K. Kt. takes K. P.

You may also play 3. P. to K. B's 4th, upon which he should take K. P. with Kt., and the game in a few moves will be equal. If Black, for his 3rd move, take P. with P., you push on the K. P., and then take P. with P.

4. Q. P. takes P.	4. P. to Q's 4th (best)

If he move 4. B. to Q. B's 4th, you play 5. Q. to K. Kt.'s 4th, and have an immediate advantage.

5. Q. B. to K's 3rd.

The game is quite even.

GAMES
ILLUSTRATIVE OF THE QUEEN'S BISHOP'S PAWN'S OPENING.

GAME I.—Between Capt. Evans and an Amateur.

WHITE. (Capt. E.)	BLACK. (Mr. P.)
1. P. to K's 4th.	1. P. to K's 4th.
2. P. to Q. B's 3rd.	2. K. Kt. to B's 3rd.
3. P. to Q's 4th.	3. P. takes P.
4. P. to K's 5th.	4. Kt. to K's 5th.
5. Q. to K's 2nd.	5. Kt. to his 4th.
6. P. takes P.	6. B. to Q. Kt.'s 5th (ch.)
7. Q. Kt. to B's 3rd.	7. Q. Kt. to B's 3rd.
8. Q. to her 3rd.	8. P. to Q's 4th.
9. P. to K. B's 4th.	9. Kt. to K's 5th.
10. K. Kt. to B's 3rd.	10. Q. B. to K. B's 4th.
11. Q. to K's 3rd.	11. Castles.

12. P. to Q. R's 3rd.	12. B. to Q. R's 4th.
13. P. to Q. Kt.'s 4th.	13. B. to Q. Kt.'s 3rd.
14. Q. B. to Kt.'s 2nd.	14. Q. B. to Kt.'s 5th.
15. Q. Kt. to Q. R's 4th.	15. B. takes K. Kt.
16. Q. Kt. takes B.	16. B. takes K. Kt. P.
17. B. takes B.	17. Q. to K. R's 5th (ch.)
18. K. to his 2nd.	18. Q. R. P. takes Kt.
19. B. takes Kt.	19. P. takes B.
20. Q. takes P.	20. Q. to Kt.'s 5th (ch.)
21. Q. to K. B's 3rd.	21. Q. to K. B's 4th.
22. Q. R. to Q. B's sq.	22. Q. Kt. takes Q. Kt. P.
23. K. R. to K. Kt.'s sq.*	23. Q. Kt. to B's 3rd.
24. K. R. to Kt.'s 5th.	24. Q. to her 2nd.
25. P. to Q's 5th.	25. Kt. to K's 2nd.
26. K. R. takes K. Kt. P. (ch.)	26. K. to R's sq.
27. Q. to her 3rd.	27. Kt. to K. Kt.'s 3rd.
28. R. takes Kt.	28. Q. R. to K's sq.
29. K. to B's 2nd.†	29. R. to K's 3rd.
30. R. to K. Kt.'s 3rd.	30. R. to Q's sq.
31. P. takes R.	31. Q. to K's 2nd.‡
32. P. takes P.	

Black surrenders.

———

GAME II.—Between Messrs. Cochrane and Staunton.

WHITE. (Mr. S.)	BLACK. (Mr. C.)
1. P. to K's 4th.	1. P. to K's 4th.
2. P. to Q. B's 3rd.	2. P. to Q's 4th.
3. K. Kt. to B's 3rd.	3. K. Kt. to B's 3rd.
4. K. Kt. takes P.	4. K. Kt. takes P.
5. P. to Q's 4th.	5. K. B. to Q's 3rd.
6. Q. Kt. to Q's 2nd.	6. Castles.
7. Q. Kt. takes K. Kt.	7. P. takes Kt.
8. Q. B. to K. B's 4th.	8. B. takes Kt.
9. Q. B. takes B.	9. Q. Kt. to B's 3rd.
10. K. B. to Q. B's 4th.	10. Q. B. to K's 3rd.
11. K. B. to Q. Kt.'s 5th.	11. Q. Kt. to K's 2nd.
12. Castles.	12. P. to Q. B's 3rd.
13. K. B. to Q. R's 4th.	13. Q. Kt. to K. Kt.'s 3rd.
14. Q. B. to K. Kt.'s 3rd.	14. P. to K. B's 4th.
15. P. to K. B's 4th.	15. P. takes P. in passing.

———

* Black played ingeniously in offering to give up the Kt If White had taken it, he must have been subjected to an embarrassing attack for some little time.

† Had he played on the P. (dis. ch.), he could not take the Q. until his King was removed.

‡ Taking the Q. would have been fatal to him.

WHITE	BLACK
16. R. takes P.	16. P. to K. B's 5th.
17. K. B. to Q. Kt.'s 3rd.*	17. Q. to her 3rd.
18. Q. B. to K. B's 2nd.	18. K. to R's sq.
19. K. B. takes B.	19. Q. takes B.
20. Q. to her 3rd.	20. Q. R. to K's sq.
21. K. R. to K. R's 3rd.	21. Q. to K. B's 4th.
22. Q. to K. B's 3rd.	22. Q. R. to K's 5th.
23. K. R. to his 5th.	23. Q. to K's 3rd.
24. P. to Q. B's 4th.	24. K. R. to K's sq.
25. P. to Q. Kt.'s 3rd.	25. Q. to K. B's 3rd.
26. Q. R. to K. B's sq.	26. Q. R. to K's 7th.
27. P. to Q. R's 4th.	27. Q. R. to his 7th.
28. P. to Q's 5th.	28. Q. R. to his 8th.
29. Q. B. takes Q. R. P.†	29. K. R. to K's 8th.
30. R. takes R.	30. R. takes R. (ch.)
31. K. to B's 2nd.	31. Q. to her R's 8th.‡
32. Q. to her 3rd.	32. R. to K. Kt.'s 8th.
33. Q. to K's 2nd.	33. Kt. to K's 2nd.
34. P. to Q's 6th.	

And wins.

GAME III.—Between Capt. Evans and M. St. Amant.

WHITE. (Capt. E.)	BLACK. (M. St. A.)
1. P. to K's 4th.	1. P. to K's 4th.
2. P. to Q. B's 3rd.	2. P. to Q. B's 4th.
3. K. Kt. to B's 3rd.	3. Q. Kt. to B's 3rd.
4. K. B. to Q. B's 4th.	4. K. Kt. to B's 3rd.
5. P. to Q's 4th.	5. Q. B. P. takes P.
6. K. Kt. to Kt.'s 5th.§	6. P. to Q's 4th.
7. P. takes P.	7. K. Kt. takes P.
8. K. Kt. takes K. B. P.	8. K. takes Kt.
9. Q. to K. B's 3rd (ch.)	9. K. to his 3rd.
10. Castles.	10. Q. Kt. to R's 4th.
11. Q. B. to K. Kt.'s 5th.	11. Q. to her 3rd.
12. P. to K. Kt.'s 4th.‖	12. Q. to her 2nd.
13. K. B. to Q's 3rd.	13. Q. to K. B's 2nd.
14. B. to K. B's 4th (ch.)	14. K. to Q's 3rd.
15. P. takes Q. P.	15. Q. B. takes B.
16. P. takes P. (ch.)	16. K. takes P.

---

* But for this move of resource, Black would evidently have gained "the exchange" at least.

† An important outlet for his King.

‡ Black has now a very menacing position.

§ We have here a position almost identical with the leading one of the "Two Knights' Game."

‖ White plays extremely well in this game.

17. P. takes B.	17. Q. Kt. to B's 3rd.
18. K. R. to K's sq. (ch.)	18. K. to Q's 3rd.
19. R. to K's 6th (ch.)	19. K. to Q. B's 4th.
20. Q. B. to K's 3rd (ch.)	20. K. Kt. takes B.
21. Q. takes K. Kt. (ch.)	21. K. to Kt.'s 4th.
22. Q. to her 3rd (ch.)	22. K. to Kt.'s 3rd.
23. Q. to her Kt.'s 3rd (ch.)	23. K. to B's 2nd.
24. R. takes Kt. (ch.), and wins.	

————

GAME IV.—Between M. St. Amant and Mr. G. Walker.

WHITE. (Mr. W.)	BLACK. (M. St. A.)
1. P. to K's 4th.	1. P. to K's 4th.
2. P. to Q. B's 3rd.	2. P. to Q's 4th.
3. P. takes P.	3. Q. takes P.
4. K. Kt. to B's 3rd.	4. K. B. to Q. B's 4th.
5. P. to Q. Kt.'s 3rd.	5. Q. B. to K. Kt.'s 5th.
6. K. B. to K's 2nd.	6. P. to K's 5th.
7. Kt. to Q's 4th.	7. B. takes B.
8. Kt. takes B.	8. Q. Kt. to B's 3rd.
9. Castles.	9. Q. Kt. to K's 4th.
10. Kt. to K. B's 4th.	10. Q. to her 3rd.
11. P. to Q's 4th.	11. P. takes P. in passing.
12. K. R. to K's sq.	12. Castles.
13. Q. Kt. to Q's 2nd.	13. P. to K. B's 4th.
14. P. to Q. R's 4th.	14. P. to Q. R's 4th.
15. P. to Q. Kt.'s 4th.	15. P. takes P.
16. P. takes P.	16. B. to Q's 5th.
17. Q. R. to Kt.'s sq.	17. K. Kt. to B's 3rd.
18. Kt. to Q. Kt.'s 3rd.	18. K. Kt. to Kt.'s 5th.
19. Kt. takes B.	19. Q. takes Kt.
20. B. to K's 3rd.	20. Q. to her 3rd.
21. B. to Q. B's 5th.	21. Q. to K. R's 3rd.
22. Kt. to K. R's 3rd.	22. K. R. to K's sq.
23. P. to Q. R's 5th.	23. P. to Q's 7th.
24. R. to K. B's sq.	24. Kt. to Q's 6th.
25. P. to Q. R's 6th.	25. P. takes P.
26. Q. to K. B's 3rd.	26. K. R. to K's 5th.
27. Q. takes P. (ch.)	27. Q. to K's 3rd.
28. Q. takes Q. (ch.)	28. R. takes Q.
29. Kt. to K. Kt.'s 5th.	29. R. to K's 8th.
30. B. to K's 3rd.	30. Kt. takes B.
31. P. takes Kt.	31. R. takes R. (ch.)
32. K. takes R.	32. Kt. to Q. B's 8th.

And Black wins.

END OF BOOK III.

SYNOPSIS OF BOOK IV.

THE KING'S GAMBIT,

1. $\dfrac{\text{P. to K's 4th.}}{\text{P. to K's 4th.}}$ 2. $\dfrac{\text{P. to K. B's 4th.}}{\text{P. takes P.}}$

WITH ITS VARIOUS MODIFICATIONS, VIZ.:—

THE KING'S KNIGHT'S GAMBIT,

1. $\dfrac{\text{P. to K's 4th.}}{\text{P. to K's 4th.}}$ 2. $\dfrac{\text{P. to K. B's 4th.}}{\text{P. takes P.}}$ 3. $\dfrac{\text{K. Kt. to B's 3rd.}}{}$

WHICH INCLUDES:—

THE CUNNINGHAM GAMBIT:—

1. $\dfrac{\text{P. to K's 4th.}}{\text{P. to K's 4th.}}$ 2. $\dfrac{\text{P. to K. B's 4th.}}{\text{P. takes P.}}$ 3. $\dfrac{\text{K. Kt. to B's 3rd.}}{\text{B. to K's 2nd.}}$

THE SALVIO AND COCHRANE GAMBITS:—

1. $\dfrac{\text{P. to K's 4th.}}{\text{P. to K's 4th.}}$ 2. $\dfrac{\text{P. to K. B's 4th.}}{\text{P. takes P.}}$ 3. $\dfrac{\text{K. Kt. to B's 3rd.}}{\text{P. to K. Kt.'s 4th.}}$

4. $\dfrac{\text{K. B. to Q. B's 4th.}}{\text{P. to K. Kt.'s 5th.}}$ 5. $\dfrac{\text{K. Kt. to K's 5th.}}{\text{Q. checks.}}$

6. $\dfrac{\text{K. to B's sq.}}{\text{K. Kt. to B's or R's 3rd.}}$ SALVIO, or 6. $\dfrac{\text{K. to B's sq.}}{\text{P. to K. B's 6th.}}$ COCHRANE.

THE MUZIO GAMBIT:—

1. $\dfrac{\text{P. to K's 4th.}}{\text{P. to K's 4th.}}$ 2. $\dfrac{\text{P. to K. B's 4th.}}{\text{P. takes P.}}$ 3. $\dfrac{\text{K. Kt. to B's 3rd.}}{\text{P. to K. Kt.'s 4th.}}$

4. $\dfrac{\text{K. B. to Q. B's 4th.}}{\text{P. to K. Kt.'s 5th.}}$ 5. $\dfrac{\text{Castles.}}{\text{P. takes Kt.}}$ or 5. $\dfrac{\text{P. to Q's 4th.}}{\text{P. takes Kt.}}$

THE ALLGAIER GAMBIT:—

1. $\dfrac{\text{P. to K's 4th.}}{\text{P. to K's 4th.}}$ 2. $\dfrac{\text{P. to K. B's 4th.}}{\text{P. takes P.}}$ 3. $\dfrac{\text{K. Kt. to B's 3rd.}}{\text{P. to K. Kt.'s 4th.}}$

4. $\dfrac{\text{P. to K. R's 4th.}}{}$

THE KING'S ROOK'S PAWN GAMBIT:—

1. $\dfrac{\text{P. to K's 4th.}}{\text{P. to K's 4th.}}$ 2. $\dfrac{\text{P. to K. B's 4th.}}{\text{P. takes P.}}$ 3. $\dfrac{\text{P. to K. R's 4th.}}{}$

THE KING'S BISHOP'S GAMBIT:—

1. $\dfrac{\text{P. to K's 4th.}}{\text{P. to K's 4th.}}$ 2. $\dfrac{\text{P. to K. B's 4th.}}{\text{P. takes P.}}$ 3. $\dfrac{\text{K. B. to Q. B's 4th.}}{}$

AND

THE GAMBIT DECLINED.

BOOK IV.

The King's Gambit.

CHAPTER I.

THIS admirable opening, in which is comprehended every variety of the game, beginning with 1. $\frac{\text{P to K's 4th}}{\text{P. to K's 4th}}$, 2. $\frac{\text{P. to K. B's 4th}}{}$, gives birth to the most intricate and beautiful combinations of which the chess-men are susceptible, and their investigation will afford you an inexhaustible fund of entertainment and instruction. To render the examination of them as intelligible as our limited space and somewhat cumbersome notation will admit, it may be well to classify the ramifications of this gambit under different heads. For this purpose I propose to divide the variations into four separate sections. The 1st will contain the manifold *débuts* which spring from THE KING'S GAMBIT PROPER, or KING'S KNIGHT'S GAMBIT, as it is sometimes called, 1. $\frac{\text{P. to K's 4th}}{\text{P. to K's 4th}}$, 2. $\frac{\text{P. to K. B's 4th}}{\text{P. takes P.}}$, 3. $\frac{\text{K. Kt. to B's 3rd}}{}$. The 2nd will treat of the modification of this opening which is generally known as THE ALLGAIER GAMBIT, 1. $\frac{\text{P. to K's 4th}}{\text{P. to K's 4th}}$, 2. $\frac{\text{P. to K. B's 4th}}{\text{P. takes P.}}$, 3. $\frac{\text{K. Kt. to B's 3rd}}{\text{P. to K. Kt.'s 4th}}$, 4. $\frac{\text{P. to K. R's 4th}}{}$, including also an attack called THE KING'S ROOK'S PAWN GAMBIT, 1. $\frac{\text{P. to K's 4th}}{\text{P. to K's 4th}}$, 2. $\frac{\text{P. to K. B's 4th}}{\text{P. takes P.}}$, 3. $\frac{\text{P. to K. R's 4th}}{}$. The 3rd will embrace the varied methods of attack and defence in the favourite KING'S BISHOP'S GAMBIT, 1. $\frac{\text{P. to K's 4th}}{\text{P. to K's 4th}}$, 2. $\frac{\text{P. to K. B's 4th}}{\text{P. takes P.}}$, 3. $\frac{\text{K. B. to Q. B's 4th}}{}$; and the 4th will be devoted to the undefinable class of moves which the second player may adopt in refusing the gambit.

GAME THE FIRST.

WHITE.	BLACK.
1. P. to K's 4th.	1. P. to K's 4th.
2. P. to K. B's 4th.	2. P. takes P.
3. K. Kt. to B's 3rd.	3. P. to K. Kt.'s 4th.

Black's third move is considered the best he can adopt after he has accepted the gambit; but he has other modes of play, which, if not equally satisfactory, may be made without disadvantage; for instance, he can play 3. P. to Q's 4th, or 3. P. to K. B's 4th, and obtain an even game. (For 3. B. to K's 2nd, see Chapter II., THE CUNNINGHAM GAMBIT.) In the first place,—

	3. P. to Q's 4th.
4. P. takes P.	4. K. B. to Q's 3rd.

(If he play 4. P. to K. Kt.'s 4th, you answer with 5. K. B. to Q. B's 4th.)

5. P. to Q's 4th.	5. P. to K. Kt.'s 4th.
6. P. to Q. B's 4th.	6. P. to Q. B's 3rd.
7. K. B. to Q's 3rd.	

The game is equal.

In the second place,—

	3. P. to K. B's 4th.
4. P. takes P.	4. P. to Q's 4th.
5. P. to Q's 4th.	5. Q. B. takes P.
6. Q. B. takes P.	6. K. Kt. to B's 3rd.

Even game.

4. K. B. to Q. B's 4th.	4. B. to K. Kt.'s 2nd (best)

In Victor Käfer's "Complete Guide to the Game of Chess," (Grätz, 1842,) the move of 4. P. to Q. B's 3rd is recommended in place of 4. K. B. to Q. B's 4th; but if Black reply with 4. K. B. to K. Kt.'s 2nd, you appear to gain nothing. (For the consequences of 4. P. to K. R's 4th, see THE ALLGAIER GAMBIT.) At the present stage of our game Black has a variety of moves at command. He may play 4. P. to K. B's 3rd, which is obviously bad, on account of 5. Kt. takes Kt. P., &c. He may also play 4. P. to Q's 3rd, but without benefit, or 4. P. to K. Kt.'s 5th, the result of which will be shown in Chapters III. and IV., THE SALVIO and COCHRANE GAMBITS, and Chapter V., THE MUZIO GAMBIT. If, instead of any one of these, he prefer 4. P. to K. R's 3rd, the game will probably be carried on as follows:—

	4. P. to K. R's 3rd.
5. Kt. to K's 5th.	5. K. R. to his 2nd.
6. P. to Q's 4th.	6. P. to Q's 3rd.

(If he play 6. Q. to K's 2nd, you can move 7. Q. to her 3rd.)

7. Kt. takes K. B. P.	7. R. takes Kt.
8. B. takes R. (ch.)	8. K. takes B.
9. P. to K. R's 4th.	9. K. Kt. to B's 3rd (best)
10. P. takes P.	10. P. takes P.
11. P. to K. Kt.'s 3rd.	11. Q. B. to K. Kt.'s 5th.
12. Q. to her 3rd.	12. Q. to K's 2nd.

Your attack will hardly compensate for the lost Piece. It would have been safer, therefore, to return the Kt. to Q's 3rd on your 7th move.

| 5. P. to Q's 4th. | 5. P. to Q's 3rd. |

It is of very little importance whether you castle at the 5th move (see Game the Third), and then play 6. P. to Q's 4th, or move as in the text, and afterwards castle. As is observed in the German "Handbuch," "the transposition of moves here produces the same result." You can, however, at this stage commence an interesting variation by playing 5. P. to K. R's 4th (see Game the Second). If you move instead 5. P. to Q. B's 3rd, Black may answer with 5. P. to K. Kt.'s 5th, and have the better game. In place of replying to your move 5. P. to Q's 4th with 5. P. to Q's 3rd, he may play 5. P. to K. R's 3rd safely, or 5. P. to K. Kt.'s 5th, but the latter would forward your game; for example:—

| | 5. P. to K. Kt.'s 5th. |
| 6. Castles. | 6. P. takes Kt. |

(You can also advantageously play 6. Q. B. takes P.)

| 7. Q. takes P. | 7. B. takes Q. P. (ch.) |
| 8. K. to R's sq. | 8. P. to Q's 3rd. |

(Should he move 8. Q. to K. B's 3rd, you reply with 9. Q. B. takes P.)

9. Q. B. takes P.	9. K. B. to his 3rd.
10. P. to K's 5th.	10. P. takes P.
11. Q. B. takes P.	11. Q. Kt. to Q's 2nd.
12. Q. B. to his 3rd.	12. Q. to K's 2nd.
13. R. to K's sq.	13. B. to K's 4th.
14. B. takes B.	14. Kt. takes B.
15. Q. to K. R's 5th.	15. K. Kt. to B's 3rd.
16. Q. takes Q. Kt.	

You have a superior game.

| 6. P. to Q. B's 3rd. | 6. P. to K. Kt.'s 5th (best) |

Black can now attack the Kt. with advantage, and by doing

so he gets the better game. He may with almost equal benefit play 6. P. to R's 3rd. (*e. g.*)

	6. P. to K. R's 3rd.
7. Q. to her Kt.'s 3rd.	7. Q. to K's 2nd.

(If you castle instead of moving the Q. thus, he answers with 7. K. Kt. to K's 2nd, and if then you attempt to open an attack by 8. P. to K. Kt.'s 3rd, he will play 8. P. to K. Kt.'s 5th, having a better game.)

8. Castles.	8. Q. Kt. to Q's 2nd.
9. P. to K. Kt.'s 3rd.	9. P. to K. Kt.'s 5th.

(If you play 9. P. to K. R's 4th, he can retort with 9. Q. Kt. to his 3rd.)

10. Q. B. takes P.	10. P. takes Kt.
11. R. takes P.	11. K. Kt. to B's 3rd.
12. P. to K's 5th.	12. P. takes P.

(Should you move 13. Q. Kt. to Q's 2nd, he castles.)

13. P. takes P.	13. K. Kt. to his 5th.
14. B. takes K. B. P. (ch.)	14. Q. takes B.
15. P. to K's 6th.	15. Q. to K. B's 4th.
16. P. takes Kt. (ch.)	16. Q. B. takes P.
17. P. to K. R's 4th.	17. Castles on Q's side.

He has a much better game than you have.

7. Kt. to his sq.	7. Q. to K. R's 5th (ch.)

If you sacrifice the Kt. by playing 7. Q. to her Kt.'s 3rd, or 7. Q. B. takes P., you must equally lose.

8. K. to B's sq.	8. K. B. to K. R's 3rd.
9. Q. to her Kt.'s 3rd.	9. Q. to K. R's 4th.

You can bring no Piece into action with advantage, while the field is all before him where to choose.

GAME THE SECOND.

WHITE.	BLACK.
1. P. to K's 4th.	1. P. to K's 4th.
2. P. to K. B's 4th.	2. P. takes P.
3. K. Kt. to B's 3rd.	3. P. to K. Kt.'s 4th.
4. K. B. to Q. B's 4th.	4. B. to K. Kt.'s 2nd.
5. P. to K. R's 4th.	5. P. to K. R's 3rd (best)

Here Black plays his best move; if he adopt instead of 5. P. to R's 3rd 5. P. to K. Kt.'s 5th, the utmost he can obtain will be an even game. (*e. g.*)

	5. P. to K. Kt.'s 5th.
6. Kt. to his 5th.	6. K. Kt. to R's 3rd.
7. P. to Q's 4th.	7. P. to K. B's 3rd.

(If he play 7. Q. Kt. to B's 3rd, you answer with 8. P. to Q. B's 3rd, and afterwards with Q. B. takes P.)

8. Q. B. takes P.	8. P. takes Kt.

(He may also play 8. P. to Q's 3rd, whereupon you move 9. Kt. to K's 6th, having an advantage; or he may play 8. P. to Q's 4th, which you take with K. B., and in a few moves the game will be equal.)

9. B. takes P.	9. B. to K. B's 3rd.
10. B. takes Kt.	10. B. takes K. R. P. (ch.)
11. K. to Q's 2nd.	11. B. to K. Kt.'s 4th (ch.)
12. K. to Q's 3rd.	

You have no disadvantage.

6. P. to Q's 4th.	6. P. to Q's 3rd.

If he play here 6. P. to K. Kt.'s 5th, you may leave the Kt. to be captured, and take P. with Q. B.

7. P. to Q. B's 3rd.	7. P. to K. Kt.'s 5th.

You may also play 7. Q. Kt. to B's 3rd, for the result of which see Var. I. Black, instead of 7. P. to K. Kt.'s 5th, may now play 7. Q. Kt. to Q's 2nd, with advantage; but if he attempt 7. Q. B. to K. Kt.'s 5th, or 7. K. Kt. to B's 3rd, the game will be less favourable for him. For example; in the first place,—

	7. Q. B. to K. Kt.'s 5th.
8. Q. to her Kt.'s 3rd.	8. Q. B. to K. R's 4th.
9. P. takes K. Kt. P.	9. P. takes P.
10. R. takes B.	

And you win.

In the second place,—

	7. K. Kt. to B's 3rd.
8. P. takes Kt. P.	8. Kt. takes K. P.

(If in place of taking the P. you play 8. P. to K's 5th, Black replies with 8. Kt. to K's 5th, and has an advantage.)

9. Q. to K's 2nd.	9. Q. to K's 2nd.

The game is even.

8. Q. B. takes P.	8. P. takes Kt

If you retreat the Kt., Black may play either 8. Q. to K's 2nd, or B. to K. B's 3rd, having a fine game. By the sacrifice of the Kt. you obtain a strong attack, but care on the part of your opponent will enable him to defend himself.

9. Q. takes P.	9. Q. B. to K's 3rd.

If instead he play 9. K. Kt. to B's 3rd, you may regain the advantage ; for instance,—

	9. K. Kt. to B's 3rd.
10. Castles.	10. Q. Kt. to B's 3rd.
11. P. to K's 5th.	11. P. takes P.

(If 11. K. Kt. to Q's 2nd, you answer with 12. Q. B. to K. Kt.'s 5th.)

12. Q. B. takes P.	12. Kt. takes B.
13. P. takes Kt.	13. Q. B. to K. Kt.'s 5th.
14. Q. to K. B's 4th.	14. P. to K. R's 4th.
15. P. takes Kt.	

You have a much better game.

10. Q. Kt. to Q's 2nd.	10. K. Kt. to K's 2nd.
11. P. to K. R's 5th.	11. B. takes B.
12. Kt. takes B.	12. P. to Q. Kt.'s 4th.
13. Kt. to K's 3rd.	13. Q. Kt. to B's 3rd.

You have no adequate compensation for the Piece you are minus.

Variation I.,

Beginning at White's 7th move.

WHITE.	BLACK.
1. P. to K's 4th.	1. P. to K's 4th.
2. P. to K. B's 4th.	2. P. takes P.
3. K. Kt. to B's 3rd.	3. P. to K. Kt.'s 4th.
4. K. B. to Q. B's 4th.	4. B. to K. Kt.'s 2nd.
5. P. to K. R's 4th.	5. P. to K. R's 3rd.
6. P. to Q's 4th.	6. P. to Q's 3rd.
7. Q. Kt. to B's 3rd.	7. P. to Q. B's 3rd.

If he attack your Kt. with the K. Kt. P., you must retreat him to his own sq. again.

8. P. takes K. Kt. P.	8. P. takes P.
9. R. takes R.	9. B. takes R.
10. K. Kt. to K's 5th.	10. P. takes Kt.

You might also play 10. K. to B's 2nd, and the following moves occur:—

| 10. K. to B's 2nd. | 10. P. to K. Kt.'s 5th. |

(Black could likewise play with advantage 10. B. to K. Kt.'s 2nd, or 10. K. Kt. to B's 3rd.)

| 11. Q. to K. R's sq. | 11. B. to K. Kt.'s 2nd. |

(His best move. 10. Q. to K. B's 3rd, or 10. P. takes K. Kt., would be in your favour.)

12. Q. to K. R's 5th.	12. P. to Q's 4th.
13. Q. Kt. takes P.	13. P. takes Kt.

(If at this crisis you play 13. P. takes Q. P., Black takes your K. Kt. with P., and then moves K. Kt. to B's 3rd.)

14. K. B. takes Q. P.	14. Q. to K's 2nd.
15. Kt. to his 5th.	15. K. Kt. to B's 3rd.
16. B. takes K. B. P. (ch.)	16. K. to B's sq.
17. Q. to K. Kt.'s 6th.	17. Kt. takes K. P. (ch.)

He now forces the exchange of Queens, and having a Piece superiority must win.

11. Q. to K. R's 5th.	11. Q. to K. B's 3rd.
12. P. takes K. P.	12. Q. to K. Kt.'s 2nd.
13. P. to K's 6th.	13. B. takes P. (best)

He may with almost equal advantage play 13. K. Kt. to B's 3rd. (*e. g.*)

	13. K. Kt. to B's 3rd.
14. P. takes P. (ch.)	14. K. to his 2nd.

(If he venture 14. K. to Q's sq., you play 15. Q. takes K. Kt. P., and win; so also, if he move 14. K. to B's sq., you may take P. with Q. B., leaving your Queen *en prise*, and if he capture either Q. or B., you mate him next move.)

15. Q. to K's 2nd.	15. Q. B. to K. Kt.'s 5th.

(Should he risk 15. Q. B. to K's 3rd, you exchange Bishops, then check with your Q. at her B's 4th, and afterwards, by playing her to Kt.'s 4th, you must gain the advantage.)

16. Q. to her 3rd.	16. Q. Kt. to Q's 2nd.
17. Q. to her 4th.	17. K. Kt. to R's 4th.

He ought to win.

14. B. takes B.	14. K. Kt. to B's 3rd.
15. B. takes K. B. P. (ch.)	15. K. to his 2nd.
16. Q. to K. Kt.'s 6th.	16. Q. takes B.

The advantage is all on Black's side.

GAME THE THIRD.

WHITE.	BLACK.
1. P. to K's 4th.	1. P. to K's 4th.
2. P. to K. B's 4th.	2. P. takes P.
3. K. Kt. to B's 3rd.	3. P. to K. Kt.'s 4th.
4. B. to Q. B's 4th.	4. B. to Q. Kt.'s 2nd.
5. Castles.	5. P. to Q's 3rd (best)

5. Castling, or 5. P. to Q's 4th, may be played indifferently. If Black, in reply to your present move, play 5. P. to K. Kt.'s

5th, you may retreat the Kt. to K's sq., and thus ensure the winning of the gambit Pawn, or you can leave the Kt. to be taken, as in the following variation:—

	5. P. to K. Kt.'s 5th.
6. P. to Q. B's 3rd.	6. P. takes Kt.
7. Q. takes P.	7. B. to K. R's 3rd.
8. P. to Q's 4th.	8. Q. to K's 2nd.
9. Q. B. takes P.	9. B. takes B.
10. Q. takes B.	10. P. to Q's 3rd.
11. B. takes K. B. P. (ch.)	11. K. to Q's sq.
12. Kt. to Q's 2nd.	

The game is even.

6. P. to Q's 4th.	6. P. to K. R's 3rd.

But for this precautionary move of his, you might get a lively but somewhat hazardous attack, by sacrificing the Kt. for the two Pawns.

7. P. to Q. B's 3rd.	7. Q. B. to K's 3rd.

If you play 7. P. to K. Kt.'s 3rd, Black replies with 7. P. to K. Kt.'s 5th, and gets the better game. Should he, in answer to your present move, play 7. P. to Q. B's 3rd, you can then advantageously move 8. P. to K. Kt.'s 3rd; for example,—

	7. P. to Q. B's 3rd.
8. P. to K. Kt.'s 3rd.	8. P. to K. Kt.'s 5th.
9. Q. B. takes P.	9. P. takes Kt.
10. Q. takes P.	10. Q. to K. B's 3rd.

(If he play 10. B. to K's 3rd, you exchange Bishops, and then take Q. P. with your Q. B. If he play 10. K. Kt. to B's 3rd, you may also take Q. P. with Q. B., and afterwards play P. to K's 5th.)

11. Q. to K. R's 5th.	11. Q. to K. Kt.'s 3rd.

(You can also obtain a powerful attack by 11. P. to K's 5th, followed by Q. to K's 3rd; the moves in the text are from the German "Handbuch.")

12. Q. takes Q.	12. P. takes Q.
13. Q. B. takes P.	13. K. Kt. to B's 3rd.
14. Q. Kt. to Q's 2nd.	

Your two central Pawns and superiority of general position are equivalent to the Piece he has gained.

8. B. takes B.	8. P. takes B.

You may here perhaps more advantageously play 8. Q. Kt. to R's 3rd.

9. Q. to her Kt.'s 3rd.	9. Q. to her B's sq.
10. P. to K. R's 4th.	10. P. to K. Kt.'s 5th.
11. Kt. to K. R's 2nd.	11. P. to K. Kt.'s 6th.

He has a Pawn more and a strong position.

GAMES
ILLUSTRATIVE OF THE FOREGOING ANALYSES.
(From the *Chess-Player's Chronicle*.)

GAME I.—Between V. H. der Laza and Dr. Bledow.

WHITE. (V. H. d. L.)	BLACK. (Dr. B.)
1. P. to K's 4th.	1. P. to K's 4th.
2. P. to K. B's 4th.	2. P. takes P.
3. K. Kt. to B's 3rd.	3. P. to K. Kt.'s 4th.
4. K. B. to Q. B's 4th.	4. K. B. to Kt.'s 2nd.
5. P. to Q's 4th.	5. Q. to K's 2nd.*
6. Castles.	6. P. to K. R's 3rd.
7. Q. Kt. to B's 3rd.	7. P. to Q. B's 3rd.
8. P. to K's 5th.	8. Q. to her Kt.'s 5th.
9. Q. Kt. to K's 4th.	9. K. B. to his sq.
10. Q. to K's 2nd.†	10. P. to K. Kt.'s 5th.
11. Kt. to Q's 6th (ch.)	11. B. takes Kt.
12. P. takes B. (dis. ch.)	12. K. to Q's sq.
13. Kt. to K's 5th.	13. R. to R's 2nd.
14. P. to Q. B's 3rd.	14. P. to K. B's 6th.
15. Q. to K's 4th.	15. K. Kt. to B's 3rd.
16. Q. takes R.	16. Kt. takes Q.

And White gave checkmate in six moves.

GAME II.—Between V. H. der Laza and Mr. H. of Berlin.

WHITE. (V. H. d. L.)	BLACK. (Mr. H.)
1. P. to K's 4th.	1. P. to K's 4th.
2. P. to K. B's 4th.	2. P. takes P.
3. K. Kt. to B's 3rd.	3. P. to K. Kt.'s 4th.
4. K. B. to Q. B's 4th.	4. B. to K. Kt.'s 2nd
5. Castles.	5. P. to K. R's 3rd.
6. P. to Q's 4th.	6. P. to Q's 3rd.
7. P. to Q. B's 3rd.	7. P. to Q. B's 3rd.
8. Q. to her Kt.'s 3rd.‡	8. Q. to K's 2nd.
9. P. to K. Kt.'s 3rd.	9. P. to K. Kt.'s 5th.
10. Q. B. takes P.	10. P. takes Kt.
11. R. takes P.	11. Q. B. to K's 3rd.

---

* The proper move, as is seen in the foregoing variations, is 5. P to Q's 3rd.

† This little game is excellently played by White.

‡ Having now your Q. P. protected, and an opening for your Queen, you can advantageously advance the K. Kt. P., and sacrifice your Kt., as in the Muzio Gambit.

12. P. to Q's 5th.	12. Q. B. to K. Kt.'s 5th.
13. P. takes Q. B. P.	13. B. takes R.
14. P. takes Kt. P.	14. Q. takes K. P.
15. P. takes R. (becoming a Q.)	15. Q. takes Q.
16. B. takes K. B. P. (ch.)	16. K. to B's sq.
17. B. takes Kt.	17. R. takes B.
18. B. takes Q. P. (ch.)	18. K. to K's sq.

White mates in three moves.*

GAME III.—Between Mr. Popert and an eminent Polish player.

WHITE. (Mr. Z.)	BLACK. (Mr. P.)
1. P. to K's 4th.	1. P. to K's 4th.
2. P. to K. B's 4th.	2. P. takes P.
3. K. Kt. to B's 3rd.	3. P. to K. Kt.'s 4th.
4. B. to Q. B's 4th.	4. B. to Q. Kt.'s 2nd.
5. P. to Q's 4th.	5. P. to Q's 3rd.
6. Castles.	6. P. to K. R's 3rd.
7. P. to K. Kt.'s 3rd.	7. P. to K. Kt.'s 5th.
8. K. Kt. to R's 4th.	8. P. to K. B's 6th.
9. Q. B. to K's 3rd.	9. Q. Kt. to B's 3rd.
10. P. to Q. B's 3rd.	10. K. B. to B's 3rd.
11. K. Kt. to K. B's 5th.	11. Q. B. takes Kt.
12. P. takes B.	12. K. Kt. to K's 2nd.
13. Q. to her Kt.'s 3rd.	13. P. to Q's 4th.
14. K. B. to Q's 3rd.	14. Q. to her 2nd.
15. Q. to her B's 2nd.	15. P. to K. R's 4th.
16. Kt. to Q's 2nd.	16. P. to K. R's 5th.
17. Q. B. to K. B's 4th.	17. Castles on Q's side.
18. P. to Q. R's 4th.	18. P. takes K. Kt. P.
19. Q. B. takes K. Kt. P.	19. K. R. to his 4th.
20. P. to Q. Kt.'s 4th.	20. K. Kt. takes K. B. P.
21. B. takes Kt.	21. Q. takes B.
22. Q. to her Kt.'s 2nd.	22. B. to K. R's 5th.
23. B. takes B.	23. R. takes B.
24. P. to Q. R's 5th.	24. R. takes K. R. P.
25. K. takes R.	

Black mates in three moves.

---

* A brilliant and amusing little skirmish.

GAME IV.

WHITE.	BLACK.
1. P. to K's 4th	1. P. to K's 4th.
2. P. to K. B's 4th.	2. P. takes P.
3. K. Kt. to B's 3rd.	3. P. to K. Kt.'s 4th.
4. K. B. to Q. B's 4th.	4. K. B. to Kt.'s 2nd.
5. P. to K. R's 4th.	5. P. to K. R's 3rd.
6. P. takes P.	6. P. takes P.
7. R. takes R.	7. B. takes R.
8. P. to Q's 4th.	8. P. to Q's 3rd.
9. Q. Kt. to B's 3rd.	9. P. to Q. B's 3rd.
10. K. Kt. to K's 5th.*	10. P. takes Kt.
11. Q. to K. R's 5th.	11. Q. to K. B's 3rd.
12. Q. P. takes P.	12. Q. to K. Kt.'s 2nd.
13. P. to K's 6th.	13. K. Kt. to B's 3rd.†
14. P. takes P. (ch.)	14. K. to B's sq.‡
15. Q. B. takes P.	15. K. to his 2nd.§
16. Q. B. takes K. Kt. P.	16. Q. Kt. to Q's 2nd.
17. Q. R. to Q's sq.‖	17. Q. Kt. to K's 4th.
18. Q. to K. R's 2nd.	18. Q. takes B.¶
19. P. to K. B's 8th, becoming a Q. (ch.)	19. K. takes Q.
20. Q. takes B. (ch.)	20. K. Kt. to his sq.
21. R. to Q's 8th (ch.)	21. Q. takes R.
22. Q. takes K. Kt. (ch.)	22. K. to his 2nd.
23. Q. to K. Kt.'s 7th (ch.)	23. K. to Q's 3rd.
24. Q. to R's 6th (ch.)	24. K. to B's 2nd.
25. Q. to K. Kt.'s 7th (ch.)	25. Kt. to Q's 2nd.
26. Q. to K. Kt.'s 3rd (ch.)	26. K. to Q. Kt.'s 3rd.

White mates in five moves.

---

* This has been shown to be an extremely hazardous mode of play, and one which can only be ventured against an inferior opponent.

† Q. B. takes P. is a better move.

‡ This is an error which should cost the game. He should move the K. to K's 2nd.

§ He would be mated directly on taking either Q. or B.

‖ Better, as the after play shows, than castling.

¶ If White had castled on the previous move, this B. would have been taken with a check.

Chapter II.

THE CUNNINGHAM GAMBIT.

THIS sparkling variation in the defence of the King's Gambit was brought into general notice from its adoption by Mr. Cunningham, the historian, one of the most eminent chess-players of his day in Europe. It differs from all other variations of the same opening, inasmuch that Black, instead of attempting to sustain the Pawn he has gained, by the customary move of 3. P. to K. Kt.'s 4th, plays his K. B. to K's 2nd, with the intention of checking at K. R's 5th, and either compelling White to move his King, or by interposing a Pawn, enable Black not only to break up the Pawns on the King's side, but to exchange his doubled P. for another of greater value and importance. The leading works to be consulted on this lively method of opposing the gambit are—Bertin (London, 1735); Stamma; Philidor (1782); Allgaier; Sarratt (1808); Lewis (1844); Walker (1846); and the German "Handbuch."

GAME THE FIRST.

WHITE.	BLACK.
1. P. to K's 4th.	1. P. to K's 4th.
2. P. to K. B's 4th.	2. P. takes P.
3. K. Kt. to B's 3rd.	3. K. B. to K's 2nd.
4. K. B. to Q. B's 4th.	4. B. to R's 5th (ch.)

Your move of B. to Q. B's 4th is the best at your command; it enables you either to play the K. to B's sq., when he is checked, or to castle at the first convenient opportunity.

5. K. to B's sq.	5. K. B. to his 3rd.

Instead of 5. K. to B's sq., which is the best move you can make, you may also play 5. P. to K. Kt.'s 3rd, as in the next game. If Black, in lieu of retreating his B. to B's 3rd, play 5. B. to K. Kt.'s 4th, you answer with 6. P. to Q's 4th, then take the K. B., and finally play Q. to K. B's 3rd, with a fine game. He may, however, move 5. K. Kt. to R's 3rd, and then the following variation is probable:—

	5. K. Kt. to R's 3rd.
6. P. to Q's 4th.	6. K. Kt. to his 5th.
7. Q. to K's 2nd.	7. K. Kt. to B's 7th.

8. K. Kt. takes B.	8. Kt. takes R.
9. Kt. to K. B's 3rd.	9. Kt. to his 6th (ch.)
10. P. takes Kt.	10. P. takes P.
11. Q. B. to K. B's 4th.	

You have a manifest advantage.

6. P. to K's 5th.	6. B. to K's 2nd.
7. P. to Q's 4th.	7. P. to Q's 4th.
8. K. B. to K's 2nd.	8. P. to K. Kt.'s 4th.
9. P. to K. R's 4th.	9. P. to K. Kt.'s 5th.
10. K. Kt. to K. R's 2nd.	10. P. to K. R's 4th.

He can also attack the Kt. by advancing the Kt. P. another sq., but the result would still be in your favour.

11. Q. B. takes P.	11. K. B. takes K. R. P.
12. P. to K. Kt.'s 3rd.	12. B. to K. Kt.'s 4th.
13. Kt. takes K. Kt. P.	

You must win.

———

GAME THE SECOND.

WHITE.	BLACK.
1. P. to K's 4th.	1. P. to K's 4th.
2. P. to K. B's 4th.	2. P. takes P.
3. K. Kt. to B's 3rd.	3. B. to K's 2nd.
4. K. B. to Q. B's 4th.	4. B. to K. R's 5th (ch.)
5. P. to K. Kt.'s 3rd.	5. P. takes P.

Your present move is not so prudent as 5. K. to B's sq., but it is one very frequently adopted, and with which you ought to be conversant.

If instead of taking the P., Black retire his B. to Kt.'s 4th, you castle, and have a good position. If he play 5. P. to Q. Kt.'s 4th, you may take the K. B. P., checking, and afterwards capture his B. with K. Kt.

6. Castles.	6. P. takes P. (ch.)
7. K. to R's sq.	7. K. B. to his 3rd.

The situation here is remarkable, and it is scarcely possible to conceive, at first sight, how such a position could occur at the sixth move of the game.

Black has all his Pawns, while on your side there is a startling deficiency; it was from this circumstance that Bertin and Stamma distinguished the opening as the "Three Pawns' Gambit." At this point Philidor observes that Black must win, and in this opinion he is seconded by Ercole Del Rio, (Lolli, p. 369); but Allgaier, on the other hand, remarks,— "With equally good players, however, White's game is not so irredeemably lost as Philidor makes it." Instead of 7. B. to K. B's 3rd, Black may play 7. P. to Q's 4th, or 7. B. to K's 2nd, for the result of which see the Variation.

8. K. Kt. to K's 5th.	8. B. takes Kt. (best)

For your 8th move, Philidor gives P. to K's 5th, pursuing the game as follows :—

8. P. to K's 5th.	8. P. to Q's 4th.
9. P. takes B.	9. K. Kt. takes P.
10. B. to Q. Kt.'s 3rd.	10. Q. B. to K's 3rd.
11. P. to Q's 4th.	11. Kt. to K's 5th.
12. Q. B. to K. B's 4th.	12. P. to K. B's 4th.
13. Q. Kt. to Q's 2nd.	13. Q. to K's 2nd.
14. P. to Q. B's 4th.	14. P. to Q. B's 3rd.
15. P. takes Q. P.	15. P. takes P.
16. Q. R. to Q. B's sq.	16. Q. Kt. to B's 3rd.
17. Q. Kt. takes K. Kt.	17. K. B. P. takes Kt.
18. Kt. takes K. R. P.	18. Castles on K's side.

(Kt. to K's 5th, for your 18th move, seems to be at least as good as taking the Pawn.)

19. Q. to her 2nd.

Philidor now makes Black play 19. P. to K. R's 3rd, and White answers with 20. Q. R. to Q. B's 5th ; but, as the "Handbuch" remarks, he overlooks the fact that White might win by 20. B. takes K. R. P.

9. Q. to K. R's 5th.	9. Q. to K's 2nd (best)
10. R. takes K. B. P.	10. Q. to her B's 4th.
11. R. to K. B's 8th (dble. ch.)	11. K. to his 2nd.
12. P. to Q's 4th.	12. Q. takes P. (best)

If he play 12. Q. takes B., you proceed thus,—

13. Q. to K's 8th (ch.)	13. K. to Q's 3rd.
14. Q. takes B. (ch.)	

Followed by Q. Kt. to R's 3rd, and Q. B. to Q's 2nd, &c.

13. Q. B. checks.	13. K. to Q's 3rd (best)
14. Q. Kt. to Q's 2nd.	14. K. Kt. to B's 3rd.
15. Q. to K. B's 7th.	15. Kt. takes K. P.

16. Q. B. to K's 3rd.	16. K. Kt. to his 6th (ch.)
17. K. to Kt.'s 2nd.	17. Q. takes B.
18. Q. to her 5th (ch.)	18. K. to his 2nd.
19. Q. to K.·B's 7th (ch.)	19. K. to Q's 3rd.

Drawn game.

VARIATION,
Beginning at Black's 7th move.

At this stage Black has at his disposal several moves beside the one of 7. B. to his 3rd, adopted in the preceding game. The most important of these are 7. P. to Q's 4th, and 7. B. to K's 2nd. In the first place, let us see the effect of 7. P. to Q's 4th.

| | 7. P. to Q's 4th. |
| 8. B. takes P. | 8. K. Kt. to B's 3rd. |

If you take the P. with P., Black retires his B. to B's 3rd and has a safe position.

| 9. B. takes K. B. P. (ch.) | 9. K. takes B. |

If instead of so playing you take B. with Kt., he also takes B. with Kt., but you may play 9. K. B. to Q. Kt.'s 3rd, with the following result:—

9. B. to Q. Kt.'s 3rd.	9. Kt. takes K. P.
10. Q. to K's 2nd.	10. Q. to K's 2nd.
11. B. takes B. P. (ch.)	11. K. to B's sq.
12. Q. takes K. R. P.	12. Kt. to Kt.'s 6th (ch.)
13. K. to Kt.'s 2nd.	13. Kt. takes K. R.

14. Q. takes K. B.	14. Q. takes Q.
15. Kt. takes Q.	15. K. takes B.
16. K. takes Kt.	

Black has obviously the advantage.

10. Kt. takes K. B.	10. K. R. to B's sq.
11. P. to Q's 4th.	11. K. to Kt.'s sq.

If, thinking to win a Piece, you advance the K. P. to K's 5th, Black will check at Q's 4th, and, on your interposing the Kt. as your best move, he will play Kt. to K. R's 4th.

12. Q. B. to K. Kt.'s 5th.	12. K. Kt. takes K. P.
13. B. takes Q.	13. R. takes R. (ch.)
14. Q. takes R.	14. Kt. to his 6th (ch.)
15. K. takes P.	15. Kt. takes Q. (ch.)

He has the Letter game.

Referring again to the diagram, let us now see the probable consequences of Black's playing 7. B. to K's 2nd.

	7. B. to K's 2nd.
8. B. takes B. P. (ch.)	8. K. takes B.

He may decline taking the Bishop, and then you pursue the game thus,—

	8. K. to B's sq.
9. Kt. to K's 5th.	9. K. Kt. to B's 3rd.
10. K. B. to Q. Kt.'s 3rd.	10. Q. to K's sq.
11. K. Kt. to B's 7th.	11. K. R. to Kt.'s sq.
12. P. to K's 5th.	12. P. to Q's 4th.
13. P. takes Kt.	13. P. takes P.
14. B. takes Q. P.	

You have a winning position.

9. Kt. to K's 5th (dble. ch.)	9. K. to his 3rd (best)
10. Q. to K. Kt.'s 4th (ch.)	10. K. takes Kt.
11. Q. to K. B's 5th (ch.)	11. K. to Q's 3rd.
12. Q. to her 5th.	

And wins.

GAMES

ILLUSTRATIVE OF THE CUNNINGHAM GAMBIT.

Game I.—Between two members of the Berlin Chess Club.

WHITE. (V. H. d. L.)	BLACK. (M. J.)
1. P. to K's 4th.	1. P. to K's 4th.
2. P. to K. B's 4th.	2. P. takes P.

3. K. Kt. to B's 3rd.   3. K. B. to K's 2nd.
4. K. B. to Q. B's 4th.   4. B. to K. R's 5th (ch.)
5. P. to K. Kt.'s 3rd.*   5. P. takes P.
6. Castles.   6. P. takes P. (ch.)
7. K. to R's sq.   7. K. B. to B's 3rd.
8. Kt. to K's 5th.   8. B. takes Kt.
9. Q. to K. R's 5th.   9. Q. to K's 2nd.
10. R. takes K. B. P.   10. Q. to her B's 4th.
11. R. to K. B's 8th (dble. ch.) 11. K. to his 2nd.
12. P. to Q's 4th.   12. Q. takes P.†
13. B. to K. Kt.'s 5th (ch.) 13. K. Kt. to B's 3rd.‡
14. B. takes Kt. (ch.)   14. P. takes B.
15. Q. to K. B's 7th (ch.) 15. K. to Q's 3rd.
16. Q. Kt. to B's 3rd.   16. R. takes R.
17. Q. takes R. (ch.)   17. K. to B's 3rd.
18. Q. to her Kt.'s 4th.   18. P. to Q's 4th.
19. B. to Kt.'s 5th (ch.)   19. K. to Kt.'s 3rd.
20. Kt. mates.

GAME II.—Between V. Bilguer and Mr. M——t.

WHITE. (V. B.)   BLACK. (Mr. M.)
1. P. to K's 4th.   1. P. to K's 4th.
2. P. to K. B's 4th.   2. P. takes P.
3. K. Kt. to B's 3rd.   3. K. B. to K's 2nd.
4. K. B. to Q. B's 4th.   4. B. checks.
5. P. to K. Kt.'s 3rd.   5. P. takes P.
6. Castles.   6. P. takes P. (ch.)
7. K. to R's sq.   7. P. to Q's 3rd.§
8. B. takes K. B. P. (ch.) 8. K. takes B.
9. Kt. takes B. (dis. ch.) 9. K. Kt. to B's 3rd.
10. P. to Q's 4th.|| 10. Q. B. to K. R's 6th.
11. R. to K. B's 3rd.   11. B. to K. Kt.'s 5th.¶
12. R. takes Kt. (ch.)   12. Q. takes R.
13. Q. takes B.   13. Q. to K. B's 8th (ch.)
14. K. takes P.   14. Q. takes Q. B.
15. Q. Kt. to B's 3rd.   15. Q. takes R.

---

* The correct reply is 5. K. to B's sq., as shown in the preceding variations.

† The best move.

‡ K. to Q's 3rd is the proper play.

§ P. to Q's 4th is far better.

|| If White checks at K. R's 5th, Black's answer is K. to Kt.'s sq.

¶ Q. to her 2nd is a better move.

16. Q. to K. B's 5th (ch.)	16. K. to his sq.*
17. Q. to Q. B's 8th (ch.)	17. K. to his 2nd.
18. Q. takes P. (ch.)	18. K. to his sq.
19. Q. to B's 8th (ch.)	19. K. to B's 2nd.
20. Q. takes P. (ch.)	20. K. to his sq.
21. Kt. to K. B's 5th.	

And must win.

CHAPTER III.

THE SALVIO GAMBIT.

So called from having first appeared in the Treatise of Salvio, 1604, is, properly speaking, like the Cochrane Gambit, a variation of the defence of the King's Gambit, which springs from the second player advancing his K. Kt. P. to Kt.'s 5th, at the 4th move, in place of posting the K's Bishop at K. Kt.'s 2nd. This method of defending the Gambit I have always regarded as somewhat hazardous, because it permits the first player to adopt the Muzio attack; but the situations arising from it are of singular interest and instruction.

The principal works which have treated of this opening are Salvio, Cozio (1st vol. p. 35); Ponziani (1782), p. 126; Cochrane (1822), pp. 171—175; Silberschmidt (1845), pp. 79—98; Lewis, (1844), pp. 338—343; Kassim (1829); Jaenisch vol. ii. p. 233; Walker (1846), p. 205; and the German "Handbuch."

GAME THE FIRST.

WHITE.	BLACK.
1. P. to K's 4th.	1. P. to K's 4th.
2. P. to K. B's 4th.	2. P. takes P.

* He must lose equally if the K. goes to his 2nd. (e. g.)

	16. K. to his 2nd.
17. Kt. to Q's 5th (ch.)	17. K. to Q's sq.
18. Q. to K. Kt.'s 5th (ch.)	18. K. to B's sq., or (A.)
19. Q. takes Kt. P.	19. Q. Kt. to R's 3rd.
20. Q. takes R. (ch.)	20. K. to Q's 2nd.
21. Q. takes R., and wins.	

(A.)

	18. K. to Q's 2nd.
19. Q. to K's 7th (ch.)	19. K. to B's 3rd.
20. Q. takes P. (ch.), and wins.	

3. K. Kt. to B's 3rd.	3. P. to K. Kt.'s 4th.
4. K. B. to Q. B's 4th.	4. P. to K. Kt.'s 5th.
5. Kt. to K's 5th.	5. Q. to K.R's 5th (ch.)

If, at your 5th move, instead of so playing, you leave the Kt. to be taken, the opening becomes the celebrated Muzio Gambit, which, with 5. B. takes K. B. P. (ch.), will form the subject of a separate Chapter. It would be bad play for Black to move Kt. to R's 3rd, before checking with his Q., because you could at once castle, and regain the given Pawn.

6. K. to B's sq.	6. K. Kt. to B's 3rd.

It is this move of Black that constitutes the Salvio defence, of which, however, Salvio was not the originator, he having taken the variation from some Portuguese work, now unknown. It is not considered so advantageous a mode of defending the game as playing 6. Kt. to K. R's 3rd, a move likewise indicated by Salvio, and the consequences of which shall be examined in the next game.

7. Q. to K's sq. (best)	7. Q. takes Q. (ch., best)

If you venture to take the K. B. P. at your 7th move with the Kt., Black replies with 7. P. to Q's 4th, and gains two Pieces for his Rook. If you take it with the Bishop, the following variation proves that the game will be also in his favour:—

7. B. takes K. B. P. (ch.)	7. K. to his 2nd (best)
8. B. to Q. Kt.'s 3rd.	8. P. to Q's 3rd.
9. Kt. to Q's 3rd.	9. Kt. to K. R's 4th.
10. Q. to K's sq.	10. P. to K. Kt.'s 6th.
11. K. to Kt.'s sq.	11. K. B. to K. Kt.'s 2nd.
12. P. to Q. B's 3rd.	12. Q. to K. Kt.'s 4th.

Black has the better game.

8. K. takes Q.	8. Kt. takes K. P.

He may also play 8. P. to Q's 3rd, as follows,—

	8. P. to Q's 3rd.
9. Kt. takes B. P.	9. P. to Q's 4th.
10. B. takes Q. P.	10. Kt. takes B.
11. Kt. takes K. R.	11. Kt. to K. B's 3rd.
12. P. to Q's 3rd.	12. B. to K. Kt.'s 2nd.
13. P. to Q. B's 3rd.	13. B. takes Kt.
14. B. takes P.	14. P. to Q. B's 3rd.
15. Q. Kt. to Q's 2nd.	

The game is about equal.

9. B. takes K. B. P. (ch.)	9. K. to his 2nd (best)
10. B. to K. R's 5th.	10. P. to K. Kt.'s 6th.

Philidor makes you play 10. B. to Q. Kt.'s 3rd, but the move in the text, which is Ponziani's, is acknowledged to be better.

11. P. to K. R's 3rd.	11. P. to Q's 3rd.
12. K. Kt. to Q's 3rd.	12. K. B. to R's 3rd.
13. Q. Kt. to B's 3rd.	13. Kt. takes Kt.

If he retire his Kt., you play B. to K. B's 3rd, and if he then move P. to Q. B's 3rd, by moving Q. Kt. to K's 2nd, you recover the P. with a better position.

14. Q. P. takes Kt.	14. R. to K. B's sq.
15. R. to K. B's sq.	15. Q. B. to K. B's 4th.
16. Kt. takes P.	16. B. takes Kt.
17. B. takes B.	17. K. R. to K. Kt.'s sq.
18. B. takes Q. P. (ch.)	18. P. takes B.
19. R. takes B.	19. K. R. to Kt.'s 2nd.

You have a Pawn more and an advantage in position.

GAME THE SECOND.

WHITE.	BLACK.
1. P. to K's 4th.	1. P. to K's 4th.
2. P. to K. B's 4th.	2. P. takes P.
3. K. Kt. to B's 3rd.	3. P. to K. Kt.'s 4th.
4. B. to Q. B's 4th.	4. P. to K. Kt.'s 5th.
5. Kt. to K's 5th.	5. Q. to K.R's 5th (ch.)
6. K. to B's sq.	6. K. Kt. to R's 3rd.

Black's present move is decidedly superior to that of Kt. to K. B's 3rd. If, in lieu of playing so, or 6. Kt. to K. B's 3rd, he move 6. P. to K. B's 6th, we have the Cochrane Gambit, which see.

7. P. to Q's 4th.	7. P. to K. B's 6th.

This is Black's best move; if he play instead 7. P. to Q's 3rd, you have the advantage, for example,—

	7. P. to Q's 3rd.
8. Kt. to Q's 3rd.	8. P. to K. B's 6th.
9. P. to K. Kt.'s 3rd.	9. Q. to K's 2nd (best)
10. Q. Kt. to B's 3rd.	10. P. to Q. B's 3rd.
11. P. to K. R's 3rd.	11. P. to K. B's 4th.

12. Q. B. takes Kt.	12. B. takes B.
13. P. takes K. B. P.	13. Q. B. takes B.
14. P. takes K. Kt. P.	14. Q. B. takes Kt. (ch.)
15. Q. takes B.	

You must win.

8. P. takes P.	8. P. to Q's 3rd.

Instead of taking the Pawn here, you may move 8. Q. B. to K. B's 4th, or 8. B. takes K. Kt. For the result of these moves, see Variation, and you can play likewise 8. P. to K. Kt.'s 3rd, or 8. Q. to K's sq., as shown in the following examples. In the first place,—

8. P. to K. Kt.'s 3rd.	8. Q. to K. R's 6th (ch.)
9. K. to B's 2nd.	9. Q. to K. Kt.'s 7th (ch.)
10. K. to his 3rd.	10. P. to K. B's 4th.

(This move of Black's we find in Silberschmidt; Salvio, Cozio, and Ponziani, play 10. P. to K. B's 3rd, which is much inferior.)

11. K. to Q's 3rd.	11. P. takes P. (ch.)

(If you play 11. P. takes K. B. P., he first dislodges your Kt. with the Q. P., and then takes P. with Kt., checking ; and if you move 11. Q. Kt to B's 3rd, he answers with 11. P. to Q. B's 3rd, and afterwards 12. P. to Q's 3rd.)

12. K. takes P.	12. P. to Q's 4th (ch.)
13. B. takes Q. P.	13. P. to K. B's 7th (dis. ch.)

He has the better game.

In the second place,—

8. Q. to K's sq.	8. Q. takes Q. (ch.)
9. K. takes Q.	9. P. takes K. Kt. P.
10. R. to K. Kt.'s sq.	10. P. to Q's 3rd.
11. Kt. to Q's 3rd.	11. K. Kt. to his sq.
12. R. takes P.	12. P. to K. R's 4th.

His game is superior to yours.

9. Kt. to Q's 3rd.	9. K. Kt. P. takes P.

If in lieu of retreating the Kt., you take his Kt. with Q. B., he takes your Kt. with Q. P.

10. K. Kt. to K. B's 2nd.	10. Q. B. to K. R's 6th (ch.)
11. Kt. takes B.	11. Q. takes Kt. (ch.)
12. K. to B's 2nd.	12. Q. to Kt.'s 7th (ch.)
13. K. to his 3rd.	13. Kt. to his 5th (ch.)
14. K. to B's 4th.	14. B. to R's 3rd (ch.)

And he mates you in two moves.

VARIATION,

Beginning from White's 8th move.

BLACK.

WHITE.

| 8. Q. B. to K. B's 4th. | 8. P. takes P. (ch.) |

It was before observed that you could also play 8. Q. B. takes
K. Kt. ; let us suppose this move,—

8. B. takes K. Kt.	8. P. takes P. (ch.)
9. K. takes P.	9. B. takes B.
10. Kt. takes K. B. P.	10. R. to K. B's sq.

Black will win.

If you take the B. P. with B., checking, instead of with the Kt., he
moves K. to his 2nd, and soon gets the better game.

9. K. takes P.	9. P. to Q's 3rd.
10. B. takes K. Kt.	10. B. takes B.
11. Kt. to Q's 3rd.	11. Q. to R's 6th (ch.)
12. K. to B's 2nd.	12. Q. to K's 6th (ch.)
13. K. to B's sq.	13. P. to Kt.'s 6th.

He has a fine attack.

CHAPTER IV.

THE COCHRANE GAMBIT.

THIS is a modification of the defence introduced by Salvio,
which we have just examined, and consists in the second
player's advancing the P. to K. B's 6th, before playing out
the K. Kt. either to B's 3rd, or to R's 3rd.   The most important

authorities upon these Gambits are Cochrane (1822), pp. 268
—276; Lewis, in whose valuable treatise is incorporated the
chief variations of Ghulam Kassim, (1844), pp. 308—343;
Calvi, in "Le Palamède" (1844); Jaenisch, vol. ii., pp. 233—
239; and the German "Handbuch." See also an interesting
article on the Cochrane Gambit, by V. H. der Laza, in the
"Chess-Player's Chronicle," vol. v., pp. 317—339.

GAME THE FIRST.

WHITE.	BLACK.
1. P. to K's 4th.	1. P. to K's 4th.
2. P. to K. B's 4th.	2. P. takes P.
3. K. Kt. to B's 3rd.	3. P. to K. Kt.'s 4th.
4. B. to Q. B's 4th.	4. P. to K. Kt.'s 5th.
5. Kt. to K's 5th.	5. Q. to K. R's 5th (ch.)
6. K. to B's sq.	6. P. to K. B's 6th.

In the previous Gambit you will remember Salvio advances
this P. one move later, that is, after his K. Kt. is moved to
B's 3rd, or R's 3rd sq.

7. P. to Q's 4th (best)	7. P. takes K. Kt. P. (ch., best.)

Instead of 7. P. to Q's 4th, you have the choice of several
moves. You may play B. takes K. B. P. (ch.); P. to K.
Kt.'s 3rd; and Kt. P. takes P.; each of which will form the
subject of a separate game. (See Games Second, Third, and
Fourth.)

If instead of any one of these you play 7. Q. to K's sq., he
takes P. with P. (ch.), and then moves Q. to K. R's 6th, with
a better game than you have. There is another move too at
your command, viz.,—7. Kt. takes K. B. P., the consequences
of which it may be well to show at once. Suppose, then,—

7. Kt. takes K. B. P.	7. K. Kt. to B's 3rd.
8. Kt. takes R.	8. Kt. takes K. P.
9. Q. to K's sq.	9. P. takes Kt. P. (ch.)
10. K. takes P.	10. Q. to R's 6th (ch.)
11. K. to Kt.'s sq.	11. B. to Q. B's 4th (ch.)

And he must win.

When at your 7th move you advance the Q. P., Black,
instead of taking the Kt. P. (ch.), may play 7. K. Kt. to
B's 3rd, to which you can reply 8. Q. Kt. to B's 3rd, and if
he attempt to dislodge your Kt. by 8. Q. P. one, you may

play 9. Kt. takes K. B. P., without danger. For the consequences of his playing at his 7th move K. Kt. to R's 3rd, his best move in the opinion of Jaenisch, see Game the Second of the Salvio Gambit, in which the same position is more safely brought about by—

1. P. to K's 4th.	1. P. to K's 4th.
2. P. to K. B's 4th.	2. P. takes P.
3. K. Kt. to B's 3rd.	3. P. to K. Kt.'s 4th.
4. K. B. to Q. B's 4th.	4. P. to K. Kt.'s 5th.
5. Kt. to K's 5th.	5. Q. checks.
6. K. to B's sq.	6. K. Kt. to R's 3rd.
7. P. to Q's 4th.	7. P. to K. B's 6th.
8. K. takes P.	8. Q. to R's 6th (ch.)
9. K. to Kt.'s sq.	9. K. Kt. to R's 3rd.

9. K. Kt. to B's 3rd would be less advantageous for him: for example,—

	9. K. Kt. to B's 3rd.
10. Kt. takes K. B. P.	10. P. to Q's 4th.

(If he play instead, 10. R. to Kt.'s sq., you move Kt. to his 5th; if 10. Kt. takes K. P., you answer with Q. to K's 2nd; and finally, if he play 10. P. to K. Kt.'s 6th, you can reply with Kt. to his 5th, or K. B. to his sq., having the better game.)

11. K. B. to his sq.	11. Q. to K. R's 5th
12. Kt. takes R.	12. Kt. takes K. P.
13. Q. to K's 2nd.	13. K. B. to Kt.'s 2nd.

(If 13. P. to K's 6th you take the P., and when he retakes, checking, you interpose the K. B.)

14. P. to Q. B's 3rd.	14. P. to K. Kt.'s 6th.
15. P. takes P.	15. Q. takes P. (ch.)
16. Q. to K. Kt.'s 2nd.	

You should win.

10. Q. to her 3rd.	10. Q. takes Q.

In this gambit if you take the Kt. with your Q. B., he attains an irresistible position. Should you at your 10th move play Q. Kt. to B's 3rd, he does the same, and will maintain the P. You may, however, move 10. K. B. to his sq., in which case this variation is probable:—

10. B. to his sq.	10. Q. to R's 5th.
11. B. takes Kt.	11. B. takes B.
12. Q. takes P.	12. B. to K's 6th (ch.)
13. K. to Kt.'s 2nd.	13. Q. takes Q. (ch.)
14. Kt. takes Q.	14. B. takes Q. P.

He has an easy game.

11. P. takes Q.	11. P. to Q's 3rd.
12. B. takes Kt.	12. B. takes B.
13. Kt. takes K. B. P.	13. B. to K's 6th (ch.)
14. K. to Kt.'s 2nd.	14. R. to B's sq.
15. R. to B's sq.	15. B. takes Q. P.

He ought to win.

The merit of working out these latter variations is due to Messrs. Henderson, Williams, and Withers, three skilful amateurs of the Bristol Chess Club, who devoted much time and attention to the analysis of this brilliant gambit.

GAME THE SECOND.

BLACK.

WHITE.

The diagram represents the position of the men up to the 6th move of the preceding game. In this and the next two games, White deviates from the former, by not playing P. to Q's 4th on his 7th move.

WHITE.	BLACK.
7. B. takes K. B. P. (ch.)	7. K. to his 2nd.
8. P. takes P.	8. P. to Q's 3rd.

If at your 8th move you play Q. to K's sq., he takes P. with P. (ch.), and then moves Q. to K. R's 6th. If 8. P. to K. Kt.'s 3rd, he checks with his Q. at R's 6th, and then moves

K. Kt. to B's 3rd, with a fine attack. And if instead of these you play 8. K. B. takes Kt., the following variation shows it will be to your disadvantage.

8. K. B. takes Kt.	8. R. takes B. (best)
9. P. takes P.	9. P. to Q's 3rd.
10. Kt. takes P.	10. B. takes Kt.
11. P. takes B.	11. R. takes P.

He has the better game.

9. B. takes Kt.	9. P. takes Kt.
10. B. to Q. B's 4th.	10. P. takes P.
11. Q. takes P.	11. B. to K. R's 6th (ch.)
12. K. to Kt.'s sq.	12. Q. to K's 8th (ch.)
13. B. to B's sq.	13. R. checks.

And wins.

GAME THE THIRD.

(Place the men again as on the diagram.)

WHITE.	BLACK.
7. P. to K. Kt.'s 3rd.	7. Q. to R's 6th (ch.)
8. K. to B's 2nd (best)	8. K. Kt. to B's 3rd.
9. P. to Q's 3rd.	9. P. to Q's 3rd.

You might here play 9. K. to his 3rd or 9. Q. Kt. to B's 3rd, for the result of which see Variations I. and II. If instead of these you preferred 9. B. takes B. P. (ch.), a few moves will show the game would be unfavourable for you. (e. g.)

9. B. takes B. P. (ch.)	9. K. to his 2nd.
10. B. to Q. Kt.'s 3rd.	10. Q. to Kt.'s 7th (ch.)
11. K. to his 3rd.	11. B. to K. R's 3rd (ch.)
12. K. to Q's 3rd.	12. R. to K. B's sq.

Black has the advantage.

10. Kt. takes K. B. P.	10. P. to Q's 4th.
11. Kt. takes R.	11. Q. to Kt.'s 7th (ch.)

If in place of taking the R. you take Q. P. with B., he first checks with his Q. and then takes B. with Kt.; or if you take the Q. P. with K. P., he can also first check with the Q., and then take your Kt. with K., regardless of the check by discovery when you play P. to Q's 6th.

12. K. to his 3rd.	12. Q. Kt. to B's 3rd.
13. Kt. to B's 7th.	13. K. takes Kt.
14. B. takes Q. P. (ch.)	14. Kt. takes B.
15. P. takes Kt.	15. B. to K. R's 3rd (ch.)

And then P. to K. B's 7th, winning.

VARIATION I.,

Beginning at White's 9th move.

WHITE.	BLACK.
9. K. to his 3rd.	9. B. to K. R's 3rd (ch.)
10. K. to Q's 3rd.	10. P. to Q's 3rd.

If you move 10. K. to Q's 4th, you have a still worse game.

11. Kt. takes K. B. P.	11. P. to Q's 4th.
12. B. takes Q. P.	12. Kt. takes B.
13. Kt. takes B.	13. Kt. to Q. Kt.'s 5th (ch.)

If you take the R. instead of the B., he plays his Q. to K. R's 4th.

14. K. to B's 4th.	14. Q. takes Kt.
15. K. takes Kt.	15. Q. Kt. to R's 3rd (ch.)
16. K. to B's 3rd.	16. Q. to her B's 3rd (ch.)
17. K. to Q's 3rd.	17. Kt. to his 5th (ch.)
18. K. to K's 3rd.	18. Kt. takes Q. B. P. (ch.)

Black must win.

VARIATION II.,

Beginning at White's 9th move.

WHITE.	BLACK.
9. Q. Kt. to B's 3rd.	9. Q. to Kt.'s 7th (ch.)
10. K. to his 3rd.	10. B. to K. R's 3rd (ch.)
11. K. to Q's 3rd.	11. Q. Kt. to B's 3rd.

If you play 11. K. to Q's 4th, the consequences are equally disastrous.

| 12. Kt. takes K. B. P. | 12. Q. Kt. to his 5th (ch.) |

Instead of taking the B. P. with your Kt., you may play 12. B. takes P. (ch.), or 12. Kt. takes Q. Kt., but with even less advantage than by the move in the text.

13. K. to Q's 4th.	13. Q. to B's 7th (ch.)
14. K. to his 5th.	14. P. to Q's 3rd (ch.)
15. K. takes Kt.	15. Q. to her 4th (ch.)

And Black wins.

GAME THE FOURTH.

(Arrange the men again according to the diagram.)

WHITE.	BLACK.
7. K. Kt. P. takes P.	7. K. Kt. to B's 3rd.
8. P. to Q's 4th.	8. P. to Q's 3rd.

Instead of 8. P. to Q's 4th, you have a variety of moves at command. For the most important of these, viz., 8. B. takes K. B. P. (ch.), 8. Kt. takes K. Kt. P., 8. Q. to K's 2nd, 8. Q. to K's sq., and P. to K. R's 3rd, see Variations I., II., III., and IV.

9. Kt. takes K. Kt. P.	9. Q. to R's 6th (ch.)
10. K. to his sq.	10. Kt. takes Kt.

If you play 10. K. to B's 2nd, your defence will be less prolonged. (*e. g.*)

10. K. to B's 2nd.	10. B. takes Kt.
11. P. takes B.	11. Kt. takes Kt. P. (ch.)
12. K. to his sq.	12. Q. to Kt.'s 7th.
13. R. to K. B's sq.	13. B. to K's 2nd.
14. B. to K's 2nd.	14. B. to K. R's 5th (ch.)
15. K. to Q's 2nd.	15. Kt. to B's 7th.

Black should win.

11. P. takes Kt.	11. B. to K's 2nd.
12. R. to B's sq.	12. B. checks.
13. K. to Q's 2nd.	13. Q. B. takes P.
14. B. to K's 2nd.	14. K.B.toKt.'s4th(ch.)
15. K. to his sq.	15. Q. to R's 5th (ch.)
16. R. to K. B's 2nd.	16. K. B. takes Q. B.
17. Q. takes B.	17. Q. B. takes K. B.
18. K. takes B.	18. Q. takes K. P. (ch.)
19. Q. to K's 3rd.	19. Q. takes Q. (ch.)

He has a Pawn more and no inferiority of position.

VARIATION I.,

Beginning at White's 8th move.

BLACK.

WHITE.

8. B. takes K. B. P. (ch.)	8. K. to his 2nd.
9. B. to Q. B's 4th.	9. P. to Q's 3rd.
10. Kt. to Q's 3rd.	10. P. takes P.

If you play 10. Kt. to K. B's 7th, he replies with 10. P. takes P., and if 10. Kt. takes Kt. P. the following moves are probable:—

10. Kt. takes Kt. P.	10. Kt. takes Kt.
11. P. takes Kt.	11. B. to K. Kt.'s 2nd.
12. P. to K. R's 3rd.	12. R. to B's sq. (ch.)
13. K. to his 2nd.	13. R. to B's 7th (ch.)

He has a winning position.

11. Kt. to K. B's 2nd.	11. Q. B. to K. R's 6th (ch.)
12. Kt. takes B.	12. Q. takes Kt. (ch.)
13. K. to his sq.	13. Kt. takes K. P

His attack is irresistible.

VARIATION II.,

Beginning at White's 8th move.—(See diagram, as before.)

WHITE.	BLACK.
8. Kt. takes K. Kt. P.	8. Kt. takes Kt.

If at move 8. you take K. B. P. with Kt., he answers with 8. P. to Q's 4th, and speedily obtains a winning game.

9. P. takes Kt.	9. Q. to R's 6th (ch.)
10. K. to his sq.	10. P. to Q's 4th.

Should you play 10. K. to his B's 2nd, Black replies with 10. Q. Kt. to B's 3rd; if then you move 11. P. to Q. B's 3rd, he plays 11. B. to K's 2nd, and wins; or if at the 11th move you play Q. to K. B's 3rd, he can exchange Queens, and then win by checking with his Kt. at K's 4th.

11. B. to K's 2nd.	11. Q. to R's 5th (ch.)
12. K. to B's sq.	12. P. to K. R's 4th.

He has an excellent game.

VARIATION III.,

Beginning at White's 8th move.—(See the diagram, as before.)

WHITE.	BLACK.
8. Q. to K's 2nd.	8. P. to Q's 3rd.

You can also move 8. Q. to K's sq. ; for example,—

8. Q. to K's sq.	8. Q. to R's 6th (ch.)
9. K. to his 2nd.	9. P. to Q's 3rd.
10. Kt. takes K. Kt. P.	10. Kt. takes Kt.
11. P. takes Kt.	11. B. takes P. (ch.)
12. K. to B's 2nd.	12. K. B. to K's 2nd.
13. Q. to K's 3rd.	13. K. B. checks.
14. K. to Kt.'s sq.	14. Q. B. to K. B's 6th.

You cannot save the game.

9. Kt. takes K. B. P.	9. P. takes P.

You may here play 9. Kt. takes K. Kt. P., and proceed thus,—

9. Kt. takes K. Kt. P.	9. Kt. takes Kt.
10. P. takes Kt.	10. Q. B. takes P.
11. Q. to B's 2nd (best)	11. Q. B. to R's 6th (ch.)
12. K. to his 2nd.	12. Q. takes K. P. (ch.)
13. Q. to K's 3rd.	13. Q. takes Q. (ch.)
14. P. takes Q.	14. Q. Kt. to B's 3rd.

He has the better game.

10. Q. to K. B's 2nd.	10. Q. B. to R's 6th (ch.)
12. K. to his sq.	12. Q. takes K. P. (ch.)
13. K. to Q's sq.	13. Q. takes B.

He must win.

VARIATION IV.,

Beginning at White's 8th move.—(Once more marshal the men according to the diagram.)

WHITE.	BLACK.
8. P. to K. R's 3rd.	8. P. takes K. R. P.
9. Q. to K's sq.	9. Q. to K. Kt.'s 4th.

Instead of 9. Q. to K's sq., you can play 9. P. to Q's 4th, or 9. Kt. takes K. B. P. For example, in the first place,—

9. P. to Q's 4th.	9. P. to Q's 3rd.
10. Kt. to Q's 3rd.	10. Kt. to K. R's 4th.
11. Q. to K's sq.	11. Kt. to Kt.'s 6th (ch.)
12. K. to Kt.'s sq.	12. R. to K. Kt.'s sq.
13. K. to R's 2nd.	13. Kt. to K's 7th.

Winning easily.

In the second place,—

9. Kt. takes K. B. P.	9. P. to Q's 4th.
10. B. takes Q. P.	10. Kt. takes B.
11. Kt. takes R.	11. Q. to Kt.'s 6th.
12. R. to K. Kt 's sq.	12. P. to K. R's 7th.
13. R. takes Q.	13. P. to R's 8th (becoming a Q.)
14. R. to Kt.'s sq.	14. B. to R's 6th (ch.)

Your game is gone.

10. Kt. to his 4th.	10. Kt. takes Kt.
11. P. takes Kt.	11. Q. takes P.
12. Q. to K's 2nd.	12. P. to K. R's 4th.
13. Q. Kt. to B's 3rd.	13. R. to K. Kt.'s sq.
14. K. to his sq.	14. B. to K's 2nd.

You might also exchange Queens, but that would unite his Pawns, and improve his game.

15. Kt. to Q's 5th.	15. Q. to R's 5th (ch.)
16. K. to Q's sq.	16. P. to Q. B's 3rd.
17. Kt. to Q. B's 7th (ch.)	17. K. to Q's sq
18. Kt. takes Q. R.	18. P. to Q's 4th.
19. Q. to K's sq.	19. P. takes B.

And wins.

An attentive consideration of the foregoing examples will lead you to the conclusion, I think, that the Salvio defence,

1. $\dfrac{\text{P to K's 4th}}{\text{P. to K's 4th}}$, 2. $\dfrac{\text{P. to K. B's 4th}}{\text{P. takes P.}}$, 3. $\dfrac{\text{K. Kt. to B's 3rd}}{\text{P. to K. Kt.'s 4th}}$, 4. $\dfrac{\text{B. to Q. B's 4th}}{\text{P. to K. Kt.'s 5th}}$,

5. $\dfrac{\text{Kt. to K's 5th}}{\text{Q. to R's 5th (ch.)}}$, 6. $\dfrac{\text{K. to B's sq.}}{\text{Kt. to K. R's 3rd}}$, 7. $\dfrac{\text{P. to Q's 4th}}{\text{P. to K. B's 6th}}$, or that of

Cochrane, which varies from it in the transposition of Black's 6th and 7th moves, 6. $\frac{\text{K. to B's sq.}}{\text{P. to K. B's 6th}}$, 7. $\frac{\text{P. to Q's 4th}}{\text{Kt. to K. R's 3rd}}$, is a safe and trustworthy method of opposing the King's Gambit, and that the danger to be apprehended by the first player, in advancing his Pawn to K. Kt.'s 5th on the 4th move, is not that his opponent should play the Kt. to K's 5th, and admit of the Salvio or Cochrane defence, but that he should leave his Kt. to be taken, and adopt the powerful and almost indefensible attack of the Muzio Gambit.

GAMES

ILLUSTRATING THE SALVIO AND COCHRANE GAMBITS.

GAME I.—Between Messrs. V. H. der Laza and H—d of Berlin.

WHITE. (Mr. H—)	BLACK. (V. H. d. L.)
1. P. to K's 4th.	1. P. to K's 4th.
2. P. to K. B's 4th.	2. P. takes P.
3. K. Kt. to B's 3rd.	3. P. to K. Kt.'s 4th.
4. K. B. to Q. B's 4th.	4. P. to K. Kt.'s 5th.
5. Kt. to K's 5th.	5. Q. to R's 5th (ch.)
6. K. to B's sq.	6. K. Kt. to R's 3rd.
7. P. to Q's 4th.	7. P. to K. B's 6th.
8. P. to K. Kt.'s 3rd.	8. Q. to R's 6th (ch.)
9. K. to B's 2nd.	9. Q. to K. Kt.'s 7th (ch.)
10. K. to his 3rd.	10. P. to K. B's 3rd.*
11. Kt. to Q's 3rd.	11. K. Kt. to B's 2nd.
12. Kt. to K. B's 4th.	12. K. B. to K. R's 3rd.
13. K. to Q's 3rd.	13. B. takes Kt.
14. Q. B. takes B.	14. P. to Q. B's 3rd.
15. Q. Kt. to B's 3rd.	15. Castles.
16. Q. B. to Q's 6th.	16. P. to Q. Kt.'s 4th.
17. B. takes Kt. (ch.)	17. R. takes B.
18. P. to K. R's 3rd.	18. P. to Q. Kt.'s 5th.
19. B. takes Q. Kt. P.	19. Q. B. to R's 3rd (ch.)
20. K. to his 3rd.	20. Q. takes K. Kt. P.
21. Q. to K. Kt.'s sq.	21. Q. to her B's 2nd.
22. Q. takes P. (ch.)	22. R. to K. Kt.'s 2nd.
23. Q. takes doubled P., and wins.	

---

* The proper move is that given by Silberschmidt, of P. to K. B's 4th.

GAME II.—Between Messrs. La Bourdonnais and Cochrane.

WHITE. (M. La B.)	BLACK. (Mr. C.)
1. P. to K's 4th.	1. P. to K's 4th.
2. P. to K. B's 4th.	2. P. takes P.
3. K. Kt. to B's 3rd.	3. P. to K. Kt.'s 4th.
4. K. B. to Q. B's 4th.	4. P. to K. Kt.'s 5th.
5. Kt. to K's 5th.	5. Q. to K. R's 5th (ch.)
6. K. to B's sq.	6. P. to K. B's 6th.
7. P. to K. Kt.'s 3rd.*	7. Q. to K. R's 6th (ch.)
8. K. to B's 2nd.	8. Q. to Kt.'s 7th (ch.)
9. K. to his 3rd.	9. B. to K. R's 3rd (ch.)
10. K. to Q's 3rd.	10. P. to Q's 4th.
11. B. takes P.	11. Q. Kt. to R's 3rd.
12. P. to Q. B's 3rd.	12. P. to Q. B's 3rd.
13. B. takes K. B. P. (ch.)	13. K. to his 2nd.
14. K. B. to Q. Kt.'s 3rd.	14. Q. Kt. to B's 4th (ch.)
15. K. to B's 2nd.	15. Q. Kt. takes K. P.
16. Q. to K. B's sq.	16. Q. B. to K. B's 4th.
17. Q. takes Q.	17. Kt. to B's 7th (dis. ch.)
18. P. to Q's 3rd.	18. P. takes Q.
19. R. to K. Kt.'s sq.	19. Q. R. to Q's sq.
20. Q. B. takes B.	20. K. Kt. takes B.
21. R. takes P.	21. Kt. takes Q. P.
22. Kt. takes Kt.	22. B. takes Kt. (ch.)
23. K. to B's sq.	23. K. R. to B's sq.
24. Q. Kt. to Q's 2nd.	24. K. Kt. to B's 4th.
25. K. B. to Q's sq.	25. Kt. to K's 6th.
26. K. R. to Kt.'s sq.	26. B. to K. B's 8th.
27. P. to Q. Kt.'s 3rd.	27. K. R. to B's 7th.
28. R. takes B.	28. Kt. takes R.
29. Kt. takes Kt.	29. Q. R. takes B. (ch.)
30. K. takes R.	30. R. takes Kt. (ch.)†

And wins.

GAME III.—From Mr. Cochrane's *Treatise*.

WHITE.	BLACK.
1. P. to K's 4th.	1. P. to K's 4th.
2. P. to K. B's 4th.	2. P. takes P.
3. K. Kt. to B's 3rd.	3. P. to K. Kt.'s 4th.
4. K. B. to Q. B's 4th.	4. P. to Kt.'s 5th.
5. Kt. to K's 5th.	5. Q. checks.

---

* P. to Q's 4th is now considered to be the best move.

† The termination is played with Mr. Cochrane's characteristic brilliancy.

6. K. to B's sq.	6. P. to K. B's 6th.
7. Q. to K's sq.	7. P. takes P. (ch.)
8. K. takes P.	8. Q. to K. R's 6th (ch.)
9. K. to his B's 2nd.	9. K. B. to Kt.'s 2nd.
10. P. to Q's 4th.	10. P. to Q's 3rd.
11. B. takes B. P. (ch.)	11. K. to his 2nd.
12. B. takes K. Kt.*	12. R. takes B.
13. K. Kt. to Q. B's 4th.	13. Q. to K. B's 3rd (ch.)
14. K. to Kt.'s sq.	14. B. takes Q. P. (ch.)
15. B. to K's 3rd.	15. P. to K. Kt.'s 6th.
16. P. to K. R's 3rd.†	16. P. to Kt.'s 7th.
17. K. R. to his 2nd.	17. Q. B. takes K. R. P.
18. Q. Kt. to Q's 2nd.‡	18. Q. to K. B's 8th (ch.)
19. Kt. takes Q.	19. P. takes Kt.

Becoming a Q., giving check, double check, and mate.

GAME IV.—Between MM. Kieseritzky and Michelet.

WHITE. (M. M.)	BLACK. (M. K.)
1. P. to K's 4th.	1. P. to K's 4th.
2. P. to K. B's 4th.	2. P. takes P.
3. K. Kt. to B's 3rd.	3. P. to K. Kt.'s 4th.
4. B. to Q. B's 4th.	4. P. to K. Kt.'s 5th.
5. Kt. to K's 5th.	5. Q. checks.
6. K. to B's sq.	6. P. to K. B's 6th.
7. P. to Q's 4th.	7. K. Kt. to B's 3rd.
8. Q. Kt. to B's 3rd.	8. K. B. to Kt.'s 2nd.
9. P. to K. Kt.'s 3rd.	9. Q. to K. R's 6th (ch.)
10. K. to B's 2nd.	10. P. to Q's 3rd.
11. Kt. takes K. B. P.	11. R. to B's sq.
12. Kt. to K. Kt.'s 5th.	12. Q. to K. Kt.'s 7th (ch.)
13. K. to his 3rd.	13. B. to K. R's 3rd.
14. K. to Q's 3rd.	14. Q. Kt. to B's 3rd.
15. P. to Q. R's 3rd.	15. B. takes Kt.
16. Q. B. takes B.	16. Kt. takes K. P.
17. Q. to K's sq.	17. B. to K. B's 4th.
18. Kt. takes Kt.	18. P. to K. B's 7th.
19. Q. to K's 3rd.	19. K. to Q's 2nd.
20. B. to Q's 5th.	20. Q. R. to K's sq.
21. Q. R. to K. B's sq.	21. B. takes Kt. (ch.)
22. B. takes B.	22. R. to K. B's 6th.

---

* If White check with his Q. B., Black interposes K. B. and wins a Piece.

† He has no better move.

‡ If the R. take the B., Black takes R. with Q., and presently wins the adverse Q. Or if, instead of taking the B., White check with his Q. at K. R's 4th, Black moves K. to his square, and wins in a few moves.

23. Q. takes R.	23. P. takes Q.
24. B. to B's 5th (ch.)	24. R. to K's 3rd.
25. P. to Q's 5th.	25. Kt. to K's 4th (ch.)
26. K. to Q's 4th.	26. P. to K. R's 4th.
27. P. takes R. (ch.)	27. K. to his sq.
28. Q. B. to K. B's 6th.	28. P. to K. R's 5th.
29. B. takes Kt.	29. P. takes B. (ch.)
30. K. takes P.	30. R. P. takes P.
31. K. to his B's 6th, and wins.	

Chapter V.

THE MUZIO GAMBIT.

In the two defences to the King's Gambit by Salvio and Cochrane just examined, when the second player for his fourth move advances his P. to K. Kt.'s 5th, attacking the Knight, White replies by moving his Knight to King's 5th, subjecting himself, as was shown, to a counter-attack, from which escape without loss is difficult if not impracticable. From this circumstance, apparently, originated the conception of the " Muzio Gambit," wherein the first player instead of removing the attacked Knight boldly abandons him, and by castling is enabled to bring an almost overwhelming array of forces to the immediate assault of the adverse King.

The earliest knowledge of this magnificent variation, the most daring and brilliant, and at the same time, as modern discoveries have shown, the most sound and enduring method of attack yet known, is derived from Salvio, (*Trattato del l'Inventione et Arte Liberale del Gioco di Scacchi.* Naples, 1604,) to whom it had been communicated by Signor Muzio as occurring in casual practice between Don Geronimo Cascio and another player. " Dirò un' altro modo di Gambitto, il quale mai fu pensato, e per quanto mi venne riferito dal Signor Muzio, d'Alessandro, gentiluomo di molto garbo, e del Giuoco molto intendente; succedè, e col Signor Don Geronimo Cascio, così gran giuocatore, con un'altro giuocatore casualmente."

The chief works to be consulted upon the Muzio Gambit are Sarratt, 1813 and 1821, p. 346; Ghulam Kassim, 1829; Lewis, 1844, pp. 348–410; Jaenisch, vol. ii, pp. 222–230; Walker, 1846, pp. 173–194, and the German " Handbuch."

GAME THE FIRST.

WHITE.	BLACK.
1. P. to K's 4th.	1. P. to K's 4th.
2. P. to K. B's 4th.	2. P. takes P.
3. K. Kt. to B's 3rd.	3. P. to K. Kt.'s 4th.
4. K. B. to Q. B's 4th.	4. P. to K. Kt.'s 5th.

In abandoning the Knight at this point you have the choice of three different methods of procedure. In the first place, to castle, which is the long established and ordinary mode of play. Secondly, to move your Q. P. to Q's 4th, as given in Koch, (*Elementarbuch der Schachspielkunst, &c.* Magdeburgh 1828,) and Ghulam Kassim (*An Analysis of the Muzio Gambit, &c.* Madras, 1829). And lastly, as suggested by the late Mr. McDonnell, to play your Q. Kt. to B's 3rd sq. Let us proceed to consider these moves in the order above given, commencing in the present Chapter with 5. Castles, and reserving 5. P. to Q's 4th and 5. Q. Kt. to B's 3rd for subsequent examination.

5. Castles.	5. P. takes Kt.
6. Q. takes P. (best)	6. Q. to K. B's 3rd (best)

If instead of taking the P. you play 6. P. to Q's 4th, Black speedily gains an advantage. (*e. g.*)

6. P. to Q's 4th.	6. P. to Q's 4th.
7. B. takes Q. P.	7. Q. B. to K. Kt.'s 5th.
8. R. to B's 2nd.	8. P. to Q. B's 3rd.
9. B. to Q. Kt.'s 3rd.	9. K. B. to Kt.'s 2nd.
10. P. to Q. B's 3rd.	10. K. B. to K. R's 3rd.
11. Q. Kt. to Q's 2nd.	11. K. Kt. to K's 2nd.

&c., &c.

Until the appearance of Mr. Sarratt's work, Black's best defence, after you have taken the P. at move 6., was considered to be 6. Q. to K's 2nd, but that and 6. P. to Q's 3rd, and 6. B. to K. R's 3rd, have given place to the move in the text of 6. Q. to K. B's 3rd, although the distinguished authors of the German "Handbuch" are of opinion that Black may adopt any one of the three former without disadvantage. The variations arising from them will be shown hereafter. (See Game the Fourth.)

7. P. to K's 5th.	7. Q. takes K. P.

If you play 7. P. to Q. B's 3rd, he replies with 7. Q. Kt. to

B's 3rd, and upon your advancing 8. P. to Q's 4th, he takes it with his Kt. and has the better game. If you play 7. P. to Q's 3rd, he will answer with 7. B. to K. R's 3rd and maintain his advantage. Black's best move apparently is to take the Pawn; if he check with the Queen at Q. Kt.'s 3rd, he takes her from the protection of his own King and drives yours to a safe refuge.

8. P. to Q's 3rd.   8. K. B. to K. R's 3rd.

The eight opening moves here given are generally allowed to be the best both for attack and defence which this remarkable Gambit admits.

Mr. McDonnell originated a variation on your 8th move of 8. P. to Q. Kt.'s 2nd; for the consequences of which see Game the Third.

If Black on his last move play 8. Q. Kt. to B's 3rd, you reply with 9. Q. B. takes P., and will have an irresistible attack.

He may play, however, 8. B. to Q. B's 4th (ch.), and afterwards 9. B. to K's 6th, upon which you can take Bishop with B., and if his Queen retake, can play Q. to K. R's 5th, and then Q. Kt. to B's 3rd, with an excellent game.

9. Q. B. to Q's 2nd.   9. K. Kt. to K's 2nd.

The best play for Black at move 9., whether you play 9. B. to Q's 2nd or 9. Q. Kt. to B's 3rd, appears to be 9. K. Kt. to K's 2nd; if he replies to both with that move, it is of course indifferent which you play first.

10. Q. Kt. to B's 3rd.   10. Q. Kt. to B's 3rd.

Opinions are divided upon Black's 10th move, some players advocating the move now given, while others prefer the more defensive one of 10. P. to Q. B's 3rd, for the consequences of which see Game the Second.

11. Q. R. to K's sq.   11. Q. to B's 4th (ch.)
12. K. to R's sq.   12. Q. Kt. to Q's 5th.

Black can also play 12. P. to Q's 3rd, but as the following train of moves will show, with less advantage.

          12. P. to Q's 3rd.
13. Q. Kt. to Q's 5th.   13. Q. Kt. to K's 4th.
14. R. takes Kt.   14. P. takes R.
15. Q. B. to Kt.'s 4th.
      You ought to win.

13. R. takes Kt. (ch.)   13. K. takes R.

He can also take the R. with his Q., as in the following:—

	13. Q. takes R.
14. Q. to K. R's 5th.	14. Kt. to K's 3rd.
15. Q. takes B.	15. Q. to K. Kt.'s 4th.
16. Q. takes Q.	16. Kt. takes Q.
17. Kt. to Q. Kt.'s 5th.	17. K. to Q's sq.
18. Q. B. to his 3rd.	

And you win.

14. Kt. to Q's 5th (ch.)   14. K. to Q's sq.

15. Q. to K. R's 5th.   15. Q. to K. B's sq.

The German "Handbuch" and other authorities now pursue the game as follows:—

16. Q. B. takes P.   16. B. takes B.

17. R. takes B.   17. Kt. to K's 3rd.

18. Q. to K. R's 4th (ch.)   18. K. to his sq.

19. Kt. to K. B's 6th (ch.)   19. K. to Q's sq.

And the game is dismissed as drawn by perpetual check. I venture to think, however, it will not be difficult to show that with a slight variation in White's play he can win instead of draw the game. Let us suppose at move 16. instead of Q. B. takes P. that you play—

16. Q. to K. R's 4th (ch.)   16. P. to B's 6th.

If he play 16. B. to K. Kt.'s 4th, you take it, checking, and ought certainly to win; and if he play K. to his sq., or Q. to K's 2nd, you obviously mate on the move.

17. Q. B. takes P.   17. B. takes B.

If instead of taking the Bishop he play 17. B. to K. Kt.'s 2nd, you win easily by 18. B. takes Q. B. P. (ch.), and 19. Q. takes Kt.; so also if he move 18. Kt. to K. B's 4th you reply with 19. B. takes Q. B. P. (ch.), followed by 19. Q. to K. R's 5th, and 20. Kt. takes K. B. P. (ch.), &c.; and if, finally, at move 18. he play otherwise, you can take B. with B., and his game is hopeless.

18. R. takes B.   18. Kt. to Q. B's 3rd.

I believe he has no better move. If 18. P. to Q's 3rd, or 18. P. to Q. B's 3rd, or 18. Kt. to K's 3rd, you can take K. B. P. with R., and the discovered check afterwards is fatal to him.

19. R. takes K. B. P.	19. Q. to K's sq.

He has no way of averting the mate.

20. R. to B's 8th (dis. ch.)	20. Kt. to K's 2nd.
21. Q. takes Kt.	

Mate.

GAME THE SECOND.

Varying from the preceding at Black's 10th move.

WHITE.

BLACK.

At this point in the prior game, Black played 10. Q. Kt. to B's 3rd: we have now to consider the effect of his moving 10. P. to Q. B's 3rd, which seems generally preferred to the former.

	10. P. to Q. B's 3rd.
11. Q. R. to K's sq.	11. Q. to her B's 4th (ch.)

Sarratt's move of 11. Kt. to K's 4th is not so strong as 11. Q. R. to K's sq.

12. K. to R's sq.	12. P. to Q's 4th.

At this stage I believe an opportunity occurs for strengthening the attack which has been overlooked. Instead of retiring the King to Rook's sq., I would suggest 12. R. to K. B's 2nd, by which you are enabled to double your Rooks at the proper moment, and continue the assault with augmented force and effect.

| 13. Q. to K. R's 5th. | 13. Q. to her 3rd. |
| 14. B. takes Q. P. | 14. P. takes B. |

If he castle at his 14th move, the chief authorities recommend you to take the Kt. with your R. Black then takes the B. with P. as his best move. You take P. with Kt., he answers with Q. Kt. to B's 3rd; you must then take the P. with your Q. B., and, after the exchange of Bishops, he will take one of the Rooks with his Q., leaving you with a Q. and Kt. against two Rooks and two minor Pieces. With the best play the game ought perhaps to be drawn. The German "Handbuch" remarks, that if Black castles at move 14., you can retire the B. to Q. Kt.'s 3rd, not having a bad game. Should Black, at his 14th move, instead of castling or playing as in the text, move Q. to K. Kt.'s 3rd, the game proceeds as follows:—

| | 14. Q. to K. Kt.'s 3rd. |
| 15. R. takes Kt. (ch.) | 15. K. takes R. |

(You may also play 15. Q. to K's 5th, and have an excellent game. If he play 15. K. to Q's sq., you move 16. Q. to K's 5th, and on his interposing the Q. B. at Q's 2nd, you can take 17. Q. B. with R., and K. R. with Q., and have a capital attack.)

| 16. Q. to K's 5th (ch.) | 16. Q. B. to K's 3rd (best) |
| 17. B. takes B. | 17. B. to K. Kt.'s 2nd. |

(If he play 17. Q. Kt. to Q's 2nd, you check, first with the Kt., then with the B., and afterwards take his K. R., having the better game. If he play 17. Q. to K. Kt.'s 2nd, you may reply with 18. Q. to her B's 5th (ch.), and win ; and if 17. P. takes B., then you take his K. R., having the advantage, play as he can.)

| 18. Q. to Q. B's 7th (ch.) | 18. K. to B's 3rd. |

(The German "Handbuch" advises you to play 18. Kt. to Q's 5th, which is a good move, but not so strong, I think, as the above. If Black now take the B. with his K., you play R. to K's sq. (ch.), and win ; if he play 18. K. to his sq., you take K. B. P. with B. (ch.), winning his Q. If he move 18. Kt. to Q's 2nd, you take the Kt. (ch.), and then play R. takes P., winning easily.)

| 19. Kt. to K's 4th (ch.) | |

And he must give up his Q. or be mated in two more moves.

| 15. Kt. takes Q. P. | 15. Q. Kt. to B's 3rd. |
| 16. Q. B. to his 3rd. | 16. Q. to K. Kt.'s 3rd. |

It is not good, at your 16th move, to play 16. B. to Q. Kt.'s 4th, or 16. R. takes Kt., because in the one case he would answer with 16. Q. Kt. takes B., and on your then taking Kt. with R., would move K. to Q's sq.; and in the other case, of immediately taking off the Kt. with R., he would first take

R. with Kt., and when you played K. R. to K's sq., he might castle, or attack your Q. with Q. B., having the better game.

If at move 16. Black castle, or move his K. R. instead of playing Q. to K. Kt.'s 3rd, you check with the Kt. at K. B's 6th, and have the advantage. He may, however, play 16. K. to B's sq., whereupon you can take Kt. with Kt., afterwards capturing his K. R. His best play appears to be that in the text.

17. R. takes Kt. (ch.)	17. K. to B's sq.

This seems stronger for you than 17. Q. takes Q. If Black play 17. Kt. takes R., you answer with Q. to K's 5th.

The move now given for your 18th is Q. takes Q., and after this exchange, with the best play on both sides, I do not think the game in your favour. In preference to repeating the leading variations from this point, all of which are well known, and may be found in Jaenisch, vol. ii. p. 228, I venture to subjoin a mode of carrying on the attack, which has at least the merit of novelty to recommend it, and which seems to present some points of interest. The following are the most important moves :—

18. R. to K's 8th (ch.)	18. K. takes R.
19. Kt. to K. B's 6th (ch.)	19. K. to B's sq.

If he play 19. K. to Q's sq., mate is inevitable in a few moves. (See the Variation.)

20. Q. to her B's 5th (ch.)	20. Kt. to K's 2nd (best)

If he play K. to Kt.'s 2nd, you have, at the very least, a drawn game through the dangerous check by discovery.

21. R. to K's sq.	21. Q. B. to K's 3rd.
22. Kt. to Q's 7th (ch.)	22. Q. B. takes Kt.

If, instead of taking the Kt., Black plays his K. to Kt.'s sq., or K's sq., you can, at least, draw the game by perpetual check.

23. Q. takes Kt. (ch.)	23. K. to Kt.'s sq.
24. Q. takes B.	24. Q. R. to K. B's sq.
25. Q. takes Q. Kt. P.	

And the game is about even.

As before remarked, I think the attack, in a majority of the variations which arise in this game, may be strengthened by your interposing the K. R. at move 12. instead of retreating the K.

VARIATION,

Beginning at Black's 19th move.

WHITE.	BLACK.
	19. K. to Q's sq.
20. Q. to her 5th (ch.)	20. K. to Q. B's 2nd.

If he move otherwise mate follows immediately.

21. B. to K's 5th (ch.)	21. Kt. takes B.

If he play 21. K. to Q. Kt.'s 3rd, you will end the game more expeditiously. (*e. g.*)

	21. K. to Kt.'s 3rd.
22. Q. to Q. Kt.'s 3rd (ch.)	22. K. to R's 3rd.

(If he move 22. K. to R's 4th, you mate in three moves. If he interpose the Kt., you take it, and then mate in three moves also.)

23. Q. to B's 4th (ch.)	23. P. to Kt.'s 4th (best)
24. Q. takes Kt. (ch.)	

And you mate in three more moves.

22. Q. takes Kt. (ch.)	22. K. to B's 3rd (best)
23. Q. to her 5th (ch.)	23. K. to Kt.'s 3rd.

K. to B's 2nd is obviously fatal, from 24. Q. to B's 5th (ch.), &c.

24. Q. to her 6th (ch.)	24. K. to R's 4th.

If 24. K. to Kt.'s 4th, you will mate in three moves.

25. Q. to her B's 5th (ch.)	25. K. to R's 3rd.

Should he play 25. P. to Q. Kt.'s 4th, your reply may be 26. P. to Q. R's 4th, with the object of afterwards advancing P. to Q. Kt.'s 5th, and then mating with the Rook or with the Queen.

26. Q. to B's 4th (ch.)	26. P. to Q. Kt.'s 4th.

If he play 26. K. to R's 4th, then follow 27. P. to Q. R's 4th, and 28. P. to Q. Kt.'s 5th. But if he move 26. K. to Kt.'s 3rd, you check with the Kt. at Q's 5th, and mate in two more moves.

27. Q. to B's 6th (ch.)	27. K. to R's 4th.
28. P. to Q. R's 4th.	

And he cannot possibly save the game.

GAME THE THIRD.

Varying from the former at White's 8th move.

BLACK.

WHITE.

8. P. to Q. Kt.'s 3rd.   8. Q. takes R. (best)

This move of 8. P. to Q. Kt.'s 3rd is a suggestion of Mr. McDonnell's. It is ingenious, but much inferior to the ordinary course of 8. P. to Q's 3rd.

Instead of capturing the R., Black may play 8. Q. Kt. to B's 3rd, and the following moves are probable :—

	8. Q. Kt. to B's 3rd.
9. Q. Kt. to B's 3rd.	9. Q. Kt. to Q's 5th.
10. Q. to K. B's 2nd.	10. K. B. to Q. B's 4th.
11. K. to R's sq.	11. Kt. to K's 3rd.

Black has the better game.

9. Q. Kt. to B's 3rd.	9. K. B. to Q. B's 4th (ch.)
10. K. to R's sq.	10. K. Kt. to K's 2nd.
11. P. to Q's 4th.	11. B. takes Q. P.

You may at move 11. play Q. takes doubled P. and proceed thus :—

11. Q. takes P.	11. R. to K. B's sq.

(The "Handbuch" suggests for Black 11. P. to K. B's 4th also.)

12. B. takes K. B. P. (ch.)	12. K. to Q's sq.
13. P. to Q's 4th.	13. P. to Q's 4th.
14. Q. to K. R's 6th.	14. R. takes B.
15. R. takes R.	15. Q. B. to Q's 2nd.

He ought to win.

12. B. takes K. B. P. (ch.)   12. K. to Q's sq.

If at move 12. you play Q. takes doubled P., he should, as his best, take Q. B. with Q.

13. B. to Q's 2nd.	13. Q. takes R. (ch.)
14. Q. takes Q.	14. R. to K. B's sq.
15. Q. takes P.	15. B. takes Kt.
16. B. takes B.	16. P. to Q's 3rd.

Black has the advantage.

GAME THE FOURTH.

WHITE.	BLACK.
1. P. to K's 4th.	1. P. to K's 4th.
2. P. to K. B's 4th.	2. P. takes P.
3. K. Kt. to B's 3rd.	3. P. to K. Kt.'s 4th.
4. B. to Q. B's 4th.	4. P. to K. Kt.'s 5th.
5. Castles.	5. P. takes Kt.
6. Q. takes P.	6. K. B. to K. R's 3rd.

In the present game our attention must be directed to the effect of Black's playing, at his 6th move, K. B. to R's 3rd, 6. P. to Q's 3rd, and 6. Q. to K's 2nd. For the two latter see Variations I. and II.

7. P. to Q's 4th.	7. Q. Kt. to B's 3rd.

You may also play, as proposed by the "Handbuch," 7. P. to K's 5th, or 7. Q. Kt. to B's 3rd.

8. Q. Kt. to B's 3rd.	8. Kt. takes Q. P.

If you move 8. Q. B. takes P., Black's reply will be 8. Q. to K. B's 3rd.

9. Q. to K. R's 5th.	9. Q. Kt. to K's 3rd.
10. Q. B. takes P.	10. B. takes B.
11. R. takes B.	11. Q. to K's 2nd.
12. B. takes Kt.	12. Q. P. takes B.
13. Q. R. to K. B's sq.	

You must win.

VARIATION I.,
Beginning at Black's 6th move.

WHITE.	BLACK.
1. P. to K's 4th.	1. P. to K's 4th.
2. P. to K. B's 4th.	2. P. takes P.

3. K. Kt. to B's 3rd.	3. P. to K. Kt.'s 4th.
4. K. B. to Q. B's 4th.	4. P. to K. Kt.'s 5th.
5. Castles.	5. P. takes Kt.
6. Q. takes P.	6. P. to Q's 3rd.

His present move, as well as 6. B. to K. R's 3rd, the German " Handbuch" observes will certainly enable Black to bring about a drawn game.

If he ventures 6. P. to Q's 4th, you can take the P. with your B., and if then he play P. to Q. B's 3rd, you should take the K. B. P. with B. (ch.), after which you would have a remarkably strong attack.

7. P. to Q's 4th.	7. B. to K. R's 3rd.
8. Q. B. takes P.	8. B. takes B.
9. Q. takes B.	9. Q. to K's 2nd.
10. B. takes K. B. P. (ch.)	10. K. to Q's sq.
11. P. to K's 5th.	

With a capital opening.

VARIATION II.,
Beginning at Black's 6th move.

WHITE.	BLACK.
1. P. to K's 4th.	1. P. to K's 4th.
2. P. to K. B's 4th.	2. P. takes P.
3. K. Kt. to B's 3rd.	3. P. to K. Kt.'s 4th.
4. K. B. to Q. B's 4th.	4. P. to K. Kt.'s 5th.
5. Castles.	5. P. takes Kt.
6. Q. takes P.	6. Q. to K's 2nd.

The move of 6. Q. to K's 2nd was first given, in this defence, by Salvio, and was long considered the best. It is now acknowledged to be inferior to 6. Q. to B's 3rd, although the authors of the " Handbuch" consider, with good play, it ought to produce a drawn game.

7. P. to Q's 4th.	7. Q. Kt. to B's 3rd.

He might also play 7. K. B. to R's 3rd, but with even less advantage.

8. Q. takes P.	8. Kt. takes Q. P.

If you play 8. P. to Q. B's 3rd, he can reply with 8. Q. Kt. to K's 4th. You may, however, play 8. Q. B. takes P., and then the following variation is probable.

8. Q. B. takes P.	8. Kt. takes Q. P.
9. Q. to K. R's 5th.	9. Kt. to K's 6th (best)
10. R. takes Kt.	10. Q. P. takes B.
11. B. to K's 5th.	11. Q. to B's 4th (ch.)
12. K. to R's sq.	12. K. Kt. to R's 3rd.
13. P. to Q. Kt.'s 4th.	13. Q. to B's 5th.
14. Q. Kt. to Q's 2nd.	14. Q. takes Q. B. P.
15. B. takes R.	15. Q. takes Kt.
16. Q. R. to Q's sq.	16. Q. to K's 6th.
17. B. to K. B's 6th.	

He has a bad game.

9. B. takes K. B. P. (ch.)	9. K. to Q's sq.
10. Q. Kt. to B's 3rd.	10. K. Kt. to R's 3rd.
11. Q. B. to K's 3rd.	11. Q. Kt. to K's 3rd.
12. K. B. takes Kt.	12. Q. takes B.
13. Q. Kt. to Q's 5th.	13. P. to Q's 3rd.
14. Q. to K. R's 4th (ch.)	

You ought to win.

GAME THE FIFTH.

KOCH AND GHULAM KASSIM'S ATTACK.

WHITE.	BLACK.
1. P. to K's 4th.	1. P. to K's 4th.
2. P. to K. B's 4th.	2. P. takes P.
3. K. Kt. to B's 3rd.	3. P. to K. Kt.'s 4th.
4. K. B. to Q. B's 4th.	4. P. to K. Kt.'s 5th.
5. P. to Q's 4th.	5. P. takes Kt.

This ingenious departure from the customary way of pursuing the attack is given by Koch, who states that it was communicated to him by the late Lieutenant-Colonel Donop, who told him that, while Commander of Brussels, he often played at the chess club there with an Englishman, who usually adopted this move, and invariably won by it. Shortly after the publication of Koch's book, Ghulam Kassim produced a more skilful and elaborate analysis of this attack, the whole of which will be found in Lewis's last treatise.

6. Q. takes P.	6. P. to Q's 4th.

You may obtain a strong but hazardous attack by castling instead of taking the Pawn. Black plays the best move. If, instead of advancing the Q. P., he move 6. Q. to K. B's 3rd, you play on the K. P. If he attempt to protect the gambit

P. by 6. B. to K. R's 3rd, you castle and reduce the game to a regular Muzio. If he bring out his Q. Kt. you can take the P. with Q. B., and when he takes Q. P. with Kt. you should capture the K. B. P. with your B. (ch.), and you will have the better game. He has, however, also the choice of 6. P. to Q's 3rd, and 6. Q. to K. R's 5th (ch.), for which see Variation II.

| 7. K. B. takes Q. P. | 7. P. to Q. B's 3rd. |

The authors of the German "Handbuch" suggest 7. K. Kt. to B's 3rd for Black's 7th move, but they have not proved its validity; but let us suppose—

| | 7. K. Kt. to B's 3rd. |
| 8. Castles. | 8. Kt. takes B. |

(If he play 8. P. to Q. B's 3rd, you may first take the K. B. P. with the B. (ch.), and then move P. to Q. B's 3rd, having a deficiency in Pieces, but a strong attack.)

| 9. P. takes Kt. | 9. Q. to K. B's 3rd. |

(He might also play 9. K. B. to Q's 3rd, but you would obtain a strong position by first checking with the R. and then playing P. to Q. B's 4th.)

| 10. B. takes P. | 10. Q. takes Q. P. (ch.) |

(You might, at your 10th move, instead of giving up the Q. P., play Q. to K's 4th (ch.), and then take the P. with Q. B.)

11. B. to K's 3rd.	11. Q. to K. R's 5th.
12. Q. Kt. to Q's 2nd.	12. K. B. to Q's 3rd.
13. Q. takes K. B. P. (ch.)	13. K. to Q's sq.
14. Kt. to K. B's 3rd.	

And you must win.

| 8. B. to Q. Kt.'s 3rd. | 8. Q. takes Q. P. |

You may likewise play 8. B. takes K. B. P. (ch.) See Variation I.

| 9. Q. B. takes P. | 9. K. Kt. to B's 3rd. |

If he take Q. Kt. P. you can play 10. Q. to K. R's 5th.

| 10. Q. Kt. to Q's 2nd. | 10. Q. B. to K. Kt.'s 5th. |
| 11. Q. to K. Kt.'s 3rd. | 11. K. Kt. takes P. |

He may at move 11. play Q. Kt. to Q's 2nd, upon which you reply with 12. P. to Q. B's 3rd, and then proceed as follows:—

	11. Q. Kt. to Q's 2nd.
12. P. to Q. B's 3rd.	12. Q. to her B's 4th.
13. P. to K's 5th.	13. Castles.
14. P. takes Kt.	14. Kt. takes P.

(Black can draw the game by checking first with his Rook at move 14, and then with the Bishop at K's 7th, on the next move.)

15. B. to K's 3rd.	15. R. to K's sq.
16. Kt. to Q. B's 4th.	

The game is equal.

12. Q. Kt. takes Kt.	12. Q. takes Kt. (ch.)

If you play 12. Q. takes B., he can then play 12. Q. to
K. B's 7th (ch.), and 13. Q. takes Kt. (ch.), followed by
14. Kt. to K. B's 7th (ch.), &c.

13. K. to Q's 2nd.

You have the better game.

VARIATION I.,

Beginning at White's 8th move.

BLACK.

WHITE.

In the previous example you adopted the safer course of
retreating the B. to Q. Kt.'s 3rd; you may, however, acquire
a very powerful attack by sacrificing the Bishop at this juncture.

8. B. takes K. B. P. (ch.)	8. K. takes B.
9. Q. B. takes P.	9. K. Kt. to B's 3rd.

You may also take the P. with your Q. (ch.), in which case
he will interpose his K. Kt. and have the better game. (*e. g.*)

9. Q. takes P. (ch.)	9. K. Kt. to B's 3rd.

(If he interpose the Q. you can check at Q. B's 7th, and get the advantage.)

10. P. to K's 5th.	10. K. B. to Kt.'s 2nd.
11. Castles.	11. K. R. to K. B's sq.
12. Q. to K. R's 4th.	12. K. to Kt.'s sq.

(Should you take the Kt. instead of playing your Q. to K. R.'s 4th, his
best move is K. to Kt.'s sq.)

13. Q. B. to K. Kt.'s 5th.   13. Q. Kt. to Q's 2nd.
14. Q. Kt. to B's 3rd.   14. P. to K. R's 3rd.

Black must win.

10. P. to Q. B's 3rd.   10. Q. B. to K. Kt.'s 5th.

I prefer Black's game.

The latter variations serve to demonstrate that the sacrifice of the Bishop at move 8. is not so good as retreating him to Q. B's 3rd. I am not sure, however, that your proper move after 8. B. takes K. B. P., and 8. K. takes B., is not 9. Q. to K. R's 5th (ch.), at least, as far as my examination goes, you obtain a more enduring attack than by the other methods, and I regret that the very limited space I have now at command, forbids the insertion of the variations.

VARIATION II.,

Beginning at Black's 6th move.

WHITE.	BLACK.
1. P. to K's 4th.	1. P. to K's 4th.
2. P. to K. B's 4th.	2. P. takes P.
3. K. Kt. to B's 3rd.	3. P. to K. Kt.'s 4th.
4. B. to Q. B's 4th.	4. P. to K. Kt.'s 5th.
5. P. to Q's 4th.	5. P. takes Kt.
6. Q. takes P.	6. P. to Q's 3rd.

As was before observed, he may also play 6. Q. to K. R's 5th (ch.), and pursue the game as follows,—

	6. Q. to K. R's 5th (ch.)
7. P. to K. Kt.'s 3rd.	7. Q. to K. R's 6th.
8. Q. B. takes P.	8. P. to K. B's 3rd.
9. Q. Kt. to Q's 2nd.	

With an excellent game.

7. Castles.	7. Q. to K. B's 3rd.
8. Q. Kt. to R's 3rd.	8. Q. takes Q. P. (ch.)
9. K. to R's sq.	9. K. B. to R's 3rd.
10. Q. B. takes P.	10. Q. to K. B's 3rd.

If he play 10. Q. takes Q. Kt. P., you get a speedier advantage by 11. Q. Kt. to his 5th.

11. Q. to K's 3rd.	11. Q. to K. Kt.'s 3rd.
12. P. to K's 5th.	12. B. takes B.
13. R. takes B.	13. B. to K's 3rd.
14. P. takes Q. P.	

You have a capital attack.

GAME THE SIXTH.

McDonnell's Attack.

WHITE.	BLACK.
1. P. to K's 4th.	1. P. to K's 4th.
2. P. to K. B's 4th.	2. P. takes P.
3. K. Kt. to B's 3rd.	3. P. to K. Kt.'s 4th.
4. K. B. to Q. B's 4th.	4. P. to K. Kt.'s 5th.
5. Q. Kt. to B's 3rd.	5. P. takes Kt.

The move of 5. Q. Kt. to B's 3rd, which Mr. McDonnell sometimes adopted instead of castling, at this stage of the opening, leads to many interesting combinations, but appears to be less advantageous to you than the old move of castling.

6. Q. takes P.	6. P. to Q's 4th.

The sacrifice of this P. is recommended by La Bourdonnais. The "Handbuch" suggests that perhaps a simple defence might be adopted by playing 6. P. to Q's 3rd, and if you then take the gambit P. with Q., he might play 7. Q. B. to K's 3rd, a move which is inadmissible in the ordinary Muzio.

He may also for his 6th move play Q. to K. B's 3rd, as in the following fragment of a game between La Bourdonnais and McDonnell, the latter playing the attack.

	6. Q. to K. B's 3rd.
7. Kt. to Q's 5th.	7. Q. to K's 4th.
8. P. to Q. B's 3rd.	8. B. to K. R's 3rd.
9. P. to Q's 4th.	9. Q. to her 3rd.
10. P. to K's 5th.	10. Q. to her B's 3rd.
11. B. to Q. Kt.'s 5th.	11. Q. to K. Kt.'s 3rd.
12. Kt. takes Q. B. P. (ch.)	

With a fine game.

7. B. takes Q. P.	7. P. to Q. B's 3rd.
8. B. to Q. Kt.'s 3rd.	8. Q. B. to K's 3rd.

You may now get a lively but not very sound attack by playing as follows, instead of 8. B. to Q. Kt.'s 3rd.

8. B. takes K. B. P. (ch.)	8. K. takes B.
9. Q. to K. R's 5th (ch.)	9. K. to Kt.'s 2nd.

(If at move 9. you advance P. to Q's 4th, he replies with 9. Kt. to K. B's 3rd; and if you then play 10. P. to K's 5th, he moves 10. K. B. to Kt.'s 2nd, and on your taking P. with Q. B., he plays 11. R. to K's sq., having a better game than you can boast.)

10. P. to Q's 4th.	10. Q. B. to K's 3rd.
11. Q. B. takes P.	11. Q. B. to K. B's 2nd.
12. B. to K's 5th (ch.)	12. Kt. to B's 3rd.
13. Q. to K. Kt.'s 5th (ch.)	13. Q. B. to K. Kt.'s 3rd.

He will soon be out of danger.

9. B. takes B.	9. P. takes B.
10. Q. to K. R's 5th (ch.)	10. K. to Q's 2nd.
11. P. to Q's 4th.	11. Q. to K. B's 3rd.
12. P. to K's 5th.	12. Q. to K. B's 4th.

You may castle at your 12th move, and proceed thus :—

12. Castles.	12. Q. to K. Kt.'s 3rd.
13. Q. to Q. R's 5th.	13. Q. Kt. to R's 3rd.
14. B. takes P.	14. K. B. to Q. Kt.'s 5th.
15. Q. to her R's 4th.	15. K. Kt. to K's 2nd.

He has the advantage.

13. Q. to K. B's 3rd.	13. K. B. to Q. Kt.'s 5th.
14. Q. B. takes P.	14. K. Kt. to K's 2nd.
15. Castles on K's side.	15. B. takes Kt.
16. P. takes B.	16. Q. Kt. to R's 3rd.

The game is in his favour.

As the " Handbuch" remarks, these variations tend to prove that Mr. McDonnell's move of 5. Q. Kt. to B's 3rd is not so potent as the usual course of castling.

Our examination of this beautiful Gambit would be imperfect without some notice of a variation in the opening, where the first player, instead of abandoning the Knight at his 5th move, sacrifices his Bishop by taking the K. B. Pawn, checking. This attack is not, strictly speaking, a part of the Muzio Gambit, but it is so intimately associated with it that I think it better to consider them both under the same head. The chief writers who have considered this sacrifice appear to be Ercole del Rio (Lolli, p. 221); Sarratt, 1808, p. 76; Allgaier, tab. v.; Lewis, 1843, p. 307; Walker, 1841, p. 116, and the German " Handbuch."

GAME THE SEVENTH.

WHITE.	BLACK.
1. P. to K's 4th.	1. P. to K's 4th.
2. P. to K. B's 4th.	2. P. takes P.
3. K. Kt. to B's 3rd.	3. P. to K. Kt.'s 4th.
4. B. to Q. B's 4th.	4. P. to K. Kt.'s 5th.
5. B. takes K. B. P. (ch.)	5. K. takes B.

This sacrifice is far less recommendable than giving up the Kt., the attack being weaker and the defence sure and not difficult to discover.

6. Kt. to K's 5th (ch.)	6. K. to his sq.

If he move, as given by Greco, 6. K. to his 3rd, you will win. (*e. g.*)

	6. K. to his 3rd.
7. Q. takes Kt. P. (ch.)	7. K. takes Kt.
8. Q. to K. B's 5th (ch.)	8. K. to Q's 3rd.
9. P. to Q's 4th.	9. K. B. to Kt.'s 2nd.
10. B. takes P. (ch.)	10. K. to his 2nd.
11. B. to K. Kt.'s 5th (ch.)	11. B. to B's 3rd.
12. Castles.	12. Q. to K. B's sq.
13. Q. to K's 5th (ch.)	

And wins.

7. Q. takes P.	7. K. Kt. to B's 3rd.

Lolli's ingenious but weaker defence consisted in now playing 7. Q. to K. B's 3rd, and pursuing the game as follows :—

	7. Q. to K. B's 3rd.
8. Q. to R's 5th (ch.)	8. K. to his 2nd.
9. Kt. to K. B's 7th.	9. Q. takes Kt.

(You can also play 9. Q. Kt. to B's 3rd.)

10. Q. to K's 5th (ch.)	10. Q. to K's 3rd (best)
11. Q. takes R.	11. K. Kt. to B's 3rd.

It was formerly considered that the White Queen could now escape only by some sacrifice, and Ponziani declared it to be impossible, after the move of 11. Kt. to K. B's 3rd, to save her. The German "Handbuch" shows, however, that she may be extricated without incurring any loss, and remarks that it is not advisable, therefore, for Black to play with the idea of winning her.

12. Castles (best)	12. P. to Q's 3rd.
13. Q. Kt. to B's 3rd.	13. P. to Q. B's 3rd.
14. R. takes K. B. P.	14. Q. Kt. to Q's 2nd.
15. P. to Q's 4th.	15. Q. to K. B's 2nd.
16. P. to K's 5th.	16. P. takes P.
17. P. takes P.	17. Q. Kt. takes P.
18. P. to Q. Kt.'s 3rd.	18. Q. Kt. to K. Kt.'s 3rd.
19. B. to Q. R's 3rd (ch.)	19. K. to his sq.
20. R. takes K. Kt.	20. Kt. takes Q.
21. R. takes Q.	21. Kt. takes R.
22. R. to K's sq. (ch.)	

With a better game.

It would thus appear that Lolli's move of 7. Q. to K. B's 3rd, however ingenious, is not so trustworthy a defence as 7. Kt. to K. B's 3rd. Let us now follow out the result of that mode of operation.

8. Q. takes K. B. P.	8. P. to Q's 3rd.
9. Kt. to Q. B's 4th.	9. Q. Kt. to B's 3rd.
10. Castles.	10. B. to K. Kt.'s 2nd.
11. P. to Q's 3rd.	11. Q. B. to K's 3rd.
12. Q. to K. Kt.'s 3rd.	12. Q. to K's 2nd.

Your attack is exhausted.

GAMES

ILLUSTRATIVE OF THE MUZIO GAMBIT.

(From the *Chess-Player's Chronicle*.)

GAME I.—Between Mr. Lewis and an Amateur of great skill.

WHITE. (Mr. L.)	BLACK. (Mr. —)
1. P. to K's 4th.	1. P. to K's 4th.
2. P. to K. B's 4th.	2. P. takes P.
3. K. Kt. to B's 3rd.	3. P. to K. Kt.'s 4th.
4. K. B. to Q. B's 4th.	4. P. to K. Kt.'s 5th.
5. Castles.	5. P. takes Kt.
6. Q. takes P.	6. K. B. to R's 3rd.
7. P. to Q's 4th.	7. Q. to K's 2nd.
8. Q. B. takes P.	8. Q. Kt. to B's 3rd.
9. Q. B. takes K. B.	9. Kt. takes B.
10. Q. to K. R's 5th.	10. Q. to K. B's sq.
11. K. R. to B's 6th.	11. Q. to K. Kt.'s 2nd.
12. Q. takes Kt.	12. Q. takes Q.
13. K. R. takes Q.	13. Q. Kt. takes Q. P.
14. Q. Kt. to Q. R's 3rd	14. P. to Q. B's 3rd.
15. K. R. to Q's 6th.	15. Kt. to K's 3rd.
16. Q. R. to Q's sq.	16. K. R. to K. Kt.'s sq.
17. K. B. takes Kt.	17. K. B. P. takes B.
18. Kt. to Q. B's 4th.	18. K. R. to K. Kt.'s 4th
19. K. to B's 2nd.	19. K. to his 2nd.
20. Kt. to K's 3rd.	20. P. to Q. R's 4th.
21. K. to his B's 3rd.	21. P. to Q. Kt.'s 4th.
22. Kt. to K. Kt.'s 4th.	22. Q. R. to his 2nd.
23. K. to B's 4th.	23. K. R. to Q. B's 4th.
24. P. to Q. B's 3rd.	24. P. to Q. Kt.'s 5th.
25. P. takes P.	25. P. takes P.
26. Kt. to K's 5th.	26. K. R. to Q. B's 7th.
27. P. to Q. R's 4th.	27. R. takes Q. Kt. P.
28. K. R. takes Q. B. P.	28. R. to K. B's 7th (ch.)
29. K. to his 3rd.	29. R. to K. B's sq.
30. Q. R. to Q. B's sq.	30. B. to Q. R's 3rd.
31. K. R. to Q. B's 7th.	31. R. takes R.
32. R. takes R.	32. K. to Q's 3rd.
33. R. to Q. R's 7th.	33. K. takes Kt.

34. R. takes B.	34. R. to Q. Kt.'s sq.
35. R. to Q. R's 5th (ch.)	35. P. to Q's 4th.
36. P. takes P.	36. P. takes P.
37. K. to Q's 3rd.	37. R. to Q. B's sq.
38. R. to Q. Kt.'s 5th.	38. R. to Q. B's 6th (ch.)
39. K. to Q's 2nd.	39. R. to Q. B's 5th.
40. P. to Q. R's 5th.	40. R. to K. B's 5th.
41. P. to Q. R's 6th.	41. R. to K. B's 7th (ch.)
42. K. to Q's 3rd.	42. R. to Q. R's 7th.
43. R. takes Q. Kt. P.	43. R. takes Q. R. P.

Drawn game.

GAME II.—Between Mr. Szen, of Hungary, and V. H. der Laza, of the Berlin Chess Club.

WHITE. (V. H. d. L.)	BLACK. (Mr. S.)
1. P. to K's 4th.	1. P. to K's 4th.
2. P. to K. B's 4th.	2. P. takes P.
3. K. Kt. to B's 3rd.	3. P. to Kt.'s 4th.
4. B. to Q. B's 4th.	4. P. to K. Kt.'s 5th.
5. Castles.	5. P. takes Kt.
6. Q. takes P.	6. Q. to K. B's 3rd.
7. P. to K's 5th.	7. Q. takes K. P.
8. P. to Q's 3rd.	8. K. B. to K. R's 3rd.
9. Kt. to Q. B's 3rd.	9. K. Kt. to K's 2nd.
10. Q. B. to Q's 2nd.	10. Castles.*
11. Q. R. to K's sq.	11. Q. to Q. B's 4th (ch.)
12. K. to R's sq.	12. P. to Q. B's 3rd.
13. K. to K's 4th.	13. Q. to K. B's 4th.
14. Q. B. to his 3rd.	14. B. to K. Kt.'s 2nd.
15. Kt. to Q's 6th.	15. Q. to K. Kt.'s 4th.
16. R. takes Kt.†	16. B. takes Q. B.‡
17. R. takes K. B. P.	17. R. takes R.
18. B. takes R. (ch.)	18. K. to Kt.'s 2nd.
19. P. takes B.	19. Kt. to Q. R's 3rd.
20. Q. takes K. B. P.	20. Q. takes Q.
21. R. takes Q.	21. Kt. to Q. B's 2nd.
22. B. to Q. Kt.'s 3rd.	22. Kt. to Q's 4th.
23. B. takes Kt.	23. P. takes B.
24. R. to B's 7th (ch.)	24. K. to Kt.'s sq.
25. R. to K's 7th.	25. P. to Q. Kt.'s 3rd.
26. R. to K's 8th (ch.)	26. K. to Kt.'s 2nd.
27. R. takes B.	

And wins.

---

* Not considered so strong a move as 10. P. to Q. B's 3rd.

† Well played.

‡ Had he taken R. with Q., White would have won a Piece by at once playing Kt. to K. B's 5th.

GAME III.—Between two Berlin players.

WHITE.	BLACK.
1. P. to K's 4th.	1. P. to K's 4th.
2. P. to K. B's 4th.	2. P. takes P.
3. K. Kt. to B's 3rd.	3. P. to K. Kt.'s 4th.
4. K. B. to Q. B's 4th.	4. P. to K. Kt.'s 5th.
5. Castles.	5. P. takes Kt.
6. Q. takes P.	6. Q. to K. B's 3rd.
7. P. to K's 5th.	7. Q. takes P.
8. P. to Q's 3rd.	8. K. B. to R's 3rd.
9. Q. B. to Q's 2nd.	9. K. Kt. to K's 2nd.
10. Q. Kt. to B's 3rd.	10. P. to Q. B's 3rd.
11. Q. R. to K's sq.	11. Q. to B's 4th (ch.)
12. K. to R's sq.	12. P. to Q's 4th.
13. Q. to K. R's 5th.	13. Q. to her 3rd.
14. K. B. takes Q. P.	14. Castles.
15. K. B. to Q. Kt.'s 3rd.	15. Q. to K. Kt.'s 3rd.
16. Q. to Q. B's 5th.	16. K. Kt. to K. B's 4th.
17. Q. B. takes P.	17. K. B. takes B.
18. K. R. takes B.	18. K. Kt. to his 2nd.
19. Kt. to K's 4th.	19. K. Kt. to K's 3rd.
20. B. takes Kt.	20. Q. B. takes B.
21. Kt. to B's 6th (ch.)	21. K. to Kt.'s 2nd.
22. R. takes B.	22. P. takes R.
23. Kt. to R's 5th (ch.)	23. K. to R's 3rd.
24. R. takes R.	24. Q. takes Kt.
25. R. to B's 6th (ch.)	25. K. to Kt.'s 2nd.
26. Q. mates.	

GAME IV.—Between Mr. Staunton and an Amateur.

WHITE. (Mr. S.)	BLACK. (Mr. —)
1. P. to K's 4th.	1. P. to K's 4th.
2. P. to K. B's 4th.	2. P. takes P.
3. K. Kt. to B's 3rd.	3. P. to K. Kt.'s 4th.
4. B. to Q. B's 4th.	4. P. to Kt.'s 5th.
5. Castles.	5. P. takes Kt.
6. Q. takes P.	6. Q. to K. B's 3rd.
7. P. to K's 5th.	7. Q. takes P.
8. P. to Q's 3rd.	8. K. B. to R's 3rd.
9. Q. Kt. to B's 3rd.	9. P. to Q. B's 3rd.
10. Q. B. takes P.	10. Q. to Q's 5th (ch.)
11. K. to R's sq.	11. B. takes B.
12. Q. R. to K's sq. (ch.)	12. K. Kt. to K's 2nd.
13. R. to K's 4th.	13. Q. to K. Kt.'s 2nd.
14. Q. takes B.	14. P. to Q's 4th.
15. B. takes Q. P.	15. P. takes B.
16. R. takes Kt. (ch.)	16. K. takes R.
17. Kt. takes P. (ch.)	17. K. to K's 3rd.

18. Q. to K's 4th (ch.)	18. K. to Q's 2nd.
19. Q. to Q's 7th (ch.)	19. K. to Q. B's 3rd.
20. Q. to B's 7th (ch.)	20. K. takes Kt.
21. P. to Q. B's 4th (ch.)	21. K. to Q's 5th.
22. Q. to Q's 6th (ch.)	22. K. to K's 6th.
23. Q. to K. B's 4th (ch.)	23. K. takes Q. P.

White mates in two moves.

GAME V.—From Ghulam Kassim.

WHITE.	BLACK.
1. P. to K's 4th.	1. P. to K's 4th.
2. P. to K. B's 4th.	2. P. takes P.
3. K. Kt. to B's 3rd.	3. P. to K. Kt.'s 4th
4. B. to Q. B's 4th.	4. P. to K. Kt.'s 5th
5. P. to Q's 4th.	5. P. takes Kt.
6. Q. takes P.	6. P. to Q's 4th.
7. B. takes P.	7. K. Kt. to B's 3rd.
8. Castles.	8. Kt. takes B.
9. P. takes Kt.	9. Q. to B's 3rd.
10. Q. to Kt.'s 4th (ch.)	10. K. to Q's sq.
11. B. takes P.	11. Q. to K's 2nd.
12. Q. to B's 3rd.	12. R. to Kt.'s sq.
13. Kt. to Q's 2nd.	13. B. to K. Kt.'s 5th.
14. Q. to B's 2nd.	14. Kt. to Q's 2nd.
15. Q. R. to K's sq.	15. Q. to B's 3rd.
16. Kt. to K's 4th.	16. Q. to K. Kt.'s 3rd
17. P. to Q. B's 4th.	17. K. B. to Q's 3rd.
18. B. takes B.	18. P. takes B.
19. P. to Q. B's 5th.	19. P. takes P.
20. P. takes P.	20. K. R. to K's sq.
21. Kt. to Q's 6th.	21. R. takes R.
22. Q. takes R.	22. K. to Q. B's 2nd.
23. Q. to her Kt.'s 4th.	23. K. to Q's sq.

White must win.

GAME VI.—Mr. Staunton gives the Queen's Rook.

(Remove White's Q. R. from the board.)

WHITE. (Mr. S.)	BLACK. (Amateur.)
1. P. to K's 4th.	1. P to K's 4th.
2. P. to K. B's 4th.	2. P. takes P.
3. K. Kt. to B's 3rd.	3. P. to K. Kt.'s 4th.
4. K. B. to Q. B's 4th.	4. P. to K. Kt.'s 5th.
5. P. to Q's 4th.	5. P. takes Kt.
6. Castles.	6. P. takes K. Kt. P.*

* P. to Q's 4th, followed by Q. B. to K. Kt.'s 5th, would have been better play.

7. B. takes K. B. P. (ch.)	7. K. takes B.
8. R. takes P. (ch.)	8. Kt. to K. B's 3rd.
9. P. to K's 5th.	9. K. to Kt.'s sq.
10. P. takes Kt.	10. P. to Q's 4th.
11. Q. to K. R's 5th.	11. Q. Kt. to B's 3rd.
12. R. to K. B's 2nd.	

Black surrendered.

GAME VII.—Mr. Staunton gives his Queen's Rook.

(Remove White's Q. R. from the board.)

WHITE. (Mr. S.)	BLACK. (Mr. —)
1. P. to K's 4th.	1. P. to K's 4th.
2. P. to K. B's 4th.	2. P. takes P.
3. K. Kt. to B's 3rd.	3. P. to K. Kt.'s 4th.
4. B. to Q. B's 4th.	4. P. to K. Kt.'s 5th.
5. P. to Q's 4th.	5. P. takes Kt.
6. Q. takes P.	6. K. B. to K. R's 3rd.*
7. Castles.	7. P. to Q's 4th.
8. B. takes Q. P.	8. P. to Q. B's 3rd.
9. B. takes K. B. P. (ch.)	9. K. takes B.
10. Q. B. takes P.	10. K. B. takes B.
11. Q. takes B. (ch.)	11. Kt. to K. B's 3rd.
12. P. to K's 5th.	12. Q. Kt. to Q's 2nd.
13. Q. Kt. to B's 3rd.	13. R. to K's sq.
14. Q. Kt. to K's 4th.	14. K. to Kt.'s sq.
15. P. takes Kt.	15. K. to R's sq.
16. P. to K. B's 7th.†	16. R. to B's sq.
17. Q. to K. R's 6th.	17. Q. to K's 2nd.
18. Kt. to Kt.'s 5th.	18. Kt. to B's 3rd.
19. P. to K. R's 3rd.‡	19. Q. B. to Q's 2nd.
20. R. takes Kt.	

And wins.

GAME VIII.—Between La Bourdonnais and Mc Donnell.

WHITE. (Mr. Mc D.)	BLACK. (M. La B.)
1. P. to K's 4th.	1. P. to K's 4th.
2. P. to K. B's 4th.	2. P. takes P.
3. K. Kt. to B's 3rd.	3. P. to K. Kt.'s 4th.
4. K. B. to Q. B's 4th.	4. P. to K. Kt.'s 5th.
5. Q. Kt. to B's 3rd.	5. P. takes Kt.

---

* If Q. to B's 3rd, White should advance P. to K's 5th.

† Better than moving the Kt. either to Q's 6th or K. Kt.'s 5th.

‡ Preferable to taking the Kt. immediately.

6. Q. takes P.	6. K. B. to K. R's 3rd.
7. P. to Q's 4th.	7. Q. Kt. to B's 3rd.
8. Castles.	8. Q. Kt. takes Q. P.
9. B. takes K. B. P. (ch.)	9. K. takes B.
10. Q. to K. R's 5th (ch.)	10. K. to his Kt.'s 2nd.
11. Q. B. takes P.	11. B. takes B.
12. K. R. takes B.	12. K. Kt. to B's 3rd.
13. Q. to K. Kt.'s 5th (ch.)	13. K. to B's 2nd.
14. Q. R. to K. B's sq.	14. K. to his sq.
15. K. R. takes Kt.	15. Q. to K's 2nd.
16. Q. Kt. to Q's 5th.	16. Q. to her B's 4th.
17. K. to R's sq.	17. Kt. to K's 3rd.
18. K. R. takes Kt.	18. P. takes R.
19. Kt. to B's 6th (ch.)	

And wins the Queen.

GAME IX.—Mr. Staunton gives his Queen's Rook.

(Remove White's Q. R. from the board.)

WHITE. (Mr. S.)	BLACK. (Mr. —)
1. P. to K's 4th.	1. P. to K's 4th.
2. P. to K. B's 4th.	2. P. takes P.
3. K. Kt. to B's 3rd.	3. P. to K. Kt.'s 4th.
4. K. B. to Q. B's 4th.	4. P. to K. Kt.'s 5th.
5. B. takes K. B. P. (ch.)	5. K. takes B.
6. Kt. to K's 5th (ch.)	6. K. to his sq.
7. Q. takes P.	7. K. Kt. to B's 3rd.
8. Q. takes P.	8. P. to Q's 3rd.
9. K. Kt. to B's 3rd.	9. Q. Kt. to B's 3rd.
10. P. to Q's 4th.	10. Q. to K's 2nd.
11. Castles.	11. Q. B. to Q's 2nd.
12. P. to K's 5th.	12. P. takes P.
13. P. takes P.	13. K. Kt. to Q's 4th.
14. Q. to K's 4th.	14. Q. B. to K's 3rd.
15. Q. B. to K. Kt.'s 5th.	15. Q. to her B's 4th (ch.)
16. K. to R's sq.	16. Q. Kt. to his 5th.
17. P. to Q. B's 4th.	17. K. Kt. to Q. Kt.'s 3rd.
18. P. to Q. Kt.'s 3rd.	18. K. B. to K's 2nd.
19. K. Kt. to Q's 4th.	19. Q. B. to K. Kt.'s sq.
20. B. takes K. B.	20. Q. takes B.
21. K. Kt. to K. B's 5th.	21. Q. to her 2nd.
22. Q. to K. R's 4th.	22. Q. R. to Q's sq.
23. Q. to K. B's 6th.	

And wins.

CHAPTER VI.

THE ALLGAIER GAMBIT.

In the preceding examples of the King's Gambit, White continues his attack after 3. Kt. to K. B's 3rd, by playing 4. K. B. to Q. B's 4th. There is, however, another not unimportant mode of operating at this point, and one which leads to situations of remarkable interest, that is, to play 4. P. to K. R's 4th, instead of 4. B. to Q. B's 4th. Black's best reply is held to be 4. P. to K. Kt.'s 5th, whereupon by your moving the endangered Knight to K's 5th, or to Kt.'s 5th, we arrive at the ALLGAIER GAMBIT, an opening once deemed invincible, at least by Allgaier himself, who devoted much attention to its details, and which still possesses attractions for many players of eminence.

The best authorities to compare upon this Gambit are Salvio (Ed. 1723), pp. 56, 58, 60; Greco (1784), p. 72; Cozio, 1st vol., pp. 48, 85, 98, 123, 165, 167, 172, 180, 196, 329; Lolli, pp. 216, 219; Mosler, tab. vii.; Allgaier, tab. vii.; Horny (1839), pp. 144—156; Lewis (1844), pp. 286—288; La Bourdonnais, pp. 91, 93, 96, 101; "Polytechnic Journal" (September, 1841), pp. 141—144; "Palamède" (1842), pp. 77—117, 298—307; and the German "Handbuch."

GAME THE FIRST.

WHITE.	BLACK.
1. P. to K's 4th.	1. P. to K's 4th.
2. P. to K. B's 4th.	2. P. takes P.
3. K. Kt. to B's 3rd.	3. P. to K. Kt.'s 4th.
4. P. to K. R's 4th.	4. P. to K. Kt.'s 5th (best)
5. Kt. to Kt.'s 5th.	5. P. to K. R's 3rd.

The present game will be devoted to the examination of what follows your move of the Kt. to Kt.'s 5th, and the next to the effects of 5. Kt. to K's 5th.

In answer to your move of Kt. to Kt.'s 5th, Black may play 5. P. to K. R's 4th, 5. P. to Q's 4th, and 5. P. to K. B's 3rd. For the two former see Variation I., the last may speedily be dismissed as bad. (*e. g.*)

	5. P. to K. B's 3rd.
6. Q. takes Kt. P.	6. P. to K. R's 4th.
7. Q. to K. B's 5th.	7. P. takes Kt.

8. Q. to Kt.'s 6th (ch.)	8. K. to his 2nd.
9. Q. takes P. (ch.)	9. K. to his sq.
10. Q. to K's 5th (ch.)	

Winning the Rook, and having the better game.

6. Kt. takes K. B. P.	6. K. takes Kt.
7. Q. takes P.	7. K. Kt. to B's 3rd.

La Bourdonnais recommends for the defence 7. Q. to K. B's 3rd, but the authors of the "Handbuch" think it inferior: you can compare both.

	7. Q. to K. B's 3rd.
8. P. to Q's 4th.	8. Q. takes Q. P.
9. Q. takes P. (ch.)	9. Q. to K. B's 3rd.

(A better move for him than 9. Kt. to B's 3rd.)

10. Q. to K. Kt.'s 4th.	10. Q. to K. Kt.'s 3rd.
11. B. to Q. B's 4th (ch.)	11. K. to Kt.'s 2nd.
12. Q. to K. B's 3rd.	12. K. Kt. to B's 3rd.
13. Q. Kt. to B's 3rd.	13. K. B. to Q. Kt.'s 5th.
14. B. to Q's 2nd.	14. P. to Q's 3rd.

Black's game is preferable.

8. Q. takes K. B. P.	8. K. B. to Q's 3rd (best)

This is Black's best move; it was first given by Horny, a German writer, and it has the effect of utterly paralyzing White's further efforts.

9. B. to Q. B's 4th (ch.)	9. K. to Kt.'s 2nd (best)

If, instead of checking with the B., you play 9. P. to K's 5th, Black takes it for nothing, as you cannot capture his B. but at the cost of your Queen. If you move 9. Q. to K. B's 2nd, he replies with 9. K. to Kt.'s 2nd, preparatory to playing R. to K. B's sq., and finally, if you move 9. Q. to K. B's 3rd, he might proceed as follows :—

9. Q. to K. B's 3rd.	9. Q. Kt. to B's 3rd.
10. P. to Q. B's 3rd.	10. Q. Kt. to K's 4th.
11. Q. to K's 2nd.	11. Q. Kt. to K. Kt.'s 5th.
12. K. R. to his 3rd.	12. Q. to K's 2nd.
13. P. to Q's 3rd.	13. P. to Q. B's 3rd.

He has obviously the better game.

10. Q. to K. B's 5th.	10. B. to Kt.'s 6th (ch.)

If you play 10. Q. to B's 2nd, he replies with 10. R. to K. B's sq., and if 10. Q. to B's 3rd, with 10. Q. Kt. to B's 3rd, as before.

11. K. to B's sq.	11. K. R. to B's sq.

Black has a winning position.

VARIATION,
Beginning at Black's 5th move.

WHITE.	BLACK.
1. P. to K's 4th.	1. P. to K's 4th.
2. P. to K. B's 4th.	2. P. takes P.
3. K. Kt. to B's 3rd.	3. P. to K. Kt.'s 4th.
4. P. to K. R's 4th.	4. P. to K. Kt.'s 5th.
5. Kt. to Kt.'s 5th.	5. P. to K. R's 4th.

When the Kt. is played to his 5th, Black's best reply is 5. P. to K. R's 3rd; and when it is played, as in the next game, to K's 5th, then the proper answering move is 5. P. to K. R's 4th. The objection to it in the present instance is the difficulty afterwards found in expelling the White Kt. from his threatening position. As was before remarked, Black may also play 5. P. to Q's 4th, the result of which it may be well to show at once. Suppose then—

	5. P. to Q's 4th.
6. P. takes P.	6. Q. takes P.

(Ponziani recommends for Black 6. K. Kt. to B's 3rd.)

7. Q. Kt. to B's 3rd.	7. Q. to K's 4th (ch.)
8. Q. to K's 2nd.	8. P. to K. B's 3rd.
9. Q. takes Q. (ch.)	9. P. takes Q.
10. B. to K. B's 4th.	10. K. Kt. to R's 3rd.
11. P. to Q's 4th.	11. P. takes P.
12. Q. Kt. to his 5th.	12. Q. Kt. to R's 3rd.
13. Q. B. takes P.	13. K. B. to Q. Kt.'s 5th (ch.)
14. P. to Q. B's 3rd.	14. P. takes P.
15. P. takes P.	15. B. to Q. R's 4th.
16. Castles on Q's side.	

With the better game.

6. K. B. to Q. B's 4th.	6. K. Kt. to R's 3rd.
7. P. to Q's 4th.	7. P. to K. B's 3rd.
8. Q. B. takes P.	8. P. takes Kt.
9. P. takes P.	9. Kt. to B's 2nd.

If he move 9. Kt. to his sq., you reply 10. Q. B. to K's 5th.

10. P. to K. Kt.'s 6th.	10. Kt. to Q's 3rd.
11. Q. B. takes Kt.	11. P. takes B.
12. B. to B's 7th (ch.)	12. K. to his 2nd.
13. Castles.	13. Q. to her R's 4th.

Allgaier's move for you is 13. Q. Kt. to B's 3rd, upon which Black plays 13. Q. to Q. R's 4th. and you answer with 14. Q.

to her 2nd.   He appears to have overlooked that Black could then play 14. K. B. to R's 3rd.

14. B. to Q's 5th.	14. K. to his sq.
15. Q. to her B's sq.	15. K. to Q's sq.
16. Q. to K. Kt.'s 5th (ch.)	16. B. to K's 2nd.
17. P. to K. Kt.'s 7th.	

And you win with ease.

GAME THE SECOND.

WHITE.	BLACK.
1. P. to K's 4th.	1. P. to K's 4th.
2. P. to K. B's 4th.	2. P. takes P.
3. K. Kt. to B's 3rd.	3. P. to K. Kt.'s 4th.
4. P. to K. R's 4th.	4. P. to K. Kt.'s 5th.
5. Kt. to K's 5th.	5. P. to K. R's 4th (best)

The playing Kt. to K's 5th gives you both a safer and more lasting attack than Kt. to Kt.'s 5th, but the advantage gained by this manner of play has been vastly overrated, since Black has at his command a sure defence, from the line of operations developed in the present game.

Black's move of 5. P. to K. R's 4th is the right one; he may, however, play 5. K. Kt. to B's 3rd, or 5. P. to Q's 3rd, without disadvantage.   For example; in the first place,—

	5. K. Kt. to B's 3rd.
6. B. to Q. B's 4th.	6. Q. to K's 2nd.

(If you play 6. P. to Q's 4th, he replies with 6. P. to Q's 3rd, and if 6. Kt. takes K. Kt. P., with 6. Kt. takes K. P., the game being even.)

7. P. to Q's 4th.	7. P. to Q's 3rd.
8. Kt. takes K. B. P.	8. Q. takes K. P. (ch.)

(If you take 8. K. B. P. with B. (ch.), Black retires his K. to Q's sq., and has the better game.)

9. Q. to K's 2nd.	9. Q. takes Q. (ch.)
10. K. takes Q.	10. P. to Q's 4th.
11. Kt. takes R.	11. P. takes B.

He has the advantage.

In the second place,—

	5. P. to Q's 3rd.
6. Kt. takes Kt. P.	6. B. to K's 2nd.
7. P. to Q's 4th.	7. B. takes K. R. P. (ch.)
8. Kt. to K. B's 2nd.	8. Q. to K. Kt.'s 4th.

(Black may also play, with apparent benefit, 8. Q. to K. B's 3rd, a move lately adopted by the leading players of Pesth.)

9. Q. to K. B's 3rd.	9. B. to K. Kt.'s 6th.
10. Q. Kt. to B's 3rd.	10. K. Kt. to B's 3rd.
11. Q. B. to Q's 2nd.	

The game is about even, but with the move given in the "Handbuch" and elsewhere for White's 11th, K. B. to Q's 3rd, Black may obtain an advantage, I think, through R. to K. Kt.'s sq., with the view to play Q. B. to K. Kt.'s 5th at the proper moment.

6. K. B. to Q. B's 4th.	6. K. Kt. to R's 3rd.

Modern authorities concur in pronouncing the move 6. K. Kt. to R's 3rd inferior to 6. R. to K. R s 2nd, and the "Handbuch" remarks, that after the former, Black must lose the gambit P. We will briefly examine the consequences arising from the defence with the Knight, and subsequently those which spring from 6. R. to K. R's 2nd. (See Game the Third.)

7. P. to Q's 4th.	7. P. to Q's 3rd.
8. Kt. to Q's 3rd.	8. P. to K. B's 6th.
9. P. to K. Kt.'s 3rd.	9. P. to Q's 4th.

If you play 9. P. takes P., he can move 9. K. B. to K's 2nd, and on your moving 10. Q. B. to K. Kt.'s 5th, take P. with P., having the advantage.

10. B. takes Q. P.	10. P. to Q. B's 3rd.

If you take Q. P. with K. P., he plays K. Kt. to B's 4th.

11. B. to Q. Kt.'s 3rd.	11. Q. takes Q. P.

He has decidedly the better game.

The ingenious variation at Black's 9th move we owe to Mr. Knight, an amateur of the London circle of chess-players; it appears as effectual in baffling all further attack in this branch of the Allgaier Gambit, as Mr. Horny's move of K. B. to Q's 3rd in the former one.

GAME THE THIRD.

WHITE.	BLACK.
1. P. to K's 4th.	1. P. to K's 4th.
2. P. to K. B's 4th.	2. P. takes P.
3. K. Kt. to B's 3rd.	3. P. to K. Kt.'s 4th.
4. P. to K. R's 4th.	4. P. to K. Kt.'s 5th.

5. Kt. to K's 5th.	5. P. to K. R's 4th.
6. K. B. to Q. B's 4th.	6. R. to K. R's 2nd.

This is the generally accepted move for Black; and prior to the discovery of Mr. Knight's defence, of which we have seen a sketch in the last game, it was, perhaps with propriety, considered preferable to 6. K. Kt. to B's 3rd.

7. P. to Q's 4th.	7. P. to K. B's 6th (best)

When the Rook is moved to his second to defend the Pawn, as in this game, you may obtain a violent but unstable attack by playing thus :—

7. Kt. takes K. B. P.	7. R. takes Kt.
8. B. takes R. (ch.)	8. K. takes B.
9. P. to Q's 4th.	9. P. to K. B's 6th.

(His best move, for if he play 9. B. to K. R's 3rd, you castle, with an improved situation.)

10. P. takes P.	10. P. to Q's 3rd.

With due care now Black must win, in spite of the exposed position of his King.

8. P. to K. Kt.'s 3rd.	8. Q. Kt. to B's 3rd.

If, instead of 8. P. to K. Kt.'s 3rd, you take the P., he may first dislodge your Kt. with 8. P. to Q's 3rd, and then play K. B. to K's 2nd.

9. Kt. takes Kt.	9. Q. P. takes Kt.

You may also play 9. Kt. to K. Kt.'s 6th, and proceed as follows :—

9. Kt. to K. Kt.'s 6th.	9. B. to K. Kt.'s 2nd.

(He might likewise take your Kt. and then move R. to his sq. again.)

10. P. to Q. B's 3rd.	10. K. Kt. to B's 3rd.
11. Q. B. to K. Kt.'s 5th.	11. P. takes Kt.
12. P. to K's 5th.	12. P. to Q's 4th.
13. B. to Q's 3rd.	13. Q. B. to K. B's 4th.
14. B. takes B.	14. P. takes B.
15. Q. to her 3rd.	15. Q. to her 2nd.
16. P. takes Kt.	16. B. to K. R's sq.

You must lose the advanced P., and Black will then have the superiority.

10. Q. B. to K. B's 4th.	10. Q. to K's 2nd.
11. Q. Kt. to B's 3rd.	11. Q. B. to K's 3rd.
12. P. to Q's 5th.	12. Castles on Q's side.

He has a little better game, but the advantage is not nearly so decisive as in the second game.

Chapter VII.

THE KING'S ROOK'S PAWN GAMBIT.

This deviation from the great parent opening consists in White's throwing forward his K. R. Pawn at the third move, instead of playing the K. Kt. to B's 3rd. The object of this move is to prevent the customary advance of Black's K. Kt. Pawn; but to attain this you sacrifice position, and if properly met, your attack is speedily foiled or turned against you.

GAME THE FIRST.

WHITE.	BLACK.
1. P. to K's 4th.	1. P. to K's 4th.
2. P. to K. B's 4th.	2. P. takes P.
3. P. to K. R's 4th.	3. K. B. to K's 2nd (best)

Black may also play with safety 3. P. to Q's 4th, but that move is not so strong as B. to K's 2nd. (See Variation.)

4. Q. to K. Kt.'s 4th.	4. P. to Q's 4th (best)

You can likewise adopt 4. K. Kt. to B's 3rd, and pursue the attack as follows :—

4. K. Kt. to B's 3rd.	4. K. Kt. to B's 3rd.

(The usual move for Black is 4. P. to Q's 3rd, that of K. Kt. to B's 3rd is given by Stamma, Jaenisch, and the German " Handbuch.")

5. P. to Q's 3rd.	5. P. to Q's 4th.

(If you play 5. P. to K's 5th, Black may reply with 5. Kt. to K. R's 4th and then Kt. to his 6th.)

6. P. takes P.	6. Kt. takes P.
7. P. to Q. B's 4th.	7. Kt. to K's 6th.
8. B. takes Kt.	8. P. takes B.
9. P. to Q's 4th.	9. Q. B. to K. Kt.'s 5th.

Black has the better game.

5. Q. takes doubled P.	5. P. takes P.

He might also play 5. K. B. to Q's 3rd, as advised by Stamma.

6. Q. takes K. P.	6. K. Kt. to B's 3rd.
7. Q. to K. B's 3rd.	7. Castles.
8. K. B. to Q. B's 4th.	8. Q. B. to K. Kt.'s 5th.
9. Q. takes Q. Kt. P.	9. Q. to her 3rd.
10. Q. to her Kt.'s 3rd,	10. Q. Kt. to B's 3rd.

If you venture to take the Rook, the following is the result :—

10. Q. takes R.	10. Q. Kt. to B's 3rd.
11. Q. to Kt.'s 7th.	11. Q. to K. Kt.'s 6th (ch.)
12. K. to B's sq.	12. K. Kt. to K's 5th.

And he must win.

11. Q. to her 3rd.	11. Q. Kt. to Q's 5th.
12. P. to Q. B's 3rd.	12. Q. to K's 4th (ch.)
13. K. to B's sq.	13. Q. Kt. to K. B s 4th.

Black has a winning game.

VARIATION,

Beginning at Black's 3rd move.

WHITE.	BLACK.
1. P. to K's 4th.	1. P. to K's 4th.
2. P. to K. B's 4th.	2. P. takes P.
3. P. to K. R's 4th.	3. P. to Q's 4th.
4. P. takes P.	4. Q. takes P.

He might also play 4. K. B. to Q's 3rd.

5. Q. to K's 2nd (ch.)	5. Q. B. to K's 3rd.
6. Q. Kt. to B's 3rd.	6. Q. to her 2nd.
7. P. to Q's 3rd.	7. K. B. to Q's 3rd.
8. K. Kt. to R's 3rd.	8. Q. Kt. to B's 3rd.
9. Q. Kt. to his 5th.	9. Castles on Q's side.
10. Kt. takes B. (ch.)	10. P. takes Kt.
11. Kt. takes P.	11. B. to K. Kt.'s 5th.
12. Q. to her 2nd.	12. R. to K's sq. (ch.)

And he has the better game.

GAMES

ILLUSTRATIVE OF THE PRECEDING ANALYSES.

GAME I.—Between two English Amateurs.

WHITE.	BLACK.
1. P. to K's 4th.	1. P. to K's 4th.
2. P. to K. B's 4th.	2. P. takes P.
3. K. Kt. to B's 3rd.	3. P. to K. Kt.'s 4th.
4. P. to K. R's 4th.	4. P. to K. Kt.'s 5th.
5. K. Kt. to his 5th.	5. P. to K. R's 3rd.
6. Kt. takes K. B. P.	6. K. takes Kt.

7. Q. takes Kt. P.	7. K. Kt. to B's 3rd.
8. Q. takes K. B. P.	8. P. to Q's 3rd.*
9. P. to Q's 4th.	9. K. to Kt.'s 2nd.
10. B. to Q. B's 4th.	10. Q. to K's sq.
11. Castles.	11. B. to K's 2nd.
12. P. to K's 5th.	12. P. takes P.
13. P. takes P.	13. B. to Q. B's 4th (ch.)
14. K. to R's sq.	14. K. Kt. to his 5th.
15. Q. Kt. to B's 3rd.	15. Q. B. to K's 3rd.
16. Kt. to K's 4th.	16. B. takes B.
17. Q. takes Kt. (ch.)	17. Q. to Kt.'s 3rd.
18. Q. takes Q. (ch.)	18. K. takes Q.
19. R. to K. B's 6th (ch.)	19. K. to Kt.'s 2nd.
20. Kt. takes K. B.	20. Q. Kt. to B's 3rd.
21. Kt. to K's 6th (ch.)	21. B. takes Kt.
22. R. takes B.	22. Q. R. to K's sq.
23. Q. B. takes K. R. P. (ch.)†	23. K. to B's 2nd.
24. R. to K. B's 6th (ch.)	24. K. to his 2nd.
25. B. to Kt.'s 5th.	25. Kt. takes K. P.
26. R. to K. R's 6th (dis. ch.)	26. K. to B's 2nd.
27. Q. R. to K. B's sq. (ch.)	27. K. to Kt.'s 2nd.
28. R. takes R.	28. K. takes R.
29. B. to B's 6th (ch.)	29. K. to Kt.'s sq.
30. R. to K's sq.	

And wins.

GAME II.—Between Messrs. Kieseritzky and Walker.

(From *Le Palamède*.)

WHITE. (M. K.)	BLACK. (Mr. W.)
1. P. to K's 4th.	1. P. to K's 4th.
2. P. to K. B's 4th.	2. P. takes P.
3. K. Kt. to B's 3rd.	3. P. to K. Kt.'s 4th.
4. P. to K. R's 4th.	4. P. to K. Kt.'s 5th.
5. Kt. to K's 5th.	5. P. to K. R's 4th.
6. K. B. to Q. B's 4th.	6. K. Kt. to B's 3rd.
7. P. to Q's 4th.	7. P. to Q's 3rd.
8. Kt. to Q's 3rd.	8. P. to K. B's 6th.
9. P. to K. Kt.'s 3rd.	9. P. to Q's 4th.‡
10. B. takes Q. P.§	10. P. to Q. B's 3rd.

---

* The correct move is that previously mentioned, by Horny, of 8. B. to Q's 3rd.

† Cleverly played.

‡ This is the principal feature of the defence, for which we are indebted to Mr. Knight.

§ If he take P. with P., then Black follows with K. Kt. to B's 4th, threatening both Q's and K. R. Pawns.

11. B. to Q. Kt.'s 3rd.	11. Q. takes Q. P.
12. Q. Kt. to B's 3rd.	12. K. B. to Q's 3rd.
13. K. Kt. to B's 4th.	13. Q. takes Q. (ch.)
14. Kt. takes Q.	14. B. takes Kt.
15. B. takes B.	15. Q. B. to K's 3rd.
16. Kt. to K's 3rd.	16. Q. Kt. to Q's 2nd.
17. B. takes B.	17. P. takes B.
18. Kt. to Q. B's 4th.	18. K. Kt. to K. B's 2nd.
19. Castles on Q's side.	19. P. to K's 4th.
20. B. to K's 3rd.	20. K. to his 2nd.
21. R. to Q's 3rd.	21. Q. Kt. to K. B's 3rd.
22. R. to Q. Kt.'s 3rd.	22. P. to Q. Kt.'s 3rd.
23. K. R. to K's sq.	23. K. R. to Q's sq.
24. P. to Q. R's 4th.	24. K. to his 3rd.
25. P. to Q. R's 5th.*	25. Kt. takes K. P.
26. P. takes P.	26. P. takes P.
27. K. to Kt.'s sq.	27. P. to Q. Kt.'s 4th.
28. Kt. to Q. R's 3rd.	28. Kt. to Q's 7th (ch.)
29. B. takes Kt.	29. R. takes B.

White surrenders.†

GAME III.—Between V. H. der Laza and Mr. H— of the Berlin Chess Club.

WHITE. (V. H. d. L.)	BLACK. (Mr. H.)
1. P. to K's 4th.	1. P. to K's 4th.
2. P. to K. B's 4th.	2. P. takes P.
3. K. Kt. to B's 3rd.	3. P. to K. Kt.'s 4th.
4. P. to K. R's 4th.	4. P. to K. Kt.'s 5th.
5. Kt. to K's 5th.	5. B. to K's 2nd.
6. B. to Q. B's 4th.	6. B. takes P. (ch.)
7. K. to B's sq.	7. K. Kt. to R's 3rd.
8. Kt. takes Kt. P.	8. Kt. takes Kt.
9. Q. takes Kt.	9. P. to Q's 4th.
10. Q. takes B. P.	10. P. takes B.
11. R. takes B.	11. Q. B. to K's 3rd.
12. P. to Q. Kt.'s 3rd.	12. Q. to her 5th.
13. Q. Kt. to B's 3rd.	13. Q. Kt. to Q's 2nd.
14. B. to Q. Kt.'s 2nd.	14. P. to K. B's 3rd.
15. Q. takes Q. B. P.	15. K. R. to Kt.'s sq.
16. R. to Q's sq.	16. P. takes P.

---

* Much better to have protected his K. P.

† This game is much below the usual standard of M. Kieseritzky's play.

17. Q. R. P. takes P.
18. Q. to K. Kt.'s 3rd.
19. Kt. to Q. R's 4th.
20. Q. R. to K's sq.
21. K. to B's 2nd.
22. B. takes Kt.
23. Q. to K. R's 2nd.
24. R. takes B.
25. Q. to K. R's 3rd (ch.)
26. Kt. to Q. B's 3rd.
27. K. to Kt.'s sq.
28. Q. to K's 3rd.
29. Kt. takes P.

17. B. to K. Kt.'s 5th.
18. Kt. to K's 4th.
19. Q. takes K. P.
20. B. to K's 2nd (ch.)
21. Q. to Q's 4th.
22. P. takes B.
23. Castles.
24. P. to Q. Kt.'s 4th.
25. K. to Kt.'s sq.
26. Q. R. checks.
27. Q. to K. B's 2nd.
28. Q. R. to K's sq.
29. R. to K. Kt.'s 3rd,

White wins.

Game IV.—Between MM. Kieseritzky and Calvi.

WHITE. (M. K.)

1. P. to K's 4th.
2. P. to K. B's 4th.
3. K. Kt. to B's 3rd.
4. P. to K. R's 4th.
5. Kt. to K's 5th.
6. K. B. to Q. B's 4th.
7. P. to Q's 4th.
8. Kt. to Q's 3rd.
9. P. takes P.
10. K. Kt. to B's 4th.
11. Q. Kt. to B's 3rd.
12. K. to B's 2nd.
13. Q. to her 3rd.
14. Q. B. to Q's 2nd.
15. Q. R. to K's sq.
16. Q. B. to K's 3rd.
17. K. B. to K's 6th.
18. P. to Q. Kt.'s 4th.
19. K. B. to Q. Kt.'s 3rd.
20. P. to Q. R's 3rd.
21. B. to Q. R's 2nd.
22. P. to K's 5th.
23. P. to K's 6th.
24. Q. B. to his sq.
25. P. takes P.
26. Q. Kt. to K's 4th.
27. Q. Kt. to K. Kt.'s 5th (ch.)
28. R. takes Kt.
29. R. to K's sq

BLACK. (M. C.)

1. P. to K's 4th.
2. P. takes P.
3. P. to K. Kt.'s 4th.
4. P. to K. Kt.'s 5th.
5. P. to K. R's 4th.
6. R. to K. R's 2nd.
7. P. to Q's 3rd.
8. P. to K. B's 6th.
9. P. to Q. B's 3rd.
10. K. Kt. to K's 2nd.
11. Q. Kt. to Q's 2nd.
12. K. to R's sq.
13. K. B. to Kt.'s 2nd.
14. K. to B's sq.
15. Q. to her Kt.'s 3rd.
16. Q. to Q. B's 2nd.
17. P. to Q. Kt.'s 4th.
18. Q. Kt. to his 3rd.
19. P. to Q. R's 4th.
20. P. to Q. R's 5th.
21. Q. B. to Kt.'s 2nd.
22. P. to Q's 4th.
23. Q. B. to his sq.
24. Q. to her 3rd.
25. K. takes P.
26. Q. to her B's 2nd.
27. K. to Kt.'s sq.
28. Q. takes R.
29. Q. to K. B's 3rd.

30. R. to K's 8th (ch.)	30. B. to K. B's sq.
31. K. Kt. to Kt.'s 6th.	31. Q. B. to K. B's 4th.
32. Q. takes B.*	32. Q. takes Q.
33. Kt. to K's 7th (ch.)	33. K. to Kt.'s 2nd.
34. Kt. takes Q. (ch.)	34. K. to B's 3rd.
35. R. to K's 6th (ch.)	35. K. takes Kt.
36. B. to Q. Kt.'s sq.	

And mates next move.

GAME V.—Between MM. Kieseritzky and Ehrman.

(From the *Chess-Player's Chronicle*.)

WHITE. (M. K.)	BLACK. (M. E.)
1. P. to K's 4th.	1. P. to K's 4th.
2. P. to K. B's 4th.	2. P. takes P.
3. K. Kt. to B's 3rd.	3. P. to K. Kt.'s 4th.
4. P. to K. R's 4th.	4. P. to K. Kt.'s 5th.
5. Kt. to K's 5th.	5. P. to K. R's 4th.
6. K. B. to Q. B's 4th.	6. K. Kt. to K. R's 3rd.
7. P. to Q's 4th.	7. P. to Q's 3rd.
8. K. Kt. to Q's 3rd.	8. P. to K. B's 6th.
9. P. to K. Kt.'s 3rd.	9. B. to K's 3rd.†
10. B. takes B.	10. P. takes B.
11. K. Kt. to K. B's 4th.	11. P. to K's 4th.
12. Kt. takes K. R. P.	12. Q. Kt. to B's 3rd.‡
13. P. to Q's 5th.	13. Q. Kt. to Q's 5th.
14. Q. Kt. to B's 3rd.	14. K. Kt. to K. B's 2nd.
15. K. Kt. to K. B's 4th.	15. Q. to K. B's 3rd.§
16. K. Kt. to Q's 3rd.	16. B. to K. R's 3rd.
17. K. to his B's 2nd.	17. Castles on Q's side.
18. P. to Q. R's 4th.	18. K. to Kt.'s sq.
19. P. to Q. Kt.'s 4th.	19. K. R. to his 2nd.
20. Q. B. takes B.	20. K. Kt. takes B.
21. Q. to her 2nd.	21. Q. R. to K. R's sq.
22. P. to Q. Kt.'s 5th.	22. Q. Kt. to K's 7th.
23. P. to Q. R's 5th.	23. K. Kt. to K. B's 2nd.
24. P. to Q. Kt.'s 6th.	24. Q. B. P. takes P
25. P. takes P.	25. P. to Q. R's 3rd.

---

* The termination of this game is very beautifully played by M. Kieseritzky.

† He should have played 9. P. to Q's 4th.

‡ Why not play King's Knight to Bishop's 2nd, winning the adverse Knight?

§ Black should have taken the Knight immediately, and then if the White Queen had taken his Knight in return, he would have won the King's Knight's Pawn, and have obtained an irresistible position.

26. Q. Kt. to his 5th.	26. Q. R. to Q. B's sq.*
27. Q. Kt. to Q. B's 7th.	27. K. Kt. to Q's sq.
28. K. Kt. to Q. Kt.'s 4th.	28. Q. R. takes Kt.
29. Q. R. takes Q. R. P.	29. Q. R. to Q. B's 5th.
30. Q. R. to Q. R's 8th (ch.)	30. K. takes R.
31. Kt. to Q. B's 6th.	31. P. takes Kt.
32. Q. to R's 5th (ch.)	32. K. to Q. Kt.'s sq.

* Badly played. In this situation he might have forced the game by two distinct modes of play.

In the first place :

26. K. R. takes K. R. P.

If White does not take the Rook, Black checks with it at Rook's 7th, and wins easily. Therefore,—

WHITE.	BLACK.
27. R. takes R., or (A.)	27. R. takes R.
28. P. takes R.	28. Q. takes P. (ch.)
29. K. to B's sq.	29. P. to K. Kt.'s 6th.

And wins.

(A.)

27. P. takes R.	27. R. takes P.
28. R. takes R.	28. Q. takes R. (ch.)
29. K. to his 3rd.	29. Q. to K. Kt.'s 4th (ch.)
30. Kt. to K. B's 4th.	30. P. takes Kt. (ch.)
31. K. to B's 2nd (or Kt. mates at K's 4th.)	31. Q. to R's 5th (ch.), &c.

If White at his 28th move refuse to capture the second Rook, and moves his Rook away instead, Black may either advance his K. Kt. P. (ch.), or play R. to R's 7th, checking, secure, in either case, of a won game.

In the second place :

	26. K. Kt. to his 4th.
27. Q. takes Kt., or (B.)	27. Q. takes Q.
28. P. takes Q.	28. R. takes R.
29. R. takes R.	29. R. takes R.
30. Q. Kt. takes Q. P. (best)	30. R. to R's 7th (ch.)
31. K. to his 3rd (best)	31. Kt. to Q's 5th.
32. K. Kt. takes K. P.	32. Kt. takes Q. B. P. (ch.)

And wins, because White must play his King to a square where he will be in check of the Queen which his opponent will make in two moves. Observe, however, that if Black advance his Bishop's Pawn before taking the Queen's Bishop's Pawn, he will probably lose the game by White's first checking with the King's Knight at Q's 7th, and then playing the other Knight to K's 8th square.

(B.)

	26. K. Kt. to his 4th.
27. P. takes Kt.	27. R. to K. R's 7th (ch.)
28. R. takes R. (best)	28. R. takes R. (ch.)

33. R. to Q. R's sq.	33. K. to Q. B's sq.
34. Q. to Q. R's 8th (ch.)	34. K. to Q's 7th.
35. P. to Kt.'s 7th.	35. Q. R. takes Q. B. P.
36. Q. P. takes P. (ch.)	36. K. to his 2nd.
37. Q. takes Kt. (ch.)	37. K. takes Q.
38. P. to Kt.'s 8th, becoming a Q. (ch.)	38. K. to his 2nd.
39. R. to Q. R's 7th (ch.)	39. K. to his 3rd.

White mates in two moves.

GAME VI.—Between Mr. Cochrane and Capt. Evans.

WHITE. (Mr. C.)	BLACK. (Capt. E.)
1. P. to K's 4th.	1. P. to K's 4th.
2. P. to K. B's 4th.	2. P. takes P.
3. K. Kt. to B's 3rd.	3. P. to K. Kt.'s 4th.
4. P. to K. R's 4th.	4. P. to K. Kt.'s 5th.
5. Kt. to K's 5th.	5. P. to K. R's 4th.
6. K. B. to Q. B's 4th.	6. K. R. to his 2nd.
7. Kt. takes K. B. P.	7. R. takes Kt.
8. B. takes R. (ch.)	8. K. takes B.
9. P. to Q's 4th.	9. B. to K. R's 3rd.*
10. B. takes P.	10. B. takes B.
11. Castles.	11. Q. takes K. R. P.
12. R. takes B. (ch.)	12. K. Kt. to B's 3rd.
13. P. to K's 5th.	13. P. to Q's 4th.
14. R. takes Kt. (ch.	14. K. to Kt.'s 2nd.
15. Q. to her 2nd.	15. Q. Kt. to Q's 2nd.
16. Q. to K. R's 6th (ch.)	

And Black resigned.

---

29. K. to his sq., or (C.)	29. P. to K. B's 7th (ch.)
30. K. takes Kt.	30. P. to B's 8th, becomes a Q. (double check), and mates next move.

(C.)

29. K. to his B's sq.	29. Kt. takes P. (ch.)
30. K. to his sq., or (D.)	30. P. to K. B's 7th (ch.)
31. Q. takes P. (best)	31. R. to R's 8th (ch.)

(If the Knight takes Pawn, Black mates in two moves.)

32. K. to Q's 2nd.	32. Q. takes P. (ch.)
33. K. to B's 3rd.	33. Kt. takes K. P. (ch.)

And wins.

(D.)

30. K. to Kt.'s sq.	30. R. takes Q.

Winning; for if White take the Queen in return, he is mated on the move.

* This is the error which loses Black's game. The correct move is 9. P. to K. B's 6th.

CHAPTER VIII.

THE KING'S BISHOP'S GAMBIT.

THE remarkable variety and power of attack obtainable by the first player from moving the K. B. to Q. B's 4th sq., instead of bringing out his K. Kt., at the 3rd move, seem hardly to have been appreciated, or rather discovered, by the earlier writers; and although we find this particular gambit to have been in vogue as far back as the time of Lopez, and to have been a good deal cultivated both in France and England in the eighteenth century, it is only of late years that its resources have been analysed and developed as they deserve. Compare the following works, which touch upon this gambit—Lopez (1584), p. 110; Gianutio (Sarratt's translation, 1817), p. 48; Salvio (Ed. 1723), p. 99; Greco (Ed. 1784), p. 85; Cozio (1st vol.), pp. 67, 334, 342; (2nd vol.) pp. 268, 322, 363; Stamma (1745), p. 43; Bertin, p. 27; Bledow (1843), p. 31; Lewis (1844), pp. 411—444; Jaenisch (who gives the most solid and complete analysis which has yet appeared), vol ii. pp. 163—212; Walker (1846), pp. 211—236; the German "Handbuch;" and the games between La Bourdonnais and McDonnell, in the "Chess-Player's Chronicle."

GAME THE FIRST.

WHITE.	BLACK.
1. P. to K's 4th.	1. P. to K's 4th.
2. P. to K. B's 4th.	2. P. takes P.
3. K. B. to Q. B's 4th.	3. Q. to K. R's 5th (ch.)

The check of the Queen is commended by Ponziani, as enabling Black to permanently protect his doubled Pawn. Instead of this move, however, he has a variety to choose from, for he may play 3. P. to K. Kt.'s 4th, 3. P. to K. B's 4th, 3. P. to Q's 4th, 3. P. to Q. B's 3rd, and 3. P. to Q. Kt.'s 4th, each of which demands examination. (See Games the First, Second, Third, and Fourth, in the next Chapter.)

4. K. to B's sq.	4. P. to K. Kt.'s 4th.

This is acknowledged to be Black's best move; for the result of his adopting instead of it 4. K. B. to Q. B's 4th, 4. K. Kt.

to B's 3rd, 4. Q. to K. B's 3rd, and 4. P. to Q's 3rd, consult Games the Fifth, Sixth, and Seventh, in the following Chapter. From this point, according to the best authorities, you have three different methods of continuing the attack, viz., 5. Q. Kt. to B's 3rd, 5. K. Kt. to B's 3rd, and 5. Q. to K. B's 3rd. The present game will exhibit the variations arising from the first, and the consequences of the latter two systems shall be shown in Games the Second and Third.

   5. Q. Kt. to B's 3rd.   5. K. B. to K. Kt.'s 2nd.

If Black at move 5. attempt to prevent the threatened advance of your Q. Kt. to Q's 5th sq., by moving either 5. K. Kt. to K's 2nd, or 5. P. to Q. B's 3rd, Major Jaenisch considers you will infallibly win the gambit Pawn. The following are his demonstrations. In the first place,—

	5. K. Kt. to K's 2nd.
6. Q. to K. B's 3rd.*	6. Q. Kt. to B's 3rd.

(If he play 6. K. B. to Kt.'s 2nd, you should move 7. P. to K. Kt.'s 3rd and if 6. K. Kt. to K. Kt.'s 3rd, play also 7. P. to K. Kt.'s 3rd.)

7. P. to K. Kt.'s 3rd.	7. Q. to K. R's 3rd.
8. P. takes P.	8. P. takes P.
9. P. to Q's 3rd.	9. K. Kt. to Kt.'s 3rd.
10. K. Kt. to K's 2nd (best)	10. K. B. to Q's 3rd.
11. P. to Q's 4th.	11. P. to K. B's 3rd.
12. Q. Kt. to Q's 5th.	12. K. R. to K. B's sq.
13. P. to Q. B's 3rd.	

You will regain the Pawn.

In the second place,—

	5. P. to Q. B's 3rd.
6. Q. to K. B's 3rd.	6. P. to Q's 3rd.

(If he play 6. K. Kt. to K's 2nd, or K. B. to Kt.'s 2nd, you again reply with 7. P. to K. Kt.'s 3rd.)

7. P. to K. Kt.'s 3rd.	7. Q. to K. Kt.'s 5th.
8. P. to Q's 3rd.	8. Q. takes Q.
9. K. Kt. takes Q.	9. K. B. to K. R's 3rd.
10. Q. Kt. to K's 2nd.	

And you win the Pawn.

---

* You may now adopt the very ingenious mode of carrying on the attack which we owe to McDonnell, viz. :—

6. P. to K. Kt.'s 3rd.	6. P. takes P.
7. K. to Kt.'s 2nd.	7. Q. to K. R's 3rd.

(Jaenisch recommends 7. Q. to K. B's 3rd, instead of 7. K. to Kt.'s 2nd.)

8. P. takes P.	8. Q. to K. Kt.'s 3rd.

Black has a slight advantage.

6. K. Kt. to B's 3rd.	6. Q. to K. R's 4th.

You may also play 6. P. to Q's 4th at least as advantageously. (For the result of that move, and of 6. P. to K. Kt.'s 3rd, see Variations I. and II.)

7. P. to K. R's 4th.	7. P. to K. R's 3rd.

It is not prudent for Black to play 7. P. to K. Kt.'s 5th, or 7. B. takes Q. Kt.

8. P. to Q's 4th.	8. P. to Q's 3rd.
9. P. to K's 5th.	9. P. takes P.

If you play 9. Q. Kt. to Q's 5th, he replies with 9. K. to Q's sq.

10. Q. Kt. to Q's 5th.	10. K. to Q's sq.
11. P. takes P.	11. B. to Q's 2nd.
12. K. to his Kt.'s sq.	12. Q. to K. Kt.'s 3rd.

If he move 12. P. to K. Kt.'s 5th, you take the doubled P. with Q. Kt., and then play B. to Q's 3rd, winning.

13. P. takes P.	13. P. takes P.
14. R. takes R.	14. B. takes R.
15. K. Kt. takes P.	15. Q. takes K. Kt.

If, instead of this sacrifice, invented by Petroff, you play, as suggested by McDonnell, 15. Q. to K's sq., Black's answer should be K. B. to K. Kt.'s 2nd again. Should Black refuse to take the Kt., and play 15. K. B. takes P., you can take the doubled P. with Q. Kt., and afterwards K. B. P. with K. Kt., having an immense attack.

16. Q. B. takes P.	16. Q. to K. Kt.'s 3rd (best)

If he play 16. Q. to K. B's 4th, or 16. Q. to K. Kt.'s 5th, or 16. Q. to K. Kt.'s 2nd, in each case you will have a good attack. In the first place,—

	16. Q. to K. B's 4th.
17. P. to K's 6th.	17. P. takes P.
18. Kt. takes Q. B. P.	18. Q. to her B's 4th (ch.)
19. K. to R's sq.	19. Q. takes B.
20. Q. to her 6th.	20. P. to K's 4th.
21. Kt. takes Q. R.	21. P. takes B.

You may now play 22. R. to K's sq., upon which he would move 22. B. to K. Kt.'s 2nd, you can then take Q. Kt. with Q., and the game is equal.

In the second place,—

	16. Q. to K. Kt.'s 5th.
17. Q. takes Q.	17. B. takes Q.
18. Kt. takes Q. B. P.	18. Q. Kt. to B's 3rd.
19. Kt. takes Q. R.	

You have the better game.

In the third place,—

| | 16. Q. to K. Kt.'s 2nd. |
| 17. Kt. takes Q. B. P. | 17. K. takes Kt. |

(He may also play 17. Q. Kt. to B's 3rd, whereupon you should retort
with 18. B. to K's 6th.)

18. P. to K's 6th (dis. ch.)	18. K. to Q's sq.
19. P. takes K. B. P.	19. Kt. to K's 2nd.
20. Q. to her 6th.	20. Q. to her 5th (ch.)
21. K. to R's 2nd.	

You ought to win.

| 17. P. to K's 6th. | 17. P. takes P. |

If you take the Q. B. P. instead of advancing this P., Black
can check with his Q. at her Kt.'s 3rd.

18. Kt. takes Q. B. P.	18. P. to K's 4th.
19. Kt. takes Q. R.	19. P. takes B.
20. B. takes K. Kt.	20. Q. takes B.
21. Q. to her 6th.	21. Q. Kt. to R's 3rd.

Jaenisch and the German "Handbuch" now suggest the
following as probable moves:—

22. R. to Q's sq.	22. Q. to K. B's 2nd.
23. P. to Q. Kt.'s 4th.	23. Q. to K's 2nd.
24. Q. takes K. B. P.	24. Q. takes Q. Kt. P.
25. Q. to K. B's 7th.	25. Q. to K's 2nd.
26. Q. to K. Kt.'s 8th (ch.)	26. Q. to K's sq.
27. Q. to K. Kt.'s 5th (ch.)	27. K. to Q. B's sq.

And Black is getting into safe quarters.

VARIATION I.,

Beginning at White's 6th move.

BLACK.

WHITE.

WHITE.	BLACK.
6. P. to Q's 4th.	6. P. to Q's 3rd.
7. P. to K's 5th.	7. P. takes P.
8. Q. Kt. to Q's 5th.	8. K. to Q's sq.
9. P. takes P.	9. B. to Q's 2nd.
10. K. Kt. to B's 3rd.	10. Q. to K. R's 4th.
11. Q. B. to Q's 2nd.	11. K. Kt. to K's 2nd.

The move of 11. Q. B. to Q's 2nd is the suggestion of Mr. Schulten, an amateur of New York, and is a singularly beautiful variation from the ordinary mode of play. If, in reply to it, Black move 11. P. to Q. B's 3rd, 11. P. to K. R's 3rd, or 11. Q. Kt. to B's 3rd, you certainly appear to obtain an excellent game. (*e. g.*) In the first place,—

	11. P. to Q. B's 3rd.
12. Q. B. to R's 5th (ch.)	12. P. to Q. Kt.'s 3rd.
13. B. to Q. B's 3rd.	13. Q. to K. Kt.'s 3rd.
14. Q. Kt. to his 4th.	14. P. to K. Kt.'s 5th.
15. K. Kt. to Q's 4th.	15. P. to Q. R's 4th.
16. K. B. to Q's 3rd.	16. Q. to K. R's 4th.
17. Q. Kt. takes P. (ch.)	

You have the better game.

In the second place,—

	11. P. to K. R's 3rd.
12. B. to Q. B's 3rd.	12. K. R. to R's 2nd.

(It is this after-move of 12. B. to Q. B's 3rd, which gives such weight to
the preliminary play of 11. B. to Q's 2nd.)

13. Kt. takes Q. B. P.	13. K. takes Kt.
14. Q. to her 6th (ch.)	14. K. to Q. B's sq.
15. P. to K's 6th.	15. P. takes P.
16. Q. B. takes K. B.	16. R. takes B.
17. Q. to K. B's 8th (ch.)	

You win at least the exchange.

Thirdly,—

	11. Q. Kt. to B's 3rd.
12. Q. B. to his 3rd.	12. K. Kt. to K's 2nd.
13. Kt. takes Kt.	13. Kt. takes Kt.
14. P. to K's 6th.	14. P. takes P.
15. K. B. takes P.	

And wins.

12. Q. B. to his 3rd.	12. K. R. to K's sq.

If he play 12. Q. to K. Kt.'s 3rd, the following moves are
probable,—

	12. Q. to K. Kt.'s 3rd.
13. Kt. takes Kt.	13. K. takes Kt.
14. Q. to her 5th.	

You ought at least to regain the P. sacrificed.

13. Kt. takes Kt.	13. R. takes Kt.
14. Q. to her 5th.	

The game is about equal.

VARIATION II.,

Beginning at White's 6th move.—(See the preceding diagram.)

WHITE.	BLACK.
6. P. to K. Kt.'s 3rd.	6. P. takes P.

This variation is one of the many felicitous inventions of
McDonnell. It is hazardous, but without the utmost exactitude in the defence, it gives you an overpowering attack on
the King's side.

If, instead of taking the P., Black retire his Q. to R's 3rd,
you take P. with P., and if he then take P. with P., you may
play Q. Kt. to Q's 5th, and afterwards P. to Q's 4th.

7. K. to Kt.'s 2nd.	7. Q. to K. R's 3rd.

Jaenisch plays 7. P. to Q's 3rd, in place of retiring the Q.,
and then pursues the game thus,—

	7. P. to Q's 3rd.
8. K. R. P. takes P.	8. Q. to K. Kt.'s 5th.

9. Q. to K. B's sq.	9. Q. to Q's 2nd.
10. K. Kt. to B's 3rd.	10. P. to K. R's 3rd.
11. Q. to K. B's 2nd.	11. P. to Q. B's 3rd.
12. P. to Q's 4th.	12. Q. to Q. B's 2nd.
13. Q. B. to Q's 2nd.	13. Q. B. to K's 3rd.

Black has the better game.

8. P. takes P.   8. Q. to K. Kt.'s 3rd.

He has the advantage.

If at move 7. Black take the Q. Kt., you should play 8. K. Kt. to B's 3rd; if he then retreat his Q. to Kt.'s 5th, you may take K. B. P. with B. (ch.), threatening the after-check with your Kt. If he retire the Queen to Q. R's 4th or 3rd, you take P. with P., and afterwards take his K. B.

GAME THE SECOND.

WHITE.	BLACK.
1. P. to K's 4th.	1. P. to K's 4th.
2. P. to K. B's 4th.	2. P. takes P.
3. B. to Q. B's 4th.	3. Q. checks.
4. K. to B's sq.	4. P. to K. Kt.'s 4th.
5. K. Kt. to B's 3rd.	5. Q. to K. R's 4th.

This method of continuing the attack is not considered quite so strong as developing your game on the Q's side before removing his Queen from her present inactive position, but it leads to many admirable combinations, and, as Major Jaenisch remarks, its resources are far from exhausted.

If Black now move his Q. to K. Kt.'s 5th, you take the K. B. P. with B. (ch.), and if he retire her to K. R's 3rd, you play 6. Kt. to K's 5th.

6. P. to K. R's 4th.   6. K. B. to K. Kt.'s 2nd.

Your present move is considered stronger than 6. P. to Q's 4th, to which Black's best reply would be also 6. B. to K. Kt.'s 2nd. If Black, instead of the move in the text, attack your Kt. with P., you should retreat him to K's sq., and then you must win the gambit Pawn.

7. P. to Q's 4th.   7. P. to K. R's 3rd.

If now at move 7. you play Q. Kt. to B's 3rd, and Black, as his best, move 7. P. to K. R's 3rd, we have the exact position which occurs in Game the First, which see. But you may also play 7. K. to Kt.'s sq., 7. K. R. to his 2nd, or 7. K. B. to K's 2nd, as in Variations I., II., and III.

Black may also play 7. P. to Q's 3rd, although it is hardly so good as the above. Let us suppose,—

	7. P. to Q's 3rd.
8. K. R. to his 2nd.	8. Q. B. to K. Kt.'s 5th.
9. K. to Kt.'s sq.	9. P. takes R. P.
10. Q. B. takes P.	10. P. to K. R's 6th.
11. P. to Q. B's 3rd.	11. Q. to K. Kt.'s 3rd.
12. P. to K. Kt.'s 3rd.	12. P. to K. R's 4th.

If he play 12. K. Kt. to K's 2nd, you answer with 8. Q. Kt. to Q's 2nd, and presently gain the P. at K. R's 6th.)

13. K. R. to K. B's 2nd.	13. P. to K. R's 5th.
14. K. to R's 2nd.	14. P. takes P. (ch.)
15. Q. B. takes P.	

The game is even.

8. P. to K's 5th.	8. K. Kt. to K's 2nd.
9. Q. Kt. to B's 3rd.	9. K. Kt. to B's 4th.

If you play 9. Q. to K's sq., or 9. K. B. to Q's 3rd, or 9. K. to Kt.'s sq., Black will have an improved game. For example; in the first case,—

9. Q. to K's sq.	9. K. Kt. to B's 4th.
10. K. to Kt.'s sq.	10. P. to K. Kt.'s 5th, &c.

Secondly,—

9. K. B. to Q's 3rd.	9. P. to Q's 3rd.
10. K. P. takes P.	10. Q. B. P. takes P.
11. P. to Q. B's 3rd.	11. Q. Kt. to B's 3rd.
12. K. to Kt.'s sq.	12. Q. to K. Kt.'s 5th.
13. Q. Kt. to Q's 2nd.	13. Q. B. to K. B's 4th.

Black has the better game.

Finally,—

9. K. to Kt.'s sq.	9. Q. to K. Kt.'s 3rd.
10. K. B. to Q's 3rd.	10. Q. to her Kt.'s 3rd, &c.

Or you may play,—

10. Q. Kt. to Q. B's 3rd.	10. P. to Q's 3rd.
11. K. P. takes P.	11. Q. B. P. takes P.
12. Q. Kt. to Q. Kt.'s 5th.	12. K. to Q's sq.

He preserves the gambit Pawn.

10. Q. Kt. to K's 4th.	10. P. to Q's 3rd.

If instead, you play 10. K. to his Kt.'s sq., he moves 10. Kt. to K. Kt.'s 6th, and proceeds as follows,—

10. K. to Kt.'s sq.	10. Kt. to his 6th.
11. K. R. to his 2nd.	11. Q. to K. Kt.'s 3rd.
12. K. B. to Q's 3rd.	12. Q. to her Kt.'s 3rd, &c., &c.

11. K. P. takes P.	11. Q. B. P. takes P.
12. Q. to K's 2nd.	12. K. to Q's sq.
13. P. to Q. B's 3rd.	13. K. R. to K's sq.

If you move 13. Q. to her 3rd, he plays 13. R. to K's sq., and on your retiring the K. to Kt.'s sq., advances P. to K. Kt.'s 5th.

| 14. K. to Kt.'s sq. | 14. P. to K. Kt.'s 5th. |
| 15. K. Kt. to Q's 2nd. | 15. P. to K. B's 6th. |

If at move 15. you retreat the Kt. to K. R's 2nd, he plays P. to B's 6th, and if you retire him to K's sq., he may then move P. to Q's 4th, in either case having a great advantage.

16. Q. to her 3rd.	16. P. takes K. Kt. P.
17. K. takes P.	17. P. to Q's 4th.
18. K. B. takes P.	18. Kt. takes K. R. P. (ch.)

And he has the better game.

VARIATION I.,

Beginning at White's 7th move.

BLACK.

WHITE.

| 7. K. to Kt.'s sq. | 7. B. to Q's 5th (ch.) |

Black's present move, and the accompanying variations, occur in a little pamphlet by Signor Dubois, lately published at Rome. Instead of checking with the B. he may play 7. P. to K. Kt.'s 5th, compelling you to move 7. Kt. to Kt.'s 5th,

or endure the dangerous check at Q. B's 4th, and then he
may play 8. K. Kt. to R's 3rd, with a fine attack in prepara-
tion.

| 8. K. to R's 2nd. | 8. P. to K. Kt.'s 5th. |

If you move 8. K. to B's sq., he plays 8. P. to Q's 3rd.

9. Kt. takes B.	9. P. to Kt.'s 6th (ch.)
10. K. to R's 3rd.	10. P. to Q's 4th (dis. ch.)
11. Kt. to K. B's 5th.	11. Q. takes Q.
12. R. takes Q.	12. Kt. to K. R's 3rd.
13. P. to K. R's 5th.	13. P. takes K. P.

If at move 13. you play B. to Q's 3rd or K's 2nd, he takes
K. P. with P., and wins easily. You may, however, play
13. Q. Kt. to B's 3rd, and the game proceed thus :—

13. Q. Kt. to B's 3rd.	13. P. takes K. P.
14. P. to K. R's 5th.	14. R. to K. Kt.'s sq.
15. Q. Kt. to Q's 5th.	15. B. takes K. Kt. (ch.)
16. K. to R's 4th.	16. K. to Q's sq.
17. Kt. to K. B's 6th.	17. K. R. to K. Kt.'s 2nd.
18. P. to Q's 4th.	

Black may now retire his B. to Q. B's sq., checking afterwards with his
Kt. at K. B's 4th. In the little work just mentioned, the variation is
carried on several moves farther, Black being made to play 18. P. to
K's 6th, which appears an unnecessary prolongation of the contest.

14. K. to R's 4th.	14. Kt. takes Kt. (ch.)
15. K. to Kt.'s 5th.	15. P. to K. B's 6th.
16. K. to B's 4th.	16. P. to K. B's 7th.

Black wins.

VARIATION II.,

Beginning at White's 7th move.

(Arrange the men as in the diagram.)

| 7. K. R. to his 2nd. | 7. P. to K. Kt.'s 5th. |

This move of the Rook was thought the best by Ponziani.

| 8. K. Kt. to Kt.'s 5th. | 8. K. Kt. to R's 3rd. |

At move 8. you may play K. Kt. to K's sq., as in the following, given by Petroff :—

| 8. K. Kt. to K's sq. | 8. Q. to her B's 4th. |
| 9. Q. to K's 2nd. | 9. K. Kt. to B's 3rd. |

10. P. to Q's 3rd.	10. K. Kt. to R's 4th.
11. Q. B. takes P.	11. Kt. takes B.
12. Q. takes P.	12. Q. to K. R's 4th.
13. Q. takes Kt.	13. K. B. to K's 4th.
14. K. B. takes P. (ch.)	14. Q. takes B.
15. Q. takes Q. (ch.)	15. K. takes Q.

And wins.

9. P. to Q's 4th.	9. P. to Q's 4th.

If instead of so playing, Black attack your Kt. with P. to K. B's 3rd, you must not retreat the Kt., but take the doubled P. with Q. B., and if then he take your Kt., you win his by K. R. P. takes P., &c. He may, however, at move 9. play P. to K. Kt.'s 6th, in which case the following variation is probable :—

	9. P. to K. Kt.'s 6th.
10. K. B. takes B. P. (ch.)	10. Kt. takes B.
11. Q. takes Q.	11. P. takes R.
12. Q. takes Kt. (ch.)	12. K. to Q's sq.
13. Q. takes K. B.	13. P. to R's 8th, becoming a Q.(ch.)
14. K. to B's 2nd.	14. Q. takes K. R. P. (ch.)
15. K. to his 2nd.	15. Q. to K. Kt.'s 5th (ch.)
16. K. to Q's 3rd.	16. Q. to K. Kt.'s 6th (ch.)
17. Q. to B's 4th.	

You have the advantage.

10. K. B. takes Q. P. (best)	10. P. to K. Kt.'s 6th.
11. B. takes K. B. P. (ch.)	11. Q. takes B.

If he take the B. with his Kt., we have a similar position to that last examined.

12. Kt. takes Q.	12. Q. B. to K. Kt.'s 5th.

If he take the R., you simply move K. to B's 2nd, and must win.

13. Q. to K's sq.	13. P. takes R.
14. K. to B's 2nd.	14. K. B. takes Q. P.(ch.)

And Black wins.

VARIATION III.,

Beginning also at White's 7th move.

(Again refer to the diagram.)

WHITE.	BLACK.
7. B. to K's 2nd.	7. P. to K. Kt.'s 5th.
8. Kt. to K's sq.	8. K. Kt. to B's 3rd.

If at move 8. you pray the Kt. to R's 2nd, he may advance the gambit P., and then take K. R. P. with his Q.

9. Q. Kt. to B's 3rd.	9. Q. to K. Kt.'s 3rd.

You may likewise move 9. P. to K's 5th, but without improving your game ; for suppose,—

9. P. to K's 5th.	9. Kt. to K's 5th.
10. K. B. takes P.	10. Kt. to his 6th (ch.)
11. K. to Kt.'s sq.	11. Q. takes K. P.
12. R. to R's 3rd.	12. P. to K. R's 4th.
13. B. to K. B's 3rd.	13. P. to Q's 4th.

Black has a capital game.

10. P. to Q's 3rd.	10. Kt. to K. R's 4th.
11. Kt. to Q's 5th.	11. Kt. to Kt.'s 6th (ch.)
12. K. to Kt.'s sq.	12. K. B. checks.
13. K. to R's 2nd.	13. Kt. takes B.

He ought to win.

GAME THE THIRD.

WHITE.	BLACK.
1. P. to K's 4th.	1. P. to K's 4th.
2. P. to K. B's 4th.	2. P. takes P.
3. B. to Q. B's 4th.	3. Q. to K. R's 5th (ch.)
4. K. to B's sq.	4. P. to K. Kt.'s 4th.
5. Q. to K. B's 3rd.	5. Q. Kt. to B's 3rd.

5. Q. to K. B's 3rd, we owe to Cozio, who first introduced this move of the Q. into the variations of the Bishop's Gambit. In answer to it Black may move 5. P. to Q's 3rd, or 5. Kt. to K. R's 3rd. (See the Variation.) If he play 5. K. Kt. to B's 3rd, or 5. K. B. to Q. B's 4th, the result will be an even game. (*e. g.*) In the first case,—

	5. K. Kt. to B's 3rd.
6. P. to K. Kt.'s 3rd.	6. Q. to K. R's 4th.
7. P. takes P.	7. Q. takes Q.
8. Kt. takes Q.	8. Kt. takes K. P.
9. P. takes P.	

The game is even.

Secondly,—

	5. K. B. to Q. B's 4th.
6. P. to K. Kt.'s 3rd.	6. Q. to K. R's 3rd.
7. P. to K. R's 4th.	7. B. takes Kt.
8. R. takes B.	

Equal game.

6. P. to K. Kt.'s 3rd.	6. Q. to K. R's 3rd.
7. P. takes P.	7. P. takes P.

If he play here 7. Kt. to Q's 5th, you gain the advantage; for example,—

	7. Kt. to Q's 5th.
8. Q. to her 3rd.	8. K. B. to Q. B's 4th.
9. P. to Q. B's 3rd.	9. Q. Kt. to K's 3rd.
10. P. to K. B's 5th.	10. Q. Kt. to K. B's 5th.
11. Q. to K. B's 3rd.	

Your game is the better.

8. P. to Q's 3rd.	8. Q. Kt. to Q's 5th.
9. Q. to K. B's 2nd.	9. K. B. to Q. B's 4th.

If instead of moving the Q. thus, you play her, as Cozio advises, to her own sq., Black replies with 9. P. to Q's 4th, and has a fine attack.

10. Q. B. takes P.	10. Q. Kt. takes Q. B. P.

Mr. Lewis suggests 10. P. to Q. B's 3rd, instead of 10. Q. B. takes P., pursuing the game as follows:—

10. P. to Q. B's 3rd.	10. Kt. to Q. Kt.'s 6th.
11. P. to Q's 4th.	11. B. takes P., or (A.)
12. P. takes B.	12. Kt. takes Q. R.
13. Q. B. takes P.	13. Q. to her B's 3rd.
14. Q. Kt. to Q's 2nd.	14. Q. Kt. to B's 7th.
15. K. Kt. to B's 3rd.	15. P. to Q's 3rd.
16. K. Kt. to his 5th.	

And Mr. Lewis prefers your game.

(A.)

	11. Kt. takes Q. R.
12. P. takes B.	12. P. to Q's 3rd.
13. Q. B. takes P.	13. Q. to K. Kt.'s 3rd.
14. P. takes Q. P.	14. P. takes P.
15. Q. Kt. to Q's 2nd.	15. Q. B. to K's 3rd.
16. K. Kt. to B's 3rd.	

You have the better game.

11. B. takes Q.	11. B. takes Q.
12. Q. B. to K. Kt.'s 7th.	12. K. B. to Q's 5th.

Black maintains his Pawn.

VARIATION,

Beginning at Black's 5th move.

WHITE.	BLACK.
1. P. to K's 4th.	1. P. to K's 4th.
2. P. to K. B's 4th.	2. P. takes P.

3. B. to Q. B's 4th.	3. Q. checks.
4. K. to B's sq.	4. P. to K. Kt.'s 4th.
5. Q. to K. B's 3rd.	5. P. to Q's 3rd.

He has also the choice of 5. K. Kt. to R's 3rd, as in the following :—

	5. K. Kt. to R's 3rd.
6. P. to K. Kt.'s 3rd.	6. P. takes P.
7. P. takes P.	7. Q. to K. Kt.'s 5th.
8. K. B. takes P. (ch.)	8. K. to his 2nd.
9. B. to K. R's 5th.	9. Q. takes Q. (ch.)
10. Kt. takes Q.	

You have the advantage.

6. P. to K. Kt.'s 3rd.	6. Q. to K. Kt.'s 5th.
7. P. to Q's 4th.	7. Q. takes Q.
8. Kt. takes Q.	8. K. B. to K. R's 3rd.

If he play 8. P. to K. Kt.'s 5th, you can move 9. K. Kt. to his 5th; and if he play 8. P. takes P., you may take K. Kt. P. with Kt.

9. P. takes P.	9. P. takes P.
10. Q. Kt. to B's 3rd.	10. Q. B. checks.
11. K. to B's 2nd.	11. K. Kt. to K's 2nd.
12. Q. Kt. to K's 2nd.	12. K. Kt. to his 3rd.
13. K. Kt. to K's sq.	

Followed by 14. K. Kt. to Q's 3rd, winning the P., with a good situation.

CHAPTER IX.

In the previous Chapter we have followed out, at some length, the most prominent variations which occur when both the attack and defence in this opening are conducted upon the principles recommended by the best authorities, and the result would seem to prove that against every system of attack in the King's Bishop's Gambit at present known, the defence, though difficult and complex in the extreme, is satisfactory.

It yet remains for us to consider what are the probable deviations from the several standard methods of defence, and in what manner these should be turned to advantage by the opening player.

GAME THE FIRST.

WHITE.	BLACK.
1. P. to K's 4th.	1. P. to K's 4th.
2. P. to K. B's 4th.	2. P. takes P.
3. B. to Q. B's 4th.	3. P. to K. Kt.'s 4th.

This mode of defence, though the best in the other gambits of the King's side, is objectionable in the Bishop's Gambit.

4. P. to K. R's 4th.	4. B. to K. Kt.'s 2nd.

If he move 4. P. to K. B's 3rd, you mate him in five moves. If he play 4. P. takes P., then—

5. Q. to K. R's 5th.	5. Q. to K's 2nd.
6. P. to Q's 3rd.	

And you win his two advanced Pawns.

So also, if he move 4. K. B. to R's 3rd, you answer with 5. Q. to K. R's 5th, and presently win the gambit P.; and finally, if he play 4. P. to K. R's 4th, the following moves will show you likewise gain the gambit P.:—

	4. P. to K. R's 4th.
5. P. takes Kt. P.	5. Q. takes P.
6. K. Kt. to B's 3rd.	6. Q. to K. Kt.'s 6th (ch.)
7. K. to B's sq.	7. P. to Q's 3rd.
8. Q. Kt. to B's 3rd.	8. K. Kt. to B's 3rd.
9. Q. Kt. to K's 2nd, &c., &c.	

Showing, as Major Jaenisch remarks, that whatever move he make, unless he checks with his Q. at the 3rd move, you win the gambit P.

5. P. to Q's 4th.	5. P. to K. R's 3rd.
6. P. takes P.	6. P. takes P.
7. R. takes R.	7. B. takes R.
8. Q. to K. R's 5th.	8. Q. to K. B's 3rd.
9. P. to K's 5th.	9. Q. to K. Kt.'s 2nd.
10. K. Kt. to K. R's 3rd.	

You have the better game.

GAME THE SECOND.

WHITE.	BLACK.
1. P. to K's 4th.	1. P. to K's 4th.
2. P. to K. B's 4th.	2. P. takes P.
3. B. to Q. B's 4th.	3. P. to K. B's 4th.

This was the favourite defence in former times. It is found in Salvio, and has been sanctioned by Philidor, Ercole del

Rio and other leading writers of the last century. Both
Jaenisch and V. H. der Laza too appear to believe it may be
adopted with perfect safety.

4. Q. to K's 2nd.   4. Q. checks.

If you play 4. B. takes Kt. or 4. P. takes P., he checks with
his Q. at K. R's 5th. You may, however, play 4. Q. Kt. to
B's 3rd, as in the variation.

5. K. to Q's sq. (best)	5. P. takes K. P.
6. Q. takes P. (ch.)	6. B. to K's 2nd.
7. P. to Q's 4th.	7. K. Kt. to B's 3rd.
8. Q. takes K. B. P.	8. Q. takes Q.

Even game.

These are the moves adopted by the chief authorities. White
would appear, however, to have a better game by taking off
the K. Kt. at his 7th move, then playing Kt. to K. B's 3rd,
followed by Q. Kt. to B's 3rd, and K. R. to K's sq.

VARIATION,

Beginning at White's 4th move.

4. Q. Kt. to B's 3rd.	4. Q. to K. R's 5th (ch.)
5. K. to B's sq.	5. K. Kt. to B's 3rd, or (A.)

Modern chess-writers are not agreed upon the best move for
Black at this point. Mr. Lewis advocates that in the
text, which he conceives to establish the opening in White's
favour, while Major Jaenisch and the German " Handbuch"
consider Black's proper play, and that which gives him an
advantage in the game, to be 5. P. takes P. I present the
leading variations on each of these moves, that you may
judge between them.

6. K. Kt. to B's 3rd.	6. Q. to K. R's 4th.
7. P. to K's 5th.	7. K. Kt. to K's 5th.

If K. Kt. to his 5th, then—

7. K. Kt. to his 5th.

8. P. to Q's 4th.	8. K. Kt. to K's 6th (ch.)
9. Q. B. takes Kt.	9. P. takes Q. B.
10. Q. Kt. to Q's 5th.	10. K. to Q's sq.
11. Q. Kt. takes K. P.	

And you have a sufficient game.

8. Q. Kt. to Q's 5th.   8. K. Kt. to his 6th.(ch.)

If he play 8. K. to Q's sq., you take the gambit P. with Kt.

9. K. to K. Kt.'s sq.   9. K. Kt. takes R.
10. Kt. takes Q. B. P. (ch.) 10. K. to Q's sq.
11. Q. Kt. takes Q. R. 11. K. Kt. to his 6th.
12. P. takes K. Kt.   12. P. takes P.
13. P. to Q's 4th.   13. K. B. to K's 2nd.
14. Q. B. to K. B's 4th. 14. Q. to K. Kt.'s 5th.
15. Kt. to K. Kt.'s 5th. 15. Q. takes Q. B.
16. Kt. to K. B's 7th (ch.) 16. K. to his sq.
17. Q. to her 3rd.   17. K. B. to Q's sq.
18. K. Kt. to Q's 6th (ch.) 18. K. to B's sq.
19. Q. R. to K. B's sq.

And you will checkmate in a few moves.

(A.)

5. P. takes K. P.

This is the move recommended by Jaenisch in preference to
Mr. Lewis's play of 5. K. Kt. to B's 3rd.

6. Q. Kt. takes P.   6. P. to Q. B's 3rd.
7. Q. to K's 2nd.   7. K. to Q's sq.
8. K. Kt. to K. B's 3rd. 8. Q. to K's 2nd.

If he play 8. Q. to K. R's 4th, you reply with Q. Kt. to
K. Kt.'s 5th; and if then he play 8. P. to Q's 4th, you move
9. K. Kt. to K's 5th.

9. Q. Kt. to K. Kt.'s 5th. 9. Q. takes Q. (ch.)
10. B. takes Q.   10. K. to his sq.
11. K. Kt. to K's 5th. 11. K. B. to K's 2nd.
12. K. Kt. to K. B's 7th. 12. B. takes Q. Kt.
13. Kt. takes B.   13. P. to K. R's 3rd.
14. B. to K. R's 5th (ch.) 14. K. to K's 2nd.
15. Kt. to K. B's 7th. 15. K. Kt. to B's 3rd.
16. Kt. takes R.   16. Kt. takes B.
17. Kt. to Kt.'s 6th (ch.) 17. K. to B's 3rd.
18. Kt. to K. R's 4th. 18. P. to K. Kt.'s 4th.
19. Kt. to K. B's 3rd.

You have the better game.
The two last variations are from Lewis's Treatise (1844).

GAME THE THIRD.

WHITE.   BLACK.
1. P. to K's 4th.   1. P. to K's 4th.
2. P. to K. B's 4th. 2. P. takes P.
3. B. to Q. B's 4th. 3. P. to Q's 4th.

This defence, although perhaps not critically sound, is preferable, I think, to either of the two last examined.

| 4. B. takes P. | 4. K. Kt. to B's 3rd. |

If you take P. with P., instead of with the B., you mask the attack of your B., and enable him more speedily to develope his forces.

| 5. Q. to K's 2nd. | 5. Kt. takes B. |

The "Handbuch" gives this as your best move; 5. Q. to B's 3rd appears to be inferior, from her occupying the sq. your Kt. is wanted on. You may, however, instead of moving the Q., play 5. Q. Kt. to B's 3rd, for which see the variation.

In place of taking the B., Black may move 5. P. to Q. B's 3rd, but you then have an immediate advantage.

| 6. P. takes Kt. (dis. ch.) | 6. B. to K's 2nd. |
| 7. Q. to K. B's 3rd. | 7. B. to K. R's 5th (ch.). |

As the "Handbuch" observes, you may also play 7. P. to Q's 3rd, but in that case, I think, Black would get the better game by castling, and threatening, at his next move, to play R. to K's sq. if you took his P., or B. to K. R's 5th if you attempted either to sustain your doubled P. or brought out your K. Kt.

8. P. to K. Kt.'s 3rd.	8. P. takes P.
9. P. takes P.	9. B. to K. Kt.'s 4th.
10. Q. Kt. to B's 3rd.	

Even game.

These are the moves which the "Handbuch" gives, but the defence has yet to be thoroughly analysed. At move 8. Black, instead of taking the K. Kt. P., and thus opening your R's file, may castle, and then, perhaps, your best move would be 9. K. Kt. to K's 2nd, but if you took either his B. or P., he would win the game, I think. For example; in the first place,—

	8. Castles.
9. P. takes B.	9. Q. takes P. (ch.)
10. Q. to B's 2nd.	10. R. to K's sq. (ch.)

(If at move 10. you play K. to B's sq., he answers with R. to K's sq., and you must lose; for if you then play 11. Kt. to K's 2nd, he attacks your Q. with his B., and if 11. Q. to B's 2nd, he checks with the B. at K. R's 6th, then, when you have taken his B., he takes the Kt. (ch.), afterwards pushing the P. to B's 6th, &c.)

| 11. Kt. to K's 2nd. | 11. Q. to K. R's 4th. |

(If, instead of interposing the Kt., you move your King to B's sq., he checks with the B., &c., as above described.)

| 12. Q. Kt. to B's 3rd. | 12. P. to B's 6th. |

And he must win.

In the second place,—

	8. Castles.
9. Q. takes P.	9. Q. takes P.
10. Kt. to K. B's 3rd.	10. K. B. to K. Kt.'s 4th.

(If you play 10. Q. to B's 3rd, he may check with his R., and will have an irresistible attack.)

| 11. Q. Kt. to B's 3rd. | 11. Q. to her B's 3rd. |

And wins.

I can see no better move for you than this of the Q. Kt. If you take the B., either with your Kt. or Q., you must infallibly lose the game in a few moves, and if you play 11. P. to Q. B's 4th, he retires his Q., as in the text.

You must not regard these deviations from the accepted series of moves as correct analyses; they are merely given to show that there is much latent resource in the present system of defence, and to pique the attention of other writers to it, who have more time and space than are afforded me in the present work.

VARIATION,

Beginning at White's 5th move.

WHITE.	BLACK.
1. P. to K's 4th.	1. P. to K's 4th.
2. P. to K. B's 4th.	2. P. takes P.
3. B. to Q. B's 4th.	3. P. to Q's 4th.
4. B. takes P.	4. K. Kt. to B's 3rd.
5. Q. Kt. to B's 3rd.	5. K. B. to Q. Kt.'s 5th.
6. K. Kt. to K's 2nd.	6. B. takes Q. Kt.

Perhaps your best move is 6. K. Kt. to B's 3rd, instead of to K's 2nd. The "Handbuch" also gives 6. P. to Q. B's 3rd for Black, and then proceeds thus,—

	6. P. to Q. B's 3rd.
7. B. to Q. B's 4th.	7. Q. B. to K. Kt.'s 5th.
8. P. to Q's 3rd.	8. K. Kt. to K. R's 4th.*

---

* Both these last moves I think may be improved. White should have castled, since pushing the Q. P. allows Black to take the K. P., and obtain a decisive advantage. (*e. g.*)

| 8. P. to Q's 3rd. | 8. Kt. takes K. P. |
| 9. P. takes Kt. | 9. Q. to K. R's 5th (ch.) |

(If you castle instead of taking his Kt., you lose a Piece.)

9. Castles.	9. K. B. takes Q. Kt.
10. P. takes B.	10. P. to K. Kt.'s 5th.

An equal game.

7. Q. P. takes B.	7. P. to Q. B's 3rd.

If you take the B. with K. Kt. instead of Q. P., Black will answer 7. Q. B. to K. Kt.'s 5th, then Kt. takes B., afterwards checking with the Q. and playing P. to K. B's 6th.

8. B. to Q. B's 4th.	8. Q. takes Q. (ch.)
9. K. takes Q.	9. Kt. takes K. P.
10. K. to his sq.	

The game is about even, since Black must eventually lose the gambit Pawn. At his 6th move, instead of taking your Q. Kt., he may get an embarrassing sort of attack on you by taking off your K. B., then checking with his Q., and afterwards advancing the P. to K. B's 6th, but with care you can defend yourself.

GAME THE FOURTH.

WHITE.	BLACK.
1. P. to K's 4th.	1. P. to K's 4th.
2. P. to K. B's 4th.	2. P. takes P.
3. B. to Q. B's 4th.	3. P. to Q. B's 3rd.

This mode of defence in the Bishop's Gambit is found in the oldest works, and may apparently be ventured without danger, but without advantage.

For the move 3. P. to Q. Kt.'s 4th, which Black may make at this point, or after giving check with the Q., see the Illustrative Games at the end of the Chapter; observing here only, that after 3. P. to Q. Kt.'s 4th, it is not prudent for you to take the K. B. P. (ch.). (*e. g.*)

	3. P. to Q. Kt.'s 4th.
4. B. takes K. B. P. (ch.)	4. K. takes B.
5. Q. to K. R's 5th (ch.)	5. P. to K. Kt.'s 3rd.
6. Q. to Q's 5th (ch.)	6. K. to Kt.'s 2nd.
7. Q. takes Q. R.	7. Q. to K. R's 5th (ch.)
8. K. to Q's sq.	8. Q. to K. Kt.'s 5th (ch.)

10. K. to B's sq.	10. P. to K. B's 6th.

(If 10. K. to Q's 2nd, Black castles, and wins easily.)

11. P. takes P.	11. B. to K. R's 6th (ch.)

And mates in five moves.

(If 8. K. to B's sq., he plays 8. K. B. to Q. B's 4th, and on your moving
9. Kt. to K. R's 3rd, he replies 9. P. to K. B's 6th, and wins.)

9. Kt. to K's 2nd.	9. Q. takes K. Kt. P.
10. R. to Kt.'s sq.	10. Q. to K. B's 7th.

He ought to win.

4. P. to Q's 4th.	4. P. to Q's 4th.
5. P. takes P.	5. P. takes P.
6. K. B. checks.	6. Q. Kt. to B's 3rd.
7. Q. B. takes P.	7. Q. to her Kt.'s 3rd.
8. Q. to K's 2nd (ch.)	8. Q. B. to K's 3rd.
9. P. to Q. B's 3rd.	9. Castles on Q's side.
10. K. Kt. to B's 3rd.	

The game is equal.

GAME THE FIFTH.

Having gone through the probable variations which Black
may adopt instead of checking with the Q., at his 3rd move,
we have now to consider those at his command, (after giving
the check,) when he does not play the usual move of 4. P. to
K. Kt.'s 4th.

WHITE.	BLACK.
1. P. to K's 4th.	1. P. to K's 4th.
2. P. to K. B's 4th.	2. P. takes P.
3. B. to Q. B's 4th.	3. Q. checks.
4. K. to B's sq.	4. B. to Q. B's 4th.

This defence is found in Greco, but is not to be commended, because it gives you a favourable opportunity to
develope your game and establish your Pawns in the centre.

5. P. to Q's 4th.	5. B. to Q. Kt.'s 3rd.
6. K. Kt. to B's 3rd.	6. Q. to K's 2nd.
7. Q. B. takes P.	7. Q. takes K. P.
8. B. takes K. B. P. (ch.)	8. K. to B's sq.
9. Q. B. to K. Kt.'s 3rd.	9. K. Kt. to R's 3rd.
10. Q. Kt. to B's 3rd.	10. Q. to K's 2nd.
11. K. B. to Q. Kt.'s 3rd.	11. P. to Q. B's 3rd.
12. Q. to her 2nd.	12. P. to Q's 4th.
13. Q. R. to K's sq.	

And you have the better game.

GAME THE SIXTH.

WHITE.	BLACK.
1. P. to K's 4th.	1. P. to K's 4th.
2. P. to K. B's 4th.	2. P. takes P.
3. B. to Q. B's 4th.	3. Q. checks.
4. K. to B's sq.	4. K. Kt. to B's 3rd.
5. K. Kt. to B's 3rd.	5. Q. to K. R's 4th.

If he play his Q. to K. Kt.'s 5th, you take his K. B. P. with B. (ch.), and if 5. Q. to K. R's 3rd, then you move 6. Kt. to K's 5th.

6. P. to K. R's 4th.	6. P. to K. Kt.'s 4th.

You may also play 6. P. to K's 5th without harm. (e. g.)

6. P. to K's 5th.	6. K. Kt. to K's 5th.
7. P. to Q's 4th.	7. Kt. to his 6th (ch.)
8. K. to Kt.'s sq.	8. Kt. takes R.
9. Q. B. takes P.	

The loss of the exchange is compensated by the superior development of your game.

If Black at move 6. take the K. P., you play 7. Q. to K's 2nd.

7. Q. Kt. to B's 3rd.	7. P. to K. R's 3rd.
8. P. to K's 5th.	8. Kt. to his sq.

If 8. Kt. to his 5th, then 9. K. to Kt.'s sq., followed by 10. P. takes K. Kt. P.

9. K. B. to K's 2nd.	9. P. to Kt.'s 5th.

You might also move 9. P. to Q's 4th.

10. Kt. to K. R's 2nd.	10. Q. takes K. P.
11. P. to Q's 4th.	

You have the advantage.

GAME THE SEVENTH.

WHITE	BLACK.
1. P. to K's 4th.	1. P. to K's 4th.
2. P. to K. B's 4th.	2. P. takes P.
3. B. to Q. B's 4th.	3. Q. checks.
4. K. to B's sq.	4. Q. to K. B's 3rd.

Although defective, this 4th move of defence is much stronger than either 4. B. to Q. B's 4th, or 4. K. Kt. to B's 3rd.

5. Q. Kt. to B's 3rd.   5. P. to Q. B's 3rd.

He may also play 5. K. Kt. to K's 2nd. (See Variation.)

6. P. to Q's 4th.	6. P. to Q's 3rd.
7. K. Kt. to B's 3rd.	7. P. to K. Kt.'s 4th.
8. P. to K. R's 4th.	8. P. to K. R's 3rd.
9. P. to K's 5th.	9. P. takes P.
10. P. takes P.	10. Q. to K. Kt.'s 2nd.
11. Q. to her 4th.	11. B. to K. Kt.'s 5th.

If he play 11. B. to K's 2nd, you move 12. P. to K's 6th, and if 11. Q. Kt. to Q's 2nd, you proceed as follows:—

                          11. Q. Kt. to Q's 2nd.

12. P. takes Kt. P.	12. P. takes P.
13. R. takes R.	13. Q. takes R.
14. P. to K's 6th.	14. Q. to K. R's 8th (ch.)
15. Q. to K. Kt.'s sq.	15. Q. takes Q. (ch.)
16. K. takes Q.	

The game is in your favour.

12. P. takes Kt. P.	12. P. takes P.
13. R. takes R.	13. Q. takes R.
14. Kt. takes K. Kt. P.	14. Q. to K. R's 8th (ch.)
15. Q. to K. Kt.'s sq.	15. Q. takes Q. (ch.)
16. K. takes Q.	

You have the superiority.

VARIATION,

Beginning at Black's 5th move.

WHITE.	BLACK.
1. P. to K's 4th.	1. P. to K's 4th.
2. P. to K. B's 4th.	2. P. takes P.
3. B. to Q. B's 4th.	3. Q. checks.
4. K. to B's sq.	4. Q. to K. B's 3rd.
5. Q. Kt. to B's 3rd.	5. K. Kt. to K's 2nd.
6. P. to Q's 4th.	6. P. to Q's 3rd.
7. K. Kt. to B's 3rd.	7. P. to K. Kt.'s 4th.

If he play 7. Q. B. to K's 3rd, you move 8. Q. to her 3rd.

8. P. to K. R's 4th.	8. P. to K. R's 3rd.
9. P. to K's 5th.	9. Q. to K. Kt.'s 2nd.

Jaenisch plays 9. P. takes K. P. The " Handbuch" gives the move in the text.

10. K. R. P. takes P.	10. K. R. P. takes P.
11. R. takes R.	11. Q. takes R.
12. Q. Kt. to K's 4th.	12. P. takes K. P.
13. P. takes P.	13. Q. to K. R's 8th (ch.)
14. K. Kt. to his sq.	14. Q. Kt. to Q's 2nd.
15. Q. Kt. takes P.	15. Q. Kt. takes K. P.
16. Q. to K's 2nd.	

You have the better position.

GAME THE EIGHTH.

WHITE.	BLACK.
1. P. to K's 4th.	1. P. to K's 4th.
2. P. to K. B's 4th.	2. P. takes P.
3. B. to Q. B's 4th.	3. Q. checks.
4. K. to B's sq.	4. P. to Q's 3rd.

This defence is considered incorrect, as it admits of your immediately recovering the Pawn by Cozio's move, 5. Q. to K. B's 3rd, nevertheless it requires to be met with circumspection.

5. Q. to K. B's 3rd.	5. P. to K. Kt.'s 4th.

Instead of 5. Q. to K. B's 3rd, you may play 5. P. to Q's 4th, as in the variation.

If you move 5. Q. Kt. to B's 3rd, his best reply is 5. Q. B. to K's 3rd.

6. P. to K. Kt.'s 3rd.	6. Q. to K. Kt.'s 5th.
7. P. to Q's 3rd.	7. K. B. to R's 3rd.
8. Q. takes Q.	8. B. takes Q.
9. P. to K. R's 4th.	9. P. takes R. P.
10. Q. B. takes P.	

Even game.

VARIATION,

Beginning at White's 5th move.

WHITE.	BLACK.
1. P. to K's 4th.	1. P. to K's 4th.
2. P. to K. B's 4th.	2. P. takes P.
3. B. to Q. B's 4th.	3. Q. checks.
4. K. to B's sq.	4. P. to Q's 3rd.
5. P. to Q's 4th.	5. Q. B. to K's 3rd.

Jaenisch recommends this move for Black; the " Handbuch" suggests, however, that his best play is perhaps 5. Q. to K. B's 3rd, and then the game proceeds as in Game the Seventh of this Chapter. Instead of either of these moves, he may play 5. P. to K. Kt.'s 4th, and the game be pursued as follows,—

	5. P. to K. Kt.'s 4th.
6. K. Kt. to B's 3rd.	6. Q. to K. R's 4th.
7. P. to K. R's 4th.	7. K. B. to Kt.'s 2nd (best)
8. K. R. to his 2nd.	8. Q. B. to K. Kt.'s 5th.
9. K. to Kt.'s sq.	9. K. Kt. to K's 2nd.

(A similar position occurs in Game the Second, Chapter VIII.)

10. P. to Q. B's 3rd.	10. B. takes Kt.
11. P. takes B.	11. R. to K. Kt.'s sq.
12. P. takes K. Kt. P.	12. Q. takes P. (ch.)
13. K. to B's sq.	13. Q. Kt. to Q's 2nd.
14. Q. to her Kt.'s 3rd.	14. P. to Q's 4th.

(You might also play 14. Q. to her 2nd, but still the advantage would be on Black's side, who could castle, with a fine game. Instead of 14. P. to Q's 4th, Jaenisch and the "Handbuch" give Black 14. B. takes Q. P., which seems premature, and leads only to an equal game, while by first advancing the Q. P., he ought, I think, to win.)

15. R. to K. Kt.'s 2nd.	15. P. takes B.

(If, instead of so playing, you take the Q. P. with P., he takes Q. P. with B., and wins; and if you take Q. P. with B., then his move, Kt. takes B., followed by B. to K's 4th, gives him an irresistible game.)

16. Q. takes Q. Kt. P.	16. Q. takes R. (ch.)
17. K. takes Q.	17. Q. R. to Kt.'s sq.
18. Q. to Q. R's 6th (best)	18. B. takes Q. P. (dis. ch.)
19. K. to B's sq. (best)	19. R. to K. Kt.'s 8th (ch.)

(If at move 19. you play the King to his R's file, then 19. Q. R. to Q. Kt.'s 3rd wins.)

20. K. to his 2nd.	20. K. R. takes B.
21. P. takes B.	21. Q. R. takes P. (ch.)
22. Kt. to Q's 2nd.	22. K. R. takes R.

Followed by K. R. takes Q. R. P., and he ought to win easily.

6. Q. to her 3rd.	6. B. takes B.
7. Q. takes B.	7. P. to Q. B's 3rd.
8. Q. to her Kt.'s 3rd.	8. P. to Q. Kt.'s 3rd.
9. Q. to K. R's 3rd.	9. Q. takes Q.
10. Kt. takes Q.	10. K. Kt. to B's 3rd.
11. Q. Kt. to B's 3rd.	11. Q. Kt. to Q's 2nd.

The game is even.

———

GAMES

ILLUSTRATIVE OF THE KING'S BISHOP'S GAMBIT.

(From the *Chess-Player's Chronicle*.)

GAME I.—Between La Bourdonnais and McDonnell.

WHITE. (Mr. McD.)	BLACK. (M. La B.)
1. P. to K's 4th.	1. P. to K's 4th.
2. P. to K. B's 4th.	2. P. takes P.
3. B. to Q. B's 4th.*	3. Q. checks.
4. K. to B's sq.	4. P. to K. Kt.'s 4th.
5. Q. Kt. to B's 3rd.	5. K. B. to Kt.'s 2nd.
6. P. to Q's 4th.	6. P. to Q's 3rd.
7. K. B. to K's 2nd.	7. Q. Kt. to B's 3rd.
8. P. to K's 5th.	8. K. Kt. to K's 2nd.
9. Q. Kt. to his 5th.	9. Castles.
10. Q. Kt. takes Q. B. P.	10. Q. R. to Q. Kt.'s sq.
11. K. Kt. to B's 3rd.	11. Q. to K. R's 3rd.
12. P. takes P.	12. K. Kt. to K. B's 4th.
13. P. to Q. B's 3rd.	13. K. Kt. to his 6th (ch.)
14. P. takes Kt.	14. Q. takes R. (ch.)
15. K. to B's 2nd.	15. P. takes P. (ch.)
16. K. takes P.	16. Q. takes Q.
17. B. takes Q.	17. P. to K. R's 3rd.
18. P. to Q. Kt.'s 3rd.	18. P. to Q. Kt.'s 4th.
19. Q. B. to K's 3rd.	19. P. to K. B's 4th.
20. P. to Q's 5th.	20. P. to K. B's 5th (ch.)
21. K. to R's 2nd.	21. P. takes B.
22. P. takes Kt.	22. P. to K. Kt.'s 5th.
23. K. Kt. to Q's 4th.	23. B. to K's 4th (ch.)
24. K. to Kt.'s sq.	24. K. B. takes Q. P.
25. Q. Kt. takes P.	25. K. B. to Q. B's 4th.
26. P. to Q. Kt.'s 4th.†	26. K. B. to Q. Kt.'s 3rd.
27. Q. Kt. to Q's 6th.	27. K. B. takes K. Kt.
28. P. takes B.	28. Q. R. takes Kt. P.
29. Kt. takes B.	29. K. R. takes Kt.
30. P. to Q's 5th.	30. K. to B's 2nd.
31. B. to Q. Kt.'s 3rd.	31. K. to K's 2nd.
32. K. to B's sq.	32. Q. R. to K's 5th.
33. K. to his 2nd.	33. K. R. to K. B's sq.
34. K. to Q's 3rd.	34. Q. R. to K's 4th.
35. R. to K's sq.	35. K. to Q's 3rd.‡

---

* This was a favourite opening of McDonnell's; he bestowed much time and labour on its analyses, and discovered many skilful methods of diversifying the attack.

† Q. B. to K's 2nd would have been better play we believe.

‡ This game is very cleverly played by La Bourdonnais.

36. R. takes P.	36. R. takes R. (ch.)
37. K. takes R.	37. P. to K. R's 4th.
38. K. to his 4th.	38. P. to K. R's 5th
39. B. to Q's sq.	39. P. to K. R's 6th.
40. P. takes P.	40. P. takes P.
41. B. to K. B's 3rd.	41. P. to K. R's 7th.
42. B. to K. Kt.'s 2nd.	42. R. to K. B's 8th.

Mr. Mc Donnell resigned.

GAME II.—Between the same players.

WHITE. (Mr. Mc D.)	BLACK. (M. La B.)
1. P. to K's 4th.	1. P. to K's 4th.
2. K. to K. B's 4th.	2. P. takes P.
3. B. to Q. B's 4th.	3. Q. checks.
4. K. to B's sq.	4. P. to K. Kt.'s 4th.
5. Q. Kt. to B's 3rd.	5. K. B. to Kt.'s 2nd.
6. P. to Q's 4th.	6. Q. Kt. to B's 3rd.
7. P. to K's 5th.	7. K. Kt. to K's 2nd.
8. K. Kt. to B's 3rd.	8. Q. to K. R's 4th.
9. Q. Kt. to K's 4th.	9. P. to K. R's 3rd.
10. Kt. to K. B's 6th (ch.)	10. B. takes Kt.
11. P. takes B.	11. P. to Q's 4th.
12. B. to Q's 3rd.	12. K. Kt. to B's 4th.
13. Q. to K's sq. (ch.)	13. K. to Q's sq.
14. Kt. to K's 5th.	14. K. Kt. takes Q. P.*
15. P. to Q. B's 3rd.	15. Q. Kt. takes Kt.
16. Q. takes Kt.	16. Kt. to Q. B's 3rd.
17. Q. takes Q. P. (ch.)	17. K. to his sq.
18. B. to Q. Kt.'s 5th.†	18. Q. B. to K's 3rd.
19. B. takes Kt. (ch.)	19. K. to K. B's sq.
20. Q. to B's 5th (ch.)	20. K. to Kt.'s sq.
21. B. to K. B's 3rd.	21. Q. to K. Kt.'s 3rd.
22. Q. to Q's 4th.	22. P. to Q. B's 4th.
23. Q. to K's 5th.	23. Q. R. to K's sq.
24. K. B. to K's 2nd.‡	24. P. to K. B's 6th.
25. K. to B's 2nd.§	25. P. takes B.
26. Q. B. to K's 3rd.	26. P. to Q. Kt.'s 3rd.
27. P. to K. R's 4th.	27. Q. B. to Q's 2nd.

---

* Had Black checked with his Kt. and taken the Rook, he would have been mated in five moves.

† This portion of the game is played by Mr. Mc Donnell with great judgment.

‡ It would have been better to take the Q. B. P. with Q.

§ It is obvious he would have lost his Q. by taking the P.

28. Q. to her 5th.	28. Q. takes P. (ch.)
29. K. takes P.	29. B. to K. Kt.'s 5th (ch.)
30. K. to Q's 2nd.	30. R. to Q's sq.

And White resigned.

GAME III.—Between the same opponents.

WHITE. (Mr. McD.)	BLACK. (M. La B.)
1. P. to K's 4th.	1. P. to K's 4th.
2. P. to K. B's 4th.	2. P. takes P.
3. B. to Q. B's 4th.	3. Q. checks.
4. K. to B's sq.	4. P. to Q's 3rd.
5. P. to Q's 4th.	5. B. to K. Kt.'s 5th.
6. Q. to her 3rd.	6. Q. Kt. to B's 3rd.
7. B. takes K. B. P. (ch.)*	7. K. takes B.
8. Q. to her Kt.'s 3rd (ch.)	8. K. to Kt.'s 3rd.
9. Q. takes Q. Kt. P.	9. Kt. takes Q. P.
10. Q. takes R.	10. K. Kt. to B's 3rd.†
11. Q. Kt. to R's 3rd.	11. P. to K. B's 6th.‡
12. P. to K. Kt.'s 3rd.	12. Q. B. checks.
13. K. to his sq.	13. Q. to K. Kt.'s 5th.
14. Q. B. to K's 3rd.	14. P. to Q's 4th.§
15. Q. takes Q. R. P.	15. Kt. to Q. B's 3rd.
16. Q. takes Q. B. P.	16. P. to Q's 5th.
17. B. to Q's 2nd.	17. Q. takes K. P. (ch.)
18. K. to Q's sq.	18. P. to K. B's 7th.
19. Kt. takes B.	19. Q. to K. B's 6th (ch.)
20. K. to Q. B's sq.	20. Q. takes R.

And wins.

GAME IV.—Between Mr. Perigal and an Amateur.

WHITE. (Mr. P.)	BLACK. (Mr. —)
1. P. to K's 4th.	1. P. to K's 4th.
2. P. to K. B's 4th.	2. P. takes P.
3. B. to Q. B's 4th.	3. Q. checks.
4. K. to B's sq.	4. P. to K. Kt.'s 4th.
5. Q. Kt. to B's 3rd.	5. B. to K. Kt.'s 2nd.
6. P. to K. Kt.'s 3rd.	6. P. takes P.
7. K. to Kt.'s 2nd.	7. K. B. takes Kt.‖

---

* This is not good play, because to recover the Piece, White is obliged to take his Queen too far from the point of action.

† Indispensable, to prevent the Q. checking at K's 8th.

‡ The winning move.

§ An excellent move to exclude the Queen.

‖ This is not advisable play.

8. K. Kt. to B's 3rd.	8. Q. to Kt.'s 5th.
9. B. takes B. P. (ch.)	9. K. to B's sq.*
10. P. to K. R's 3rd.	10. Q. takes K. P.
11. Q. P. takes B.	11. K. takes B.
12. K. R. to K's sq.	12. Q. to her B's 3rd.
13. Q. to her 4th.	13. K. Kt. to B's 3rd.
14. Q. B. takes K. Kt. P.	14. R. to K's sq.
15. R. takes R.	15. Kt. takes R.
16. Q. to K. B's 4th (ch.)	16. Kt. to K. B's 3rd.
17. K. takes P.	17. Q. to her 3rd.
18. Kt. to K's 5th (ch.)	18. K. to Kt.'s 2nd.
19. B. to R's 6th (ch.)	19. K. to Kt.'s sq.

White mates in two moves.

GAME V.—Played some years ago between one of the best players of the day and Mr. Staunton.

WHITE. (Mr. —)	BLACK. (Mr. S.)
1. P. to K's 4th.	1. P. to K's 4th.
2. P. to K. B's 4th.	2. P. takes P.
3. B. to Q. B's 4th.	3. P. to Q's 4th.
4. P. takes P.†	4. K. Kt. to B's 3rd.
5. Q. to K. B's 3rd.	5. K. B. to Q's 3rd
6. P. to K. R's 3rd.	6. Castles.
7. P. to Q. B's 3rd.	7. P. to Q. B's 3rd.
8. P. takes P.	8. Q. Kt. takes P.
9. P. to Q's 4th.	9. K. Kt. to K's 4th.
10. Q. B. takes P.	10. Q. to K. R's 5th (ch.)
11. P. to K. Kt.'s 3rd.	11. K. Kt. takes P.
12. Q. B. takes K. B.	12. Kt. takes R. (dis. ch.)
13. K. to B's sq.	13. Q. B. to K's 3rd.
14. K. B. to Q's 3rd.	14. Q. R. to Q's sq.
15. Q. B. to K. R's 2nd.	15. Q. B. to Q's 4th.
16. Q. to K. B's 4th.	16. Q. to K. R's 4th.
17. Q. Kt. to Q's 2nd.	17. Q. Kt. to K's 2nd.
18. P. to Q. B's 4th.	18. Q. Kt. to K. Kt.'s 3rd.
19. Q. to K. Kt.'s 4th.	19. Q. to K. R's 3rd.
20. Q. R. to Q's sq.	20. Q. to K's 6th.
21. Q. to K. B's 5th.	21. B. to K. Kt.'s 7th (ch.)
22. K. takes B.	22. Kt. to K. R's 5th (ch.)

And Black wins.

---

* Taking the Bishop would evidently involve the loss of the Queen.
† It is better to take the Pawn with the Bishop.

GAME VI.—Between MM. Kieseritzky and Devinck.

WHITE. (M. D.)	BLACK. (M. K.)
1. P. to K's 4th.	1. P. to K's 4th.
2. P. to K. B's 4th.	2. P. takes P.
3. B. to Q. B's 4th.	3. P. to Q. Kt.'s 4th.
4. B. takes Kt. P.	4. Q. checks.
5. K. to B's sq.	5. Q. B. to Q. Kt.'s 2nd.
6. Q. Kt. to B's 3rd.	6. K. B. to Q. Kt.'s 5th.
7. Q. to K. B's 3rd.	7. P. to K. B's 4th.
8. P. to Q's 3rd.	8. B. takes Kt.
9. P. takes B.	9. P. takes P.
10. P. takes P.	10. K. Kt. to B's 3rd.
11. K. B. to Q's 3rd.	11. Castles.
12. Q. B. to Q. R's 3rd.	12. P. to Q's 3rd.
13. B. to Q. B's 4th (ch.)	13. K. to R's sq.
14. B. to Q's 5th.	14. Kt. takes B.
15. P. takes Kt.	15. Q. Kt. to Q's 2nd.
16. P. to Q. B's 4th.	16. Kt. to K's 4th.
17. Q. to her B's 3rd.	17. P. to K. B's 6th.
18. P. to K. Kt.'s 3rd.	18. Q. takes Q. B. P. (ch.)
19. Q. takes Q.	19. Kt. takes Q.
20. B. to Q. Kt.'s 4th.	20. P. to K. B's 7th.
21. K. Kt. to R's 3rd.	21. B. takes Q. P.

Black wins.

GAME VII.—Between MM. Kieseritzky and Desloges.

WHITE. (M. D.)	BLACK. (M. K.)
1. P. to K's 4th.	1. P. to K's 4th.
2. P. to K. B's 4th.	2. P. takes P.
3. B. to Q. B's 4th.	3. P. to Q. Kt.'s 4th.
4. B. takes Kt. P.	4. Q. to K. R's 5th (ch.)
5. K. to B's sq.	5. P. to K. Kt.'s 4th.
6. K. Kt. to B's 3rd.	6. Q. to K. R's 4th.
7. K. B. to K's 2nd.	7. P. to K. Kt.'s 5th.
8. Kt. to Q's 4th.	8. P. to Q's 3rd.
9. P. to K. R's 3rd.	9. K. B. to Kt.'s 2nd.
10. K. Kt. to Q. Kt.'s 3rd.	10. P. to K. B's 6th.
11. P. takes P.	11. P. takes K. R. P.
12. P. to K. B's 4th.	12. Q. to K. R's 5th.
13. P. to Q's 3rd.	13. P. to K. R's 7th.
14. K. B. to B's 3rd.	14. Q. Kt. to B's 3rd.
15. P. to Q's 4th.	15. Q. B. to Q. R's 3rd (ch.)
16. K. to Kt.'s 2nd.	16. K. Kt. to R's 3rd.
17. R. takes P.	17. Q. to K. B's 3rd.
18. Q. B. to K's 3rd.	18. K. R. to Kt.'s sq.
19. Q. to K. R's sq.	19. Kt. takes Q. P.
20. Kt. takes Kt.	20. Q. takes Kt.

21. B. takes Q.	21. B. takes B. (dis. ch.)
22. K. to R's 3rd.	22. Q. B. to his sq. (ch.)
23. K. to R's 4th.	23. K. B. to his 3rd (ch.)
24. K. to R's 5th.	24. R. to K. Kt.'s 3rd.
25. R. to K. Kt.'s 2nd.	25. Kt. to his sq.
26. P. to K. B's 5th.	26. R. to his 3rd (ch.)
27. K. to Kt.'s 4th.	27. R. takes Q.
28. P. to Q. B's 3rd.	28. K. B. to K's 4th.
29. K. B. to K's 2nd.	29. Kt. to K. B's 3rd (ch.)
30. K. to his B's 3rd.	30. Kt. takes K. P.
31. R. to Kt.'s 8th (ch.)	31. K. to his 2nd.
32. R. takes Q. B.	32. Kt. to K. Kt.'s 4th (ch.)
33. K. to Kt.'s 4th.	33. P. to K. R's 4th (ch.)
34. K. takes Kt.	34. P. to B's 3rd (ch.)
35. K. to Kt.'s 6th.	35. R. to K. Kt.'s 8th (ch.)
36. K. to R's 7th.	36. Q. R. takes R.
37. P. to Q. R's 3rd.	37. Q. R. to K. Kt.'s sq.
38. B. to Q. B's 4th.	

And Black mates in three moves.

CHAPTER X.

THE GAMBIT DECLINED.

IF Black does not choose to accept the Gambit he has several modes of defence, which may be briefly noticed. They present, in fact, no particular difficulty of analysis, and none of those complicated and brilliant combinations that arise from taking the Pawn and maintaining it, and it may be remarked generally that, by refusing the Gambit, Black subjects himself to some disadvantage of position, though, probably, not so much as to influence materially the result of the game.

GAME THE FIRST.

WHITE.	BLACK.
1. P. to K's 4th.	1. P. to K's 4th.
2. P. to K. B's 4th.	2. B. to Q. B's 4th.

This appears to be Black's best move, if he declines taking P. with P.

We shall examine, in subsequent games, the consequences of his moving 2. P. to Q's 3rd, and 2. P. to Q's 4th. (See Games the Second and Third.) Black has also several other defences, which are but rarely adopted; for instance, he may play 2. K. Kt. to B's 3rd, on which you take P. with P., and on his taking K. P. with Kt., move out K. Kt. to B's 3rd.

He may also play 2. Q. Kt. to B's 3rd, and you reply
3. K. Kt. to B's 3rd; if he then play 3. B. to Q. B's 4th, you
may move 4. B. to Q. Kt.'s 5th, &c.

If Black move 2. P. to Q. B's 3rd, your best move, as
recommended by Jaenisch, is 3. P. to Q's 4th.

If he play 2. Q. to K. B's 3rd, your best move, according
to the "Handbuch," is 3. P. to Q's 3rd.

And finally, if he play 2. Q. to K. R's 5th (ch.), you play
3. P. to K. Kt.'s 3rd, and afterwards P. takes K. P., and you
have a better game.

3. K. Kt. to B's 3rd.	3. P. to Q's 3rd.
4. P. to Q. B's 3rd.	4. B. to K. Kt.'s 5th.

Your 4th move, P. to Q. B's 3rd, is considered stronger than
4. B. to Q. B's 4th, in which case he replies 4. K. Kt. to
B's 3rd, and the game is about equal. By playing 4. P. to
Q. B's 3rd, you threaten to establish your Pawns in the
centre.

5. B. to K's 2nd (best)	5. B. takes Kt.

This is apparently your best move, but you may also play
5. P. to Q's 4th, for which see the variation.

6. B. takes B.	6. Q. Kt. to B's 3rd.
7. P. to Q. Kt.'s 4th.	7. B. to Q. Kt.'s 3rd.
8. P. to Q. Kt.'s 5th.	8. Q. Kt. to K's 2nd.
9. P. to Q's 4th.	

And the position is, perhaps, a little in your favour.

VARIATION,

Beginning at White's 5th move.

WHITE.	BLACK.
1. P. to K's 4th.	1. P. to K's 4th.
2. P. to K. B's 4th.	2. B. to Q. B's 4th.
3. K. Kt. to B's 3rd.	3. P. to Q's 3rd.
4. P. to Q. B's 3rd.	4. B. to K. Kt.'s 5th.
5. P. to Q's 4th.	5. P. takes P.
6. P. takes P.	6. B. takes Kt.
7. P. takes B.	7. Q. to K. R's 5th (ch.)
8. K. to his 2nd.	8. B. to Q. Kt.'s 3rd.
9. B. to K's 3rd.	9. Kt. to K. B's 3rd.
10. Kt. to Q. B's 3rd.	10. Kt. to Q. B's 3rd.

Equal game.

GAME THE SECOND.

WHITE.	BLACK.
1. P. to K's 4th.	1. P. to K's 4th.
2. P. to K. B's 4th.	2. P. to Q's 3rd.

This move is objectionable, as unnecessarily confining the King's Bishop.

3. K. Kt. to B's 3rd.	3. B. to K. Kt.'s 5th.

Instead of this move you have the choice of 3. B. to Q. B's 4th, the result of which will be shown in the variation.

4. B. to Q. B's 4th.	4. Q. Kt. to B's 3rd.
5. P. to Q. B's 3rd.	5. B. takes Kt.
6. Q. takes B.	6. Kt. to K. B's 3rd.

The game is slightly in your favour.

VARIATION,
Beginning at White's 3rd move.

WHITE.	BLACK.
1. P. to K's 4th.	1. P. to K's 4th.
2. P. to K. B's 4th.	2. P. to Q's 3rd.
3. B. to Q. B's 4th.	3. P. takes P.

If Black does not take this P., you can play 4. P. to Q's 3rd, or 4. K. Kt. to B's 3rd, and the position becomes the same as in the foregoing game. At this point, Jaenisch makes him play 3. P. to K. B's 4th.

4. K. Kt. to B's 3rd.	4. B. to K's 3rd.

Q. to K. B's 3rd would also be a good move for you. If Black now play 4. P. to K. Kt.'s 4th, you reply 5. P. to K. R's 4th, and we have a position which occurs in the All-gaier Gambit.

5. B. takes B.	5. P. takes B.
6. P. to Q's 4th.	6. P. to K. Kt.'s 4th.
7. P. to K. R's 4th.	7. P. to K. Kt.'s 5th.
8. Kt. to K. Kt.'s 5th.	8. Q. to K. B's 3rd
9. Q. takes P.	

You have the advantage.

GAME THE THIRD.

WHITE.	BLACK.
1. P. to K's 4th.	1. P. to K's 4th.
2. P. to K. B's 4th.	2. P. to Q's 4th.

This is the customary mode of declining the King's Gambit, but it appears to be less advantageous for the second player than 2. B. to Q. B's 4th.

3. P. takes Q. P.	3. Q. takes P.

In lieu of taking the Q. P. he can play 3. P. takes K. B. P., as in the variation.

4. Q. Kt. to B's 3rd.	4. Q. to K's 3rd.

Ponziani advises, for your 4th move, 4. Q. to K's 2nd.

5. K. Kt. to B's 3rd.	5. P. takes P. (dis. ch.)

You may likewise take P. with P. and have a good game. Black can move also 5. P. to K's 5th, when the following moves are probable:—

	5. P. to K's 5th.
6. Kt. to K's 5th.	6. K. Kt. to R's 3rd.
7. B. to Q. B's 4th.	7. Q. to K's 2nd.
8. B. to Q. Kt.'s 3rd.	8. P. to K. B's 3rd.
9. K. Kt. to Q. B's 4th.	9. B. to K's 3rd.
10. Q. to K's 2nd.	

The game is even.

At move 9. instead of Kt. to Q. B's 4th, in actual play you would perhaps venture 9. Q. to K. R's 5th (ch.), &c.

6. K. to B's 2nd.	6. P. to Q. B's 3rd (best)

He plays thus to prevent the check of your B., and the subsequent loss of the Q., by your moving R. to K's sq.

7. P. to Q's 4th.	7. B. to Q's 3rd.
8. B. to Q's 3rd.	8. K. Kt. to K's 2nd.
9. R. to K's sq.	

You have a fine game.

VARIATION,

Beginning at Black's 3rd move.

WHITE.	BLACK.
1. P. to K's 4th.	1. P. to K's 4th.
2. P. to K. B's 4th.	2. P. to Q's 4th.

3. P. takes Q. P.
4. B. to Q. Kt.'s 5th (ch.)

3. P. takes K. B. P.
4. B. to Q's 2nd.

Instead of checking with your B., let us suppose 4. K. Kt. to B's 3rd.

4. K. Kt. to B's 3rd.
5. P. to Q's 4th.

4. Q. takes P.
5. P. to K. Kt.'s 4th.

(You may also attack the Q. with Q. Kt., and have the better game shortly.)

6. P. to Q. B's 4th.

You have certainly the advantage.

5. Q. to K's 2nd (ch.)
6. Kt. to Q. B's 3rd.
7. B. takes B. (ch.)
8. P. to Q's 4th.
9. Q. takes Q.
10. B. takes P.

5. Q. to K's 2nd.
6. Kt. to K. B's 3rd.
7. Q. Kt. takes B.
8. Castles.
9. B. takes Q.
10. Q. Kt. to his 3rd.

Equal game.

GAMES

ILLUSTRATIVE OF THE GAMBIT DECLINED.

GAME I.—Between Mr. G. Walker and Mr. Tuckett.

WHITE. (Mr. G. W.)
1. P. to K's 4th.
2. P. to K. B's 4th.
3. K. Kt. to B's 3rd.
4. K. B. to Q. B's 4th.
5. P. to Q's 4th.
6. P. to K's 5th.
7. P. takes P.
8. P. to K. R's 3rd.
9. Q. B. to K. Kt.'s 5th.
10. B. takes Kt.
11. Q. Kt. to Q's 2nd.
12. B. to Q's 3rd.
13. Q. Kt. to K's 4th.
14. P. to Q. B's 3rd.
15. K. to B's sq.
16. Q. Kt. to B's 6th (ch.)
17. Q. Kt. to Q's 5th.
18. Kt. takes B.
19. Q. R. to Kt.'s sq.
20. Q. to her B's 2nd.

BLACK. (Mr. T.)
1. P. to K's 4th.
2. K. B. to Q. B's 4th.
3. P. to Q's 3rd.
4. K. Kt. to B's 3rd.
5. P. takes Q. P.
6. P. takes P.
7. Kt. to his 5th.
8. Kt. to K. R's 3rd.
9. Q. to her 2nd.
10. P. takes B.
11. Q. to K. B's 4th.
12. Q. to B's 5th.
13. B. to Q. Kt.'s 5th (ch.)
14. Q. to K's 6th (ch.)
15. P. takes P.
16. K. to B's sq.
17. Q. to her B's 4th.
18. P. takes P.
19. Q. takes Kt.
20. Kt. to Q. B's 3rd.

21. R. takes P.	21. Q. to K. B's 5th.
22. K. to B's 2nd.	22. K. R. to Kt.'s sq.
23. B. takes K. R. P.	23. R. to K. Kt.'s 4th.
24. K. R. to K's sq.	24. K. to Kt.'s 2nd.
25. P. to K. Kt.'s 4th.	25. Kt. to Q's 5th.
26. Q. to her B's 3rd.	26. Q. takes Kt. (ch.)
27. Q. takes Q.	27. Kt. takes Q.
28. K. takes Kt.	28. K. takes B.
29. K. to B's 4th.	29. P. to Q. Kt.'s 3rd.
30. Q. R. to K. Kt.'s 2nd.	30. B. to Q. Kt.'s 2nd.
31. Q. R. to Q's 2nd.	31. B. to his sq.
32. Q. R. to Q's 8th.	32. K. R. to Kt.'s sq.
33. K. R. to Q's sq.	33. B. to K's 3rd.

And after several more moves White resigned.

GAME II.—Between MM. Devinck and Kieseritzky.

(From the *Cinquante Parties par L. Kieseritzky*, p. 11.)

WHITE. (M. D.)	BLACK. (M. K.)
1. P. to K's 4th.	1. P. to K's 4th.
2. P. to K. B's 4th.	2. P. to Q's 3rd.
3. K. Kt. to B's 3rd.	3. Q. Kt. to B's 3rd.
4. K. B. to Q. B's 4th.	4. Q. B. to K's 3rd.
5. B. takes B.	5. P. takes B.
6. P. takes K. P.	6. Q. Kt. takes P.
7. P. to Q's 4th.*	7. Kt. takes Kt. (ch.)
8. Q. takes Kt.	8. Q. to K. B's 3rd.
9. Castles.	9. Q. takes Q.†
10. R. takes Q.	10. B. to K's 2nd.
11. Q. B. to K's 3rd.	11. B. to K. B's 3rd.
12. Kt. to Q's 2nd.	12. Kt. to K's 2nd.
13. Q. R. to K. B's sq.	13. Kt. to K. Kt.'s 3rd.
14. P. to K. Kt.'s 3rd.	14. P. to K's 4th.
15. P. to Q. B's 3rd.	15. R. to K. B's sq.
16. Kt. to Q. B's 4th.	16. K. to K's 2nd.
17. P. to K. R's 4th.	17. P. to Q. Kt.'s 4th.
18. P. takes K. P.	18. Kt. takes K. P.
19. Kt. takes Kt.	19. B. takes Kt.
20. R. takes R.	20. R. takes R.
21. R. takes R.	21. K. takes R.
22. K. to K. B's 2nd.	22. P. to Q. R's 4th.
23. B. to Q's 4th.	23. P. to Q. B's 4th.
24. B. takes B.	24. P. takes B.

---

* If Kt. takes Kt., Q. checks at K. R's 5th.

† Taking the P. would be wrong, on account of 10. B. to K's 3rd, 11. Q. to R's 5th (ch.), and 12. Q. to Q. Kt.'s 5th (ch.), &c.

25. K. to K. B's 3rd.	25. P. to K. R's 4th.
26. P. to K. Kt.'s 4th.	26. P. to K. Kt.'s 3rd.
27. P. takes P.	27. P. takes P.
28. K. to K's 3rd.	28. P. to Q. B's 5th.
29. P. to Q. R's 3rd.	29. K. to K's 2nd.
30. K. to Q's 2nd.	30. K. to Q's 3rd.
31. K. to Q. B's 2nd.	31. K. to Q. B's 4th.
32. P. to Q. Kt.'s 4th (ch.)	32. R. P. takes P.
33. R. P. takes P. (ch.)	33. K. to Q. B's 3rd.

A drawn game.

GAME III.

(From *Philidor*.)

WHITE.	BLACK.
1. P. to K's 4th.	1. P. to K's 4th.
2. P. to K. B's 4th.	2. P. to Q's 4th.
3. P. takes Q. P.	3. Q. takes P.
4. P. takes P.	4. Q. takes K. P. (ch.)
5. B. to K's 2nd.	5. B. to Q's 3rd.
6. K. Kt. to B's 3rd.	6. Q. to K's 2nd.
7. P. to Q's 4th.	7. B. to K's 3rd.
8. Castles.	8. Q. Kt. to Q's 2nd.
9. P. to Q. B's 4th.	9. P. to Q. B's 3rd.
10. Q. Kt. to B's 3rd.	10. K. Kt. to B's 3rd.
11. B. to Q's 3rd.	11. Castles on K's side (best.)
12. Q. B. to K. Kt.'s 5th.	12. P. to K. R's 3rd.
13. B. to K. R's 4th.	13. Q. to her sq.
14. Q. Kt. to K's 4th.	14. K. B. to K's 2nd.
15. Q. to K's 2nd.	15. Q. to Q. B's 2nd.
16. Kt. takes Kt. (ch.)	16. Kt. takes Kt.
17. B. takes Kt.	17. B. takes B.
18. Q. to K's 4th.	18. P. to K. Kt.'s 3rd.
19. Kt. to K's 5th.	19. B. takes Kt.
20. P. takes B.	20. Q. R. to Q's sq.*
21. K. R. to B's 6th.	21. Q. to her 2nd.
22. R. takes Kt. P. (ch.)	22. P. takes R.
23. Q. takes P. (ch.)	23. K. to R's sq.
24. Q. takes P. (ch.)	

And draws the game by perpetual check.

---

* If Black attack the Q., by playing B. to K. B's 4th, you take the B. with R.

END OF BOOK IV.

SYNOPSIS OF BOOK V.

THE QUEEN'S GAMBIT,

1. $\dfrac{\text{P. to Q's 4th.}}{\text{P. to Q's 4th.}}$ 2. $\dfrac{}{\text{P. to Q. B's 4th.}}$

ACCEPTED AND DECLINED.

IRREGULAR OPENINGS,

INCLUDING

THE FRENCH GAME:—

1. $\dfrac{\text{P. to K's 4th.}}{\text{P. to K's 3rd.}}$

THE SICILIAN GAME:—

1. $\dfrac{\text{P. to K s 4th.}}{\text{P. to Q. B's 4th.}}$

THE CENTRE COUNTER GAMBIT:—

1. $\dfrac{\text{P. to K's 4th.}}{\text{P. to Q's 4th.}}$

THE FIANCHETTO:—

1. $\dfrac{\text{P. to K's 4th.}}{\text{P. to Q. Kt.'s 3rd.}}$

WITH OTHER LESS PRACTISED DÉBUTS, VIZ.:—

1. $\dfrac{\text{P. to Q's 4th.}}{\text{P. to K. B's 4th.}}$ 1. $\dfrac{\text{P. to Q's 4th.}}{\text{P. to Q. B's 4th.}}$ 1. $\dfrac{}{\text{P. to K. B's 4th.}}$

AND

1. $\dfrac{}{\text{P. to Q. B's 4th.}}$

BOOK V.

The Queen's Gambit.

___

CHAPTER I.

THE QUEEN'S GAMBIT.

THE Queen's Gambit, or, as it was sometimes called, the
"Aleppo Gambit," from its having been the favourite game
of Stamma, of Aleppo, is a very sound and instructive method
of opening the game; less brilliant, because less hazardous,
than the gambits on the King's side, but especially improving
to the student, from the nicety and correctness of play on
both sides which it demands. We find it noticed as early
even as Damiano and Lopez, and to have been subsequently
examined by Salvio, Gianutio, and Carrera—by Stamma (who
eulogizes it as the best of all openings), by Cozio, Philidor,
Lolli, Ercole del Rio, Sarratt, Lewis, La Bourdonnais, Petroff,
Jaenisch, Walker, the German "Handbuch," the "Chess-
Player's Chronicle," and admirably illustrated in the games
between McDonnell and La Bourdonnais.

GAME THE FIRST.

WHITE.	BLACK.
1. P. to Q's 4th.	1. P. to Q's 4th.
2. P. to Q. B's 4th.	2. P. takes P.

These moves form the Queen's Gambit. But the best authorities have decided that it is unadvisable for Black to take
the Pawn, and that his most prudent play is 2. P. to K's 3rd,
(see Game the Fifth). The refusal of the gambit is in accordance with the example of Salvio; but in declining it he proposes a less recommendable move, namely, 2. P. to Q. B's 4th.
(See Salvio, Ed. 1723, p. 104.)

3. P. to K's 3rd.	3. P. to K's 4th.

Your move of 3. P. to K's 3rd is that adopted in La Bourdonnais and McDonnell's games, and appears to be at least as
good s 3 P. to K's 4th, although it is denounced by the older

writers.   You may also play without disadvantage 3. Q. Kt.
to B's 3rd.   (See Game the Third.)

Black plays correctly here in advancing his K. Pawn.   If
instead of this move he play 3. P. to K. B's 4th, you may
answer 4. K. B. takes P., and on his then playing 4. P. to K's
3rd, 5. Q. to her Kt.'s 3rd.   For the move 3. P. to Q. B's
4th, see the variation.   And if he attempt to sustain the gambit Pawn, you will easily obtain an advantage; for instance,—

		3. P. to Q. Kt.'s 4th.
4. P. to Q. R's 4th.		4. P. to Q. B's 3rd, or (A.)
5. P. takes P.		5. P. takes P.
6. Q. to K. B's 3rd.		

And you win a Piece.

(A.)

		4. B. to Q's 2nd.
5. P. takes P.		5. B. takes P.
6. P. to Q. Kt.'s 3rd.		6. Q. to her 4th.
7. P. takes P.		7. B. takes P.
8. Q. to her R's 5th (ch.)		

And again you win a Piece.

4. K. B. takes P.	4. P. takes Q. P.

If you play 4. P. takes K. P., Black will have the better
game; for example,—

4. P. takes K. P.	4. Q. takes Q. (ch.)
5. K. takes Q.	5. Q. Kt. to B's 3rd.
6. K. Kt. to B's 3rd.	6.. Q. B. to K's 3rd.
7. Q. Kt. to Q's 2nd.	7. Castles.
8. K. to Q. B's 2nd.	8. Q. Kt. to his 5th (ch.)
9. K. to Q. B's 3rd.	9. Kt. to Q's 6th.
10. B. takes Kt.	10. R. takes B. (ch.)

And the game is in Black's favour.

5. P. takes P.	5. K. Kt. to B's 3rd.
6. Q. Kt. to B's 3rd.	6. K. B. to Q's 3rd.
7. K. Kt. to B's 3rd.	7. Q. Kt. to B's 3rd.
8. Castles.	8. Castles.
9. P. to K. R's 3rd.	9. P. to K. R's 3rd.

The game is equal; but your P. is well placed, and you have
still the move.

VARIATION,

Beginning at Black's 3rd move.

WHITE.	BLACK.
1. P. to Q's 4th.	1. P. to Q's 4th.
2. P. to Q. B's 4th.	2. P. takes P.

3. P. to K's 3rd.	3. P. to Q. B's 4th.
4. B. takes P.	4. P. takes Q. P.
5. P. takes P.	5. Q. Kt. to B's 3rd.
6. K. Kt. to K's 2nd.	6. P. to K's 4th.
7. Q. B. to K's 3rd.	7. P. takes P.
8. Kt. takes P.	8. Kt. takes Kt.
9. B. takes Kt.	9. Q. to K's 2nd (ch.)
10. K. B. to K's 2nd.	10. Q. to her Kt's 5th (ch.)
11. Q. to her 2nd.	11. Q. takes Q. (ch.)
12. Kt. takes Q.	12. Kt. to K's 2nd.

You have the superiority.

GAME THE SECOND.

WHITE.	BLACK.
1. P. to Q's 4th.	1. P. to Q's 4th.
2. P. to Q. B's 4th.	2. P. takes P.
3. P. to K's 4th.	3. P. to K's 4th.

You may without danger play your K. P. to K's 4th, but it is difficult to sustain the two Pawns abreast in the centre, and hence P. to K's 3rd, as in the previous game, or Q. Kt. to B's 3rd, is more generally adopted.

Black's move in reply is the correct one, as he thus ensures the breaking up of your centre. If he play 3. P. to Q. Kt.'s 4th, you answer with 4. P to Q. R's 4th, as in the variation given in the preceding game; and for the result of 3. P. to K. B's 4th, see the fourth game. He may, however, play without much disadvantage 3. P. to Q. B's 4th, as in the following:—

	3. P. to Q. B's 4th.
4. P. to Q's 5th.	4. P. to K's 3rd.
5. B. takes P.	5. P. takes Q. P.
6. K. P. takes P.	6. K. B. to Q's 3rd.

Your Pawn is passed, and will serve to obstruct the approach of his Pieces, but the advantage is very slight.

4. P. to Q's 5th.	4. P. to K. B's 4th.

Many players prefer P. takes P. for your 4th move, and the German "Handbuch" remarks, that although it has been censured by some authors, it is as good as 4. P. to Q's 5th. The following moves will enable you to judge:—

4. P. takes P.	4. Q. takes Q. (ch.)
5. K. takes Q.	5. Q. Kt. to B's 3rd.
6. P. to K. B's 4th.	6. Q. B. to K. Kt.'s 5th (ch.)

(If you play 6. Q. B. to K. B's 4th, he answers with 6. Q. B. to K's 3rd.)

7. B. to K's 2nd.	7. Castles (ch.)
8. Q. B. to Q's 2nd.	8. B. takes K. B. (ch.)
9. K. Kt. takes B.	9. K. B. to Q. Kt.'s 5th.
10. Q. Kt. to B's 3rd.	10. K. Kt. to K's 2nd.

The game is even.

5. K. B. takes P.	5. K. Kt. to B's 3rd.

You can also play 5. Q. Kt. to B's 3rd, or 5. P. takes K. B. P., without harm. For example; in the first place,—

5. Q. Kt. to B's 3rd.	5. K. Kt. to B's 3rd.
6. P. takes B. P.	6. Q. B. takes P.

(You might without danger play 6. P. to K. B's 3rd.)

7. K. B. takes P.	7. K. B. to Q's 3rd.
8. K. Kt. to K's 2nd.	8. Castles.
9. Castles.	9. Q. Kt. to Q's 2nd.

The game is equal.

In the second place,—

5. P. takes K. B. P.	5. Q. B. takes P.
6. Q. Kt. to B's 3rd.	6. Q. Kt. to Q's 2nd.
7. K. B. takes P.	7. Q. Kt. to his 3rd.
8. Q. B. to K's 3rd.	

An even game.

He would obviously lose by taking the K. P., on account of your playing 6. Q. to K. R's 5th (ch.).

6. K. Kt. to B's 3rd.	6. K. B. to Q's 3rd.
7. P. takes P.	7. Q. B. takes P.
8. Castles.	8. Castles.
9. Q. Kt. to B's 3rd.	9. Q. Kt. to Q's 2nd.

The positions are pretty equal, but you have still an advantage in the move.

GAME THE THIRD.

Before proceeding to the consideration of games wherein Black refuses the gambit, it may be well to give a brief example of a different mode of carrying on the opening in the regular gambit which is at your command, and often adopted.

WHITE.	BLACK.
1. P. to Q's 4th.	1. P. to Q's 4th.
2. P. to Q. B's 4th.	2. P. takes P.
3. Q. Kt. to B's 3rd.	3. K. Kt. to B's 3rd.

For the consequences of his playing 3. P. to Q. B's 4th, or

3. P. to Q. B's 3rd, see the variation. He might also play
3. P. to K's 4th, and the game proceed as follows:—

3. P. to K's 4th.

4. P. to Q's 5th.	4. P. to Q. B's 3rd.

(You could here too play 4. P. to K's 3rd.)

5. P. to K's 4th.	5. K. Kt. to B's 3rd.

(If he move 5. P. to Q. Kt.'s 4th, you will have the advantage.)

6. Q. B. to K. Kt.'s 5th.	6. P. takes Q. P.
7. P. takes P.	7. Q. B. to K. B's 4th.
8. B. takes P.	8. K. B. to Q's 3rd.

The game is about equal.

4. P. to K's 3rd.	4. P. to K's 4th.
5. K. B. takes P.	5. P. takes P.
6. P. takes P.	6. K. B. to Q's 3rd.

The game may be called even.

VARIATION,
Beginning at Black's 3rd move.

WHITE.	BLACK.
1. P. to Q's 4th.	1. P. to Q's 4th.
2. P. to Q. B's 4th.	2. P. takes P.
3. Q. Kt. to B's 3rd.	3. P. to Q. B's 4th.

If he move this Pawn to Q. B's 3rd only, the following moves are likely:—

3. P. to Q. B's 3rd.

4. P. to Q. R's 4th.	4. P. to K's 4th.
5. P. takes P.	5. Q. takes Q. (ch.)
6. Kt. takes Q.	

The game is quite even.

4. P. to Q's 5th.	4. P. to K's 3rd.
5. P. to K's 4th.	5. P. takes P.
6. P. takes P.	6. K. B. to Q's 3rd.
7. K. B. takes P.	7. K. Kt. to K's 2nd.

Equal game.

GAME THE FOURTH.
THE SCHWARTZ DEFENCE.

WHITE.	BLACK.
1. P. to Q's 4th.	1. P. to Q's 4th.
2. P. to Q. B's 4th.	2. P. takes P.
3. P. to K's 4th.	3. P. to K. B's 4th.
4. P. to K's 5th.	4. Q. B. to K's 3rd.

This mode of defence is the invention of Mr. W. Schwartz, of Livonia; it is novel and ingenious, but if properly opposed, leaves an evident advantage in the hands of the opening player.

Instead of playing 4. P. to K.'s 5th, you may nullify the defence, apparently, by taking the doubled P. with your Bishop, and, if Black takes K. P. with P., moving Q. to her Kt.'s 3rd, or, if he bring K. Kt. to B's 3rd, by advancing K. P. to K's 5th. You may also at the 4th move take K. B. P. with P., and obtain a fine game.

WHITE	BLACK
5. Q. Kt. to R's 3rd.	5. Q. Kt. to B's 3rd.
6. Q. B. to K's 3rd.	6. Q. Kt. to R's 4th.
7. Q. to Q. R's 4th (ch.)	7. P. to Q. B's 3rd.
8. B. to Q's 2nd.	8. Q. takes Q. P.
9. Q. takes Kt.	9. Q. takes Q. Kt. P.
10. Q. B. to his 3rd.	10. Q. to her Kt.'s 3rd.
11. Q. takes Q.	11. P. takes Q.
12. Q. Kt. takes P.	12. P. to Q. Kt.'s 4th.
13. Q. Kt. to K's 3rd.	13. P. to K. B's 5th.
14. Q. Kt. to Q. B's 2nd.	14. R. takes P.
15. K. B. to Q's 3rd.	15. R. takes R. (ch.)
16. B. takes R.	

You have much the better game.

GAME THE FIFTH.
THE GAMBIT REFUSED.

WHITE.	BLACK.
1. P. to Q's 4th.	1. P. to Q's 4th.
2. P. to Q. B's 4th.	2. P. to K's 3rd.

Black's move of 2. P. to K's 3rd, I agree with Major Jaenisch in thinking the best he can adopt; P. to Q. B's 4th, and P. to Q. B's 3rd, are certainly inferior. (See Variations I. and II. in the present game.) When the game is opened by the first player with 1. P. to Q's 4th, a very common rejoinder among leading practitioners is 1. P. to K. B's 4th, or 1. P. to Q. B's 4th, the consequences of which will be shown under the head of "Irregular Openings."

| 3. Q. Kt. to B's 3rd. | 3. K. Kt. to B's 3rd. |
| 4. P. to K's 3rd. | 4. P. to Q. B's 4th. |

It is a curious feature in this description of "close" game, that the Queen's Bishop can rarely be played over to the King's side with advantage.

5. K. Kt. to B's 3rd.	5. Q. Kt. to B's 3rd.
6. P. to Q. R's 3rd.	6. P. to Q. R's 3rd.

And the positions are quite even.

VARIATION I.,

Beginning at Black's 2nd move.

WHITE.	BLACK.
1. P. to Q's 4th.	1. P. to Q's 4th.
2. P. to Q. B's 4th.	2. P. to Q. B's 4th.

By this move of Black's you obtain a slight advantage of position.

3. P. takes Q. B. P.	3. P. to Q's 5th (best)

Major Jaenisch counsels you take the Q. P., and not the Q. B. P., and his variation proceeds thus,—

3. P. takes Q. P.	3. Q. takes P.
4. P. to K's 3rd.	4. P. takes P.
5. Q. Kt. to B's 3rd.	5. Q. to her sq.
6. P. takes P.	6. P. to K's 3rd.

And the second player has lost time.

I believe you may obtain at least as good a position, however, by taking the Q. B. P.

4. P. to Q. Kt.'s 4th.	4. P. to Q. R's 4th.

You may play too 4. K. Kt. to B's 3rd, and then 5. P. to Q. R's 3rd. If he play 4. P. to K's 4th, the following is a probable result:—

	4. P. to K's 4th.
5. K. Kt. to B's 3rd.	5. P. to K. B's 3rd.
6. P. to K's 3rd.	6. P. takes P.
7. Q. takes Q. (ch.)	7. K. takes Q.
8. Q. B. takes P.	8. P. to Q. R's 4th.
9. P. to Q. Kt.'s 5th.	9. Q. Kt. to Q's 2nd.
10. P. to Q. B's 6th.	10. P. takes P.
11. P. to Q. R's 4th.	11. P. to Q. B's 4th.
12. Q. Kt. to Q's 2nd.	

With a better game.

5. P. to Q. Kt.'s 5th.	5. P. to K's 4th.
6. K. Kt. to B's 3rd.	6. P. to K. B's 3rd.
7. P. to K's 3rd.	7. B. takes doubled P.
8. P. takes Q. P.	8. P. takes P.

If he take with the Bishop, you take B. with Kt., and he cannot save the Pawn.

    9. B. to Q. Kt.'s 2nd.

        And you have certainly the advantage.

VARIATION II.,

Beginning at Black's 2nd move.

WHITE.	BLACK.
1. P. to Q's 4th.	1. P. to Q's 4th.
2. P. to Q. B's 4th.	2. P. to Q. B's 3rd.

Black's second move here is even weaker aparently than P. to Q. B's 4th.

3. P. to K. B's 3rd.	3. K. Kt. to B's 3rd.

If instead of bringing out his Kt. he play 3. P. takes P., you move 4. P. to K's 3rd, and if then he support his Pawn with 4. P. to Q. Kt.'s 4th, you can reply with 5. P. to Q. R's 4th.

4. Q. Kt. to B's 3rd.	4. Q. B. to K. B's 4th.
5. P. to K's 3rd.	5. P. to K's 3rd.
6. K. B. to Q's 3rd.	6. B. takes B.
7. Q. takes B.	7. K. B. to Q. Kt.'s 5th.
8. P. to K's 4th.	8. B. takes Kt. (ch.)
9. P. takes B.	9. Q. Kt. to Q's 2nd.
10. Q. B. P. takes Q. P.	10. Q. B. P. takes P.
11. P. to K's 5th.	11. Kt. to K. R's 4th.
12. K. Kt. to K's 2nd.	

        The game is in your favour.

GAMES

ILLUSTRATIVE OF THE FOREGOING ANALYSIS.

(From the *Chess-Player's Chronicle*.)

GAME I.—Between M. De la Bourdonnais and Mr. McDonnell.

WHITE. (M. De la B.)	BLACK. (Mr. Mc D.)
1. P. to Q's 4th.	1. P. to Q's 4th.
2. P. to Q. B's 4th.	2. P. takes P.
3. P. to K's 3rd.	3. P. to K's 4th.
4. K. B. takes P	4. P. takes P.
5. P. takes P.	5. K. Kt. to B's 3rd.

6. Q. Kt. to B's 3rd.	6. K. B. to K's 2nd.*
7. K. Kt. to B's 3rd.	7. Castles.
8. P. to K. R's 3rd.†	8. Q. Kt. to Q's 2nd.
9. Q. B. to K's 3rd.	9. Q. Kt. to his 3rd.
10. K. B. to Q. Kt.'s 3rd.	10. P. to Q. B's 3rd.
11. Castles.	11. K. Kt. to Q's 4th.
12. Q. to K's 2nd.	12. P. to K. B's 4th.
13. K. Kt. to K's 5th.	13. P. to K. B's 5th.
14. Q. B. to Q's 2nd.	14. P. to K. Kt.'s 4th.‡
15. Q. R. to K's sq.	15. K. to his Kt.'s 2nd.
16. Q. Kt. takes Kt.	16. Kt. takes Kt.
17. K. Kt. takes Q. B. P. §	17. Q. Kt. P. takes Kt.
18. B. takes Kt.	18. Q. takes B.
19. Q. takes B. (ch.)	19. R. to K. B's 2nd.
20. Q. to her Kt.'s 4th.	20. Q. B. to K. B's 4th.
21. R. to K's 5th.	21. Q. to her 2nd.
22. P. to Q's 5th. ‖	22. P. takes P.
23. Q. to her 4th.	23. K. to R's 3rd.
24. P. to K. R's 4th.	24. Q. B. to K's 3rd.
25. K. R. to K's sq.	25. Q. R. to K's sq.
26. Q. R. takes Kt. P.¶	26. Q. R. to K. B's sq.
27. Q. to K's 5th.	27. Q. B. to K. Kt.'s 5th.
28. R. to K. R's 5th (ch.)	28. B. takes R.
29. Q. mates.	

GAME II.—Played by correspondence some years since between the Amateurs of Bristol and Mr. Staunton.

WHITE. (The Amateurs.)	BLACK. (Mr. S.)
1. P. to Q's 4th.	1. P. to Q's 4th.
2. P. to Q. B's 4th.	2. P. takes P.
3. P. to K's 3rd.	3. P. to K's 4th.
4. B. takes P.	4. P. takes P.
5. P. takes P.	5. K. Kt. to B's 3rd.
6. K. Kt. to B's 3rd.	6. K. B. to Q. Kt.'s 5th (ch.)
7. Q. Kt. to B's 3rd.	7. Castles.
8. Castles.	8. Q. B. to K. Kt.'s 5th.
9. Q. B. to K's 3rd.	9. Q. Kt. to Q. B's 3rd.
10. K. B. to K's 2nd.**	10. K. Kt. to Q's 4th.

---

* This is a fault. The Bishop should always be played to Q's 3rd at the present stage.

† An indispensable move in this opening.

‡ The advance of these Pawns should rarely be ventured by any but the experienced player.

§ Capitally played.

‖ An excellent move.

¶ The best mode of taking the Pawn.

** The best move apparently to preserve the Q. P.

11. Q. to Q. B's 2nd.*	11. Q. B. to Q. R's 4th.†
12. P. to Q. R's 3rd.	12. K. B. to Q. R's 4th.
13. K. Kt. to K's 5th.	13. K. Kt. takes Q. Kt.
14. K. B. takes B.	14. Q. Kt. takes Kt.
15. Q. P. takes Kt.	15. Kt. to Q's 4th.
16. Q. B. to Q. B's 5th.	16. K. R. to K's sq.
17. P. to K. B's 4th.	17. P. to Q. B's 3rd.
18. Q. R. to Q's sq.	18. Q. to K. R's 5th.
19. Q. to K's 2nd.	19. P. to K. Kt.'s 3rd. ‡
20. K. B. to K. Kt.'s 4th.	20. B. to Q. Kt.'s 3rd. §
21. B. takes B.	21. Q. R. P. takes B.
22. P. to K. B's 5th. ‖	22. Q. R. to Q. R's 5th.¶
23. P. takes K. Kt. P.	23. K. R. P. takes P.
24. B. to K. B's 3rd.	24. Kt. to K. B's 5th.**
25. Q. to K's 3rd.	25. P. to Q. Kt.'s 4th.
26. R. to Q's 7th.	26. Q. to K. Kt.'s 4th.††
27. K. to R's sq.‡‡	27. Q. takes K. P.
28. Q. takes Q.	28. R. takes Q.
29. Q. R. takes Q. Kt. P.	29. Kt. to Q. B's 5th.
30. P. to K. R's 3rd.	30. Kt. to Q's 6th.
31. B. to Q's sq.	31. Q. R. to K. B's 5th.
32. R. takes R.	32. Kt. takes R.
33. B. to K. B's 3rd.§§	33. Kt. to Q's 4th.
34. K. to Kt.'s sq.‖‖	34. K. to Kt.'s 2nd.

* Good play, threatening to move K. Kt. to Kt.'s 5th, which might cost the Black a Piece.

† Correctly played; by this simple move he utterly disconcerts the meditated attack on his K. R. P.

‡ Had Black, instead of this move, 'taken K. B. P. with his Kt., the opponents, by capturing K. B. P. with Bishop (giving check at the same time), would have obtained a winning position.

§ Far better than playing P. to K. R's 4th, in which case White would have moved the B. to Q's 7th, attacking the Rook.

‖ By this move the Bristolians appear to have weakened their game.

¶ This Rook is admirably posted.

** A fine position for the Kt. also. Had the Kt. remained at Q's 4th, White might have taken him with K's Bishop, and then by playing Q. to K. B's 3rd, would have won a Pawn.

†† Threatening to win the Queen by checking with the Kt. at K. R's 6th.

‡‡ But for the necessity of making this defensive move, there is every probability that the Bristol players would have acquired the better game. If, however, instead of moving the King, they had proceeded with their attack, playing Q. to Q. Kt.'s 6th, their adversary would have moved his Q. R. to Q. B's 5th, and afterwards checked with Kt., and thus have been enabled at least to draw the game.

§§ This is stronger than B. to Q. Kt.'s 3rd.

‖‖ These moves are to bring the King within reach of the adverse Pawn on Q's side.

35. K. to B's 2nd.	35. K. to B's 3rd.*
36. P. to Q. Kt.'s 3rd.	36. Kt. to K's 2nd.
37. P. to Q. R's 4th.	37. P. takes P.
38. P. takes P.	38. R. to Q. R's 4th.

The game was resigned as a drawn battle.

GAME III.—Played in Paris by three members of the Chess Cercle, MM. Harrwitz, Sasias, and another, in consultation, against MM. Kieseritzky, Henderson, and Kling, in the Café de la Régence.

WHITE. (Allies of the Cercle.)	BLACK. (Allies of the Café.)
1. P. to Q's 4th.	1. P. to Q's 4th.
2. P. to Q. B's 4th.	2. P. takes P.
3. P. to K's 4th.	3. P. to K. B's 4th.†
4. P. takes P.‡	4. Q. B. takes P.
5. K. B. takes P.	5. K. Kt. to B's 3rd.
6. K. Kt. to K's 2nd.	6. Q. B. to K's 5th.
7. Castles.	7. Q. Kt. to B's 3rd.
8. Q. to Kt.'s 3rd.	8. B. to Q's 4th.
9. B. takes B.	9. Q. takes B.
10. Q. takes Q. Kt. P.	10. Q. Kt. takes Q. P.§
11. Q. to R's 6th.	11. P. to K's 4th.
12. Q. Kt. to B's 3rd.	12. Q. to her B's 3rd.
13. Q. takes Q.	13. Kt. takes Q.
14. P. to K. B's 4th.	14. B. to Q. B's 4th (ch.)
15. K. to R's sq.	15. Castles on K's side.
16. P. to K. R's 3rd.	16. Q. R. to K's sq.
17. P. takes P.	17. Q. Kt. takes P.
18. Q. B. to K. Kt.'s 5th.	18. Q. R. to K's 3rd.
19. Q. R. to Q's sq.	19. Q. Kt. to B's 5th.
20. P. to Q. Kt.'s 3rd.	20. Q. Kt. to K's 6th.
21. B. takes Q. Kt.	21. Q. R. takes B.
22. K. R. to B's 3rd.	22. K. R. to K's sq.
23. K. Kt. to K. B's 4th.	23. Kt. to K's 5th.
24. Q. Kt. takes Kt.	24. K. R. takes Kt.‖
25. R. takes R.	25. B. takes R.
26. R. to Q's 8th (ch.)	26. K. to B's 2nd.
27. Kt. to Q's 5th.	27. R. to Q's 5th.

---

* This appears to be the only move by which Black can prevent his opponents obtaining a "passed" Q. R. P.

† This leads to the objectionable defence of Mr. Schwartz, which has been previously examined.

‡ Bishop takes Pawn would be likewise good play.

§ Very neatly played.

‖ It would have been better perhaps to have taken this Kt. with the Queen's Rook.

28. R. to Q's 7th (ch.)	28. K. to his 3rd.
29. R. to K's 7th (ch.)	29. K. takes Kt.
30. R. takes B.	30. R. to K's 5th.
31. R. to Q's 3rd (ch.)	31. K. to Q. B's 3rd.
32. K. to R's 2nd.	32. R. to K's 7th.
33. P. to Q. R's 3rd.	33. P. to Q. R's 4th.
34. P. to K. R's 4th.	34. R. to K's 5th.
35. K. to R's 3rd.	35. K. to Q. Kt.'s 4th.
36. P. to K. Kt.'s 4th.	36. P. to Q. B's 4th.
37. K. to Kt.'s 3rd.	37. P. to Q. R's 5th.
38. P. takes P. (ch.)	38. K. takes P.
39. R. to Q's 7th.	39. P. to Q. B's 5th.
40. R. takes K. Kt. P.	40. P. to Q. B's 6th.

The players of the Black men win.

GAME IV.—Between M. St. Amant and Mr. Staunton.

WHITE. (M. St. A.)	BLACK. (Mr. S.)
1. P. to Q's 4th.	1. P. to Q's 4th.
2. P. to Q. B's 4th.	2. P. to K's 3rd.
3. Q. Kt. to B's 3rd.	3. K. Kt. to B's 3rd.
4. K. Kt. to B's 3rd.	4. P. to Q. R's 3rd.
5. P. to Q. B's 5th.	5. K. B. to K's 2nd.
6. Q. B. to K. Kt.'s 5th.*	6. Castles.
7. P. to K's 3rd.	7. P. to Q. Kt.'s 3rd.†
8. P. to Q. Kt.'s 4th.	8. Q. B. to Q. Kt.'s 2nd.
9. Q. B. takes Kt.	9. B. takes B.
10. K. B. to Q's 3rd.	10. P. to Q. R's 4th.
11. P. to Q. R's 3rd.	11. Kt. to Q's 2nd.‡
12. Q. B. P. takes P.	12. P. takes P.
13. Castles.	13. Q. to K's 2nd.§
14. Q. to her Kt.'s 3rd.‖	14. P. takes P.
15. P. takes P.	15. K. R. to Q. B's sq.
16. B. to Q. Kt.'s 5th.¶	16. Kt. to K. B's sq.

---

* It has been previously remarked that the Q. B. in these games can seldom be advantageously played to the King's side.

† This appears the only safe and effectual way of bringing the Queen's Bishop into play.

‡ Threatening to gain a Pawn.

§ A much better move than advancing the King's Pawn one step, which would have cost Black at least a Pawn. (*e. g.*)

	11. P. to K's 4th.
12. P. takes P.	12. Kt. takes P.
13. Kt. takes Kt.	13. B. takes Kt.
14. B. takes K. R. P. (ch.)	14. K. takes B.
15. Q. to K. R's 5th (ch.)	15. K. to Kt.'s sq.
16. Q. takes B., &c.	

‖ Well played.

¶ A lost move.

17. K. R. to Q. B's sq.	17. Kt. to K. Kt.'s 3rd.
18. B. to K's 2nd.	18. Q. to her sq.
19. Kt. to Q. Kt.'s 5th.	19. B. to K's 2nd.
20. K. Kt. to K's sq.	20. B. to Q. R's 3rd.*
21. P. to K. B's 4th.	21. Kt. to R's 5th.
22. K. to B's 2nd.	22. Kt. to K. B's 4th.
23. K. Kt. to B's 3rd.	23. B. takes Q. Kt.
24. Q. R. takes R.	24. R. takes Q. R.
25. B. takes B.	25. Kt. to Q's 3rd.
26. B. to Q's 3rd.	26. P. to Q. Kt.'s 4th.
27. Kt. to K's 5th.	27. Kt. to Q. B's 5th.
28. Kt. to Q. B's 6th.	28. Q. to her 3rd.
29. Kt. takes B. (ch.)	29. Q. takes Kt.
30. B. takes Kt.	30. Q. P. takes B.†
31. Q. to Kt.'s 2nd.	31. R. to Q. R's 5th.
32. R. to Q. Kt.'s sq.	32. Q. to her R's 2nd.
33. Q. to her B's 2nd.	33. P. to K. Kt.'s 3rd.
34. P. to K. R's 4th.	34. Q. to K's 2nd.
35. R. to K. R's sq.	35. Q. takes Q. Kt. P.
36. Q. to K's 4th.	36. Q. to her Kt.'s 7th (ch.)
37. K. to Kt.'s 3rd.	37. R. to Q. R's 7th.
38. R. to K. B's sq.	38. P. to Q. Kt.'s 5th.
39. Q. to her Kt.'s 7th.	39. P. to K. R's 4th.
40. K. to R's 3rd.	40. P. to Q. B's 6th.
41. R. to K. Kt.'s sq.	41. Q. to K. B's 7th.
42. Q. to her Kt.'s 8th (ch.)	42. K. to R's 2nd.
43. Q. to K. B's 8th.	43. Q. takes K. P. (ch.)
44. P. to K. Kt.'s 3rd.	44. R. to Q. R's 2nd.
45. R. to Q. R's sq.‡	45. Q. takes Q. P.§
46. R. takes R.	46. Q. takes R.
47. Q. takes Q. Kt. P.	47. Q. to K. Kt.'s 8th.
48. Q. to her Kt.'s 7th.	48. K. to Kt.'s 2nd.
49. Q. to K's 4th.	49. Q. to her B's 4th.
50. Q. to K's sq.	50. P. to Q. B's 7th.
51. Q. to her R's sq. (ch.)	51. K. to R's 2nd.
52. Q. to her B's sq.	52. Q. to K. B's 4th (ch.)
53. K. to R's 2nd.	53. Q. to her 6th.
54. P. to K. B's 5th.	54. Q. to K's 7th (ch.)
55. K. to R's 3rd.	55. Q. to her 8th.
56. P. takes P. (ch.)	56. P. takes P.

And White surrendered.

---

* From this point the game is in Black's favour.

† Black properly takes with the Q. P., foreseeing, in the event of the capital Pieces being changed off, that a White passed P. on the Q. Kt.'s file, would be out of reach of his King.

‡ High praise is due to White for the pertinacious ingenuity with which he struggled to draw the game.

§ Had he taken the R., White would have drawn the game.

CHAPTER II.

IRREGULAR OPENINGS.

THOSE methods of commencing the game, in which the first or second player moves otherwise than $1.\frac{\text{P. to K's 4th}}{\text{P. to K's 4th}}$, or $2.\frac{\text{P. to Q's 4th}}{\text{P. to Q's 4th}}$, are usually designated "Irregular." Without assenting to the propriety of this distinction, I have thought it advisable, for the sake of perspicuity, to adopt a general and well known classification in preference to arranging these peculiar *débuts* under separate and less familiar heads.

Of the "Irregular Openings," the most important are,— First, the different modes of defence which Black may adopt in answer to your 1st move of $1.\overline{\text{P. to K's 4th}}$, when he declines playing $1.\overline{\text{P. to K's 4th}}$; also, viz. :—$1.\overline{\text{P. to K's 3rd}}$, $1.\overline{\text{P. to Q. B's 4th}}$, $1.\overline{\text{P. to Q's 4th}}$, and $1.\overline{\text{P. to Q. Kt.'s 3rd}}$; together with $1.\overline{\text{P. to K. B's 4th}}$, and $1.\overline{\text{P. to Q. B's 4th}}$, in reply to $1.\overline{\text{P. to Q's 4th}}$; and Secondly, two ways of beginning the contest, which are at your command, beside the customary $1.\overline{\text{P. to K's 4th}}$, or $1.\overline{\text{P. to Q's 4th}}$, viz. :—$1.\overline{\text{P. to K. B's 4th}}$, and $1.\overline{\text{P. to Q. B's 4th}}$.

The present Chapter shall be devoted to the consideration of the irregular defences in question, and the next to the examination of these two unusual systems of attack. The leading authorities to consult upon these openings are—Bertin (1735); Ponziani (1782), p. 78; Lolli, pp. 134, 140; Cochrane, p. 261; La Bourdonnais, p. 114; Mòuret (1838); Jaenisch, 1st vol., pp. 42—59, 74; Lewis (1844), and the German "Handbuch."

GAME THE FIRST.

THE FRENCH GAME.

Throughout the whole of the preceding Chapters of this work which treat of the opening on the King's side, Black's reply to your first move, of 1. P. to K's 4th, has invariably been 1. P. to K's 4th also; and this mode of defence has subjected him, in every case, to an attack of more or less intensity and duration, according to the particular course you have afterwards chosen to pursue. It is needful now to direct attention to those defences by which, as far as present experience teaches us, the advantage of the first move is sooner neutralized, and the combatants are placed upon a fairer footing of equality at starting.

WHITE.	BLACK.
1. P. to K's 4th.	1. P. to K's 3rd.

This manner of defence brings us nearer to the form of the ancient game, before the innovation in the march of the Pawn was introduced, than any other, and by nullifying the advantage of the first move, gives a higher tone and character to the game than it possesses while chance is an admitted element in the struggle.

2. P. to Q's 4th (best)	2. P. to Q's 4th.

You can also answer with 2. P. to K. B's 4th, as in the variation.

3. P. takes P. (best)	3. P. takes P.

If, instead of taking the P., you play 3. P. to K's 5th, the game will be in favour of Black; for example,—

3. P. to K's 5th.	3. P. to Q. B's 4th.
4. B. to Q. Kt.'s 5th (ch.)	4. Q. Kt. to B's 3rd.
5. B. takes Kt. (ch.)	5. P. takes B.

(In place of taking the Kt., you may play 5. P. to Q. B's 3rd, but he still obtains an advantage.)

6. P. to Q. B's 3rd.	6. Q. to her Kt.'s 3rd.
7. K. Kt. to B's 3rd.	7. Q. B. to Q. R's 3rd.
8. Q. Kt. to Q's 2nd.	8. P. takes Q. P.
9. P. takes P.	9. P. to Q. B's 4th.
10. Q. Kt. to his 3rd.	10. P. takes Q. P.
11. K. Kt. takes P.	11. K. B. checks.
12. B. to Q's 2nd.	12. K. Kt. to K's 2nd.
13. K. Kt. to K's 2nd.	13. Kt. to Q. B's 3rd.
14. P. to K. B's 4th.	14. Q. to K's 6th.
15. Q. Kt. to B's sq.	15. Castles.

He has a manifest advantage.

(See also the Illustrative Games at the end of the Chapter.)

4. P. to Q. B's 4th.	4. K. B. checks.

If 4. P. takes P., you reply with 5. K. B. takes P., and on his then playing 5. B. to Q's 3rd, the game is quite equal.

5. B. to Q's 2nd.	5. Q. to K's 2nd (ch.)

Interposing the Q. Kt. is not so good for you. (*e. g.*)

5. Q. Kt. to B's 3rd.	5. K. Kt. to B's 3rd.
6. Q. to her Kt.'s 3rd.	6. Q. Kt. to B's 3rd.
7. K. Kt. to B's 3rd.	7. Q. B. to K's 3rd.
8. B. to Q's 2nd.	8. Castles.
9. P. to Q. R's 3rd.	9. P. takes P.
10. K. B. takes P.	10. Q. B. takes B.
11. Q. takes Q. B.	11. R. to K's sq. (ch.)
12. B. to K's 3rd.	12. B. takes Kt. (ch.)
13. P. takes B.	13. K. Kt. to Q's 4th.

He has an embarrassing attack upon you.

5. Q. to K's 2nd.	5. Q. B. to K's 3rd.
6. P. takes P.	6. B. takes B. (ch.)
7. Q. Kt. takes B.	7. B. takes P.

The game is equal.

VARIATION,

Beginning at White's 2nd move.

WHITE.	BLACK.
1. P. to K's 4th.	1. P. to K's 3rd.
2. P. to K. B's 4th.	2. P. to Q's 4th.
3. P. takes P.	3. P. takes P.

You can also advance your K. P. to K's 5th, as in the following:—

3. P. to K's 5th.	3. P. to Q. B's 4th.
4. K. Kt. to B's 3rd.	4. Q. Kt. to B's 3rd.
5. P. to Q. B's 3rd.	5. P. to K. B's 3rd.
6. Q. Kt. to R's 3rd.	6. K. Kt. to R's 3rd.
7. Q. Kt. to B's 2nd.	7. Q. B. to K's 2nd.
8. P. to Q's 4th.	8. Castles.

I prefer his game.

4. K. Kt. to B's 3rd.	4. P. to Q. B's 4th.
5. P. to Q's 4th.	5. Q. Kt. to B's 3rd.

To check with your B. would be unavailing.

6. P. to Q. B's 3rd.	6. K. Kt. to B's 3rd.
7. Q. B. to K's 3rd.	7. Q. to her Kt.'s 3rd.
8. Q. to her Kt.'s 3rd.	8. Q. Kt. to R's 4th.
9. Q. takes Q.	9. P. takes Q.

Instead of exchanging Queens you may play,—

9. K. B. checks.	9. B. to Q's 2nd.
10. B. takes B. (ch.)	10. K. Kt. takes B.

There is little advantage on either side, but I like the disposition of his forces.

10. K. B. checks.	10. Q. B. to Q's 2nd.
11. B. takes B. (ch.)	11. K. Kt. takes B.

The game is even.

GAME THE SECOND.

THE SICILIAN GAME.

WHITE.	BLACK.
1. P. to K's 4th.	1. P. to Q. B's 4th.

In the opinion of Jaenisch and the authors of the German "Handbuch," with which I coincide, this is the best possible reply to the move of 1. P. to K's 4th, "as it renders the formation of a centre impracticable for White and prevents every attack." This defence is found in the earlier Italian works, and has been analysed by Philidor in the second edition (1777) of his treatise. In the appendix to Sarratt's translation of Damiano, Lopez, and Salvio, mention is made of some games at this opening, which the author had received as an extract from an old Italian MS. Sarratt has given us neither the name of the writer nor the date of the MS., but merely says: "These games are extracted from a scarce and valuable MS., which has been obligingly communicated to the editor by E. Morris, Esq., M.P., indisputably one of the ablest chess-players of the present day. This opening is called the 'GUIOCO SICILIANO.'"

In answer to this move you have several ways of playing. You may move 2. K. Kt. to B's 3rd, which Major Jaenisch formerly thought your best; or 2. P. to Q's 4th, which he now prefers; or 2. P. to K. B's 4th; or 2. P. to Q. B's 4th; or 2. P. to Q. Kt.'s 4th. The present game shall be devoted to the examination of the first of these, and the consequences of the others shall be shown in Games the Third, Fourth, Fifth, and Sixth.

2. K. Kt. to B's 3rd.	2. P. to K's 3rd.

He can likewise play 2. Q. Kt. to B's 3rd, and proceed thus:—

	2. Q. Kt. to B's 3rd.
3. P. to Q's 4th.	3. P. takes P.
4. Kt. takes P.	4. P. to K's 4th.
5. K. Kt. to B's 3rd.	5. K. Kt. to B's 3rd.

(Taking his Kt. would perhaps be imprudent, from its drawing his side Pawns to the centre, but 5. K. Kt. to Q. Kt.'s 3rd would prevent his B. taking the customary station at Q. B's 4th, and would cramp his game a little.)

6. K. B. to Q's 3rd.   6. B. to Q. B's 4th.

And the game is even.

3. P. to Q's 4th.	3. P. to Q's 4th.
4. P. takes Q. P.	4. K. P. takes P.
5. P. to Q. B's 4th.	5. P. takes Q. P.

Your can check with your B., instead of throwing forward the Q. B. P., and equalise the game; for instance,—

5. B. to Q. Kt.'s 5th (ch.)	5. Q. Kt. to B's 3rd.
6. Q. B. to K's 3rd.	6. P. takes P.
7. K. Kt. takes P.	7. Q. B. to Q's 2nd.
8. P. to Q. B's 4th.	8. P. takes P.
9. K. B. takes P.	9. K. B. checks.
10. Q. Kt. to B's 3rd.	10. K. Kt. to K's 2nd.
11. Castles.	11. B. takes Q. Kt.
12. P. takes B.	12. Castles.

The advantages are pretty equally balanced.!

6. P. takes Q. P.	6. Q. takes P.
7. Q. takes P.	7. Q. takes Q.
8. Kt. takes Q.	8. K. B. to Q. B's 4th.
9. Kt. to Q. Kt.'s 3rd.	9. B. to Q. Kt.'s 3rd.
10. B. to Q. B's 4th.	10. K. Kt. to B's 3rd.
11. Castles.	11. Castles.

Equal game.

———

GAME THE THIRD.

WHITE.	BLACK.
1. P. to K's 4th.	1. P. to Q. B's 4th.
2. P. to Q's 4th.	2. P. takes P.

If he move 2. P. to K's 3rd, you can play the P. on to Q's 5th.

3. Q. takes P.   3. Q. Kt. to B's 3rd.

Instead of taking the P. you have a choice of two other moves, viz., 3. K. Kt. to B's 3rd, or 3. K. B. to Q. B's 4th, which it may be well to examine; suppose then, in the first place,—

3. K. Kt. to B's 3rd.   3. P. to K's 4th.

(He can obtain a perfectly equal game also by giving up the P., and playing 3. P. to K's 3rd, and 4. P. to Q's 4th, instead of bringing out his Kt.)

4. B. to Q. B's 4th.	4. K. Kt. to B's 3rd.

(The "Handbuch" suggests 4. K. B. to K's 2nd, as Black's best move.)

5. K. Kt. to his 5th.	5. P. to Q's 4th.
6. P. takes P.	6. P. to K. R's 3rd.
7. Kt. to K. B's 3rd.	7. Q. B. to K. Kt.'s 5th.
8. P. to K. R's 3rd.	8. Q. to her B's 2nd.
9. P. takes B.	9. Q. takes B.
10. Kt. takes K. P.	10. Q. takes Q. P.
11. Castles.	11. B. to Q's 3rd.
12. B. to K. B's 4th.	12. Castles.
13. P. to Q. B's 4th.	13. Q. to K's 5th.
14. Q. to K. B's 3rd.	14. Q. takes Q.
15. P. takes Q.	15. Q. Kt. to B's 3rd.
16. Kt. takes Kt.	16. B. takes B.

The game is even, for White dare not take the Q. P.

This variation is taken from the "Handbuch;" the first 12 moves are the opening of a game between Mr. Cochrane and the writer.

In the second place,—

3. B. to Q. B's 4th.	3. P. to K's 4th.
4. P. to K. B's 4th.	4. Q. Kt. to B's 3rd.
5. K. Kt. to B's 3rd.	5. K. Kt. to B's 3rd.
6. Q. to K's 2nd.	6. B. to K's 2nd.

(If you take the P., at move 6., with your Kt., he takes Kt. with Kt. and then checks with his Q. at her R's 4th, &c.)

7. Castles.	7. P. to Q's 3rd.

His position is preferable.

4. Q. to her sq.	4. K. Kt. to B's 3rd.

The "Handbuch" proposes 4. P. to K. B's 4th for Black, following it out thus:—

	4. P. to K. B's 4th.
5. P. takes P.	5. K. Kt. to B's 3rd.

(He can also check with his Q., and take the P.)

6. P. to K. Kt.'s 4th.	6. Q. checks.
7. Q. Kt. to B's 3rd.	7. P. to K. R's 4th.

(If you interpose the Q. B. P. instead of the Kt., he checks at K's 4th, and on your playing, for the best, Q. B. to K's 3rd, he moves Q. to K's 5th, &c.)

8. P. to K. Kt.'s 5th.	8. K. Kt. to K's 5th.
9. Q. to her 3rd.	9. Kt. takes Q. Kt.
10. P. takes Kt.	10. P. to Q's 3rd.
11. B. to K. R's 3rd.	11. Kt. to K's 4th.
12. Q. to her 2nd.	12. Q. B. to Q's 2nd.

Black has the better game.

5. Q. Kt. to B's 3rd.	5. P. to K's 3rd.
6. Q. B. to K. Kt.'s 5th.	6. K. B. to K's 2nd.

The game appears to be equal.

GAME THE FOURTH.

WHITE.	BLACK.
1. P. to K's 4th.	1. P. to Q. B's 4th.
2. P. to K. B's 4th.	2. P. to K's 3rd.

In reply to your advance of the K. B. P., he may also play
2. Q. Kt. to B's 3rd, as in the variation.

3. K. Kt. to B's 3rd.	3. P. to Q's 4th.

The "Handbuch" recommends for you 3. B. to K's 2nd, in
preference to bringing out the Kt.

4. P. to K's 5th.	4. Q. Kt. to B's 3rd.

You can take the P. instead of passing it, but the opening
will still be rather unfavourable for you. (*e. g.*)

4. P. takes Q. P.	4. P. takes P.
5. B. to K's 2nd.	5. K. B. to Q's 3rd.
6. P. to Q. B's 3rd.	6. Q. Kt. to B's 3rd.
7. P. to Q's 3rd.	7. Q. to her B's 2nd.

He has the better game.

5. P. to Q. B's 3rd.	5. P. to K. B's 3rd.
6. K. B. to Q's 3rd.	6. K. Kt. to R's 3rd.
7. K. B. to Q. B's 2nd.	7. Q. to her Kt.'s 3rd.

Black has the advantage.

VARIATION,
Beginning at Black's 2nd move.

WHITE.	BLACK.
1. P. to K's 4th.	1. P. to Q. B's 4th.
2. P. to K. B's 4th.	2. Q. Kt. to B's 3rd.
3. K. Kt. to B's 3rd.	3. P. to K's 3rd.
4. B. to K's 2nd.	4. P. to Q's 4th.

Your 4th move is advised by the authors of the " Handbuch."
The usual play has been 4. P. to Q. B's 3rd, or as Philidor
proposes, 4. P. to Q's 4th. In the latter case, his best reply
appears to be 4. P. to Q's 4th, and your position is inferior to

his. If you play the former move, 4. P. to Q. B's 3rd, the game is one of difficulty for both parties, but he acquires a situation which is less assailable than yours. (*e. g.*)

4. P. to Q. B's 3rd.	4. P. to Q's 4th.
5. P. to K's 5th.	5. P. to K. B's 3rd.
6. Q. Kt. to R's 3rd.	6. K. Kt. to R's 3rd.

(If you play 6. B. to Q's 3rd, the position is the same as one we have previously been looking at.)

7. Q. Kt. to Q. B's 2nd.	7. Q. to her Kt.'s 3rd.
8. P. to Q's 4th.	8. Q. B. to Q's 2nd.

Black will presently play his Q. R. to B's sq., and castle afterwards, having a good game.

5. P. to Q's 3rd.	5. P. takes P.

This is the mode of play given in the "Handbuch," from whence these moves are taken, but I think Black's best policy, in similar situations, is not to exchange his men, but to develope his game as rapidly as possible. 5. P. to K. Kt.'s 3rd, followed by K. B. to K. Kt.'s 2nd, would greatly strengthen his game, by preventing the advance of your Pawns on the King's side, and by bringing his K. B. into commanding play.

6. P. takes P.	6. Q. takes Q. (ch.)
7. B. takes Q.	7. K. Kt. to B's 3rd.
8. Q. Kt. to B's 3rd.	8. Q. B. to Q's 2nd.
9. Q. B. to K's 3rd.	9. Castles.

The game is even.

GAME THE FIFTH.

WHITE.	BLACK.
1. P. to K's 4th.	1. P. to Q. B's 4th.
2. P. to Q. B's 4th.	2. P. to K's 3rd.

I agree in opinion with Major Jaenisch, that this rejoinder of yours is objectionable. With two Pawns so circumstanced your chief Bishop is absolutely shut in, play him where you will; and you can never advance the Q. P. to Q's 4th without your centre being broken up, while the enemy's remains intact and impregnable. Another disadvantage attending the present position of your K. P. and Q. B. P., is the facility afforded the adversary to post either his Q. Kt. or K. B. in the very heart of your encampment.

3. K. Kt. to B's 3rd.	3. Q. Kt. to B's 3rd.
4. Q. Kt. to B's 3rd.	4. P. to K. Kt.'s 3rd.
5. P. to Q's 3rd.	5. B. to K. Kt.'s 2nd.
6. B. to K's 2nd.	6. K. Kt. to K's 2nd.

I much prefer his game.

GAME THE SIXTH.

WHITE.	BLACK.
1. P. to K's 4th.	1. P. to Q. B's 4th.
2. P. to Q. Kt.'s 4th.	2. P. takes P.

This mode of attack, which Jaenisch calls "The Wing Gambit," is found in Sarratt; if properly opposed, the result is favourable to the second player.

Black may either take the offered P., as in the text, or simply play 2. P. to Q. Kt.'s 3rd, with a safe game.

3. P. to Q's 4th.	3. P. to Q's 4th.

He can also play 3. P. to K's 3rd, and frustrate all attack. (*e. g.*)

	3. P. to K's 3rd.
4. P. to Q. R's 3rd.	4. P. takes Q. R. P.
5. Q. B. takes P.	5. B. takes B.
6. Q. R. takes B.	6. Q. Kt. to B's 3rd.
7. P. to K. B's 4th.	7. P. to Q's 4th.
8. P. to K's 5th.	8. K. Kt. to R's 3rd.
9. K. Kt. to B's 3rd.	9. Castles.

He has gained a clear Pawn, without any inferiority of position.

4. P. to K's 5th.	4. Q. B. to K. B's 4th.
5. P. to Q. R's 3rd.	5. P. takes P.
6. Q. B. takes P.	6. Q. Kt. to B's 3rd.

You have no equivalent for the lost Pawn.

GAME THE SEVENTH.

WHITE.	BLACK.
1. P. to K's 4th.	1. P. to Q's 4th.

The defence of Q. P. *versus* K. P., or "The Centre Counter Gambit," as Major Jaenisch terms it, is not often practised, although it presents many features of interest; and if not opposed with care and judgment, will frequently turn the scale in favour of the second player.

2. P. takes P. (best)	2. Q. takes P.

If instead of taking P. with P., you play 2. P. to K's 5th, the opening is shortly resolved into a position of the French game which is not advantageous to the first player. Black, in place of re-taking the P., may move 2. K. Kt. to B's 3rd. (See Variation I.)

3. Q. Kt. to B's 3rd	3. Q. to her sq. (best)

If you play 3. P. to Q's 4th, he should answer with 3. P. to K's 4th, or Q. Kt. to B's 3rd.

4. P. to Q's 4th.	4. Q. B. to K. B's 4th.
5. K. Kt. to B's 3rd.	5. P. to K's 3rd.
6. K. B. to Q. B's 4th.	

You have a better opened game.

VARIATION I.,

Beginning at Black's 2nd move.

WHITE.	BLACK.
1. P. to K's 4th.	1. P. to Q's 4th.
2. P. takes P.	2. K. Kt. to B's 3rd.
3. B. to Q. Kt.'s 5th (ch.)	3. B. to Q's 2nd.
4. K. B. to Q. B's 4th.	4. P. to Q. Kt.'s 4th.

Instead of 4. P. to Q. Kt.'s 4th, Black might play as follows:—

	4. Q. B. to K. B's 4th.
5. Q. Kt. to B's 3rd.	5. P. to Q. B's 3rd.
6. P. takes P.	6. Q. Kt. takes P.
7. P. to Q's 3rd.	

Your game is preferable.

5. K. B. to Q. Kt.'s 3rd.	5. Q. B. to K. Kt.'s 5th.

For the result of his playing 5. P. to Q. R's 4th, see Variation II.

6. P. to K. B's 3rd.	6. Q. B. to his sq.

At move 6. you might also play, as given in the "Chess-Player's Chronicle," vol. viii. p. 44,—

6. K. Kt. to B's 3rd.	6. Kt. takes P.
7. Q. Kt. to B's 3rd.	7. Kt. takes Kt.
8. K. Kt. to K's 5th.	8. Q. to her 5th.

(If he take the Q. with either Piece, you mate him at once.)

9. Q. takes B.	9. Q. takes Kt. (ch.)

10. K. to B's sq.	10. P. to K. B's 4th.
11. Q. to K. B's 3rd.	11. K. Kt. to K's 5th.
12. P. to Q's 3rd.	

And you have a fine game.

7. Q. to K's 2nd.	7. P. to Q. R's 3rd.
8. P. to Q. B's 4th.	8. P. to Q. B's 3rd.
9. Q. P. takes P.	9. Q. Kt. takes P.
10. Q. B. P. takes P.	10. Q. Kt. to Q's 5th.
11. Q. to K's 3rd.	11. Q. R. P. takes P.

If he play 11. Q. B. to K's 3rd, you still reply with 12. Kt. to K's 2nd.

12. Kt. to K's 2nd.	12. Kt. takes Kt.
13. K. takes Kt.	13. Q. B. to Q. R's 3rd.
14. K. R. to Q's sq.	14. P. to Q. Kt.'s 5th (dis. ch.)
15. P. to Q's 3rd.	15. P. to K's 3rd.
16. P. to Q. R's 3rd.	

You have a good game, and a Pawn superiority.

VARIATION II.,

Beginning at Black's 5th move.

WHITE.	BLACK.
1. P. to K's 4th.	1. P. to Q's 4th.
2. P. takes P.	2. K. Kt. to B's 3rd.
3. B. to Q. Kt.'s 5th (ch.)	3. B. to Q's 2nd.
4. B. to Q. B's 4th.	4. P. to Q. Kt.'s 4th.
5. B. to Q. Kt.'s 3rd.	5. P. to Q. R's 4th.
6. P. to Q. R's 3rd.	6. Q. B. to K. Kt.'s 5th.
7. P. to K. B's 3rd.	7. B. to his sq.
8. Q. Kt. to B's 3rd.	8. Q. B. to Q. R's 3rd.
9. P. to Q's 3rd.	9. P. to Q. Kt.'s 5th.

If he move 9. Q. Kt. to Q's 2nd, White answers with 10. Q. B. to K's 3rd.

10. Q. R. P. takes P.	10. Q. R. P. takes P.
11. Q. Kt. to R's 4th.	11. Q. B. to Q. Kt.'s 2nd.
12. Q. B. to Q's 2nd.	

Black's position is inferior.*

* For an interesting analysis of this opening, see the Berlin " Schach-zeitung" for September, 1846.

GAME THE EIGHTH.
The Fianchetto.

WHITE.	BLACK.
1. P. to K's 4th.	1. P. to Q. Kt.'s 3rd.

Black's present move, which the Italians call "Il Fianchetto di Donna," although disapproved of by the earlier writers, may be made by the second player without harm, if followed speedily by P. to K's 3rd, and P. to Q. B's 4th. It is not, however, so advisable a mode of opening the game for the first player as the more customary moves, from its being essentially defensive.

2. P. to Q's 4th.	2. Q. B. to Q. Kt.'s 2nd.
3. K. B. to Q's 3rd.	3. P. to K's 3rd.

For the consequences of his now playing 3. P. to K. Kt.'s 3rd, followed by 4. K. B. to K. Kt.'s 2nd, see the variation. He may, however, but without advantage, move 3. P. to K. B's 4th, instead of the move in the text. (*e. g.*)

	3. P. to K. B's 4th.
4. P. takes P.	4. B. takes K. Kt. P.
5. Q. to K. R's 5th (ch.)	5. P. to K. Kt.'s 3rd.
6. P. takes P.	6. B. to K. Kt.'s 2nd.

(If 6. K. Kt. to B's 3rd, you mate him in two moves.)

7. P. takes P. (dis. ch.)	7. K. to B's sq.
8. P. takes Kt., becoming a Q. (ch.)	8. K. takes Q.
9. Q. to K. Kt.'s 4th.	9. B. takes R.
10. P. to K. R's 4th.	10. P. to K's 3rd.
11. P. to K. R's 5th.	

You have a better game than he has.

4. P. to K. B's 4th.	4. P. to Q's 4th.

If he play 4. P. to K. B's 4th, you answer with 5. Q. to K's 2nd, and soon obtain an advantage.

5. P. to K's 5th.	5. P. to Q. B's 4th.
6. P. to Q. B's 3rd.	6. K. Kt. to K. R's 3rd.

The game appears to be equal.

Variation,
Beginning at Black's 3rd move.

WHITE.	BLACK.
1. P. to K's 4th.	1. P. to Q. Kt.'s 3rd.
2. P. to Q's 4th.	2. B. to Q. Kt.'s 2nd.
3. B. to Q's 3rd.	3. P. to K. Kt.'s 3rd.

4. P. to K. B's 4th.	4. B. to K. Kt.'s 2nd.
5. K. Kt. to B's 3rd.	5. P. to Q's 3rd.

If he play 5. P. to K's 3rd, then Jaenisch proceeds thus:—

	5. P. to K's 3rd.
6. P. to Q. B's 3rd.	6. P. to Q. B's 4th.
7. Q. B. to K's 3rd.	7. P. to Q's 3rd.
8. Q. Kt. to Q's 2nd.	8. K. Kt. to K's 2nd.
9. Castles.	

With a good game.

6. Q. B. to K's 3rd.	6. Q. Kt. to Q's 2nd.
7. P. to Q. B's 4th.	7. P. to K's 3rd.
8. Q. Kt. to B's 3rd.	8. K. Kt. to K's 2nd.
9. Q. to K's 2nd.	9. Castles.
10. Castles on Q's side.	10. P. to K. B's 4th.
11. K. Kt. to his 5th.	11. P. takes K. P.
12. B. takes P.	12. B. takes B.
13. Q. Kt. takes B.	

You have the better game.

GAME THE NINTH.

WHITE.	BLACK.
1. P. to Q's 4th.	1. P. to K. B's 4th.

This is a very common defence to the openings on the Queen's side, yet, if properly taken advantage of, the premature advance of his K. B. P. may cause Black a good deal of subsequent embarrassment. It is found in Stein's "Nouvel Essai sur le Jeu des Echecs," (1789). (For 1. P. to Q. B's 4th, see the next game.)

2. P. to Q. B's 4th.	2. K. Kt. to B's 3rd.

You might also play 2. P. to K's 4th, or 2. P. to K. R's 3rd, as in Variations I. and II.

If Black, at his 2nd move, play 2. P. to K's 3rd, the game is likely to proceed as follows:—

	2. P. to K's 3rd.
3. P. to Q. R's 3rd.	3. K. Kt. to B's 3rd.
4. Q. Kt. to B's 3rd.	4. B. to K's 2nd.
5. P. to K. B's 3rd.	5. P. to Q's 4th.
6. P. takes P.	6. P. takes P.
7. Q. B. to K. B's 4th.	7. Castles.

Even game.

3. Q. Kt. to B's 3rd.	3.. P. to Q's 3rd.
4. Q. B. to K. B's 4th.	4. P. to Q. B's 3rd.

5. P. to K's 3rd.	5. Q. to her B's 2nd.
6. K. Kt. to B's 3rd.	6. K. Kt. to K. R's 4th.
7. Q. B. to K. Kt.'s 5th.	7. P. to K. R's 3rd.
8. B. to K. R's 4th.	8. P. to K. Kt.'s 4th.
9. K. Kt. to Q's 2nd.	9. K. Kt. to B's 3rd.
10. B. to K. Kt.'s 3rd.	10. P. to K's 4th.

Equal game.

VARIATION I.,
Beginning at White's 2nd move.

WHITE.	BLACK.
1. P. to Q's 4th.	1. P. to K. B's 4th.
2. P. to K's 4th.	2. P. takes P.

Your present move first occurred in a game between Mr. Horwitz and the writer, and seems to be a recommendable mode of carrying on the attack.

If Black refuse to take the P., you can take P. with P., and then play K. B. to Q's 3rd.

3. Q. Kt. to B's 3rd.	3. K. Kt. to B's 3rd.

If he advance the Q. P. to Q's 4th, you check with the Q., and then take the Q. P.

4. Q. B. to K. Kt.'s 5th.	4. P. to Q. B's 3rd.
5. B. takes Kt.	5. K. P. takes B.
6. Q. Kt. takes K. P.	6. P. to Q's 4th.
7. Q. Kt. to K. Kt.'s 3rd.	7. B. to Q's 3rd.
8. B. to Q's 3rd.	8. Castles.

I prefer your position.

VARIATION II.,
Beginning at White's 2nd move.

WHITE.	BLACK.
1. P. to Q's 4th.	1. P. to K. B's 4th.
2. P. to K. R's 3rd.	2. K. Kt. to B's 3rd.
3. P. to K. Kt.'s 4th.	3. P. to Q's 4th (best)

If he take the K. Kt. P., you will have the better game. (*e.g.*)

	3. P. takes P.
4. P. takes P.	4. Kt. takes P.
5. P. to K's 4th.	5. P. to Q's 3rd.
6. B. to K's 2nd.	6. P. to K. R's 4th.
7. Q. B. to K. Kt.'s 5th.	7. P. to K. Kt.'s 3rd.

You have the advantage.

4. P. to K. Kt.'s 5th.   4. K. Kt. to K's 5th.
5. P. to K. R's 4th.   5. P. to Q. B's 4th.
6. P. to Q. B's 3rd.   6. P. to K's 3rd.
7. K. Kt. to B's 3rd.   7. Q. Kt. to B's 3rd.
8. Q. B. to K. B's 4th.   8. K. B. to Q's 3rd.
9. B. takes B.   9. Q. takes B.

Even game.

GAME THE TENTH.

WHITE.   **BLACK.**
1. P. to Q's 4th.   1. P. to Q. B's 4th.

Black now adopts a move which is given in Ben-Oni,* and
which occurs in two of the games between M. St. Amant and
the writer.

2. P. to Q's 5th.   2. P. to K's 4th.

Your move of 2. P. to Q's 5th, yields you an immediate
advantage in position, while taking the P. would only result
in an even game.

Instead of 2. P. to K's 4th, Black may play 2. P. to K. B's
4th, as in Ben-Oni, upon which the following moves will probably occur :—

                                 2. P. to K. B's 4th.
3. Q. Kt. to B's 3rd.   3. P. to Q's 3rd.
4. P. to K's 4th.   4. K. B. P. takes P.
5. Kt. takes P.   5. P. to K's 4th.
6. B. to K. Kt.'s 5th.   6. Q. to her R's 4th (ch.)

[If he interpose either B. or Kt., you have a fine game. (*e. g.*)

                                 6. Kt. or B. to K's 2nd.
7. K. B. checks.   7. Q. Kt. or B. to Q's 2nd (best)
8. Kt. takes Q. P. (ch.), &c.]

7. P. to Q. B's 3rd.   7. Q. B. to K. B's 4th.
8. Kt. to K. Kt.'s 3rd.   8. B. to K. Kt.'s 3rd.
9. B. to Q's 3rd.   9. B. takes B.
10. Q. takes B.

You have much the better game.

3. P. to Q. B's 4th.   3. P. to K. B's 4th.
4. Q. Kt. to B's 3rd.   4. P. to Q's 3rd.

You have the advantage.

---

* "Ben-Oni, oder die vertheidigungen die Gambit-zuge im Schache,
&c., von Aaron Reinganum," Frankfort, 1825.

CHAPTER III.

GAME THE FIRST.

WHITE.	BLACK.
1. P. to K. B's 4th.	1. P. to Q's 4th.

This way of opening may be ventured without much danger, and unless it is properly met, will give your adversary some trouble ; it is not, however, so advantageous for the first player as 1. P. to K's 4th.

Black's best reply appears to be the move in the text, but he may play 1. P. to K. B's 4th also, and equalize the game. (*e. g.*)

	1. P. to K. B's 4th.
2. K. Kt. to B's 3rd.	2. K. Kt. to B's 3rd.
3. P. to Q's 4th.	3. P. to Q's 4th.

Even game.

2. K. Kt. to B's 3rd.	2. Q. B. to K. Kt.'s 5th.

He may also play 2. P. to Q. B's 4th, and the game then proceeds as follow :—

	2. P. to Q. B's 4th.
3. P. to K's 3rd.	3. Q. Kt. to B's 3rd.
4. K. B. to Q. Kt.'s 5th.	4. P. to Q. R's 3rd.

(If he play 4. B. to Q's 2nd, you may castle.)

5. B. takes Kt. (ch.)	5. P. takes B.
6. Castles.	6. P. to K's 3rd.
7. P. to Q. B's 4th.	7. K. Kt. to R's 3rd.
8. Q. to K's 2nd.	8. K. B. to Q's 3rd.
9. Q. Kt. to B's 3rd.	9. Q. to K's 2nd.
10. P. to Q. Kt.'s 3rd.	10. P. to K. B's 3rd.
11. P. to Q's 3rd.	11. Castles.
12. P. to K's 4th.	12. P. takes K. P.
13. Q. P. takes P.	13. P. to K's 4th.
14. P. to K. B's 5th.	

You have the advantage.

The above are the opening moves of a game played by the writer many years ago against the leading amateurs of Bristol.

3. K. Kt. to K's 5th.	3. B. to K. B's 4th.
4. P. to K. Kt.'s 4th.	4. P. to K's 3rd.

Your third move is thus given by the " Handbuch," and in Lewis, but I think the attack is needlessly hazardous, and that 4. P. to Q's 3rd, or 4. P. to Q. B's 4th, would be more to the purpose.

5. P. to K. Kt.'s 5th.	5. P. to K. B's 3rd.

6. Kt. to K. B's 3rd.	6. P. takes P.
7. Kt. takes P.	7. K. B. to K's 2nd.
8. P. to K. R's 4th.	8. P. to K. R's 3rd.
9. Kt. to K. B's 3rd.	9. Q. B. to K. Kt.'s 5th.

Black has the better game, owing to your premature attack at
the 4th move.

GAME THE SECOND.

WHITE.	BLACK.
1. P. to Q. B's 4th.	1. P. to Q. B's 4th.

This is an opening which may be adopted with perfect security, either by the first or second player.

The move recommended by modern authors for Black's
reply is 1. P. to K's 4th, and we have then of course the
same position as if Black had commenced the game with
1. P. to K's 4th, and you had replied with 1. P. to Q. B's 4th,
with this difference, that in the present instance *you have the
advantage of the move*, a circumstance which seems to have
escaped the notice of some writers, since, with a strange
inconsistency, they carry on the game from this position, and
decide it in favour of the defending player, who is a move
behind; while in the " Sicilian Game," 1. $\frac{\text{P. to K's 4th.}}{\text{P. to Q. B's 4th}}$, when
the position is reversed, and you have Black's position, and
in addition the advantage of the move, you can barely make
an even game. For the effect of his defending with 1. P. to
K's 4th, see the variation.

2. P. to K. B's 4th.	2. P. to K. B's 4th.

These moves are extracted from the " Handbuch." Jaenisch
gives for your second 2. P. to K's 4th, pursuing the game as
follows :—

2. P. to K's 4th.	2. P. to K's 4th.

(I prefer 2. P. to K's 3rd for your 2nd move.)

3. P. to Q's 3rd.	3. P. to Q's 3rd.
4. P. to K. B's 4th.	4. K. Kt. to B's 3rd.
5. K. Kt. to B's 3rd.	5. Q. Kt. to B's 3rd.

The game is even.

3. P. to Q's 3rd	3. K. Kt. to B's 3rd.
4. Q. Kt. to B's 3rd.	4. P. to Q's 3rd.

5. P. to K's 4th.	5. Q. Kt. to B's 3rd.
6. K. Kt. to B's 3rd.	6. P. to K's 4th.
7. B. to Q's 2nd.	7. Q. to K's 2nd.
8. P. to Q. R's 3rd.	8. P. to K. Kt.'s 3rd.
9. P. to K. Kt.'s 3rd.	9. K. B. to Kt.'s 2nd.
10. Q. Kt. to Q's 5th.	10. Kt. takes Kt.
11. Q. B. P. takes Kt.	11. Q. Kt. to Q's 5th.
12. Kt. takes Kt.	12. Q. B. P. takes Kt.

Equal game.

VARIATION,

Beginning at Black's 1st move.

WHITE.	BLACK.
1. P. to Q. B's 4th.	1. P. to K's 4th.
2. Q. Kt. to B's 3rd.	2. P. to K. B's 4th.
3. P. to K's 3rd.	3. K. Kt. to B's 3rd.

The "Handbuch" and Lewis give you 3. P. to Q's 4th, following it thus,—

3. P. to Q's 4th.	3. P. to K's 5th.
4. P. to Q's 5th.	4. P. to Q. B's 3rd.
5. P. to Q's 6th.	5. Q. to K. B's 3rd.
6. P. to Q. B's 5th.	6. P. to Q. Kt.'s 3rd.
7. P. takes P.	7. Q. R. P. takes P.
8. Q. Kt. to R's 4th.	8. B. takes Q. P.
9. Kt. takes P.	9. B. checks.
10. B. to Q's 2nd.	10. Q. takes Q. Kt. P.
11. Kt. takes Q. R.	11. B. takes B. (ch.)
12. Q. takes B.	12. Q. takes R. (ch.)
13. Q. to Q's sq.	13. Q. takes Q. R. P.

Black has the better game by far.

4. P. to Q's 4th.	4. P. to K's 5th.
5. K. Kt. to R's 3rd.	

You have the advantage in position.

For additional examples of this fine opening, see the Illustrative Games at the end of the Chapter.

GAMES

ILLUSTRATIVE OF THE PRECEDING ANALYSES.

(From the *Chess-Player's Chronicle*.)

GAME I.—In a match between the Paris and Westminster
Chess Clubs.

WHITE. (Westminster.)	BLACK. (Paris.)
1. P. to K's 4th.	1. P. to K's 3rd.
2. P. to Q's 4th.	2. P. to Q's 4th.
3. P. takes P.	3. P. takes P.
4. K. Kt. to B's 3rd.	4. K. Kt. to B's 3rd.
5. K. B. to Q's 3rd.	5. P. to Q. B's 4th.
6. Q. to K's 2nd (ch.)*	6. K. B. to K's 2nd.
7. P. takes P.	7. Castles.
8. Q. B. to K's 3rd.	8. K. R. to K's sq.
9. K. B. to Q. Kt.'s 5th.	9. Q. Kt. to B's 3rd.
10. Kt. to Q's 4th.	10. B. takes P.
11. B. takes Kt.†	11. P. takes B.
12. P. to Q. B's 3rd.	12. B. takes Kt.
13. P. takes B.	13. P. to Q. B's 4th.
14. Q. to her 3rd.	14. Q. to her Kt.'s 3rd.
15. Castles.	15. Q. B. to R's 3rd.
16. Q. to her Kt.'s 3rd.	16. Q. takes Q.
17. P. takes Q.	17. B. takes R.
18. K. takes B.	18. Kt. to his 5th.
19. P. takes P.	19. Kt. takes B.
20. P. takes Kt.	20. K. R. takes P.
21. Kt. to Q's 2nd.	21. Q. R. to K's sq.
22. P. to K. Kt.'s 4th.	22. K. R. to Q's 6th.
23. R. takes Q. R. P.	23. R. takes Kt.
24. P. to Q. Kt.'s 5th.	24. K. R. takes Q. Kt. P.
25. P. to Q. Kt.'s 6th.	25. P. to Q's 5th.
26. P. to Q. Kt.'s 7th.	26. P. to Q's 6th.
27. R. to Q. R's 8th.	27. K. to B's sq.

And White surrendered.

GAME II.—Between Messrs. Szen and Boncourt.

WHITE. (Mr. S.)	BLACK. (M. B.)
1. P. to K's 4th.	1. P. to K's 3rd.
2. P. to Q's 4th.	2. P. to Q's 4th.
3. P. takes P.	3. P. takes P.

---

* This move was the primary cause of all White's subsequent difficulties.

† If they had taken Kt. with Kt., Black would have played Q. to
her Kt.'s 3rd.

4. P. to Q. B's 4th.	4. K. Kt. to B's 3rd.
5. Q. Kt. to B's 3rd.	5. K. B. to Q. Kt.'s 5th.
6. P. to Q. R's 3rd.	6. B. takes Kt. (ch.)
7. P. takes B.	7. Kt. to K's 5th.
8. Q. to her Kt.'s 3rd.	8. P. to Q. B's 3rd.
9. K. B. to Q's 3rd.	9. Castles.
10. K. Kt. to K's 2nd.	10. P. takes P.
11. K. B. takes P.	11. P. to Q. Kt.'s 4th.
12. K. B. to Q's 3rd.	12. Q. B. to K. B's 4th.
13. Q. to her B's 2nd.	13. R. to K's sq.
14. Castles.	14. B. to K. Kt.'s 3rd.
15. Kt. to K. B's 4th.	15. K. Kt. to Q's 3rd.
16. Kt. takes B.	16. K. R. P. takes Kt.
17. Q. B. to K. B's 4th.	17. Q. Kt. to R's 3rd.
18. K. R. to K's sq.	18. Q. to Q's 2nd.
19. P. to Q. R's 4th.	19. Q. Kt. to B's 2nd.
20. Q. B. takes K. Kt.	20. Q. takes B.
21. R. takes R. (ch.)	21. R. takes R.
22. P. takes P.	22. P. takes P.
23. R. takes P.	23. R. to K's 8th (ch.)
24. B. to his sq.	24. Q. to her B's 3rd.
25. Q. to her 2nd.	25. R. to Q. Kt.'s 8th.
26. Q. to her 3rd.	26. R. to Q. B's 8th.
27. Q. R. to his 3rd.	27. Kt. to Q's 4th.
28. Q. to K. B's 3rd.	28. P. to K. B's 3rd.
29. Q. to her 3rd.	29. Kt. to K. B's 5th.
30. P. to Q's 5th.	30. Q. takes Q. P.
31. Q. takes Q. (ch.)	31. Kt. takes Q.
32. P. to K. Kt.'s 3rd.	32. Kt. takes Q. B. P.

Black wins.

GAME III.—Between MM. St. Amant and Kieseritzky.

WHITE. (M. K.)	BLACK. (M. St. A.)
1. P. to K's 4th.	1. P. to K's 3rd.
2. P. to K. B's 4th.*	2. P. to Q's 4th.
3. P. takes P.	3. P. takes P.
4. P. to Q's 4th.	4. P. to Q. B's 4th.
5. P. takes P.†	5. K. B. takes P.
6. K. B. checks.	6. Q. Kt. to B's 3rd.
7. Q. to K's 2nd (ch.)	7. K. Kt. to K's 2nd.
8. K. Kt. to B's 3rd.	8. Q. B. to K. Kt.'s 5th.
9. Q. B. to K's 3rd.	9. Q. to her Kt.'s 3rd.
10. Q. B. takes B.	10. Q. takes Q. B.

---

* This is not so good a reply as P. to Q's 4th.

† P. to Q. B's 4th, or K. Kt. to B's 3rd, is better, because the present move brings the adverse B. into powerful play.

11. Q. Kt. to B's 3rd.	11. Castles on K's side.
12. Castles on Q's side.	12. Q. R. to Q's sq.
13. B. to Q's 3rd.*	13. K. to R's sq.
14. P. to K. R's 3rd.	14. B. to K. B's 4th.
15. P. to K. Kt.'s 4th.	15. B. takes B.
16. Q. takes B.	16. Kt. to Q. Kt.'s 5th.
17. Q. to her 4th.	17. Q. to R's 4th.
18. P. to Q. R's 3rd.	18. Q. Kt. to B's 3rd.
19. Q. to her 3rd.	19. P. to Q. R's 3rd.
20. K. R. to K's sq.	20. P. to Q. Kt.'s 4th.
21. Kt. to Q's 4th.	21. P. to Q. Kt.'s 5th.
22. Kt. to Q. Kt.'s 3rd.	22. Q. to B's 2nd.
23. Kt. to K's 2nd.	23. P. takes P.
24. P. takes P.	24. Kt. to Q. R's 4th.
25. Q. to Q. B's 3rd.	25. Kt. to Q. B's 5th.
26. Q. to Q. Kt.'s 4th.†	26. R. to Q. Kt.'s sq.
27. Q. to Q. R's 4th.	27. K. R. to Q. B's sq.
28. P. to K. B's 5th.	28. Q. to K's 4th.‡

The game was prolonged for many moves, but finally won by Black.

GAME IV.—Between McDonnell and La Bourdonnais.

WHITE. (McD.)	BLACK. (La B.)
1. P. to K's 4th.	1. P. to Q. B's 4th.
2. K. Kt. to B's 3rd.	2. Q. Kt. to B's 3rd.
3. P. to Q's 4th.	3. P. takes P.
4. Kt. takes P.	4. Kt. takes Kt.§
5. Q. takes Kt.	5. P. to K's 3rd.
6. K. B. to Q. B's 4th.	6. K. Kt. to K's 2nd.
7. Q. Kt. to B's 3rd.	7. Kt. to Q. B's 3rd.
8. Q. to her sq.	8. K. B. to Q. B's 4th.
9. Castles.	9. Castles.
10. K. to R's sq.	10. P. to K. B's 4th.
11. P. takes P.	11. R. takes P.
12. K. B. to Q's 3rd.	12. R. to K. B's sq.
13. Q. to K. R's 5th.	13. R. to K. B's 4th.‖
14. B. takes R.	14. P. takes B.
15. Q. takes B. P.	15. P. to Q's 3rd.
16. Q. to her 5th (ch.)	16. K. to R's sq.

---

* Threatening to take the K. R. P. (ch.), and if the K. took the B., to check with the Kt. at his 5th.

† Badly played, as it enables Black to strengthen his attack without losing time.

‡ Overlooking the obvious move of Kt. to Q. Kt.'s 3rd, which wins at once.

§ This is not so good as P. to K's 4th.

‖ He appears to have no better move.

17. B. to K. Kt.'s 5th.
18. Kt. to K's 4th.
19. Q. to her Kt.'s 3rd.
20. Q. R. to K's sq.
21. P. to Q. R's 4th.

17. Q. to K. B's sq.
18. Kt. to Q. Kt.'s 5th.
19. Q. B. to K. B's 4th.
20. Q. B. to Q's 2nd.

And White wins.

GAME V.—Between Messrs. Cochrane and Staunton.

WHITE. (Mr. C.)	BLACK. (Mr. S.)
1. P. to K's 4th.	1. P. to Q. B's 4th.
2. P. to Q's 4th.	2. P. takes P.
3. Q. takes P.	3. Q. Kt. to B's 3rd.
4. Q. to her sq.	4. P. to K's 4th.
5. K. B. to Q. B's 4th.	5. K. Kt. to B's 3rd.
6. K. Kt. to B's 3rd.	6. K. B. to Q. B's 4th.*
7. Castles.	7. Castles.
8. Q. Kt. to B's 3rd.	8. P. to K. R's 3rd.
9. P. to Q. R's 3rd.†	9. P. to Q. R's 3rd.
10. K. B. to Q's 5th.	10. P. to Q's 3rd.
11. B. takes Kt.	11. P. takes B.
12. K. Kt. to K's sq.	12. Kt. to his 5th.
13. P. to K. R's 3rd.	13. Kt. to K. B's 3rd.
14. K. to R's sq.	14. Kt. to K. R's 2nd.
15. K. Kt. to Q's 3rd.	15. B. to Q. R's 2nd.
16. P. to K. B's 4th.	16. Q. to K. R's 5th.
17. Q. to K. B's 3rd.	17. P. to K. B's 4th.
18. P. takes K. B. P.	18. Q. B. takes P.
19. P. to K. Kt.'s 4th.	19. Kt. to his 4th.
20. Q. to K. Kt.'s 2nd.‡	20. Kt. takes K. R. P.
21. Q. to K. R's 2nd.	21. Q. takes K. Kt. P.
22. Q. to K. Kt.'s 2nd.	22. Q. to K. R's 5th.
23. Q. to K. R's 2nd.	23. P. to K's 5th.
24. Kt. to K's sq.	24. K. B. to K. Kt.'s 8th.
25. R. takes B.	25. Kt. to B's 7th (ch.)
26. K. to Kt.'s 2nd.	26. B. to K. R's 6th (ch.)

And White resigned.

---

* Had he taken the K. P., White would have taken the K. B. P. with his B., checking, and then played Q. to her 5th.

† With the intention of advancing the Q. Kt. P. and removing the adverse Kt. from the support of the K. P.

‡ If White had ventured to take the Kt., Black would have played the Q. B. to K's 5th, winning the Q.

GAME VI.—Between the same players.

WHITE. (Mr. C.)	BLACK. (Mr. S.)
1. P. to K's 4th.	1. P. to Q. B's 4th.
2. P. to Q's 4th.	2. P. takes P.
3. K. Kt. to B's 3rd.	3. P. to K's 4th.
4. K. B. to Q. B's 4th.	4. K. Kt. to B's 3rd.
5. K. Kt. to Kt.'s 5th.	5. P. to Q's 4th.
6. P. takes P.	6. P. to K. R's 3rd.
7. K. Kt. to B's 3rd.	7. Q. B. to K. Kt.'s 5th.
8. P. to K. R's 3rd.	8. Q. to her B's 2nd.
9. P. takes B.	9. Q. takes B.
10. Kt. takes K. P.	10. Q. takes Q. P.
11. Castles.	11. B. to Q's 3rd.
12. B. to K. B's 4th.	12. Castles.
13. R. to K's sq.*	13. R. to K's sq.
14. P. to Q. B's 4th.	14. Q. to her R's 4th.
15. B. to Q's 2nd.	15. Q. to her B's 2nd.
16. Kt. to Q's 3rd.	16. R. takes R. (ch.)
17. B. takes R.	17. Q. takes P.
18. Q. to K. B's 3rd.	18. Q. Kt. to B's 3rd.
19. B. to Q's 2nd.	19. R. to K's sq.
20. P. to K. Kt.'s 5th.	20. P. takes P.
21. B. takes P.	21. Q. Kt. to Q. Kt.'s 5th.†
22. B. to K. B's 4th.	22. B. takes B.
23. Kt. takes B.	23. Q. to her B's 8th (ch.)
24. K. to R's 2nd.	24. Q. takes Q. Kt. P.

White abandoned the game.

GAME VII.—Between Messrs. Horwitz and Staunton.

WHITE. (Mr. H.)	BLACK. (Mr. S.)
1. P. to K's 4th.	1. P. to Q. B's 4th.
2. K. B. to Q. B's 4th.	2. P. to K's 3rd.
3. Q. Kt. to B's 3rd.	3. Q. Kt. to B's 3rd.
4. P. to K. B's 4th.	4. P. to Q. R's 3rd.
5. P. to Q. R's 4th.	5. P. to K. Kt.'s 3rd.
6. K. Kt. to B's 3rd.	6. K. B. to K. Kt.'s 2nd.

---

* P. to Q. B's 4th would, perhaps, have been better play.
† Black might also have secured the game thus :—

	21. Q. takes Kt.
22. Q. takes Q.	22. R. to K's 8th (ch.)
23. Q. to K. B's sq.	23. B. to K. R's 7th (ch.)
24. K. takes B.	24. R. takes Q.

Locking up White's remaining Pieces, and winning easily.

7. Castles.	7. K. Kt. to R's 3rd.
8. P. to Q's 3rd.	8. P. to K. B's 4th.
9. Q. to K's sq.	9. Castles.*
10. Q. B. to K's 3rd.	10. P. to Q. Kt.'s 3rd.
11. P. to K. R's 3rd.	11. Q. Kt. to K's 2nd.†
12. P. to K's 5th.	12. Q. B. to Kt.'s 2nd.
13. P. to Q's 4th.	13. P. takes P.
14. Kt. takes P.	14. Q. to her B's 2nd.
15. P. to Q. Kt.'s 3rd.	15. Q. Kt. to B's 3rd.
16. Q. to K. B's 2nd.	16. Q. R. to Q. Kt.'s sq.‡
17. Q. R. to Q's sq.§	17. Kt. takes Kt.
18. B. takes Kt.	18. B. to Q. B's sq.‖
19. Q. to K's 2nd.	19. Q. to her Kt.'s 2nd.¶
20. B. to K. B's 2nd.**	20. Kt. to K. B's 2nd.
21. R. to Q's 3rd.	21. K. R. to K's sq.
22. K. R. to Q's sq.	22. B. to K. R's 3rd.††
23. P. to K. Kt.'s 3rd.	23. K. B. to his sq.
24. K. to R's 2nd.	24. Q. to B's 3rd.‡‡
25. Q. R. to Q's 2nd.	25. B. to Q. Kt.'s 5th.

---

* This game is opened with remarkable care and prudence on both sides.

† Threatening to win a Piece shortly, by advancing the Q. P. two squares.

‡ Imperative, for preserving the Kt. P.

§ He might have gained three Pawns for a Piece by taking the K. P. with his Kt.

‖ The only move to save the P., for Q. to her B's 3rd would have been unavailing.

¶ Black is driven to this abject defence for a time to preserve his Pawns.

** Well played. To understand the merit of this move, the student should observe that during the whole of the attack and defence on the Q's side, Black has been looking for that moment to throw forward his Q. P., when White, by taking it *en passant*, would expose an unprotected Piece to the range of the Black K. B. Hitherto White has very cleverly thwarted him, and effectually prevented his advancing the P. beneficially; but now, having his Q. R. bearing on the file, he changes his tactics, and seemingly affords his adversary the very opportunity desired; since if Black at this point plays on his Q. P., White cannot take it in passing without losing his Kt. Upon looking into the position, however, it will be seen that if Black throws forward his Q. P., White, instead of taking it *en passant*, would simply take it with his Kt.; and if the Kt. were taken, would win the adverse Queen by the check of the Bishop.

†† An important move, far better than playing the Bishop to his square at once, because it compels his adversary to make a move in some degree prejudicial to his game.

‡‡ Black has now an irresistible position. He threatens to gain a Piece by pushing on the Q. Kt. P., and also to play his B. to Q. Kt. s 2nd.

26. B. to Q's 4th.	26. B. takes Kt.
27. B. takes B.	27. P. to Q. Kt.'s 4th.
28. R. to Q's 6th.*	28. Kt. takes R.
29. P. takes Kt.	29. B. to Q. Kt.'s 2nd.†
30. P. takes P.	30. P. takes P.
31. K. B. takes P.	31. Q. takes Q. B.
32. B. takes P.	32. B. to K. B's 6th.
33. R. to Q's 3rd.	33. B. takes Q.
34. R. takes Q.	34. K. R. to Q's sq.
35. B. takes P. (ch.)	35. K. to B's sq.
36. P. to Q's 7th.	36. B. to Q. Kt.'s 4th.
37. P. to K. R's 4th.	37. B. takes P.
38. B. to Q. B's 4th.	38. B. to Q. Kt.'s 4th.
39. B. takes B.	39. R. takes B.
40. K. to R's 3rd.	40. P. to K. R's 4th.
41. R. to Q. B's 6th.	41. K. to Kt.'s 2nd.
42. R. to B's 7th (ch.)	42. K. to R's 3rd.
43. R. to Q. B's 4th.	43. K. R. to Q's 8th.
44. P. to Q. Kt.'s 4th.	44. Q. R. to Q's 4th.
45. K. to Kt.'s 2nd.	45. Q. R. to Q's 7th (ch.)
46. K. to B's 3rd.	46. Q. R. to Q's 5th.
47. R. to Q. B's 8th.	47. Q. R. takes P.
48. K. to his 3rd.	48. K. R. to Q's 5th.

And after a few more moves, White surrendered.

GAME VIII.—Between the same players.

WHITE. (Mr. H.)	BLACK. (Mr. S.)
1. P. to K's 4th.	1. P. to Q. B's 4th.
2. P. to K. B's 4th.	2. P. to K's 3rd.
3. K. Kt. to B's 3rd.	3. Q. Kt. to B's 3rd.
4. P. to Q. B's 4th.	4. P. to Q's 3rd.
5. K. B. to K's 2nd.	5. K. Kt. to K's 2nd.
6. Castles.	6. K. Kt. to his 3rd.
7. P. to Q's 3rd.	7. K. B. to K's 2nd.
8. Q. Kt. to B's 3rd.	8. B. to K. B's 3rd.
9. Q. to K's sq.	9. P. to Q. R's 3rd.
10. K. to R's sq.	10. Castles.
11. Q. B. to K's 3rd.	11. Q. R. to Kt.'s sq.
12. P. to Q. R's 4th.	12. Kt. to Q's 5th.
13. K. B. to Q's sq.	13. Q. B. to Q's 2nd.‡

* The ingenuity of desperation; he sacrifices "the exchange," for the purpose, if possible, of playing his Q. to K's 5th.

† He would evidently have lost the game by taking the Bishop. The present move not only gives White no time to plant his Q. at the K's 5th, but prevents another very dangerous move, viz., R. to Q's 5th.

‡ It would, perhaps, have been prudent to return the Kt. to Q. B's 3rd.

14. Q. B. takes Kt.	14. P. takes B.
15. Q. Kt. to K's 2nd.	15. P. to Q. Kt.'s 4th.
16. Q. B. P. takes P.	16. P. takes P.
17. P. to Q. R's 5th.	17. P. to K's 4th.*
18. P. to K. B's 5th.	18. Kt. to K's 2nd.
19. P. to K. Kt.'s 4th.	19. Kt. to Q. B's 3rd.
20. K. R. to Kt.'s sq.	20. B. to K. Kt.'s 4th.
21. B. to Q. Kt.'s 3rd.†	21. B. to K's 6th.
22. K. R. to Kt.'s 2nd.	22. Q. R. to his sq.
23. P. to Q. R's 6th.	23. Kt. to Q. Kt.'s sq.
24. P. to K. Kt.'s 5th.	24. K. to R's sq.‡
25. Q. to K. R's 4th.	25. Q. R. takes P.
26. Q. R. to K. B's sq.§	26. Kt. to Q. B's 3rd.
27. K. R. to Kt.'s 3rd.	27. Kt. to Q. Kt.'s 5th.
28. B. takes K. B. P.‖	28. K. R. takes B.
29. Q. to K. R's 5th.	29. Q. to K. Kt.'s sq.¶
30. Kt. to R's 4th.	30. P. to Q's 4th.**
31. R. to K. R's 3rd.	31. P. to K. Kt.'s 3rd.††
32. Q. to Kt.'s 4th.	32. Kt. takes Q. P.
33. Q. to Kt.'s 2nd.	33. Q. P. takes P.
34. Kt. takes P. (ch.)‡‡	34. R. takes Kt.
35. P. takes R.	35. R. takes R. (ch.)
36. Q. takes R.	36. Kt. to B's 7th (ch.)§§

* Black's necessity to sustain the doubled Pawn gave White an opportunity of opening a powerful attack on the King's side.

† Very well played.

‡ A little examination will show that this was indispensable.

§ White plays here with becoming care and foresight. He knew well the importance of getting his K. R. to Kt.'s 3rd, with the object of afterwards placing it behind the Q. on the R's file, and he saw the difficulty of accomplishing it while Black's B. could be played to K. B's 7th, a move effectually barred by the Q. R. being stationed at K. B's sq.

‖ This is an error. White forgot that on pushing forward his Kt. P., as he meditated, Black could exchange Queens. His best move, we believe, was P. to K. B's 6th, from which many beautiful variations spring. He might also have played K. R. to his 3rd, and in either case would have had an irresistible attack.

¶ Played with the conviction that White, overlooking the Q. R. in reserve, would dash at a mate with his Kt.

** This may be called "The game move." By bringing the banished Rook into operation at the proper moment, Black completely paralyses his opponent's attack.

†† Leaving White nothing but to retreat.

‡‡ He would obviously have lost his Q. had he taken the doubled P. with her.

§§ We have here one of those positions, where the young player, flushed with success, is too apt to suffer a victory within his reach to elude him. Nine out of ten inexperienced amateurs would now snatch at

37. Q. takes Kt.	37. B. takes Q.
38. R. takes P. (ch.)	38. Q. takes R.
39. P. takes Q.	39. K. takes P.
40. K. to Kt.'s 2nd.	40. P. to K's 6th.
41. K. to B's 3rd.	41. B. to Q. B's 3rd (ch.)
42. K. to Kt.'s 4th.	42. P. to Q's 6th.

White resigns.

GAME IX.—Between the same players.

WHITE. (Mr. H.)	BLACK. (Mr. S.)
1. P. to K's 4th.	1. P. to Q. B's 4th.
2. P. to Q. B's 4th.	2. P. to K's 3rd.
3. P. to K. B's 4th.	3. P. to Q's 3rd.
4. K. Kt. to B's 3rd.	4. K. Kt. to R's 3rd.
5. K. B. to K's 2nd.	5. P. to K. Kt.'s 3rd.
6. P. to K. R's 3rd.	6. P. to K. B's 4th.
7. P. to K's 5th.	7. Q. Kt. to Q. B's 3rd.
8. P. takes P.	8. B. takes P.
9. P. to Q's 3rd.	9. Q. to B's 2nd.
10. Q. to her 2nd.	10. Castles.
11. Castles.	11. K. Kt. to B's 2nd.
12. Q. Kt. to B's 3rd.	12. P. to Q. R's 3rd.
13. K. to R's sq.	13. Q. R. to Kt.'s sq.
14. P. to Q. Kt.'s 3rd.	14. P. to Q. Kt.'s 4th.*
15. P. takes P.	15. P. takes P.
16. P. to Q's 4th.	16. Q. Kt. to R's 2nd.†
17. P. takes P.	17. B. takes Q. B. P.
18. Q. B. to Kt.'s 2nd.	18. K. R. to Q's sq.
19. Q. to B's 2nd.‡	19. B. to K's 6th.§
20. P. to Q. Kt.'s 4th.	20. Q. B. to Kt.'s 2nd.‖

---

the R., conceiving the check with the Kt. sheer loss of time; and would be astounded to learn that they had lost the game by their impetuosity. Let us suppose Black to have played in this manner :—

	36. B. takes R.
37. Q. to B's 6th (ch.)	37. Q. to Kt.'s 2nd.
38. Q. to her 8th (ch.)	38. Q. to Kt.'s sq.
39. P. to K. Kt.'s 7th (ch.)	39. K. must take P.
40. Q. to K. B's 6th.	

Mate ! !

* This move was not sufficiently considered. B. to Q's 2nd would have been better play.

† By taking the Q. P. he would have lost two Pawns for one.

‡ If properly taken advantage of, this move should have lost the game.

§ With the intention of winning the Kt. by playing the P. to Q. Kt.'s 5th.

‖ It would have been better play to take the K. B. P., we think.

21. Q. to Kt.'s 3rd.	21. Q. takes K. B. P.
22. Q. takes K. P.	22. K. R. to K's sq.
23. Q. to K. B's 6th.*	23. Q. to K. R's 3rd.
24. Kt. takes Q. Kt. P.	24. B. takes K. Kt.†
25. R. takes B.	25. B. to K. Kt.'s 4th.
26. Q. to her B's 3rd.	26. Kt. takes Kt.
27. B. takes Kt.	27. R. takes B.‡
28. P. to Q. R's 4th.	28. Q. R. to K's 4th.
29. P. to Q. Kt.'s 5th.	29. B. to Q's 7th.
30. Q. to her B's 6th.	30. Q. R. to K's 3rd.
31. Q. to B's 4th.	31. B. to Q. R's 4th.
32. B. to Q. B's 3rd.	32. R. to K's 5th.
33. Q. to her B's 5th.	33. B. takes B.
34. Q. takes B.	34. Kt. to K's 4th.
35. Q. to Kt.'s 3rd (ch.)	35. K. to Kt.'s 2nd.
36. Q. to Kt.'s 2nd.	36. Q. to K. R's 5th.
37. P. to Q. R's 5th.	37. K. to R's 3rd.
38. K. R. to B's sq.	38. Kt. to K. Kt.'s 5th.
39. Q. to her 2nd (ch.)	39. K. to R's 4th.
40. K. to Kt.'s sq.§	40. Kt. to K's 6th.
41. K. R. to Q. Kt.'s sq.	41. Kt. to Q. B's 5th.‖
42. Q. to K. B's 2nd.	42. Q. to K. Kt.'s 4th.
43. P. to Q. R's 6th.	43. R. to K's 7th.
44. Q. to B's 3rd (ch.)	44. K. to R's 3rd.
45. P. to Q. R's 7th.	45. Kt. to Q. Kt.'s 3rd.
46. P. to Q. R's 8th (becoming a Q.)	46. Kt. takes Q.
47. R. takes Kt.	47. Q. takes K. Kt. P. (ch.)
48. Q. takes Q.	48. R. takes Q. (ch.)
49. K. takes R.	49. R. takes R.
50. K. to B's 3rd.	50. K. to Kt.'s 4th.
51. K. to his 3rd.	51. K. to R's 5th.

---

* Threatening to win at least a Piece by playing Q. Kt. to Q's 5th next move.

† If he had taken the Q. Kt., White would have won the game by moving K. B. to Q. B's 4th.

‡ Black has now the advantage of a Kt. for a P., quite sufficient, with ordinary care, to win the game.

§ Intending to take the Kt. (checking) next move.

‖ Instead of this move he should have taken the K. Kt. P. with his Kt., and then he must have won easily. (*e. g.*)

	41. Kt. takes K. Kt. P.
42. Q. takes Kt., or (A.)	42. Q. R. to K's 6th.

And White cannot save the game.

(A.)

42. Q. to her sq. (ch.)	42. R. to K's 7th, &c.

White has many ways of playing besides the two given, but none which can prevent the ultimate loss of the game.

52. P. to Q. Kt.'s 6th.	52. P. to K. Kt.'s 4th.
53. P. to Kt.'s 7th.	53. R. to Q. Kt.'s sq.
54. K. to B's 3rd.	54. P. to K. R's 4th.
55. K. to Kt.'s 2nd.	55. P. to Kt.'s 5th.
56. P. takes P.	56. R. P. takes P.
57. R. to Kt.'s 5th.	57. P. to B's 5th.
58. K. to B's 2nd.	58. P. to B's 6th.
59. R. to Q. Kt.'s sq.	59. K. to Kt.'s 4th.
60. K. to Kt.'s 3rd.	60. K. to B's 4th.
61. R. to Kt.'s 4th.	61. K. to his 4th.
62. R. takes P.	

Drawn game.

GAME X.—Between V. H. der Laza and Mr. H. of Berlin.

WHITE. (Mr. H.)	BLACK. (V. H. d. L.)
1. P. to K's 4th.	1. P. to Q's 4th.
2. P. takes P.	2. K. Kt. to B's 3rd.
3. K. B. checks.	3. B. to Q's 2nd.
4. B. to Q. B's 4th.	4. P. to Q. Kt.'s 4th.
5. B. to Q. Kt.'s 3rd	5. B. to K. Kt.'s 5th.
6. P. to K. B's 3rd.	6. B. to his own sq.
7. Q. Kt. to B's 3rd.*	7. P. to Q. Kt.'s 5th.
8. Q. Kt. to K's 4th.	8. Kt. takes P.
9. B. takes Kt.	9. Q. takes B.
10. K. Kt. to K's 2nd.	10. P. to K. B's 4th.
11. K. Kt. to B's 4th.	11. Q. to her Kt.'s 4th.
12. Q. Kt. to K. Kt.'s 3rd.	12. P. to K's 4th.
13. K. Kt. to K's 2nd.	13. K. B. to Q. B's 4th.†
14. P. to Q's 4th.	14. P. takes P.
15. K. Kt. takes Q. P.	15. B. takes Kt.
16. Q. takes B.	16. Castles.
17. Q. B. to K. B's 4th.‡	17. Q. Kt. to B's 3rd.
18. Q. to her 3rd.	18. K. R. to K's sq. (ch.)
19. K. to B's 2nd.	19. Q. to Kt.'s 3rd (ch.)
20. B. to K's 3rd.§	20. R. takes B.
21. Q. takes R.	21. P. to K. B's 5th.
22. Q. takes Q.	22. P. takes Kt. (ch.)
23. P. takes P.	23. Q. R. P. takes Q.
24. K. R. to Q's sq.	24. B. to K. B's 4th.
25. K. R. to Q's 2nd.	25. K. to B's 2nd.

---

* Instead of this move, he ought to have played Q. to K's 2nd.

† By this move, White is deprived of the power to castle.

‡ He has perhaps no better move in his present bad position.

§ To avoid the shutting up of his K. R., he is obliged to sacrifice two minor Pieces for a R. and P.

26. P. to K. Kt.'s 4th.	26. B. to K's 3rd.
27. P. to Q. R's 3rd.	27. P. takes P.
28. P. takes P.	28. Kt. to K's 4th.
29. K. to Kt.'s 3rd.	29. P. to K. R's 3rd.
30. K. to R's 4th.	30. Q. R. to his 5th.
31. K. R. to K's 2nd.	31. Kt. takes K. Kt. P.
32. P. takes Kt.	32. R. takes P. (ch.)
33. K. to R's 5th.	33. R. to Kt.'s 4th (ch.)
34. K. to R's 4th.	34. R. to Kt.'s 5th (ch.)*

Drawn game.

GAME XI.—Between the same players.

WHITE. (Mr. H.)	BLACK. (V. H. d. L.)
1. P. to K's 4th.	1. P. to Q's 4th.
2. P. takes P.	2. K. Kt. to B's 3rd.†
3. B. checks.‡	3. B. to Q's 2nd.
4. B. to Q. B's 4th.	4. P. to Q. Kt.'s 4th.
5. B. to Q. Kt.'s 3rd.	5. B. to K. Kt.'s 5th.§
6. P. to K. B's 3rd.	6. B. to his own sq.
7. Q. to K's 2nd.‖	7. P. to Q. R's 3rd.
8. P. to Q. B's 4th.¶	8. P. to Q. B's 3rd.
9. Q. Kt. to B's 3rd.**	9. P. takes Q. P.
10. P. takes Q. P.††	10. B. to Q. Kt.'s 2nd.

---

* Here Black proffered to make the game drawn, remarking that he might perhaps win by venturing R. to K. B's 5th.

† It is with this move the Centre Gambit begins : if, instead of playing the Kt., the first player takes the P. with his Q., he is obliged by Q. Kt. to B's 3rd, to retreat his Q., which is followed by Q. P. two ; and his opponent has the superior game.

‡ It may be remarked here, that if the first player wishes to avoid the complicated manœuvres of this Gambit, and prefers giving up the gained P., which will probably be the case in actual games, he should play for his 3rd move Q. P. two ; and, when the Kt. takes the gambit P., bring K. Kt. to B's 3rd.

§ Black might play P. to Q. R's 4th (and White must answer with P. to Q. R's 3rd), then Q. B. to K. Kt.'s 5th, then Q. B. to his own sq., and afterwards B. to Q. R's 3rd, by which he acquires another position, presenting new difficulties for the defence of the gambit P., which are not easily got over.

‖ This is better than the move of the Kt. in the last game.

¶ Better than P. to Q. R's 4th, as in the first of these games.

** He might also take Q. B. P. with Q. P.

†† If Q. B. P. takes Q. Kt. P., Black plays—

	10. P. to Q's 5th.
11. Q. Kt. to K's 4th.	11. P. to Q's 6th.
12. Kt. takes Kt. (ch.)	12. K. Kt. P. takes Kt

11. Q. to K's 5th.*	11. Q. Kt. to Q's 2nd.
12. Q. to her 4th.	12. Q. to her Kt.'s 3rd.†
13. Q. to K's 3rd.‡	13. P. to Q. Kt.'s 5th.
14. Kt. to Q. R's 4th.	14. Q. to her R's 4th.
15. P. to Q's 6th.§	15. Q. B. to his 3rd.
16. P. to Q. R's 3rd.‖	16. P. to K's 3rd.¶
17. Q. R. P. takes P.**	17. Q. takes P.
18. Q. to her B's 3rd.††	18. Q. takes P.
19. P. to Q's 4th.‡‡	19. K. Kt. to Q's 4th.
20. B. takes Kt.	20. Q. takes B.
21. K. Kt. to K's 2nd.	21. B. to Q. Kt.'s 4th.§§
22. K. Kt. to K. B's 4th.	22. Q. to K. B's 4th.
23. K. to B's 2nd.	23. K. B. to Q's 3rd.
24. P. to K. Kt.'s 4th.	24. Q. to K. B's 3rd.
25. Q. to K's 3rd.‖‖	25. Castles on K's side.
26. P. to K. R's 4th.¶¶	26. P. to K's 4th.
27. K. Kt. to R's 5th.	27. Q. to K. Kt.'s 3rd.
28. Q. to K's 4th.	28. P. to K. B's 4th.
29. Q. to her 5th (ch.)	29. K. to R's sq.
30. P. to K. Kt.'s 5th.	30. P. to K. B's 5th.

---

13. Q. to K's 4th.	13. Q. R. to Q. R's 2nd.
14. K. B. to Q. B's 4th.	14. Q. R. to Q's 2nd.

and White will not he able to rid himself of the P. at his Q's 3rd, which completely locks up his game.

* To defend the P. If he attempts to do so by Q. to her 3rd, Black plays K. P. one.

† If Black replies with Q. Kt. to his 3rd, White may play Q. R. P. two.

‡ White retires his Q., that if Black exchanges he may unite his P's— K. Kt. to K's 2nd would, however, have been better, the P. at Q's 5th being no longer defensible.

§ The only way to preserve the P. for a move or two.

‖ By this move the Kt., which appears to be lost, is indirectly but yet securely defended.

¶ If Black persevere in his endeavours to win a Piece by playing Q. R. to Q. Kt.'s sq., White can answer with—

17. Q. R. P. takes P.	17. R. takes P.
18. Q. to Q. B's 3rd,	

having a better position.

** It would be unsound to sacrifice the B. now by taking the K. P.

†† To drive Black to take the P. at Q's 6th, by which the development of his Pieces is somewhat retarded.

‡‡ K. Kt. to K's 2nd appears to be better.

§§ The best move—preventing White from castling.

‖‖ The Q. is not well placed—Kt. to K. Kt.'s 2nd would have prolonged the defence.

¶¶ He might also have played Q. Kt. to B's 3rd, or K. R. to K's sq.; but neither would have been of much avail.

31. K. R. to Q's sq.	31. Q. takes Kt.
32. Q. takes K. B.	32. Q. takes K. R. P. (ch.)
33. K. to Kt.'s sq.	33. Q. takes P. (ch.)
34. K. to R's sq.	34. Q. to R's 5th (ch.)
35. K. to Kt.'s 2nd.	35. Q. to Kt.'s 6th (ch.)
36. K. to R's sq.	36. K. R. to B's 4th.

And White loses the game.

GAME XII.—Between Messrs. Horwitz and Staunton.

WHITE. (Mr. S.)	BLACK. (Mr. H.)
1. P. to Q's 4th.	1. P. to K. B's 4th.
2. P. to K's 4th.*	2. P. takes P.
3. Q. Kt. to B's 3rd.	3. K. Kt. to B's 3rd.
4. Q. B. to K. Kt.'s 5th.	4. P. to Q. B's 3rd.
5. B. takes Kt.	5. K. P. takes B.
6. Kt. takes P.	6. P. to Q's 4th.
7. Kt. to K. Kt.'s 3rd.	7. B. to Q's 3rd.
8. B. to Q's 3rd.	8. Castles.
9. K. Kt. to K's 2nd.	9. P. to K. B's 4th.
10. P. to K. B's 4th.	10. P. to Q. B's 4th.
11. P. to Q. B's 3rd.	11. P. takes P.
12. P. takes P.	12. B. to Q. Kt.'s 5th (ch.)
13. K. to B's 2nd.	13. Q. Kt. to B's 3rd.
14. K. R. to K. B's sq.	14. B. to Q. R's 4th.†
15. K. to Kt.'s sq.	15. B. to Q. Kt.'s 3rd.
16. B. to Q. Kt.'s 5th.‡	16. Q. to K. B's 3rd.
17. B. takes Kt.	17. P. takes B.
18. R. to K. B's 3rd.§	18. P. to Q. B's 4th.‖
19. P. takes P.	19. B. takes P. (ch.)
20. K. to R's sq.	20. Q. B. to Kt.'s 2nd.
21. K. R. to Q. Kt.'s 3rd.	21. K. B. to Q. Kt.'s 3rd.¶
22. P. to Q. R's 4th.	22. P. to Q. R's 4th.**
23. Kt. takes K. B. P.	23. Q. takes Kt.
24. R. takes B.	24. B. to Q. R's 3rd.
25. Kt. to K. Kt.'s 3rd.	25. Q. takes K. B. P.
26. Q. takes Q. P. (ch.)	26. K. to R's sq.

---

* This strikes us as a novelty not to be found in " the books."

† Preparatory to an attack on the Q. P. with B. and Q.

‡ The only move apparently to save the Q. P.

§ Partly in anticipation of Black's playing Q. B. to R's 3rd.

‖ To get the advantage of a " passed" Pawn, and give free range presently to his Q. B.

¶ Had he protected the Q. B. with either of his Rooks, White would have won both Bishops for his Rook.

** By this mode of play Black loses a Pawn, but we doubt if he had any other less disadvantageous to him.

27. Q. takes Q. R. P.*	27. Q. R. to Q. B's sq.†
28. Q. to K's sq.‡	28. K. R. to K's sq.
29. Q. to K. Kt.'s sq.	29. B. to Q's 6th.§
30. P. to Q. R's 5th.	30. B. to Q. B's 5th.
31. P. to Q. R's 6th.‖	31. B. to Q's 4th.
32. Q. R. to Q's sq.	32. Q. to K's 4th.
33. Kt. to B's sq.	33. R. to Q. B's 7th.
34. R. takes B.	34. Q. takes R.
35. Kt. to K's 3rd.	35. Q. to her 7th.
36. Kt. takes R.	36. Q. takes Kt.
37. P. to Q. R's 7th.	37. Q. to her B's 2nd.
38. R. to K's 6th.	38. R. to Q. R's sq.
39. Q. to K's 3rd.	39. P. to K. R's 3rd.
40. R. to K's 8th (ch.)	40. R. takes R.
41. Q. takes R. (ch.)	41. K. to R's 2nd.
42. Q. to K's 4th (ch.)	42. P. to K. Kt.'s 3rd.
43. Q. to K's 3rd.	43. Q. to her Kt.'s 2nd.
44. P. to K. R's 3rd.	44. P. to K. R's 4th.
45. P. to Q. Kt.'s 4th.	

And White won the game.

- - -

GAME XIII.—Played some years since, in a match by correspondence, between the leading players of Bristol and Mr. Staunton.

WHITE. (Mr. S.)	BLACK. (Bristol.)
1. P. to K. B's 4th.	1. P. to Q's 4th.
2. K. Kt. to B's 3rd.	2. P. to Q. B's 4th.
3. P. to K's 3rd.	3. Q. Kt. to B's 3rd.
4. K. B. to Q. Kt.'s 5th.	4. P. to Q. R's 3rd.
5. B. takes Kt. (ch.)	5. P. takes B.
6. Castles.	6. P. to K's 3rd.
7. P. to Q. B's 4th.¶	7. K. Kt. to R's 3rd.
8. Q. to K's 2nd.	8. K. B. to Q's 3rd.
9. Q. Kt. to B's 3rd.	9. Q. to K's 2nd.

---

* This move involved so many remote contingencies, that it required some nerve and the nicest calculation to venture on it.

† Ingeniously played.

‡ His only safe move.

§ Black's game was to bring this B. to bear on the adverse K. Kt. P.; he would have saved time, therefore, by moving it at once to its 5th.

‖ If White had played his R. to Q. Kt.'s 7th, with the view of winning the K. Kt. P., Black might have played R. to K's 3rd, leaving the P. to be taken, and then R. to K. R's 3rd.

¶ If Black take this P., their opponent obtains more than an equivalent, as he separates their Pawns, and gains one of them immediately.

10. P. to Q. Kt.'s 3rd.	10. P. to K. B's 3rd.
11. P. to Q's 3rd.*	11. Castles.
12. P. to K's 4th.	12. Q. P. takes K. P.
13. Q. P. takes P.	13. P. to K's 4th.
14. P. to K. B's 5th.†	14. Kt. to B's 2nd.
15. K. Kt. to K. R's 4th.	15. Q. B. to Q's 2nd.
16. R. to B's 3rd.	16. K. R. to Q's sq.‡
17. Q. B. to K's 3rd.	17. Q. B. to K's sq.
18. Q. R. to K. B's sq.	18. K. Kt. to K. Kt.'s 4th.
19. R. to K. Kt.'s 3rd.	19. P. to K. R's 3rd.
20. Q. to K. Kt.'s 4th.	20. K. R. to Q's 2nd.
21. K. Kt. to B's 3rd.	21. K. to B's sq.
22. K. Kt. takes Kt.§	22. K. R. P. takes Kt.
23. P. to K. R's 4th.	23. B. to K. B's 2nd.
24. P. takes P.	24. K. to his sq.
25. P. to K. Kt.'s 6th.	25. B. to K. Kt.'s sq.
26. K. R. to his 3rd.	26. K. to Q's sq.
27. Q. to K's 2nd.	27. K. to Q. B's 2nd.
28. Kt. to Q. R's 4th.	28. K. R. to Q's sq.
29. Q. to her B's 2nd.	29. K. to Q. Kt.'s 2nd.
30. P. to K. Kt.'s 4th.	30. Q. to Q. B's 2nd.
31. B. takes P.	31. B. takes B.
32. Kt. takes B. (ch.)	32. K. to Q. B's sq.
33. R. to Q's 3rd.	33. R. takes R.
34. Kt. takes R.	34. Q. to her 3rd.
35. R. to Q's sq.	35. K. to B's 2nd.
36. R. to Q's 2nd.	36. Q. to her 5th.
37. Q. takes Q.	37. P. takes Q.
38. K. to B's 2nd.	38. R. to Q's sq.
39. K. to his B's 3rd.	

And wins.

---

* Better than moving the P. to Q's 4th, as Black would then have released the doubled Pawns.

† Far more effective than taking the K. P.

‡ Q. R. to Q's sq. would, perhaps, have improved their game.

§ If White had attacked the Kt. with K. R. P., instead of taking it, he would have lost his Queen.

END OF BOOK V.

SYNOPSIS OF BOOK VI.

ENDINGS OF GAMES.

CHAPTER I.

King and Queen against King.
King and Rook against King.
King and two Bishops against King.
King, Bishop, and Knight against King.
King and two Knights against King.
King and Pawn—King, Bishop, and Pawn—and King, Knight, and
    Pawn, against King.

CHAPTER II.

Queen against a Knight or Bishop.
Queen against Rook.
Queen against Rook and Pawn.
Queen against two Bishops.
Queen against two Knights.
Queen against Knight and Bishop.
Queen against Queen and Pawn.
Queen against Pawn.

CHAPTER III.

Rook against Bishop.
Rook against Knight.
Rook and Pawn against Bishop.
Rook against three minor Pieces.
Rook and Pawn against Rook.
Rook against one or more Pawns.
Rook against two Rooks.
Rook against Rook and Bishop.
Rook against Rook and Knight.

CHAPTER IV.

Endings of games with Kings and Pawns only.
King and Pawn against King and Pawn.
King and two Pawns against King and Pawn.
King and two Pawns against King and two Pawns.
King and two Pawns against King and three Pawns.
King and Pawns against King and three Pawns.

CHAPTER V.

Chess Notation adopted in Germany and France.
Chess Problems

BOOK VI.

Endings of Games.

To play with correctness and skill the ends of games, is an important but a very rare accomplishment, except among the magnates of the game. To the inexperienced player, a want of knowledge of the principles which should govern the action of his forces when the field is comparatively vacant, is a constant source of embarrassment and mortification. How often, while he is exulting in a fancied victory, when in fact it seems within his grasp, and he is dismissing the last uncertainty of its result, do we see it snatched from him in a moment! The well-timed advance of some unheeded Pawn—the perpetual and unavoidable check of the sole remaining Piece of his opponent—or the still more tantalizing dilemma of a forced stalemate—will often reverse the fortunes of the day or make the contest null. You should, therefore, make it an especial point of study, to comprehend the various classes of positions which most frequently occur towards the terminating stages of the conflict. To enable you to do so, we will now begin with the simpler class of checkmates, consisting of the King alone against an adverse force of different degrees, proceeding onward to the more difficult and complex situations which arise, when both parties are left with nearly equal forces at the end.

Chapter I.

KING AND QUEEN AGAINST KING.

This is one of the simplest of all checkmates. It is only necessary to force the single King to the nearest side of the chess-board, and then bringing up your own King, you mate in a very few moves. There is, however, one danger to be guarded against, viz., that of *stalemating* your adversary. The power of the Queen being so great, renders you very liable to this error. Place your Pieces as in Diagram 1, and find how to effect mate in two moves—observing the probability there is of your giving stalemate.

KING AND ROOK AGAINST KING.

This is also a very easy checkmate, though less so than the preceding one. A little practice, however, will enable you readily to master it. In fact, in the most favourable position for the single King, he cannot protract mate beyond eighteen or nineteen moves. As before, he must be driven to the side of the board, and then your King being placed in front of him, with one square between, mate is given by a check from the Rook on the same side line upon which the King stands. An example (see Diagram 2) will make this quite plain.

WHITE.	BLACK.
1. R. to K. R's 7th.	1. K. to K. B's sq.
2. K. to K's 2nd.	2. K. to K. Kt.'s sq.
3. R. to Q. R's 7th.	3. K. to K. B's sq.
4. K. to K's 3rd.	4. K. to K's sq.
5. K. to K's 4th.	5. K. to Q's sq.
6. K. to Q's 5th.	6. K. to Q. B's sq.
7. K. to Q's 6th.	7. K. to Q. Kt.'s sq.
8. R. to K. R's 7th.	

(8. R. to Q. B's 7th is still better, but the present move exhibits the principle more clearly.)

	8. K. to Q. B's sq.
9. R. to K. Kt.'s 7th.	9. K. to Q. Kt.'s sq.
10. K. to Q. B's 6th.	10. K. to R's sq.
11. K. to Q. Kt.'s 6th.	11. K. to Kt.'s sq.
12. R. to K. Kt.'s 8th (checkmate.)	

Diagram 1.   Diagram 2.

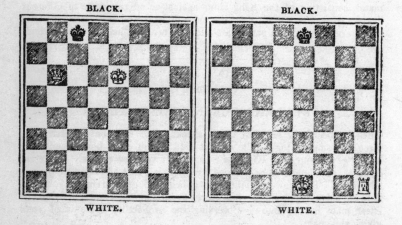

BLACK.   BLACK.

WHITE.   WHITE.

In the following situation (see Diagram 3), examine how to give mate in three moves.

KING AND TWO BISHOPS AGAINST KING.*

THE two Bishops also win, without much difficulty, against the King alone; but in this case the King must be forced, not only to a side of the board, but into one of the corners, or, at any rate, into a square adjoining a corner one. The following example (see Diagram 4) will be a sufficient illustration :—

WHITE.	BLACK.
1. K. B. to K. R's 3rd.	1. K. to Q's sq.
2. Q. B. to K. B's 4th.	2. K. to K's 2nd.
3. K. to his 2nd.	3. K. to K. B's 3rd.
4. K. to K. B's 3rd.	4. K. to K's 2nd.
5. K. B. to K. B's 5th.	5. K. to K. B's 3rd.
6. K. to his Kt.'s 4th.	6. K. to his 2nd.
7. K. to his Kt.'s 5th.	7. K. to Q's sq.
8. K. to his B's 6th.	8. K. to K's sq.
9. Q. B. to Q. B's 7th.	9. K. to B's sq.
10. K. B. to Q's 7th.	10. K. to Kt.'s sq.
11. K. to his Kt.'s 6th.	11. K. to B's sq.
12. Q. B. to Q's 6th (ch.)	12. K. to Kt.'s sq.
13. K. B. to K's 6th (ch.)	13. K. to R's sq.
14. Q. B. checkmates.	

Diagram 3.   Diagram 4.

BLACK.   BLACK.

WHITE.   WHITE.

---

* Chess Chronicle, vol. ii. p. 184.

KING, BISHOP, AND KNIGHT AGAINST KING.*

THIS is a much more difficult checkmate than any of the preceding ones, and should you be left with such a force at the termination of a game, you would probably find it quite impossible to win within the stipulated number of moves. This position merits a close examination, and you will then see that in this case, the King must not only be driven into a corner of the board, but into one of them which is commanded by your Bishop.

You will observe in this position (see Diagram 5), that the Black King is in the most unfavourable situation for you, since he occupies a corner square which is not commanded by your Bishop.

WHITE.	BLACK.
1. Kt. to K. B's 7th (ch.)	1. K. to Kt.'s sq.
2. B. to K's 4th.	2. K. to B's sq.
3. B. to K. R's 7th.	3. K. to his sq.
4. Kt. to K's 5th.	4. K. to his B's sq., or (A.)
5. Kt. to Q's 7th (ch.)	5. K. to his sq.
6. K. to his 6th.	6. K. to Q's sq.
7. K. to Q's 6th.	7. K. to his sq. (best.)
8. B. to K. Kt.'s 6th (ch.)	8. K. to Q's sq.
9. Kt. to Q. B's 5th.	9. K. to Q. B's sq.
10. K. B. to his 7th.	10. K. to Q's sq.
11. Kt. to Q. Kt.'s 7th (ch.)	11. K. to Q. B's sq.
12. K. to Q. B's 6th.	12. K. to Q. Kt.'s sq.
13. K. to Q. Kt.'s 6th.	13. K. to Q. B's sq.
14. B. to K's 6th (ch.)	14. K. to Q. Kt.'s sq.
15. Kt. to Q. B's 5th.	15. K. to Q. R's sq.
16. B. to Q's 7th.	16. K. to Q. Kt.'s sq.
17. Kt. to Q. R's 6th (ch.)	17. K. to Q. R's sq.
18. B. to Q. B's 6th (checkmate.)	

(A.)

	4. K. to Q's sq.
5. K. to his 6th.	5. K. to Q. B's 2nd.
6. Kt. to Q's 7th.	6. K. to Q. B's 3rd.

(This is his best move, to avoid the corner square; if, instead of this, he play his K. to Q. Kt.'s 2nd, your best move is the B. to Q's 3rd, and if he then play K. to Q. B's 3rd, you can move your B. to Q. B's 4th, and after his next move, B. to Q. Kt.'s 5th.)

7. B. to Q's 3rd.	7. K. to Q. B's 2nd (best.)
8. B. to Q. Kt.'s 5th.	8. K. to Q's sq.
9. Kt. to K's 5th.	9. K. to B's 2nd.
10. Kt. to Q. B's 4th.	10. K. to Q's sq.
11. K. to Q's 6th.	11. K. to Q. B's sq.

---

* Chess Chronicle, vol. ii. p. 185.

12. Kt. to Q. R's 5th.	12. K. to Q's sq.
13. Kt. to Q. Kt.'s 7th (ch.)	13. K. to Q. B's sq.
14. K. to Q. B's 6th.	14. K. to Kt.'s sq.
15. Kt. to Q's 6th.	15. K. to R's 2nd.
16. K. to Q. B's 7th.	16. K. to R's sq.
17. B. to Q. B's 4th.	17. K. to R's 2nd.
18. Kt. to Q. B's 8th (ch.)	18. K. to R's sq.
19. B. to Q's 5th (checkmate.)	

It not unfrequently happens, however, that when your opponent has a Pawn besides the King, checkmate can be given without the necessity of driving him to the corner commanded by your Bishop, because you do not then incur the risk of stalemating him. The following position, from the "Palamède," (December, 1842, p. 288,) illustrates this. (See Diagram 6.)

Diagram 5.   Diagram 6.

BLACK.   BLACK.

WHITE.   WHITE.

White to move, and give mate in six moves.

WHITE.	BLACK.
1. B. to Q. Kt.'s 4th.	1. K. to Q. R's 2nd.
2. B. to Q. B's 5th (ch.)	2. K. to R's sq. (best.)
3. K. to Q. Kt.'s 6th.	3. P. to Q. Kt.'s 5th.
4. K. to Q. R's 6th.	4. P. to Q. Kt.'s 6th.
5. B. to Q's 6th.	5. P. to Q. Kt.'s 7th.
6. Kt. mates.	

KING AND TWO KNIGHTS AGAINST KING.

THE two Knights, with the assistance of the King, cannot force checkmate; unless, indeed, the adversary has a Pawn, which may sometimes be made the means of effecting it with only a single Knight, as will be seen hereafter. Many singular positions occur with the Knights, where the adverse Pawns, or even Pieces, may be made to assist in crowding, and finally in checkmating, their own monarch. The following is an example :—

Diagram 7.

BLACK.

WHITE.

White mates in six moves, thus :—

WHITE.	BLACK.
1. Kt. from K's 3rd to Q. B's 4th.	1. P. to Q. B's 4th.
2. P. to Q. Kt.'s 4th.	2. P. takes P.
3. K. to his 2nd.	3. P. to Q. Kt.'s 6th.
4. K. to his sq.	4. P. to Q. Kt.'s 7th.
5. Kt. to K's 5th.	5. P. Queens.
6. Kt. to Q's 3rd (checkmate.)	

KING AND PAWN,—KING, BISHOP, AND PAWN,—AND KING, KNIGHT, AND PAWN,—AGAINST KING.

WHEN one Pawn only is left on the board, supported by its King, and the adverse King is either in front of the Pawn, or within such distance as to be able to intercept it, it becomes a point of great nicety in some cases, to calculate whether or not you have the power of Queening the Pawn, and therefore of winning the game. This frequently depends upon your gaining the opposition, which you cannot always do.

In the annexed position (see Diagram 8) you have the opposition, and if Black have to play you will win. Thus :—

	1. K. to his sq.
2. P. to K's 7th.	2. K. to his 2nd.
3. K. to B's 7th, and	
4. P. Queens.	

But if you move first, the game is drawn; for if you play P. to K's 7th (ch.), Black moves King to his square, and you must either abandon the Pawn or give stalemate. You will find, on trial, that any other mode of play on your part will produce the same result,—from which is deduced this important general rule : That if you can advance the Pawn to its 7th sq., *not giving check*, you will win; but that if the Pawn checks at this point, you will only draw.

Diagram 8.	Diagram 9.
BLACK.	BLACK.

| WHITE. | WHITE. |

In this position (see Diagram 9) you will win either with or without the move; for if Black have to play, he is forced to allow your King to be moved either to B's 7th or Q's 7th sq.; and if you move you gain the opposition, by playing K. to B's 6th or Q's 6th, and then P. to K's 6th. It is evident that this would equally hold good if your Pawn were any number of squares less advanced; so that you invariably win, if you can succeed in placing your King on the sixth square of the file occupied by your Pawn, and in front of it; providing, of course, that the single King cannot attack the Pawn, so as to compel you to retreat in order to support it. It is perhaps scarcely necessary to observe, that if the Pawn be upon either of the Rooks' files, these remarks will not apply—this contingency will be considered hereafter.

Recurring to the last position (Diagram 9), place your King and Pawn each one square further back, that is, King at his 5th, and Pawn at King's 4th square. If now you have to move you win, by playing King to his 6th as before; but if Black play first he will draw the game. (*e. g.*)

WHITE.	BLACK.
	1. K. to his 2nd.
2. K. to K. B's 5th.	2. K. to B's 2nd.
3. P. to K's 5th.	3. K. to K's 2nd.
4. P. to K's 6th.	4. K. to K's sq.

It is obvious, that if instead he had moved K. to Q's or K. B's sq., you would have won, as in the first example.

5. K. to B's 6th.	5. K. to B's sq.

And draws as before.

The student is recommended to devote a little time to the careful examination of the preceding positions and variations, with such others arising out of them, as will readily suggest themselves; after which, he will not find much difficulty in understanding the following one. (See Diagram 10.)

This position was first given by Lolli, and has been subsequently quoted by most of the later authors. An analysis of it will exhaust the principal varieties of this branch of the subject. The winning of it for White, depends altogether upon his having the move or the contrary. In the first place, suppose White plays first:—

WHITE.	BLACK.
1. K. to Q's 2nd.	1. K. to his 2nd.
2. K. to his 3rd.	2. K. to his 3rd.
3. K. to his 4th.	3. K. to B's 3rd.
4. K. to Q's 5th.	4. K. to K's 2nd.
5. K. to his 5th.	5. K. to B's 2nd.
6. K. to Q's 6th.	

If he play K. to B's 3rd, you advance P. to K's 4th, then to K's 5th, and on his afterwards moving K. to his sq., you gain the opposition, as shown before.

	6. K. to his sq., or to B's sq.
7. K. to K's 6th.	

And then advance Pawn, winning.

Next, suppose Black has the move, and he will draw :—

WHITE.	BLACK.
	1. K. to K's 2nd.
2. K. to Q's 2nd.	2. K. to his 3rd.
3. K. to his 3rd.	3. K. to his 4th.
4. K. to Q's 3rd.	4. K. to Q's 4th.
5. P. to K's 3rd, or to K's 4th (ch.)	5. K. to K's 4th.

And it is clear that, play as you may, you can only draw the game.

The only exception in all the foregoing cases is to be found, as has already been remarked, when the Pawn is upon either of the Rooks' files. In these instances, Black will invariably draw the game when his King can be placed on any part of the file in front of the Pawn, it being quite immaterial at what distance the adverse King and Pawn may be. Even, as in the next example, which is to be found in Ponziani, the player of the single King will draw the game, if he have not the move, against two Pawns in a somewhat similar position. For White being to move, he can only play K. to R's 8th, to which Black must reply by K. to B's sq.; and if White then advance B's Pawn, it will be taken; or if he play R's Pawn, Black returns K. to B's 2nd, and his adversary is stalemated. (See Diagram 11.)

Diagram 10.   Diagram 11.

BLACK.   BLACK.

WHITE.   WHITE.

Two *united* Pawns, with their King, always win against King alone. Another advantage in having two Pawns thus situated is, that they can always maintain themselves until the arrival of the King to their support, for should one be taken, the other will advance to Queen. In the next position (see Diagram 12), White wins by advancing K. to Kt.'s 6th, then Queening Rook's Pawn, and upon that being taken, playing K. to R's 6th, or B's 6th, having the opposition. It is curious, however, that if White had a Bishop in place of a Pawn, at his R's 7th sq., he could only draw the game, for he could not drive the adverse King from the corner;

and should he sacrifice the Bishop at Kt.'s 8th, he could not afterwards gain the opposition.

Of course, in all ordinary cases, a Pawn, with the support of one of the minor Pieces in addition to the King, must win with ease. Besides the case just mentioned, however, there are one or two important exceptions to this rule,—an acquaintance with which will sometimes enable you to save an otherwise desperate game. Of these, the one of most consequence has reference to the Bishop, and may be thus expressed : That if you are left with a Pawn on the Rooks' file, and a Bishop which does not command the 8th square of that file, or, in other words, the square on which your Pawn should go to Queen, you will not be able to win, unless the adverse King can be prevented from getting before the Pawn.

Diagram 12.   Diagram 13.

BLACK.   BLACK.

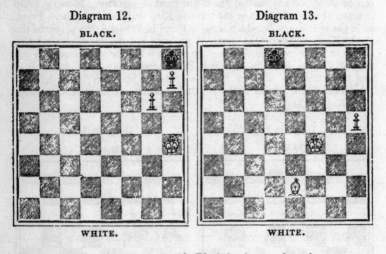

WHITE.   WHITE.

In this position (see Diagram 13), Black having to play, the game, you will find, can only be drawn. Thus :—

WHITE.	BLACK.
	1. K. to his sq.
2. K. to Kt.'s 5th.	2. K. to B's sq.
3. K. to R's 6th.	3. K. to Kt.'s sq.
4. K. to Kt.'s 6th.	4. K. to R's sq.
5. P. to R's 6th.	5. K. to Kt.'s sq.
6. B. to Q's 3rd.	6. K. to R's sq.
7. K. to B's 6th.	7. K. to Kt.'s sq.
8. P. to R's 7th. (ch.)	8. K. to R's sq.
9. K. to Kt.'s 5th.	9. K. to Kt.'s 2nd.

And play as you may, the game is drawn.

We may conclude this Chapter with two ingenious positions from the excellent German Treatise so often referred to already, (see Book II., page 11,) in which a single King draws the game against Knight and Pawn.

Diagram 14.   Diagram 15.

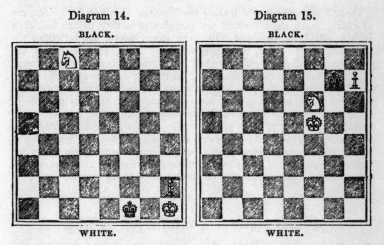

The first of these positions (Diagram 14) strikingly exemplifies an important peculiarity of the Knight, viz., that he can never gain a move. White would now win if Black had to move; but having himself to play, the case is different; for in order to force away the Black King, the Knight must be able to occupy one of the squares commanding King's Bishop's square, or King's Bishop's 2nd square, not giving check, which, (since the moves required by a Knight to reach a given point cannot be altered from an even to an odd number) you will find he can never do. Suppose,—

WHITE.	BLACK.
1. Kt. to Q's 6th.	1. K. to B's 7th.
2. Kt. to K's 4th (ch.)	2. K. to B's 8th.
3. Kt. to Q's 2nd (ch.)	3. K. to B's 7th.

&c., &c.

Diagram 15. Here also it is clear that White cannot win, for the Knight cannot command the Rook's 8th square without leaving the Pawn to be taken, and should the King attempt to support it, you inevitably give stalemate.

CHAPTER II.

ENDINGS of games in which there are Pieces or Pawns on both sides, are of course much more difficult and complicated in their nature than such as have yet been examined. In many cases, indeed, the variations are too numerous to admit of complete demonstration, whilst in others, the result continually changes according to the different parts of the board which the same Pieces may occupy. All that we can attempt here, therefore, is to mention the principal instances, in which the issue is determinate and fixed; and to give as accurate an approximation as possible in those that remain. We need only premise further, that the reader will find a careful study of these peculiar endings of the greatest advantage, not, only as regards his acquaintance with the positions actually given, many of which in play may never occur, but still more particularly as to his general knowledge of the powers and range of the various Pieces, and of the methods of most effectually combining and playing them.

QUEEN AGAINST A KNIGHT OR BISHOP.

(IN all cases, each party is of course understood to have a King in addition to the Pieces named.)

The Queen wins easily against one of the minor Pieces, except when in such a position that the weaker party, by the sacrifice of the Piece, may force a stalemate. As an example, see Diagram 16.

WHITE.	BLACK.
1. Q. to her 4th (ch.)	1. K. to his 3rd.
2. K. to his 4th.	

If he move the Kt. to Q. B's 3rd, you should check with your Q. at her 5th, and then take the Kt.; but if he play—

	2. Kt. to K. Kt.'s 3rd.
3. Q. to her Kt.'s 6th (ch.)	3. K. to B's 2nd.
4. K. to B's 5th.	4. Kt. to K's 2nd (ch.)
5. K. to Kt.'s 5th.	5. Kt. to Q's 4th.
6. Q. to her 6th.	6. Kt. to K's 2nd.
7. Q. to K. B's 6th. (ch.)	7. K. to his sq.
8. Q. to K's 6th.	8. K. to Q's sq.
9. K. to B's 6th.	9. Kt. to Q. B's sq.
10. Q. to Q. B's 6th.	

And you must win the Kt.

Whenever the Knight is at a distance from the King, you may generally win it in a few moves by a divergent check, or by attacking and confining the Knight; but you must always be careful to prevent your King and Queen being attacked at the same time by the adverse Knight; and to avoid positions in which Black may draw by giving up his Knight, as in the following (see Diagram 17), where Black having to move, can make a drawn game.

Diagram 16.   Diagram 17.

BLACK.   BLACK.

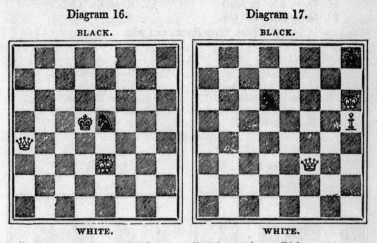

WHITE.   WHITE.

In the same manner, the Queen easily wins against a Bishop.

QUEEN AGAINST ROOK.

HERE also, as in the last case, the Queen wins in all general positions, the exceptions being of the same nature as before, viz., being founded on the possibility of making a stalemate,—an instance of which has been given in the Introduction (see page 33).

Philidor gives this position (see Diagram 18), and the method of playing it. Black being already in check, he plays :—

WHITE.	BLACK.
	1. K. to Kt.'s 6th.
2. K. to Q's 6th.	2. R. to Q. B's 7th.

(Should Black play 2. R. to B's 5th, White's reply is 3. Q. to K's sq., and then to advance his King.)

3. K. to Q's 5th.

(To check would be a loss of time.)

	3. K. to Kt.'s 7th.
4. K. to Q's 4th.	4. K. to R's 8th.

(Inviting White to take the Rook, and thus give stalemate.)

5. K. to Q's 3rd.	5. R. to Kt.'s 7th.
6. Q. to K. R's 4th (ch.)	6. K. to Kt.'s 8th, or (A.)
7. K. to B's 3rd.	7. R. to K. R's 7th.

8. Q. to Kt.'s 5th (ch.)	8. K. to R's 8th.
9. Q. to R's 6th (ch.)	9. K. to Kt.'s 8th.
10. Q. to Kt.'s 6th (ch.)	10. K. to R's 7th.
11. Q. to R's 7th (ch.)	11. K. to Kt.'s 8th.
12. Q. to Kt.'s 8th (ch.)	

Then takes Rook, and wins.

(A.)

	6. R. to Q. R's 7th.
7. Q. to Q's sq. (ch.)	7. K. to Kt.'s 7th.
8. Q. to Q. B's 2nd (ch.)	8. K. to R's 6th.
9. Q. to Q. B's 3rd (ch.)	9. K. to R's 5th.
10. K. to Q. B's 4th.	

And wins.

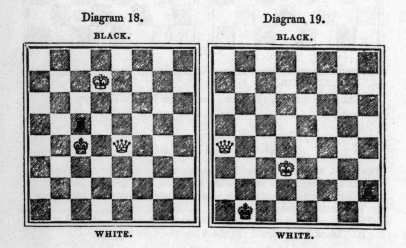

Diagram 18.   Diagram 19.

BLACK.   BLACK.

WHITE.   WHITE.

With the exceptions already referred to, you can always force the single King to a side of the board, and afterwards win the Rook, either by a divergent check, or as in the last variation. We give one other example of the same kind (see Diagram 19), with the method of playing it.

| WHITE. | BLACK. |
| 1. Q. to K. Kt.'s 4th. | |

If he play R. to K. R's 2nd, White moves Q. to K. B's 5th, and if;

	1. R. to Q. B's 7th.
2. Q. to Q's sq. (ch.)	2. R. to Q. B's 8th.
3. Q. to Q. Kt.'s 3rd (ch.)	3. K. to R's 8th.
4. Q. to Q. R's 4th (ch.)	

If instead you play K. to his 2nd, Black moves R. to B's 7th (ch.), and will draw the game.

5. K. to Q's 2nd.
6. Q. to Q. Kt.'s 5th (ch.)
7. Q. to Q. R's 6th (ch.)
8. Q. to Q. R's 5th.
9. K. to Q's 3rd.
10. Q. to Q. Kt.'s 5th (ch.)
11. Q. to Q. R's 4th (ch.)
12. K. to Q's 2nd.

4. K. to Kt.'s 7th.
5. R. to Q. Kt.'s 8th.
6. K. to R's 7th.
7. K. to Kt.'s 6th.
8. R. to Q. Kt.'s 7th (ch.)
9. R. to Q. Kt.'s 8th.
10. K. to R's 7th.
11. K. to Kt.'s 7th.

And wins.

Diagram 20.

BLACK.

WHITE.

In this position (see Diagram 20), which is given by Ponziani, Black having the move, will draw the game; thus,—

WHITE.	BLACK.
	1. R. to R's 2nd (ch.)
2. K. to Kt.'s 2nd.	2. R. to Kt.'s 2nd (ch.)
3. K. to B's 3rd.	3. R. to B's 2nd (ch.)
4. K. to Kt.'s 4th.	4. R. to Kt.'s 2nd (ch.)
5. K. to B's 5th.	5. R. to B's 2nd (ch.)
6. K. to Kt.'s 6th.	6. R. to Kt.'s 2nd (ch.)
7. K. to R's 6th.	7. R. to R's 2nd (ch.)

&c., for if White should take the Rook, his adversary is stalemated.

QUEEN AGAINST ROOK AND PAWN.

WITH few exceptions, arising from peculiar situations, the Queen wins also against a Rook and Pawn, though with greater difficulty than before. The two following positions, illustrating both a won and a drawn game, are from Philidor.

Diagram 21.

BLACK.

WHITE.

Here White having to play, will win. The following is Philidor's analysis, and seems satisfactorily to prove this :—

WHITE.	BLACK.
1. Q. to R's 7th (ch.)	1. K. to K's 3rd (best.)
2. Q. to Q. B's 7th.	2. R. to Q. B's 4th.
3. Q. to Q's 8th.*	3. R. to K's 4th.
4. Q. to K's 8th (ch.)	4. K. to Q's 4th.
5. Q. to Q. B's 8th:	5. R. to K's 5th (ch.)

(Had the Rook instead been played to his 4th square, White would have checked with Queen at her Rook's 8th, and in two or three more moves would win the Pawn at least.)

6. K. to K. B's 5th.	6. R. to K's 4th (ch.)
7. K. to K. B's 6th.	7. R. to K's 5th.

(If instead he had played K. to Q's 5th, the Queen would advance to her Bishop's 6th.)

---

* This is the position which White must endeavour to gain, in order that he may force the King to his Queen's 4th, in front of the Pawn.

8. Q. to K. B's 5th (ch.)	8. R. to K's 4th.
9. Q. to Q's 3rd (ch.)	9. K. to Q. B's 4th.
10. Q. to Q's 2nd.	10. K. to Q. B's 3rd.
11. Q. to Q's 4th.	11. K. to Q's 2nd.

(He might also have played to Q. B's 2nd.   See Variation.)

12. Q. to Q. B's 4th.	12. R. to Q. B's 4th.
13. Q. to K. B's 7th (ch.)	13. K. to Q. B's 3rd.
14. K. to his 7th.	

(This is the important point, to be able to play the King behind the Pawn.)

	14. R. to K's 4th (ch.)
15. K. to Q's 8th.	15. R. to Q. B's 4th.
16. Q. to Q's 7th (ch.)	16. K. to Q's 4th.
17. K. to K's 7th.	17. R. to Q. B's 3rd.
18. Q. to K. B's 5th (ch.)	18. K. to Q. B's 5th.
19. K. to Q's 7th.	19. R. to Q. B's 4th.
20. Q. to K's 4th (ch.)	20. K. to Kt.'s 6th.
21. K. takes P.	

And wins.

VARIATION

On Black's 11th move.

WHITE.	BLACK.
	11. K. to Q. B's 2nd.
12. Q. to Q. R's 4th.	12. R. to Q. B's 4th.
13. Q. to Q. R's 7th (ch.)	13. K. to Q. B's 3rd.
14. K. to his 7th.	

And wins, as above.

In the next position (see Diagram 22) Black may draw the game either with the move or without it, for his King cannot be forced in front of the Pawn, as in the last example.   Suppose,—

WHITE.	BLACK.
1. Q. to Q. Kt.'s 8th (ch.)	1. K. to his 2nd.
2. Q. to K. Kt.'s 8th.	2. R. to Q. B's 3rd.
3. K. to his 5th.	3. R. to K's 3rd (ch.)
4. K. to Q's 5th.	

And the game is drawn.

The Rook, with the aid of two united Pawns, will frequently draw against the Queen, and still more easily with one or both of the minor Pieces. In the latter case they may sometimes win, as in the following situation (see Diagram 23) from Ponziani.

WHITE.	BLACK.
	1. B. to Q. R's 5th (ch.)
2. K. to Q. B's sq.	2. R. to K's sq.
3. Q. to Q. Kt.'s 4th.	

(Or P. to K. Kt.'s 6th.   See A.)

	3 B. to Q. B's 7th.

4. P. to K. B's 7th.	4. R. to Q. R's sq.
5. Q. takes Kt. (ch.)	5. K. takes Q.
6. K. takes B.	6. K. to Q's 4th.
7. P. to K. Kt.'s 6th.	7. K. to K's 3rd.
3. P. to K. R's 5th.	8. K. to B's 3rd.

And wins.

(A.)

3. P. to K. Kt.'s 6th.	3. R. takes Q.
4. P. takes Q.	4. Kt. to Q's 6th.
5. P. to K. Kt.'s 7th. ·	5. B. to Q. Kt.'s 3rd.

And wins.

Diagram 22.   Diagram 23.

QUEEN AGAINST TWO BISHOPS.

THE Queen usually wins against two of the minor Pieces, at least, if they are on different parts of the board, or at a distance from their King. There are, however, many instances in which, by skilful play, the weaker force may draw the game, nor are the principal writers by any means yet agreed as to the number and description of such cases. The examination is a difficult one, and we shall here present the latest discoveries.

The two Bishops will be able to draw when they can assume a position similar to the following (see Diagram 24), or in other words, such a position in front of their King, that the adverse King cannot approach.

This situation is from Lolli, who gives the following moves to prove that White cannot win; and, indeed, it is pretty evident that the White King can never cross the line formed by the two Bishops.

Diagram 24.

BLACK.

WHITE

White moves first.

WHITE.	BLACK.
1. Q. to Q's 7th (ch.)	1. K. to B. or Kt.'s sq. (best)
2. Q. to K's 6th.	2. K. to Kt.'s 2nd.
3. K. to K. B's 4th.	3. B. to K. R's 2nd.
4. Q. to Q's 7th (ch.)	4. K. to Kt.'s 3rd.
5. Q. to K's 8th (ch.)	5. K. to Kt.'s 2nd.
6. K. to Kt.'s 4th.	6. B. to Kt.'s 3rd.
7. Q. to K's 6th.	7. B. to R's 2nd.
8. Q. checks at Q's 7th.	8. K. to Kt.'s 3rd.
9. Q. to K's 8th (ch.)	9. K. to Kt.'s 2nd.
10. K. to R's 5th.	10. Q. B. to K. B's 4th.

The game is drawn.

In the "Handbuch" the above moves are quoted, and the author then proceeds to show, at some length, and by a detailed examination, that should Black on his first move play a Bishop in place of the King, he would lose. The reason is, that your King could then be played to his Bishop's 5th; for instance,—

WHITE.	BLACK.
1. Q. to Q's 7th (ch.)	1. B. to K. B's 2nd.
2. K. to K. B's 5th.	2. B. to Q. B's 6th.
3. Q. to Q. B's 7th.	3. B. to Q. R's 8th.
4. Q. to Q. R's 7th.	4. B. to Q. Kt.'s 7th.
5. Q. to Q. Kt.'s 6th.	5. B. to Q. R's 6th.
6. Q. to Q's 4th (ch.)	6. K. to Kt.'s sq
7. K. to K. B's 6th.	7. K. to B's sq.
8. Q. to Q's 8th (ch.)	8. Q. B. to K's sp.

9. K. to K's 6th.	9. K. B. to Q. Kt.'s 5th.
10. Q. to K. B's 6th (ch.)	10. K. to Kt.'s sq.
11. Q. to K. Kt.'s 5th (ch.)	11. K. to B's sq.
12. Q. to K. B's 4th (ch.)	

And wins a Bishop.

And although Black may vary his defence in many parts, you will find that in a similar manner you can always, after his first error of B. to K. B's 2nd, force him to assume a position of the same kind, and win one of the Bishops.

QUEEN AGAINST TWO KNIGHTS.

THE power of the Queen against the two Knights has of late years been a subject of considerable discussion. It had been laid down by Lolli and other old authors that, with one or two exceptions only, the Queen could always win in these cases, and this opinion was entertained until recently by all succeeding analysts. MM. V. H. d. Laza and Bilguer, however, consider this decision to rest on no sufficient grounds, and with the spirit of patient research which distinguishes the whole of their treatise, have succeeded, if not in demonstrating, yet in showing a very high degree of probability in support of their opinion.

The kind of exception already referred to as having been so long supposed the only one in which the Knights could draw, is the following (see Diagram 25) :—

Diagram 25.　　　　　　　　Diagram 26.

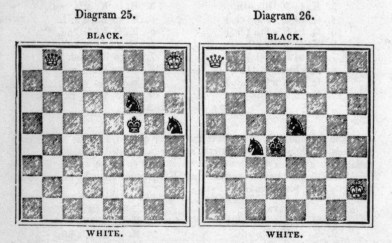

BLACK.　　　　　　　　BLACK.

WHITE.　　　　　　　　WHITE.

Here it is obvious that the White King can never move from the corner, and you will find that so long as Black keeps his King near the Knights, and does not play him on to the Rook's file (in which case White might, by occupying the Knight's file with his Queen, break up the position) the game is only drawn. Should Black leave the Knights with his King, the latter would speedily be forced into one of the Rook's squares, and prevented from moving, and then being compelled to move a Knight, would lose at once.

Another position, strictly analogous to the above, and which, therefore, does not invalidate the general principle, has more recently been made public by Mr. Walker.

Leaving those few instances in which the King of the stronger party can be prevented from moving out of the corner and coming into play, it was always considered that the strongest situation in which the Black force could be placed, was one where the two Knights should mutually defend each other, and be within reach of their King. The opinion, however, or we may rather say the discovery, of Von H. d. Laza is, that, to use his own words, " it is even more easy to draw the game against the Queen with two Knights than with two Bishops, and the whole secret consists in placing the Knights before their King in the same position as the Bishops, that is to say, side by side, and not so that they may defend each other."

He then proceeds to support his assertion thus :—" In the well-known position examined by Lolli (see his valuable treatise, p. 427), and pronounced by subsequent writers as one in which the Queen must win, I think the game ought to be drawn."[*] The position alluded to is given above (see Diagram 26) :—

WHITE.	BLACK.
" 1. K. to Kt.'s 3rd.	1. K. to Q's 6th.

(It would be equally good to play K. Kt. to Q's 6th.)

2. Q. to her 5th (ch.)	2. K. to Q. B's 6th.
3. K. to B's 4th.	3. K. Kt. to Q's 6th (ch.)
4. K. to B's 3rd.	

" Lolli now makes Black play K. Kt. to K's 4th, checking, a move which speedily loses him the game. Suppose him, however, to play—

	4. K. Kt. to Q. Kt.'s 5th.
5. Q. to her sq.	5. Q. Kt. to Q's 7th (ch.)
6. K. to his 2nd.	6. Q. Kt. to his 6th.
7. Q. to K's sq. (ch.)	7. K. to Q. B's 5th.
8. Q. to K. R's 4th (ch.)	8. K. to B's 6th.
9. Q. to K. B's 6th (ch.)	9. Q. Kt. to Q's 5th (ch.)
10. K. to B's 2nd.	10. K. Kt. to Q's 4th.

And I cannot discover how White will win the game.

" The two following positions (see Diagrams 27 and 28) are certainly very favourable for the Q. and K., and yet it is, if not quite impossible, at least extremely difficult, to bring the K. into action and win the game.

WHITE.	BLACK.
1. Q. to K's 6th.	1. K. to Kt.'s 2nd.
2. K. to his B's 3rd.	2. Q. Kt. to K. R's 2nd.

This appears to be a better move than K. Kt. to R's 5th (ch.)

---

[*] See " Chess Chronicle," vol. iii. p. 79.

3. K. to Kt.'s 4th.
4. Q. to her 6th.
5. Q. to her 5th (ch.)
6. K. to Kt.'s 5th (a bad move.)

3. Q. Kt. to K. B s sq.
4. K. to B's 2nd.
5. K. to Kt.'s 2nd.
6. Q. Kt. to K. R's 2nd (ch.)

Winning the Q. next move."

In Diagram 28 the best mode of defence is the following :—

WHITE.

2. K. to Q. B's 6th.
3. K. to Kt.'s 5th.

BLACK.

1. Q. Kt. to Q. B's sq. (ch.)
2. Q. Kt. to K's 2nd (ch.)
3. K. Kt. to Q's 3rd (ch.)

And I know not how White can win.

Diagram 27.

BLACK.

WHITE.

Diagram 28.

BLACK.

WHITE.

Our author then proceeds to show, with great minuteness of detail, that in this last instance Black has no other successful method of defence. All the variations will be found fully given in the "Chess-Player's Chronicle," vol. iii. pp. 79—91, to which we refer those of our readers who may be desirous of further investigating the subject.

QUEEN AGAINST KNIGHT AND BISHOP.

THIS kind of ending is analogous in character to the last, and the discovery of MM. V. H. d. Laza and Bilguer equally applies to it. Except in some few positions, such as the following (see Diagram 29), where, as with the two Knights, the White King can be imprisoned in the corner, and that of the adversary is in the neighbourhood of his two Pieces, it has always been laid down that the Queen wins. Again, however, we incline to agree with V. H. d. Laza, that, though with greater difficulty, "a King with Bishop and Knight can in many cases draw the game against a King and Queen." "The system of defence which I am about to lay down," he says, "is the invention of my late friend, Von Bilguer, and has hither-to been known only to himself and me."

"Let us suppose the Black King to stand on his Rook's 8th sq., then if we place his Kt. on K. R's 7th, the latter attacks three squares, viz., King's Knight's 5th, King's Bishop's 6th, and King's Bishop's 8th, and it is evident that the adverse party can only win by bringing his King near the other, which is to be effected by passing over his Rook's 4th, Bishop's 4th, or Bishop's 2nd squares; but if we now place Black's Bishop at K. Kt.'s 6th, all the squares around are for a moment defended, and before mate could be given, Black must be compelled to quit his entrench-ments, and then it remains to be shown that it is impossible for him to take up a similar position."

Diagram 29.　　　　　　　Diagram 30.

Diagram 30.

WHITE.	BLACK.
1. Q. to her 5th (ch.)	1. K. to his Kt.'s 3rd.
2. Q. to K. Kt.'s 2nd (ch.)	2. K. to his B's 2nd.

(If instead of this move White play his Q. to K. Kt.'s 8th, Black must move his B. to K. Kt.'s 4th, or R's 5th, and then again back to B's 3rd, as circumstances may require.)

3. Q. to K. Kt.'s 4th.	3. B to K's 4th.

(Since it is of great importance to defend the K. Kt.'s 3rd sq. against the Q., Black can only move his B., which he must play to K's 2nd or 4th sq.)

4. Q. to her B's 4th (ch.)	4. K. to his Kt.'s 3rd.
5. Q. to K's 4th (ch.)	5. K. to his B's 3rd.

It must now be examined whether White can force the game, **or if** Black cannot again take up a safe position.

6. K. to Q. B's 6th.	6. Kt. to K. B's 4th.

(In order to cut off afterwards the White squares from the adverse King.)

7. Q. to K. B's 3rd.	7. K. to his 3rd.
8. Q. to K's 4th.	8. K. to his B's 3rd.

(Should White play his K. to Q. B's 5th, Black, by answering with B. to Q's 3rd (ch.), would gain a position similar to the primitive situation of the Pieces, and if he play Q. to her 5th (ch.), the Black K. must be moved to his B's 3rd, the result of which shall be analysed in the accompanying variation.)

9. K. to Q's 5th.	9. Kt. to K's 2nd (ch.)
10. K. to Q. B's 4th.	10. Kt. to K. B's 4th.
11. K. to Q's 3rd.	11. Kt. to Q's 3rd.
12. Q. to her 5th.	12. K. to his B's 4th.
13. K. to his 3rd.	13. K. to B's 3rd.
14. K. to his B's 3rd.	14. Kt. to K. B's 4th.
15. Q. to her B's 6th (ch.)	15. Kt. to Q's 3rd.
16. K. to his Kt.'s 4th.	16. K. to his 3rd.

VARIATION,

Beginning at White's 8th move.

WHITE.	BLACK.
8. Q. to her 5th (ch.)	8. K. to his B's 3rd.
9. K. to Q's 7th.	9. Kt. to K. Kt.'s 2nd.
10. K. to Q's 8th.	10. Kt. to K's 3rd (ch.)
11. K. to Q. B's 8th.	11. K. to his B's 4th.
12. K. to Q's 7th.	12. Kt. to K. B's 5th.

And White has gained nothing.

In this position (see Diagram 31) also it would appear that Black, with the move, may draw the game, or at any rate the contrary vet remains to be proved. Suppose,—

WHITE.	BLACK.
	1. B. to Q. Kt.'s 2nd.

(B. to Q. R's sq. would be equally good.)

2. Q. to K. R's 4th.	2. K. to Q's 7th.
3. Q. to K. Kt.'s 5th (ch.)	3. K. to Q. B's 7th.

(By returning to K's 7th, the Bishop would obviously be lost.)

4. Q. to Q. Kt.'s 5th.	4. B. to K. R's 8th.
5. Q. to Q. B's 4th (ch.)	5. K. to Q's 7th.
6. Q. to Q. R's 2nd (ch.)	6. K. to his 6th.
7. Q. to Q. R's 7th (ch.)	7. K. to Q's 7th.
8. Q. to Q. R's 5th (ch.)	8. K. to Q. B's 7th.

And we do not see that White can win.

Diagram 31.

BLACK.

WHITE.

In a situation of this kind, however, the nicest play is absolutely essential on the part of the two Pieces, as the slightest error would inevitably lead to a speedy defeat. Suppose in the last example Black should play for his first move B. to K. R's 8th, M. Von H. d. Laza proves that he must then lose.

WHITE.	BLACK.
	1. B. to K. R's 8th.
2. Q. to K. R's 4th.	2. B. to Q. R's sq.

If in place of his last move, the Bishop is played to K. B's 6th, he is lost by the check at K's 7th; if to Q's 4th, or Q. Kt.'s 2nd, White equally wins him by a divergent check; and if to Q. B's 3rd, the result is as follows :—

	2. *B. to Q. B's 3rd.*
3. *Q. to K. R's 5th (ch.)*	3. *K. to his 8th.*

If to B's 8th, White's reply is Q. to her sq. (ch.)

4. *Q. to K. Kt.'s 6th.*	4. *B. to Q. Kt.'s 4th.*
5. *Q. to K. B's 5th.*	

And wins.

3. Q. to K. R's 5th (ch.)	3. K. to his 6th.

(If K. to B's 8th, White moves Q. to her sq. (ch.), and then **Q. to her 2nd**.)

4. Q. to K. R's 6th (ch.)	4. K. to his 7th.

(If to his 5th sq., the Queen checks at K. R's sq. and takes B.)

| 5. Q. to K's 6th (ch.) | 5. K. to Q's 8th. |

(If the King is played to his B's 8th, the Queen is moved to her B's 4th,
and then checks at her R's 2nd.)

| 6. Q. to Q. Kt.'s 3rd (ch.) | 6. K. to Q's 7th. |
| 7. Q. to Q. R's 2nd (ch.) | |

And wins.

On the whole, as regards this part of the subject, it may be safely
assumed, that when you are left, at the end of a game, with the Queen
against any two of the minor Pieces, the probability is very great in
favour of your easily gaining it, and that this probability is converted
almost into certainty, when the two Pieces are far removed from each
other or from their King, or when they cannot prevent your King from
entering into their game. At the same time there appear to be many
positions that the weaker force may occasionally take up, in which by a
very careful and accurate system of defence, they may succeed in maintaining their entrenchments, and thus produce a drawn game. The innu-
merable variations, however, are very far from being exhausted, and leave
ample scope for the researches of future analysts.

QUEEN AGAINST QUEEN AND PAWN.

In cases of this kind the game is usually drawn without difficulty, and
most generally so by means of a perpetual check, though the same object
may sometimes be attained by an exchange of Queens, when your King is
able to stop the Pawn. When, however, the Pawn is advanced to its 7th
square, and more particularly if defended by its King, the task is one of
more difficulty, and many instructive situations occur where the Pawn
may be Queened and the game therefore won. We subjoin an example
or two of each kind, by way of illustration.

Diagram 32.   Diagram 33.

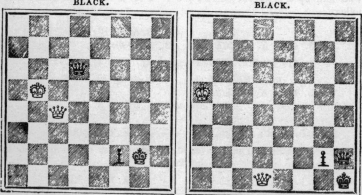

BLACK.   BLACK.

WHITE.   WHITE.

Here (see Diagram 32), with the move, White will draw the game; for suppose,—

WHITE.	BLACK.
1. Q. to K. Kt.'s 4th (ch.)	1. Q. to K. Kt.'s 6th.
2. Q. to K's 4th (ch.)	2. K. to Kt.'s 8th.
3. Q. to Q's 4th.	3. K. to R's 7th.
4. Q. to K. R's 8th (ch.)	4. Q. to R's 6th.
5. Q. to K's 5th (ch.)	5. K. to Kt.'s 8th.
6. Q. to Kt.'s 5th (ch.)	6. Q. to Kt.'s 7th.
7. Q. to K's 3rd.	

And he will always be able to make a drawn game.

In the next case (see Diagram 33), you would be ready to suppose that, as Black must Queen the Pawn, he will win; it will be seen on examination, however, that the game is really drawn. Black being in check plays—

	1. P. Queens.
2. Q. to K. B's 3rd (ch.)	2. Q. from R's 7th to Kt.'s 7th.
3. Q. to K. R's 5th (ch.)	3. Q. from Kt.'s 8th to R's 7th.
4. Q. to K's sq. (ch.)	4. Either Queen interposes.

And you evidently give a perpetual check.

The ingenious position Diagram 34 is given by Mr. Lewis; Black, with the move, ought to win. You are recommended to endeavour to discover the method of doing so before looking at the solution.

WHITE.	BLACK.
	1. Q. to her Kt.'s 4th.
2. K. moves.	

(For it is clear that the Queen cannot move without allowing the Pawn to advance.)

	2. K. to Q's 8th.
3. Q. to Q. R's sq. (ch.)	3. P. Queens.

And wins.

Diagram 34.   Diagram 35.

BLACK.   BLACK.

WHITE.   WHITE.

White moves and wins.   (See Diagram 35.)

WHITE.	BLACK.
1. P. Queens (ch.)	1. K. to K. B's 5th.

(If instead the King is moved to B's 4th, White checks at Q's 5th, and then forces the exchange of Queens.)

2. Q. to K. B's 8th (ch.)	2. K. to his 5th.
3. Q. to K's 7th (ch.)	3. K. to K. B's 6th.

(If to B's 5th, the Queen checks at K. B's 7th.)

4. Q. to K. B's 6th (ch.)	4. K. to his 5th.
5. Q. to K's 6th (ch.)	5. K. to K. B's 6th.
6. Q. to K. B's 5th (ch.)	6. K. to his 7th.
7. Q. to her 3rd (ch.)	

Then forces an exchange of Queens, and wins with his remaining Pawn.

QUEEN AGAINST PAWN.

IN all ordinary situations, the Queen of course easily stops a single Pawn and wins against it; if, however, the latter has reached its 7th square, and has the support of its King, there are instances in which the game must be drawn. Our first position (see Diagram 36) will show the method of winning, and we shall afterwards point out the exceptions.

Diagram 36.

BLACK.

WHITE.

WHITE.	BLACK.
1. Q. to K. B's 5th (ch.)	1. K. to K. Kt. s 7th.
2. Q. to K's 4th (ch.)	2. K. to B's 7th.
3. Q. to K. B's 4th (ch.)	3. K. to Kt.'s 7th.
4. Q. to K's 3rd.	4. K. to B's 8th.
5. Q. to K. B's 3rd (ch.)	5. K. to his 8th.

6. K. to Q's 4th.	6. K. to Q's 8th.
7. Q. to her 3rd (ch.)	7. K. to his 8th.
8. K. to his 3rd.	8. K. to B's 8th.
9. Q. takes P. (ch.), and wins.	

The same mode of procedure can always be adopted, unless the single Pawn should be either on the Bishop's or Rook's file, in which case Black may usually make a drawn game, owing to the power which he then has of making a stalemate. His having this alternative, however, altogether depends upon the distance which the adverse King may chance to be from the scene of action. In the next position (Diagram 37) the game is drawn.

WHITE.	BLACK.
1. Q. to K. Kt.'s 4th (ch.)	1. K. to R's 8th.
2. Q. to K. B's 3rd (ch.)	2. K. to Kt.'s 8tn.
3. Q. to K. Kt.'s 3rd (ch.)	3. K. to R's 8th.

And it is evident, that if White take the Pawn, his adversary is stalemated.

The result is the same when the Pawn is on the Rook's file, as you will at once see by making the experiment.

The following position (see Diagram 38), from Lolli, is a very ingenious exception to this rule, and will well repay your attention.

WHITE.	BLACK.
1. K. to Q. B's 5th (ch.)	1. K. to Q. B's 7th (best.)
2. Q. to K. Kt.'s 2nd (ch.)	2. K. to Q. B's 6th.
3. Q. to K. B's sq.	3. K. to Q. Kt.'s 7th.
4. Q. to K's 2nd (ch.)	4. K. to Q. Kt.'s 6th.
5. Q. to her sq. (ch.)	5. K. to Q. Kt.'s 7th.
6. Q. to her 2nd sq. (ch.)	6. K. to Q. Kt.'s 8th.
7. K. to Q. Kt.'s 4th.	7. P. Queens.
8. K. to Q. Kt.'s 3rd.	

And wins.

Diagram 37.   Diagram 38.

WHITE.   WHITE.

CHAPTER III.

ROOK AGAINST BISHOP.*

It is not very difficult to draw the game with a Bishop against a Rook. As it is necessary that the two Kings should be opposite each other (except in the corners of the board), before checkmate can be given with the Rook, it follows, that if you can so play your Bishop as to prevent his King facing yours, the game will be drawn. It is seldom good play to interpose the Bishop when the King is checked, and your Bishop should generally be at a distance from your King. (See Diagram No. 39.)

WHITE.	BLACK.
1. B. to Q. Kt.'s 7th.	1. R. to Q. Kt.'s 3rd.
2. B. to Q's 5th.	2. R. to Q. Kt.'s 7th.
3. B. to Q. B's 6th.	3. R. to K. B's 7th (ch.)
4. K. to Kt.'s sq.	

If instead you had played K. to his sq., you would have lost the game. See (A.)

	4. K. to his 7th.
5. B. to Q's 5th.	5. K. to his 8th.
6. B. to Q. B's 6th.	6. R. to K. B's 3rd.
7. B. to Q. Kt.'s 7th.	7. R. to K. Kt.'s 3rd (ch.)
8. K. to K. R's 2nd.	

(Not to K. R's sq., because he would play K. to K. B's 7th, and win the game.)

	8. K. to K. B's 7th.
9. K. to K. R's 3rd, &c.	

And the game is drawn.

(A.)

WHITE.	BLACK.
4. K. to his sq.	4. R. to Q. B's 7th.
5. B. to Q. R's 4th.	5. R. to Q. B's 8th (ch.)
6. B. interposes.	6. R. to Q. Kt.'s 8th.

And wins.

The most secure position, though not, as Philidor asserts, the only safe one, for the weaker force, is that where the King can be played to a corner square of a different colour to that on which the Bishop runs, as in this situation you have only to move your King or Bishop to Kt.'s sq. or Rook's 2nd, and cannot be compelled to leave the corner.

White with the move gives mate in seven moves.† (See Diagram 40.)

WHITE.	BLACK.
1. R. to Q. B's 2nd.	1. B. to Q. Kt.'s 6th.‡
2. R. to B's 8th (ch.)	2. B. to K. Kt.'s sq.

---

* See " Chess Chronicle," vol. ii. p. 278.   † Ibid, p. 145.
‡ If the Pawn is moved instead, the result is the same.

3. K. to Q's 6th.

4. R. to Q. B's 7th.

5. K. takes B.

6. K. to his 6th.

7. R. mates.

3. P. to Q. Kt.'s 6th.

4. B. to Q's 4th (best.)

5. K. to Kt.'s sq.

6. K. moves.

Diagram 39.   Diagram 40.

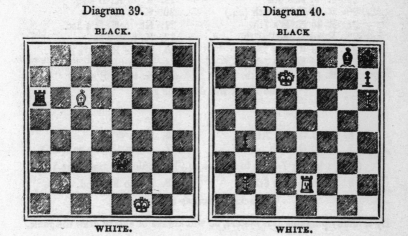

BLACK.   BLACK

WHITE.   WHITE.

ROOK AGAINST KNIGHT.

In ordinary positions, and where the Knight is near to, or cannot be prevented approaching, his King, the weaker party will be able to draw the game. The method of doing so, however, is not very easy, and there are many positions (of which we shall give some examples) where the Rook can win.

Diagram 41.

White to play.

WHITE.	BLACK.
1. R. to Q. R's 8th.	1. K. to Q's sq.
2. R. to Q. Kt.'s 8th.	2. K. to Q. B's 2nd.
3. R. to Q. Kt.'s 4th.	3. K. to Q's sq.
4. R. to Q. Kt.'s 7th.	4. K. to his sq.
5. R. to Q's 7th.	5. Kt. to Q. Kt.'s 3rd.
6. R. to Q. Kt.'s 7th, or (A.)	6. Kt. to Q. B's sq.
7. R. to K. B's 7th.	7. K. to Q's sq.
8. R. to K. R's 7th.	8. Kt. to Q. Kt.'s 3rd.
9. K. to Q's 6th.	9. Kt. to Q. B's sq. (ch.)
10. K. to Q. B's 6th.	10. Kt. to K's 2nd (ch.)
11. K. to Q. Kt.'s 7th.	11. K. to his sq.
12. K. to Q. B's 7th.	12. K. to his B's sq.
13. K. to Q's 7th.	13. Kt. to K. Kt.'s sq.

14. K. to Q's 8th.	14. Kt. to K. B's 3rd.
15. R. to K. R's 8th (ch.)	15. Kt. interposes.
16. R. to K. R's 4th.	16. K. to K. Kt.'s 2nd.
17. K. to K's 8th.	17. Kt. to K. B's 3rd (ch.)
18. K. to K's 7th.	18. Kt. to Kt.'s sq. (ch.)
19. K. to K's 6th.	19. K. to K. B's sq.
20. R. to K. B's 4th (ch.)	20. K. to his sq.
21. R. to K. B's 7th.	21. Kt. to K. R's 3rd.
22. R. to K. Kt.'s 7th.	22. K. to B's sq.
23. R. to K. R's 7th.	23. Kt. to K. Kt.'s sq.
24. R. to K. B's 7th (ch.)	24. K. to his sq.
25. R. to Q. Kt.'s 7th.	25. K. to K. B's sq.

And Black will draw the game.

(A.)

6. R. to Q. B's 7th.	6. K. to Q's sq.
7. K. to Q's 6th.	7. Kt. to Q. B's sq. (ch.)

(If Black play 7. Kt. to Q. R's sq., he would lose the game.)

8. K. to Q. B's 6th.	8. Kt. to K's 2nd.

Checking, &c., as before.

By carefully pursuing this system, he will always be able to draw the game.

Diagram 41.   Diagram 42.

BLACK.   BLACK.

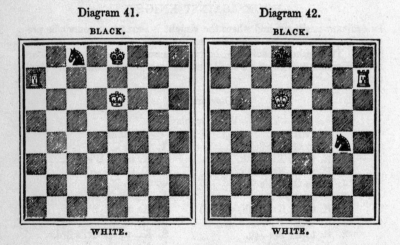

WHITE.   WHITE.

Diagram 42.

This position, Black having the move, was considered for some time a drawn game. The late lamented Mr. Forth, however, proves that White can win. (See Mr. R. A. Brown's "Collection of Problems," p. 73.)

WHITE.   BLACK.

1. K. to K's sq. (best.)

(For if he play Kt. to K. B's 3rd, you check with Rook, and then play K. to his 6th; and if instead he move K. to Q. B's sq., you play R. to R's 4th, and in a few moves will equally win the Knight.)

2. K. to his 6th sq.	2. K. to B's sq.
3. R. to R's 4th.	3. Kt. to K's 6th.

(Any other move loses the Kt. at once.)

4. R. to K's 4th.	4. Kt. to Q. B's 7th.

(If to K. Kt.'s 7th, White moves K. to K. B's 6th.)

5. K. to Q's 5th.	5. K. moves.
6. K. to Q. B's 4th.	6. K. moves.
7. R. to K's 2nd.	7. Kt. to Q. R's 6th (ch.)
8. K. to Kt.'s 4th.	8. Kt. to Kt.'s 8th.
9. R. to Q. Kt.'s 2nd.	

And wins.

In the following position (see Diagram 43) White will win either with the move or without it.

Diagram 43.

BLACK.

WHITE.

WHITE.	BLACK.
	1. Kt. to R's 2nd (ch.)
2. K. to K. B's 7th.	2. Kt. to Kt.'s 4th (ch.)

(If he move Kt. to B's sq., you play R. to Q. R's 8th, for if you at once take the Kt. he is stalemated.)

3. K. to K. Kt.'s 6th.

And wins.

The two last examples forcibly illustrate the importance of keeping the Knight near his King, and of not playing either the King or Knight to a corner square, or even to a Knight's square, if it can be avoided. In all cases the danger increases to the weaker force, as he is compelled to recede from the centre squares of any of the side lines. The principle to be observed is, therefore, precisely opposite to the one recommended in the case of Bishop against Rook, where the corner squares are the most secure of any.

ROOK AND PAWN AGAINST BISHOP.

NOTWITHSTANDING that the Rook is much more powerful than the Bishop, and more particularly so towards the end of a game, it is singular that there are many positions in which the former cannot do more than draw the game. We give some examples of both results.

Diagram 44.   Diagram 45.

BLACK.   BLACK.

WHITE.   WHITE.

Diagram 44.

This situation is given by Philidor, and may either be won by White or only drawn, accordingly as he plays correctly or otherwise. In the first place, suppose—

WHITE.	BLACK.
1. R. to Q. R's sq.	1. B. to Q. Kt.'s sq.

(This is his best mode of play.)

| 2. R. to R's 6th (ch.) | 2. B. to Q's 3rd. |

(The object of White is to be able to play his King in front of the Pawn, which, as you will see, speedily gives him the victory.)

3. R. to Q. Kt.'s 6th.	3. K. to Q's 2nd.
4. K. to Q's 5th.	4. B. to K. Kt.'s 6th.
5. R. to Q. Kt.'s 7th (ch.)	5. B. to Q. B's 2nd.
6. R. to Q. R's 7th.	6. K. to Q. B's sq., or Q's sq.
7. K. to Q. B's 6th.	

And then advances the Pawn, winning easily.

But if White for his first move had played P. to Q's 5th (ch.), Black might have drawn the game as follows :—

WHITE.	BLACK.
1. P. to Q's 5th (ch.)	1. K. to Q's 2nd.
2. K. to Q's 4th.	2. B. to K. Kt.'s 6th.
3. R. to Q. R's sq.	3. B. to K. B's 5th.
4. R. to Q. R's 7th (ch.)	4. K. to Q's 3rd.
5. K. to his 4th.	5. B. to K. Kt.'s 6th.

(Black must exercise great care here; had he played 5. B. to R's 7th, White would have moved R. to K. Kt.'s 7th, and won the game.)

6. R. to K. Kt.'s 7th.	6. B. to K's 8th.
7. R. to Kt.'s 6th (ch.)	7. K. to Q's 2nd.
8. P. to Q's 6th.	

(Were he to attempt first to support the Pawn by playing King to his 5th, is is evident that the check from the Bishop would force him to retire.)

	8. K. to Q. B's 3rd.
9. K. to his 5th.	9. B. to Q. Kt.'s 5th.

And it is obvious that White can never advance the Pawn without immediately losing it.

Diagram 45.

In this situation, for which we are indebted to Mr. Lewis, ("First Series of Lessons," &c., 1833, p. 316,) Black draws the game, either with the move or without it. Suppose White begins,—

WHITE.	BLACK.
1. R. to Q. Kt.'s 7th.	1. B. to Q. B's 5th.
2. R. to Q. B's 7th.	2. B. to Q. Kt.'s 4th.

(Had he instead played B. to Q. Kt.'s 6th, you would have won the game by moving first K. to his Kt.'s 6th, and then checking with Rook.)

3. K. to K. B's 5th.	3. B. to K's 7th.
4. K. to his 6th.	4. B. to K. Kt.'s 5th (ch.)
5. K. to his 5th.	5. B. to K's 7th.
6. K. to B's 5th.	6. B. to Q's 6th (ch.)
7. K. to K. Kt.'s 5th.	7. B. to K's 7th.
8. R. to Q. R's 7th.	8. B. to Q. B's 5th.
9. P. to K. B's 7th.	9. K. to Kt.'s 2nd.

(Had he taken the Pawn, White would have won the game by moving K. to B's 6th.)

10. K. to B's 5th.	10. B. takes P.
11. R. to Q. Kt.'s 7th.	11. K. to K. Kt.'s sq.
12. K. to K. B's 6th.	12. B. to Q. B's 5th.
13. R. to K. Kt.'s 7th (ch.)	13. K. to K. R's sq.
14. K. to K. Kt.'s 6th.	14. B. to K. Kt.'s sq.

And draws easily.

" You will perceive," adds Mr. Lewis, " from the foregoing, that the principal difficulty consists in playing your Bishop properly, so that when he plays his King to either side of the Pawn, you may be able to check him off."

When, however, the Pawn is on the Knight's file, the Rook, in a similar position, will win.   (See Diagram 46.)

WHITE.   BLACK.
1. P. to K. Kt.'s 7th (ch.)

Should he take the Pawn, White wins by advancing K. to K. Kt.'s 6th, therefore,—

1. K. to R's 2nd.
2. R. to Q. Kt.'s sq.

If he take P. with Bishop, you check with R. at K. R's sq., and then play K. to Kt.'s 6th, therefore,—

	2. B. to Q's 5th.
3. R. to Q. Kt.'s 4th.	3. B. to K. B's 7th.
4. R. to K. Kt.'s 4th.	4. K. to Kt.'s sq.
5. K. to K. Kt.'s 6th.	5. B. to Q's 4th.
6. R. to K. B's 4th.	6. B. takes P.
7. R. to Q. B's 4th, &c.	

Winning.

Diagram 46.	Diagram 47.
BLACK.	BLACK.

WHITE.	WHITE.

Diagram 47.

(White having to play, is to give mate in 10 moves.)

We close this part of the subject with the above beautiful stratagem of the Rev. H. Bolton, which first appeared in the "Chess-Player's Chronicle," vol. i. p. 305.

SOLUTION.

WHITE.	BLACK.
1. P. to Q. Kt.'s 7th (ch.)	1. K. to Q. Kt.'s sq.
2. B. to K. B's 4th (ch.)	2. R. to Q. B's 2nd.
3. K. to his Kt.'s 6th.	3. P. to K. R's 4th.
4. B. to K's 5th.	4. P. to K. R's 5th.
5. K. to K. R's 7th.	5. P. to K. Kt.'s 4th (dis. ch.)
	(best.)
6. K. to Kt.'s 8th.	6. P. to K. R's 6th.
7. K. to B's 8th.	7. P. to K. R's 7th.
8. B. takes R. P.	8. P. to K. Kt.'s 5th.
9. B. to K's 5th.	9. P. to K. Kt.'s 6th.
10. K. to his 8th.	10. P. to K. Kt.'s 7th.
11. K. to Q's 8th.	11. P. to K. Kt.'s 8th.
12. B. takes R.	(Queens.)

Checkmate.

ROOK AGAINST THREE MINOR PIECES.

THREE minor Pieces are much stronger than a Rook, and in cases where two of them are Bishops will usually win without much difficulty, because the player of the Rook is certain soon to be compelled to lose him for one of his adversary's Pieces. If, however, there are two Knights and one Bishop opposed to a Rook, the latter may generally be exchanged for the Bishop, and as two Knights are insufficient of themselves to force checkmate, the game will be drawn.

Diagram 48.

Black will win. For suppose,—

WHITE.	BLACK.
1. R. to Q. R's 3rd (ch.)	1. B. to K's 6th.
2. R. to Q. R's 2nd.	2. K. to Kt.'s 6th.
3. R. to K. R's 2nd.	3. B. to K. B's 5th.
4. R. to Q. R's 2nd.	4. B. to K. R's 6th.
5. R. to Q. R's 3rd (ch.)	5. B. to K's 6th.
6. R. to Q. R's 2nd.	6. Kt. to K. B's 7th (ch.)
7. K. to Kt.'s sq.	7. B. to K. Kt.'s 7th.
8. R. to K's 2nd.	8. Kt. to K. R's 6th (checkmate.)

Diagram 48.   Diagram 49.

Diagram 49.

In this position also Black, with the move, will win, as his adversary will not be able to exchange his Rook for the Bishop.

WHITE.	BLACK.
	1. K. to K. B's 7th.
2. R. to Q's sq.	2. Kt. to Q. Kt.'s 6th (ch.)
3. K. to Q. Kt.'s 2nd.	

(Had he played K. to Q. B's 2nd, Black would have taken the Rook, checking, and if White retook, have given mate next move.)

	3. B. takes R.
4. P. to Q. R's 7th.	4. B. to K. B's 6th.
5. K. takes Kt.	5. K. to K. Kt.'s 8th.
6. P. to K. R's 4th.	6. Kt. takes P.
7. K. to Q. B's 4th.	7. Kt. to K. Kt.'s 3rd.
8. K. to Q. B's 5th.	8. Kt. to K. B's 5th.
9. K. to Q's 6th.	9. Kt. to Q's 6th.
10. K. to Q. B's 7th.	10. Kt. to Q. Kt.'s 5th.
11. K. to Q. Kt.'s 8th.	11. Kt. to Q. R's 6th (ch.)

And will win.

ROOK AND PAWN AGAINST ROOK.

This is a more important ending, as being one of more probable occurrence in actual play than many of those we have been examining. The single Rook will frequently draw against Rook and Pawn when his King is in front of the Pawn.

The first position (see Diagram 50) is given by Philidor, and is intended to show the method by which Black may draw the game, and also the mode of play which White must adopt should his adversary not play the correct defence. White, having to play, moves—

WHITE.	BLACK.
1. P. to K's 5th.	1. R. to Q. Kt.'s 3rd.

(If he play R. to Q. R's 8th, Philidor thinks he ought to lose the game. See Variation.)

2. R. to Q. R's 7th.	2. R. to Q. B's 3rd.
3. P. to K's 6th.	3. R. to Q. B's 8th.
4. K. to K. B's 6th.	4. R. to K. B's 8th (ch.)

And will draw.

VARIATION.

WHITE.	BLACK.
1. P. to K's 5th.	1. R. to Q. R's 8th.
2. K. to K. B's 6th.	2. R. to K. B's 8th (ch.)
3. K. to his 6th.	3. K. to K. B's sq.
4. R. to K. R's 8th (ch.)	4. K. to K. Kt.'s 2nd.
5. R. to K's 8th.	5. R. to K's 8th.
6. K. to Q's 7th.	6. K. to K. B's 2nd.

(If Black here check with the Rook, White must move K. to his 7th.)

7. P. to K's 6th (ch.)	7. K. to K. Kt.'s 2nd.
8. K. to his 7th.	8. R. to K's 7th.
9. R. to Q's 8th.	9. R. to K's 8th.
10. R. to Q's 2nd.	10. R. to K's 6th.
11. R. to K. Kt.'s 2nd (ch.)	11. K. to R's 2nd.
12. K. to K. B's 7th.	12. R. to K. B's 6th (ch.)
13. K. to his 8th.	13. R. to K's 6th.
14. P. to K's 7th.	14. R. to Q's 6th.
15. R. to Q. B's 2nd.	15. K. to K. Kt.'s 2nd.
16. R. to Q. B's 7th.	16. R. to Q's 7th.
17. R. to Q's 7th.	17. R. to Q. Kt.'s 7th.
18. R. to Q's sq.	18. R. to Q. Kt.'s sq. (ch.)
19. K. to Q's 7th.	19. R. to Q. Kt.'s 2nd (ch.)
20. K. to K's 6th.	20. R. to Q. Kt.'s 3rd (ch.)
21. R. to Q's 6th.	21. R. to Q. Kt.'s sq.
22. R. to Q's 8th.	

And wins.

Diagram 50.

BLACK.

WHITE.

Diagram 51.

BLACK.

WHITE.

In the next case, according to Del Rio (see Diagram 51), Black will draw the game, even against two Pawns.

WHITE.	BLACK.
	1. K. to Q. B's 4th.
2. K. to Q's 3rd.	2. R. to Q's 3rd (ch.)
3. K. to Q. B's 3rd.	3. R. to Q. R's 3rd.
4. R. to K. B's 4th.	4. R. to Q. R's 6th (ch.)

Drawn game; and you will find, that whatever mode of play White may adopt, the result will be the same.

Diagram 52.

BLACK.

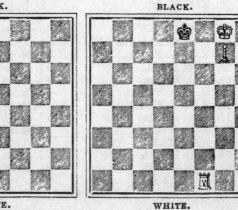

WHITE.

Diagram 53.

BLACK.

WHITE.

Diagram 52.

Black, having to move, the game is drawn.

WHITE.	BLACK.
	1. R. to Q. R's 7th (ch.)
2. K. to Q. Kt.'s 6th.	2. R. to Q's 7th.

And Black has only to persist in placing his Rook in front of that of his adversary, as if the latter takes it, he gives stalemate.

Diagram 53.

In this instructive position White, with the move, will win the game.

WHITE.	BLACK.
1. R. to K. B's 4th.	1. R. to K. R's 8th.
2. R. to K's 4th. (ch.)	2. K. to Q's 2nd.
3. K. to K. B's 7th.	3. R. to K. B's 8th (ch.)
4. K. to K. Kt.'s 6th.	4. R. to K. Kt.'s 8th (ch.)
5. K. to K. R's 6th.	5. R. to K. R's 8th (ch.)
6. K. to K. Kt.'s 5th.	6. R. to K. Kt.'s 8th (ch.)
7. R. to K. Kt.'s 4th.	

And White wins.

ROOK AGAINST ONE OR MORE PAWNS.

We have already seen (p. 430) that a Pawn at its 7th square, defended by its King, and with the adverse King at a distance, may in some cases draw the game against the Queen. It will be obvious that, in a similar position, it must be much more easy to do so against a Rook. The latter, indeed, must speedily be sacrificed for the Pawn to prevent the loss of the game. When, however, the Pawn is not quite so far advanced, and especially if supported by a second one, many cases of the greatest difficulty occur, and which demand the utmost nicety and precision of calculation.

The following examples will serve in some degree to illustrate this, and they might easily be varied and increased to an indefinite extent.

Diagram 54.

White must lose, even with the move.

Suppose :—

WHITE.	BLACK.
1. R. to K's 8th.	1. K. to Q's 2nd.
2. K. to his 3rd.	2. P. "Queens."

&c., &c.

Diagram 54. Diagram 55.

Diagram 55.

Here White will win the Pawn, and therefore the game.

WHITE.	BLACK.
1. R. to K. Kt.'s 6th (ch.)	1. K. to Q's 4th.
2. K. to Q's 2nd.	2. P. to Q. B's 4th.
3. R. to Q's 6th (ch.)	3. K. to Q. B's 5th.
4. K. to Q. B's 6th.	4. K. to Q. Kt.'s 5th.
5. K. to Q's 5th.	5. P. to Q. B's 5th.
6. R. to K. Kt.'s 6th (ch.)	6. K. to Q. B's 6th.
7. R. to Q. B's 6th.	

And White wins.

Two united Pawns at their 6th square, supposing the Kings to be at a distance, will win against a Rook if they have the move, or even without the move, providing they are not at the moment attacked. (See Diagram 56.)

Black having to play, moves :—

WHITE.	BLACK.
	1. P. to Q. Kt.'s 7th.
2. R. to K. B's sq.	2. P. to Q. B's 7th.
3. R. to K. Kt.'s sq. (ch.)	3. K. to K. R's 6th.
4. K. to K. B's 3rd.	4. Either Pawn " Queens."

&c., &c.

Diagram 56.   Diagram 57.

Three united Pawns, defended by their King, must win against a Rook, unless the adverse King can be brought at an early period in front of the Pawns. In the present instance (see Diagram 57) the Pawns win, even under that disadvantage.

WHITE.	BLACK.
	1. P. to K. B's 6th (ch.)
2. R. takes P.	2. R. P. "Queens" (ch.)
3. K. takes Q.	3. K. takes R.
4. K. to K. Kt.'s sq.	4. P. to K. Kt.'s 7th.
5. K. to K. R's 2nd.	5. K. to B's 7th, and wins.

Or,

	1. P. to K. B's 6th (ch.)
2. K. to R's sq.	2. P. to K. Kt.'s 7th (ch.)
3. K. takes R. P.	3. P. takes R., and becomes a Kt. (ch.), and wins.

It is evident that were Black to make a Queen, his opponent would be stalemated.

Even when, as in the next position (see Diagram 58), the Pawns are one step less advanced, Black, by careful play, will be able to draw the game.

WHITE.	BLACK.
1. R. to K. B's 2nd.	1. K. to K. B's 3rd.
2. K. to K. B's 4th.	2. K. to K. Kt.'s 3rd.
3. R. to K's 2nd.	3. K. to K. B's 2nd.
4. R. to K's 5th.	4. K. to K. Kt.'s 3rd.
5. R. to K's 6th (ch.)	5. K. to K. Kt.'s 2nd.
6. R. to Q's 6th.	

(White dare not play K. to Kt.'s 5th, as Black would then advance R's Pawn, afterwards supporting it with Kt.'s Pawn.)

6. K. to K. B's 2nd.

His best move; were he to play K. to R's 2nd he would lose; thus,—

6. *K. to R's 2nd.*

7. *K. to Kt.'s 5th.*	7. *K. to K. Kt.'s 2nd.*
8. *R. to Kt.'s 6th (ch.)*	8. *K. to K. R's 2nd.*
9. *R. to K. R's 6th (ch.)*	9. *K. to K. Kt.'s 2nd.*
10. *R. to K. R's 5th.*	

And will win.

7. R. to K. R's 6th.	7. K. to K. Kt.'s 2nd.
8. R. to K. R's 5th.	8. K. to K. Kt.'s 3rd.
9. R. to K. Kt.'s 5th (ch.)	9. K. to K. R's 3rd.
10. R. to K. Kt.'s 8th.	

(It is clear that, if White take the Pawn, Black must win, through the advance of R's Pawn.)

	10. K. to K. R's 2nd.
11. R. to Q's 8th.	11. K. to K. Kt.'s 3rd.
12. R. to Q's 6th (ch.)	

And cannot do more than draw the game.

Diagram 58.

BLACK.

WHITE.

Diagram 59.

BLACK.

WHITE.

Had Black, however, played up his King to support the Pawns, he must have lost. (*e. g.*)

WHITE.	BLACK.
1. R. to K. B's 2nd.	1. K. to K. Kt.'s 3rd.
2. K. to K. B's 4th.	2. K. to K. R's 4th.
3. R. to Q's 2nd.	3. K. to K. R's 5th.
4. R. to Q's 6th.	4. K. to K. R's 4th.

5. R. to K's 6th.	5. P. to K. R's 7th.
6. R. to K's 8th.	6. P. "Queens."
7. R. to K. R's 8th (ch.)	

And wins.

Diagram 59.

With the move Black wins.

WHITE.	BLACK.
	1. R. to Q. B's sq.
2. K. to Q. R's 6th.	2. K. to Q. B's 3rd.
3. R. takes R.	3. P. to Q. R's 7th.
4. K. to Q. R's 7th.	4. P. "Queens" (ch.)
5. K. to Q. Kt.'s sq.	5. Q. to Q. R's 3rd.
6. R. moves.	6. Q. checkmates.

ROOK AGAINST TWO ROOKS.

THE two Rooks, in all ordinary cases, win with ease against one Rook, for you are speedily able to force an exchange of the single Rook for one of yours. As in almost every rule which can be laid down in chess, however, occasional exceptions occur.

Diagram 60.

BLACK.

WHITE.

This ingenious position is first given by Stamma, and has been copied by many subsequent writers. With the move, Black gives checkmate at once; and even without this advantage, it would at first sight appear that he may draw the game, because White cannot at the same time defend the checkmate and protect his attacked Rook. By the following mode of play, however, it will be seen that, having to play, White may win the game.

WHITE.	BLACK.
1. R. to K. R's 5th.	1. R. takes R.
2. R. to Q. R's 6th (ch.)	2. K. moves.
3. R. to Q. R's 5th (ch.)	3. K. moves.
4. R. takes R.	

And wins.

The most important class of cases in which the single Rook is enabled to draw the game, is that where his King is placed in a position of stalemate by the two Rooks; the weaker force has then only to persist in giving a perpetual check, and offering to sacrifice his Rook as often as the opportunity arises. Diagram 61 is an example. Suppose:—

WHITE.	BLACK.
	1. R. to Q. Kt.'s 2nd (ch.)
2. K. to his 8th.	2. R. to Q. Kt.'s sq. (ch.)
3. K. to Q's 7th.	3. R. to Q's sq. (ch.)
4. K. to Q. B's 7th.	4. R. to Q. B's sq. (ch.), &c.

And it is obvious that White cannot avoid the check without stalemating his adversary.

Diagram 61.   Diagram 62.

BLACK.   BLACK.

WHITE.   WHITE.

Diagram 62.

Here, with the move, White wins the game.

WHITE.	BLACK.
1. P. to K. B's 7th.	1. R. to K. B's sq.

(Had he moved instead, P. to Q. B's 7th, White would win by 2. P. to
K. B's 8th, becoming a Queen.)

2. R. to K. B's 2nd.	2. R. takes K. B. P.

(In lieu of 2. R. takes P. Black might have played P. to Q. B's 7th; had he done so, White would have taken the Pawn, and then moved R. to K's 2nd.)

3. R. takes R.   3. K. to Kt.'s sq.
4. R. to Q. B's 7th.

And wins.

ROOK AND BISHOP AGAINST ROOK.

THE long pending controversy, whether the King, Rook, and Bishop can win by force from any indifferent position against the King and Rook alone, appears at length to be definitively settled in the negative. The merit of this interesting discovery, which may be said to set at rest a question upon which the leading players of Europe have been at issue for above two hundred years, is mainly due to the unwearying industry and penetration of Mr. Kling, a German amateur, long domiciled in England.

Before proceeding to the consideration of the many beautiful variations adduced by Mr. Kling to establish his conclusion, we should recommend the student who is desirous of comprehending the peculiar difficulties which beset this remarkable enigma, to make himself perfect master of the celebrated position from which Philidor so admirably demonstrates that the superior forces win.   (See Diagram 63.)

PHILIDOR'S POSITION.
Diagram 63.

BLACK.

WHITE.

WHITE.	BLACK.
1. R. to Q. B's 8th (ch.)	1. R. to Q's sq.
2. R. to Q. B's 7th.	2. R. to Q's 7th.

(This is his only play to prevent your winning immediately, for as will be seen presently, when once you can compel him to move the Rook to

your Q's sq., or to your Q's 3rd, the only two other squares open to
him, the game must be won in a few moves.)

    3. R. to Q. Kt.'s 7th.   3. R. to Q's 8th.

(Here you observe that he was obliged to occupy one of the objectionable
    squares, since if he played his R. off the file, you mated at once.)

    4. R. to K. Kt.'s 7th.   4. R. to K. B's 8th (or Var. I.)
    5. B. to K. Kt.'s 3rd.   5. K. to B's sq. (or Var. II.)

(You play the B. thus to prevent his checking when he moves the Rook,
    and at the same time to force him to take up a less advantageous
    position.)

    6. R. to K. Kt.'s 4th.   6. K. to his sq. again.

(He returns his King thus, because you now threaten to win directly by
    playing the B. to Q's 6th (ch.), and afterwards R. to K. Kt.'s 8th,
    &c.)

    7. R. to Q. B's 4th.   7. R. to Q's 8th (or Var. III.)
    8. B. to K. R's 4th.   8. K. to B's sq.
    9. B. to K. B's 6th.   9. R. to K's 8th (ch.)
   10. B. to K's 5th.   10. K. to Kt.'s sq.
   11. R. to K. R's 4th.

       And he cannot possibly save the game.

Variation I.,

Beginning at Black's 4th move.

WHITE.   **BLACK.**
4. R. to K. Kt.'s 7th.   4. K. to B's sq.
5. R. to K. R's 7th.   5. R. to K. Kt.'s 8th.

(By this move he is compelled to play his R. to Kt.'s 8th, in order to
    interpose when you check with yours, and the result is that you win
    his R. by force.)

    6. R. to Q. B's 7th.   6. K. to Kt.'s sq.

(This is his best move; if he check with the R. at K. Kt.'s 3rd, you
    interpose the Bishop, and he cannot escape.)

    7. R. to Q. B's 8th (ch.)   7. K. to R's 2nd.
    8. R. to K. R's 8th (ch.)   8. K. to Kt.'s 3rd.
    9. R. to K. Kt.'s 8th (ch.)

           Winning his Rook.

Variation II.,

Beginning at Black's 5th move.

WHITE.   **BLACK.**
5. B. to K. Kt.'s 3rd.   5. R. to K. B's 6th.
6. B. to Q's 6th.   6. R. to K's 6th (ch.)
7. B. to K's 5th.   7. R. to K. B's 6th.

(If he move the K. to B's sq., instead of playing the R. thus, you have only to place your R. on K. R's 7th to ensure the game.)

8. R. to K's 7th (ch.)   8. K. to B's sq.

(If K. to his Q's sq., your reply must be R. to Q. Kt.'s 7th.)

9. R. to Q. B's 7th.	9. K. to Kt.'s sq.
10. R. to K. Kt.'s 7th (ch.)	10. K. to B's sq.
11. R. to K. Kt.'s 4th.	11. K. to his sq.

(If he play R. to K's 6th, instead of returning the K. to his sq., you answer with R. to K. R's 4th, &c.)

12. B. to K. B's 4th.

And you must win easily.

VARIATION III.,

Beginning at Black's 7th move.

WHITE.	BLACK.
7. R. to Q. B's 4th.	7. K. to B's sq.
8. B. to K's 5th.	8. K. to Kt.'s sq.
9. R. to K. R's 4th.	

Winning.

In playing over the variations just submitted, it is impossible to avoid being struck by the elegance and accuracy of this analysis, but, as Lolli and other writers observe, " the general proposition laid down by Philidor, of the Rook and Bishop winning against a Rook, can only be sustained on the supposition that the adversary can always be forced into this or a similar position," and this, though attempted by Philidor in his edition of 1777, has never been demonstrated, and in the opinion of every player who is conversant with the subject, is an impossibility.

Lolli has subsequently given three positions, in two of which White can win by force, but the third is one where, with the best possible play, he can only draw. As these positions are well known, and are besides comprehended in one or other of the categories in Mr. Kling's demonstration, it is not necessary to give them again. In addition to these, Mr. Cochrane has given three situations, which it appears were sent by two players of Lolli to the Café de la Régence, in Paris, as examples where White can only draw the game. (See Cochrane, p. 341.)

In later times Mr. Szen, the celebrated player of Hungary, has also put forth a position wherein Black can maintain his defence and draw the game. (See Diagram 64.)

But, still more recently, we have had the admirable analysis of Mr. Zytogorski, in which an attempt, all but successful, has been made to prove that the superior force should always win. (See the " Chess-Player's Chronicle," vol. ii. p. 427, and vol. iii. pp. 13, 45, 74, and 289.) From this able article we take one of the most important positions, where Mr. Z. conceives he demonstrates that White can win, but which Mr. Kling has shown to be an error. (See Diagram 65.)

MR. ZZEN'S POSITION.   MR. ZYTOGORSKI'S POSITION.

Diagram 64.   Diagram 65.

BLACK.   BLACK.

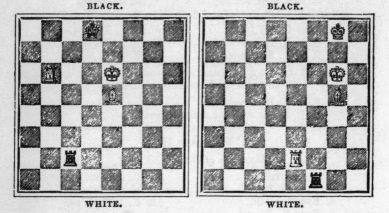

WHITE.   WHITE.

As these positions are included in one or other of the classes into which Mr. Kling divides the subject, it is needless to append their manifold variations, but the particular one of Mr. Zytogorski's in which the error before alluded to occurs, it may be well to give. Place the Pieces as in Diagram 65.

WHITE.	BLACK.
1. R. to K's 8th (ch.)	1. R. to K. B's sq.
2. R. to K's 7th.	2. R. to K. B's 8th.
3. R. to Q's 7th.	3. R. to K. B's 7th.
4. R. to Q. B's 7th.	4. R. to K. B's 8th.
5. B. to K. B's 6th.	5. R. to K. Kt.'s 8th (ch.)
6. K. to B's 5th.	6. R. to K. Kt.'s 7th.
7. B. to K's 5th.	7. R. to Q. R's 7th.
8. R. to K. Kt.'s 7th (ch.)	8. K. to B's sq.
9. R. to Q's 7th.	9. K. to Kt.'s sq.
10. K. to B's 6th.	10. R. to Q. R's 3rd (ch.)
11. B. to Q's 6th.	11. R. to Q. R's 8th.
12. R. to K. Kt.'s 7th (ch.)	12. K. to R's sq.
13. R. to K. Kt.'s 2nd.	13. R. to K. B's 8th (ch.)
14. K. to K. Kt.'s 6th.	14. K. to Kt.'s sq.
15. B. to Q. B's 5th.	15. R. to K. B's 5th.
16. R. to K. Kt.'s 5th.	16. R. to Q. R's 5th.
17. K. to B's 6th (dis. ch.)	17. K. to R's 2nd.
18. B. to K's 3rd.	18. R. to Q. B's 5th.
19. R. to K. Kt.'s 7th (ch.)	19. K. to R's sq.
20. R. to Q. Kt.'s 7th.	20. K. to Kt.'s sq.

It is at this 20th move of Black, according to Mr. Kling, that Mr. Zytogorski's mistake occurs.

Nothing can be more beautiful and correct than the foregoing play, but at this point, instead of directing Black to move his King as above, he makes him give check with his R. at Q. B's 3rd, and by that means lose the game.

21. R. to Q. Kt.'s 8th (ch.)	21. K. to R's 2nd.
22. R. to Q. Kt.'s 6th.	22. R. to Q. B's 2nd.
23. B. to Q's 4th.	23. R. to K. B's 2nd (ch.)

This is his only move to draw the game; and now, whether you take the Rook or not, he will succeed in preventing your winning.

Mr. Kling's "Analysis."

FIRST CHAPTER.

THE positions found in the following Chapter will show how the player with the Rook and Bishop can drive his adversary to the end of the board, and at the same time will point out the surest method that Black can adopt to arrive at a position for drawing the game.

FIRST POSITION. (Diagram 66.)

BLACK.

WHITE.

We start from a position which the Black can always be compelled to occupy.

WHITE.	BLACK.
1. B. to K's 5th.	1. R. to Q. Kt.'s 2nd.
2. R. to K. R's 6th.	2. R. to Q's 2nd.
3. B. to Q's 6th.	3. R. to Q's sq. (see Var. I. and III.)
4. R. to K. B's 6th (ch.)	4. K. to K. Kt.'s 2nd.
5. B. to K. B's 4th.	5. R. to Q's 2nd.
6. K. to K's 6th.	6. R. to Q's 8th.

(This move is bad, and loses the game. See Variation II.)

7. B. to K's 5th.	7. K. to K. R's 2nd.
8. R. to K. B's 7th (ch.)	8. K. to Kt.'s 3rd.
9. R. to K. Kt.'s 7th (ch.)	9. K. to K. R's 3rd.
10. R. to K. Kt.'s 4th.	10. K. to K. R's 2nd.
11. K. to K. B's 7th.	11. R. to Q's 2nd (ch.)
12. K. to K. B's 6th.	12. R. to Q. Kt.'s 2nd.
13. K. to K. B's 5th.	13. R. to Q's 2nd.
14. K. to K. Kt.'s sq.	14. R. to K. B's 2nd (ch.)
15. B. to K. B's 6th.	15. R. to Q's 2nd.
16. R. to K. R's sq. (ch.)	16. K. to Kt.'s sq.
17. K. to K's 6th.	17. R. to K. R's 2nd.
18. R. to K. Kt.'s sq. (ch.)	18. K. to K. B's sq.
19. R. to Q's sq.	

And wins.

This variation shows that Black's 6th move loses the game; the other variations lead to drawn games.

VARIATION I.

WHITE.	BLACK.
	3. K. to K. Kt.'s 2nd.
4. R. to K. Kt.'s 6th (ch.)	4. K. to K. B's 2nd.
5. R. to K. B's 6th (ch.)	5. K. to Kt.'s sq.
6. K. to K's 6th.	6. R. to Q. R's 2nd.
7. R. to K. B's 8th (ch.)	7. K. to K. R's 2nd.
8. R. to K. B's sq.	8. K. to Kt.'s sq.
9. B. to K's 5th.	9. R. to Q. R's 3rd (ch.)
10. K. to K. B's 5th.	10. K. to K. R's 3rd.
11. R. to K. Kt.'s sq. (ch.)	11. K. to K. B's 2nd.
12. R. to K. Kt.'s 7th (ch.)	12. K. to K. B's sq.
13. B. to K. B's 6th.	13. R. to K. R's 7th.
14. R. to Q. R's 7th.	14. R. to Q. B's 7th.
15. B. to K's 7th (ch.)	15. K. to K's sq.
16. R. to Q's 6th.	16. K. to Q's sq.
17. K. to K's 6th.	17. K. to Q. B's sq.

It now becomes a position of the second class, the defence of which will be found in the Third Chapter.

VARIATION II.

WHITE.	BLACK.
	6. R. to Q. R's 2nd.
7. B. to K. R's 6th (ch.)	7. K. to Kt.'s sq.
8. B. to K. B's 8th.	8. R. to Q. R's 3rd (ch.)
9. B. to Q's 6th.	9. R. to Q. R's 2nd.
10. R. to K. B's 8th (ch.)	10. K. to R's 2nd.
11. R. to K. B's sq.	11. R. to Q. R's 3rd.
12. R. to K. Kt.'s sq.	12. K. to K. R's 3rd.

This is now a position of the first class, the defence of which will be found in the following Chapter.

Variation III.

WHITE.	BLACK.
	3. K. to K's sq.
4. R. to K's 6th (ch.)	4. K. to Q's sq.
5. R. to K. B's 6th.	5. K. to Q. B's sq.*
6. R. to K. B's 8th (ch.)	6. K. to Q. Kt.'s 2nd.
7. K. to K's 6th.	7. R. to K. R's 2nd.
8. K. to Q's 5th.	8. R. to K. R's 4th (ch.)
9. B. to K's 5th.	9. K. to Q. Kt.'s 3rd.
10. R. to Q. Kt.'s 8th (ch.)	10. K. to Q. R's 4th.

Again a position of the first class.

Second Chapter.

First Class.

The division of the different positions into classes is made to estimate their value with regard to the possibility of defence.

The first and second class give us the easiest method of defence, and we shall see that we can arrive at the one or the other by playing the correct moves; we shall also show that one can be changed to the other. If, however, the second player does not play very well, he can be forced into a position belonging to the other classes, which gives to the first player a better chance of forcing the game.

We have only made use of the Queen's Bishop in the several positions —it being evident that the King's Bishop would lead to similar positions on squares of the other colour.

Diagram 67.
BLACK.

Diagram 68.
BLACK.

1   2 WHITE. 3

WHITE.

First, Second, and Third Position.—The White Rook occupying the same square in the three positions.

Fourth Position.—This last position is the only exception in the first class, in which White can win by playing K. to Kt.'s 6th.

---

* If Black play R. to K. R's 2nd, it will still resolve into a position of the first class.

The other positions are played as follows.

FIRST POSITION.

This is the one of the most difficult of this class for the defence, the Black King being so near the Rook's square. It is evident that White would win, were the Black King placed on Q. R's square, and his Rook on Q. R's 8th—and White's King on Q. R's 5th—B. on Q. R's 4th—K. R. on K. R's 7th, the position being the same on the left side of the board as that of the fourth position on the right.

WHITE.	BLACK.
1. K. to Q. B's 5th.	1. K. to Q. R's sq. (or Var. I.)
2. B. to Q's 2nd.	2. R. to Q. Kt.'s 2nd.
3. R. to K. R's sq.	3. R. to K's 2nd.
4. R. to K. Kt.'s 5th.	4. R. to Q. Kt.'s 2nd.
5. B. to K. B's 6th.	5. R. to Q. R's 2nd.
6. B. to Q's 4th.	6. R. to Q. B's 2nd (ch.)
7. K. to Q's 5th.	7. K. to Q. Kt.'s 2nd.
8. B. to K's 5th.	8. R. to K. B's 2nd.
9. K. to K's 6th.	9. R. to K. B's 7th.
10. R. to Kt.'s sq. (ch.)	10. K. to Q. B's 3rd.
11. R. to B's sq. (ch.)	11. K. to Q. Kt.'s 4th.
12. K. to Q's 5th.	12. R. to K. B's 4th.
13. R. to Kt.'s sq. (ch.)	13. K. to Q. R's 4th.

This is a position of the same class, and one more favourable for the defence than the first position.

VARIATION I.

WHITE.	BLACK.
	1. R. to Q. B's 8th (ch.)
2. K. to Q. Kt.'s 6th.	2. K. to B's sq.
3. B. to Q. B's 5th.	3. K. to Q's sq.
4. K. to Q. B's 6th.	4. R. to K's 8th.
5. R. to K. B's 7th.	5. R. to K's 3rd (ch.)
6. B. to Q's 6th.	6. R. to K's 8th.
7. R. to K. B's 6th.	

This is not so well defended as the other, but it is still a drawn game, as we shall see in the third position of the third class. The best method of defence is only given, the variations being too numerous and too similar to excite any interest.

THIRD CHAPTER.

Second Class.

In this class there is only one position won for the White. Besides the five regular positions, we have added one where the White King attacks the adverse Rook at the first move, which gains White a move and the game.

This position is solely to show with what precision the Black Rook ought to be played.

FIRST POSITION. (Diagram 69.)   SECOND POSITION. (Diagram 70.)

THIRD POSITION. (Diagram 71.)   FOURTH POSITION. (Diagram 72.)

FIFTH POSITION. (Diagram 73.)   SIXTH POSITION. (Diagram 74.)

This fifth position is the only one of this class which is lost for Black. The Black Rook is placed on K. Kt.'s 5th—the game being lost on any other square on the same line; were he on the K. Kt.'s 3rd, White could give mate in three moves, which would be still worse.

White to play.

WHITE.	BLACK.
1. R. to Q. R's 8th (ch.)	1. K. to K. R's 2nd.
2. K. to K. B's 5th.	2. R. to Kt.'s sq.
3. R. to Q. R's 7th (ch.)	3. K. to R's 3rd.
4. R. to Q. R's sq.	

Winning.

The third of these positions (Diagram 71) may be played in the following manner :—

WHITE.	BLACK.
1. R. to K. Kt.'s 7th.	2. K. to Q's sq.

By this move Black loses the position of the second class and is obliged to take one of the third, which however is still defensible.

SIXTH POSITION.

WHITE.	BLACK.
1. K. to Q's 5th.	1. B. to Q. B's 8th.
2. B. to Q. B's 5th.	2. K. to Kt.'s sq.*
3. R. to K. R's 7th.	3. R. to K's 8th.
4. K. to Q. B's 6th.	4. R. to K's 3rd (ch.)
5. B. to Q's 6th (ch.)	5. K. to R's sq.
6. R. to K. R's sq.	

Winning.

---

* If Black play to Q's sq., White plays his King to Q. B's 6th, and can occupy a winning position in four moves.

FOURTH CHAPTER.

Third Class.

Although there is only one winning position in the five given in this class, the defence is more difficult than those of the preceding classes.

FIRST POSITION.   (Diagram 75.)

BLACK.

WHITE.

White plays in this position,

WHITE.	BLACK.
1. R. to Q's 7th.	1. R. to Q. B's 7th.
2. R. to K. R's 7th.	2. K. to Q. B's sq.

This is now a position of the second class, and can be resolved into a position similar to the one we start from.

SECOND POSITION. (Diagram 76.)   THIRD POSITION. (Diagram 77.)

BLACK.	BLACK.

WHITE.	WHITE.

FOURTH POSITION. (Diagram 78.)

BLACK.

WHITE.

This fifth position is lost for the Black. (*e. g.*)

WHITE.	BLACK.
1. R. to K. R's 8th (ch.)	1. R. to K. Kt.'s sq.
2. R. to K. R's 4th.	2. R. to K. Kt.'s 6th.
3. R. to Q. R's 4th.	3. K. to Kt.'s sq.
4. R. to Q. R's 8th (ch.)	4. K. to K. R's 2nd.
5. R. to K. R's 8th.	

Winning.

It is won, because the Black Rook has not so many squares to play to as in the preceding variations.

FIFTH POSITION. (Diagram 79.)

BLACK.

WHITE.

FIFTH CHAPTER.

Fourth Class.

In this Chapter two positions out of five are favourable for White, the third and fifth.

FIRST POSITION. (Diagram 80.)

BLACK.

WHITE.

WHITE.	BLACK.
1. R. to Q. B's 7th.	1. R. to K's 3rd.
2. R. to Q's 7th.	2. R. to Q. B's 3rd.
3. R. to Q's 2nd.	3. R. to Q. B's 8th.
4. R. to Q's 6th.	

It is now a position of the third class; but if Black for his first move play R. to Q's 8th, White can win.

SECOND POSITION. (Diagram 81.)   THIRD POSITION. (Diagram 82.)

BLACK.   BLACK.

WHITE.   WHITE.

In this third position, White can win in the following manner :—

WHITE.	BLACK.
1. R. to Q. B's 2nd.	1. R. to Q. R's 3rd.
2. R. to K. R's 2nd.	2. K. to Q. B's sq.
3. R. to Q. Kt.'s 2nd.	3. R. to Q. R's sq.
4. R. to Q. Kt.'s 6th.	4. K. to Q's sq.
5. R. to Q. B's 6th.	5. K. to K's sq.*
6. R. to Q. B's sq.	6. K. to Q's sq.
7. B. to K's 7th (ch.)	7. K. to K's sq.
8. R. to K. B's sq.	8. R. to Q. R's 3rd (ch.)
9. B. to Q's 6th.	9. R. takes B.
10. K. takes R.	10. K. to Q's sq.
11. Rook mates.	

SIXTH CHAPTER.

Fifth Class.

FIRST POSITION. (Diagram 83.)   SECOND POSITION. (Diagram 84.)

BLACK.   BLACK.

WHITE.   WHITE.

* The game is equally lost if Rook moves to Q. R's 2nd. This move gives rise to many variations, which are given in "Le Palamède" for 1846, page 493, &c.

THIRD POSITION. (Diagram 85.)   FOURTH POSITION. (Diagram 86.)

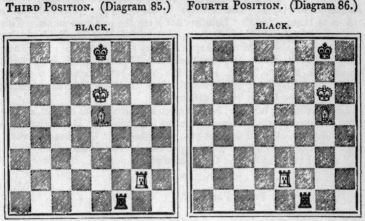

BLACK.   BLACK.

WHITE.   WHITE.

All the positions of this class are won for White, with the exception of the last, which, however, is the most difficult to defend. Some of these positions have been analysed by Philidor and Lolli. The last may be found in the " Chess Chronicle," and at the time it was thought to be a won game by Mr. Kling, and many of our best players ; a profound analysis has demonstrated the impossibility of winning. Mr. Kling now agrees in the opinion of Lolli, La Bourdonnais, and others, who have declared the following position a drawn game.

Diagram 87.

BLACK.

WHITE.

We shall see that this position is nearly the same as No. 4 of this class.

Lolli, as also La Bourdonnais, give no instruction with regard to the manner of playing it. The last says, in his work, pp. 186, 187 (1833): "It is to be regretted that Lolli has not given the principal moves. This position of Lolli is fertile of 'pats,' and I think that Black, by playing correctly, can always hinder their adversary from occupying, with their King and their Bishop, the position where the winning of the game is shown (viz. K. on K's 6th, B. on K's 5th); but I conceive also that White can easily force the Black King on the other line, in a position where he will no longer have a defence."

La Bourdónnais, however, has not given any proof of his opinion, and we show the manner which demonstrates the impossibility. He continues:— "It is a pity that Lolli has not proved his assertion by a demonstration. That would have facilitated the study of this difficult position."

We are now going to give the defence of this position.

FIRST POSITION.   (Diagram 88.)

BLACK.

WHITE.

Here White forces Black to take the first position of the fifth class in two moves, and wins the game.

WHITE.	BLACK.
1. R. to Q. Kt.'s 6th (ch.)	1. K. to Q. R's sq.
2. R. to K. R's 6th.	2. R. to Q. Kt.'s 8th.
3. R. to K. R's 8th (ch.)	3. R. to Kt.'s sq.
4. R. to K. R's 4th.	4. R. to Q. Kt.'s 8th.*

---

* Had Black played R. to K's sq. the game would equally have been lost, and had he moved the R. to Q. Kt.'s 2nd, the game would continue thus,—

WHITE.	BLACK.
5. R. to K. Kt.'s 4th.	5. R. to Q. R's 2nd (ch.)

5. B. to Q. Kt.'s 4th.
6. K. to Q. Kt.'s 6th.
7. K. to Q. B's 6th, wins.

5. K. to Q. Kt.'s sq.
6. K. to B's sq.

It is evident that had Black played K. to Q. B's sq. on the first move, White would win by playing R. to Q's 6th.

In the SECOND POSITION of this Class (see Diagram 84, page 462) White plays,—

WHITE.	BLACK.
1. R. to K's 8th (ch.)	1. R. to Q's sq.
2. R. to K's 7th.	2. R. to Q's 7th.
3. R. to K. B's 7th.	3. R. to Q's 8th.
4. R. to Q. R's 7th.	4. R. to Q. Kt.'s 8th.
5. R. to K's 7th.	5. R. to Q's 8th.
6. B. to K's 3rd.	6. R. to Q's 6th.

(If Black play 6. R. to Q's sq., White replies with R. to K's 4th, and wins more speedily.)

7. B. to Q. Kt.'s 6th.	7. R. to Q. B's 6th (ch.)
8. B. to Q. B's 5th.	8. R. to Q's 6th.
9. R. to Q. B's 7th (ch.)	9. K. to Q's sq.
10. R. to Q. R's 7th.	10. K. to K's sq.
11. R. to K's 7th (ch.)	11. K. to Q's sq.
12. R. to K's 4th.	12. K. to Q. B's sq.
13. B. to Q's 4th.	

And wins.

THIRD POSITION. (See Diagram 85, page 463.)

WHITE.	BLACK.
1. R. to K. Kt.'s 8th (ch.)	1. R. to K. B's sq.
2. R. to K. Kt.'s 7th.	2. R. to K. B's 7th.
3. R. to K. R's 7th.	3. R. to K. B's 8th.
4. R. to Q. B's 7th.	4. R. to Q's 8th.
5. B. to Q. B's 3rd.	5. R. to Q's 6th.

(If Black play instead 5. R. to Q's sq., the answer is 6. R. to Q. B's 4th, winning more easily.)

---

6. K. to Q. Kt.'s 6th.	6. R. to Q. Kt.'s 2nd (ch.)
7. K. to Q. B's 6th.	7. R. to Q. Kt.'s sq.[1]
8. B. to Q. B's 7th.	8. R. to Q. Kt.'s 2nd.
9. R. to K. R's 4th, and wins.	

---

[1] If Black move—

	K. to Q. R's 2nd.
B. to Q. B's 7th.	K. to Q. R's sq.
R. to K. R's 4th, and wins.	

For several interesting variations to this first position see " Le Pala-mède," 1841, pp. 531, 532.

6. B. to K. B's 6th.	6. R. to K's 6th (ch.)
7. B. to K's 5th.	7. R. to Q's 6th.
8. R. to K's 7th (ch.)	8. K. to Q's sq.
9. R. to K. R's 7th.	9. K. to Q. B's sq.
10. R. to Q. B's 7th (ch.)	10. K. to Q's sq.
11. R. to Q. B's 4th.	

And wins.

FOURTH POSITION.   (See Diagram 86.)

[This position, with the leading variation, which deserves the most attentive consideration, has already been given in the introductory observations to Mr. Kling's Analysis.   (See page 452, and Diagram 65.)]

The variations springing from this last position are so numerous that
it would be impossible to give them all; we only add two, where Black
having played incorrectly, has taken a lost position.

Diagram 89.   Diagram 90.

Diagram 89.

WHITE.	BLACK.
1. R. to Q. R's 3rd.	1. R. to K. Kt.'s 7th (ch.)
2. B. to K. Kt.'s 3rd.	2. K. to B's sq.
3. K. to K. B's 6th.	3. K. to Kt.'s sq.
4. R. to Q. R's 8th (ch.)	4. K. to R's 2nd.
5. R. to Q. R's 7th (ch.)	5. K. to R's 3rd (or Var. I.)
6. R. to K. Kt.'s 7th.	6. K. to R's 4th.
7. R. to K. Kt.'s 5th (ch.)	7. K. to R's 3rd.
8. R. to K. Kt.'s 4th.	8. K. to R's 2nd.
9. K. to K. B's 7th, and wins.	

VARIATION I.,
From Black's 5th move.

	5. K. to Kt.'s sq.
6. R. to K. Kt.'s 7th (ch.)	6. K. to R's sq.
7. R. to K. Kt.'s 4th.	7. R. to Q. R's 7th.

8. B. to K's 5th.	8. K. to K. R's 2nd.*
9. R. to K. Kt.'s 7th (ch.)	9. K. to R's sq.
10. R. to Kt.'s sq.	10. K. to R's 2nd.
11. R. to K. R's sq. (ch.)	11. K. to Kt.'s sq.
12. B. to Q's 4th.	12. R. to Q. R's 3rd (ch.)
13. K. to K's 7th.	13. R. to K. R's 3rd.
14. R. to Kt.'s sq. (ch.)	14. K. to K. R's 2nd.
15. White gives mate in six moves.	

Diagram 90.

WHITE.	BLACK.
1. R. to K. Kt.'s 7th (ch.)	1. K. to B's sq.
2. R. to Q. B's 7th.	2. R. to Q. Kt.'s 8th.
3. B. to Q's 4th.	3. R. to Q's 8th.
4. B. to K's 5th.	4. R. to Q. Kt.'s 8th.
5. R. to Q's 7th.	5. K. to Kt.'s sq.
6. K. to K. B's 6th.	6. R. to Q. Kt.'s 3rd (ch.)
7. B. to Q's 6th.	7. R. to Q. Kt.'s 8th.
8. B. to Q. B's 5th.	8. R. to Q. Kt.'s 6th.
9. R. to K. Kt.'s 7th (ch.)	9. K. to R's sq.
10. R. to Kt.'s sq.	10. R. to K. B's 6th (ch.)
11. K. to K. Kt.'s 6th.	11. K. to Kt.'s sq.
12. R. to K. Kt.'s 4th.	12. R. to Q. B's 6th.
13. B. to Q's 6th.	13. R. to Q. B's 3rd.
14. K. to K. B's 6th (dis. ch.)	14. K. to K. R's 2nd.
15. R. to K. Kt.'s 7th (ch.)	15. K. to R's sq.
16. R. to Q's 7th.	16. R. to Q. B's 8th.
17. B. to K's 5th.	17. R. to Q. B's 3rd (ch.)
18. K. to K. B's 7th (dis. ch.)	18. K. to R's 2nd.
19. R. to Q's 8th.	19. K. to R's 3rd.
20. B. to K. B's 6th.	20. R. to Q. B's 2nd (ch.)
21. B. to K's 7th.	21. K. to R's 2nd.
22. R. to Q's 4th.	22. R. to Q. B's 3rd.
23. B. to Q's 6th.	

And wins.

There are many other methods of varying the moves, but those given are the most interesting, and sufficiently develope the principle of the defence.

From these it is evident that White can force his adversary's King to the extreme line of the board, but it is equally apparent that he cannot win, if the defence be correctly played,—it is also shown that Black can always make a drawn game, even after losing the advantage of the positions of the first and second class, and being driven into one of the other less favourable situations; those are only exceptions where White has won.

Mr. Kling concludes his very able and interesting examen (which leaves little to be desired beyond a more distinct and methodical arrange-

---

* If he play R. to K. B's 7th (ch.), he is equally lost. See "Pala-mède," 1846, pp. 535, 536.

ment of the matter), by declaring his conviction, after the most laborious investigation of the subject, that "*the Rook and Bishop against the Rook constitute a drawn game.*"

ROOK AGAINST ROOK AND KNIGHT.

THIS species of termination has not received one tithe of the attention and study which has been bestowed on the very similar one we have just been discussing. It seems to have been taken for granted that the single Rook, in such positions, can draw the game. The late Mr. Forth, however, gave much consideration to the subject, and is of opinion, and, we think, has satisfactorily proved, that "the Rook and Knight exercise a more effective power against the Rook than that Piece does in opposition to the Knight, or than King and two Knights can do against King and Pawn."

We proceed to give a few examples, for which we are mainly indebted to the demonstrations of Mr. Forth, and we commend this particular study, as one still fertile in discoveries, to the consideration of amateurs.

Diagram 91.
White, with the move, will win the Rook in four moves.

WHITE.	BLACK.
1. Kt. to K's 6th (ch.)	1. K. to Q's 4th.

(If instead he play K. to his 5th, White will check with R. at Kt.'s 4th.)

2. R. to Q's 8th (ch.)	2. K. to his 5th.
3. R. to Q's 4th (ch.)	3. K. moves.
4. K. takes R.	

Diagram 91.	Diagram 92.
BLACK.	BLACK.

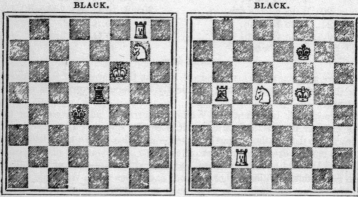

WHITE.	WHITE.

Many instances of this kind might obviously be given if necessary, but it is more important to understand the mode of action when the Pieces are at the side of the board, or may be driven there.

Diagram 92.

In this instance, White, with the move, will win in ten moves.

WHITE.	BLACK.
1. R. to Q. B's 7th (ch.)	1. K. to his sq. (best.)
2. K. to his 6th.	2. K. to Q's sq.

(If to K. B's sq., White checks with R. at K. B's 7th, and on the K. moving to Kt.'s sq., gives mate in two more moves.)

3. R. to Q's 7th (ch.)	3. K. to Q. B's sq.
4. Kt. to K's 7th (ch.)	4. K. to Kt.'s sq.
5. K. to Q's 6th.	5. R. to Q. Kt.'s 3rd (ch.)

(His best move to delay the mate.)

6. Kt. to Q. B's 6th (ch.)	6. R. takes Kt. (ch.)

(If he play K. to Q. B's sq., White may move R. to Q. R's 7th.)

7. K. takes R.

And mates in three more moves.

Diagram 93.	Diagram 94.
BLACK.	BLACK.

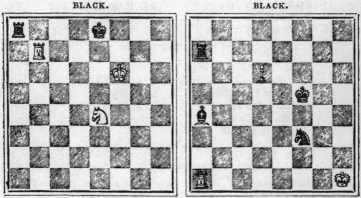

WHITE.	WHITE.

Diagram 93.

This example is much more difficult than the preceding one. "It will be seen," says Mr. Forth, "that when the Black King is on the Rook's, Knight's, or Bishop's squares, it is comparatively easy to force the game, but the difficulty is materially enhanced when he is on the King's or Queen's squares, where it is, at present, an undecided question whether mate can be forced in general situations. The positions where the Rook and Knight exercise the greatest power, are those in which the adverse Rook is on the same half of the board as that on which the Kings stand, and the White Knight can be moved to the next square to his King for the purpose of interposing when check is given. Such situations are, for the most part, decisive; care, however, must be taken to keep the Kings near each other, that time may not be lost in gaining the opposition at the proper moment."

In the present position White can win in twenty moves. (*e. g.*)

WHITE.	BLACK.
1. Kt. to Q's 6th (ch.)	1. K. to B's sq. (best.)
2. R. to Q's 7th.	2. R. to Q. Kt.'s sq., or (A.)
3. R. to Q. R's 7th.	3. R. to Q's sq.

(It is necessary to force the Black Rook on to this square, in order to prevent his checking the King when White removes his Knight.)

4. Kt. to K. B's 5th.	4. R. to Q. Kt.'s sq. (best.)
5. Kt. to K. Kt.'s 7th.	5. R. to Kt.'s 3rd (ch.)
6. Kt. to K's 6th (ch.)	6. K. to Kt.'s sq.
7. R. to K's 7th.	7. R. to Q. Kt.'s 6th.
8. K. to Kt.'s 6th.	8. R. to Q. Kt.'s sq.
9. R. to Q's 7th.	9. R. to Q. R's sq.
10. R. to Q's 6th.	10. R. to K's sq.
11. R. to Q. B's 6th.	11. R. to Q. R's sq.
12. Kt. to Kt.'s 5th.	12. K. to B's sq.
13. R. to K's 6th.	13. K. to Kt.'s sq.
14. Kt. to K. R's 7th.	14. R. to Q. Kt.'s sq.
15. R. to K's 7th.	15. R. checks.
16. Kt. to K. B's 6th (ch.)	16. R. takes Kt. (ch.)

And White wins in four more moves.

(A.)

	2. K. to his Kt.'s sq.
3. K. to his Kt.'s 6th.	3. K. to B's sq.
4. R. to B's 7th (ch.)	4. K. to Kt.'s sq.
5. Kt. to K's 4th.	5. Moves where he can.
6. Kt. to B's 6th.	

&c., &c.

Diagram 94.

This position is from Lolli, and is an example of a drawn game. White having to move plays,—

WHITE.	BLACK.
1. P. to Q's 7th.	1. R. takes P.
2. R. takes B.	2. R. to Q's 7th.
3. R. to K. B's 4th (ch.)	3. K. takes R.

And White is stalemated.

CHAPTER IV.

ENDINGS OF GAMES WITH KINGS AND PAWNS ONLY.

WHEN, towards the end of a game, a few Pawns only, with their respective Kings, are left upon the board, it might at first sight be supposed, from the limited nature, and the simplicity and uniformity of their moves, that little difficulty could arise, and no great study or examination be necessary. If, indeed, the value of the Pawns, like that of the superior Pieces, were to be estimated only by the power they originally possessed, such a supposition would doubtless be correct; but the peculiar privilege by which, under certain conditions, they may be elevated to the rank of the most valuable Pieces, brings a new and very interesting element into the calculation, and renders this particular species of termination at once one of the most difficult and most important branches of chess strategy. It is at the same time one which is generally very imperfectly understood by amateurs; and perhaps it is amongst finished players only that its essential importance is fully recognised, because from that class chiefly those well-contested and equal games proceed which are most frequently brought to similar conclusions. And even amongst the very first-rate practitioners numerous instances occur, where the slightest miscalculation leads to the loss of an otherwise secure battle. Nothing can well be conceived more trying to the nerves and temper, than after hours of the intensest mental effort, and when a difficult game has been successfully conducted through danger, and against a superior force, until it is safely reorganised with victory in view, to see the well-earned conquest suddenly fall from your hands by some momentary lapse of the overstrained attention, or some paltry artifice which a tyro would have penetrated.

A remarkable example of this kind occurs in the eleventh game of the great match played in Paris in the year 1843. After a long and severe struggle, conducted by the English player with some inferiority of force (his opponent having gained an advantage at the commencement), the following position (see Diagram 95) occurred; Black (Mr. S.) having to play.

Diagram 95.

BLACK.

WHITE.

There can we think be little doubt that, under ordinary circumstances,

Black would at once have played the correct move of K. takes Q. P., and by so doing have won the game with ease. Instead of this, however, from momentary inadvertence, the consequence of nine or ten hours' incessant mental exertion, he moved K. to his 5th, and the game was pursued as follows :—

WHITE.	BLACK.
	1. K. to his 5th.
2. K. to Q's sq.	2. K. to Q's 6th.
3. P. to Q's 5th.	3. P. to K's 7th (ch.)
4. K. to his sq.	4. K. to Q. B's 7th.
5. P. to Q's 6th.	5. K. takes P.
6. P. to Q's 7th.	6. P. to Q. B's 6th.
7. P. to Q's 8th and "Queens."	7. P. to Q. B's 7th.
8. Q. to her 2nd.	

And wins.

But had Black, on the contrary, played as already suggested, he would have won the game ; thus,—

WHITE.	BLACK.
	1. K. takes P.
2. K. to Q's sq.	

(If, in place of this move, he advance K. Kt. P., Black will equally win by playing K. to his 5th, then taking the Knight's Pawn in another move or two, and afterwards returning with his King in sufficient time to defend his own King's Pawn.)

WHITE.	BLACK.
	2. K. to Q's 6th.
3. P. to K. Kt.'s 4th.	3. P. to K's 7th (ch.)
4. K. to his sq.	4. K. to Q. B's 7th.
5. P. to K. Kt.'s 5th.	5. K. takes Q. Kt. P.
6. P. to K. Kt.'s 6th.	6. P. to Q. B's 6th.
7. P. to K. Kt.'s 7th.	7. P. to Q. B's 7th.
8. P. "Queens."	8. P. "Queens" (ch.)
9. K. takes P.	9. Q. to Q. B's 5th (ch.)
10. Q. takes Q.	10. P. takes Q.

And must evidently win.

The student will naturally enquire how a proficiency in the art of playing Pawns may be best attained ? And whether he can hope to gain much benefit in it from books ? We can only say, that it is a matter exceedingly difficult to generalize upon, or to reduce to rules, and that, therefore, great and incessant practice is the grand requisite ; but it should never be forgotten that the required practice may be obtained equally, and perhaps even in a superior degree, by the study of those critical and ingenious positions which are given by our best authors, as by actual play, and we strongly recommend attention, therefore, to the selection of situations which form the subject of the present Chapter.

KING AND PAWN AGAINST KING AND PAWN.

WE have already seen (p. 409) the method of playing a single King against a King and Pawn. When a Pawn is left on each side, and both are able to Queen at the same time, the result is usually a drawn game; there are, however, exceptions of some importance which, before exchanging the last Pieces, it is necessary to bear in mind. These may arise either through one of the Pawns giving check at the time it becomes a Queen, or from the King of the party "Queening" last being on the same file as his Pawn, so that his opponent, by a simple check, forces the King to move and wins the Queen. The following, from Lolli, will be a sufficient illustration.

Diagram 96.

BLACK.

WHITE.

Here, Black having the move, may draw the game by advancing P. to Q's 7th; if, on the contrary, he take P. with R. (ch.), expecting to Queen his Pawn, he will lose it. (*e. g.*)

WHITE.	BLACK.
	1. R. takes P. (ch.)
2. R. takes R.	2. P. to Q's 7th.
3. R. to Q's 5th.	

(A remarkably neat *coup*.)

	3. K. takes R.
4. P. to Q's 7th.	4. P. "Queens."
5. P. "Queens" (ch.)	

And wins.

KING AND TWO PAWNS AGAINST KING AND PAWN.

MOST commonly the two Pawns win, but many cases occur where the game is drawn.

Diagram 97.   Diagram 98.

BLACK.   BLACK.

WHITE.   WHITE.

The first position (see Diagram 97) is by Philidor. If Black have to play, White will win, but if otherwise the game is drawn. This instance forcibly exemplifies the importance in similar cases of gaining the opposition with your King, or of so placing him opposite the adverse one, with one square between them, that he, having to play first, is compelled to retreat and leave you to take up the position you may require.

First, suppose White moves :—

WHITE.	BLACK.
1. K. to Q's 4th.	1. K. to Q's 3rd.

(Had he played K. to B's 4th, you would have won by moving K. to his 3rd.)

2. K. to Q's 3rd.	2. K. to Q's 2nd.
3. K. to K's 3rd.	3. K. to K's 2nd.
4. K. to Q's 4th.	4. K. to Q's 3rd.
5. K. to K's 4th.	5. K. to K's 3rd.

And the game must be drawn.

But suppose Black have to play :—

WHITE.	BLACK.
	1. K. to Q's 3rd.
2. P. to K. B's 5th.	2. K. to K's 2nd.

(Had he taken the Pawn you would have retaken his, and have then easily Queened your Kt.'s Pawn, first placing your King on his R's 7th sq.)

3. P. to K. B's 6th (ch.)

(If you had taken his Pawn, he would have drawn the game.)

4. K. to Q's 4th.	3. K. to his 3rd.
5. P. to K. B's 7th.	4. K. to Q's 3rd.
6. K. to his 5th.	5. K. to his 2nd.
7. K. to Q's 6th.	6. K. takes P.
8. K. to his 6th.	7. K. to B's sq.
9. K. to his 7th.	8. K. to Kt.'s 2nd.
10. K. to B's 6th.	9. K. to Kt.'s sq.
11. K. to B's 7th.	10. K. to R's 2nd.
12. K. takes P.	11. K. to R's sq.
13. K. to B's 6th.	12. K. to Kt.'s sq.
14. K. to B's 7th.	13. K. to R's 2nd.
15. K. to Kt.'s 6th.	14. K. to R's sq.
16. K. to R's 6th.	15. K. to Kt.'s sq.
17. P. to Kt.'s 6th.	16. K. to R's sq.

And wins.

Diagram 98.

Here White wins by sacrificing at the proper moment his Queen's Pawn; thus,—

WHITE.	BLACK.
1. K. to K. B's 6th.	1. K. to Q's sq.
2. P. to Q's 7th.	2. K. takes P.
3. K. to B's 7th.	3. K. to Q's sq.
4. K. to his 6th.	4. K. to Q. B's 2nd.
5. K. to his 7th.	5. K. to Q. B's 8th.
6. K. to Q's 6th.	6. K. to Q. Kt.'s 7th.
7. K. to Q's 7th.	7. K. to Q. Kt.'s sq.
8. K. takes P.	

And wins.

Diagram 99.	Diagram 100.
BLACK.	BLACK.

WHITE.	WHITE.

The chance of a drawn game is greater for the single Pawn when that is a Rook's Pawn opposed to the adverse Rook's and Knight's Pawns. In the present instance (see Diagram 99) White, however, wins, but had the Pawns and Kings been one step further advanced, the game would only have been drawn.

WHITE.	BLACK.
	1. K. to Q. B's 4th.
2. K. to Q's 3rd.	2. K. to Q's 4th.
3. K. to his 3rd.	3. K. to his 4th.
4. K. to K. B's 3rd.	4. K. to Q's 4th.

(Black still keeps up the opposition, but dare not move any further from the Pawns.)

5. K. to K. B's 4th.	5. K. to Q's 3rd.
6. K. to his 4th.	6. K. to his 3rd.
7. K. to Q's 4th.	7. K. to Q's 3rd.
8. K. to Q. B's 4th.	8. K. to Q. B's 2nd.
9. K. to Q's 5th.	9. K. to Q. Kt.'s 3rd.
10. K. to Q's 6th.	10. K. to Q. Kt.'s 2nd.
11. K. to Q. B's 5th.	11. K. to Q. B's 2nd.
12. P. to Q. Kt.'s 6th (ch.)	

And must win.

Diagram 100.

The game is drawn. If Black have to move he takes up the opposition, and suppose, on the contrary, White play,—

WHITE.	BLACK.
1. K. to Q's 4th.	1. K. to his 3rd.

(Any other move would lose the game.)

2. K. to his 4th.	2. K. to Q's 3rd.

And White cannot do more than draw the game.

Diagram 101.   Diagram 102.

BLACK.   BLACK.

WHITE.   WHITE.

Diagram 101.

The move is quite immaterial, the game in either case being easily drawn. If White have to play, and move P. to R's 6th, he can never force his adversary to abandon the possession of the Rook's and Knight's squares, and if he play,—

WHITE.	BLACK.
1. P. to K. Kt.'s 6th.	1. P. to K. R's 3rd.

(By taking the Pawn he would lose the game.)

2. P. to Kt.'s 7th (ch.)	2. K. to Kt.'s sq.

And the game is drawn.

From this it will appear that in nearly all cases, when the Rook's and Knight's Pawns are advanced to their fifth squares, the opposite Rook's Pawn, with its King near, will draw the game. The only exception appears to be when the White King is on his Rook's 6th sq., and the Black King occupying the corner, as in the present diagram, White has to play. Thus, suppose White's King here to be on his Rook's 6th sq., he will play,—

WHITE.	BLACK.
1. P. to K. Kt.'s 6th.	1. K. to his Kt.'s sq.

(If he take the Pawn, the result is obviously the same.)

2. P. to K. Kt.'s 7th.	2. K. to B's 2nd.
3. K. takes R. P., &c.	

Winning.

But if Black had the move, in this same position, the game would be drawn, because, after the exchange of Pawns, White's remaining Pawn, on being advanced to its 7th sq., would give check, after which White cannot win, as already shown (p. 409).

Diagram 102.

Here also the game is drawn, whoever moves first. Suppose Black has to play,—

WHITE.	BLACK.
	1. K. to R's sq.

(Had he played the Pawn, or moved K. to Kt.'s sq., he would have lost.)

2. K. to R's 6th.	2. K. to Kt.'s sq.
3. P. to R's 5th.	3. K. to R's sq.
4. P. to Kt.'s 5th.	

(Had this Pawn been unmoved, or moved only one square, White would now have won. This applies to many similar cases, and proves that if White can place his King at R's 6th, with either of his Pawns unmoved, he must win, because he has then the option of moving them one or two squares at pleasure, and thus gaining a move.)

	4. K. to Kt.'s sq.
5. P. to Kt.'s 6th.	

And the game is drawn, as in the last example.

Diagram 103.   Diagram 104.

BLACK.   BLACK.

WHITE.   WHITE.

Diagram 103.

This position was given by some of the earliest writers, who, however, erroneously supposed that in all cases the game should be drawn. The error was clearly demonstrated by Lolli, who shows that, with the move, White must win. We give some of the principal variations, the minor details will be easily supplied.

WHITE.	BLACK.
1. K. to his 5th.	1. P. to R's 4th, or (A.)
2. P. to K. Kt.'s 5th.	2. K. to B's 2nd.
3. K. to Q's 6th.	3. K. to B's sq.

(It is quite immaterial, as you will readily discover, where the King is played to.)

4. K. to his 6th.	4. K. to Kt.'s 2nd.
5. K. to B's 5th.	5. K. to B's 2nd.
6. P. to Kt.'s 6th (ch.), &c.	

And wins.

(A.)

1. K. to his 5th.	1. K. to Kt.'s 2nd.
2. P. to R's 5th.	

(Had Black, instead of his last move, played K. to B's 2nd, your reply must have been 2. K. to B's 5th.)

	2. K. to B's 2nd.
3. K. to B's 5th.	3. K. to Kt.'s 2nd.
4. K. to his 6th.	4. K. to R's sq.
5. K. to B's 6th.	5. K. to R's 2nd.
6. K. to B's 7th.	6. K. to R's sq.
7. K. to Kt.'s 6th.	

Winning.

Diagram 104.

This situation has been the occasion of much discussion. The older writers, by whom it was introduced, considered that White ought to win, but this opinion has of late been controverted, at least so far as relates to cases where White has the move. We are indebted to the indefatigable authors of the "Handbuch" for a copious analysis, which appears to us to set the question at rest, and to prove, that with proper play, the game must always be drawn, it being only requisite for the weaker party to advance at the critical moment his Rook's Pawn.

First, suppose White moves,—

WHITE.	BLACK.
1. K. to Kt.'s 3rd.	

(This is the move usually given to White, and it does not appear that he has anything better.)

	1. K. to K. Kt.'s 4th.
2. P. to R's 3rd, or (A.)	2. P. to R's 3rd.
3. K. to B's 3rd.	3. K. to B's 4th.
4. P. to Kt.'s 4th (ch.)	4. K. to B's 3rd.

(If instead you play this Pawn one square only, Black advances his Pawn another square, and maintains the opposition.)

5. K. to B's 4th.	5. K. to Kt.'s 3rd.
6. K. to Kt.'s 3rd.	6. K. to Kt.'s 4th.
7. R. P. checks.	7. K. to Kt.'s 3rd.
8. K. to B's 3rd.	8. K. to B's 2nd.
9. K. to K's 4th.	9. K. to K's 3rd.

Drawn game.

(A.)

WHITE.	BLACK.
1. K. to Kt.'s 3rd.	1. K. to Kt.'s 4th.
2. P. to R's 4th (ch.)	2. K. to B's 4th.
3. K. to B's 3rd.	

(Should you instead play K. to R's 3rd, he will equally advance P. to R's 4th.)

	3. P. to R's 4tn.
4. P. to Kt.'s 3rd.	4. K. to his 4th.
5. K. to his 3rd.	5. K. to B's 4th.

And Black must draw.

Now, suppose Black plays first,—

WHITE.	BLACK.
	1. K. to B's 5th.
2. K. to his 2nd, or (A.)	2. K. to his 5th.
3. P. to R's 3rd.	3. P. to R's 3rd.
4. K. to B's 2nd.	4. K. to B's 5th.
5. P. to Kt.'s 3rd (ch.)	5. K. to B's 4th.
6. K. to B's 3rd.	6. P. to R's 4th.

Drawn game.

(A.)

WHITE.	BLACK.

2. P. to R's 3rd.

Lolli now makes Black move K. to B's 4th, and then shows that he must lose. It is evident that he ought to play—

2. P. to R's 3rd.

And will always be able to draw the game.

We cannot here afford space to follow the "Handbuch" through all the details, but what we have now given will be a sufficient clue to the student, and enable him to discover, without much difficulty, the proper defence for Black in any given variation.

Diagram 105.   Diagram 106.

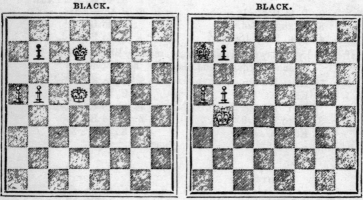

Diagram 105.

White having to play, the game is drawn.

WHITE.	BLACK.
1. K. to B's 5th.	1. K. to Q. B's 2nd.
2. P. to Q. Kt.'s 6th (ch.)	2. K. to Kt.'s sq.
3. K. to Q's 6th.	3. K. to B's sq.
4. K. to his 7th.	4. K. to Kt.'s sq.
5. K. to Q's 7th.	5. K. to R's sq.
6. P. to R's 6th.	6. K. to Kt.'s sq.

And draws.

Diagram 106.

If Black move, he draws the game by playing K. to Kt.'s sq., but if White play first, he wins as follows :—

WHITE.	BLACK.
1. K. to B's 5th.	1. K. to Kt.'s sq.
2. K. to Kt.'s 6th.	2. K. to R's sq.
3. K. to B's 7th.	3. K. to R's 2nd.
4. P. to R's 6th.	

And will win.

Had Black on his first move played K. to R's sq., you still move 2. K. to Kt.'s 6th, Black must then move 2. K. to Kt.'s sq., and you advance R. P., and if he refuse to take it, play K. to B's 7th.

Diagram 107.   Diagram 108.

BLACK.   BLACK.

WHITE.   WHITE.

Diagram 107.

White wins either with the move or without it.

First, suppose he has the move :—

WHITE.	BLACK.
1. K. to Q. B's 5th.	1. P. to Kt.'s 3rd (ch.)
2. K. to Q's 5th.	2. K. to Q's 2nd.
3. P. to Kt.'s 5th.	3. K. to B's 2nd.
4. K. to his 6th.	

And wins.

If Black move first :—

	1. K. to B's sq.
2. K. to Kt.'s 6th.	2. K. to Kt.'s sq.
3. P. to Kt.'s 5th.	3. K. to R's sq.
4. K. to B's 7th.	4. K. to R's 2nd.
5. P. to R's 5th.	5. K. to R's sq.
6. K. to Q's 8th.	

(By this you gain a move, and place your King in the proper position before advancing the Pawn.)

7. K. to Q's 7th.	6. K. to Kt.'s sq.
8. K. to B's 8th.	7. K. to R's 2nd.
9. P. to R's 6th.	8. K. to R's sq.
10. K. to B's 7th.	2. P. to Kt.'s 3rd.
11. K. to B's 6th.	10. K. to R's 2nd.

Winning.

Diagram 108.

White wins with or without the move.

WHITE.	BLACK.
	1. K. to Kt.'s 5th.
2. K. to his 4th.	2. K. to B's 5th.
3. K. to his 3rd.	3. P. to Kt.'s 5th.
4. K. to his 4th.	4. P. to Kt.'s 6th.
5. P. to R's 3rd.	

White wins.

Diagram 109.	Diagram 110.
BLACK.	BLACK.

WHITE.	WHITE.

Diagram 109.

In this position also White wins.

WHITE.	BLACK.
1. P. to Q. B's 5th.	1. K. to B's sq.

(Had he advanced the Pawn, White would not have taken it, but moved P. to B's 6th.)

2. K. to Kt.'s 6th.	2. K. to Kt.'s sq.
3. P. to B's 6th.	3. K. to R's sq.

(He would equally lose by taking the **Pawn.**)

4. K. to B's 7th.

And wins.

Diagram 110.

With the move Black may draw the game, without it he must lose. White having the move plays :—

WHITE.	BLACK.
1. K. to Q. B's 3rd.	1. P. to Q's 4th, or (A.)
2. P. to K's 3rd.	2. K. to B's 3rd.
3. K. to Q's 4th.	3. K. to Q's 3rd.
4. P. to Q. B's 3rd.	4. K. to B's 3rd.
5. P. to Q. B's 4th.	5. P. takes P.
6. K. takes P.	

And will win.

(A.)

WHITE.	BLACK.
	1. K. to Q's 4th.
2. K. to Q's 3rd.	2. P. to Q's 3rd.
3. P. to Q. B's 3rd.	3. K. to Q. B's 4th.
4. P. to K's 4th.	4. P. to Q's 4th.
5. P. to K's 5th.	

And wins.

But if Black move first, he plays :—

WHITE.	BLACK.
	1. K. to Q. B's 5th.
2. P. to Q. B's 3rd.	2. P. to Q's 4th.
3. P. to K's 3rd.	3. K. to B's 4th.
4. K. to Q's 3rd.	4. K. to B's 3rd.
5. P. to B's 4th.	5. K. to Q's 3rd.

And the game is drawn.

KING AND TWO PAWNS AGAINST KING AND TWO PAWNS.

SOME interesting cases occur under this head, where the game may be won or drawn by correct play.

Diagram 111.

This is a well-known position of Philidor's, who supposed, that if Black had the move, he would lose the game. This opinion, however, has been proved to be erroneous, the game being drawn whoever plays first. If White move, he plays :—

WHITE.	BLACK.
1. K. to his 3rd.	1. K. to his 4th.
2. K. to B's 3rd.	2. K. to B's 4th.

3. K. to Kt.'s 3rd.

3. K. to K's 4th.

4. K. to Kt.'s 4th.

4. K. to B's 3rd.

5. K. to Kt.'s 3rd.

5. K. to K's 4th.

And the game is drawn.

If Black move, he plays :—

1. K. to his 4th.

2. K. to his 3rd.

2. K. to Q's 4th.

(Were he to move K. to B's 4th, you would win by 3. K. to Q's 4th.)

3. K. to B's 3rd.

3. K. to his 4th.

4. K. to Kt.'s 3rd.

4. K. to his 3rd.

5. K. to Kt.'s 4th.

5. K. to B's 3rd.

And by continuing to play thus, Black may always draw the game.

Diagram 111.   Diagram 112.

BLACK.   BLACK.

WHITE.   WHITE.

Diagram 112.

Black moves and wins.

WHITE.   BLACK.

1. K. to Q. B's 6th.

2. K. to his 2nd.   2. K. to Q. Kt.'s 7th.

3. K. to Q's 2nd.   3. K. takes P.

4. K. to Q. B's 2nd.   4. P. to K. B's 5th.

And must evidently win.

Diagram 113.

White, with the move, will win.

WHITE.   BLACK.

1. Kt. to Q's 7th (ch.)   1. K. to his 2nd.

2. Kt. takes B.	2. B. P. takes Kt.
3. P. to Q. Kt.'s 5th.	3. K. to B's 2nd.

(If to B's 3rd, White moves K. to his 4th, and the position becomes the same as under in another move.)

4. K. to his 5th.	4. K. to his 2nd.
5. P. to B's 6th (ch.)	5. K. to B's 2nd.
6. K. to Q's 6th or B's 5th.	

And wins.

Diagram 113.

BLACK.

WHITE.

Diagram 114.

BLACK.

WHITE.

Diagram 114.

White moves and wins.

WHITE.	BLACK.
1. P. to Q. Kt.'s 7th.	1. P. to Q. R's 7th.
2. P. "Queens."	2. P. "Queens" (ch.)
3. Q. to K's 5th (ch.)	3. Q. takes Q. (ch.)
4. P. takes Q.	4. P. to Q. Kt.'s 5th.
5. P. to K's 6th.	5. P. to Kt.'s 6th.
6. P. to K's 7th.	6. P. to Kt.'s 7th.
7. P. "Queens" (ch.)	

And wins.

KING AND TWO PAWNS AGAINST KING AND THREE PAWNS.

Diagram 115.

BLACK.

Diagram 116.

BLACK.

WHITE.

WHITE.

Diagram 115.

With or without the move Black wins.

First, with the move,—

WHITE.	BLACK.
	1. P. to K. Kt.'s 6th.
2. P. to R's 3rd, or (A.)	2. K. to Q's 5th.
3. K. to B's 3rd.	

(If you play instead K. to Q's 2nd, he advances B's Pawn.)

	3. K. to his 4th.
4. K. to his 2nd.	

(Had you here moved K. to Kt.'s 4th, he would win by playing K. to his 5th, then to his 6th, and afterwards advancing B's Pawn.)

	4. K. to his 5th.
5. K. to B's sq.	5. K. to Q's 6th.
6. K. to his sq.	6. K. to K's 6th.
7. K. to B's sq.	7. K. to Q's 7th.
8. K. to Kt.'s sq.	8. K. to his 7th.
9. K. to R's sq.	9. P. to B's 6th.
10. P. takes P.	10. K. to B's 7th.

Winning.

(A.)

2. P. takes P.	2. R. P. takes P.
3. K. to B's sq.	3. K. to his 6th.
4. K. to his sq.	4. K. to Q's 6th.
5. K. to B's sq.	5. K. to Q's 7th.
6. K. to Kt.'s sq.	6. K. to his 7th.
7. K. to R's sq.	7. P. to B's 6th.

And wins.

Next, if White move first he must equally lose.

WHITE.	BLACK.
1. K. to B's 2nd.	

(You have nothing better; if you had moved P. to Kt.'s 3rd, Black would have taken P. with R. P., and have won as before.)

	1. P. to Kt.'s 6th (ch.)
2. K. to Kt.'s sq.	2. K. to his 6th.
3. K. to R's sq.	3. P. to B's 6th.
4. P. takes B. P.	4. K. to B's 7th, &c.

Winning.

Diagram 116.

The game is drawn.

WHITE.	BLACK.
1. K. to Kt.'s 4th.	1. K. to Kt.'s 3rd.
2. K. to B's 4th.	2. K. to B's 2nd.
3. K. to B's 5th.	3. K. to K's 2nd.
4. K. to Kt.'s 4th.	4. K. to his 3rd.
5. K. to B's 4th.	5. K. to his 2nd.

Drawn game.

KING AGAINST THREE PASSED PAWNS.

WE now come to a species of termination which has latterly occupied very much of the attention of the chess world, viz., the power of the King as opposed to three united Pawns, the opposite King not being able to come to their aid. Without going through the multitude of positions and variations which have appeared on the subject, we shall endeavour to make it as clear as our space will permit. The first question to be considered, and it is one which well understood will very much simplify and render easy all the rest, is the proper method of playing the King in situations such as the following (see Diagram 117), or where the White King is on any square in front of the Pawns. Formerly it was supposed that the three Pawns could advance to Queen by their own force, when thus opposed to a King only, but this opinion is now shown to have been incorrect. The fact is, that the King, when he occupies any square in front of the Pawns, or when he is within three moves of his Kt.'s 3rd square, which from its importance has been called the master square of the position, can invariably stop the Pawns. (It is important to recollect that Black is always understood to be unable to move his King so as to gain a move when necessary.)

Diagram 117.

BLACK.

WHITE.

We now proceed to analyse some of the situations arising from this description of end game, beginning with the one above given. The White King, being here less than three moves from his Kt.'s 3rd, wins in all cases.

WHITE.	BLACK.
	1. P. to B's 4th (see Var.)
2. K. to Kt.'s 2nd.	2. P. to R's 4th (B.)
3. K. to Kt.'s 3rd.	3. P. to Kt.'s 4th (A.)
4. K. to Kt.'s 2nd.	

(In all cases like this, where the King is in front of the three equally advanced Pawns, with one square between, he immediately arrests them by retreating one square, providing they are not further advanced than to their fifth squares.)

4. P. to B's 5th.

(If P. to R's 5th, the King is played to R's 3rd; and if P. to Kt.'s 5th, to Kt.'s 3rd.)

5. K. to B's 3rd.	5. P. to R's 5th.
6. K. to Kt.'s 4th.	

And wins; because whatever Pawn is moved, the King takes it.

(A.)

3. P. to Kt.'s 3rd.

(This is the strongest position (the adversary having to move) the Pawns can assume, and were they one step further advanced, White could not stop them.)

4. K. to Kt.'s 2nd.   4. P. to Kt.'s 4th.

Had he moved 4. P. to B's 5th, or R's 5th, you win thus :—

	4. *P. to B's 5th.*
5. *K. to B's 3rd.*	5. *P. to Kt.'s 4th.*
6. *K. to B's 2nd.*	6. *P. to R's 5th.*
7. *K. to Kt.'s 2nd.*	7. *P. to Kt.'s 5th.*
8. *K. to Kt.'s sq., &c.*	

5. K. to Kt.'s 3rd.   5. P. to Kt.'s 5th.

(If he play P. to R's 5th, or B's 5th, you play King in front of it.)

6. K. to Kt.'s 2nd.   6. P. to B's 5th.
7. K. to B's 2nd.

If he move P. to Kt.'s 6th, you play K. to B's 3rd, and if

                     7. P. to R's 5th.

8. K. to Kt.'s sq., &c.

(B.)

                     2. P. to Kt.'s 4th.
3. K. to Kt.'s 3rd.

(If 3. P. to R's 4th, see first variation, if P. to R's 3rd, White moves
4. K. to B's 3rd.)

                     3. P. to Kt.'s 5th.
4. K. to B's 4th.   4. P. to R's 3rd.

(If to R's 4th, White wins at once by 5. K. to Kt.'s 3rd.)

5. K. to Kt.'s 3rd.   5. P. to R's 4th.
6. K. to Kt.'s 2nd.

                 And wins, as before.

VARIATION

On Black's 1st move.

It is obvious that the moves already given will equally apply if Black
play P. to R's 4th, or P. to B's 4th; therefore, suppose,—

WHITE.	BLACK.
	1. P. to Kt.'s 4th.
2. K. to Kt.'s 2nd.	2. P. to Kt.'s 5th.
3. K. to Kt.'s 3rd.	3. P. to B's 4th.
4. K. to B. or R's 4th.	

And the position is the same as in Variation (B.)

A careful examination of this analysis will speedily enable the student
to understand the proper method of playing the King so as to prevent the
Pawns advancing to Queen.

We give a few more positions by way of illustration.

Diagram 118.   Diagram 119.

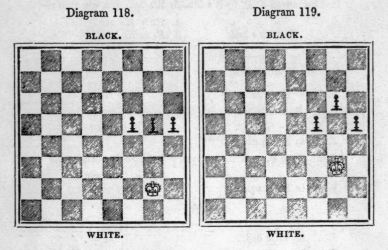

In these four instances, the King wins either with or without the move, but in all of them he does so most readily if the Pawns play first; and in all of them, if the Pawns were one square further advanced, with the King in the same relative position, the party having to move would lose. Suppose, then, the King moves:—

Diagram 118.

WHITE.	BLACK.
1. K. to Kt.'s 3rd.	1. P. to Kt.'s 5th.
2. K. to Kt.'s 2nd.	2. P. to B's 5th.
3. K. to B's 2nd.	3. P. to R's 5th.

(If instead he had played P. to Kt.'s 6th, you move K. to B's 3rd, or if P. to B's 6th, K. to Kt.'s 3rd.)

4. K. to Kt.'s sq.	4. P. to B's 6th.
5. K. to B's 2nd, &c.	

Diagram 119.

WHITE.	BLACK.
1. K. to Kt.'s 2nd.	1. P. to B's 5th.

(If he advance Kt. P., the position is the same as the last.)

2. K. to B's 3rd.	2. P. to Kt.'s 4th.
3. K. to B's 2nd.	

(If to Kt.'s 2nd, the Pawns win.)

3. P. to R's 5th.

(If to Kt.'s 5th, see Diagram 121.)

4. K. to Kt.'s 2nd.　　　　　4. P. to Kt.'s 5th.
5. K. to Kt.'s sq.

And wins.

Diagram 120.　　　　　　　　Diagram 121.

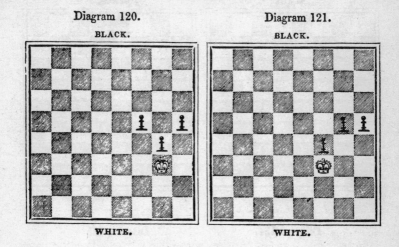

Diagram 120.

WHITE.　　　　　　　　　　　　BLACK.
1. K. to Kt.'s 2nd.

And the situation is the same as at the 2nd move of Diagram 118.

Diagram 121.

WHITE.	BLACK.
1. K. to B's 2nd.	1. P. to Kt.'s 5th.
2. K. to Kt.'s 2nd.	2. P. to Kt.'s 6th.

(If P. to R's 5th, see Diagram 119.)

3. K. to B's 3rd.	3. P. to R's 5th.
4. K. to Kt.'s 2nd.	

Black must lose.

We have already observed that in similar positions, but one step further advanced, the King, if he have to move, would lose. The student having examined the above will find the solution easy. We only, therefore, give four more examples, where in all cases the Pawns win.

Diagram 122.

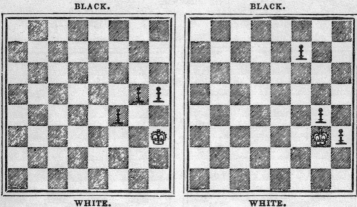

Diagram 123.

Diagram 124.

Diagram 125.

Diagram 122. If the Pawns move, they play P. to K. B's 6th, or, if K. moves, and is played to Kt.'s 2nd, they advance R. P., if to R's 2nd, they move B. P.

Diagram 123. The Pawns having to play, move P. to B's 4th; on the contrary, had the King the first move, this Pawn would play to B's 3rd only, thereby gaining a move.

Diagram 124. Here also the unmoved Pawn advances one or two squares, accordingly as the King has or has not the first move. If the Pawns move first,—

WHITE.	BLACK.
	1. P. to B's 3rd.
2. K. to B's 3rd.	2. P. to B's 4th.
3. K. to Kt.'s 2nd.	3. P. to B's 5th, &c.

Winning.

Diagram 125. The position is similar to the two preceding ones. The Pawns winning by their power of playing the unmoved Pawn one or two squares at pleasure. For example,—

WHITE.	BLACK.
	1. P. to Kt.'s 3rd.
2. K. to Kt.'s 2nd.	2. P. to Kt.'s 4th.

&c., &c.

Had the King here originally stood at B's 3rd, or R's 3rd, the party moving first would have won.

It would obviously be easy to multiply these examples to an indefinite extent; the foregoing, however, will be sufficient to exemplify the principle with which we set out, viz., that the King can always stop the Pawns when he is originally upon any square in front of them, or when he can reach his Kt.'s 3rd sq. within three moves. It will also be clear (from the three last positions) that whenever two of the Pawns can succeed in advancing unattacked to their fifth squares, with the third unmoved, they invariably win, wherever the adverse King may be.

Suppose, then, that the White King originally stood on his Queen's square, (the Pawns being unmoved,) it follows that whoever has the move must win; because, if the King move he has time to place himself on the Kt.'s 3rd sq. within three moves, but if the Pawns move they will be able to prevent his doing so; thus:—

WHITE.	BLACK.
	1. P. to R's 4th.
2. K. to his 2nd.	2. P. to B's 4th.
3. K. to B's 3rd.	3. P. to R's 5th.
4. K. to B's 4th.	

(If the King retreat, Black will play P. to B's 5th, &c.)

	4. P. to Kt.'s 4th (ch.)
5. K. to B's 3rd.	

&c., &c.

The Pawns win as in a former example.

The foregoing examples naturally lead us to the consideration of the still more complex positions arising from King with Rook's, Knight's, and Bishop's Pawns unmoved, against a similar opposing force.

KING AND THREE PASSED PAWNS AGAINST KING AND THREE PASSED PAWNS.

Diagram 126.

BLACK.

WHITE.

Diagram 126.

With the Pawns placed as in the Diagram above, the two Kings may occupy a great variety of situations on the board, producing, of course, different results, according as they may relatively be more or less advantageously situated. However varied the position of the two Kings, either player may, nevertheless, readily discover whether his position be a winning or a losing one, by observing the following rules.

To simplify the matter, all the possible positions that may be assumed for the two Kings are divided and classed under the two following cases:—

Case 1. When both the Kings are more than three moves distant from their respective master squares.

Case 2. When one or both Kings are within three moves of their master squares.

With respect to the first case, it has already been shown that, under the conditions named, the King cannot prevent the adverse Pawns from going to Queen. Each party will, therefore, make a Queen, and the game ought to be drawn, unless one of the Kings happen to occupy a square in the royal rank, in which case he would lose, as the adversary would Queen a Pawn, checking, &c. None of the positions falling under the first case produce any interesting situations, nor afford much scope for play.

The game, however, becomes totally altered in its character in all the numerous situations included in *Case* 2, wherein the party should win whose King is most advanced in the game, and to ascertain which of the two Kings is so in advance, observe the following General Rule.* " Victory

---

* An exception to this Rule is, when one of the Kings stands so near the adversary's Pawns as to prevent them being moved two squares without being captured.

will be in the hands of the party who can first play his King into its master square.'' The power of arriving first to this square will result either from the advantage of the first move, or from being originally placed nearer to it.

The proper mode of play is the following:—The player having the winning position (which suppose to be the White), should have in view to advance his Pawns until they are stopt by the Black King. White will then stop the Black Pawns, which will compel the Black King to move out of position, and the White Pawns will afterwards go forcedly to Queen. (This will be shown in the 1st Example.)

In cases where the Black (when losing player) would force his Pawns to be stopt first, the White would still win, for the Black would not afterwards be able to stop the White Pawns. This is shown in the 1st Variation to the 1st Example.

In conducting his game the player having the winning position must be cautious of two things, and which, it is probable, were the chief difficulties that had so long retarded the solution of the '' Three Pawn Problem.''

1st. Before advancing his Pawns he must take care that his King be near enough to the adverse Pawns to prevent two of them reaching their fifth squares with the third Pawn unmoved. Were this permitted, the game would be drawn, as shown in the 1st Variation to the 2nd Example. When, therefore, his King is three moves distant from the master square, he must begin by moving his King, and not his Pawns, as the 2nd Example and its 1st Variation will prove.

2nd. The winning player must be careful when advancing his King to oppose the adverse Pawns, to stop them in the fewest possible number of moves, for the loss of a move would be the loss of the game. As an error of this kind may be easily committed, two examples are given as illustrations. (See 2nd and 3rd Variations to 1st Example.)

FIRST EXAMPLE.

GRECO'S POSITION. Diagram **127.**

BLACK.

WHITE.

Diagram 127.

This situation has been handed down to us by Greco, in his "Treatise on Chess." It was considered by him, and until recently by all chess-players since his time, to be a drawn game, whoever had the move.

This fallacy was first discovered by M. Szen, the celebrated Hungarian player, and afterwards by others. On viewing the position, it will be perceived that the White King can first reach the master square, even if the Black begin. White should therefore, according to the rule, win the game, whether he move first or not.

Suppose, then, Black to have the first move, and to play :—

WHITE.	BLACK.
	1. K. to Q's 2nd.
(As he might have played a Pawn.	See Variations.)
2. P. to R's 4th.	2. K. to Q. B's 3rd.
3. P. to R's 5th.	3. K. to Kt.'s 4th.
4. P. to Kt.'s 4th.	4. P. to R's 4th.
5. P. to B's 4th (ch.)	5. K. to R's 3rd.
6. P. to B's 5th.	6. K. to Kt.'s 4th.
7. K. to B's 2nd.	7. P. to R's 5th.
8. K. to Kt.'s 2nd.	8. P. to Kt.'s 4th.
9. K. to R's 3rd.	9. P. to B's 4th.

(Better than P. to B's 3rd; but it may be observed here, that no advantage can be derived from playing an unmoved Pawn one or two squares, unless the other two Pawns have reached their 5th square.)

10. K. to R's 2nd.

(K. to Kt.'s 2nd would lose the game.)

	10. P. to B's 5th.
11. K. to Kt.'s 2nd.	11. P. to Kt.'s 5th.
12. K. to Kt.'s sq.	12. P. to B's 6th.
13. K. to B's 2nd.	13. P. to R's 6th.
14. K. to Kt.'s 3rd.	14. Is obliged to move his King, and one of the White Pawns will Queen.

Variation I.

WHITE.	BLACK.
	1. P. to R's 4th.
2. K. to B's 2nd.	2. P. to R's 5th.
3. K. to Kt.'s 2nd.	

(If 3. K. to B's 3rd, you would lose the game ; see 2nd Variation.)

	3. P. to Kt.'s 4th.
4. K. to R's 3rd.	4. P. to B's 4th.

5. P. to R's 4th.	5. P. to B's 5th.
6. K. to Kt.'s 4th.	6. K. to Q's 2nd.
7. P. to R's 5th.	7. K. to B's 3rd (best, as
8. P. to B's 4th.	most likely to mislead.)

P. to Kt.'s 4th would have lost the game. See (A.)

8. K. to Kt.'s 2nd.

(If K. to B's 4th, you check with Kt. P., and then advance R. P.)

9. P. to B's 5th.

Two of the Pawns being now at their 5th squares, with the third unmoved, one of them must Queen. If Black now play K. to Kt.'s sq., you move P. to Kt.'s 3rd, not 4th, and if K. to any other square, you advance B. or R. P. according to circumstances.

(A.)

8. P. to Kt.'s 4th.	8. K. to Kt.'s 4th.
9. P. to B's 3rd (best.)	9. K. to R's 3rd.
10. P. to B's 4th.	10. K. to R's 2nd.
11. P. to Kt.'s 5th (has nothing better.)	11. K. to Kt.'s 2nd.
12. P. to R's 6th (ch.)	12. K. to Kt.'s 3rd.
13. P. to B's 5th (ch.)	13. K. to R's 2nd.
14. P. to B's 6th.	14. K. to Kt.'s 3rd.

White is now forced to move his King, and cannot afterwards stop the Pawns.

VARIATION II

WHITE.	BLACK.
	1. P. to R's 4th.
2. K. to B's 2nd.	2. P. to R's 5th.
3. K. to B's 3rd.	

This move loses the game.)

3. K. to Q's 2nd.

(No other move would win.)

4. K. to Kt.'s 4th.	4. P. to Kt.'s 4th.
5. P. to R's 4th.	5. P. to B's 4th (ch.)
6. K. to R's 3rd.	6. K. to B's 3rd.
7. P. to R's 5th.	7. K. to Kt.'s 4th.
8. P. to Kt.'s 4th.	8. P. to B's 5th.
9. K. to Kt.'s 4th.	9. K. to R's 3rd.
10. P. to B's 4th.	10. K. to R's 2nd.
11. P. to B's 5th.	11. K. to Kt.'s 2nd.

Stops the Pawns, and wins.

VARIATION III.

WHITE.	BLACK.
	1. P. to R's 4th.
2. K. to B's 2nd.	2. P. to Kt.'s 4th.
3. K. to Kt.'s 3rd.	3. P. to R's 5th (ch.)
4. K. to Kt.'s 4th.	

(This move loses, because Black gains a move by checking with B. P.;
you ought to have played K. to R's 3rd.)

	4. P. to B's 4th (ch.)
5. K. to R's 3rd.	5. K. to Q's 2nd.

(He might also play P. to B's 5th.)

6. P. to R's 4th.	6. K. to B's 3rd.
7. P. to Kt.'s 4th.	7. P. to B's 5th.
8. K. to Kt.'s 4th.	

(Unless you made this move, you could not stop the Black Pawns.)

	8. K. to Kt.'s 3rd.
9. P. to Kt.'s 5th.	9. K. to B's 4th.
10. P. to B's 3rd (best.)	10. K. to Kt.'s 3rd.
11. P. to B's 4th.	11. K. to Kt.'s 2nd.
12. P. to B's 5th.	12. K. to R's 2nd or B's 2nd.

Stops the Pawns, and wins.

Diagram 128.

SECOND EXAMPLE.

Diagram 128.

SZEN'S POSITION.

This position was first introduced to the notice of chess-players by
M. Szen. It only differs from that of Greco in the situation of the White

King. Here the two Kings are equidistant from their master square, *i. e.*, the K. Kt.'s 3rd for White, and Q. Kt.'s 3rd for Black. According to the rule, therefore, the first player must win. Suppose White begin :—

WHITE.	BLACK.
1. K. to his 2nd.	

(This is the only winning move; had a Pawn been played, the game would have been drawn. See 2nd Variation.)

1. P. to R's 4th.

(As he might have played the King. See 1st Variation.)

2. K. to B's 3rd.	2. P. to Kt.'s 4th.
3. P. to R's 4th.	3. P. to R's 5th.
4. K. to Kt.'s 4th.	4. P. to B's 4th (ch.)
5. K. to R's 3rd.	5. P. to B's 5th.
6. K. to Kt.'s 4th.	6. K. to Q's 2nd.
7. P. to R's 5th.	7. K. to B's 3rd.
8. P. to B's 4th.	

And the Pawns will Queen, as in the 1st Variation of the last Example.

VARIATION I.

WHITE.	BLACK.
1. K. to his 2nd.	1. K. to Q's 2nd.
2. P. to R's 4th.	2. K. to B's 3rd.
3. P. to R's 5th.	3. K. to Kt.'s 4th, or (A.)
4. P. to Kt.'s 4th.	4. P. to R's 4th.
5. P. to B's 4th (ch.)	5. K. to R's 3rd.
6. P. to B's 5th.	6. K. to Kt.'s 4th.
7. K. to B's 3rd.	7. P. to R's 5th.
8. K. to Kt.'s 4th.	

And will stop the Black Pawns, throwing the move upon Black, who must then lose.

(A.)

3. P. to R's 5th.	3. P. to R's 4th.
4. K. to B's 3rd.	4. P. to R's 5th.
5. K. to Kt.'s 4th.	5. P. to Kt.'s 4th.
6. P. to B's 4th.	6. P. to B's 4th (ch.)
7. K. to R's 3rd.	7. P. to B's 5th.
8. K. to Kt.'s 4th.	8. K. to Kt.'s 2nd.
9. P. to B's 5th.	9. He cannot stop the White Pawns.

VARIATION II.

WHITE.	BLACK.
1. P. to R's 4th.	1. P. to R's 4th.

(Had he played the King, he would not have taken proper advantage of the error of White's first move.)

2. P. to R's 5th.	2. K. to Q's 2nd.
3. P. to Kt.'s 4th.	3. K. to B's 3rd.
4. P. to R's 6th.	4. K. to Kt.'s 3rd.

5. P. to Kt.'s 5th.	5. P. to R's 5th.
5. K. to his 2nd.	6. P. to Kt.'s 4th.
7. K. to B's 2nd.	7. P. to R's 6th.
8. K. to Kt.'s 3rd.	8. P. to Kt.'s 5th.
9. K. to R's 2nd.	9. K. to R's 2nd.

The party who first plays his unmoved Pawn will lose, because his adversary will gain the move by advancing his unmoved Pawn either one or two squares. As, therefore, each party will play the King only, the game will be drawn.*

CHAPTER V.

CHESS NOTATION.

THE system of notation in general use in this country has been explained in the Introductory Chapter, and fully exemplified in the subsequent analyses of the different openings, but a short sketch of the arbitrary systems which are more or less adopted in standard chess works on the continent, may prove of service to the inexperienced amateur.

The squares of the chess-board and the chess-men themselves may be denoted by various methods, but the moves of the men can be indicated only in two ways.

1st. By giving the square from which a Piece is played and that to which it is moved, without naming the Piece itself; and it is here understood that the Piece to be moved stands on the first-mentioned square, and is to be placed on the second, any adverse Piece on the latter square to be, of course, removed from the board.

2nd. By indicating both the Piece to be moved and the square to which it is played, superadding also the operation of taking an opposing man. The Piece may be designated by its initials, as in the English and the French notations, or by some letter of the alphabet, as is done by Kieseritzky and others. In the former the move is frequently indicated by simply mentioning the operation of taking, as " K. B. takes Q. Kt.," or " F. du R. prend le C.," but this is never the case in any of the arbitrary systems alluded to.

When the first-mentioned plan of stating the move is adopted, viz., by giving the square from which and to which a Piece is moved, the name of the Piece to be moved is sometimes given, and the act of taking is also indicated, out these are quite unnecessary.

So also, under the second method, if the Piece to be played and the square to which it goes are given, the operation of taking need not be expressed any more than in the first, although it is customary to have it so.

In Alexandre, Jaenisch, the " Handbuch," and in Germany generally, the squares are marked as in Diagram No. 1.

---

* For this clear and simple resolution of the celebrated problem " King and Three Pawns versus King and Three Pawns," we are indebted to the skilful industry of Capt. W. D. Evans, the inventor of the beautiful opening called the Evans' Gambit.

NOTATION ADOPTED BY ALEXANDRE, JAENISCH, "THE HANDBUCH,"
AND THE GERMAN WRITERS GENERALLY.

(No. 1.)

BLACK.

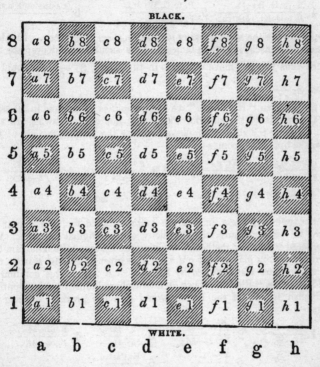

WHITE.

Here the Black corner square, which is occupied by the Q's Rook at the beginning of a game, is marked "*a* 1," Q. R's 2nd is "*a* 2," and so on to Q. R's 8th, which is known as "*a* 8." Q. Kt.'s square, in like manner, is "*b* 1." Q. B's square is "*c* 1." Q's square is "*d* 1." K's square is "*e* 1." K. B's square is "*f* 1." K. Kt.'s square is "*g* 1," and K. R's square is "*h* 1," and each of these go on of course from the first square of the file to the 8th, in the same direction. In the adoption of this notation, it is usual to give merely the square from which a Piece is moved, and that to which it goes, a small sign (✕) being used to denote check, ○—○ to denote castling on the King's side, and ○—○—○ to denote the same operation on the Queen's side.

The following will serve as an example of this description of notation:—

1. $\dfrac{e\,2-e\,4.}{e\,7-e\,5.}$ 2. $\dfrac{g\,1-f\,3.}{b\,8-c\,6.}$ 3. $\dfrac{d\,2-d\,4.}{e\,5-d\,4.}$ 4. $\dfrac{f\,1-c\,4.}{f\,8-b\,4✕.}$

5. $\dfrac{c\,2-c\,3.}{d\,4-c\,3.}$ 6. $\underline{○—○}$

In the English notation these moves would be given thus :—

1. $\dfrac{\text{P. to K's 4th.}}{\text{P. to K's 4th.}}$
2. $\dfrac{\text{Kt. to K. B's 3rd.}}{\text{Kt. to Q. B's 3rd.}}$
3. $\dfrac{\text{P. to Q's 4th.}}{\text{P. takes P.}}$

4. $\dfrac{\text{B. to Q. B's 4th.}}{\text{B. to Q. Kt.'s 5th (ch.)}}$
5. $\dfrac{\text{P. to Q. B's 3rd.}}{\text{P. takes P.}}$
6. $\dfrac{\text{Castles on K's side.}}{}$

We shall give the same opening in all our other specimens. In Alexandre and Jaenisch, *taking* is indicated by a small ○ placed over the last cypher; thus the 3rd move of Black in the above, 3. $\dfrac{}{e\,5-d\,4}$, would be written 3. $\dfrac{}{e\,5-d\,4°}$.

In the German "Handbuch" we find : signifies *takes;* and in the same work the initials of the superior Pieces, but not of the Pawns, are also given. Taking the above example, and giving the English initials of the Pieces, the opening becomes—

1. $\dfrac{e\,2-e\,4.}{e\,7-e\,5.}$
2. $\dfrac{\text{Kt. }g\,1-f\,3.}{\text{Kt. }b\,8-c\,6.}$
3. $\dfrac{d\,2-d\,4.}{e\,5-d\,4\;:}$
4. $\dfrac{\text{B. }f\,4-c\,4.}{\text{B. }f\,8-b\,4\times.}$

5. $\dfrac{c\,2-c\,3.}{d\,4-c\,3\;:}$
6. $\dfrac{\text{○—○.}}{}$ &c.

In our opinion, these initials are quite uncalled for, and appear to destroy, in some measure, the simplicity of the original notation. We now proceed to another method of denoting the squares. (See Diagram 2.)

Here we find, in place of *a b c d e f g h,* as given in the last system, the same squares are distinguished by 1 2 3 4 5 6 7 8. This notation is found in Koch's "Elementarbuch der Schachspielkunst," and, adopting the English initials of the Pieces, would give the previous opening as follows :—

1. $\dfrac{52-54.}{57-55.}$
2. $\dfrac{\text{Kt. }71-63.}{\text{Kt. }28-36.}$
3. $\dfrac{42-44.}{55-44.}$
4. $\dfrac{\text{B. }61-34.}{\text{B. }68-24\times.}$

5. $\dfrac{32-33.}{44-33\text{ P.}}$
6. $\dfrac{\text{K. Cast.}}{}$

Kieseritzky has adopted this plan of denoting the squares, but with the difference of placing the figures which indicate the *columns* or *files* before those which denote the *ranks.* (See Diagram 3.) His method, however, of giving the moves is different to Koch's, and we think unquestionably preferable. He denotes the officers or Pieces by the capitals A B C D E F G H, beginning in order from Q. R., and the Pawns standing before them by the small letters *a b c d,* &c. He then gives the Piece or Pawn to be moved, and the square to which it goes, and if any capture is made, the Piece or Pawn taken is also mentioned. (*e. g.*)

1. $\dfrac{e\,45.}{e\,55.}$
2. $\dfrac{\text{G. }36.}{\text{B. }63.}$
3. $\dfrac{d\,44.}{c\,44\,d.}$
4. $\dfrac{\text{F. }43.}{\text{F. }32\times.}$
5. $\dfrac{c\,33.}{e\,33\,c.}$
6. $\dfrac{\text{○—○.}}{}$

This, it must be admitted, leaves nothing to be desired on the score of conciseness, but it would have been easier for players accustomed to our notation, if he had marked the squares as in Diagram 2, and grafted on that plan his own method of indicating the men.

The above would then stand thus,—

1. $\dfrac{e\ 54.}{e\ 55.}$ 2. $\dfrac{G.\ 63.}{B.\ 36.}$ 3. $\dfrac{d\ 44.}{e\ 44\ d.}$ 4. $\dfrac{F\ 34.}{F\ 23\times.}$ 5. $\dfrac{c\ 33.}{e\ 33\ c.}$ 6. $\overline{\text{ó—ó}}$

and in this form is more intelligible to Englishmen, because 1. $\overline{e\ 54}$ reads

1. $\overline{\text{K. P. to K's 4th}}$, but $\overline{e\ 45}$ is 1. $\overline{\text{K. P. to the 4th of the K.}}$ But it is probable

in this instance M. K. consulted the convenience of the French players, who express themselves in the manner objected to.

KOCH'S NOTATION.

(No. 2.)

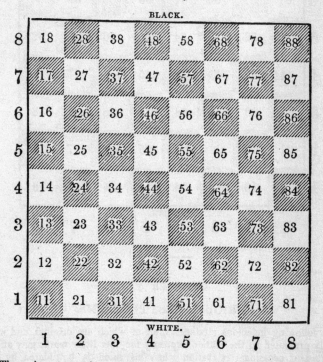

There is yet another manner of notation, in which the squares are numbered 1 2 3 4 5, &c., up to 64, but this method seems to offer no advantages of any kind, and therefore needs no further mention.

In conclusion, we may remark, that it is easy enough to invent new chess notations, or vary the old, but extremely difficult to discover anything likely to supersede that already in use,—for our own notation, with some slight modifications or abbreviations, may be rendered almost as concise, and certainly more expressive, than any of the arbitrary systems above described.

KIESERITZKY'S NOTATION.*

(No. 3.)

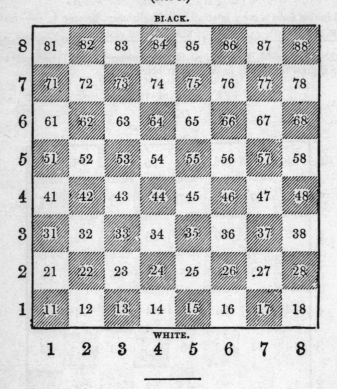

BLACK.

8	81	82	83	84	85	86	87	88
7	71	72	73	74	75	76	77	78
6	61	62	63	64	65	66	67	68
5	51	52	53	54	55	56	57	58
4	41	42	43	44	45	46	47	48
3	31	32	33	34	35	36	37	38
2	21	22	23	24	25	26	.27	28
1	11	12	13	14	15	16	17	18

WHITE.

1   2   3   4   5   6   7   8

CHAPTER VI.

CURIOUS CHESS PROBLEMS.

THE following ingenious stratagems, all of which are original, and were kindly presented to the author expressly for this little work, may afford the student occasional relaxation when his mind is bewildered by the inexhaustible variations which spring from the openings of games.

For the assistance of those readers who want leisure or patience to unravel the intricacies of these positions, the solutions are appended.

* For a more detailed description of M. Kieseritzky's method of indicating the moves, the student is referred to the prefatory address in his "Cinquante Parties," and the opening chapters of Witcomb's translation of Mr. Lewis's last Chess Treatise.

FIRST POSITION.

By Mr. Mc G—y.

BLACK.

WHITE.

White playing first checkmates
in four moves.

SECOND POSITION.

By Mr. Mc G—y.

BLACK.

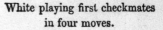

WHITE.

White playing first checkmates
in four moves.

THIRD POSITION.

By Mr. Mc G—y.

BLACK.

WHITE.

White playing first checkmates
in four moves.

FOURTH POSITION.

By the Rev. H. Bolton.

BLACK.

WHITE.

White playing first checkmates
in five moves.

FIFTH POSITION.

By Herr Kling.

BLACK.

WHITE.

White playing first checkmates
in five moves.

SIXTH POSITION.

By Mr. Mc G—y.

BLACK.

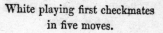

WHITE.

White playing first checkmates
in five moves.

SEVENTH POSITION.

By the Rev. H. Bolton.

BLACK.

WHITE.

White playing first checkmates
in six moves.

EIGHTH POSITION.

By the Rev. H. Bolton.

BLACK.

WHITE.

White playing first checkmates
in six moves.

NINTH POSITION.

By the Rev. H. Bolton.

BLACK.

WHITE.

White playing first checkmates
in six moves.

TENTH POSITION.

By the Rev. H. Bolton.

BLACK.

WHITE.

White playing first checkmates
in seven moves.

ELEVENTH POSITION.

By the Rev. H. Bolton.

BLACK.

WHITE.

White playing first checkmates
in seven moves.

TWELFTH POSITION.

By the Rev. H. Bolton.

BLACK.

WHITE.

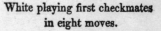

White playing first checkmates
in eight moves.

THIRTEENTH POSITION.

By the Rev. H. Bolton.

BLACK.

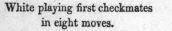

WHITE.

White playing first checkmates
in eight moves.

FOURTEENTH POSITION.

By the Rev. H. Bolton.

BLACK.

WHITE.

White playing first checkmates
in nine moves.

FIFTEENTH POSITION.

By the Rev. H. Bolton.

BLACK.

WHITE.

White playing first checkmates
in nine moves.

SIXTEENTH POSITION.

By the Rev. H. Bolton.

BLACK.

WHITE.

White playing first checkmates
in ten moves.

SEVENTEENTH POSITION.

By the Rev. H. Bolton.

BLACK.

WHITE.

White playing first checkmates
in thirteen moves.

EIGHTEENTH POSITION.

By Mr. McG—y.

BLACK.

WHITE.

White playing first compels Black
to checkmate him in four moves.

NINETEENTH POSITION.

By Mr. McG—y.

BLACK.

WHITE.

White playing first compels Black
to checkmate him in five moves.

TWENTIETH POSITION.

By Mr. McG—y.

BLACK.

WHITE.

White playing first compels Black
to checkmate him in five moves.

TWENTY-FIRST POSITION.

By Mr. Mc G—y.

BLACK.

WHITE.

White playing first compels Black
to checkmate him in six moves.

TWENTY-SECOND POSITION.

By Mr. Mc G—y.

BLACK.

WHITE.

White playing first compels Black
to checkmate him in six moves.

TWENTY-THIRD POSITION.

By Mr. Mc G—y.

BLACK.

WHITE.

White playing first compels Black
to checkmate him in seven moves.

TWENTY-FOURTH POSITION.

By Mr. Mc G—y.

BLACK.

WHITE.

White playing first compels Black
to mate him in eight moves.

TWENTY-FIFTH POSITION.
By Mr. Mc G—y.

BLACK.

WHITE.

White playing first compels Black to checkmate him in fourteen moves.

TWENTY-SIXTH POSITION.
By the Rev. H. Bolton.

BLACK.

WHITE.

White undertakes to compel Black to checkmate him on his (White's) Q. R's sq. in twenty-five moves.

SOLUTIONS TO THE CHESS PROBLEMS.

FIRST POSITION.

WHITE.	BLACK.
1. Kt. to Q's 8th (ch.)	1. K. to Q's 4th.
2. Castles (giving ch.)	2. B. interposes.
3. B. to Q. B's 5th.	3. Any move.
4. R. takes B. Mate.	

SECOND POSITION.

WHITE.	BLACK.
1. R. takes B. (ch.)	1. Kt. takes R. (best.)
2. Kt. takes Kt. (ch.)	2. K. to Q's 5th.
3. R. takes R. (ch.)	3. R. to Q's 4th.
4. R. takes R. Mate.	

THIRD POSITION.

WHITE.	BLACK.
1. Q. to K. B's 5th (ch.)	1. K. takes Q. (best.)
2. Kt. takes Kt. (ch.)	2. K. to K's 4th (best.)
3. Kt. from K. B's 2nd to K. Kt.'s 4th (ch.)	3. K. to Q's 5th.
4. Kt. to K. B's 5th (ch.) Mate.	

Fourth Position.

WHITE.	BLACK.
1. Kt. to Q's 5th.	1. Kt. takes B., or (A.)
2. Kt. takes Q. Kt. P. (ch.)	2. K. is moved.
3. Q. to Q. R's 7th (ch.)	3. K. removes.
4. Kt. to Q. R's 8th.	4. Plays as he can.
5. White mates.	

(A.)

	1. P. takes Kt.
2. Q. B. to Q's 6th (dis. ch.)	2. Kt. to Q. Kt.'s sq.
3. K. B. to B's 5th (ch.)	3. R. to Q's 2nd.
4. Q. takes Kt. Mate.	

Fifth Position.

WHITE.	BLACK.
1. Castles.	1. P. to K. R's 4th.
2. K. to R's 2nd.	2. P. to K. R's 5th.
3. B. to K. Kt.'s sq.	3. P. to K. R's 6th.
4. R. to B's 2nd.	4. K. to Q's 4th.
5. R. to K. B's 4th.	

Double check, and mate.

Sixth Position.

WHITE.	BLACK.
1. P. takes P. (ch.)	1. K. takes P. on his Q. B's 4th, or (A.)
2. Q. takes R. (ch.)	2. K. to Q's 3rd (best.)
3. Q. takes B. (ch.)	3. K. takes Q., or (B.)
4. B. takes P. (ch.)	4. P. to K. B's 5th.
5. B. takes P. Mate.	

(A.)

	1. K. takes P. on his Q. B's 5th.
2. Q. to her B's 3rd (ch.)	2. K. to Q's 4th.
3. Q. takes P. (ch.)	3. K. takes P.
4. Q. to Q. Kt.'s 4th.	

Mate.

(B.)

	3. Q. to Q's 2nd.
4. Q. to K's 6th. Mate.	

Seventh Position.

WHITE.	BLACK.
1. R. to Q. Kt.'s 4th.	1. Kt. takes R. (best.)
2. P. takes Kt. (ch.)	2. K. to B's 5th.
3. Q. to her R's 3rd.	3. P. to Q. B's 4th.
4. K. to his 4th.	4. P. takes P.
5. Q. to K's 3rd.	5. P. to Q. Kt.'s 6th.
6. Q. to her 4th. Mate.	

EIGHTH POSITION.

WHITE.	BLACK.
1. P. to Q. Kt.'s 7th (ch.)	1. B. takes P.
2. R. to Q's 7th.	2. Kt. takes Kt. (best.)
3. R. takes B.	3. Kt. to Q's sq.
4. R. to Q. Kt.'s sq. (dis. ch.)	4. Kt. to Q. Kt.'s 2nd.
5. R. takes Kt.	5. Moves as he will.
6. R. to Q. Kt.'s sq. (dis. ch.)	

Mate.

NINTH POSITION.

WHITE.	BLACK.
1. R. takes Kt.	1. Q. to her R's 4th (best.)
2. Q. to her 5th.	2. Q. takes Q. (best.)
3. R. takes Q. (dis. ch.)	3. K. takes P.
4. K. to K. B's sq.	4. Kt. P. takes B.
5. R. to Q's 4th.	5. P. to Q. Kt.'s 7th.
6. R. to K. B's 4th.	

Mate.

TENTH POSITION.

WHITE.	BLACK.
1. Q. to her B's 8th (ch.)	1. K. to his 2nd.
2. Q. to K's 8th (ch.)	2. K. to Q's 3rd, or (A.)
3. Kt. to Q. Kt.'s 5th (ch.)	3. K. to Q's 4th.
4. Q. to K's 4th (ch.)	4. K. to Q. B's 5th (best.)
5. Kt. to Q's 6th (ch.)	5. K. removes.
6. Q. to her Kt.'s sq. (ch.)	6. K. takes R. P.
7. Kt. to Q. Kt.'s 5th.	

Mate.

(A.)

	2. K. to his B's 3rd.
3. Q. to K's 5th (ch.)	3. K. removes.
4. Q. to K. B's 5th (ch.)	4. K. removes.
5. P. to K. Kt.'s 5th.	

Mate.

ELEVENTH POSITION.

WHITE.	BLACK.
1. Kt. to Q's 6th (ch.)	1. K. to Q's 6th.
2. P. to Q. R's 3rd.	2. R. to Q's sq.
3. P. to K. Kt.'s 8th, becoming a Q.	3. R. takes Q., or (A.)
4. Kt. to Q. B's sq. (ch.)	4. K. removes.
5. K. to Q's 2nd.	5. P. to Q. B's 5th.
6. Q. R. P. takes P.	6. Where he will.
7. White mates.	

(A.)

	3. R. takes Kt.
4. Kt. to Q. B's sq. (ch.)	4. K. to Q's 5th.
5. Kt. to K's 2nd (ch.)	5. K. to Q's 6th.
6. Q. to Q. Kt.'s 3rd.	

Mate.

TWELFTH POSITION.

WHITE.	BLACK.
1. P. takes R. (ch.)	1. P. takes P.
2. Q. to her B's 3rd.	2. K. to Q. R's 3rd (best.)
3. Kt. from Q's 3rd to Q.B's 5th (ch.)	3. K. removes.
4. Q. takes P. (ch.)	4. K. takes Q.
5. Kt. to Q's 3rd (ch.)	5. K. takes R. P. (best.)
6. P. to Q. Kt.'s 3rd (ch.)	6. K. to Q. R's 4th.
7. P. to Q. Kt.'s 4th (ch.)	7. K. removes.
8. White mates with one of the Knights.	

THIRTEENTH POSITION.

WHITE.	BLACK.
1. Q. to K's 5th (ch.)	1. K. takes R., or (A.)
2. Kt. to Q's 6th (ch.)	2. K. removes.
3. Kt. to Q's 3rd (ch.)	3. K. removes.
4. Kt. to K's 4th.	4. B. takes Q. R. P.
5. Q. to Q's 4th (ch.)	5. B. interposes (best.)
6. Q. takes B. (ch.)	6. K. removes.
7. Q. to her Kt.'s 4th (ch.)	7. K. removes.
8. Kt. to Q. B's 5th.	

Mate.

(A.)

	1. K. takes Q.
2. Kt. to Q's 3rd (ch.)	2. K. removes.
3. R. to Q's 4th.	

Mate.

FOURTEENTH POSITION.

WHITE	BLACK.
1. Q. to her B's 4th (ch.)	1. K. to Q. R's 4th, or (A.)
2. Kt. to Q. B's 5th.	2. R. to Q. Kt.'s 3rd (best.)
3. Q. to her R's 2nd (ch.)	3. K. removes.
4. Q. to K's 2nd (ch.)	4. K. removes.
5. Kt. to Q. Kt.'s 3rd (ch.)	5. K. to Q. R's 5th.
6. Q. to her R's 2nd (ch.)	6. K. removes.
7. Kt. to Q. B's 5th.	7. Where he will.
8. White mates in two moves.	

(A.)

	1. K. to Q. R's 5th.
2. Kt. to Q. Kt.'s 7th.	2. R. to Q. Kt.'s 3rd.
3. Kt. to Q's 6th.	3. Anywhere.
4. White mates.	

FIFTEENTH POSITION.

WHITE.	BLACK.
1. R. takes Kt. (ch.)	1. K. takes R.
2. Q. to Q. B's 3rd (ch.)	2. K. to K's 2nd.
3. Q. to Q. B's 7th (ch.)	3. K. to his B's 3rd.
4. R. to K. B's 5th (ch.)	4. K. to Kt.'s 3rd (best.)
5. Q. to K. B's 4th.	5. R. to K. Kt.'s 2nd.
6. R. to K. Kt.'s 5th (ch.)	6. K. to K. R's 2nd (best.)
7. Q. to K. R's 2nd.	7. R. takes R.
8. B. takes R. (dis. ch.)	8. K. removes.
9. Q. to K. R's 6th.	

Mate.

SIXTEENTH POSITION.

WHITE.	BLACK.
1. Kt. takes B. (dis. ch.)	1. K. to R's 2nd.
2. Kt. to K. B's 8th (ch.)	2. K. removes.
3. Kt. to Q's 7th (dis. ch.)	3. K. removes.
4. R. takes B. (ch.)	4. K. takes B.
5. Kt. takes R.	5. P. takes R.
6. Kt. takes Q. Kt. P.	6. P. to K. R's 5th.
7. Kt. to Q's 4th.	7. P. to K. R's 6th.
8. Kt. to Q. B's 6th.	8. P. to K. R's 7th.
9. Kt. to K's 5th.	9. P. to K. R's 8th, becoming
10. Kt. takes B. P.	a Q.

Mate.

SEVENTEENTH POSITION.

WHITE.	BLACK.
1. Kt. to Q's 8th (ch.)	1. K. to Q. B's sq.
2. Kt. to K. B's 7th (dis. ch.)	2. K. to Q. Kt.'s 2nd (best.)
3. P. to Q. B's 6th (ch.)	3. K. takes P.
4. Q. to K's 8th (ch.)	4. K. to Q. Kt.'s 2nd.
5. Kt. to Q's 8th (ch.)	5. K. removes.
6. Kt. takes K. P. (dis. ch.)	6. K. to Q. Kt.'s 2nd.
7. Kt. to Q's 8th (ch.)	7. K. removes.
8. Kt. to Q. B's 6th (dis. ch.)	8. K. removes.
9. K. B. takes P.	9. P. to Q. Kt.'s 4th (best.)
10. P. to Q. R's 4th (ch.)	10. K. to Q. Kt.'s 3rd (best.)
11. P. to Q. R's 5th (ch.)	11. K. to Q. Kt.'s 2nd.
12. Kt. to K's 7th (dis. ch.)	12. P. to Q. B's 3rd.
13. Q. mates.	

EIGHTEENTH POSITION.

WHITE.	BLACK.
1. B. takes R. (ch.)	1. R. to K's 7th.
2. Q. R. takes P. (ch.)	2. Kt. takes R.
3. K. R. takes Kt. (ch.)	3. Q. to K's 6th.
4. Q. to K. R's 5th.	4. Black must give mate with Kt. or Q

Nineteenth Position.

WHITE.	BLACK.
1. B. takes Kt. (ch.)	1. K. R. to B's 6th.
2. Q. to K's 6th (ch.)	2. B. to K's 4th.
3. Q. to her 5th (ch.)	3. K. takes Q.
4. Kt. to Q. Kt.'s 4th (ch.)	4. K. to K's 5th.
5. R. to K's 6th.	5. Kt. must mate.

Twentieth Position.

WHITE.	BLACK.
1. Kt. takes Kt. (ch.)	1. K. to Q's 8th.
2. R. to R's sq. (ch.)	2. K. takes P.
3. K. to K's 4th (dis. ch.)	3. K. to Q. B's 7th.
4. K. to B's 3rd (dis. ch.)	4. K. takes Q. Kt. P.
5. R. to Q. B's 6th.	5. Kt. must mate.

Twenty-First Position.

WHITE.	BLACK.
1. Kt. at K's 5th takes Kt. (ch.)	1. Kt. takes Kt.
2. B. takes B. (ch.)	2. R. to K's 2nd.
3. B. takes R. (ch.)	3. K. to his sq.
4. Kt. takes B. (dis. ch.)	4. Kt. to Kt.'s sq.
5. Q. takes Q. (ch.)	5. K. to Q's 2nd.
6. K. takes R.	6. Kt. must take Kt.

Mate.

Twenty-Second Position.

WHITE.	BLACK.
1. R. to Q. B's 8th (ch.)	1. B. to Q. B's 2nd.
2. R. to Q. B's 2nd (ch.)	2. B. to Q. B's 5th.
3. B. to K. B's 2nd (ch.)	3. Kt. to K's 6th.
4. Q. to K. B's 5th (ch.)	4. Kt. to Q's 4th.
5. K. to his 4th.	5. P. to K. Kt.'s 3rd.
6. Kt. to K. B's 3rd.	6. P. must take Q.

Mate.

Twenty-Third Position.

WHITE.	BLACK.
1. Q. to her B's 8th (ch.)	1. Kt. to Q. B's 2nd.
2. P. takes P. (ch.)	2. K. to Q's 4th (best.)
3. R. to Q. Kt.'s 4th (dis. ch.)	3. K. to Q. B's 4th.
4. Q. to K. B's 5th (ch.)	4. Kt. to Q's 4th.
5. Q. to K. B's 2nd (ch.)	5. Kt. to K's 6th.
6. R. to Q. B's 4th (ch.)	6. K. takes R.
7. Q. to her B's 2nd (ch.)	7. Kt. must take Q.

Mate.

Twenty-Fourth Position.

WHITE.	BLACK.
1. Q. to Q. R's 8th (ch.)	1. K. to Kt.'s 3rd.
2. R. takes Kt. (ch.)	2. K. removes.
3. B. takes R. (ch.)	3. K. takes Kt.
4. Castles (ch.)	4. Q. to her 6th.
5. Q. takes R. (ch.)	5. Kt. to Q. Kt.'s 5th.
6. K. to Kt.'s sq.	6. Q. to her 7th (best.)
7. P. to Q. B's 3rd (ch.)	7. K. to Q's 6th.
8. Q. takes Kt.	8. Q. must take R.

Mate.

Twenty-Fifth Position.

WHITE.	BLACK.
1. Q. takes P. (ch.)	1. K. to Q's sq.
2. B. takes B. (ch.)	2. Kt. to Q. Kt.'s 3rd.
3. B. takes Kt. (ch.)	3. K. to Q. B's sq.
4. Q. to K. B's 8th (ch.)	4. R. to K's sq.
5. Q. takes R. (ch.)	5. Q. takes Q.
6. Kt. at B's 5th to Q's 7th (dis. ch.)	6. K. to Kt.'s 2nd.
7. B. takes Kt. (dis. ch.)	7. K. to R's sq.
8. B. takes R. (ch)	8. Q. interposes.
9. P. takes B.	9. Q. to Q's 4th.
10. B. to K's 4th.	10. Q. to Q. B's 3rd.
11. B. to Q's 5th.	11. Q. to Q. Kt.'s 2nd.
12. R. to Q's sq.	12. Q. to her B's 3rd.
13. Kt. to Q. R's 6th.	13. Q. to Kt.'s 2nd.
14. B. to Q. B's 6th.	14. Q. must take Bishop.

Mate.

Twenty-Sixth Position.

WHITE.	BLACK.
1. Q. to Q. R's sq.	
2. B. to K's 4th.	
3. R. to Q's 2nd.	
4. Q. to Q's sq.	
5. R. to Q. R's 2nd.	
6. B. to Q. Kt.'s sq.	
7. P. to Q. Kt.'s 4th.	
8. Q. to her 7th (ch.)	
9. P. to Q. Kt.'s 6th.	Black's moves are all forced.
10. K. to Q. Kt.'s 5th.	
11. K. to Q. B's 4th.	
12. K. to Q. Kt.'s 3rd.	
13. R. to Q. B's 2nd.	
14. K. to Q. R's 2nd.	
15. K. to Q. R's sq.	
16. Q. to her B's 8th (ch.)	
17. R. to Q. R's 2nd (ch.)	

18. R. to Q. R's 6th (ch.)   ⎞
19. Q. to Q. B's 6th (ch.)   ⎟
20. R. to Q. Kt.'s 6th (ch.) ⎟
21. Q. to her B's 5th (ch.)   ⎬   Black's moves are all forced.
22. R. to Q. Kt.'s 4th (ch.) ⎟
23. R. to K's 4th (dis. ch.) ⎟
24. Q. to Q. Kt.'s 5th (ch.) ⎠
25. Q. to Q. Kt.'s 2nd (ch.)   25. P. takes Q., giving check-
                                      mate.

SOLUTION OF THE FRONTISPIECE.

WHITE.	BLACK.
1. Q. to her B's 4th (ch.)	1. R: to K. B's 2nd.
2. B. to K. Kt.'s 7th.	2. K. takes B. (best.)
3. Q. to her 4th (ch.)	3. K. to Kt.'s sq. (best.)
4. Q. to her 8th (ch.)	4. R. to B's sq.
5. Q. to her 5th (ch.)	5. R. to B's 2nd.
6. K. to K. R's 6th.	6. P. to K. Kt.'s 6th.
7. Q. to her 8th (ch.)	7. R. to B's sq.
8. Q. to K's 7th.	8. R. to K. B's 2nd.
9. Q. to K. Kt.'s 5th (ch.)	9. K. to R's sq.
10. Q. to her 8th (ch.)	10. R. to B's sq.
11. Q. takes R.	

Mate.

FINIS.